D0706590

The Westminster Confession into the 21st Century

Essays in Remembrance of the 350th Anniversary of the Westminster Assembly

Volume 2

'Maintaining proper Christian faithfulness to historic Christian confessions has become exceedingly difficult in the modern world. Increased transience, growing inter-Christian (and inter-religious) awareness, heightened media saturation‹all work against the edifying transmission of inherited confessional standards. If the historic confessions are to be preserved for the future, it will take the kind of sympathetic historic description and effective doctrinal argumentation displayed in this book. It is a volume that Christians who adhere to other confessions, or those who feel that Westminster did not say the last word, should value as much as those who believe in the entire adequacy of Westminster for today.'

Mark A. Noll
McManis Professor of Christian Thought
Wheaton College, Illinois

The Westminster Confession into the 21st Century

Essays in Remembrance of the 350th Anniversary of the Westminster Assembly

Volume 2

General Editor
J. Ligon Duncan, III

Associate Editors
W. Duncan Rankin
Derek W. H. Thomas
Robert C. "Ric" Cannada, Jr.
Stephen R. Berry
Stephen E. Tindall

MENTOR

© J. Ligon Duncan III

ISBN 1-85792-878-4

Published in 2004,
Reprinted 2005
in the
Mentor Imprint
by
Christian Focus Publications,
Geanies House, Fearn,
Ross-shire, IV20 1TW, Scotland, UK

www.christianfocus.com

Cover design by Alister MacInnes

Printed and bound by
W.S. Bookwell, Finland

Contents

Foreword

Almost a decade ago we marked the 350th anniversary of the English Parliament's ordinance calling for the historic Westminster Assembly (1643-1649/52). Reformed Theological Seminary (RTS) has a special interest in the promotion of the study of the Assembly since the Confession serves as our basic doctrinal position. Because we passionately believe these truths, RTS has aimed to produce pastors who believe and promote them in a way that is warmly and winsomely Reformed and biblically ecumenical, spreading the influence of these truths as broadly as possible.

This set of books is published with a view to introducing the student to some of the main issues in the history, theology and literature of the Assembly, and in hopes of spurring new interest in the work of the Westminster divines. Our aims, however, are not merely academic. They are also pastoral and devotional. We hope to provide material that will prove both interesting and helpful to the scholars, ministers, elders, candidates and congregations of the various evangelical churches influenced by the Westminster Assembly.

We catch something of the pastoral and devotional heart of the Assembly in the words of Samuel Rutherford (a Scottish commissioner to the Assembly), speaking of his Savior, Jesus Christ: "I am so in love with His love, that if His love were not in heaven, I should not be willing to go thither." This kind of passionate adoration of Christ is at the heart of Reformed theology at its best, and that is the sort of devotion we seek to promote through the work of Reformed Theological Seminary: love for God, love for his truth, love for Christ, love for people. Our message is "A mind for truth, a heart for God."

There is much indeed to feed our souls (as well as to strengthen our minds) which we can learn from these forefathers in the faith. The Westminster Assembly has provided for us both a profound, reverent, moving exposition of the doctrines of the Bible, and a worthy model of the function of truth in the pursuit of godliness.

Personally, my parents led me to memorize the Westminster Shorter Catechism when I was a young boy. Later I was given a copy of the complete Westminster Standards by my home church, First Presbyterian Church in Jackson, Mississippi, along with all others in that congregation when we completed our secondary education. My parents made sure that copy was packed in my luggage when I left home for undergraduate studies. A number of times as I discussed issues with others at Vanderbilt University, I turned to the Westminster Confession for guidance into the truths of Scripture. In particular the Confession was a great help to me in those days in my understanding and teaching on the subject of assurance of salvation and for my own personal comfort and encouragement in this vital area of the Christian life.

May our Sovereign God use these volumes to reacquaint His people with the rich spiritual heritage bequeathed to them by their Puritan forefathers and to spur them on to further study of their "affectionate, practical" theology.

Dr. Robert C. "Ric" Cannada, Jr.
    President, Reformed Theological Seminary
        Jackson, MS; Orlando, FL; Charlotte, NC; Washington, DC; Atlanta, GA, USA
    Associate Editor, Westminster Assembly Project

Introduction

This volume is the second in a series of four, all part of a larger scholarly initiative known as the "Westminster Assembly Project," begun in the early 1990s, with the encouragement of the administration of Reformed Theological Seminary (Jackson, Mississippi; Orlando, Florida; Charlotte, North Carolina; Washington, DC; Atlanta, Georgia). As a part of this project, a group of eminent scholars from around the world was approached to participate in the production of literature (both popular and academic) designed to discuss and debate the most important issues in current post-Reformation studies, as well as promote interest in the Westminster Assembly and its work. For more information about the literary products of this project, the reader is referred to the introduction of the first volume.

Suffice it to say that we have been busy for over a decade researching, producing literature and preparing for this multi-volume set of scholarly essays on various subjects related to the work of the Westminster Assembly. Our aim has been to produce something of a symposium on the theology of the Assembly. Perhaps it should be said clearly that not all the contributors are in agreement, though all of us have a regard for the product and importance of the Assembly. Most of us do, however, have a positive assessment of how the Westminster theology (and the larger Puritan/Protestant Scholastic stream) relates to the Reformed tradition as a whole. Consequently, we would argue for the basic continuity between Calvin and Calvinism, without ignoring developments and discontinuities.

Our purpose is to **inform**, **challenge**, **evaluate**, and **commend**. We aim (1) to inform the reader about the Assembly in is historical, theological, political and social setting, (2) to challenge inaccurate assertions commonly made about Westminster in its relation to both earlier and later Reformed theology, (3) to provide fresh evaluation of its place in and contribution to the Calvinian tradition, and (4) to commend the Westminster theology as a faithful expression of clear-headed Christian thinking for our own generation.

There are many reasons why it is beneficial for the scholars, ministers, elders, students and congregations of the various Reformed churches to study the Westminster Assembly. We have already articulated some of those reasons in the introduction to the first volume. And precisely because such a study is worthwhile, we have assembled contributions from an impressive list of students of Westminster and its context, to provide a window into its work and world.

In this volume, the essays commence with R. Scott Clark's and Joel Beeke's "Ursinus, Oxford and the Westminster Divines." These two outstanding scholars of post-Reformation studies trace an important stream of influence on the federal theology of the Westminster Assembly, and in so doing simultaneously debunk the idea that covenant theology somehow reintroduced medieval "works soteriology" into the Reformed tradition, and show the reformational and continental rootage of the idea of the covenant works (over against those who would either jettison it as scholastic or mistakenly assert it to be late).

David B. Calhoun, master teacher and historian from Covenant Theological Seminary contributes "Old Princeton Seminary and the Westminster Standards." This fine chapter gives a fair and sympathetic presentation of the reception of the

Westminster Standards in the halcyon days of orthodoxy at Princeton. While many polemicists use Princeton like a football or a wax nose, to establish the legitimacy of whatever contemporary views they are seeking to justify or condemn, Calhoun lets Princeton speak for itself.

Douglas F. Kelly tackles the issue of "The Puritan Regulative Principle and Contemporary Worship" deftly and graciously. Kelly, while appreciating historical and theological insights from John Frame and Hughes Old, and allowing for some discontinuity between Calvin and the Puritans on the application of the regulative principle, retains confidence in the language and idea of "the historic regulative principle" (RPW) and then proceeds to apply it to matters of great moment in the modern church, without a hint of the censoriousness that often attends discussions of the RPW and its application, or Reformed evaluations of contemporary worship, for that matter.

Paul Helm's chapter on "Westminster and Protestant Scholasticism" addresses the oft-heard charge that the Confession's theology is a degenerate, abstract, arid, philosophical version of the robust, concrete, warm, biblical thought of the Reformers, and Calvin especially. Helm, looking hard at the Confession's doctrine of providence and comparing it with Calvin, says "not guilty." Indeed, this whole chapter is a nice entry into a corrective view of the relation of the theology of Calvin and Westminster.

David W. Hall reminds us of the profound piety of the Assembly's constituents in "Westminster Spirituality." His chapter is helpful in at least two directions. First, it is another rebuttal of the view that Westminster is all about dead and dry theologizing, rather than "the life of God in the soul of man." In other words, this chapter reveals in the Assembly a depth of devotion to Christ, enjoyment of God, spiritual experience that dwarfs today's gurus of spirituality—and yet it displays a solidly grounded, theologically anchored, biblically derived piety (in contrast to the fluff of today). Second, it challenges contemporary Reformed anti-piety—an anti-piety that parades itself as truly Reformed while at the same time wanting to jettison "piety" as the product of degenerate, Great Awakening era Reformed theology.

Joseph Hall, in "The Westminster Shorter and the Heidelberg Catechisms Compared," demonstrates the folly of pitting these two catechetical systems of theology over against one another. Rejecting both Schaff's estimation of the Shorter Catechism and Warfield's critique of the Heidelberg, Hall appreciatively surveys both and shows the basic continuity as well as some interesting discontinuities.

In "The Erosion of Calvinist Orthodoxy," Ian Hamilton traces the sad decline of confessional orthodoxy and biblical fidelity in the Scottish Presbyterian tradition. This is a morality tale for all contemporary Reformed confessional communions. Hamilton is an expert in the history of Scottish subscription, and this is a distillation of his larger thesis on this subject.

Hugh Cartwright "Westminster and Establishment: A Scottish Perspective" introduces non-British Reformed and Presbyterian audiences to the issue of the establishment principle. Establishment is often viewed by, say, American Presbyterians (at least by some of the few who know anything of it at all) as tantamount to theocracy, inherently Erastian, subversive of religious toleration and the source of all Scottish Presbyterianism's problems for the last 300 years. But the establishment principle is important for understanding anything of the Scottish Presbyterian tradition. By the establishment principle, we mean the view of church-state relations in which the state is considered to be under obligation to establish a particular church (for example, in England—the Church of England or in Scotland—The Church of Scotland) and work with it for the advancement of the cause of religion in the realm. We may paraphrase William

Cunningham's description of the principle behind this view in this way: the obligation to advance the cause of God and the Kingdom of Christ lies not only with individuals, but also with rulers and nations.

Professor Nick Needham tackles the tricky issues of "Westminster and Worship: Psalms, Hymns? And Musical Instruments?" He is particularly concerned to give an accurate historical judgment relating to the Assembly's views and deliverances relating to exclusive psalmody and non-instrumental worship (two aspects of worship held to be essential to "regulative principle" directed corporate worship by many Presbyterian and Reformed bodies). Needham's conclusions will enlighten and, perhaps, surprise many.

Derek W. H. Thomas addresses "The Eschatology of the Westminster Confession and Assembly" and provides what is perhaps the best concise overview and evaluation of the Assembly's eschatology available. Thomas is not afraid to probe and critique, but his presentation is as sympathetic as it is informative and is as comprehensive as the constraints of his word limit will allow. It is the perfect entry-point for an intelligent discussion of Westminster eschatology for the student who wants a faithful and judicious guide, and to be pointed to the right questions and categories.

Chi Mo Hong introduces us to "The Influence of the Westminster Confession on the Korean Presbyterian Church." As the first look at this subject that many of us will have ever read, this chapter helpfully leads us into *terra incognita* and gives us an appreciation for the fruits of faithful, conservative, evangelical, Reformed missionaries to Korea, and more, for the gracious work of the Holy Spirit in establishing and growing Christ's church.

Philip G. Ryken's "Oliver Bowles and the Westminster View of Gospel Ministry" reveals to us a little masterpiece of pastoral theology, Oliver Bowles' treatise on the evangelical pastor. This chapter, like David Hall's, gives us yet another glimpse of the "affectionate, practical theology" of the Assembly, and the warmth and wisdom of their whole approach to the work of the minister.

My chapter on "True Communion with Christ: Calvin, Westminster and Consensus on the Lord's Supper" argues that the Confession helpfully captures the consensus of the Reformed tradition on the much-disputed issue of the nature of the presence of Christ in the Lord's Supper. Over against current neo-Reformed sacerdotalism's attempt to highjack Calvin as a proto-advocate of its eccentric view, I suggest that we look at the continuity of Calvin, Tigurinus and Westminster for consensus, and evaluate all historic Reformed teaching on this subject in light of a faithful submission to Scripture (lest we fall prey to an unhealthy traditionalism).

John V. Fesko writes on "The Westminster Confession and Lapsarianism"—a précis of his larger important study of lapsarianism from Calvin to Westminster. Dr. Fesko sketches a picture of the history of lapsarianism in the Reformation and post-Reformation periods. As we have noted before, there is a school of historiography that argues that the post-Reformation Reformed theologians under the influence of Ramist logic distorted Calvin's doctrine of predestination through an arid blend of scholastic rationalism. Beza, Turretin, Perkins, Ames, Dort and Westminster usually figure as bad guys who ossified the warm, pastoral, dynamic biblical-theological approach of Calvin into a cold, abstract, metaphysical, schematized system of decrees. Now, let's be clear, this analysis is bunk; and recently a string of outstanding church historians have ably demonstrated its deficiency. Dr. Fesko's work contributes to this historiographical rectification. Indeed, his thesis will catch many by surprise: "the post-Reformation Reformed theologians (the Protestant scholastics) did not distort Calvin's doctrine of predestination but rather moderated it." Fesko will argue that Calvin was supralapsarian, while Dort and Westminster are infralapsarian. The former assertion will, no doubt, raise far more eyebrows than the latter, but Fesko's constructively provocative argument is more than worth the time to ponder, whether you agree with him at every point or not.

The magnitude of the Assembly and its work, the quality of its product, and its significance for the English-speaking world and beyond in successive generations should not be underestimated, but often is today. The Assembly's theological formulations are a landmark of pastoral theology and the work of the Assembly marks the highpoint of Reformed confessionalism, and thus warrants the further study and consideration that these essays of ours intend to promote.

J. Ligon Duncan, III, BA, MDiv, MA, PhD
    General Editor, The Westminster Assembly Project
    Senior Minister, First Presbyterian Church (PCA), Jackson,
        Mississippi, USA
    Adjunct Professor, Reformed Theological Seminary
    Convener, Twin Lakes Fellowship
    Council, Alliance of Confessing Evangelicals
    Chairman, Council on Biblical Manhood and Womanhood
    Secretary of the Board, Belhaven College
    Editorial Director, Reformed Academic Press

Acknowledgments

This second volume of the Westminster Assembly Project's essays on the Assembly has, like its predecessor, been waiting to see the light of day for more than half a decade. The General Editor wishes to express his appreciation to the authors, who have so patiently awaited its arrival, for their outstanding work. Also, on behalf of my fellow editors (W. Duncan Rankin, Derek W. H. Thomas, Robert C. "Ric" Cannada, Jr., Stephen Berry and Stephen Tindall), I want to thank Hunter Bailey (who is now a doctoral student at the University of Edinburgh, New College, Scotland), and Jonathan Stuckert (who is currently serving in the administration of Reformed Theological Seminary in Atlanta, Georgia). These are my two former interns, and they have greatly aided me in this work. Thank you for your partnership in this work. Thank you for your partnership in this work, and your friendship, men. Jennifer Redd of Reformed Theological Seminary in Orlando, Florida, has done the indexing of this volume under the supervision of John R. Muether. We offer our thanks to them as well.

Collectively, the whole editorial team here expresses our thanks to the Executive Committee of RTS for its ongoing encouragement and support. Many congregations and individuals have given financially toward the work of the Westminster Assembly Project, among them, the First Presbyterian Church of Yazoo City, Mississippi, James R. "Sonny" Peaster (a trustee of the Banner of Truth Trust) and A. William May (a Ruling Elder of First Presbyterian Church, Jackson) stand out. Without their gifts, we could not have brought this work to completion.

The good folk of A Press, Inc., Reformed Academic Press and Word Association in Greenville, South Carolina, USA, also deserve our unceasing gratitude. They undertook the considerable labor of the typesetting and layout task.

We all also here express our appreciation to our publisher, William Mackenzie, Managing Director of Christian Focus Publications, and to our Editorial Manager, Willie Mackenzie (not to be confused with his aforementioned uncle!).

All of the editors are grateful to God for our wives and families—all of whom have made their own contribution to this work in different ways. Each of us has been gifted by God with an extraordinary woman with whom we share life and partnership in the work of the Gospel. I'm moved to the realization of that again, even as I write these words. Anne Duncan, Shirley Rankin, Rosemary Thomas, Rachel Cannada, Dana Berry and Sara Tindall have each gladly borne the costs of ministry and have enriched our lives through their self-giving. We rise up and call you blessed.

Soli Deo Gloria
L. D.

Ursinus, Oxford, and the Westminster Divines

R. Scott Clark
Joel R. Beeke

Introduction

"The first covenant made with man was a covenant of works; wherein life was promised to Adam, and in him to his posterity, upon condition of perfect and personal obedience" (WCF 7.2). That the Westminster Assembly of Divines chose to express its doctrine of redemption by using the notion of the *foedus operum* troubles many contemporary theologians and historians of doctrine. Since the rise of Neo-orthodoxy many scholars have come to believe that the Westminster formulation erroneously diverges from Calvin's emphasis on God's undeserved sovereign grace.[1] The question has naturally arisen regarding the source of the alleged error. A number of scholars have regarded Calvin's successor in Geneva, Theodore Beza, to be the primary culprit.[2] Recently,

---

[1] John Metcalfe, *The Westminster Confession Exploded: Deliverance From the Law* (Tylers Green, 1991); R. T. Kendall, *Calvin and English Calvinism to 1649* (Oxford, 1979); Holmes Rolston III, "Responsible Man in Reformed Theology: Calvin versus the *Westminster Confession*," *Scottish Journal of Theology* 23 (1970): 129-55; Basil Hall, "Calvin Against the Calvinists," *John Calvin: A Collection of Essays* (Grand Rapids, 1966).

[2] Heinrich Heppe, *Geschichte des deutschen Protestantismus in den jahren 1555-1581*, 4 vol. (Marburg, 1852-59); Hans Emil Weber, *Reformation,*

however, some scholars have turned their attention increasingly away from Beza toward Zacharias Ursinus (1534-83).[3]

According to R. T. Kendall, Ursinus was guilty of preparationism and assurance-destroying legalism.[4] Kendall theorizes that William Perkins drew his doctrine of faith in part from the Heidelberg theologians; consequently, it was through Perkins that Ursinus' theology was communicated to the Westminster Assembly.[5] R. W. A. Letham says that Ursinus thought of the covenant of works in a "reciprocal, mutual, contractual sense" such that "participation in the covenant was

---

Orthodoxie und Rationalismus (Gütersloh, 1951); Otto Gründler, "Thomism and Calvinism in the Theology of Girolamo Zanchi" (Th.D. Thesis, Princeton Theological Seminary, 1961); Ernst Bizer, *Frühorthodoxie und Rationalismus* (Zurich, 1963); Walter Kickel, *Vernunft und Offenbarung bei Theodor Beza* (Neukirchen, 1967); Brian G. Armstrong, *Calvinism and the Amyraut Heresy* (Madison, 1969); David C. Steinmetz, *Reformers in the Wings* (Philadelphia, 1971), 169; John S. Bray, *Theodore Beza's Doctrine of Predestination* (Nieuwkoop, 1975); A. E. McGrath, *Institia Dei*, 2 vol. (Cambridge, 1986), 2.40; David A. Weir, *The Origins of Federal Theology in Sixteenth Century Reformation Thought* (Oxford, 1990); Michael Jinkins, "Theodore Beza: Continuity and Regression in the Reformed Tradition," *Evangelical Quarterly* 64 (1992); 140-154. For a response to this interpretation of Beza see Richard A. Muller, "The Use and Abuse of a Document: Beza's *Tabula praedestinationis*, the Bolsec Controversy, and the Origins of Reformed Othodoxy," in Carl R. Trueman and R. Scott Clark, ed., *Protestant Scholasticism: Essays in Reassessment* (Carlisle, UK, 1999).

[3] Kendall, 38-41, 197-208; R. W. A. Letham, "Saving Faith and Assurance in Reformed Theology: Zwingli to the Synod of Dort," 2 vol. (Ph.D. Thesis, Aberdeen, 1979), 1.187-95; Weir, vii, 101, 3; Stephen Strehle, *Calvinism, Federalism and Scholasticism: A Study of the Reformed Doctrine of the Covenant* (Bern, 1988), 165. The best biography of Ursinus in English is Derk Visser, *Zacharias Ursinus: The Reluctant Reformer, His Life and Times* (New York, 1983). See also, idem, "Zacharias Ursinus," *Shapers of Religious Traditions*, ed. Jill Raitt (New Haven, 1981), 121-39. Lyle Bierma, has responded to the claim of legalism in Ursinus' doctrine of the covenant of works in "Law and Grace in Ursinus' Doctrine of the Natural Covenant," in Trueman and R. Clark, ed., *Protestant Scholasticism*. The present essay takes a somewhat differant approach, however.

[4] Kendall, 39, 41.

[5] Kendall, 41, 56, 58, 62, 74, 210.

dependent upon embracing and serving Christ, so that the accent was on the responsibility of man rather than on the enabling grace of God."[6] Letham comes close to describing Ursinus' soteriology as synergistic. According to D. A. Weir, who also locates the source of the difficulty in Ursinus, "Zacharias Ursinus was the first theologian who first utilized the idea of a prelapsarian covenant to any great extent in the sixteenth century."[7] The prelapsarian covenant was a "novel idea . . . associated with the Decalogue," the conditions of which were the same as the "postlapsarian covenant."[8] Such federalism departed from Calvin's paradoxical theology.[9] Upon this federalist theology the "Westminster Assembly put the stamp of orthodox approval."[10] The strongest

---

[6] Letham, 1.187-95, See also Michael McGiffert, "From Moses to Adam: The Making of the Covenant of Works," *The Sixteenth Century Journal* 19 (1988): 132-34.

[7] Weir, 101.

[8] Weir, 105-106.

[9] Weir, 15-16. For the opposite point of view see Peter A. Lillback, "Ursinus' Development of the Covenant of Creation: A Debt to Melanchthon or Calvin?" *Westminster Theological Journal* 43 (1981): 247-88; Christopher J. Burchill, "On the Consolation of a Christian Scholar: Zacharias Ursinus (1534-1583) and the Reformation in Heidelberg," *Journal of Ecclesiastical History* 37 (1986): 565-83; Derk Visser, "The Covenant in Zacharias Ursinus," *The Sixteenth Century Journal* 18 (1987): 531-44.

[10] Weir, 157. For a general critique of the principles behind Weir's thesis see R. Scott Clark, *The Substance of the Covenant: Caspar Olevion ofn the double Benefit of Christ* (Carlisle and Edinburgh, 2004). Lyle D. Bierma, *German Calvnism in the Confessional Age: The Covenant Theology of Caspar Olevianus* (Grand Rapids, 1996); idem, "Federal Theology in the Sixteenth Century: Two Traditions?," *Westminster Theological Journal*, 45 (1983): 304-321; idem, "The Role of Covenant Theology in Early Reformed Orthodoxy," *The Sixteenth Century Journal* 21 (1990): 453-462; Mark W. Karlberg, "Covenant Theology and the Westminster Tradition," *Westminster Theological Journal* 54 (1992): 135-152. For a view of Puritan federalism which views it as Protestant, see John von Rohr, *The Covenant of Grace in Puritan Thought* (Atlanta, 1986). Donald K. McKim, "William Perkins and the Theology of the Covenant," *Studies of the Church in History*, ed. Horton Davies (Allison Park, 1983), sees Perkins' federalism as Protestant. For an

criticism of Ursinus, however, has come from Stephen Strehle who regards him as a purveyor of a sub-Protestant contract theology. For example, he says that Ursinus' theology of the sacraments was a regression to the Franciscan pledge of divine favor to those who do their best.[11]

This essay will argue that though these critics have misunderstood Ursinus, the Westminster Standards, and their interrelatedness, they are right to draw the connection. The nexus lies in what Warfield called "the architectonic principle of the Westminster Confession," namely, "the Federal theology."[12] We will argue (1) that Ursinus' Calvinism was a notable part of the stream of continental Reformed theology that flowed into England in the late sixteenth century and nourished young English Calvinists who would later take their places in the Assembly of the Divines; (2) that one medium by which Ursinus' theology was communicated to English Calvinism was Oxford University; and (3) that properly understood, his federalism, and by implication that of the Westminster divines, was Protestant, gracious, and Calvinist.

---

interpretation of the Puritans which strongly dissents from Kendall see Paul Helm, *Calvin and the Calvinists* (Edinburgh, 1982); idem, "Calvin and the Covenant: Unity and Continuity," *The Evangelical Quarterly* 55 (1983): 65-82; Joel Beeke, *Assurance of Faith: Calvin, English Puritanism and the Dutch Second Reformation* (New York, 1991); idem, "Faith and Assurance in the Heidelberg Catechism and its Primary Composers: A Fresh Look at the Kendall Thesis," *Calvin Theological Journal* 27 (1992): 39-67; idem, "Does Assurance Belong to the Essence of Faith? Calvin and the Calvinists," *The Master's Seminary Journal* 5 (1994): 43-71; Paul R. Schaefer, "The Spiritual Brotherhood on the Habits of the Heart: Cambridge Protestants and the Doctrine of Sanctification from William Perkins to Thomas Shepard" (D.Phil., Thesis, Oxford University, 1994).

[11] Strehle, 165.

[12] Benjamin B. Warfield, *The Westminster Assembly and Its Work* (New York, 1931), 56.

Ursinus, the Oxford Calvinists, and the Westminster Divines

Until recently the existence of a dynamic and influential group of theologians whom we shall call the Oxford Calvinists has been a secret well kept by historians. From the accession of Elizabeth (1558) until the appointment of William Laud as her Chancellor (1630), Oxford University was dominated by Calvinist theologians.[13] This period of influence was even longer if one considers that the great Italian Reformed theologian Peter Martyr Vermigli (1491-1562) was Regius Professor of Divinity under Edward VI (1548-53).[14] C. M. Dent and Nicholas Tyacke have recently documented the rise and predominance of Calvinism in Oxford.[15] Under Martyr's influence, Reformed theology gained a foothold in Oxford. Though its prospects diminished considerably under Mary Tudor, the planted seed was watered with the blood of the Marian martyrs. Upon Elizabeth's accession the Reformed contingent, which had flourished under Edward, was slow to return; consequently there was a shortage of Protestant preachers. "There were only three Protestant preachers in the University of Oxford in the year 1563, and they were all Puritans, viz., Dr. Humphrys, Mr. Kingsmill, and Mr. Sampson."[16] Not until

---

[13] Patrick Collinson, *The Elizabethan Puritan Movement* (London, 1967), 129.

[14] On early English Protestantism see Carl R. Trueman, *Luther's Legacy*: *Salvation and the English Reformers 1525-1556* (Oxford, 1994). On Vermigli see John Patrick Donnelly, *Calvinism and Scholasticism in Vermigli's Doctrine of Man and Grace* (Leiden, 1976); Frank A. James III, "A Late Medieval Parallel in Reformation Thought: *Gemina Praedestinatio* in Gregory of Rimini and Peter Martyr Vermigli," *Via Augustini: Augustine in the Later Middle Ages, Renaissance and Reformation,* ed. Heiko A. Oberman, Frank A. James (Leiden, 1991).

[15] C. M. Dent, *Protestant Reformers in Elizabethan Oxford* (Oxford, 1983); Nicholas Tyacke, *Anti-Calvinists:The Rise of English Arminianism* (Oxford, 1987), 4-16.

[16] Daniel Neal, *History of the Puritans,* (London, 1822), 1.145. On some of the difficulties attending the use of the word "Puritan," see Dent, 2-3.

5

the visitation of 1568 did Calvinism begin to flourish again in Oxford.[17] By the mid 1570s students from Zurich, Geneva, and Heidelberg were venturing back to Oxford, bringing their Reformed theology with them.[18]

The leading Oxford Calvinist of the late sixteenth century was John Reynolds (1549-1607) who was President of Corpus Christi College and Dean of Lincoln.[19] The Presbyterian activist John Field (1545-88) proceeded M. A. in 1567.[20] Patrick Collinson has traced forty-two Puritan ministers in Oxford in the decade 1565-75.[21] Other outstanding Oxford Calvinists were, Laurence Humphrey (c.1527-90), Edmund Bunney (1539-c.1618), William Twisse (c.1578-1646), Daniel Featley (1582-1645),[22] and Cornelius

---

[17] Dent, 44ff. Henry VIII, Edward VI, and Elizabeth I sent ecclesiastical "visitors" to ensure that the colleges and University were conforming to the Protestant regime. Often royal visitors were rewarded with permanent posts in prominent colleges.

[18] Dent, 74-102.

[19] Sidney Lee, ed. *Dictionary of National Biography*, vol. 16 (London, 1909). Hereafter *DNB*.

[20] Collinson, 85-86. Field was the co-author of the *Admonition to Parliament* (1572) for which part he served a year in prison. Collinson, 153, speculates that after imprisonment, Field fled to Heidelberg in 1573. This hypothesis explains his close connections to the Continental Reformed movement and how he became the translator of Caspar Olevian's *An Exposition of the Symbole of the Apostles or Rather the Articles of Faith* (London, 1581) and J. Piscator's *Aphorismes of the Christian Religion* (London, 1596). Dan G. Danner, s.v. "Field, John," *Encyclopedia of the Reformed Faith*, ed. Donald K. McKim (Edinburgh, 1992). On the Presbyterian "radicals" at Oxford, see Dent, 131-45; Mark H. Curtis, *Oxford and Cambridge in Transition 1558-1640* (Oxford, 1959), 199-203; Roland G. Ussher, *The Presbyterian Movement in the Reign of Elizabeth* (London, 1905).

[21] Collinson, 129. Collinson does not indicate how many of these ministers were attending Oxford.

[22] It is true that Featley did not sit the entire session. However, A. F. Mitchell, ed. *Minutes of the Sessions of the Westminster Assembly* (Edinburgh, 1874), xxxii, lxvi, says that he played a significant role in the abortive revision of the Thirty-Nine Articles, even defending against Twisse, the doctrine of the

Burgess (c.1589-1665).[23] The latter three sat in the Assembly.

Incepting Doctors routinely defended stoutly Calvinist theses from the 1590s until the 1630s and Oxford preaching was largely Calvinist in the 1590s.[24] However, not only preachers were attracted to Calvinism. The official structures of the University were largely controlled by Calvinists. As the semi-Pelagian backlash developed, it was quite likely that the offending Oxonian preacher could find himself explaining his views to a rigorously Calvinist vice-chancellor.[25] Whereas in Cambridge explicit Calvinism was banned from Commencement by Royal proclamation in 1626, such was not the case in Oxford until 1632.[26] From 1613 Abbot lectured regularly in Oxford against the Dutch Arminians.

For most of the period from 1548-1654 the Regius Professorship of Divinity was held by Calvinists.[27] In addition, many Oxford Calvinists served as heads of colleges and in other positions of authority.[28] Oxford was only part of the larger trend

---

imputation of Christ's active obedience. See also, Charles Davis Cremeans, *The Reception of Calvinistic Thought in England* (Urbana, 1949), 84-85.

[23] To be sure, present in the Oxford contingent, if we include Thomas Goodwin (1600-80), who was later President of Magdalen College, were the additional independents, Philip Nye and Joseph Caryl (James Reid, *Memoirs of the Westminster Divines* 2 vol. [London, 1811] 1.37-98; Warfield, 37).

[24] Dent, 222. To incept is to commence one's degree by defending theses.

[25] Tyacke, 58-76. See also Curtis, 177.

[26] Tyacke, 76. On Calvinism at Cambridge, see Schaefer, 10-21.

[27] Peter Martyr, 1548-54; Laurence Humphrey, 1560-89; Thomas Holland, 1589-1612 (Anthony á Wood, *Athenae Oxonienses* [London, 1815], 2.111, does not say if Holland was a Calvinist); Richard Abbot, 1612-15; John Prideaux, 1615-41; Joshua Hoyle, 1648-54. See *The Historical Register of the University of Oxford* (Oxford, 1900), 48; *DNB*, vol. 10; Joseph Foster, ed., *Alumni Oxonienses* (London, 1892), vol. 2.

[28] Francis Cheynell, a member of the Assembly, was Lady Margaret Professor of Divinity from 1648-52. John Wallis, Clerk of the Assembly, was Savilian Professor of Geometry, 1649-1704. Edward Corbet was University Orator in 1648 (*The Historical Register*, 39, 52-53).

toward the dominance of Calvinism in Elizabethan England.[29] The Calvinist Edmund Grindal (c.1519-83) was Archbishop of Canterbury for thirteen years (1570-83) and the Oxonian Calvinist George Abbot (1562-1633) was Archbishop of Canterbury for twenty-two years (1611-33). Mark Curtis notes that the leading Puritan spokesmen at the Hampton Court Conference (1604) were Oxonians.[30] Undoubtedly the major impetus for Calvinism in England was the Geneva Bible. Between 1579-1615 thirty-nine quarto editions were printed bound with a Calvinist catechism.[31] Calvin's *Institutes* were first translated in 1561 by Thomas Norton; more of Calvin was published in England than of any other Protestant writer from 1548 to 1600.[32]

Of the approximately 108 delegates who actively worked to shape the Westminster Confession, about one third received their theological training at Oxford.[33] Both the Prolocutors of the Assembly, Twisse and Charles Herle (1598-1659) were Oxford men.[34] Many of the Assembly's Oxonians began their academic careers in colleges such as All-Souls or Queens but eventually were "translated" (to borrow Thomas Reid's term) to what was

---

[29] Tyacke, 3.

[30] Curtis, 197.

[31] Tyacke, 2.

[32] Cremeans, 65-66.

[33] The actual number of participants is hard to reckon since many who were called to serve did not attend the Assembly. Here is a partial list of the Oxford Calvinists who sat in the Assembly: William Twisse, Cornelius Burgess, John White, Thomas Baylie, Richard Byfield, Joseph Caryl, Thomas Case, Humphrey Chambers, Francis Cheynell, Thomas Coleman, John Conant, Edward Corbet, Calibute Downing, John Drury, Thomas Ford, John Foxcroft, Hannibal Gammon, William Greenhill, Robert Harris, Charles Herle, Richard Heyrick, Gaspar Hickes, Joshua Hoyle, John Ley, John Maynard, Philip Nye, William Rathband, Edward Reynolds, Obadiah Sedgwick, Edmund Stanton, John Strickland, Thomas Temple, Christopher Tesdale, John Wallis, Henry Wilkinson, Francis Woodcock.

[34] Reid, 1.37; 2.25, 208.

then Magdalen Hall (now Hertford College), so that Oxford had its own Puritan enclave.[35] According to Tyacke, the Calvinist atmosphere at Oxford might have been even more rigorous than at Cambridge. Unlike Cambridge, there was no dispute at Oxford in the 1590s between "Arminians" (speaking anachronistically) and Calvinists. "Arminianism" had "been checked" in the 1580s.[36]

Ursinus played a significant role in mediating Calvinism to Oxford. His connection with English Calvinism and with the Westminster Confession lies first of all in the Heidelberg Catechism itself and secondarily in his lectures on the Heidelberg Catechism. Two months after it was first published in German, in 1563, the Heidelberg Catechism was translated into Latin by Joshua Lagus and Lambertus Pithopoeus.[37] This was the version defended by Ursinus and Olevianus in the University of Heidelberg and in the seminary (*Collegium Sapientiae*), as well as the version which first reached international Calvinism. The first English translation, *The catechisme, or maner to teach children and others the Christian fayth: vsed in all the landes and dominions that are vnder the mighty prince Frederike, the palsgraue of the Rhene* was completed by the non-conformist William Turner (1510-1568) in 1568 and published in 1572.[38]

---

[35] Hertford College absorbed Magdalen Hall in the mid- nineteenth century. Magdalen Hall was a medieval hall among whose alumni was William Tyndale. John Owen graduated B.A. from Queens College in 1628 and proceeded M.A. in 1635. He was later Dean of Christ Church and Vice-Chancellor of the University.

[36] Tyacke, 58-59.

[37] Fred H. Klooster, "The Heidelberg Catechism. Origin and History" (Calvin Theological Seminary, Grand Rapids, 1989), 187.

[38] London, 1572. J. I. Good, *The Heidelberg Catechism in Its Newest Light* (Philadelphia, 1914), 22-25. Turner was a physician, botanist, Dean of Wells, a friend of Nicholas Ridley, and attended the "religious conference" at the White Horse Inn. He was exiled under Mary and returned upon Elizabeth's accession (*DNB*, vol. 19).

The Catechism was widely used in England and, in January 1579, Oxford University required that it "should be used for the extirpation of every heresy and the preparation of the youth in true piety."[39] It was the only catechism printed by the University. It was re-translated by John Seddon and published twice in 1588 with the arms of the University on the title page.[40] English Puritanism found the Heidelberg Catechism congenial; in fact, it was still being published in 1804, by Oxford University Press.[41] Cambridge too was feeling the impact of the Catechism. In recounting his spiritual experience at age fourteen while a scholar in Christ's Cambridge, Thomas Goodwin (1600-80) described in passing the use of the Catechism among Puritans:

> I received the sacrament at Easter when I was fourteen years old, and for that prepared myself as I was able. I set myself to examine whether I had grace or not, and by all the signs in Ursin's Catechism, which was in use among the Puritans in the College, I found them all, as I thought in me.[42]

---

[39] Good, 26; Dent, 88. Dent, 92-93, rather inaccurately characterizes the Heidelberg Catechism as "anthropocentric" in contrast to Bullinger's "theocentric" *Cathechesis pro adultoribus scripta* (Zurich, 1559). Warfield, 379-400, made the same sort of dichotomy between the Heidelberg Catechism and the Westminster Shorter Catechism. In the first place, this sort of analysis is unhistorical and misleading. Bullinger wrote for a community which had benefited from three decades of Reformed teaching. The Westminster Shorter Catechism was written for a nation which had enjoyed a century of Reformed teaching. In contrast, the Heidelberg Catechism was written to a largely Lutheran audience with virtually no prior Reformed instruction. Secondly, as Fred Klooster has ably shown, even the Heidelberg Catechism's first question, which appears at first glance to be anthropocentric, is actually answered within a theocentric, Trinitarian framework. Finally additional questions and answers of the Heidelberg Catechism clearly posit theoncentric principles, e.g., Questions 6, 50, 52, 53, 58, 86, 122, 123, 128.

[40] Dent, 91. *A catechisme, or short kind of instruction, whereby to teach children and the ignoraunter sort, the Christian religion,* trans. J. Seddon (Oxford, 1588).

[41] *Sylloge confessionum sub tempus reformandfi Ecclesifi editarum. Subjiciuntur Catechismus Heidelbergensis et canones Synodi Dordrechtanfi,* ed. J. Randolph (Oxford, 1804).

[42] *The Works of Thomas Goodwin* (Edinburgh, 1861), 2.lii.

The other major source of Ursinus' influence on the development of English Calvinism was his lectures on the Catechism. They were first edited by his student David Pareus and published by Simon Goulart in Geneva in 1584.[43] The *Compendium Christinae Doctrinae* was translated into English in 1587 by Henry Parry, a young Calvinist Oxford undergraduate, later Greek reader at Corpus Christi College, Bishop of Worcester and Gloucester, and Chaplain to the Queen.[44] Parry's translation went through seven editions in Oxford from 1587 to 1633.[45] The *Compendium* was not only reprinted seven times in Oxford, but also enjoyed almost constant use in the University Library in the last two decades of the sixteenth century. The 1585 edition was also printed in Cambridge and was held in the libraries of three Oxford Colleges. Later additions were held in six other Oxford colleges.[46] Quirinus Reuter published Ursinus' collected works in 1612, in which the lectures on the Catechism were expanded and retitled *Explicationes Catecheseos*.[47] Later editions of Pareus' edition of Ursinus' lectures on the Catechism were published in Heidelberg (1621), Frankfurt (1627), and Hanau

---

[43] *Doctrinae christianae compendium, seu commentarii catechetici* (Geneva, 1584).

[44] *The Summe of Christian Doctrine*, trans. Henry Parrie (Oxford, 1587). On Henry Parry see Wood, *Athenae Oxonienses* 2.102-3. Wood incorrectly attributed to Parry the 1591 translation of "a catechism . . . by Zacharias Ursinus." The entry under "Parry, Henry" in *DNB*, vol. 15 repeats this error.

[45] See John Platt, *Reformed Thought and Protestant Scholasticism* (Leiden, 1982), 49-56.

[46] A. W. Pollard and R. R. Redgrave, *A Short Title Catalogue of Books Printed in England, Scotland, & Ireland and English Books Printed Abroad 1475-1640*, 2 vol., 2nd ed. (London, 1976); Paul Morgan et al., "Holdings of STC Books in Oxford Libraries other than the Bodleian" (1985, Unpublished Typescript in the Lower Reading Room of the Bodleian Library, Oxford).

[47] Zacharias Ursinus, *Opera theologica*, 3 vol., ed. Quirinus Reuter (Heidelberg, 1612). An earlier collection of Ursinus' shorter writings had already been published by Ursinus' son from 1584-89 (Zacharias Ursinus, *Volumen tractationem*, 2 vol., ed. Joanes Ursinus [Neustadt, 1584-89]).

(1634) while miscellaneous catechetical works as *Corpus Doctrine Ecclesiarum* were added to the Bodleian Library.[48]

Besides the *Compendium*, several of Ursinus' smaller works were quickly translated into English, which indicates that there was a demand for Ursinus in Oxford in this period. John Stockwood, "a schoole teacher," translated Ursinus' exposition of the Fourth Commandment from his *Loci Theologici* as *A Verie Profitable and Necessary Discourse Concerning the Observation and Keeping of the Sabbath Day*.[49] Several other shorter works were published in Oxford in 1600 as *A Collection of Certain Learned Discourses*.[50] According to Dent, Ursinus' lectures were, in this period, "a standard textbook" in Oxford.[51] He was certainly

---

[48] Zacharias Ursinus, *Corpus doctrinfi Christianfi Ecclesiarum à papatu reformatarum, continens explicationes catecheticas d. Zacharifi Ursini, denuò recogn. studio D. Parei. Accesserunt Miscellanea catechetica diligenter recognita* (Heidelberg, 1621). Bodleian Library, *The first printed catalogue of the Bodleian Library 1605, a facsimile: Catalogus librorum bibliothecae publicae quam . . . Thomas Bodleius eques auratus in academia Oxoniensi nuper instituit* (Oxford, 1986) .

[49] London, 1584. Zacharias Ursinus, *Loci theologici traditi in academia Heidelbergensi, expositio decalogi, quartum praeceptum. Tractationem*, vol. 1. This treatise can also be found in *Opera* 1.713-25.

[50] Zacharias Ursinus, *A collection of certaine learned discourses, written by Zachary Vrsine. For explication of divers difficult points, laide downe in his Catechisme*, trans. I. H. (Oxford, 1600). The shorter writings of Ursinus included were, *An Exhortation to Study Christianity* (*In paranesi ad sacrae theologiae studium* [*Opera*, 1.3-9]); *The Antiochian Beliefe Touching the Incarnation of the Word* . . . (*De verbi incarnatione. symbolum patrum antiochinorum adversus Paulus Samosatenum* [*Opera*, following vol. 3 under *Miscellenea catechetica seu collectio D. Paraei D.* 27-8]); *An Epistle of Ursin upon Predestination* (*Epistola D. Zachariae Ursini ad amicum, de praedestinatione* [*Misc. Cat.* 28-44]); *A Brief Exposition of the controversie about the Lordes supper: between the Consubstantialists, and the maintainers of the truth* (*Compendiosa explicatio totius de coena domini controversiae inter synusiastas et orthodoxos* [*Misc. Cat.* 47-53]); *Rules and Axiomes of certain chiefe pointes of Christianitie* . . . (*Theses theologicae de parcipuis aliquot doctrinae Christianae* [*Misc. Cat.* 53-83]).

[51] Dent, 186.

perceived as a threat by the Archbishop of York who, in 1630, banned the sale of his books along with those of William Perkins.[52] Thus, by the time the Westminster Assembly was convened, Ursinus' commentary and Opera were a fixture in the English Reformed theological landscape, particularly in Oxford.

Through the Catechism and the Compendium there is a definite link between Ursinus and Oxford, and through the latter to the Assembly. However, it is difficult to document this link more precisely. For example, though Thomas Goodwin mentioned "Ursin's catechism" (the Heidelberg Catechism), we were unable to find any explicit references to Ursinus in several of Goodwin's major works, e.g., *Christ Set Forth*—not even when he discusses the covenant, where one might expect at least a passing reference to Ursinus.[53] This omission can be explained in part by the fact that writers of this period did not usually cite sources extensively. It is striking, however, that when Goodwin does refer to other sixteenth century continental theologians such as Wollebius, Keckermann, Piscator, Polanus, and Calvin, he omits Ursinus. Christ's role as Mediator is a prominent theme in Ursinus, but he is not mentioned in Goodwin's, *A Discourse of Christ the Mediator*.[54] Cornelius Burgess, in his *Baptismal Regeneration of Infants*, appeals to Calvin, Peter Martyr, Zanchi, Junius, Bucer, and Beza as authorities who support his position, but not to Ursinus.[55] Nor does Daniel Featley, in *Pelagius Redivivus*,[56] or William Twisse, in *The Riches of God's Love*, appeal to Ursinus, despite the fact that Ursinus wrote explicitly on predestination.[57] In

---

[52] Tyacke, 182.

[53] Thomas Goodwin, *Christ Set Forth in his Death, Resurrection, Ascension, Sitting at God's Right Hand, Intercession as the Cause of Justification, Object of Justifying Faith* (London, 1642), 52-66.

[54] London, 1692 (reprinted, Edinburgh, 1863).

[55] Oxford, 1629.

[56] London, 1626.

[57] Oxford, 1653.

his lecture on the question of the Sabbath, at the Act of 1622, John Prideaux did cite Ursinus (along with Calvin, Bullinger, Bucer, and several other continental theologians) in support of his position.[58] Yet he did not cite Ursinus either in his lectures *de iustificatione* or *de Christi satisfactione*.[59] Nor did George Abbot cite Ursinus in his *Quaestiones Sex*, a collection of lectures delivered in the Divinity schools in 1597.[60] A second partial explanation for Ursinus' absence in these authors is that, in a sense, the major theological controversies had passed him by. The Remonstrant controversy and resurgent Catholicism were the issues of the day.[61]

Ursinus and Reformed Federalism

It is the contention of this essay that the attempt by Kendall, Letham, Weir, and Strehle to characterize Ursinus' and

---

[58] John Prideaux, "Oratio VII inauguralis in promotione doctorum Christ," in *Viginti-duae Lectiones de totidem Religionis capitibus praecipue hic tempore controversis, prout publice habebantur oxoniae in vesperiis* (Oxford, 1643), 1.67; *The Doctrine of the Sabbath* (London, 1634), 34.

[59] *Viginti-duae Lectiones*, 1.60-76; 1.294-308.

[60] George Abbot, *Quaestiones Sex, totidem praelectionibus, in schola theologica, oxoniae, pro forma, habitis, discussae, et discetptae. Anno 1597* (Oxford, 1598). Abbot cited the following sixteenth century Protestants: Calvin, 91; John Whitgift, 98; Thomas Cartwright, 99; Bucer, 107, 108; Melanchthon, 113, 116, 125; Chemnitz, 151; Peter Martyr, 162, 165, 167, 177, 200; Whittaker, 200. He wrote against Edmund Çampion and cited mainly patristic authors, usually Augustine.

[61] These writers followed the trend observed by Dent, 93-102. However, Dent mistakes the move of Reformed theology from the pulpit to the classroom for a decline. See Richard A. Muller, *Post-Reformation Reformed Dogmatics* 4 vol. (Grand Rapids, 2003). For the point of view that Ursinus' scholastic method did adversely affect his theology, see John Platt, *Reformed Thought and Protestant Scholasticism* (Leiden, 1982), 49-59; Patrick J. Donnelly, "Immortality and Method in Ursinus's Theological Ambiance," *Controversy and Conciliation: The Palatinate Reformation, 1559-1618*, ed. Derk Visser (Pittsburgh, 1986).

Westminster's federalism as sub-Protestant will not stand close scrutiny of the sources. For example, though Kendall acknowledges that Ursinus defined faith as a "certain knowledge" and "an assured trust," he also asserts that Ursinus made the practical syllogism the ground of faith.[62] However, this is a dubious reading of Ursinus. The definition of faith in Ursinus' commentary parallels his definition given in Question 38 of the *Summa*, *"What is faith?"*

> It is to assent strongly to everything delivered to us in the word of God and to have a firm trust by which each one stands, that remission of sins, righteousness and life eternal, are gracious gifts from God to us, for the sake of Christ's merit and through him. This faith having been kindled in the hearts of the elect by the Holy Spirit, makes us living members of Christ and produces in us true love for and calling upon God.[63]

Later in the *Summa* he augmented this definition by placing it within the framework of Calvin's Prophet-Priest-King scheme. *"What is it therefore to believe in Jesus Christ?"*

> It is to have this comfort, that just as by our King himself, we are given and ruled by the Holy Spirit, and defended against all dangers; even so by our High Priest, we are reconciled and led to the Father, so that from him we might be able to seek and expect all good things; so likewise by the prophets we are illumined with the true knowledge of the Father. Finally, that we and all ours might be made kings and priests with him for ever, with him ruling over all creatures and making thankful offerings to God, and be made prophets truly knowing and worshipping God.[64]

---

[62] Kendall, 40-41.

[63] Question 38: *Quid est fides?* Est firmiter assentiri omni verbo Dei nobis tradito: & firma fiducia qua singuli statuunt, sibi donatam esse a Deo remissionem peccatorum, iustitiam & vitam aeternam, gratis, propter meritum Christi & per eum: accensa in electorum cordibus a Spiritu sancto: faciens nos viva Christi membra & gignens in nobis veram dilectionem & invocationem Dei (*Summa, Opera,* 1, 14). All English translations in this essay are the authors' unless otherwise indicated. The authors gratefully acknowledge the assistance of Ray Lanning, Charles Krahe, and Steven M. Baugh with translations incorporated into this essay.

[64] Question 64: *Quid est igitur in Iesum Christum credere?* Est consolationem hanc habere, quod ab ipso tanquam rege nostro donemur & regamur Spiritu

In Question 66 Ursinus again turns to the mystical witness of the Spirit. *"What is it to believe in the Son of God?* It is to feel in the heart, by the testimony of the Holy Spirit, that we are adopted by God as sons, for the sake of his only begotten Son."[65] Ursinus made frequent use of both the *syllogismus practicus* and the *syllogismus mysticus*. One's election is known by one's faith, and progress in piety, which is buttressed by good works.[66] These syllogistic aids, however, were not intended to function outside a gracious, Trinitarian, Christ-centered structure of salvation.[67] To believe in Christ as *Lord* is to have confidence that we will never be snatched from his hand.[68] It is difficult to see what in this definition of faith would tend toward an undue emphasis on the will, preparationism, or the like. It would appear that Kendall has also caricatured Ursinus, just as his analysis of Calvin and English Protestantism has been criticized as a caricature. In contrast to Kendall, one should remember that for Ursinus faith is first of all a sovereign gift of grace, not the act of an unregenerate human will. As in the Heidelberg, so also in the *Summa*, faith is informed by the Word, and it is personal—"kindled in the hearts

---

sancto, & defendamur adversus omnia pericula tanquam a summo sacerdote nostro, reconcilemur & adducamur Patri, ut ab eo petere & expectare omnia bona possimus: tanquam a Propheta, vera Patris agnitione illuminemur: Efficiamur denique cum ipso reges, in aeternum cum ipso dominantes omnibus creaturis: & sacerdotes, nos & nostra omnia, gratas iam hostias Deo offerentes: & Prophetae DEUM vere agnoscentes & celebrantes (*Summa, Opera,* 1, 16).

[65] Question 66: *Quid est in Filium Dei credere?* Est in corde, Spiritus sancti testimonio, sentire, nos a Deo propter Filium eius unigenitum in filios adoptatos esse (*Summa, Opera,* 1, 16).

[66] See *Opera* 1.21, 3.44; Beeke, "Faith and Assurance," 56-57.

[67] Beeke, "Faith and Assurance," 59-60. Ursinus rejected in the strongest terms the Roman Catholic doctrine that assurance of election is not possible (Otto Thelemann, *An Aid to the Heidelberg Catechism* [Grand Rapids, 1959], 452-53).

[68] *Summa, Opera,* 1, 16.

of the elect" (*accensa in electorum cordibus*); its object is Christ and his *meritum* and benefits graciously given. At the same time the regenerate person does strongly assent. This balance is very similar to Calvin's definition of faith in *Institutes* 3.2.7.

Conditionality in the Compendium *and the* Summa Theologiae

The approach represented by Kendall, Letham, Weir, and Strehle, has also unnecessarily muddied the water by consistently failing to distinguish between *covenant conditionality* by which human beings are accepted by God only after they have met certain conditions and *covenant obligations* which God places on his redeemed people.[69] Were Ursinus' federal theology to require human cooperation with divine grace for acceptance with God, then it could be fairly described as a regression to the Pelagian-Nominalist *pactum* theology of Gabriel Biel (c.1415-95).[70] But this was demonstrably not the case in Ursinus. This criticism confuses obligations imposed upon the elect *after* redemption with conditions required *before* redemption.[71] The critics have taken hold of the definition of *foedus* which Ursinus gave in his lectures on the catechism:

> What is this covenant?
>
> A covenant in general is a mutual contract, or agreement between two parties, in which the one party binds itself to the other to accomplish something upon certain conditions, giving or receiving something, which is accompanied with certain outward signs and

---

[69] On Calvin and conditionality see Peter A. Lillback, "The Continuing Conundrum: Calvin and the Conditionality of the Covenant," *Calvin Theological Journal* 29 (1994): 42-74.

[70] See Gabriel Biel, *Quaestiones de justificatione*, ed. Carol Feckes (Münster, 1929); John L. Farthing, *Thomas Aquinas and Gabriel Biel: Interpretations of St. Thomas Aquinas in German Nominalism on the Eve of the Reformation* (Durham, NC, 1988).

[71] Derk Visser, "The Covenant," 532.

symbols, for the purpose of ratifying in the most solemn manner the contract entered into, and for the sake of confirming it, that the engagement may be kept inviolate.[72]

In order to properly understand Ursinus' definition of the covenant, it is important to note the distinction which Ursinus himself implied in his answer. This answer defines a covenant *in genere* which concept is controlled by his understanding of the covenant of works. We will see that when Ursinus describes the covenant of works, however, he has in view the federal representatives who as public persons possessed unique abilities. He saw Christ accomplishing for elect humanity what Adam had failed to accomplish for all humanity: perfect obedience to God's law over a probationary period.[73] He distinguished clearly between the covenant as it considers the federal heads and the covenant as it respects sinners. The criticisms of Ursinus which we have noted fail to observe this crucial distinction between *genus* and *species*.

Ursinus' notion of the covenant of grace cannot be separated from his Calvinist soteriology. He defined covenant as a *mutua pactio* because when he thought of covenant, he thought first of all of the covenant as it was conceived in the natural prelapsarian state, in which Adam had the ability not to sin. The prelapsarian covenant controlled his definition of covenant. This is why when

---

[72] Zacharias Ursinus, *The Commentary of Dr. Zacharias Ursinus on the Heidelberg Catechism,* trans. George Willard (Columbus, 1852), 97. *Quod sit foedus Dei?* Foedus in genere est mutua pactio duarum partium, qua altera alteri se certis condtionibus obligat ad aliquid facidendum, dandum vel accipiendum, adhibitis signis et symbolis externis ad solennem testifactionem, confirmationis causa, ut promissio sit inviolabilis (Zacharias Ursinus, *Explicationes Catecheseos Palatinae, sive corpus Theologiae* in *Opera*, 1, 99).

[73] Geerhardus Vos, "The Doctrine of the Covenant in Reformed Theology," *Redemptive History and Biblical Interpretation*, ed. Richard B. Gaffin (Phillipsburg, 1980), 242-45, reminds us that it is this attribute which distinguished the Reformed conception of creation and covenant from the Lutheran conception.

defining the law, Ursinus returns to the prelapsarian covenant between God and Adam. *"What does the divine law teach?"*

> The sort of covenant which God began with man, in creation; by which man should have carried himself in serving God; and what God would require from him after beginning with him a new covenant of grace; that is, how and for what [end] man was created by God; and to what state he might be restored; and by which covenant one who has been reconciled to God ought to arrange his life.[74]

Ursinus conceived of sin and redemption in terms of a broken covenant of works and a gracious covenant of redemption. The Sinaitic law is not read back into creation. Rather, the Sinaitic law is a reflection of God's prelapsarian intention. Thus the law was said to apply in the New Covenant, not however as a condition of righteousness, but as a guide to life for the redeemed. This is standard Protestant teaching. Consequently, original sin is defined in terms of willful unbelief of God's probationary promise of blessing.[75] For Ursinus, sin is a contradiction of our created status as obedient bearers of the divine image (the *qualis* of creation) and it is the status to which we have been graciously returned in Christ. For Ursinus *"conditus"* and *"redactus,"* and *"reconciliatus"* are parallel terms.[76] God sovereignly, graciously creates, redeems and renews without our assistance. This question which has been taken as a stark indicator of Ursinus' legalism is actually a powerful example of the radical graciousness and divine monergism of his federalism.

---

[74] *Quid docet lex divina?* Quale in creatione foedus cum homine Deus iniverit; quo pacto se homo in eo servando gesserit: & quid ab ipso Deus post initium cum eo novum foedus gratiae, requirat: hoc est, qualis & ad quid conditus sit homo a Deo, in quem statum sit redactus: et quo pacto vitam suam Deo reconciliatus debat institutere (*Summa*, Question 10, *Opera*, 1, 10).

[75] Question 25: *Quid est peccatum originis?* Est reatus propter lapsum primorium parentum & ignorantiae & dubitatio de Deo & eius voluntate, & inclinatio ad ea quae Deus prohibuit, propter lapsum primorum parentum omnib. innascens, & causa omnium malarum actionum internarum & externarum (*Opera*, 1, 11).

[76] They are both carefully expressed in the passive voice.

A quick series of subsequent questions on the *imago Dei* confirm that Ursinus is thoroughly Protestant and Reformed. *"How was man created?"* We were made in God's image.[77] What was this image? "The true knowledge of God and of the divine will, and the inclination and desire of the whole man to live solely according to this image."[78] What was the goal of the prelapsarian covenant? That man "might worship God his entire life, in eternal blessedness."[79] The doctrine that one is created *ad imaginem Dei* is organically related to the eschatological orientation of the prelapsarian covenant. In Ursinus' theology, to be God's image means to be fit *ad aeternitatem*. For Ursinus, there was looming before Adam, in the prelapsarian *foedus*, a state of final blessedness and communion with God, conditioned upon his obedience to the probationary command or the *lex naturale*. The corollary of this promised eternal beatitude is the promised eternal suffering upon transgression of the terms of the covenant.[80]

In this light we may understand the rest of his definition of the covenant. What he meant by *mutua pactio* is a *foedus* in which "God gives assurance to men that he will be merciful to them, forgive their sins, grant unto them a new righteousness, the Holy Spirit, and eternal life by and for the sake of his Son, our Mediator."[81] It is the office of

---

[77] Question 11: *Qualis est homo conditus?* Ad imaginem Dei (*Opera*, 1, 10).

[78] Question 12: *Quae haec est imago?* Vera Dei & divinae voluntatis agnitio & secundum hanc solam vivendi, totius hominis inclinatio & studium (*Opera*, 1, 10).

[79] Question 13: *Ad quid autem est conditus?* Ut universa vita sua Deum in aeterna beatudine colat (*Opera*, 1, 10).

[80] "However, every sin is infinitely culpable, because the offense was against God, that is, against infinite good; therefore it merits infinite punishment." (Question 30, Est autem omne peccatum culpa infinitia; quia Dei, id est boni infiniti offensio est itaque poenam infinitam meretur [*Summa, Opera*, 1, 11]).

[81] Hinc facile colligitur definitio foederis Dei. Est enim mutua pactio inter Deum et hmines, qua Deus confirmat hominibus, se futurum eis propitium, remissurum peccata, donaturum iustitiam novam, spiritum sanctum, & vitam aetermam, per & propter filium mediatorem . . . (*Explicationes, Opera*, 1, 99).

the Mediator, not of sinners, to restore the Covenant broken in the fall and to redeem the lost.[82] The covenant of grace is not possible without the Mediator to satisfy God's justice in place of the elect.[83] It should be carefully noted that, for Ursinus, it is God who initiated the *foedus* (*Deus confirmat*) and God who graciously granted its benefits, all of which are granted "for the sake of the Son" (*propter filium*). It would appear that Ursinus' critics have ignored the *propter filium* or *propter Christum* of Ursinus' covenant theology.[84]

The blessings of the covenant are secured for the elect by the "merit and efficacy" of Jesus, the "author of perfect and eternal salvation for all who believe in him."[85] God's function *in foedere* is primary and our part is secondary. Our part of the covenant is a matter of responding thankfully, by divine grace, to God's initiative.

> And, on the other side, men bind themselves to God in this covenant that they will exercise repentance and faith, or that they will receive with a true faith this great benefit which God offers, and render such obedience as will be acceptable to him. This mutual engagement of God and man is confirmed by these outward signs which we call sacraments, which are holy signs, declaring and sealing unto us God's good will, and our thankfulness and obedience.[86]

---

[82] Question 72: *Quod ergo est Mediatoris officium?* Foedus inter Deum & homines, qui a Deo desecrant, restituere (*Summa, Opera*, 1, 16).

[83] Question 73: *Cur foedus hoc sine Mediatore saneiri non poterat?* Quia iustitia Dei postulabat, ut Deus hominibus propter peccatum esset in aeternum iratus, cum igitur esset impossibile, ut contra suam iustitiam DEUS ullam cum genere humano societatem iniret; necesse fuit aliquem intervenire, qui Deum nobis exorans iustitiae Dei satisfaciens, & omnem in posterum offensionem tollens, homines a Deo avulsos, rursus cum eo coniungeret (*Opera*, 1, 16).

[84] For the same reasons, John Farthing has also identified the theme *propter Christum* as important for interpreting the covenant theology of Girolamo Zanchi. See John Farthing, "Jerome Zanchi on the Covenant," *Calvin Theological Journal* 29 (1994), 152-53.

[85] Question 58: *Quare Iesus dicitur?* Quia merito & efficacia sua, salutis perfectae atque aeternae autor est omnibus in ipsum credentibus (*Summa, Opera*, 1, 15).

[86] . . . Vicissim homines se obligant Deo ad fidem & poenitentiiam, hoc est, ad recipiendum vera fide hoc tantum beneficium, & ad praestandum Deo veram

It is noteworthy that there is an important difference between the text of the 1584 edition of the *Compendium* (Geneva, 1584), edited by Simon Goulart (1543-1628), and the text of the same commentary entitled *Explicationes Catecheseos* and published in Ursinus' *Theologica Opera* (Heidelberg, 1612), edited by Quirinus Reuter (1558-1613).[87] In the 1612 text, the first line of the answer to the question, "What is the covenant?" (*Quid sit foedus?*) was: "The covenant in general is a mutual pact of two parties. . . ." (*Foedus in genere est mutua pactio duarum partium . . .*), whereas in the 1584 text, the first line of the answer read: "The covenant generally signifies a mutual promise or pact between two parties. . . ." (*Foedus in genere signficat mutuam promissionem vel pactionem inter duas partes . . .*). In fact, the phrase *promissio vel pactio mutua* occurred twice in the 1584 definition but not at all in the 1612 definition. In the Reuter edition, the word *promissio* does not even occur in the answer to the question. Thus, the impact upon the reader of the 1584 Goulart text is somewhat different from that of the 1612 Reuter text. In the Reuter text, one is struck by the obligations of the covenant while the former text seems to balance promise and obligation. It was solely the Goulart text by which the Oxford divines had access to Ursinus' lectures for twenty-five years. Moreover, the definition as found in the Reuter edition is also considerably longer than

---

obedientiam. Haec pactio mutua Dei & hominum symbolis externis confirmatur, quae vocamus ssacramenta, hoc est, sacra signa testifcantia de hac Dei ergo nos voluntate, & nostra erga Deum gratitudne atque officiis (*Opera*, 1, 99).

[87] For biographical details on Reuter see Melchior Adam, *Vitae Germanorum Theologorum* (Heidelberg, 1620), 819-27; s.v. Reuter, Quirinus, Freiherr R. Filiencron, ed., *Allgemeine Deutsche Biographie*, 55 vol. (Leipzig, 1875-1910), 28.328-9. For Goulart, see Leonard C. Jones, *Simon Goulart, étude biographique et bibliographique* (Geneva, 1917); J-Fr. Gilmont, "Goulart, Simon," *Dictionnaire d' Histoire et de Geographie Ecclesiastiques*, ed., R. Aubert, 25 vol. (Paris, 1912-), 21.939-46.

that found in the Genevan edition of 1584. Clearly the text was rearranged and enlarged by Reuter. On this particular point, we cannot know with certainty which text most closely resembled Ursinus' lectures on the catechism. Still, this textual variant should give pause to the critics of Ursinus' federalism.[88]

One should also remember that Ursinus' definition of the covenant in his lectures occurred in his explication of the *second* section of the Heidelberg Catechism—which focuses on grace and salvation—not in the first which focuses on guilt and the convicting character of the Law. He spent nearly four folio columns on Christ as the Mediator of redemption.[89] Thus, Ursinus was lecturing his students about the role of the Mediator in redeeming his people, not about our role in negotiating *quid pro quo* with God for salvation. This is an essentially Protestant *ordo*. He was emphasizing Christ's priestly-mediatorial office against the Roman sacerdotal system. Prior to the question "What is the covenant of God?" (*Quid sit foedus Dei?*), he linked the doctrine of the covenant explicitly and closely with Christ's office as Mediator under the heading *De foedere*.

> It has been shown, that a Mediator is one who reconciles parties that are at variance, as God and men. This reconciliation is called in the Scriptures a Covenant, which has particular reference to the Mediator, inasmuch as every mediator is the mediator of some covenant, and the reconciler of two opposing parties. Hence the doctrine of the Covenant which God made with man, is closely connected with the doctrine of the Mediator.[90]

---

[88] Zacharias Ursinus, *Opera* 1, 99; cf. idem, *Doctrinae Christianae*, 138: Foedus in genere significat mutua, promissionem vel pactionem duas partes, qua utraque pars alteri se certis conditionibus obligat ad aliquid faciendum, dandum, vel accipiendum, adhibitis ceremoniis & Symbolis ad solemnem testificationem.

[89] Richard A. Muller, *Christ and the Decree: Christology and Predestination in Reformed Theology from Calvin to Perkins* (Durham, NC, 1986), 96-97, noted that Ursinus' doctrine of the Mediator preceded and governed his covenant theology, indeed the gospel, the doctrine of faith, and his credal exposition.

[90] Ursinus, *Commentary*, 96; Dictum est, quod mediator sit persona reconcilians partes diffidentes, Deum & homines. Ista autem reconciliatio in scripturis

Informed by the broader context of this definition, we see that for Ursinus *foedus* is not about two equal parties, but about the work of Christ reconciling sinners to God through his mediatorial work.[91] Richard A. Muller observes that in Ursinus, "Christ is both mediator and *medius*. . . ."[92] This is made explicit in the second part of the section when Ursinus asked, "How could this covenant between God and man be made?" (*Quomodo foedus inter Deum & homines iniri possit?*)

> This covenant could not have been made without a Mediator. For we could neither satisfy nor return to favor with God, nor indeed receive the benefit of redemption [purchased] by another. For, at that time, God would not, on account of his justice, admit us into his favor without sufficient satisfaction. We were enemies of God, and hence access to God shall not stand open to us, except through the interceding of Christ the Mediator. . . . This reconciliation was not possible without the satisfaction and death of the Mediator.[93]

For Ursinus to think *de foedere gratiae* was to think about the Mediator and his *satisfactio* and *intercessio* on behalf of the people of God. Another way of expressing the relationship between the covenant of works and the covenant of grace is to say that he used the doctrine of the covenant to express the Protestant distinction between law and gospel.

---

dicitur foedus, quod est correlativum mediatoris. Omnis enim mediator est alicuius foederis mediator, & duarum partiam conciliator. Quare cum doctrina de mediatore cohaeret doctrina de foedere Dei (*Opera*, 1, 98-99).

[91] Mark W. Karlberg, "The Mosaic Covenant and the Concept of Works in Reformed Hermeneutics: A Historical-Critical Analysis with Particular Attention to Early Covenant Eschatology" (Ph.D. Diss. Westminster Theological Seminary, 1980), 92, has noted that "this mutuality, however, was *never* construed in terms of equality."

[92] Muller, *Christ and the Decree*, 98.

[93] Hoc foedus non potuit fieri sine mediatore. Nam neque nos satisfacere poteramus: neque redire in gratiam cum Deo, imo nec accipere beneficium reconciliationis ab alio partum. Tum etiam Deus propter iustitum suam noluit nos absque satisfactione sufficiente admittere. Eramus hostes Dei: ideo aditus ad Deum nobis non patebat, nisi intercedente pro nobis Christo mediatore. . . . Non potuit reconciliatio haec fieri sine satisfactione & morte mediatoris (*Opera*, 1, 99).

Q. 36 *What distinguishes law and gospel?*

The law contains a covenant of nature begun by God with men in creation, that is, it is a natural sign to men, and it requires of us perfect obedience toward God. It promises eternal life to those keeping it, and threatens eternal punishment to those not keeping it. In fact, the gospel contains a covenant of grace, that is, one known not at all under nature. This covenant declares to us fulfillment of its righteousness in Christ, which the law requires, and our restoration through Christ's Spirit. To those who believe in him, it freely promises eternal life for Christ's sake.[94]

The law contained a *foedus naturale* initiated by God in creation. When Ursinus speaks of "creation" he is speaking of the prelapsarian world. When he speaks of "us" we are considered federally, that is, in our representative Adam. He conceived of the prelapsarian arrangement with sinless Adam as a probationary matter. Failure results in judgment. Obedience results in life. The gospel, i.e., covenant of grace, does not have those marks because the terms of the covenant of works were satisfied by Christ.[95]

The critics also fail to account for Ursinus' entire definition of the covenant, or they focus only on the first line of his answer. The words *mutua pactio* must be understood in light of the words *propter Christum*. Ursinus worked out his covenant theology in the context of two catechisms, the *Summa Theologiae* (*Catechesis Maior*) and his *Compendium* of the Heidelberg Catechism. In

---

[94] Question 36: *Quod est discrimen legis et evangelli?* Lex continet foedus naturale, in creatione a Deo cum hominibus initium, hoc est, natura hominibus nota est; & requirit a nobis perfectam obedientiam erga Deum, praestantibus eam promittit vitam aeternam, non prestantibus minatur aeternas poenas. Evangelium vero continet foedus gratiae, hoc est, minime natura notum existens: ostendit nobis eius iustitiae, quam Lex requirit, impletionem in Christo, & restitutionem in nobis per Christi Spiritum; & promittit vitam aeternam gratis propter Christum, his qui in eum credunt (O*pera*, 1, 14).

[95] Question 32: *Quare hoc foedus etiam testamentum dicitur?* Primo; quia in Ecclesia usurpari coepit nomen testamenti pro foedere. Secundo; quia sicut testamentum non est ratum, nisi interveniente morte testatoris: ita foedus hoc sanciri non potuit nis morte Christi (O*pera,* 1, 14).

their nature, catechisms are cumulative. Thus the only proper place to begin in interpreting catechisms is with the first question. In the interpretation of Ursinus' covenant theology this pedagogical principle has been forgotten. Nor does it appear to be the case that Ursinus was schizophrenic, i.e., Protestant in his formal doctrine of justification and substantially sub-Protestant in his doctrine of sanctification. According to Question 86 of the Heidelberg Catechism we are redeemed "for the sake of Christ without any merit of ours" (*propter Christum sine ullo nostro merito*). For Ursinus, salvation is always *sola gratia* and *sola fide*.[96] Question 1 of the *Summa* asked,

What firm comfort do you have in life and in death?

That I was created by God in his image and for eternal life. After I, of my own accord, lost this image in Adam, God out of his immense and gracious mercy, received me into his covenant of grace, so that, on the basis of the obedience and death of his Son, who was sent in the flesh, he gave to me, a believer, righteousness and eternal life. Moreover, He sealed his covenant in my heart through his Spirit (who renews me in God's image and who cries in me "Abba, Father"), and through his Word and the visible signs of his covenant.[97]

Clearly this answer, like the first answer of the Heidelberg Catechism, to which the *Summa* is organically connected, did not begin with conditions of entrance into the covenant, but with God and man as the image of God. The ground of confidence is God's "immense and gracious mercy." The object of faith is the obedience of the incarnate Son. The bond of one's union with

---

[96] See *Heidelberg Catechism*, Question 87.

[97] *Quam habes firmam in vita & morte consolationem?* Quod a Deo ad imaginem eius & vitam aeternam sum conditus: & postquam hanc volens in Adamo amiseram, Deus ex immensa & gratuita misericordia me receipt in foedus gratiae suae, ut propter obedientiam & mortem Filii sui missi in carnem, donet mihi credenti iustitiam & vitam aeternam: atque hoc foedus suum in corde meo per Spiritum suum, ad imaginem Dei me reformantem & clamantem in me Abba Pater, & per verbum suum & sogma juius foederis visibilia obsignavit (*Summa, Opera*, 1, 10).

Christ is God's Spirit, who is the power of sanctification. Building on this divine monergism, Question 2 asked, "How do you know that this sort of covenant was begun by God with you?" The answer: "Because I am truly a Christian."[98] By *christianus* he plainly means "elect," as is made clear in the following question: "Whom do you call truly Christian? Those who by faith are truly engrafted into Christ and baptized into him."[99] Note that he carefully expressed this most Calvinist idea of union with Christ in the passive voice. Questions 4 and 5 function as a unit to seal Ursinus' commitment to a thoroughly Augustinian view of salvation. Question 4 argued for the uniqueness of Christianity among world religions. "*Is therefore none but the Christian religion true?* None."[100] Question 5 continued, "*Why do you assert this?* Because to this religion only the Holy Spirit bears witness in believing hearts. This religion alone declares sure liberation from sin and death."[101] The federal structure of Ursinus' understanding of fall and redemption does not result in a higher estimation of human ability, but repeatedly sends one back to Christ. When he asks, "Who can offer this obedience?," the answer is "Christ alone." It is not and never has been possible to go to anyone else for the obedience necessary for redemption.[102] If one's

---

[98] Question 2: *Qui scis tale foedus a Deo tecum esse initum?* Quia vere Christianus sum (*Opera*, 1, 10). We are not saved because we are sanctified but sanctified because we are saved.

[99] Question 3: *Quem dicis vere Christianum?* Qui vere fide Christo insitus, & in eum baptizatus est (*Opera*, 1, 10).

[100] Question 4: *Nulla ne igitur nisi Christiana religio est vera?* Nulla (*Opera*, 1, 10).

[101] Question 5: *Qua ratione hoc aseveras?* Quia huic soli Spiritus sanctus in credentium cordibus testimonium perhibet: Haec sola liberationem certam a peccato & morte ostendit (*Opera*, 1, 10).

[102] Question 18: *Potestne quisquam nostrum hanc obedientiam praestare?* Solo Christo excepto, nullus unquam hominum in hac vita eam praestare neque potuit, neque poterit (*Opera*, 1, 11).

position before God was measured by his status as image-bearer before the fall, *post lapsum* it is measured by its absence.[103]

When Ursinus' definition of the covenant has Christ as the Second Adam in view, it is controlled by the probationary prelapsarian covenant. The covenant as it has the sinner in view, however, is purely gracious. "From where therefore do you conceive the hope of eternal life? From the covenant of grace, which God initiated afresh with believers in Christ."[104] *What is this covenant?*

> It is reconciliation with God, having been secured by the intercession of Christ, in which God promises believers, always to be a Father near to them for the sake of Christ and to give them eternal life; and they themselves promise in turn that they will accept these benefits by true faith in him, and as becomes grateful and obedient sons, worship God for ever, and under both visible signs (which we call sacraments) publicly attest this mutual promise.[105]

The covenant of grace, as respects fallen sinners, is a distinct species of covenant. Elect sinners are viewed as those for whom the terms of the covenant have been met in their federal head, Christ. Thus, for Ursinus, gospel and *foedus* are synonymous in Christ. "What does the gospel teach?"

> What God promises to us in his gracious covenant: how in this covenant we might be received, and how we might know ourselves to be in this covenant, that is, how we might be delivered from sin and death, and how we might be sure of this liberation.[106]

---

[103]Question 19: *Cur autem praestare non possumus?* Quia imaginem Dei amisimus (*Opera*, 1, 11).

[104]Question 30: *Unde igitur spem vitae aeternae concipis?* Ex foedere gratuito, quod DEUS denuo cum credentib. in Christum init (*Opera*, 1, 11).

[105]Question 31: *Quod est illud foedus?* Est reconciliatio cum Deo, Christi intercessione impetrata, in qua Deus promittit, se credentibus, propter Christum perpetuo fore Patrem propicium, ac daturum vitam aeternam et ipsi vicissim spondent, se haec beneficia vera fide accepturos, & sicut gratos & obedientes filios decet, perpetuo celebraturos: & utrique hanc promissionem mutuum signis visibilibus, quae sacramenta vocamus, publice contestantur (*Opera*, 1, 11).

[106]Question 35: *Quid docet evangelium?* Quid promittat nobis Deus in fodere gratiae suae: quomodo in illud recipiamur; & in eo nos esse sciamus, hoc

In his *ordo salutis* Ursinus left no room for human initiative, not even in the exercise of faith. By nature "we were enemies of God" (*eramus hostes Dei*), unwilling and unable to accept the benefits of redemption so graciously purchased. Thus any interpretation of Ursinus' *de conditionibus* must be interpreted in the light of his thoroughgoing Calvinism.

> There is but one covenant, because the principal conditions, which are called the substance of the covenant, are the same before and since the incarnation of Christ; for in each testament God promises to those that repent and believe, the remission of sin; whilst men bind themselves, on the other hand, to exercise faith in God, and to repent of their sin.[107]

The "conditions" of which Ursinus wrote should be made clear. If, by conditions, he meant law-keeping, then he was teaching a sort of conditionality strange to the Reformation. This, however, is not the case. He defended the unity of the substance of the covenant (*substantia foederis*), distinguishing between *substantia* and *circumstantias*. The *conditiones* are equated with the *substantia*, i.e., the promise of the remission of sins (*remissionem peccatorum*) of those who believe, who as we have seen, are those who have been regenerated by sovereign grace. It was in this context that he raised the question of human responsibility to the call of the gospel. The offer of the gospel to all is sincere since "none were made participants until they embrace and keep that covenant, that is, who by true faith receive Christ and his benefits for themselves."[108] The

---

est, quomodo a peccato & morte liberemus, & huius liberatinis certi simus (*Opera*, 1, 14).

[107] *Commentary*, 99; cf. *The Summe*, 256. Unum dumtaxat est, quia conditiones principales, quae substantia foederis dicuntur, eadem sunt ante Christum & post Christum exhibitum. Deus credentibus & poenitentiam agentibus promittit remissionem peccatorum & homines se obligant ad credendum Deo, & ad poenitentiam agendam (*Opera*, 1,100).

[108] Question 37: *Nunquid Evangelium docet, foedus gratia Dei ad omnes homines pertinere?* Omnes quidem ad illud vocat: sed nulli eius fiunt participes, nisi qui illud amplectuntur & servant, hoc est, qui vera fide oblatum sibi Christum & beneficia eius accipiunt (*Opera*, 1, 14).

divine monergism extends to the preservation of the redeemed. He defined God's kingdom in terms of the Son's preservation of the elect through the ministry of the gospel, against the devil, *in conspectum Patris.*[109]

For Ursinus, good works are an "internal and external cooperation with the precepts in the Decalogue."[110] This definition might be Gabriel Biel's, except that unlike Biel, Ursinus is *not* writing *de merito congruo.* Rather, he is affirming the place of the law in the life of the believer *after renewal.* The purpose of the law is that the elect

> . . . [first] may know the worship which God approves and requires from his confederates [i.e., those in covenant with him]. Next, seeing how far they are from the perfect fulfillment of the law in this life, that they might be kept in humility and aspire to heavenly life.[111]

Ursinus moved to good works *only after* establishing Christ as the federal head of the redeemed and the gracious nature of the covenant by which the elect are saved. The "covenant of God's grace" was said to "obligate" believers to manifest "fruit of faith," i.e., "true conversion to God."[112] Conversion is "mortification of the flesh" and "vivification of the spirit,"[113] or regeneration.

---

[109] *Summa, Opera,* 1.15-6.

[110] *Summa, Opera,* 1, 21.

[111] Question 150: *Cur autem post evangelium praedicatum, conversis etiam proponenda est?* Primum, ut discant, quos cultus probet DEUS & a confoederatis suis requirat. Deinde ut videntes quam procul in hac vita absint a perfecta legis impletione, in humilitate contineantur, & ad vitam coelestem aspirent (*Summa, Opera,* 1, 21).

[112] Question 142: *Quis est ergo fructus fidei, ad quem foedus gratiae Dei nos obligat, & ex quo vera fides agnoscitur?* Vera ad Deum conversio (*Summa, Opera* 1, 21).

[113] Question 143: *Quid est conversio ad Deum? Mortificatio carnis & vivficatio spiritus* (*Summa, Opera* 1, 21). In this section, as well as others, it is clear that there is little difference between Ursinus' view of the importance of sanctification and that of the mainstream of Puritanism.

Regeneration is the renewal of the divine image lost in the fall. "*What is the quickening of the Spirit?* It is joy in God who is reconciled to us through Christ, and love and ardent zeal for righteousness for the sake of God's glory."[114]

Conclusion

Undoubtedly many streams of thought and practice converged at the assembly of divines at Westminster. One significant stream was the Protestant, gracious, and holy federalism of Zacharias Ursinus, mediated to the divines in part through the Oxford Calvinists. We have surveyed Ursinus on the questions of conditionality in the covenant, and on the covenant of works. We have found him to teach that in the beginning God instituted a covenant of works. Since it was a creational arrangement with humanity in its original state, it was a *foedus naturale*. The prelapsarian covenant was not only natural but probationary and made with Adam as the federal head of the entire human race. In Ursinus' view, Adam was created fully capable of meeting the conditions of the covenant and of entering into eternal blessedness with God. In our examination of conditionality in Ursinus' view of the covenant, we have found him to distinguish between the probationary prelapsarian covenant of works and the covenant of grace instituted after the fall. In his double covenant scheme, the only conditions which adhere to the covenant are those obligations which the believer takes upon himself subsequent to election, faith and renewal. It is the Holy Spirit who, together with the Word and sacraments, meets these conditions in the believer.[115]

---

[114]Question 145: *Quid est vivificatio Spiritus?* Est laetitia in Deo per Christum in nobis propitio, & amor ac studium ardens iustitiae propter gloriam Dei (*Opera* 1, 21).

[115]Contra Robert Kolb, "Luther, Augsburg, And the Concept of Authority in the Late Reformation Ursinus vs. The Lutherans," *Controversy and Conciliation: The Palatinate Reformation, 1559-1618,* ed. Derk Visser (Pittsburgh, 1986).

We have found no evidence that Ursinus renewed the medieval *pactum* theology or taught a covenant theology which imposed conditions on sinful human beings prior to entrance into the covenant, which they must meet on their own or even with the assistance of grace, *de merito congruo*. We have argued that, rather, his doctrine of the covenant should be interpreted in the broader context of both the Heidelberg Catechism, of which he was a major author in the light of his *Compendium* and of the *Summa*. In short, Ursinus' doctrine of justification and of the covenant is profoundly Protestant. It is: Christ for me (*Christus pro me*).[116]

---

[116]*Opera*, 1, 230.

Old Princeton Seminary and the Westminster Standards

D. B. CALHOUN

Princeton Seminary was founded in 1812 by the General Assembly of the Presbyterian Church. Following a period of unrest at the seminary and turmoil in the church, the General Assembly "reorganized" Princeton in 1929, combining its two boards to give control to the liberal, or moderate, element. "Old Princeton," as it has come to be called, was a remarkable place of personal devotion to God, commitment to his inspired word, and zeal for the worldwide spread of the gospel. Its faculty, from Archibald Alexander and Samuel Miller to Benjamin Breckinridge Warfield and J. Gresham Machen, were bound together by kinship and friendship and by theological conviction. Samuel Miller wrote in 1849, "The union in our faculty has been complete. And the solid basis of the whole has been a perfect agreement, on the part of all of us, in an honest subscription to our doctrinal formularies."[1]

Value of the Confessions of Faith and Catechisms

During the period of his Philadelphia pastorate, Archibald Alexander, who had been somewhat influenced by New England

---

[1] Samuel Miller, [Jr.], *The Life of Samuel Miller* (Philadelphia: Claxton, Remsen and Haffelfinger, 1869), vol. 2, 513.

theological ideas, began to settle "more definitely in the direction of the common Westminster theology." His study led him to the conclusion that the Reformed writers of the sixteenth and seventeenth centuries had "pushed theological investigation to its greatest length, and compacted its conclusions into the most symmetrical method." By 1812, when he was chosen by the Presbyterian church as the first professor at its new seminary, Alexander had acquired a "reputation as a theologian of original and clear views and strict adherence to the Reformed tenets."[2] Of the Westminster Confession and Catechisms he wrote:

> We venerate these standards, partly because they embody the wisdom of an august Synod; because they come down to us associated with the memory and faith of saints and martyrs and embalmed with their blood; but we love them most of all because they contain the truth of God—that truth which forms the foundation of our hopes. As our fathers prized them, and we prize them, so may our children and our children's children love and preserve them.[3]

To ensure that Presbyterian children knew the teachings of the Westminster Confession, the Princetonians urged careful and regular use of the catechisms by parents and pastors. Ashbel Green—one of Princeton Seminary's "founders" and for thirty-six years president of its board of directors—systematically taught the catechism to the children of his Philadelphia congregation. Dr. Green believed that "a thorough acquaintance with the Shorter Catechism should form an indispensable part" of the Sunday school plan of the church. When the children of Second Presbyterian memorized answers to the Shorter Catechism, they joined a Bible class that met weekly in the pastor's study. The older children received instruction from Dr. Green's series of lectures on the Shorter Catechism. Later these lectures appeared

---

[2] James W. Alexander, *The Life of Archibald Alexander* (New York: Charles Scribner, 1854), 295; A. A. Hodge, *The Life of Charles Hodge* (New York: Charles Scribner's Sons, 1880), 47, 48

[3] *Biblical Repertory and Princeton Review* (1843), 586.

in the *Christian Advocate*, which Green edited, and were published in two volumes (916 pages) by the Presbyterian Board of Publication, with the title *Lectures on the Shorter Catechism of the Presbyterian Church in the United States of America Addressed to Youth*.[4]

Reviewing Dr. Green's Lectures on the Shorter Catechism, Archibald Alexander urged that every Presbyterian family have at least one copy of Green's book. Dr. Alexander noted that "creeds and catechisms, so highly appreciated by our ancestors, are in danger of being cast aside like old-fashioned furniture, which is too cumbersome for modern use." He urged parents to regularly catechize their children from their youngest days on, taking "great pains . . . to explain the doctrines in the catechism and to illustrate them in a way adapted to [children's] capacity." The secret of catechizing, Alexander added, was to give "a little at a time, and often repeated." Children who memorize the catechism acquire "a treasure which may be to them of more value than silver or gold," the Princeton professor stated. It will enable them to understand sermons and religious books better than other people do and will equip them to "obey the apostle's exhortation, 'Prove all things, hold fast that which is good.'"[5]

The Princeton professors, from Archibald Alexander to Gresham Machen, learned the catechisms as children—"an educational process of priceless value," according to Charles Hodge. Hodge explained:

> The principles of moral and religious truth contained in that sublime symbol [the Westminster Catechism], when once imbedded in the mind, enlarge, sustain, and illuminate it for all time. . . . A series of such precise, accurate, luminous propositions, inscribed on the

---

[4] Ashbel Green ended his second volume with the comment that the Lord had spared and strengthened him to complete "this laborious undertaking," which may be, he added, "the most important . . . of my ministerial life" (vol. 2, 469).

[5] *Biblical Repertory and Theological Review* (1830), 300, 304, 305.

understanding of a child, is the richest inheritance which can be given to him. They are seeds which need only the vivifying influence of the Spirit of life, to cause them to bring forth the fruits of holiness and glory.[6]

The Princeton Seminary students were expected to be familiar with the Westminster Standards and to have memorized at least the Shorter Catechism. According to the seminary's Plan, written by Dr. Green, every student, before graduating, had to be able also to support the doctrines of the Confession of Faith and Catechisms by "a ready, pertinent, and abundant quotation of Scripture texts."

Samuel Miller, the seminary's teacher of church polity, was especially concerned to stress the importance of confessions. In 1824 the Reverend John Duncan, a Presbyterian pastor from Baltimore, was elected to the board of Princeton Seminary. On the day that he took his seat, Duncan preached a sermon before the directors, faculty, and students, in which he attacked creeds and confessions. Samuel Miller responded by giving the introductory lecture at the opening of the summer session on "The Utility and Importance of Creeds and Confessions."[7] Creeds and confessions, Miller said, do not claim to be in themselves "laws of Christ's house" but simply "a list of the leading truths which the Bible teaches." He answered a number of objections commonly brought against creeds—including the charges that they supersede the Bible, interfere with the rights of conscience,

---

[6] *Biblical Repertory and Princeton Review* (1855), 143, 144. Hodge is writing about Archibald Alexander's childhood experience of learning the catechisms.

[7] The lecture formed the basis of Miller's published work *The Utility and Importance of Creeds and Confessions* (Philadelphia: Presbyterian Board of Publication, 1824). It was revised, enlarged, and reprinted several times. Combined with another of Miller's works, it has been reprinted by Presbyterian Heritage Publications under the title *Doctrinal Integrity: On the Utility and Importance of Creeds and Confessions and Adherence to our Doctrinal Standards* (1989).

discourage free inquiry, fail to achieve their purpose, and promote discord and strife. A full confession, such as the Westminster Confession of Faith, Dr. Miller stated, was indispensable for harmony and purity in the church. He urged the students to "strive to promote" among their church members "a general and intimate acquaintance with our Confession of Faith and Form of Government and Discipline, as well as our Catechisms."[8]

Samuel Miller and the Princetonians did not see a contradiction between their wholehearted commitment to the Scripture alone as the source of all theological truth and their advocacy of a confessional statement. Confessions and catechisms, wrote Ashbel Green, "endeavour to provide for the maintenance of an orthodox scriptural creed; and yet they leave a full and complete opening for all real improvements in biblical learning and theological knowledge."[9] A major treatise on this subject appeared in the April 1832 issue of the *Biblical Repertory and Princeton Review*, written by J. W. Alexander, then pastor in Trenton, New Jersey, and one of the "association of gentlemen" responsible for the journal. Alexander argued for the propriety and necessity for "systems" in every department of knowledge. Sound philosophy teaches us, he wrote, "not to reject system, but to systematize wisely." Alexander, like all the Princetonians, championed the inductive method of Newton as set forth by Bacon, in which the scientist and the theologian "classify and arrange the fruits of their observation and gather from them new proofs of that general system which has previously commended itself to their faith." He asked whether or not, "in pursuing this method, it is absolutely necessary to reject all the results of precedent labours." His answer was: "The true light in which a system of theology should be viewed by one who uses it as an aid

---

[8] Miller, *The Utility and Importance of Creeds and Confessions*, 7, 8, 114.

[9] Green, *Lectures on the Shorter Catechism*, vol. 1, 26.

in scriptural study is as a simple hypothesis, an approximation to the truth, and a directory for future inquiries."[10]

The Princeton professors taught and defended the Westminster Standards. Archibald Alexander Hodge, Charles Hodge's son who came to Princeton Seminary in 1877 to assist his father in teaching theology, published the first edition of his *Commentary on the Confession of Faith* in 1869. It became one of the standard expositions of the Westminster Confession.[11] Alexander McGill's lectures on church government, published in 1888, set forth his views of polity based on "the Bible as interpreted by Westminster literature of the seventeenth century."[12]

Benjamin Breckinridge Warfield wrote numerous scholarly and popular articles expounding and defending the Westminster Confession of Faith. Some of these writings were collected in the volume entitled *The Westminster Assembly and its Work*.[13] This book contains Warfield's masterful treatment of the history and work of the assembly and his invaluable survey of the printing of the Westminster Confession. In weighty articles on "The Westminster Doctrine of Holy Scripture" and "The Doctrine of Inspiration of the Westminster Divines," Dr. Warfield—against Charles Briggs and others who were attempting to capture the Westminster divines for their critical view of Scripture—showed

---

[10] *Biblical Repertory and Theological Review* (1832), 179, 184, 185, 187.

[11] The introduction to The Banner of Truth Trust reprint, *The Confession of Faith: A Handbook of Christian Doctrine Expounding the Westminster Confession* (1958), states: "This book provides probably the finest concise exposition of the greatest systematic Confession of Faith in the English language" (xii, xiii).

[12] Alexander T. McGill, *Church Government: A Treatise Compiled from His Lectures in Theological Seminaries* (Philadelphia: Presbyterian Board of Publication and Sabbath-School Work, 1888).

[13] B. B. Warfield, *The Westminster Assembly and its Work* (New York: Oxford University Press, 1931). This volume was reprinted in 1972 by Mack Publishing Company and in 1981 by Baker Book House.

that the Confession of Faith taught that the vernacular translations competently transmitted the Word of God for all practical purposes; that the transmitted text of the originals has been kept so pure as to retain full authoritativeness in all controversies of religion; and that the original text itself was "immediately inspired of God"—a technical expression in common theological use at the time of the Westminster divines, by which the idea of divine authorship, in the highest sense of the word, was conveyed. Warfield's article on the Westminster divines and inspiration included an exhaustive survey of the writings on scripture by John Lightfoot—"probably the greatest Biblical scholar that took any large part in the discussions of the Assembly." Warfield concluded:

> Here we may bring our study of Lightfoot to a close. It is perfectly evident that his fundamental conception of Scripture was that it is the Book of God, the "dictates of the Holy Spirit," of every part and every element of which—its words and its very letters—God is Himself the responsible author. It is perfectly evident that he would have considered it blasphemy to say that there is anything in it—in the way of falseness of statement, or error of inadvertence—which would be unworthy of God, its Author, who as Truth itself, lacks neither truthfulness nor knowledge. It is perfectly evident, in a word, that he shared the common doctrine of Scripture of the Reformed dogmaticians of the middle of the seventeenth century. It is perfectly evident also, we may add, that his doctrine of Scripture is generally that of the Westminster Confession; and that he could freely and with a good conscience vote for every clause of that admirable—the most admirable extant—statement of the Reformed doctrine of Holy Scripture. It is a desperate cause indeed, which begins by misinterpreting that statement, and then seeks to bolster this obvious misinterpretation by asserting that men like Lightfoot, and Rutherford, and Lyford, and Capel, and Ball, and Baxter, did not believe in the doctrines of verbal inspiration and the inerrancy of Scripture. If they did not believe in these doctrines, human language is incapable of expressing belief in doctrines. Is it not a pity that men are not content with corrupting our doctrines, but must also corrupt our history?[14]

Other writings of Dr. Warfield on the Westminster Standards are found in the two volumes of *Selected Shorter Writings of*

---

[14] Warfield, *The Westminster Assembly and its Work*, 332, 333.

Benjamin B. Warfield. These include his powerful statement of "The Significance of the Confessional Doctrine of the Decree" and his moving answer to the question "Is the Shorter Catechism Worthwhile?"[15] On November 8, 1897, Dr. Warfield made one of his rare trips from Princeton to speak to the Presbytery of New York on the occasion of the celebration of the 250th anniversary of the completion of the Westminster Standards. He declared that "in these forms of words we possess the most complete, the most fully elaborated and carefully guarded, the most perfect, and the most vital expression that has ever been framed by the hand of man, of all that enters into what we call evangelical religion." "To read over a chapter or two of the Westminster Confession," he told the presbyters, "gives one fresh from the obscurities and confusions of much modern theological discussion a mental feeling very nearly akin to the physical sensation of washing one's hands and face after a hot hour's work."[16]

Dr. Warfield's Princeton colleague, New Testament professor J. Gresham Machen, upheld the Westminster doctrines in his battle with modern religious thought. In 1923 Machen wrote:

> Certainly the essentially creedal character of evangelical churches is firmly fixed. A man may disagree with the Westminster Confession, for example, but he can hardly fail to see what it means; at least he can hardly fail to understand the "system of doctrine" which is taught in it. The Confession, whatever its faults may be, is certainly not lacking in definiteness. And certainly a man who solemnly accepts that system of doctrine as his own cannot at the same time be an advocate of a non-doctrinal religion which regards as a trifling thing that which is the very sum and substance of the Confession and the very centre and core of the Bible upon which it is based.[17]

---

[15] *Selected Shorter Writings of Benjamin B. Warfield*, ed. John E. Meeter (Nutley, New Jersey: Presbyterian and Reformed Publishing Company, 1970, 1973).

[16] B.B. Warfield, *The Significance of the Westminster Standards as a Creed* (New York: Charles Scribner's Sons, 1898), 2, 22.

[17] J. Gresham Machen, *Christianity and Liberalism* (Grand Rapids: Wm. B. Eerdmans, 1946), 170.

Not only the directors and faculty but also the benefactors of Princeton agreed in their determination to keep the seminary committed to the Westminster Standards. The deed of May 5, 1843—when donor James Lenox transferred title of the new library to the seminary—set forth the requirement that Princeton Seminary permanently teach these doctrines:

> PROVIDED ALWAYS AND NEVERTHELESS and upon this condition that if at any time or times hereafter the said parties of the second part shall pass from under the supervision and control of the General Assembly of the Presbyterian Church in the United States of America now commonly known and distinguished as the Old School General Assembly and its successors, or if at any time or times hereafter the leading doctrines declared as the confession of faith, and catechisms of the Presbyterian Church, such as the doctrines of universal and total depravity, the doctrine of election, the doctrine of the atonement, the doctrines of the imputation of Adam's sin to all his posterity and of the imputation of Christ's righteousness to all his people for their justification, the doctrine of human inability and the doctrine of the necessity of the influence of the Holy Spirit in the regeneration, conversion, and sanctification of sinners, as these doctrines are now understood and explained by the aforesaid Old School General Assembly, shall cease to be taught and inculcated in the said Seminary, then and in either case the Grant and Conveyance, hereby made, shall cease and BECOME NULL AND VOID.[18]

In 1876 Alexander and Robert L. Stuart donated Stuart Hall to Princeton on the condition that the seminary remain under the control of the Presbyterian church and that the Old School interpretation of the doctrines of the Westminster Standards continue "to be taught and inculcated."[19]

Earlier Scottish emigrants Robert and Marian Hall gave $2500 to endow a scholarship at Princeton. When it was suggested that the scholarship be called the Hall Scholarship, Marian Hall replied, "I dinna wish my worthless name to be remembered after I am dead and gone, but I do wish to do something for the cause of

---

[18] William K. Selden, *Princeton Theological Seminary: A Narrative History*, 1812-1992 (Princeton: Princeton University Press, 1992), 39.

[19] *Presbyterian Encyclopedia*, 724.

true religion, which shall maintain the truth, as long as the Kirk shall lead, and, therefore, I wish the Scholarship to be named Ed." When asked for the meaning of the name, she said, "And dinna ye ken, young mon? E'en go and read your Bible." She directed the questioner to Joshua 22:34, in which the children of Reuben and the children of Gad called the altar at the Jordan Ed, "for it shall be a witness between us that the Lord is God." "I believe in the doctrines of the Bible, as expressed in the Confession of Faith, the Larger and Shorter Catechisms of the Presbyterian Church," said the old lady, "and I wish that the Scholarship be called Ed, as a witness between us and the Theological Seminary, that the Lord is God."[20]

During Old Princeton's history, the theological opinions of the church, including the Presbyterian church, shifted dramatically. What Ashbel Green, Archibald Alexander, and Samuel Miller set forth, and James Lenox, the Stuarts, and the Halls sought to perpetuate, B.B. Warfield and Gresham Machen fought to save. They did not win that battle in the Presbyterian church; but their writings, like the confession itself, refresh us with cool, clear water in contrast to the murkiness and tepidness of much of modern Christianity.

Subscription to the Confession of Faith

The Princeton professors were required by the General Assembly to subscribe to the Westminster Confession of Faith, the Catechisms, and the Form of Church Government of the Presbyterian Church, according to a prescribed and strictly worded formula:

> In the presence of God and of the Directors of this Seminary, I do solemnly, and *ex animo* adopt, receive, and subscribe the Confession of Faith, and the Catechisms of the Presbyterian Church in the United States of America, as the confession of my faith; or as a summary

---

[20] *Presbyterian Magazine* (1857), 24, 25.

and just exhibition of that system of doctrine and religious belief which is contained in the Holy Scripture, and therein revealed by God to man for his salvation; and I do solemnly, *ex animo* profess to receive the Form of Government of said Church, as agreeable to the inspired oracles. And I do solemnly promise and engage, not to inculcate, teach, or insinuate any thing which shall appear to me to contradict or contravene, either directly or impliedly, any thing taught In the said Confession of Faith or Catechisms; nor to oppose any of the fundamental principles of Presbyterian Church Government, while I shall continue a Professor in this Seminary.[21]

Samuel Miller set forth what remained the position of Old Princeton Seminary on the matter of subscription in his *Utility and Importance of Creeds and Confessions*. Miller held that "common honesty" and "Christian truth" made subscription "a weighty transaction, which really means what it professes to mean; that no man is ever at liberty to subscribe articles which he does not truly and fully believe; and that, in subscribing, he brings himself under a solemn, covenant engagement to the church which he enters, to walk with it 'in the unity of faith,' and 'in the bond of peace and love.'" If the "candidate for admission" agrees with the Confession of Faith "in all its fundamental articles" but not with some of "its minor details," he is to state to the presbytery "all his doubts and scruples, with perfect frankness; opening his whole heart, as if on oath; and neither softening nor concealing any thing." Following the traditional American Presbyterian approach to subscription, Miller explained: "If the Presbytery . . . should be of the opinion that the excepted points were of little or no importance, and interfered with no article of faith, and should be willing to receive his subscription in the usual way, he may proceed."[22]

Subscription became an issue during the 1830s as the "Old School" and "New School" parties within the Presbyterian church moved toward division. Old School leader Ashbel Green believed

---

[21] *Life of Samuel Miller*, vol. 1, 357.

[22] Miller, *The Utility and Importance of Creeds and Confessions*, 100-102.

that the major difference was that the "New School" allowed "a far greater latitude of construction" in its view of subscription to the Westminster Confession of Faith. Dr. Green stated that "in the Presbyterian church, at the present time, doctrines not in accordance with our public standards are freely promulgated, both from the pulpit and the press."[23] He began to push for heresy trials and, if necessary, the division of the church.

Despite their esteem for Ashbel Green and their love for the Westminster Standards, the Princeton professors refused to condemn those who in their opinion did not deny teachings central to the "system of doctrine" of the Westminster Standards. Charles Hodge explained in 1831 that two extremes concerning subscription were "equally to be lamented."

> On the one hand, there are some who seem inclined to give the phrase [system of doctrine] such latitude as that any one who holds the great fundamental doctrines of the Gospel, as they are recognized by all evangelical denominations, might adopt it; while on the other, some are disposed to interpret it so strictly as to make it not only involve the adoption of all doctrines contained in the Confession, but to preclude all diversity in the manner of conceiving and explaining them.

Hodge pointed out that those of the second persuasion regarded "those who do not in this sense adopt the Confession of Faith and yet remain in the Church as guilty of a great departure from moral honesty." This, according to Charles Hodge, was "an extreme and mischievous" view, because "it tends to the impeachment of the character of many upright men, and because its application would split the Church into innumerable fragments." "Such a degree of uniformity never was exacted, and never has existed," Hodge stated.

> The Confession, as framed by the Westminster Divines, was an acknowledged compromise between different classes of theologians. When adopted by the Presbyterian Church in this country, it was

---

[23] *The Spruce Street Lectures: by several clergymen. Delivered during the years 1831-2* (Philadelphia: Presbyterian Board of Publication, 1841), 14.

with the distinct understanding that the mode of subscription did not imply strict uniformity of views. And from that time to this, there has been an open and avowed diversity of opinion on many points, among those who adopted the Confession of Faith, without leading to the suspicion of insincerity or dishonesty.[24]

Hodge believed that he was one of less than a dozen ministers in the Presbyterian church who actually accepted every proposition of the confession, but that most ministers, not even Ashbel Green, could have subscribed under the strict view.[25]

Charles Hodge held that in subscribing to the Confession of Faith one professed to believe "the whole series of doctrines which go to make up the Calvinistic system, in opposition to the Socinian, Pelagian, Semi-Pelagian, Arminian, or any other opposite and inconsistent view of Christianity." But he also believed that "with respect to each of these several points, there are, and safely may be, various modes of statement and explanation consistent with their sincere reception." After hearing all the candidate has to say about his views, the presbytery has the responsibility of deciding whether or not he truly accepts the doctrines of the Confession of Faith. "And here the matter must be left," Hodge added. Although Hodge believed that "the great mass of Presbyterians" agreed with this view of subscription, he feared that "this is not the ground always acted upon with impartial fidelity. While some may be disposed to resort to the discipline of the Church to correct mere diversity of explanation; others seem disposed to wink at the rejection of acknowledged constituent doctrines of the Calvinistic system."[26]

In 1833, Samuel Miller contributed to the *Presbyterian* a series of letters on the growing crisis in the Presbyterian church.[27] Dr.

---

[24] *Biblical Repertory and Theological Review* (1831), 520, 521.

[25] *Biblical Repertory and Princeton Review* (1858), 686.

[26] *Biblical Repertory and Theological Review* (1831), 522-25.

[27] Samuel Miller, *Letters to Presbyterians on the Present Crisis in the Presbyterian Church in the United States* (Philadelphia: Anthony Finley,

Miller's first letter dealt with "Adherence to our Doctrinal Standards." Miller rejected both "absolute uniformity in the mode of explaining every minute detail of truth," which some advocated, and the acceptance of "all sorts of unscriptural opinion, except the extreme of heresy," which others apparently held. "If we cannot adopt some course between these ruinous extremes, and with a spirit of mutual affection and accommodation walk in it," Dr. Miller stated, "there is an end of our long-cherished union." The Westminster divines, added Miller, had minor differences among themselves; but they were "all substantial and sincere Calvinists, and framed the Confession in such a manner as that those who differed, in respect to these minor shades of opinion, might all honestly adopt it." Samuel Miller put the issue clearly before the church:

> And now, at the close, I ask, "What will you do?" The question is not, whether, in opposing erroneous opinions, you will patronize a system of "ultra" rigor, of inquisitorial strictness. This I have never approved, and have no wish to see applied. But the question is, whether you will honestly and with good faith maintain the system of doctrine which every minister elder of the Presbyterian Church has solemnly engaged to sustain?[28]

The Princetonians maintained their moderate and conciliatory attitude as the church moved toward division. "It is not enough that a doctrine be erroneous, or that it be dangerous in its tendency," stated Charles Hodge; "if it be not subversive of one or more of the constituent elements of the Reformed faith, it is not incompatible with the honest adoption of our Confession."[29] Princeton did not approve of the Hopkinsian peculiarities in

---

1833). Letters 6-8 were reprinted, under the title *Doctrinal Integrity*, by the Presbyterian Heritage Publications in 1989.

[28] Miller, *Doctrinal Integrity,* 75-77, 129.

[29] Charles Hodge, "Retrospect of the History of the Princeton Review," in *The Biblical Repertory and Princeton Review. Index Volume from 1825 to 1868,* 22, 23.

theology, but "none of the sober-minded among the Old School," A. A. Hodge wrote, "had ever deliberately regarded" the views of the Hopkinsians "as putting a man beyond the pale."[30] The more extreme New Haven theology, however, with its denial of the inability of fallen man, was another matter.

At the division of the church in 1837 the Princetonians without hesitation allied themselves with the Old School. Charles Hodge wrote his *Constitutional History of the Presbyterian Church in the United States* to show the continuity in American Presbyterianism with Old School views. He argued that "the terms of ministerial communion among us have been from the beginning and by the constitution of the Church continue to be, the real belief and honest profession that 'the system of Doctrine taught In the Holy Scriptures' is the one contained in the Westminster Confession of Faith and Catechisms."[31] Hodge's statements in his *Constitutional History* that appear to demand a stricter position than he advocates elsewhere must be interpreted in the context of his polemic against what he saw as the New School view of subscription to the essential doctrines of the gospel only.

Charles Hodge objected to the 1858 General Assembly's plan to produce a commentary on the Bible governed by the teaching of the Confession of Faith. While the confession is the rule controlling ministerial communion, Hodge wrote, it had never been made the rule for the interpretation of Scripture. Furthermore, he argued, agreement is not perfect even as to the Confession of Faith. "We could not hold together a week if we made the adoption of all its professions a condition of ministerial communion," Hodge asserted.[32] Hodge's comments were criticized by what he

---

[30] *Life of Charles Hodge*, 289

[31] Charles Hodge, *The Constitutional History of the Presbyterian Church in the United States of America*, 2 vols. (Philadelphia: William S. Martien, 1839, 1840); *Life of Charles Hodge*, 281.

[32] *Life of Charles Hodge*, 406.

called the "the Old School-press" as teaching the loose view that the standards were subscribed only in the sense of agreement with their substance of doctrine. Hodge set forth his position on the "Adoption of the Confession of Faith" in the October 1858 issue of the *Biblical Repertory and Princeton Review*. He stated that he had nothing new to say on this subject, having as long ago as 1831 expressed the views which he still held. Hodge once again asked what the Presbyterian church understands the candidate to profess when he receives and adopts the Confession of Faith as containing the system of doctrine taught in the Holy Scriptures. He suggested three possible answers. First, "system of doctrine" means "substance of doctrine." From the beginning of American Presbyterianism, Hodge argued, "the mind of our church has been that 'system of doctrine' in its integrity, not the substance of those doctrines, was the term of ministerial communion."[33] Charles Hodge had dealt in detail with his objections to this view in his *Constitutional History*.[34] Second, subscription means adopting every proposition contained in the confession. This, Hodge stated, was "a new rule of subscription," which would brand with infamy or exclude from the church hundreds of Presbyterian ministers who did not receive all the propositions contained in the Confession of Faith and Catechisms. Hodge added:

> There doubtless have been, and there still may be, men who would do all this, and in the mingled spirit of the Pharisee and Dominican, rejoice in the desolation they had wrought, and shout, "The temple of the Lord, the temple of the Lord are we." God forbid that such spirit should ever gain the ascendancy in our church. Let us keep our hands off of God's ark, and not assume to be more zealous for his truth, or more solicitous for the purity of his church, than he is himself.

This view of subscription, Hodge asserted, leads to other great evils. It hurts the conscience and "fosters a spirit of evasion and subterfuge." "The overstrict, the world over," Hodge asserted,

---

[33] *Biblical Repertory and Princeton Review* (1858), 672, 678.

[34] See *Constitutional History*, vol. 1, chap. 3.

"are the least faithful."[35]

Rejecting these two views, he set forth a third: "system of doctrine" is to be intelligently and honestly taken in its "fixed, historical meaning."

> It presupposes belief in all those truths which are common to all Christians, and those common to all evangelical Protestants, and embraces in addition all those special doctrines by which the Reformed or Calvinistic Churches are distinguished from the Lutherans and Arminians and other Protestants. This system is well known, and easily ascertainable; it is clearly taught in the Confession, and is professed by all who adopt this as the standard of their faith.[36]

"If we are not satisfied with this," Hodge concluded, "we shall soon split into insignificant sects, each contending for some minor point, and all allowing 'the system of doctrine' to go to destruction. If there is any dependence to be placed on the teachings of history, the men who begin with making the tithing of anise and cummin of equal importance with justice and mercy, are sure in the end to cling to the anise, and let mercy go."[37]

Subscription to the Westminster Standards again became an issue in the New School-Old School merger negotiations. In 1864 New School theologian Henry B. Smith, professor at Union Theological Seminary in New York, set out three conditions for reunion of the two branches of the Presbyterian church: a spirit of mutual concession, commitment to Presbyterian polity, and acceptance of the Westminster Confession, interpreted in its "legitimate grammatical and historical sense, in the spirit of the original Adopting Act, as containing the system of doctrine taught in the Holy Scriptures."[38] Smith believed that his church was closer

---

[35] *Biblical Repertory and Princeton Review* (1858), 685, 687-89.

[36] *Life of Charles Hodge*, 407, 408. The quotation is A. A. Hodge's summary of his father's view, expressed in his article of 1858.

[37] *Biblical Repertory and Princeton Review* (1858), 691, 692.

[38] Robert T. Handy, *A History of Union Theological Seminary in New York* (New York: Columbia University Press, 1987), 42, 43.

to its standards than it had ever been. Most Old School Presbyterians were convinced that the New School had indeed become more conservative theologically since 1837; but some, including Charles Hodge, opposed reunion. He did not believe that the New School brethren were heretical; but they maintained and practiced, he thought, "a principle and latitude of toleration" different from that of the Old School. While carefully repudiating a rigid confessionalism, as he had done in 1831 and in 1858, Hodge feared that reunion with the New School would commit the Old School to "a latitudinarian principle of subscription" that required nothing more than the acceptance of the essential doctrines of Christianity. In the July 1867 issue of the *Biblical Repertory and Princeton Review*, Hodge set forth again the three possible views of subscription, in order to illustrate "the principle of interpretation for which Old School-men contend." "We do not expect that our ministers should adopt every proposition contained in our standards. This they are not required to do. But they are required to adopt the system; and that system consists of certain doctrines, no one of which can be omitted without destroying its identity."[39] In a long list of three pages—beginning with the plenary inspiration of the Scriptures and ending with the final judgment—Hodge stated what he believed to be essential doctrines of the confession.

Henry Smith replied, in the *American Presbyterian and Theological Review* of October 1867, that the New School had "uniformly repudiated" the principle of subscription ascribed to it by Hodge and held a view precisely the same as the Princeton professor's. A. A. Hodge agreed with Smith. The 1885 edition of his *Commentary on the Confession of Faith* included an appendix with statements from Charles Hodge and Henry Smith "as to the sense in which the historical Presbyterian church understands entrants into her ministry to accept the 'Confession of Faith as

---

[39] *Biblical Repertory and Princeton Review* (1867), 505, 509.

containing the system of doctrine taught in the Holy Scriptures.'" These quotations showed, A. A. Hodge stated, that "the two branches of the Presbyterian Church are thus shown to have been perfectly agreed" on the matter of subscription.[40]

In their view of subscription the Princetonians avoided the extremes of overstrict intolerance and casual latitudinarianism. They championed the historic position of American Presbyterianism. They were faithful to the Westminster divines' understanding of theological confessions. And they set an example of a faithful and honest adoption of the Westminster Standards.

Revision of the Confession of Faith

The First General Council of the new Alliance of Reformed Churches Throughout the World Holding the Presbyterian System—meeting in Edinburgh under Free Church of Scotland auspices in 1877—revealed that most of the European Presbyterian and Reformed churches had already revised their confessions. Some American Presbyterians were anxious to do the same. They were especially unhappy with the Westminster Confession's chapters on "God's Eternal Decree" and "Effectual Calling" and wanted statements that placed more emphasis on God's love and on human responsibility.

Charles Briggs of Union Seminary in New York championed the revision movement in the Presbyterian church by appealing to the history of the development of the Reformed confessions. In an article in *The Presbyterian Review*, "The Consensus of the Reformed Confessions," A. A. Hodge claimed that the sudden interest in and appeal to the development of the Reformed creeds— "ostensibly for the sake of Presbyterian unity and evangelical truth" —actually masked heterodox impulses desiring to be "relieved from

---

[40] A. A. Hodge, *A Commentary on the Confession of Faith* (Philadelphia: Presbyterian Board of Christian Education, 1940 [1885]), 539-43.

the pressure of the old creeds" and evinced a cowardly "restlessness under the obligation of subscription." In a brief outline of the confessional history of the Reformed churches, Hodge showed that there was not an evolving, developmental pattern, as Briggs had argued, but an impressive identity, or "consensus."[41]

The 1889 General Assembly, meeting in Philadelphia, voted by an overwhelming majority to submit two questions to the 209 presbyteries of the church: "Do you desire a revision of the Confession of Faith? If so, in what respects, and to what extent?" This decision set off a paper war that was "unrivaled in American Presbyterian (and perhaps evangelical) history."[42] Princeton Seminary—especially B. B. Warfield and Francis L. Patton—led the conservative movement that opposed revision.[43]

In September 1889, Charles Briggs published his strongest attack on Princeton in his book *Whither? A Theological Question for the Times*.[44] He identified the confessionalist "betrayers" of Reformed orthodoxy by name—the Princeton professors, Robert L. Dabney of Union Seminary in Virginia, and his own colleague William G. T. Shedd. "It is the theology of the elder and younger Hodge," Briggs wrote, "that has in fact usurped the place of the Westminster theology in the minds of a large portion of the ministry of the Presbyterian Churches, and now stands in the way of progress in theology and of true Christian orthodoxy; and there is no other way of advancing in truth except by removing the errors that obstruct our path." In another place he asked

---

[41] *The Presbyterian Review* (1884), 269.

[42] Mark S. Massa, *Charles Augustus Briggs and the Crisis of Historical Criticism* (Minneapolis: Fortress Press, 1990), 77, 78.

[43] Thirty-two separate articles on confessional revision by Warfield are listed in *A Bibliography of Benjamin Breckinridge Warfield 1651-1921*, ed. John E. Meeter and Roger Nicole (Nutley, New Jersey: Presbyterian and Reformed Publishing Company, 1974).

[44] Charles Briggs, *Whither? A Theological Question for the Times* (New York: Charles Scribner's Sons, 1889).

rhetorically, "Will you follow Calvin or Dr. Shedd, the Reformers or the Hodges, Westminster theology or Princeton theology?" He claimed that the Princetonians and their supporters—the confessionalists—were not champions of orthodoxy at all but of what he called "orthodoxism." He described it harshly:

> Orthodoxism is unwilling to learn; it is haughty and arrogant; assuming the divine prerogatives of infallibility and inerrancy refuses to accept the discoveries of science or the facts of history on the pretense that [these] conflict with the orthodoxy of the standards, preferring the traditions of man to the truth of God.[45]

The October 1889 issue of *The Presbyterian Review* contained two articles on the revision issue. Philip Schaff, Briggs's Union Seminary colleague, supported revision, concluding his argument with these words:

> We need a theology and a confession that is more human than Calvinism, more divine than Arminianism, and more Christian and catholic than either; a confession as broad and deep as God's love, and as strict and severe as God's justice. We need a theology and a confession that will not only bind the members of one denomination together, but be also a bond of union between the various folds of the one flock of Christ, and attract the ungodly world, that it may be converted by the regenerating and sanctifying power of the everlasting gospel.[46]

John DeWitt, professor at McCormick Theological Seminary, was opposed to revision. DeWitt, who would come to Princeton in 1892 to teach church history, concluded by asking the following questions concerning the suggested changes in the confession:

> Will they remove great evils? Will they secure great benefits? Are they sufficiently valuable to overbear the strong presumption against the amendment of this most beneficent document, which, ancient as it is, is still instinct with a vitality so commanding? These, after all, are the important and determining questions. Deeply impressed by the considerations, which I have inadequately set forth in this paper, I expect to cast my vote in behalf of the Confession as it is.[47]

---

[45] Briggs, *Whither?* 7, 8.

[46] *The Presbyterian Review* (1889), 552.

[47] *The Presbyterian Review* (1889), 588, 589.

Caspar Wistar Hodge, son of Charles Hodge and New Testament professor at Princeton Seminary from 1860 to 1891, also opposed the revision movement. According to Francis Patton:

> It was not because he felt that in minor statements [the Westminster Confession] was incapable of improvement, but because he knew that our terms of subscription were liberal enough to remove every burden from the conscience of any man who heartily believed in generic Calvinism. He also felt, as others did, that it would be hard to arrest a movement after it had begun; and, moreover, that while older men might be satisfied with a softening of the harder lines of Calvinism, there would be no inconsiderable number of younger men who would be willing to see the Calvinistic elements eliminated.[48]

For B. B. Warfield, who declined to sit on the revision committee, it was "an inexpressible grief" to see the Presbyterian church "spending its energies in a vain attempt to lower its testimony to suit the ever-changing sentiment of the world about it." Warfield was not opposed to revision of the confession in principle. "If there is a call for revision at all," Warfield wrote, "it is obviously for even clearer and more precise definition, for even higher and more finished construction, than the Westminster divines have given us in their noble formulation of the truth." Warfield feared, however, that the committee was rejecting the demands made on it "for progress in the doctrinal statement of our orthodox truth in relation to our present-day needs" and was requesting "the Church to lower its voice in telling the world the truth!" "It is not a time in which to whisper the truth in doubtful phrases," he wrote, "but to shout it from the housetops in the clearest and sharpest language in which it can be framed."[49]

---

[48] Francis L. Patton, *Caspar Wistar Hodge: A Memorial Address* (New York: Anson D. F. Randolph & Co., 1891), 56, 57.

[49] *The Presbyterian and Reformed Review* (1892), 329, 330. Thirty-two separate articles by Warfield on confessional revision are listed in *A Bibliography of Benjamin Breckinridge Warfield 1851-1921,* ed. John E. Meeter and Roger Nicole (Nutley, NJ: Presbyterian and Reformed Publishing Company, 1974).

The first attempt at revision failed, but at the turn of the century a new movement to revise the Westminster Confession of Faith arose suddenly in the Presbyterian church. The 1900 General Assembly appointed a committee to draft amendments to the confession and to draw up a brief, nontechnical statement of the Reformed faith.

Once again, the Princeton faculty was opposed to confessional revision. Geerhardus Vos, professor of biblical theology at Princeton since 1893, argued that one of the gravest symptoms of the revision movement was its lack of serious appeal to scriptural authority for the confessional changes it advocated. Vos had the revision movement in mind when he chose for his address at the opening of the seminary in the fall of 1901 the topic "The Scriptural Doctrine of the Love of God." He warned that the new ideas would lead to "extravagant, unCalvinistic, unscriptural notions on the subject" and a confusion between God's "general benevolence" and his "special affection" for his own. He claimed that although in the period of its supremacy orthodoxy did not stress the love of God exclusively as was now the tendency, it did in those days appreciate more fully "the infinite complexity and richness of the life of God."[50]

B. B. Warfield feared that revision would mar and weaken the work of the Westminster divines. He was not impressed by the criticism that the Confession of Faith was deficient in not having a chapter specifically devoted to "the Holy Spirit and His Work." It was, "as a Puritan document was sure to be," already "very much a treatise on the work of the Spirit," he argued. "The sole reason why it does not give a chapter to this subject . . . is because it prefers to give nine chapters to it."[51] Warfield went so far as to tell the New York Presbytery in his address on November

---

[50] *The Presbyterian and Reformed Review* (1902), 1-37.

[51] *Selected Shorter Works of Benjamin B. Warfield*, vol. 1, 205.

8, 1897, that the Westminster Confession was "the final fixing in confessional language of the principles and teachings of evangelical religion." He believed that all subsequent attempts to restate the doctrines of the confession could only "repeat these older statements—which were struck out when the fires were hot and the iron was soft—or else fall helplessly away from the purity of their conceptions or the justness of their language."[52]

The General Assembly of 1902 acclaimed, but did not adopt as the creed of the church, the "Brief Statement" of the Reformed faith written largely by Henry van Dyke of Princeton University, whose father had been a leader in the earlier revision movement. The assembly transmitted eleven overtures dealing with confessional revision to the presbyteries—two new chapters, entitled "Of the Holy Spirit" and "Of the Love of God and Missions"; a declaratory statement which explained that Chapter 3, "Of God's Eternal Decree," was to be interpreted in harmony with the belief that God loves all mankind, and that Chapter 10, Section 3, which speaks of "elect infants," is not to be regarded as teaching that any who die in infancy are lost; and a number of textual modifications, such as dropping from Chapter 25, Section 6, the statement that "the Pope of Rome" is "antichrist." All eleven overtures were approved by well over the necessary two-thirds majority of the presbyteries.

While some saw the revision of 1903 as "a definite toning down of the Calvinistic emphasis of the Confession of Faith," Dr. Warfield—who had remained in opposition to confessional revision to the end—was surprisingly positive in his judgment of the "revision material."[53] The "Declaratory Statement," in Warfield's opinion, "reaffirmed" while it "explained" the third

---

[52] *The Significance of the Westminster Standards as a Creed*, 13, 25.

[53] *Selected Shorter Works of Benjamin B. Warfield*, vol. 2, 370-410. "The Confession of Faith as Revised in 1903" first appeared as a pamphlet published in Richmond, Virginia, 1904.

chapter ("Of God's Eternal Decree") and the third section of the tenth chapter (on "elect infants"). Eight doctrinal propositions are declared in the "Declaratory Statement" to be in harmony with the doctrine of the decree as set forth in Chapter 3 of the Confession. Warfield describes the statement as "the common Calvinistic response" to Arminian attacks on the doctrine of God's decree. He defends them with quotations from Calvin, Turretin, Edwards, the Puritans, the Hodges, Shedd, and Southern Presbyterian theologians. The "Declaratory Statement" also sets forth an interpretation of Chapter 10, Section 3, of the Confession. This section, it states, "is not to be regarded as teaching that any who die in infancy are lost. We believe that all dying in infancy are included in the election of grace. . . ." Warfield believed that this statement went beyond the teaching of the confession, which confined itself "strictly to the way in which dying infants are saved, without any implication whatever as to the number of them that are saved." The new teaching, however, Warfield believed to be "logically altogether hospitable" to Calvinism. It had been the teaching, he claimed, of "some of the best of Calvinists, and for the last hundred years by practically all Calvinists."

Two new chapters were added to the Confession of Faith— Chapter 34 ("Of the Holy Spirit") and Chapter 35 ("Of the Love of God, and Missions"). Chapter 34 is "a compact summary of the ordinary Calvinistic doctrine of the Holy Spirit and his work." The first section "merely repeats what the Confession has already said," but Section 2 is largely new and gives "a comprehensive statement of a great and distinctively Calvinistic doctrine" of common grace. The third section of the new chapter "evinces no great firmness or precision of touch" but manages, "even in its somewhat bungling way, to set forth . . . a very tolerable account of the progressive stages through which (in the Calvinistic view) a sinner passes as he is brought into the experience of salvation by the Holy Spirit." Warfield praised the fourth section of the new chapter that develops the doctrine of "the Holy Spirit in the

Church." He criticized the title of Chapter 35 "as not perfectly appropriate to its contents." "It is a development of the doctrine of the Gospel," he wrote, "which it very properly represents as originating in and proclaiming the love of God, and as issuing in missions." This chapter "incorporates into the Confession a rather full exposition of the doctrine of the External Call, sufficiently clear, calmly stated, and thoroughly sound."

The three alterations were made to the actual text of the confession. The omission in Chapter 22, Section 3 (of the single sentence "Yet it is a sin to refuse an oath touching anything that is good and just, being imposed by lawful authority") does not deny what the confession had stated, but simply leaves it an open matter. Chapter 25, Section 6, is rewritten in order to avoid calling the pope of Rome "'that antichrist, that man of sin, and son of perdition, that exalteth himself in the Church against Christ and all that is called God,' which does seem rather strong language," Dr. Warfield commented. The "remodeling" of Chapter 16, Section 7—the section in the chapter on "Good Works" that treats the works of the unregenerate—Dr. Warfield believed to be "a positively bad piece of work." The new section is neither "untrue" nor "unsound" but creates the suspicion that the determining motive for the remodeling may have been to avoid affirming that works done by unregenerate men "are sinful and cannot please God."

Warfield summarized his position:

> Certainly new doctrines [common grace, the external call, infant salvation, and the work of the Holy Spirit in the church] have been inserted into the Confession by the Revision of 1903; and we have no disposition to minimize the importance of these new doctrines. But there is something else that must be said about them also. These new doctrines are true doctrines—good, sound, Calvinistic doctrines, which taking their places in a statement of the Calvinistic system, simply expand it into greater completeness of treatment, and in no sense modify either it or any of the doctrines that enter into it.[54]

---

[54] *Selected Shorter Works of Benjamin B. Warfield*, vol. 2, 398.

Warfield and Princeton Seminary took comfort that the matter was settled and that "no doctrine has been touched, so the church stands just where it did before." Radical revision of the Westminster Confession of Faith was successfully resisted, but the danger was not over. In 1906 the Presbyterian church merged with the majority of the Cumberland Presbyterian Church, a denomination which had broken away almost a hundred years earlier in rejection of the Presbyterian insistence on an educated ministry and the Westminster Confession's "fatalistic" doctrine of election. Although the revision of 1903 did not move the Presbyterian church from its Calvinistic confessional stance, it apparently did help prepare the way for reunion with the Cumberland Presbyterians. The addition of the Cumberland churches strengthened substantially the growing movement in the Presbyterian church to understand subscription to the Westminster Confession in a "broader" or "looser" way. Dr. Patton and his colleagues at Princeton Seminary had opposed the merger with the Cumberland Presbyterian Church. Patton said, "It is more important than revision, far more important, for it is, in effect, not necessarily in intention, an indirect way of revising the Confession of Faith on radical grounds."

William B. Greene, Princeton professor of apologetics and Christian ethics, criticized what he called "broad churchism"—the tendency to regard church union as more important than church distinctions. By its indifference to truth "broad churchism," Greene wrote, is "a grievous sin, indeed, a direct insult to God." There would be no "revival of religion" in the churches, Greene maintained, "until there has been a revival of doctrinal instruction."[55]

"Broad churchism" became, however, more and more the direction of the Presbyterian church, further weakening the church's commitment to the Westminster Standards. Princeton

---

[55] *The Princeton Theological Review* (1906), 306, 313, 316.

Seminary's conservatives did all they could to prevent this theological and confessional drift. The church's constitution bound its ministers to teach and defend the Westminster Confession of Faith, they tirelessly pointed out. After solemnly subscribing to the Bible as "the only infallible rule of faith and practice," and the Westminster Confession as containing "the system of doctrine taught in the Holy Scriptures," it was dishonest for a Presbyterian minister to view the Bible as a collection of inspirational writings and the Confession as outdated. Gresham Machen urged the Presbyterian church to reaffirm "the absolute exclusiveness of the Christian religion" and suggested that those who did not hold to this conviction withdraw from its jurisdiction.

Dr. Machen objected to the "Philadelphia Plan" of church union and, during 1921, put forth his views in three articles written for *The Presbyterian*. The plan contained "great Christian truths," according to Machen, but omitted "not some, but practically all, of the great essentials of the Christian faith"—including "the transcendence and omnipotence of God, the deity of Christ, the virgin birth, the resurrection, the atoning death."[56] Its basis, Machen argued, was "couched in the vague language of modern naturalism." By stating that creeds were "purely nominational affairs," the "Philadelphia Plan," Machen wrote, "clearly relegated to the realm of the nonessential our historic Confession of Faith."[57]

The "Auburn Affirmation" of 1924 stated that certain doctrines held by conservatives were in reality "theories" that were not required for ministers in the Presbyterian church. In a "Counter-affirmation," Dr. Machen stated that the so-called "theories" of the "Auburn Affirmation" were not theories at all but "facts upon which Christianity is based and without which Christianity would

---

[56] Ned B. Stonehouse, *J. Gresham Machen: A Biographical Memoir* (Grand Rapids: Wm. B. Eerdmans, 1954), 306, 312.

[57] Ronald Thomas Clutter, "Reorientation of Princeton Theological Seminary 1900-1929" (Ph.D. diss., Dallas Theological Seminary, 1982), 111.

fall." The "Auburn Affirmation" really advocates "the destruction of the confessional witness of the Church," he wrote, "to allow interpretations which reverse the meaning of a confession is exactly the same thing as to have no confession at all."[58]

As the Presbyterian church moved to reorganize Princeton Seminary to silence its persistent conservative voice, Dr. Machen set forth the facts of the struggle in a booklet entitled *The Attack upon Princeton Seminary: A Plea for Fair Play*. Machen pled with the Presbyterian church to allow Princeton to maintain its adherence to "the complete truthfulness of the Bible as the Word of God," its commitment to "the Reformed or Calvinistic faith as being the system of doctrine that the Bible contains," and its insistence on a scholarly defense of the Bible and the Westminster Standards. That was not to be, and "Old Princeton" came to an end. Its influence and power, however, live on and encourage us to stand strong in our allegiance to the historic Calvinism of the Westminster Standards, which is, as B. B. Warfield wrote, religion come fully "to its rights in our thinking, and feeling, and doing."[59]

---

[58] D. G. Hart, "'Doctor Fundamentalis': An Intellectual Biography of J. Gresham Machen, 1881-1937" (Ph.D. diss., The Johns Hopkins University, 1988), 239.

[59] *Selected Shorter Writings of Benjamin B. Warfield*, vol.1, 392.

The Puritan Regulative Principle and Contemporary Worship

DOUGLAS KELLY

I approach this subject of the Puritan regulative principle and contemporary worship with solemnity, joy and humility. It is a solemn subject because true worship of the infinitely holy and inexpressibly beautiful Triune God is the highest exercise in which a human being can ever be involved. Kneeling at His footstool in submission and adoration we find our highest dignity and truest humanity. It is a subject to be approached with great joy as we think of the thrill and gladness with which our heavenly Father welcomes His returning prodigal son, and the gladness in the presence of the angels over the one sinful sheep who repents. Psalm 51 demonstrates the joy which follows penitence as David prays: "Restore unto me the joy of thy salvation" and Psalm 43 exults in God as "our chiefest joy." Shorter Catechism question one sums up this connection of putting the God we worship first and then discovering joy appositely: "Man's chief end is to glorify God and enjoy him forever."

We must speak of divine worship with solemnity and joy, but also with a strong dose of humility, for as St. Paul reminds us in 1 Cor. 13, "For we know in part and we prophesy in part. . . . For now we see through a glass darkly. . . ." (vss. 9, 12). That God is to be worshiped, all Christians agree on; how He is to be worshiped is another matter. And it is this more difficult and controversial matter as to HOW God is to be worshiped that we shall be examining together. And although it is inherently a difficult and controversial matter, I wish to do my best to approach it not controversially or censoriously, but with devotion and humility.

In many ways, possibly the greatest revival after Pentecost, the sixteenth century Protestant Reformation, came about as the Holy Spirit, through the rediscovered teachings of the Word of God written, answered the questions of longing hearts as to how a holy God may be approached by sinners who wish to be put in the right with Him and devote their lives to His worship and service. The Reformation was characterized by a burning zeal to be "put in the right" with God (or justified) so that the redeemed could then consecrate all their ransomed powers to glorifying God first in worship and then in every other area of life and thought.

The Reformation, of course, took place in a fallen world and therefore was not an idealistically golden era. How far to go in reforming all elements of traditional Medieval Catholic worship and practice was a question that would engage the best minds and highest energies of countless Reformers and their spiritual heirs for several generations. None of their spiritual offspring entered into this task with more faith, enthusiasm, intelligence and self-sacrifice than the British Puritans, our own ecclesiastical forefathers. The Puritans were working through questions of worship with heart, mind and soul from approximately the late 1550s (when Elizabeth I came to the throne) until the 1660s (when Charles II returned to the throne after the Commonwealth and by force of government excluded the Puritans from the Church of England).

It is to this period of biblical exegesis and theological thought that we must turn (while always keeping an eye on Calvin and the earlier Reformation) in order to think through the contemporary significance of the Puritan regulative principle.

At the very heart of the Puritan Movement was a determination to regulate worship and church government by the Word of God. In one sense they were merely carrying out what the earlier generation of classical Protestant Reformers such as Luther, Zwingli, Bullinger and Calvin had contended for over against traditional Roman Catholicism: that the Church—and all of life —are to be reformed in terms of the revealed will of God, and that this meant throwing off the human inventions of church tradition.

For instance, the famous and able protagonist against the Protestant Reformation, Cardinal Bellarmine, stated the issue quite clearly:

> The controversy between us and heretics consists in this—that we assert that all necessary doctrine concerning faith and morals is not expressly contained in Scripture, and consequently, besides the written Word there is needed an unwritten one; whereas they teach that in the Scriptures all such necessary doctrine is contained, and consequently there is no need of an unwritten word.[1]

Over against this elevating of church tradition to the level of divine authority, Martin Luther had protested at the Diet of Worms at risk of his life:

> Unless I am refuted and converted by testimonies of the Scriptures or by clear arguments (since I believe neither the Pope nor councils alone; it being evident that they have often erred and contradicted themselves), I am conquered by the Holy Scriptures quoted by me, and my conscience is bound in the word of God: I can not and will not recant anything, since it is unsafe and dangerous to do anything against the conscience.[2]

In a word, the early Protestant Reformers believed in the *sufficiency of Scripture*. They would have agreed with the words of the later Westminster Confession of Faith (composed long after their deaths in the late 1640s) that: "The whole counsel of God,

---

[1] Bellarimine, De V. D., lib.iv, c.2.

[2] Quoted in Philip Schaff, *History of the Christian Church*, (Grand Rapids: Eerdmans, 1969), Vol. 8, 601.

concerning all things necessary for his own glory, man's salvation, faith, and life, is either expressly set down in Scripture, or by good and necessary consequence may be deduced from Scripture: unto which nothing at any time is to be added, whether by new revelations of the Spirit, or traditions of men. . . ." (1.6).

John Calvin had said much the same in his *Institutes of the Christian Religion* (written in 1536 and revised until 1559):

> In his law the Lord has included everything applicable to the perfect rule of the good life, so that nothing is left to men to add to that summary. He did this for two reasons. The first is that he wants us to regard himself as the master and guide of our life. This we shall do if all our actions conform to the standard of his will, for in it all righteous living consists. The second is that he wants us to realize there is nothing he requires of us more than obedience. . . . We hear that God claims this one prerogative as his very own—to rule us by the authority and laws of his Word. . . . If we duly weigh this, that it is unlawful to transfer to man what God reserves for himself, we shall understand that the whole power of those who wish to advance themselves to command anything in the church apart from God's Word is thus cut off. (4.10.7)

A clear, one-sentence summary of Calvin's central concern in this matter is found in his 1547 tract, "The True Method of Reforming the Church and Healing Her Divisions." He simply says: "Let it, I say, be our fixed principle, that the voice of the Shepherd alone is to be heard, that of strangers guarded against and rejected."[3]

Calvin was particularly concerned about the innate tendency of the fallen human mind to idolatry. He spoke of the mind of man as an idol factory.[4] He believed that in the Roman Church this idol-making propensity of the human spirit had triumphed, and in so doing had corrupted the pure, apostolic worship of God with "human inventions" and had polluted and perverted the true

---

[3] *Selected Works of John Calvin: Tracts and Letters,* Edited by Beveridge and Bonnet (Baker: Grand Rapids, 1983 reprint), Vol. 3, 242.

[4] See, for instance, Calvin, *Institutes,* 1.11.8 and 2.8.17.

Gospel of salvation by grace through faith with unscriptural, and sometimes pagan attempts to establish works' righteousness. Hence, the only solution was to bring the entire church back to the voice of her shepherd, speaking in inspired Scripture. Thus, by avoiding the voice of corrupt man, the Lord alone would be heard, and so could reform His own church in accordance with His own Word.

Commenting on II Kings 17 and 16, Calvin summarizes his position:

> From this we gather that a part of the reverence that is paid to him consists simply in worshiping him as he commands, mingling no inventions of our own . . .we see how the Spirit loathes this insolence solely because the inventions of men in the worship of God are impure corruptions.[5]

The Puritans Go Further than Calvin

As we noted earlier, the Puritans were much like the original Reformers in wishing to liberate and reform the Church by the Word of God. But the Puritans also represented a development beyond the first generation of Reformers. Clearly Calvin had held that ceremonies in worship which obscure the Gospel and further superstition must be cut out. However, at the same time, he allowed some freedom in the ordering of public worship in terms of "subservient ceremonies."

He brings out this distinction in his tract "The true method of giving peace and of reforming the Church," as follows:

> But lest anyone should cavil and say, that we are too rigid in external matters when we thus expressly destroy all freedom, I would here protest to the pious reader that I am not now debating about ceremonies which are only subservient to decency and order, or which are signs of and incitements to that reverence which we pay to God. We are disputing about works which the mediators pretend to be pleasing to God in themselves, and by which they affirm that he is duly worshipped . . . if works undertaken by us without the command

---

[5] Ibid., 4.10.23.

of God are allowed to creep in and form part of divine worship and spiritual righteousness, the chief thing in religion is overthrown.[6]

It would appear that Calvin was prepared to allow rather more freedom in national churches arranging their patterns of worship than were many of the later Puritans. James I. Packer discusses this difference between Calvin and the Puritans, when he mentions ". . . Calvin's judgment that the second Edwardian Prayer Book of 1552 contained *multas tolerabiles ineptias* ("many bearable pieces of foolishness"), whereas the later Puritans were much less ready to tolerate set forms of worship such as the Anglican Prayer Book.[7]

Norman Shepherd also notes a certain difference between Calvin and the Puritans (in his discussion of the conscience clause of chapter 20.2 of the Westminster Confession of Faith). Shepherd writes:

> It appears, however, that the focus of Calvin's concern is opposition to the <u>imposition</u> of novel forms of worship, forms which as a matter of fact obscured the doctrine of Christ. It is not clear that Calvin was opposed to the <u>institution</u> of new forms of worship, assuming, of course, that these forms did not obscure Christ. Calvin writes, "there is a great difference between instituting some exercise of piety, which believers may use with a free conscience, or may abstain from if they think the observance may not be useful, and enacting a law which brings the conscience into bondage." (Calvin, *Institutes* 4.10.20).[8]

Shepherd adds (in his discussion of Chapter XXI.1 of the Westminster Confession of Faith): "The Confession allows no room for what Calvin calls the institution of exercises of piety

---

[6] Calvin, "The True Method of Giving Peace. . . .", 263.

[7] J. I. Packer, "The Puritan Approach to Worship," *Diversity in Unity*. Papers read at the Puritan and Reformed Studies Conference, December 1963, 4. This appears as chapter 15 of Packer's *A Quest For Godliness: The Puritan Vision of the Christian Life* (Crossway Books: Wheaton, IL, 1990).

[8] Norman Shepherd, "The Biblical Basis for the Regulative Principle of Worship," *The Biblical Doctrine of Worship* (Committee on Worship of the RPCNA, 1974), 49.

which believers may use with a free conscience. What is without scriptural warrant is forbidden [i.e., by the Confession]."[9]

There were historical/theological reasons for the Puritans' greater stringency on such matters. Because of the peculiar nature of the English Reformation under Henry VIII, many medieval Roman elements had been left unreformed in the church. During the persecution of the English Reformers under Queen Mary Tudor, who attempted to force England to return wholesale to Catholicism, many leaders fled to the Continent, where they took refuge with Calvinist churchmen and scholars. When these English churchmen could safely return home after the death of Mary, many of them brought an experience of a much more thoroughgoing reformation (as in Calvin's Geneva) with them. They set to work to apply a deeper, fuller reformation of the English church in terms of regulation by the Scriptures of every aspect of its life. In a sense, the main impetus of the Puritan movement comes into prominence at this time during the early reign of Queen Elizabeth I.

This is not to deny that there were already convictions of what would later be termed a Puritan nature even before Elizabeth's reign (as in the Bible translator, Tyndale, in John Knox, who served as chaplain to Edward VI—who forced some changes in the 1552 Prayer Book—and in Bishop Hooper, who had at great cost to himself opposed the usage of church vestments). But the major program of the Puritans to reform the entire church by the Word of God came into public notice during the early reign of Elizabeth.

As Principal Alexander Mitchell in his classical work on the Westminster Assembly brought out long ago, at the beginning of the controversy, there was not too large a distance between the Puritans and their opponents in the Church of England. He writes:

> The points of difference between the Puritans and those who fall to be distinguished from them in the Reformed Church of England seem at first to have been few in number, and of minor importance. . . . So

---

[9] Ibid., 50.

far again as concerned matters of worship and church polity, the only expression at variance with the principle of Puritanism in the Articles of the Church was the first clause of the XXth Article, asserting the power of the Church to decree rites and ceremonies. This clause was not contained in the corresponding article as framed in the time of Edward VI; and the Puritans strenuously contended it had been foisted in, somewhat inconsiderately, in the time of Queen Elizabeth.[10]

Hetherington, another nineteenth century authority on the Westminster Assembly, outlined these differences as they were brought out in the Anglican Convocation of 1562:

Six alterations were proposed [i.e., to the Prayer Book], to the following purport:—The abrogation of all holidays, except Sabbaths, and those relating to Christ,—that in prayer the minister should turn his face to the people, so that they might hear and be edified,—that the sick and aged might not be compelled to kneel at the communion, —that the partial use of the surplice might be sufficient, and that the use of organs be laid aside.[11]

The famous apologist for the Anglican "via media" compromise between Roman Catholicism and the Reformation, Richard Hooker, in Book V of his Ecclesiastical Polity (written in the late 1590s) argued strongly against the scriptural regulative principle of the Puritans. Hooker grounded his argument in the broad concept of divine law which is expressed in nature and discovered by man through the use of his reason. While Scripture clearly states what is essential to salvation, it does not definitely prescribe how God is to be worshiped (other than in the most general terms). The specifics of divine worship must be determined by man's reason in accordance with his particular culture and time. Man's reason comes to its highest expression in the state/church synthesis, which therefore has divine authority to legislate as to particulars in ordering worship. Scripture and church tradition are important elements in

---

[10] Alexander F. Mitchell *The Westminster Assembly Its History and Standards* (Philadelphia: Presbyterian Board of Publication, second edition, 1897), 3, 4, 5.

[11] W. M. Hetherington (Robert Williamson, ed.), *History of the Westminster Assembly of Divines* (Edinburgh: James Gemmell, 1878, 4th ed.), 23.

working this out; but, according to Hooker, they may not be pleaded as detriments to the national church/state leadership's deciding how best to worship God in their own time and place. In other words, as cultures change, the national leadership may appropriately adjust the worship in accordance with the underlying divine laws of nature, discoverable by reason.

The continuation of this controversy over reforming or "purifying" (hence the term "Puritan") the church led to an increase and clarification of the differences between Puritans and non-Puritans. The Puritans stated the differences this way. They (especially Cartwright and Travers) maintained that the non-reforming Anglicans were following Martin Luther's approach to liturgy in holding that "whatever is not forbidden in Scripture is allowed." On the contrary, the Puritans maintained that their regulative principle was based on the much stricter maxim: "whatever is not commanded in Scripture (or warranted by it) is not allowed."

It is much easier to state these two varying rules for regulating church worship and government than to decide exactly how to work either of them out! Indeed, some scholars deny that either of the two statements is an accurate characterization of Calvin, Bullinger and the other "High Rhenish" Reformers.

Hughes O. Old, in his recent book, *The Shaping of the Reformed Baptismal Rite in the Sixteenth Century* states:

> The Reformers did not intend to make a choice between 'what is not forbidden is allowed' and 'what is not commanded is not allowed.' Neither did the High Rhenish Reformers apply the principle of *adiaphora* the way Luther did. They appreciated Luther's point but they saw the problem in a different way. As Oaecolampadius formulated it in his defense of infant baptism, those questions about which Scripture does not specifically speak should be answered in a way consistent with the fundamental teachings of Scripture.[12]

According to Old, to Calvin, Bullinger, Oecolampadius and other "High Rhenish Reformers": "The principle of 'what is

---

[12] Hughes O. Old, *The Sharing of the Reformed Baptismal Rite in the Sixteenth Century* (Wm. B. Eerdmans: Grand Rapids, 1992), 283.

forbidden is allowed' as well as its opposite, 'what is not commanded is forbidden,' were equally unacceptable. They were determined to find a third principle, the reform of the church 'according to God's Word.'"[13]

Olds' observation that the Puritan regulative principle, encapsulated in the phrase: "whatever is not commanded or warranted by Scripture is forbidden" goes beyond John Calvin, is confirmed by J.I. Packer, who refers to Horton Davies' *The Worship of the English Puritans*:

> When the Puritans singled out some of the *ineptiae* of the *Prayer Book* as intolerable, when they challenged the principle that each church has liberty to ordain non-biblical ceremonies in worship where these seem conducive to edification and reverence, when they repudiated all set prayers, when they rejected kneeling in public worship, the Christian year, weekly Communion, and the practice of confirmation, they were not in fact reverting to Calvin, but departing from him, though as Horton Davies says, it is doubtful whether they realized this.[14]

But for the purposes of this paper, whether or not the Puritans realized they were going further than Calvin is not so important. As Packer rightly adds: "Even if they had realized it, however, it would not have affected their position; for their basic concern was not to secure Reformed solidarity . . . but simply to obey God's authoritative Word."[15]

Details of the Regulative Principle

Before we look at the historical details and theological ramifications of the Puritan regulative principle, it is appropriate to remind ourselves of the reason why the Puritans did go into such precise details about worship, and indeed, were prepared to go to war over such matters (as evidenced in the liturgical riots in

---

[13] Ibid., 102, n.77.

[14] Packer, *A Quest For Godliness*, 248.

[15] Ibid.

Edinburgh during the reign of Charles I). Unless we appreciate the heart of their concern, we may have little patience with them, and thus deprive ourselves of thought-provoking guidance for the worship of the church in our own day.

They were so concerned with worship because they were so concerned with God. Puritanism budded during a revival movement, an outpouring of the Holy Spirit, which gave them an immediate sense of the nearness, the holiness, the beauty and the grace of the Triune God. They had experienced for themselves the truth of the words of Jesus, that "this is eternal life, to know thee, the only true God, and Jesus Christ whom thou has sent" (John 17:3). Therefore, their priorities were truly scriptural. Everything less than God was secondary to knowing and serving Him aright. Worship was first; even the most legitimate concerns were second. If worship then was of such supreme significance, what could matter more than to do it in a way that would please God?

Another crucial element in the Puritan determination to have worship regulated by Scripture alone was their devotion to Christ "as the only lawgiver in Zion," or as the Scottish Covenanters would have it in the "killing times" of the 1680s, they stood "for Christ's crown and covenant." That is, they understood that Christ's direct and continuing authority as Head of his church precluded contemporary church government from overstepping its bounds and prescribing new laws for worship or government, which had not been laid down by the 'one mediator between God and man.' For Calvin that meant a continuing polemic against the false authority of the Medieval Roman Church to prescribe a plethora of ceremonies that obscured Christ, especially in the Mass and penitential system of the Church. Book IV of his Institutes fights this necessary battle valiantly, as do many of his Tracts and Treatises such as his 1539 "The Necessity of Reforming the Church."

Always Calvin's central concern in this polemic is that ceremonies which obscure Christ must be excluded. In *Institutes*

4.10.29, arguing against "the theatrical pomps that the papists use in their sacred rites," he states that "(For) ceremonies to be exercises of piety, they ought to lead us straight to Christ." When prescribed ceremonies do not lead to the Savior, they thereby obscure the Gospel and must hence be excluded.

A hundred years after Calvin, the great Puritan John Owen is dealing with the regulative principle in a rather different context. His "Discourse Concerning Liturgies and Their Imposition" was written in 1662, after some two thousand pro-Puritan clergymen had been forced out of the Church of England by the restored, High Church government of Charles II. Owen and the Puritans had paid a high price for their convictions: loss of manses, salaries, and freedom of assembly and speech. Indeed, his 1662 "Discourse" had to be published anonymously. Because they would not conform to the Book of Common Prayer (and the Episcopal system), their religious and civil liberties were severely restricted until after the "Glorious Revolution" of 1688.

The grief of this experience must be born in mind in assessing Owen's polemic against all set liturgies. While Calvin opposes ceremonies that obscure Christ, Owen opposes any set formulary for public worship (other than the preaching of the Word, singing of Psalms and extemporaneous prayer). Much of his argument against liturgies comes from their being (to use the word in his title) "Imposed"; that is, he sees any formal ritual as a civil or ecclesiastical imposition on the believer's conscience. This goes much further than Calvin. For instance, in chapter 3 of this "Discourse," Owen actually tries to prove that it is wrong for a congregation to pray the Lord's Prayer in unison, because it would be an imposition on the conscience. His reasoning here, I feel, is not up to his usually superbly high standard. (In my opinion, for what it may be worth, he employs in this chapter a sort of dispensational argument—unlike most of his covenantal thinking, as well as a strong element of atomistic individualism). Elsewhere, much of his argumentation is based on historical abuses that have accompanied liturgies (and certainly he has an important point here), but even so, I am inclined to say with Thomas Aquinas: "abusus non tollit usum" ("abuse does not remove use").

At any rate, while I may be wrong, I do not feel that either here in Volume 15 of his *Works* or in Volume 16 on "The True Nature of a Gospel Church," Owen has conclusively demonstrated that it is wrong to have an order of service with some set prayers (including the Lord's Prayer). Calvin, I think, is much more convincing in proving the necessity of excluding all ceremonies that obscure Christ. But more to our point today, nearly eighty years after the death of Calvin, and almost twenty years before the Puritans were forced out of the Church of England, the Westminster Assembly dealt with this question.

Probably the finest and most succinct statement of the Puritan regulative principle is given in three different places in the Westminster Confession of Faith (completed in 1647). The central formulation of the principle is found in chapter 21.1:

> But the acceptable way of worshiping the true God is instituted by himself, and so limited by his own revealed will, that he may not be worshiped according to the imaginations and devices of men, or the suggestions of Satan, under any visible representation, or any other way not prescribed in Scripture.

Chapter 20.2 looks at this matter of divine regulation of worship (and life) in light of the conscience: "God alone is Lord of the conscience, and hath left it free from the doctrines and commandments of men, which are, if any thing, contrary to His Word; or beside it, in matters of faith, or worship."

Norman Shepherd points out that "The semi-colon is essential to the thought,"[16] and John Frame calls it "an eloquent semicolon."[17] Both properly point out that the believer is given even greater freedom from lesser human authorities in matters of

---

[16] Shepherd, op cit., 48.

[17] John M. Frame, "Some Questions About the Regulative Principle," *Westminster Theological Journal* 54 (1992), 358.

faith and worship than anywhere else, because in faith and worship "We are free to reject not only what is contrary to Scripture, but also what comes from outside Scripture."[18] The distinction made by the semicolon is that in general human life we are free to reject what is contrary to Scripture, whereas in matters of faith and worship, we are free not only to reject what is contrary to Scripture, but also what is beside Scripture.

Confessional Modifications of the Regulative Principle

These two texts of the Westminster Confession therefore mean, in the words of William Cunningham, "That nothing should be introduced into the government and worship of the church, unless a positive warrant for it could be found in Scripture."[19] But there is a third text in the same Confession, which, as Cunningham states, constitutes an "obvious modification" of the regulative principle.[20] Cunningham saw this modification to be a necessary one, since "The principle must be interpreted and explained in the exercise of common sense."[21]

The text in question, chapter 1.6 of the Westminster Confession says: "The whole counsel of God, concerning all things necessary for his own glory, man's salvation, faith, and life, is either expressly set down in Scripture, or by good and necessary consequence may be deduced from Scripture . . . and that there are some circumstances concerning the worship of God, and government of the church, common to human actions and

---

[18] Ibid.

[19] William Cunningham, "The Reformers and the Regulative Principle" in *Historical Theology* (London: Banner of Truth Trust reprint, 1960), Vol.1, 64.

[20] Ibid., 65.

[21] Ibid.

societies, which are to be ordered by the light of nature and Christian prudence, according to the general rules of the word, which are always to be observed."

Two qualifications are implied here: first, one can logically deduce some proper element of worship through "good and necessary consequence," or in the words of John Frame, "from Scripture's implicit teaching as well as from its explicit teaching."[22] And one might well add here, that it has been the general historical Puritan position that a valid inference from Scripture is just as binding as a specific statement, as James Henley Thornwell contended against Charles Hodge in the mid-nineteenth century debates over the scriptural validity of church boards.[23]

The second qualification of the regulative principle concerns "circumstances . . . which are to be ordered by the light of nature and Christian prudence. . . ." Thornwell explained this second modification as follows:

> In public worship, indeed in all commanded external actions, there are two elements—a fixed and a variable. The fixed element, involving the essence of the thing, is beyond the discretion of the Church. The variable, involving only the *circumstances* of the action, its separable accidents, may be changed, modified, or altered, according to the exigencies of the case. The rules of social intercourse and of grave assemblies in different countries vary. The Church accommodates her arrangements so as not to revolt the public sense of propriety. Where people recline at their meals, she would administer the Lord's Supper to communicants in a reclining attitude. Where they sit, she would change the mode.[24]

But how to decide between what is "fixed and variable" or in other terms, how to decide between what is a commanded element and a changeable circumstance seems to be more difficult than one might assume from reading Thornwell at this point.

---

[22] Frame, op. cit.

[23] *The Collected Writings of James Henley Thornwell*: Vol.4. Ecclesiastical (The Banner of Truth Trust reprint, 1974), 255.

[24] Ibid., 248.

Cunningham is realistic about the difficulty:

> But even this distinction between things and circumstances cannot
> always be applied very certainly; that is, cases have occurred in which
> there might be room for a difference of opinion, whether a proposed
> regulation or arrangement was *a distinct thing* in the way of
> innovation, or merely a *circumstance* attaching to an authorized thing
> and requiring to be regulated. Difficulties and differences of opinions
> may arise about details, even when sound judgment and good sense
> are brought to bear upon the interpretation and application of the
> principle. . . .[25]

John Frame, in my opinion, is not overstating the case when
he comments on the difficulty of knowing what these
modifications to the regulative principle mean in specific cases.
"It appears that we must determine God's will for worship by the
same hermeneutically problematic methods by which we seek to
discover God's will in other areas of life."[26] He goes on to say
that these qualifications of the regulative principle made by the
Westminster Confession "entail areas of freedom analogous to
those we enjoy as we apply the word to other areas of life," and
shows that they serve "as a warning against applying the principle
in a wooden manner, such as by demanding specific proof texts
to justify worship practices."[27]

The difficulty of discerning the detailed outworking of this
principle in light of its modifications by the Confession helps us
understand both historical and contemporary differences among
Reformed believers in what they think is scripturally proper in
worship services. As Packer writes:

> On these issues, evangelicals would differ now, as the Puritans differed
> in their day. Baxter, for instance, like Calvin and Knox, approved of
> a liturgy with room for extempore prayer at the minister's discretion;
> but Owen maintained that "all liturgies, as such, are . . . false worship
> . . . used to defeat Christ's promise of gifts and God's Spirit." Which

---

[25] Cunningham, op. cit., 65.

[26] Frame, op. cit., 361.

[27] Ibid., 366.

was right? Here again is an issue which is not simple, and cannot be regarded as dead.[28]

Some Reformed theologians have maintained that the Puritan regulative principle excludes the use of musical instruments in proper Christian worship (as John L. Girardeau).[29] Others have held that the principle requires the exclusive singing of Psalms in Christian worship.[30] But the majority of Reformed Churches today, even those professing the Westminster Confession of Faith, do not agree that the regulative principle requires either non-instrumental music or exclusive psalmody.

Some followers of the regulative principle interpret it in such a way as to allow for the possibility of drama in worship as a circumstance or "mode" of preaching.[31] Others have argued that far from excluding the Christian year, a true view of the regulative principle allows Christians the freedom to observe holy days or not to do so, since "the Church has indeed a greater freedom in determining worship practices than was given to the Old Creation, precisely because the Spirit has come, we are in Christ, we have the fullness of revelation, and we have a greater access to God."[32]

Principal Cunningham is certainly right that "difficulties and differences of opinion . . . afford no ground for denying or doubting the truth or soundness of the principle itself."[33] He goes on to add that "The right course is to ascertain, if possible, whether or not the principle be true; and if there seem to be sufficient evidence

---

[28] Packer, op. cit., 248.

[29] John L. Girardeau, *Instrumental Music in Public Worship* (New Covenant Publication Society: Havertown, PA, 1983 reprint of 1888 edition).

[30] Good representative pieces are to be found in *Worship in the Presence of God*, Frank J. Smith and David C. Lachman, eds. (Greenville Seminary Press: Greenville, SC, 1992) .

[31] Frame, op. cit., 366.

[32] James B. Jordan, *Rite Reasons: Studies in Worship*, Feb. 1993 (Biblical Horizons: Niceville, FL), 4.

[33] Cunningham, op. cit., 65.

of its truth, then to seek to make a reasonable and judicious application of it."[34]

Here is the right place to pose this most basic question: is the Puritan regulative principle actually found in Scripture? If Thornwell is right concerning the trans-temporal nature of the Scripture, then we would properly expect it to address specifically how God's people are to worship Him to the end of time. If Christ is the continuing head of His church, then we do expect Him through the inspired writings of His apostles to have given sufficient instruction on ordering His house in worship and government.

Writers on the regulative principle have done serious exegetical work in establishing the canon that only what God prescribes (explicitly or implicitly) is acceptable in worship. Cunningham, Girardeau, Shepherd, Smith and Lachman, and Frame (in the works already referred to in this paper) mention scores of relevant passages, which clearly seem to teach this point. John Owen does likewise in "Discourse Concerning Liturgies," especially chapter 7, and John Calvin does so, particularly in *Institutes,* Book IV, chapter 10, and to some degree in chapter 19, as well as in "The Necessity of Reforming the Church" and "Reply to Sadoleto."

All of these theologians properly focus on the significance of the Second Commandment with its prohibition of graven images, and on such incidents as the death of Uzzah and Nadab and Abihu for tampering with God's clearly prescribed way of worship. They also emphasize the significance of Christ's once-for-all Lordship, and the sufficiency of Scripture, with the prohibition not to add to or take from the divinely imposed covenant words.

Certainly, it is difficult for me to see how anyone who cordially holds to the doctrine of Scripture taught in the Westminster Standards (which, I think, merely teach what the Scripture teaches about itself) would have a problem with the heart of the regulative

---

[34] Ibid.

principle. Namely, *elements* which are not prescribed by Scripture (i.e., either commanded directly or by good and necessary inference) are proscribed from the worship of God. The difficulty however arises with the *circumstances* of worship (or in Thornwell's terms, between the "variable" as opposed to "fixed" elements).

It is rather disappointing to find in so much that has been written on this significant distinction between element and circumstance or fixed and variable, a lack of careful discussion and a paucity of illustrations to help us distinguish the two. One has the impression that many who assert this distinction, fly from it as quickly as possible. Thornwell, for instance, mentions as a circumstance either reclining or sitting at the Lord's Supper, and quickly moves on (see Thornwell, Vol. 4, 248). Others illustrate "circumstantial" by referring to hours when divine service is performed, type of building or seating or possibly number of services a week, etc.

But the more difficult and important question does not seem to be addressed by most who draw this legitimate distinction. Are the following things fixed or variable (an element or a circumstance): the actual order of service, praying of the Lord's Prayer and other written prayers, recitation of the Apostles' Creed, and singing of the Doxology and Gloria? Undoubtedly John Owen deals with this in chapters 3 and 7 of "Discourse Concerning Liturgies," but most of the other works do not appear to answer this question. But, as we have seen, Cunningham—greatly to his credit—is very open about the difficulty of carrying through this distinction.

Perhaps as a way out of this difficulty, Professor John Frame has made the following intriguing suggestion. He proposes essentially two *different strains of worship* in Scripture bearing on worship, and that one of these firmly and plainly indicates the traditional understanding of the Puritans that what is not commanded in worship is forbidden as "will-worship'" (Col. 2:22f.). These passages require explicit and specific divine warrant for worship, such as Exodus 25:40, where God commands Moses to construct the tabernacle "according to the pattern shown thee on the mount."[35]

But Frame points to another strand of worship:

> Beside the tabernacle/temple worship, there is another strain of worship in the OT. On weekly sabbaths and feast days, God commanded the people to have "holy convocations" or "assemblies" (Exod. 12:16; Lev. 23:2ff., 7f, 21, 24, 27, 35ff.; Num. 28:18, 25f.; 29:1, 7, 12). We know very little of what was done at those convocations. Surely there is no revelation about them comparable to the detailed teachings about the tabernacle, sacrifices, and priesthood. . . .
>
> With regard to the tabernacle/priesthood worship, we might say [that the Puritan regulative principle] could have been applied almost without our first qualification ("good and necessary consequence"). For that kind of worship, God indeed provided a detailed book of commands, a sort of Directory of Worship. . . . But with regard to the "holy convocations," there is almost no specific revelation. . . . Apparently, God left these matters in the hands of the religious leaders, as those appointed to apply the broader commands of the word.[36]

Frame then goes on to make the fruitful suggestion that "This system of holy convocations, I would assume, was the ancestor of the synagogue worship. God's approval upon that system can be verified through Jesus' regular attendance at the synagogue (Luke 4:16). . . . But this is worship without a divinely revealed Directory. It is worship which simply applies the general principles of the word to various human circumstances."[37]

Specific Application of the Regulative Principle Today

As one who cordially holds to the continuing relevance of the regulative principle as to the elements of divine worship for all times, I wish to look at some of these elements and their circumstances in contemporary Reformed worship. I do not wish

---

[35] Frame, op. cit., 364-366.

[36] Ibid., 365.

[37] Ibid.

to avoid any important points just because it may be difficult to decide whether they are fixed or variable. Remembering "that we know in part . . . and see through a glass darkly," I am eager to admit at the outset that my answers may be partial or incorrect. But we have to start somewhere, and I am asking you to think through these matters with me. I shall welcome critique, suggestions, and further discussion. Only together can we approach such holy ground.

The One High Priesthood of Jesus

Foundational to the vital practice of scripturally mandated divine worship is the crucial biblical insight of John Calvin that we approach God always and only in and through the one Priesthood of the Lord Jesus Christ. Drawing on St. Cyprian's teaching that there is only one Bishop of the Church, Christ, and that all earthly bishops or elders merely participate in that one bishopric, Calvin thinks through this truth in terms of the one priesthood of Christ in which all true worshipers participate. Calvin particularly thinks through Christ's one Priesthood in his *Commentary on the Epistle to the Hebrews*, especially chapters 7 through 10, and he expounds what this means in his *Institutes*, Book II, chapters 9-11 and Book IV, chapters 14-17.

Let me attempt to collapse a few hundred pages of richest theological insight into a few lines. Christ is "the leader of our worship" (*Leitourgos*)—Heb. 8:2, "the minister of the true sanctuary which the Lord pitched and not man." In His incarnation, atonement and coronation, He has fulfilled and replaced the Old Testament priesthood, and abides as "the High Priest over the House of God." (see Heb. 9). This Christ is the sum and substance of our worship, its High Priest, its leader. Or put in covenantal terms, He fulfills the obligations of God towards us and of us towards God as Representative Head of the Covenant of Grace. As Christ "through the eternal Spirit offered himself"

(Heb. 9:14), so we still have nothing more nor less to offer in our worship than Him.

As Calvin notes in his Commentary on Hebrews 6:19, even as in the Old Testament, when the High Priest entered into the Holy of Holies, all Israel entered with him, so in Christ's priestly work "in the person of one man all entered the sanctuary together." Even as God accepted Israel in the person of the High Priest bearing the sacrificial blood to the mercy seat, so God accepts all true worshipers as His crucified, risen Son now represents them in the heavenly sanctuary. Our earthly worship only has validity because it is the counterpart of His heavenly worship. In worship, as in justification, sanctification, adoption and glorification, "we are accepted in the Beloved" (Eph. 2:6).

I quote here a few selection from Calvin's Hebrews commentary (using the old translation in the Baker reprint):

Commenting on Heb. 9:11 "of good things to come," he writes —"The meaning is, that we are led by Christ's priesthood into the celestial kingdom of God, and that we are made partakers of spiritual righteousness and of eternal life so that it is not right to desire anything better. Christ alone, then, has that by which he can retain and satisfy us in himself."[38]

On Heb. 9:13,14, he says—"Besides, he teaches us that nothing can proceed from us that can be pleasing to God until we are purified by the blood of Christ; for as we are all enemies to God before our reconciliation, so he regards as abominable all our works; hence the beginning of acceptable service is reconciliation. And then, as no work is so pure and free from stain, that it can of itself please God, it is necessary that the purgation through the blood of Christ should intervene, which alone can efface all stains."[39]

---

[38] John Calvin, *Commentaries on the epistle to the Hebrews* (Baker: Grand Rapids, 1981) 201.

[39] Ibid., 205.

On Heb. 9:18, he writes—"For the majesty of God is justly to be dreaded by us, and the way to his presence is nothing to us but a dangerous labyrinth, until we know that he is pacified towards us through the blood of Christ, and that this blood affords to us a free access. All kinds of worship are then faulty and impure until Christ cleanses them by the sprinkling of his blood."[40]

Finally, commenting on Heb.10:19, he says—(contrasting animal blood and the blood of Christ) "But the blood of Christ, which is subject to no corruption, but flows ever as a pure stream, is sufficient for us even to the end of the world. It is no wonder that beasts slain in sacrifice had no power to quicken, as they were dead; but Christ who arose from the dead to bestow life on us, communicates his own life to us. It is a perpetual consecration of the way, because the blood of Christ is always in a manner distilling before the presence of the Father, in order to irrigate heaven and earth."[41]

What joyful liberation such teaching brings and what rich praise it should inspire! One can fully appreciate Calvin's determination to cut out all man-made Medieval ceremonies, pomps and trifles which obscured the way home through such a High Priest, who ever lives to make intercession for us.

This insight is always the ground of vital, biblical worship in its every element and circumstance. The divine worship required of us (and provided for us in our Covenant Head) is not a human work; it is always the work of Christ for us and through us. This bears the closest relationship to the biblical teaching of justification by faith in Christ on the ground of grace alone. We are justified in Christ; we worship in Christ. Worship is not primarily self-expression. Rather it is the groaning, praising and interceding of

---

[40] Ibid., 210.

[41] Ibid., 235.

the Holy Spirit within us, taking us back to the One who sent Him to us on the basis of His finished work (see Rom. 8:14-17).

The nineteenth-century Southern Presbyterian preacher and theologian, B. M. Palmer, works out this insight of Calvin (and the Epistle to Hebrews) of our participation in the one priesthood of Christ in terms of prayer in his *Theology of Prayer*. In one place he insightfully speaks of the Holy Spirit (as in Romans 8) "re-echoing" inside of us the intercessions of our great High Priest in the presence of the Father.

This firm foundation then of our worship not being a human good work, but rather a gracious participation in the one Priesthood of Christ (through "the priestly Spirit" as the third-century Church Father, Hippolytus of Rome, called Him) is at the heart of all true worship. In my view, everything that we can say about elements and circumstances, things fixed and variable, is quite beside the point until we are clear on this. As long as we keep our eyes and hearts on Christ's one priesthood, I do believe that essential matters regarding the right ordering of His worship can substantially be worked out (though some not-unimportant differences are likely to remain amongst Christian until we see Him "face to face").

Even though Christ does not give us anything approaching a detailed worship formulary in the New Testament (unlike the Old), His apostles have certainly drawn back the curtain on their post-Pentecostal worship to let us behold its major elements. Acts 2:42 says: " And they continued steadfastly in the apostles' doctrine and fellowship, and in breaking of bread, and in prayers." From many other apostolic texts, we know that there were other elements of worship such as singing, baptism, offerings and vows. Let us now look at some of these major elements with an eye on Christ's priesthood, the regulative principle and today's situation.

Elements of Worship

The Reformation was perhaps above all else a recovery of the centrality of the preaching of the Word of God as the ordained way of converting the soul (Ps. 19:7) and building up the body in Christ (Eph. 2:15-23). The false way of salvation through participation in the mass as a meritorious repetition of the once-for-all sacrifice, together with the medieval penitential system and all the related "theatrical trifles" of worship (as Calvin calls them) had crowded out the preaching of the Word and deeply obscured the Gospel.

Dr. Hughes Oliphant Old has two outstanding chapters on the Reformational rediscovery and practice of preaching the Word: chapter 5 in *Worship* (Guides to the Reformed Tradition Series), Leith & Kuykendall, eds. (John Knox Press: Atlanta, 1984) and pp.194-202 on "The Lectio Continua" in *The Patristic Roots of Reformed Worship* (Theologischer Verlag: Zurich, 1970). And Professor John H. Leith's *The Reformed Imperative: What the Church Has to Say That No One Else Can Say* (The Westminster Press: Philadelphia, 1988) is of highest quality.

I quote one passage from Dr. Old's *The Patristic Roots of Reformed Worship:*

> One of the most prominent features of the worship of the Reformed Church has always been the preaching of the biblical books in course, that is preaching through a book of the Bible or a major section of a book of the Bible starting at the beginning and continuing through, chapter by chapter or even verse by verse, in such a way that the whole message of the sacred writing is presented in an orderly fashion over a series of weeks or months. Zurich, Basel, Strasbourg and Geneva all adopted the *lectio continua* at an early date in the Reformation and it is unquestionably one of the most clear restorations of the form of worship of the early Church.[42]

---

[42] Hughes Oliphant Old, *The Patristic Roots of Reformed Worship* (Theologischer Verlag: Zurich, 1970), 194-95.

The Rev. James Philip of Holyrood Abbey Parish Church in Edinburgh, a contemporary expositor of great note in the Church of Scotland, wrote a powerful article on exposition in the Reformation and today in a 1984 issue of *The Journal of Christian Reconstruction,* which I strongly recommend to us all. Perhaps the whole point of the Reformational insistence of the central of expository preaching has been best summed up by another Scottish minister, the Rev. William Still, who had been pastor of the same church in Aberdeen from 1945 to 1997 (yes, fifty-two years)! In his significant booklet *The Work of the Pastor,* he shows that the whole Christ is to be found in the whole Word, and that therefore our people need to be exposed regularly and systematically to all parts of Scripture. They will go astray, he argues, commensurately to the areas of biblical truth left out in our preaching. Thus Proverbs, Genesis, Haggai and so forth are all needed as well as John 3:16.

Without further comment, this should show that those of us who intend to be regulated by Scripture in our worship services must ever resist the temptation to base our preaching on anything but the Scripture or to shorten the time allotted for it in the service to such a degree that our people cannot have the various parts of it explained to them over the years, week by week.

The Sacraments

The Reformation considered the pure administration of the Sacraments to be one of the marks of the true church, as well as preaching of the Word and discipline. It is neither necessary nor possible in this already long paper to discuss the theology of the sacraments of baptism and the Lord's Supper. Gladly do I commend Dr. Old's chapters on these subjects in the books I referred to, as well as Dr. John Leith's *Introduction to the Reformed Tradition* (John Knox Press: Atlanta, 1978) and his *The Reformed Imperative.*

All I want to draw attention to here is the centrality of the two sacraments in Christian worship. Calvin eloquently shows (following St. Augustine) that the sacraments are *visible words*: another divinely appointed way of presenting the mystery (the Greek word *mysterion* is the word translated *sacramentum* in the Vulgate, from whence we derive "sacrament") of our union with Christ. Baptism is the sign and seal of our once-for-all incorporation into Him, and the Lord's Supper is the continuing sign and seal of feeding upon Him and being strengthened in Him. Calvin considers our participation in the sacraments to be a strengthening of the bonds of our union with our risen Lord, through faith through the operation of the Holy Spirit.

Once we understand what the sacraments are, therefore, we will immediately perceive that they are not optional extras added to worship.

We humans in the body need a visible, tangible word as well as the audible word of preaching. For that reason, Calvin wanted to celebrate the Lord's Supper every Sunday, though the Town Council of Geneva was not ready for this (and apparently we are still not ready, some 450 years later!).

Let me draw two contemporary lessons from the Reformation's understanding of the cruciality of the sacraments. First, it is disturbing to see some of our larger Presbyterian Churches in America decision not to celebrate the Sacraments during regular Sunday worship services in favor of placing them to a week night, where only Christians will be present, rather than unbelievers, who might find them strange and be made to feel uncomfortable.

Now let me make it clear that I am not trying "to take a dig" at true church growth, and I sincerely applaud every attempt to incorporate modern secular pagans into our worship services by rethinking what we do, why we do it, and how unbelievers will likely react to it. To think I am against growth through making every endeavor to bring in the non-churched would be to miss the precise point I wish to make here.

On the contrary, the pagans, as well as the Christians need to see visible words as well as to hear audible words. To cut out the sacraments from the services they attend will be to deprive them of something essential to the Gospel. Moreover, there is nothing wrong in showing them a line of demarcation between the flock and those who do not yet know the Shepherd. Indeed, in Scottish communion seasons (which are really the background of both Scottish and American colonial revivals), it has often been the administration of the sacrament of the Lord's Supper, which has been so attended by the effusion of the Spirit that multitudes have been savingly awakened. I would say to all pastors and church leaders: do not try to improve on God's appointed means of grace. Not only can you not do it any better than His ordained way, you cannot do it so well.

Secondly, the scriptural regulative principle in regard to both Word and Sacraments reminds us that the means of grace are truly sufficient. That is why Calvin cut out all other "theatrical trifles." Once you have tasted the real thing, who needs a paltry substitute? Thus we do not need in Reformed worship either images or dramatic presentations.

David Willis-Watkins of Princeton recently wrote these words which are as much needed by modern evangelical Protestants as they were by Medieval Catholics:

> Part of Calvin's teaching is just the orthodox understanding that God is immeasurable. . . . Calvin concludes that not only are depictions of God prohibited but there is no place in true worship for images of Christ, or of the saints, or of events that make up sacred narratives. Calvin does indeed make a distinction between images of God and images of other subjects; but that distinction is not sufficient for him to give a positive role to any images, *other than that of the living Word,* in worship. Any other images are false because they do not represent a reality; they are false because they represent an illusion, a deceit.[43]

This, to my mind at least, raises a serious question about the propriety of various sorts of dramatic presentations as elements

---

[43] "The Second Commandment and Church Reform: The Colloquy of St. Germain-en-Laye, 1562" in *Studies in Refomed Theology and History,* Vol. 2, No. 2, Spring, 1994: Princeton Theological Seminary, 40.

of a Reformed worship service. What Dr. Hughes Old says about the celebration of the Passover bears repetition here:

> An important part of the rite of Passover was recounting the saving acts of God which the meal celebrated.
>
> "And you shall tell your son on that day, 'It is because of what the LORD did for me when I came out of Egypt.'" (Exodus 13:8)
>
> The account in Exodus carefully provides the retelling of the story of God's redemption of Israel from servitude in Egypt. Three times the account directs that the father on the day of the feast is to tell his children the story of the deliverance from Egypt (Exod. 12:26; 13:8; 13:14). It should be carefully noted, however, that the father is to *tell* his son. Nothing is said about dramatizing the event. Nothing is said about redoing the Exodus in our day.[44]

I do not have statistics on this matter, but I wonder if the increase of dramatic presentations in churches may not be in direct proportion to the decrease of strong expository preaching and regular celebration of the Sacraments. As Augustine and Calvin have noted, the human heart longs for a tangible, visible word as well as an audible. To remove or play down either preaching or the Sacraments makes it all the more likely that what Calvin terms "theatrical trifles" will not be long in filling the vacuum.

By the same token, it seems to me that the introduction of incense into Reformed congregational worship is another "theatrical trifle;" a turning back to shadows, after the full-bodied reality has come in the one whose "rich wounds, yet visible above in beauty glorified" make all the offerings of our worship acceptable. As I contemplate the eclipse of serious expository preaching and regular administration of the sacraments by "theatrical trifles" of dramatic presentations and incense, I cannot think of a better practical argument for the continuing relevance of the scriptural regulative principle in contemporary worship.

---

[44] Old, *Worship*, 105, 106.

Prayer

I will say little about that essential means of grace and ordained element of worship: prayer. In passing I will say that you could do worse than reading B. M. Palmer's substantial *Theology of Prayer* or Calvin's *Institutes,* Book III, chapter 20. These texts have helped revitalize the personal and congregational praying of many ministers over the generations.

All I will emphasize here is that personal and congregational prayer is an aspect of our participation in the one Priesthood of Christ. Just the fact that we conclude our prayers "In Jesus' name" or "Through Jesus Christ our Lord" indicates something of surpassing importance: we do not pray in our own name or worthiness; we pray in and through the Lord Jesus Christ, "who ever liveth to make intercession for us" (Heb. 7:25). Romans 8 indicates how His Spirit literally prays within us, so that true prayer starts from the mediatorial throne, comes into the believer, and then goes back up to that throne with divine acceptance and power.

One other matter must be addressed concerning the public practice of prayer; a matter of much more concern to some of the Puritans than to Calvin and Knox. Must all prayer be extemporaneous? Is it against scriptural regulations to have set prayers which are read? It seems to me that the very Lord's Prayer itself indicates that set prayers are fully proper (and I have already indicated that I do not accept the arguments of Owen against its use in public worship). The Psalms are surely meant to be prayed as well as sung. God gives us the Scriptures as away of putting His own words into our mouths that He may the more readily answer us, thus shaping our intercessions in accordance with His will, which He always gladly does in His wise timing and fashion.

At the same time, I am in close accord with the Westminster Directory of Worship, which rather than giving us a written prayer book, instead provides elements that should be included in the minister's extemporaneous prayer. In sum, I think Dr. Samuel

Miller of nineteenth-century Princeton was right: there is a place in the public worship of God for both kinds of prayers, and certainly I would give preeminent position to the extemporaneous, and not seek to bind a minister's conscience to even a worthy ecclesiastical formulary.

The Church Year

Let me make a few brief remarks about the revival of the church year in modern Reformed Churches in light of the Calvinist Reformation and Puritan Movement (out of which our understanding of the regulative principle comes). Calvin believed that the old Medieval Church year obscured Christ and turned people from the Gospel with its emphasis on something like 150 saints' days or other ecclesiastical celebrations. The Calvinist wing of the Reformation threw out everything but the dominical celebrations of Christmas, Circumcision, Good Friday, Easter, Ascension and Pentecost.

The great Scottish Reformer, and disciple of Calvin, John Knox went further than that. When Theodore Beza (Calvin's assistant, and later his successor in Geneva) wrote to Knox seeking approval of the General Assembly of the Church of Scotland for the Second Helvetic Confession in 1566, the Assembly replied that they generally approved it with the exception of chapter 24. That chapter upheld these six dominical church holidays, and the Scots (including Knox) answered, ". . . that these festivals at the present time obtain no place among us; for we dare not religiously celebrate any other feast-day than what the divine oracles have prescribed."[45] The Puritans throughout Britain generally followed the stricter interpretation of Knox, and most American Presbyterians did so as well until the very late nineteenth or early twentieth century.

---

[45] John Knox, *Works* (New York: AMS Press, 1966), Vol. 6, 547-48.

Who was right: Calvin, Beza and the vast majority of twentieth century American Presbyterians on the one side, or Knox, the British Puritans and our own eighteenth and nineteenth American Presbyterian forefathers on the other side? I am personally unsure that the regulative principle gives a definitive answer one way or the other. Following a remark that Professor John Leith recently made, I would suggest that the missing key to the whole matter of bringing back more and more of the church year within Reformed circles is our having dropped our forefathers' profoundly biblical appreciation and practice of the Sabbath Day.

Our desperate need of recovering the Sabbath is much more pressing, I believe, than whether or not we do or do not encourage yearly celebrations of the dominical feasts. By giving up Sabbath observance for whatever reasons, we have unwittingly contributed to the quicker secularization of our culture, and have in so doing left a deep gap or vacuum in the spirit of both churched and unchurched people for some kind of touch with traditional transcendent realities. If Sabbath observance is of no real consequence to church people, then the world has yet another practical argument for the peripheral nature of God and the transcendent (an argument that used to be given every week by millions in the contrary direction). And more to our concern here, if we neglect a whole-hearted observance of the Christian Sabbath, the Lord's Resurrection Day, we do lose something of the transcendent: indeed, we lose a great deal of it in the very church itself.

Why fill in this deep, hurting gap with attempts at resuscitating ever more of the church year? Is there anything wrong with humbling ourselves and repenting of our abuse of the Lord's Day, and seeking to return to a happy keeping of it? I suspect that would make the currently popular bringing in of church seasons such as Advent and Lent quite superfluous. After all, these seasons were historically closely tied in to the Medieval Penitential System. Who needs them, when hearts and eyes of faith are turned Sabbath by Sabbath to our great High Priest, who through the power of His atoning blood and resurrection, continually presents us to the Father?

But even if the desires of my heart were granted in my own lifetime, that the Lord's people would once again delight to honor His day, still that does not fully settle the question of whether a vitally Reformed Church could celebrate such dominical holidays as Christmas and Easter. I personally think that there is something to be said for Calvin's celebration of these feasts, which are so closely tied to significant events in the Lord's life and ministry.

At very least, I fail to see why a minister is prohibited from preaching on Christ's birth in December, His passion and resurrection around traditional Easter time, and the Holy Spirit around Pentecost. As long as the various church seasons are not imposed on congregations, I do not think the regulative principle can properly be used to keep a minister from preaching on such subjects at such times (as well as at other times if he wishes).

A major proviso here would be to guard against the church year (or individual dominical holidays, which stretch beyond one Sunday) bringing in a sort of preaching lectionary, which prevents ministers from regular, sequential expository preaching throughout most of the year. In my view, lectionary preaching is better than disconnected topical preaching, but not nearly so good as systematic expository preaching through books of the Bible as the core of one's pulpit work.

In sum, many of you will appreciate Dr. Hughes Old's remarks on the church year:

> The recent efforts to bring back the celebration of the old liturgical calendar has suspicious similarities to a revival of the nature religions, natural theology, a cyclical interpretation of life, and the resurgence of the religions of fortune and fertility. One does penance in Advent when winter sets in and then one rejoices at Easter when the flowers reappear in the spring. It is all quite natural, but this fascination with liturgical seasons sometimes not much more than a revival of Canaanitism. One thing should be clear, the primary emphasis of any Reformed liturgical calendar should be the weekly observance of the Lord's Day. Very significantly, the seven day cycle of the biblical

week is not related to any of the nature cycles! The celebration of the resurrection is primarily the weekly celebration of the Lord's Day, not the yearly celebration, which in certain parts of the world is connected with spring. To drape the worship of any Sunday in penitential purple is contrary to the best our tradition teaches us.[46]

Singing

Scripture commands singing as an essential element of divine worship. The Reformation brought singing back from the Cathedral choir to the people of the congregation. All of Northern Europe experienced an outburst of joyful song as the Gospel was rediscovered. The primary songbook of both ancient and Reformed Church was clearly the 150 Psalms of David. Calvin preferred the singing of Psalms to uninspired hymns, although he did compose some hymns himself, and had the Apostles' Creed, as well as certain portions of Scripture outside the Psalms (such as *Mary's Magnificat* and Simeon's *Nunc Dimittis*) sung in divine worship.

We shall deal with only two questions here as regards singing and the regulative principle. First, is the church prohibited from singing anything other than Psalms? It is important to state unequivocally that Psalms should constitute the bulk of the church's praises. We evangelical Protestants have much ground to recover in this regard. I have been encouraged by the work of the Worship Committee of the Presbyterian Church in America, chaired by the Rev. Terry Johnson of Savannah, which has published the Psalms of David set to metre, with appropriate, singable tunes. This new Psalter, which is well adapted to our own musical culture, could help get people singing the Psalms once again.

The piety and strength that can come from Psalm singing will truly surprise you in its effects (not to speak of what matters most: the glory it will bring to the God who gave these Psalms in the first place, to inform His peoples praises). I lived for some four

---

[46] Old, *Worship*, 161.

years in Scotland, and regularly attended a church where the Scottish metrical Psalms were sung. Experiencing such praise has deeply shaped my inner life for the better all the years since then. It has been my hope and prayer to see the Psalms restored to our own American Presbyterianism ever since.

So you will not think, I hope, that I have a low view of Psalm singing. Nevertheless, I am not at all convinced that the regulative principle calls for exclusive psalmody. It seems likely that the New Testament itself contains fragments of hymns (some of them substantial), and covenantally speaking, after we have experienced the bodily reality of the Incarnate Lord, who was pointed forward to so eloquently by the Psalms, it seems proper that new songs should be forthcoming, which reflect the greater knowledge we have of Him, His names, person and work. That is definitely the case in the last book of the Bible, where they sing "the song of Moses and the Lamb." If the saints and angels are singing a new song above, could it be wrong for the believers below to sing new songs based on His completed work and continuing ministry?

Secondly, what about the accompaniment of church praises by musical instruments? Calvin disapproved of organs, as he mentions in one of his sermons on 2 Samuel and in several other places, and the Puritans followed him in this. The great Calvinist theologian and saint of nineteenth century South Carolina, John L. Girardeau wrote an entire volume against the use of musical instruments in Christian worship. As greatly as I admire and follow the teachings of Dr. Girardeau, I think that here (though not elsewhere), he employs a basically dispensational argument to cut out instruments from New Testament worship.

He says that instruments were connected with temple worship, and, that now since the temple has passed away and been replaced by Christ, instruments, which were an accompaniment of that older order of worship have also passed away. I do not think there is that much clear-cut discontinuity between Old and New Testaments for one matter, and secondly, what do we make of the prominent use of instruments in the heavenly worship in the New Testament book of Revelation? If the church above uses instruments, why is it wrong for the church below to do so?

Whether we employ instruments or not, these remarks of Calvin in his preface to the Genevan Psalter of 1542 will be appropriate in every worship service:

> And in truth, we know through experience, that singing has a grand force and vigor in moving and inflaming the hearts of men to invoke and praise God with more zeal and ardor. One should always take care that the music is not light and flighty, but rather has gravity and majesty as Saint Augustine tells.[47]

A truly systematic paper on the regulative principle in contemporary worship would need to cover among other things, the charismatic movement, and also art and dance, all of which I have chosen to omit because of space and time, and because I felt they would be of less concern than the topics I addressed. I would like to have covered more points and to have done so in much more detail. Nevertheless, if in any sense these thoughts have stimulated you to seek the face of God in order the more effectually to present yourselves and your people to the Father in your great High Priest as "those who are alive from the dead" (Rom. 6:13) and seated with the one you worship in heavenly places" (Eph. 2:6), then I shall deem my frail efforts well worthwhile.

---

[47] John Calvin, *Opera Selecta*, II, 15.

Westminster and Protestant Scholasticism

Paul Helm

"Scholastic" and "Scholasticism," at least when used of Reformed theology, are frequently terms of abuse. They imply degeneracy and deformation a theological fall from the purity of the creative theological genius of John Calvin. Those who charge the later generations of Reformed theologians with scholasticism do so in the spirit of Ecclesiastes 7:29 "God made mankind upright, but men have gone in search of many schemes." And the schemes allegedly searched out by the Reformed scholastics *are* many. They are variously accused of arid rationalism, of adopting a theological methodology which was deductive and foundational, based upon the divine decrees; of evolving a natural theology in the place of the revelational theology of the Reformers; of replacing Calvin's humanist-style warm, direct Christocentrism with speculative hair splitting; and of compromising Calvin's gospel of unconditional grace. Thus

> later Reformed writers are better described as philosophical, rather than biblical theologians . . . concerned with metaphysical and speculative questions.[1]

> With Perkins we can see, as with Beza, a more severe, more speculative and less biblical version of the doctrine of grace, lacking

---

[1] Alistair E. McGrath, *A Life of John Calvin*, (Oxford: Blackwell, 1990), 212.

Calvin's attempt to give it christocentric emphasis.[2]

Most of these charges are ill-defined, and some of them cancel each other out. For example, it has been pointed out by Richard Muller that the federal theology of later Calvinism, championed as a movement away from rationalism to a more biblical, historically orientated theological method, in fact was sympathetic to Cartesianism, at the same time that Cartesianism was being excoriated by high Calvinists such as Voetsius. So on the not unreasonable test of sympathy for Descartes, the allegedly non-rationalist federal theologians were rationalistically inclined, while those accused of being rationalists, the high Calvinists, were not.[3] Other charges of rationalism are clearly at odd with the facts; with the fact, for example, that some of the divines who stand accused of aridity reveal themselves as masters of experiential divinity. They then stand accused in court of another set of charges —introspectionism, legalism, preparationism, and much else.

Other writers on the Reformed theology of this period, without using the term "scholastic," have claimed to discern sharp discontinuity, and even a theological reaction, between the theology—particularly the soteriology—of Calvin and the Westminster divines.[4]

In the space of a short article it is not possible to address all these charges as they related to the Westminster Confession of

---

[2] Basil Hall, 'Calvin against the Calvinists' in *John Calvin* ed. G. E. Duffield (Appleford, 1966) 29. Quote by Richard A. Muller, *Christ and the Decree*, (Durham, NC: Labyrinth Press, 1986), 8. On this charge see Richard A. Muller "Perkins *A Golden Chaine:* Predestinarian System or Schematized *Ordo Salutis?*" (*Sixteenth Century Journal*, IX.I. 1978).

[3] Richard A. Muller, *Christ and the Decree*, (Durham, NC: Labyrinth Press, 1986), 7.

[4] See, for example, R. T. Kendall, *Calvin and English Calvinism to 1649*, (Oxford: Clarendon Press, 1979). For critical comment on Dendall's claims, see Paul Helm, *Calvin and the Calvinists,* (Edinburgh: Banner of Truth Trust, 1982).

Faith. The charges as they relate to Reformed theology more generally are in any case now being given a fair assessment in the literature. What I shall endeavour to do is to consider one or two of the most prominent of these charges as they relate to one prominent chapter in the Westminster Confession of Faith, Chapter Five, "Of Providence."[5] I shall evaluate the charge by a comparative study of the Westminster document, the writing of John Calvin on the theme, and the writing of one of the Westminster Divines, John Arrowsmith on the same theme.

I.

One of the most frequent and serious charges leveled against the later Reformed theologians is that they perverted the biblically based approach of John Calvin into a system which deduced certain Christian doctrines, if not all doctrines, from the divine decree. It is said that this perversion is signaled by the way in which Calvin, having treated providence and predestination together in the editions 1539-1554 of the *Institutes* later unceremoniously separates them. Calvin's discussion of predestination was moved about from one edition of the *Institutes* to another. It started, in the edition of 1536, as part of his discussion of the church, then became in 1539 part of Calvin's treatment of divine providence until it finally, in 1559, came to rest as part of Calvin's soteriology. By contrast, it is alleged, the doctrine of the

---

[5] According to B. B. Warfield the chapter "Of Providence" went through the hands of the Assembly of Divines in the following order. "On July 16, 1645, it was '*Ordered* — The first Committee to prepare the Confession of Faith upon . . . the works of Creation and Providence.' On November 27, there was 'report made from the First Committee about Providence.' It was debated November 28, December 2 and 4; and reviewed and ordered June 19, 1646. The Scriptural proofs were debated on January 28, 29 and February 1; and they were reviewed April 6, 1647." The chapter was debated in the House of Commons, October 2, 1647. (B. B. Warfield, *The Westminster Assembly and Its Work*, New York: Oxford University Press, 1931), 108.

divine decree takes first place in the writings of the Reformed scholastics, becoming of first, axiomatic importance in their work, a veritable theological *cogito ergo sum.* This fact has been alleged as evidence that Calvin was in no sense a scholastic in his theological method, though Richard Muller has provided a valuable service in showing that Reformed theologians of scholastic stripe varied considerably in their views about where treatments of predestination were to be placed.[6]

Why, in a piece on providence, entertain these reflections on predestination? The answer is that while Calvin's treatment of predestination occupies a fairly subordinate place in the final edition of the *Institutes,* his treatment of providence remains appropriately early, and remains noticeably predestinarian in character. According to Calvin there, all events are governed by the secret plan of God, nothing takes place without his deliberation, and God so attends the regulation of individual events that nothing takes place by chance. These are familiar points. But there is more. It has become customary to distinguish between providence and predestination, but here Calvin mingles the two. For in his treatment of providence thus early on in the *Institutes* he is unembarrassed by references to the church (e.g., 1.17.1), for God has a special care for his church "which he deigns to watch more closely," and it is only the believer who can make the proper use of the doctrine of divine providence.

So predestination is implied not only by the doctrine of providence itself, but also by the proper use of that doctrine. There is no reason, therefore, given Calvin's insistence that divine providence is *particular* providence, and given the place of divine providence in the structure of the *Institutes,* why providence/predestination could not have functioned as a single theological

---

[6] Richard A. Muller, *Christ and the Decree*, (Durham, NC: Labyrinth Press, 1986).

axiom from which all other doctrines are derivable more *geometrico,* should Calvin have chosen to adopt such a perverse theological method. There is nothing in the location of providence/ predestination in the system of the *Institutes* to prevent this use. We must therefore conclude that the place that a theologian chooses to give to providence in any systematic theology he writes is only contingently related to whether that person is or is not a scholastic in method, where this means "adopts a method of deducing all theological conclusions from one axiom." Whether there ever were such theologians is another matter, one that happily we can avoid considering here.

II.

The Confession's treatment of divine providence follows on from the chapters on God, God's eternal decree and His work as Creator. So there is a logical, natural order: each of the Chapters 2 through 5 presupposes the material of the immediately earlier chapter. But it does not follow from this that each chapter is *deduced from* the earlier material. The framers of the Confession sought to ground each of their assertions in the text of Scripture, while recognizing that in our thought about these matters there is a logical order. One cannot sensibly consider the decree of God without first establishing the existence of God, and his work of creation and providence is the unfolding of his decree. So if "scholasticism" means "deduction from an axiom asserting the eternal decree of God" the chapter on providence in the Confession is emphatically not a piece of scholastic theology.

But is the chapter scholastic in some other sense which reveals its degeneracy from primitive Calvinism? We shall attempt to answer this question by first briefly summarizing what the chapter on providence asserts.

To begin with, it maintains the theocentric teaching of the earlier chapters. Providence is an expression of the creatorship of God; the Lord governs the creation to the praise of His glory. All events, whether they are instances of laws of nature ("necessarily"), or of human choices ("freely"), or of unforseen happenings ("contingently"), or miracles (3), and including the Fall itself, are in the direct control of God. So the Confession asserts that providence is all-encompassing and particular; nothing escapes, nor ever has or can; divine providence is both microscopic and macroscopic in its scope. The wording of the Confession is emphatic on this point, for having stated that God "doth uphold, direct, dispose and govern all creatures, actions and things, from the greatest even to the least" (1) it goes on to stress (4) that this control, even where it extends to the "first fall, and all other sins of angels and men" is not a bare permission, "but such as hath joined with it a most wise and powerful bounding, and otherwise ordering and governing of them."

So God governs every minute particular of his creation, even the sins of men and angels, without himself being tainted by sin or approving of it. At the same time the wording of the chapter strongly affirms the responsibility and culpability of the wicked. The sinfulness of sin proceedeth only from the creature, and not from God (4).

The concluding paragraphs (5-7) make three practical applications of the doctrine set forth. The first asserts that the providence of God is not at odds with the fact that at times the children of God suffer. In his wisdom God by his providence may order suffering in order to chastise, to humble them, to increase their dependence on God and to make them more watchful. Similarly God hardens "wicked and ungodly men" by withholding grace and withdrawing gifts from them. Finally, and by way of summary, the Confession asserts (7) that while the providence of God extends to all, He takes particular care of His church, for whom all things are made to work together for their good. Far from presenting the doctrine of providence in an arid or a merely academic way, the divines strive to relate it to the practicalities of Christian life and experience.

So far we have seen that the treatment of providence cannot fairly be accused of scholasticism in that it is not deductive, nor is it dry and theoretical in temper. There is a further noteworthy feature of this chapter which marks it off from certain kinds of scholasticism in theology. At no point in their treatment of providence do the divines offer a *theory* of divine providence; an account of how it can be that God can remain pure while ordaining the minutest particulars of evil actions, or of how men and women remain responsible for their actions even though all they do is governed by divine providence.

Why is this? I suggest that it is because the divines, in their concise summaries of Christian doctrine, wished to adhere as closely as possible to Scripture. And because they could find no theory of providence in Scripture, no statement of how it is that God is both the governor or all things good and evil and yet remains untainted, and evil men are still responsible for those sins which God in his providence ordains, they did not offer a theory as part of the Church's public confession of faith. In this respect the chapter on providence may be said to be resolutely *a posteriori* in intent. The divines do not produce an a *priori* theory of divine providence which they impose on Scripture, but seek, by induction, to formulate such a doctrine from the canonical documents, going as far as, but no farther than they judge those documents to warrant.

This is also the reason why the chapter on providence cannot be thought of as scholastic in yet another sense, in the sense that it depends upon a natural theology, a theology arrived at by some generic appeal to what all men consider to be true or reasonable. It is certainly possible to attempt to build up an account of providence in this way, and the attempt has been made; in deism, for example. But there is not a trace of such an approach in the Confession. There is nothing, for example, that approaches the language of David Hume's *Cleanthes*

> Look around the world: Contemplate the whole and every part of it:
> You will find it to be nothing but one great machine, subdivided into

an infinite number of lesser machines, which again admit of subdivisions to a degree beyond what human senses and faculties can trace and explain. All these various machines, and even their most minute parts are adjusted to each other with an accuracy which ravishes into admiration all men who have ever contemplated them.[7]

There is no appeal to what is reasonable, to clear and distinct ideas, to natural light, or to what may be judged to be probable on the basis of human experience alone. Rather, in a way which no doubt some regard as tedious and hidebound, the compilers of the Confession seek to ground their assertions about divine providence on the assertions of Holy Scripture, and as a consequence they give prominence to the "unsearchable wisdom" of God.

Thus, in asserting that God orders all things to fall out according to the natures of second causes, either necessarily, freely, or contingently (2) the authors of the Confession cite Gen. 8:22 and Jer. 31:35 as proof of God's ordering of necessary secondary causes; Exod. 21:13, Deut. 19:5and I Kings 20:34 as his ordering of contingent secondary causes; and Isa. 5:6, 7 as his ordering of free secondary causes.

It is at this point in the chapter on providence that the only concession that is made in the direction of theorizing about divine providence, namely the use of the distinction between primary and secondary causes. As we have just noted according to the Confession God "ordereth them (*viz.*, all things) to fall out according to the nature of second causes, either necessarily, freely, or contingently" (2). Thus the Confession asserts that natural events and human actions are the secondary causes of what they bring to pass, while it implies (though it does not assert) that God is the primary cause. Is the use of the distinction between primary and secondary causes an evidence of scholasticism? Perhaps it is. Certainly the medieval scholastics used it. But if it is evidence of scholasticism then John Calvin is also a scholastic, since (as

---

[7] David Hume, *Dialogues Concerning Natural Religion*, (1779), Dialogue II.

we shall shortly see) he also uses the distinction in his elucidation of the doctrine of providence.

So far we have briefly surveyed some of the ways in which the Confession's chapter on providence might be said to be scholastic, and the reasonable conclusion is that it is scholastic in none of these ways. But there is one way in which the influence of scholasticism may be discerned. One of the characteristics of scholasticism in the medieval period is that it developed theology in a highly technical way; by means of question and answer, and the use of carefully formulated distinctions, and by the use of definition and argument, theological topics were carefully discriminated, and discussed with equal care. There is no doubt that the influence of scholasticism in this sense may be discerned in the chapter on providence. For in that chapter, as throughout the Confession, there is a premium placed on precise and economical turns of phrase. Central Christian doctrines are defended against many errors in few words. As B.B. Warfield judged the compilers of the Confession of Faith.

> The authors were men of learning and philosophic grasp; but above all of piety. Their interest was not in speculative construction, but in the protection of their flocks from deadly error. It results from the very nature of the case, therefore, that it is a religious document which they have given us. And the nicety of its balance in conceiving and the precision of its language in stating truth, will seem to us scholastic only in proportion as our religious life is less developed than theirs.[8]

So there is little by way of rhetorical flourish. Issues are stated —or rather understated—in a calm and concise way. In this sense —but in this sense only—can the Confession, including its chapter on providence, be regarded as "scholastic." But it is precisely as used in this sense that scholastic is a presentational matter rather than theologically substantive.

---

[8] "The Significance of the Westminster Standards as a Creed" in *The Selected Shorter Writings of B.B. Warfield,* ed. John E. Meeter, (Nutley, New Jersey: Presbyterian and Reformed Publishing Co., 1973), 662.

III.

Calvin's most significant teaching on divine providence is to be found in Book I of the *Institutes,* 16-18.[9] It therefore forms part of what Calvin refers to as our knowledge of God the Creator, and follows on from his teaching on the character of God, and the creation. Unlike the Confession, as we noted earlier, Calvin does not treat here of the divine decree, not until much later in the *Institutes.* Much has been made of this omission by commentators on Calvin who wish to emphasize the difference between him and later Reformed theologians. But it is easy to overemphasize this difference. Once it is appreciated that neither Calvin nor the Westminister divines intend to deduce their teaching on providence from anything than the text of Scripture, and that (as we have already noted) in Calvin's treatment of providence there are prominent predestinarian elements, then the significance of this fact is greatly diminished.

If Calvin may be said to deduce his doctrine of providence from anything (other than Scripture) it is from the omnipotence of God. He writes

> And truly God claims, and would have us grant him, omnipotence —
> not the empty, idle, and almost unconscious sort that the Sophists
> imagine, but a watchful, effective, active sort, engaged in ceaseless
> activity. Not, indeed, an omnipotence that is only a general principle
> of confused motion, as if he were to command a river to flow through
> its once-appointed channels, but one that is directed toward individual
> and particular motions. For he is deemed omnipotent, not because he
> can indeed act, yet sometimes ceases and sits in idleness, or continues
> by a general impulse that order of nature which he previously
> appointed; but because governing heaven and earth by his providence,

---

[9] But it is by no means the only place. One other significant source of information on Calvin's views on providence is his treatise *The Secret Providence of God,* written as a rebuttal of the views of Albertus Pighius (1490-1542), a Dutch Roman Catholic theologian. For a recent examination of Calvin's arguments in this treatise see Paul Helm, "Calvin (and Zwingli) on Divine Providence," *Calvin Theological Journal* 29, (1994): 388-405.

he so regulates all things that nothing takes place without his deliberation.[10] *(Institutes* 1.16.3)

Yet it is clear from this quotation that for Calvin providence is not so much a deduction from divine omnipotence as an expression of it. And in any case, divine omnipotence is not considered by Calvin as an abstract divine perfection, but its lines are drawn from Scripture. Later on he is clear that we should not draw our view of providence from *a priori* views of what God should and should not do.

> Hence it happens that today so many dogs assail this doctrine with their venomous biting, or at least with barking: for they wish nothing to be lawful for God beyond what their own reason prescribes for themselves. Also they rail at us with as much wantonness as they can; because, we, not content with the precepts of the law, which comprise God's will, say also that the universe is ruled by his secret plans. As if what we teach were a figment of our brain, and the Holy Spirit did not everywhere expressly declare the same thing and repeat it in innumerable forms of expression. (*Institutes* 1.17.2)

Such passages effectively rule out the idea that Calvin derives his view of providence from natural theology.

In *Institutes* 1.16.1-4 Calvin sets out his view of providence. It is all embracing control of all aspects of the creation, God's personal governing of his world, not to be confused with an impersonal fate (p. 207). Calvin proceeds to show that "God so attends to the regulation of individual and they all so proceed from his set plan, that nothing takes place by chance" (p. 203). He does so by considering, in order, God's providential rule over nature, over human actions, and over chance events. Let us glance at each of these in turn.

In the case of God's government of nature, Calvin emphasises that this is not partial or half-hearted, as if God sets up the natural order but that its seasonal and other variations are left outside

---

[10] All quotation from and page references to the *Institutes* are taken from the translation by F. L. Battles (London: S. C. M. Press, Library of Christian Classics, Vol. XX, 1960).

His control. Not only does the sun shine by the will of God, but when it burns, or when it is hidden these particular events are also from His hand. "Surely if the flight of birds is governed by God's definite plan, we must confess with the prophet that he so dwells on high as to humble himself to behold whatever happens in heaven and on earth" (p. 204). And miraculous events involving nature, such as the stirring of the wind that enabled the Children of Israel to cross the Red Sea, are equally from God's hand.

And what is true of nature is also true of human affairs. Quoting Proverbs 20:24 and 16:1, 9 Calvin says "It is an absurd folly that miserable men take it upon themselves to act without God, when they cannot even speak except as he wills" (p. 205) Even further, Calvin emphasises that events which are seemingly chancy and fortuitous are subject to the Lord. "Who does not attribute lots to the blindness of fortune? But the Lord does not allow this, claiming for himself the determining of them. Some events may seem to us to be fortuitous, without apparent rhyme or reason,

> But since the order, reason, end, and necessity of those things which happen for the most part lie hidden in God's purpose, and are not apprehended by human opinion, those things, which it is certain take place by God's will, are in a sense fortuitous. . . . As all future events are uncertain to us, so we hold them in suspense, as if they might incline to one side or the other. Yet in our hearts it nonetheless remains fixed that nothing will take place that the Lord has not previously foreseen. (*Institutes* 1.16.9)

In brief, Calvin recognizes, as does the Westminster Confession of Faith, that the providence of God extends to what happens by the necessity of nature, to miracles, to human choices and to seemingly chancy or fortuitous events.

Such providence does not relieve us of our responsibility. Though God ordains all events, including all human actions, it is nevertheless vain to attribute these to God in such a way as to evade responsibility.

> For he was has set the limits to our life has at the same time entrusted
> to us its care; he has provided means and helps to preserve it; he has
> also made us able to foresee dangers; that they may not overwhelm
> us unaware, he has offered precautions and remedies *(Institutes* 1.17.4)

In these ways does Calvin safeguard his doctrine of particular
providence against the charge of fate. God has not willed ends
irrespective of means, and has provided men and women with
powers and opportunities to effect certain ends. Yet even in the
exercise of these powers God's providence rules.

The final phase of Calvin's treatment of divine providence
concerns moral responsibility. Because human beings are responsible
for bringing about changes through their actions, they are responsible
for those actions when they are done wickedly. Though the wicked
carry out their nefarious doings by the providence of God,
nevertheless God is not himself tainted by their sin.

Is this because God merely permits their wickedness? No. In
language that the Confession was to echo nearly a century later
Calvin insists that the providence of God does not extend to the
wicked by a "bare permission."

> Hence the distinction was devised between doing and permitting
> because to many this difficulty seemed inexplicable, that Satan and
> all the impious are so under God's hand and power that he directs
> their malice to whatever end seems good to him, and uses their wicked
> deeds to carry out his judgments. . . . However, that men can
> accomplish nothing except by God's secret command, that they cannot
> by deliberating accomplish anything except what he has already
> decreed with himself and determines by his secret direction, is
> provided by innumerable and clear testimonies. *(Institutes* 1.18.1)

The fact that all things are controlled by God is a matter of
great comfort for the believer, who recognizes that both prosperity
and adversity are from the hand of God, and that the wicked are
in His hand.

> Therefore the Christian heart, since is has been thoroughly persuaded
> that all things happen by God's plan, and that nothing takes place by
> chance, will ever look to him as the principal cause of things, yet will
> give attention to the secondary causes in their proper place. Then the
> heart will not doubt that God's singular providence keeps watch to

preserve it, and will not suffer anything to happen but what may turn out to its good and salvation. *(Institutes* 1.17.6)

Note that Calvin here, as elsewhere,[11] uses the distinction between primary and secondary causes in exactly the way the Confession of Faith was later to do.

When comparing the treatment of providence in Chapter III of the Confession with that of Calvin in the *Institutes* certain differences are readily apparent. The Confession is concise and nuanced. Calvin has a more personal, direct and engaging style. The order of treatment of the various aspects of the topic is different. The Westminster Confession states the doctrine, denies that it carries the consequence that God is the author of sin, and then draws consequences of a practical kind. Calvin states the doctrine, then draws out practical consequences, finally safeguarding the doctrine from the consequence that it makes God the author of sin. But although the order of their treatment of the doctrine is different, as is the style, the doctrine itself is substantially the same.

IV.

So far we have compared Calvin and the Westminster Confession in direct fashion. Additional collateral evidence for the claim that there is no substantive theological difference between the Westminster Confession of Faith's teaching on providence and the earlier teaching of John Calvin, none, at least, due to the malign influence of "scholasticism," can be obtained in less direct fashion.

---

[11] "Nevertheless, that difference of causes, on which I have before dwelt, is by no means to be forgotten—that one causes is proximate, another remote. The careful observance of this distinction is indispensable, that we may clearly understand how wide a difference there is, and how momentous a distinction between the just and equal Providence of God and turbulent impetuosities of men" (*The Secret Providence of God*, trans. Henry Cole, in *Calvin's Calvinism* (London: Sovereign Grace Union, 1927) 251.

John Arrowsmith[12] was a leading Westminster divine. His *A Chain of Principles* contains a treatment of divine providence. Unlike either the Calvin or the Confession, Arrowsmith begins his treatment of divine providence from the fact that human life is a mixture of prosperity and adversity, and draws some lessons from this; for example, that God allows such a mixture to magnify His goodness, and to be known to be the Sovereign Lord of all persons and things (p. 389), and draws practical lessons for the life of faith in typically Puritan fashion.

Then, in the last aphorism of the work, he proceeds to discuss providence in a more formal way. "Providence extends itself, not only to all created beings, and to all human affairs, especially those that concern the Church: but even to the sins of Angels and men" (p. 400). This as we have seen, is essentially the same teaching as Calvin's and the Confession's. Arrowsmith proceeds to "demonstrate" these claims, this demonstration consisting of the provision of scriptural proofs. For example, the proposition that divine providence extends itself to all created beings is

---

[12] John Arrowsmith (1602-1659), a preacher at King's Lynn, Norfolk, was called to sit in the Assembly when it met in 1643, and was one of the committee of nine appointed to draw up a confession of faith, and later (17th June 1646) was added to the committee for "perfecting" the Confession. He was appointed Master of St. John's College, Cambridge, in 1644. William Hetherington states that following this appointment Arrowsmith attended the Assembly only occasionally. (*History of the Westminster Assembly of Divines),* Edinburgh 1878, 306). However, the Minutes of the Assembly record that he delivered the report "Of Justification and adoption" (11 and 12) which was agreed July 23, 1646 (*Minutes of the Sessions of the Westminster Assembly of Divines* edd. A. F. Mitchell and J. Struthers (Edinburgh and London: William Blackwood, 1874, 259) and that on Christian Liberty (289). While Master of St. John's (he was later to be Master of Trinity College, Cambridge and also Regius Professor of Divinity), he began to write a systematic theology designed in the form of thirty aphorisms with corresponding exercitations. Only six aphorisms and sets of exercitations were finished at his death. The work was posthumously published as *Armilla Catechetica. A Chain of Principles* (Cambridge, 1659).

demonstrated from Neh. 9:6 and a number of other texts. He then proceeds in a similar fashion to demonstrate the truth of the proposition that divine providence extends to all human affairs (p. 405), distinguishing between Economical, Civil, Military, Moral and Ecclesiastical affairs. These are treated in turn in the same way, scriptural proofs being adduced for each.

In Exercitation 2 God's providential care over the church is given the same treatment. The third exercitation concerns God's concurrence with sinful actions. "Divine providence is an actor even in sin itself. I shall single out hardness of heart, a sin common to all sorts of men, though in different degrees." (p. 438) Partial hardness may occur in the elect, total in the reprobate; in each degree of hardness "the providence of God is an actor" (p. 451). Arrowsmith goes into some detail as to how this can be. Among the ways he mentions are that God hardens hearts by "privation," and by denying his blessing, by permitting evil ("Although he frequently permit it, yet we must say he is not altogether willing to have it, however willing to suffer it" [p. 455]).

There is undoubtedly some development here, and in a way in which perhaps Calvin himself would not have altogether welcomed. For Calvin did not favour Augustine's idea of evil as a privation,[13] but Arrowsmith relies on that idea here. There is also a tendency to offer explanations of *how* it can be that God's providence extends to evil, a tendency that we saw was absent in both the Confession and in Calvin. For even where Calvin appears to intend to tell us how God's impulse comes to pass in men (as in *Inst.*1.18.2) he does so not by using a metaphysical idea such

---

[13] "I will not say, with Austine—which, however, I readily acknowledge to have been truly said by him—'In sin or in evil, there is nothing positive.' For this is an acuteness of argument which, to many, may not be satisfactory. I would rather assume another principle of argument, and say, 'Those things which are vainly or unrighteously done by man are, rightly and righteously, the works of God.'" (*The Secret Providence of God*), 233.

as the privative nature of evil, but by reaffirming the scriptural teaching (as Calvin saw it) that God works inwardly in men's minds.

Yet the significance of this use of the Augustinian idea of evil as a privation (a development [or degeneracy], as you prefer) ought not to be exaggerated. For in going into further, and perhaps questionable, detail as to how it is possible for the providence of God to encompass the evil actions of men, Arrowsmith is explicitly endorsing the doctrine of both Calvin and the Confession. For by his use of the idea of evil as a privation he could be said to be offering a gloss on 5.3 of the Confession, or on Book I, Chapter 18, of the *Institutes*. For what he is making use of here is not the scholasticism of natural theology, nor is he attempting to make deductions from the divine decree treated in axiomatic fashion, nor is he attempting a rationalistic reconstruction of the faith, but he is endeavouring by this distinction to gain further understanding of what he already firmly believes.

And what he believes, in common both with John Calvin and the Confession of Faith which he helped to compile, is that no event or action, not even the actions of the wicked, fall outside God's providential ordering.

V.

Although in the space available we have been able to examine only one chapter of the Confession of Faith, our findings are surely not without more general significance. For what we have seen is that there is no substance to the charge that, in this area at least, the Confession expresses a degenerate form of Reformed theology. It may be that the topic of divine providence is unique in this respect, and that the degeneracy which it escapes is present elsewhere in the Confession. This is possible, but not likely. It is more likely that what we have discovered when considering

Chapter 5 of the Confession is also true of the other chapters, making reasonable the conclusion that the Confession as a whole is an expression of Calvinism that John Calvin himself would recognize to be such.

Westminster Spirituality

David W. Hall

Frequently the claim that the authors of the Westminster Confession were spiritual giants is met with either looks of horror, disbelief, shock, or bursts of laughter. Sadly, few moderns are aware of the depth and breadth of spirituality in these divines. The unawareness of that is both our own loss, and due to no fault of the divines. The footprints of their spirituality are not beyond tracing out.

Perhaps only an age like our own—which so loathes so much of the past—would make this mistake. However, Christians will have broader horizons than the narrow confines of any single age and desire to benefit from the examples of any who have gone before us. Indeed, a perennial challenge is to identify mentors or those whose spirituality surpasses our own to emulate. I modestly suggest that we begin our search for such spiritual role models not so much with our own contemporaries as we are apt to do, but with some who may have superseded our own spirituality. It may be put this way: If we desire to imitate the best of orthodox spirituality, why not study the lives and practices of the best of Christians? Until we surpass the divines of Westminster in spirituality, or until our age on the whole possesses more innate spiritual vitality, until we find deeper and cooler wells of spiritual refreshment, why not consider the lives and spiritual disciplines of these divines to glean patterns?

If we find that they grasped things that we have not realized, or if perhaps their insights were deeper than the average contemporary Christian paperback, then there is no compulsion to cling merely to an unreasonable bias for the modern. Our century has shown us how dangerous that is. Jeremiah spoke of the "ancient paths" (Jer. 6:16) as those tried and trusted ruts of life, which rebels sought to overturn because they were routine. Indeed, some ancient Christian examples are preferable to many unproven modern ones. C. S. Lewis believed we could learn much from earlier works: "The only palliative is to keep the clean sea breeze of the centuries blowing through our minds, and this can be done only by reading [the old]. Not, of course, that there is any magic about the past. People were no cleverer then than they are now; they made as many mistakes as we. But not the same mistakes. . . ."

Much has been recorded for us, and if we have ears to hear, we can hear some of the richest testimonies from exemplary Christians of an earlier age. In fact, these testimonies are more God-centered and dripping with grace-filled piety than many of the standard testimonies we hear today. Why not have the best? Not to disparage any modern testimonies, but the truth of the matter is that these Puritans, on the average, were more—not less— advanced than the average evangelical today. After all, the New Testament on occasion reminds us of the value of imitation. Of course, Christians are to imitate Christ, first and foremost. But after that, it is permissible to follow others who imitate Him.

Nearly a century earlier, G. K. Chesterton gave testimony about the value of rediscovering our past Christian heritage, when he found that the best truths had already been mined:

> I did, like all other solemn little boys, try to be in advance of the age. Like them I tried to be some ten minutes in advance of the truth. And I found that I was eighteen hundred years behind it. . . . When I fancied that I stood alone I was really in the ridiculous position of being backed up by all Christendom. It may be, Heaven forgive me, that I did try to be original; but I only succeeded in inventing all by

myself an inferior copy of the existing traditions of civilized religion
. . . It might amuse a friend or an enemy to read how I gradually
learnt from the truth of some stray legend or from the falsehood of
some dominant philosophy, things that I might have learnt from my
catechism—if I had ever learnt it. . . . I found at last what I might
have found in the nearest parish church.[1]

Critics of Westminster Spirituality

Critics, of course, would be hesitant to agree with our study.
Certain personalities and images from the past sometimes stand in
dire need of rehabilitation. The divines, too, suffer outside the camp
as some of the most maligned in history, being ranked with the
likes of Calvin, Beza, Turretin, and a few others. Sadly, most of the
modern world (and it should not be so in an informed church) think
of these divines as machine-tooled, robo-theologians, bereft of heart,
passion, emotion, and maybe even soul. That is a caricature
underivable from the best of historical review.

Images accrued through history are often hard to jettison.
Sometimes even if accrued images are not in accord with actual
history, it is difficult to reclaim reputations. Unfortunately these
divines of Westminster have been tarred and feathered (normally
by opponents), such that they are frequently perceived to be devoid
of feeling, compassion, or spirituality. They have frequently been
caricatured as "black hats" by those who did not understand or
agree with them. With even the slightest bit of archaeological
digging, however, it can be seen that these Westminster men—
far from being spiritually sterile—expressed their spirituality of
the highest order. It simply is not the case that these divines were
spiritual dwarves. It is time to help rehabilitate these saints. Any
who slander them without reviewing the record first are guilty of
false witness, not to mention ignorance. These divines were deeply
spiritual. And most of us could learn from them.

---

[1] G. K. Chesterton in *Orthodoxy* (New York: Doubleday, 1990), 12.

Of the Confession as an accurate and vital compilation of Christian truth, Warfield contended, that as such, the Westminster Confession of Faith could not in its influence, "lack in spiritual quality. . . . Their authors were men of learning and philosophic grasp; but above all of piety. Their interest was not in speculative construction, but in the protection of their flocks from deadly error."[2]

On the group as a whole, biographer James Reid commented:

> There were never, perhaps, men of holier lives than the generality of the Puritans and Nonconformists of this period. Their piety and devotedness to God were very remarkable. Their ministers made considerable sacrifices for God and religion. They spent their lives, in sufferings, in fastings, in prayers, in walking closely with God in their families, and among their people who were under their pastoral care, in a firm adherence to their principles, and in a series of unremitted labors for the good of mankind. They were indefatigably zealous in their Master's service.[3]

In order to benefit, many of the critics' barbs must be dismissed. For example, Sidney Ahlstrom marveled, "That so many learned and contentious men in an age of so much theological hair-splitting could with so little coercion establish so resounding a consensus on so detailed a doctrinal statement is one of the marvels of the century."[4] But criticism of the divines is certainly not a twentieth century sport.

A great tradition of slandering the divines exists. In his 1647 burlesque, *The Assembly-Man*,[5] John Birkenhead (1616-1679) illustrates the accusation of the divines for intolerance: "The onely difference 'twixt the Assembler and a Turk, is, that one plants

---

[2] Cited in Shedd, *Calvinism: Pure and Mixed* (Edinburgh: Banner of Truth Trust, 1986), 116.

[3] James Reid, *Memoirs of the Westminster Assembly of Divines* (Edinburgh: Banner of Truth Trust, 1986), 130.

[4] *A Religious History of the American People* by Sydney Ahlstrom (New York: Doubleday, 1975), vol. I, 136.

[5] Found in *Journal of Presbyterian History*, Vol. xxi, nos. 2 and 3, June and September, 1943, 133-147.

Religion by the power of the Sword, and the other by the power of the scimitar." He proceeded to allege that, "Nay, the greatest strife in their whole Conventicle, is who shall do worst; for they all intend to make the Church but a Sepulchre, having not onely plundered, but anatomized all the true Clergy."[6]

These godly men were unfortunately but frequently accused of intoleration and the desire to seize power tyrannically to persecute their opponents. In response Hetherington wisely noted, "that both the principles and the constitution of a rightly formed Presbyterian Church render the usurpation of power and the exercise of tyranny on its part wholly impossible."

Fairborn alleged that "to the Presbyterians, toleration was the very man of sin" and Masson, Milton's biographer, accused the Assembly as follows: "Toleration to them was a demon, a chimera, the Great Diana of the Independents."[7] They were also accused of immoderation in seeking to elucidate so many biblical truths. However, the Confession of Faith is quite moderate and non-inventive in its formulation of biblical truth.

A witness to the moderation of this Assembly is the observation that the Assembly did not seek to settle the speculative controversy about the order of God's decrees in salvation (lapsarianism), instead referring those debatable matters to the seminaries. Although the moderator (Twisse) had well-formed opinions on this subject, such specificity did not imprint the Confession. Rather than taking out absolutist positions on every subject, this Assembly was guided by the biblical mandate of moderation. The Confession does not lay out an elaborate end-time scheme, nor treat complex ethical issues. Neither does it attempt to settle all conceivable issues. It is restrained and moderate in scope. Still, criticisms endure.

---

[6] *Journal of Presbyterian History*, xxi, nos. 2 and 3, 140.

[7] William Beveridge, *A Short History of the Westminster Assembly* (1904; rpr. Greenville, SC: A Press, 1991), 86.

John Milton even roasted the divines in his most famous epic. One scene from *Paradise Lost* was based on the sitting of the Assembly, as angry Milton compared the divines with the fallen angels in the infernal world. Milton likely had the Assembly in mind when he wrote:

> Others, apart, sat on a hill retired,
> In thought more elevate, and reasoned high
> Of Providence, foreknowledge, will and fate;
> Fixed fate, free will, foreknowledge absolute;
>   And found no end, in wandering mazes lost[8]

Other similar doggerls were composed for the Synod as well:

> Pretty Synod doth it sit,
> Void of grace, as well of wit, . . .
>   Thereby to end us;
> From Synod's nonsense and their treason,
> And from their catechistic reason,
>   Good heaven, defend us![9]

One of the most stinging critics of the Assembly was Royalist sympathizer John Birkenhead. While the Assembly was sitting, his anonymously published tract, *The Assembly-Man*, contained some of the bitterest scorn for the Assembly. Birkenhead alleged that they sat "four years towards a new Religion, but in the interim left none at all."[10] Moreover, he esteemed the divines as "Atoms; petty small Levites, whose parts are not perceptible," and as those who "follow the Geneva Margin, as those Seamen who understand not the Compass crept along the shore."[11]

Birkenhead, the critic, assessed the Shorter Catechism as "paultry," accused the divines of being materially motivated, only interested in "silver chains," and satirized that "though the

---

[8] Cited in *Memorial Volume of the Westminster Assembly, 1647-1897*, ed. by Francis Beattie, Charles Hemphill, and Henry Escott (Richmond: Presbyterian Committee for Publication, 1897), 81.

[9] Cited in *Memorial Volume,* 81.

[10] Cf. *Journal of Presbyterian History*, xxi, nos. 2 and 3, 137.

[11] *Journal of Presbyterian History,* Ibid., 138.

Assembler's Brains are Lead, his Countenance is Brass; for he condemned such as held two Benefices, while he himself has four or five, besides his Concubin-Lecture."[12] Contemporary critics did not avoid personal criticism as Assembly divine, John Arrowsmith, an eminent Professor of Theology at Cambridge, was castigated along with his fellow assemblymen as: "So that Learning now is so much advanced, as Arrowsmith's Glass-eye sees more than his Natural."[13]

The Puritan traits of the divines are mocked, as well as charged with effeminacy: "His [a divine] two longest things are his Nails and his Prayer. But the cleanest thing about him is his Pulpit cushion, for he still beats the dust out of it."[14] Of the Puritan long-windedness, Birkenhead ridicules a divine, "Yet though you heard him three hours, he'll ask a fourth, . . . If he has got any new Tale or Expression, 'tis easier to make Stones speak than him to hold his peace. He hates a Church where there is an Echo for it robs him of his dear Repetition, and confounds the Auditory as well as he," and their sermons: "had they the art to shorten it into Sense, they might write his whole Sermon on the back of their Nail."[15] Bitter criticisms were often set forth, citing the divines as the dupes of Parliament: "At Fasts and Thanksgivings the Assembler is the States' Trumpet; . . . proclaim News, very loud, the Trumpet and his Forehead both of one metal."[16]

Birkenhead's summation of the character of the divines is that they have "the Pride of three Tyrants, the Forehead of six Gaolers, and the Fraud of twelve Brokers. Or take him in the Bunch, and their whole Assembly is a Club of Hypocrites, where

---

[12] *Journal of Presbyterian History,* Ibid., 139.

[13] *Journal of Presbyterian History,* Ibid., 141.

[14] *Journal of Presbyterian History,* Ibid., 142.

[15] *Journal of Presbyterian History,* Ibid., 145.

[16] *Journal of Presbyterian History,* Ibid., 146.

six dozen schismatics spend two hours for four shillings apiece."[17]

Is this an accurate description of their spirituality? Or is it a caricature? If accurate, then by all means these lives should not be spiritual guides. But if inaccurate, we might still learn from these. Whatever the conclusion, it is important for anyone claiming the heritage of Westminster to do so without naivete. Exposure to criticism can also help avoid idolizing Westminster.

The Spirituality of the Westminster Assembly

This survey briefly considers fasting, spiritual warfare, preaching, confession of sins, testimonies about the family's nurture of children, as well as missionary zeal, reliance on Scripture, and last-breath testimonies of faith from the lips of these previous saints.

Beecher never spoke more truly than when he said of Calvinism: "There never was a system since the world stood which put upon man such motives to holiness, or which builds batteries which sweep the whole ground of sin with such terrible artillery. As a matter of fact, wherever this system of truth has been embraced it has produced a noble and distinct type of character—a type so clearly marked that secular historians, with no religious bias, have recognized it, and pointed to it as a remarkable illustration of the power of religious training in the formation of character."[18] At the 250th anniversary of this Assembly it was noted: "We claim, then, for our venerable creed, that whatever the world may say of it, it is fitted to be, and according to the testimony of impartial history, has proved itself to be a *character-making* creed.[19]

---

[17] *Journal of Presbyterian History,* Ibid., 147.

[18] *Memorial Volume of the Westminster Assembly, 1647-1897*, ed. by Francis Beattie, Charles Hemphill, and Henry Escott (Richmond, VA: Presbyterian Committee for Publication, 1897), 261-262.

[19] *Memorial Volume*, 265.

From the outset of the Assembly these participants wanted it known how unworthy they saw themselves to be, and correspondingly, how much they depended on the grace of God from first to last. In the wording of the Solemn League and Covenant, adopted first in Scotland, and later introduced on August 17, 1643, to the Assembly, they expressed their inner longings: "we profess . . . our unfeigned [sincere] desire to be humbled for our own sins . . . especially that we have not as we ought valued the inestimable benefit of the gospel; that we have not labored for the purity and power thereof; and that we have not endeavored to receive Christ in our hearts, nor to walk worthy of him in our lives; which are the cause of other sins and transgressions so much abounding amongst us; and our true and unfeigned purpose, desire, and endeavor for ourselves, and all others under our charge . . . to amend our lives, and each one to go before another in the example of a real reformation; that the Lord may turn away his wrath and heavy indignation, and establish these churches and kingdoms in truth and peace."[20]

The genuine piety of the membership of the Assembly is exemplified in a speech by Philip Nye. While urging adoption of the Solemn League and Covenant, he spoke of the fear of the Lord, the humility requisite for their task, and the necessary simplicity of spirit. Nye called for "courage, spirits that are bold and resolute . . . not amazed amidst much stirs . . . wise statesmen, like an experienced seaman, [who] knows the compass of this vessel, and though it heave and toss, and the passengers cry out about him, yet in the midst of its all, he is himself, turning not aside from his work, but steering on his course."[21] As a prototype of the pathos and piety of this group. Nye urged:

---

[20] Anon., *A History of the Westminster Assembly of Divines* (Philadelphia, 1841), 38.

[21] Reid, 1982, 379.

I beseech you, let it be seriously considered, if you mean to do any such work in the house of God as this is; if you mean to pluck up what many years ago was planted, or to build up what so long ago was pulled down, and to go through with this work, and not be discouraged, you must beg of the Lord this excellent spirit, this resolute stirring spirit, otherwise you will be outspirited, and both you and your cause slighted and dishonored.[22]

Nye also went on immediately to charge, "On the other hand, we must labor for humility, prudence, gentleness, meekness. A man may be very much zealous and resolute, and yet very meek and merciful: Jesus Christ was a Lion and yet a Lamb also."[23] Philip Nye concluded his exhortation to adopt the Solemn League in a fashion indicative of the Assembly's goal:

Grant unto us also, that when this life is finished, and we gathered to our fathers, there may be a generation out of our loins to stand up in this cause, that his great, and reverend name may be exalted from one generation to another, until he himself shall come, and perfect all with his own wisdom: even so come Lord Jesus, come quickly. Amen.[24]

These were hearts held out sincerely and promptly to serve God, just as aflame with zeal for the Lord and his house as Calvin and other fathers of the faith had been. These were not sterile academics; rather they possessed a passionate zeal for the Lord's honor.

At the very service of covenanting, the following expressions of prayer and worship were evident: Mr. Wilson expounded verses in the Psalms, with Mr. White praying nearly an hour, followed by another hour-long exhortation by Nye. The commissioners raised their hands as in pledging, after each clause of the Covenant was read. This was followed by another prayer by Dr. Gouge, finalized by adjournment to observe the fast.[25]

---

[22] Reid, 1982, 380.

[23] Reid, 1982, 380.

[24] Reid, 1982, 381.

[25] Summarized from Beveridge (1904), 47.

Another historian comments on another characteristic of the spirituality of the divines:

> The sense of humble dependence on God, as seen in the prominence given to prayer. Not only were the daily sessions opened and closed with prayer, and often interspersed with prayer for specific objects, but once a month all business was regularly suspended, that a day of fasting and prayer might be observed in concert with the two houses of Parliament. And what days they were! We read, for instance, in Lightfoot's Journal, that on Friday, October 13, 1643, the order is taken for the fast on the following Monday in these words: "The time to be from nine to four; the exercises to be the word and prayer, three to pray and two to preach. Dr. Burgess, Mr. Goodwin, and Dr. Stanton to pray, and Mr. Palmer and Mr. Whittacre to preach."[26]

Fasting

It became a frequent staple of the Assembly to fast. While in the heat of the debate on the form of government, this Assembly was neither oblivious of prayer concerns, nor unmindful of the prayers of the saints poured out on the altar. On May 17, 1644, the Assembly adjourned this controversy to fast and pray for the needs of the nation and the army. According to Baillie, the "sweetest day ever seen in England" saw the divines begin a day of prayer with Dr. Twisse leading, followed by two hours of prayers by Mr. Marshall, confessing the sins of the Assembly in a passionate, yet prudent manner. Two hours! The fast continued with preaching by John Arrowsmith, succeeded by another two-hour prayer by Mr. Vines. Another sermon was offered, and yet another two-hour prayer was offered by Mr. Seaman. This particular fast led Baillie to say, "God was so evidently in all this exercise, that we expect certainly a blessing both in our matter . . . and in the whole kingdom."[27]

Immediately prior to collecting the Scripture proofs, the Assembly felt an ominous pressure from Parliament. When asked

---

[26] *Memorial Volume*, 82-83.

[27] Beveridge (1904), 81-82.

to present their final versions with Scripture references, the Assembly hastily "appointed a day of fasting and humiliation for themselves. . . . The fast was observed within their own walls on the 6th of May."[28] This Assembly did not trust in their own strength, nor behave as if they needed no Divine assistance. Rather, they frequently resorted to prayer and fasting. Upon returning to Scotland, the Scottish ambassadors, keenly aware of the impending storm in England, being "deeply sensible of their own defects, the first thing which they did after returning home was to hold a solemn fast to lament their own defection from the solemn league and covenant."[29]

On one occasion Henry Hall led a solemn fast, just prior to the convening of the Assembly (May 29, 1643). On that opportunity he preached on suffering as an aid to sanctification, difficult though it be. Said Hall, "A Christian is never so glorious, as when he suffers most reproach and ignominy for Christ's sake . . . keep alive this sacred fire, upon the altar of our hearts, that it may inflame our devotion toward God, kindle our love toward men, and burn out all our corruptions."[30]

An early historian said: "We often find this Assembly engaging in the self-denying duty of fasting; and once a month regularly, they united with the Parliament in observing a solemn fast. On these occasions, nearly the whole day was spent in the public exercises of religion. It is noted by Baillie, that on these solemn occasions, one minister would sometimes pray, without ceasing, for two whole hours. The godly men of that day seem to have been mighty in prayer, and to have known what it was to pray without fainting. Their preaching too, we have reason to believe,

---

[28] Anon. *A History of the Westminster Assembly of Divines* (Philadelphia, 1841), 124.

[29] Anon. *A History of the Westminster Assembly of Divines* (Philadelphia, 1841), 165.

[30] Reid, Vol. 2, 6.

from the specimens which have come down to us, was solemn, searching, evangelical, pungent, and powerful. Mr. Baillie incidentally observes, in one of his letters, that "Mr. Marshall was reckoned to be the best preacher, and Mr. Palmer the best catechist, in England."[31] Most of the sermons preached before the Parliament on these fast days were printed later.

Furthermore, the very Directory for Worship produced by this Assembly included separate chapters on fasting and thanksgiving, so important were they as spiritual basics. The original drafts of these were drawn up by the pious Goodwin (fasting) and the moderator, Herle (thanksgiving). Samuel Carruthers described one fast:

> The first of these [fasts] was Monday, 25 September, the day when the Commons and the Divines took the Covenant; they met in St. Margaret's Church, White leading in prayer, Nye speaking a word of exhortation, and Gouge concluding with prayer. Three weeks later (16 October) there was again a day of fasting and prayer, this time in their usual meeting place. It was from nine till four, and during these seven hours (probably not actually continuous) three men (Burges, Goodwin, and Staunton) prayed, and two (Palmer and Whitaker) preached. Lightfoot records that Burges' prayer took an hour, as did also Staunton's. There were four intervals of psalm-singing, but it is not recorded that Scripture was read; and Twisse concluded with prayer. There was a collection (£3 15s.) for maimed soldiers; but next day it was voted to be given to Mrs. Rood, widow of a minister, in straitened circumstances.[32]

Again the leading historian of the Assembly in the early twentieth century noted:

> On 14 May, 1644, the Lord General, Essex, informed the Divines that he had appointed a fast for the army to be held three days later, and asked them to appoint preachers. They resolved, also at his request, to keep that day as an Assembly fast. Accordingly, Twisse opened with a brief prayer. Then, after singing part of Psalm xxvii,

---

[31] Anon., *A History of the Westminster Assembly of Divines* (Philadelphia, 1841), 177-178.

[32] Samuel Carruthers, *The Everyday Work of the Westminster Assembly* (London: Presbyterian Historical Society, 1943), 65.

Marshall said, "Let me speak a few words." He declared that the nation "had not had so troublous times for many hundred years"; reminded them that they had been preserved in safety, and that upon them "the eyes, not only of the kingdom, but of all the churches in Christendom" were fixed. They had expected that much would have been done by now; but "for some cause or other it pleaseth God that we have had many a sad breach that we cannot drive on so cheerfully." That was reason enough for humiliation; let each one look into his own heart and see whether he were to blame. Then there was "common and almost general apostasy in the kingdom"; had they done enough about that? If they did some heart-searching, then, said he, "we shall find more fruit of one day's musing than of many days' disputing." He then led in prayer "for two hours, most divinely, confessing the sins of the members of Assembly in a wonderfully pathetic and prudent way."[33]

At one fast, John Arrowsmith preached for an hour, from Haggai 2:4-5, and Richard Vines led in prayer for nearly two hours, followed by a second sermon which also lasted an hour. Samuel Carruthers's details after three centuries are worth hearing again to capture partially some of the Westminster spirituality:

> On 30 June, 1645, the Commons asked the Divines to make the next day a day of prayer. There was no session of the Assembly the next day. Once more ten churches were named, the occasion being made a public one. On 26 September, 1645, the Divines once more resolved to have a day of humiliation for themselves. This was prompted more by the condition of their own business than by that of public affairs. They appointed Wednesday, 1 October, from 9 a.m. to 4 p.m., and appointed two members "for exhortation" and three 'for prayer.'[34]

The scope and manner of keeping theses fasts is also interesting: "In addition to the regular monthly fast, established by Parliament before the Assembly met, special fasts and thanksgivings were held. The suggestion for these came sometimes from Parliament and sometimes from the Assembly; they were sometimes country-wide (so far at least as the authority of the Parliament might at the time extend), usually a week or more later in the provinces than in London, to allow the

---

[33] Carruthers, 65-66.

[34] Carruthers, 69-70.

instructions to be forwarded; at other times only in certain districts or in certain churches." For example, "On 18 July, 1643, the Assembly suggested a fast 'for the two late disasters in the North and in the West,' but the next day, before they communicated with the Houses, they were informed that one had been fixed for the 21st, and certain divines were asked to preach."[35]

If most critics of the Assembly knew more about the prayer lives and fasting of these divines, criticisms might be withheld until their godliness was surpassed.

Spiritual Battle

In one letter, these divines disclosed their hearts' passion in terms of spiritual warfare: "We doubt not, but the sad reports of the miseries under which the church and kingdom of England do bleed, and wherewith we are ready to be swallowed up, is long since come to your ears; and it is probable, the same instruments of Satan and Antichrist have, by their emissaries, endeavored to present us as black as may be among yourselves."[36]

It is instructive to note their cognizance of the satanic and the presence of antichristian opposition. As this letter to Belgic, French, and Swiss churches of the reformation continues, the authors' spirituality is seen when they say,

> But though we hoped through the goodness of God, and his blessing . . . that our winter had been past, yet alas! we find it to be quite otherwise. We know our sins have deserved all, and if we die and perish, the Lord is righteous; to his hand we submit, and to him alone we look for healing. The same antichristian faction not being discouraged, by their want of success in Scotland, have stirred up a bloody rebellion in Ireland, wherein above one hundred thousand Protestants have been destroyed in one province. . . ."[37]

---

[35] Carruthers, 73.

[36] Anon., *A History of the Westminster Assembly of Divines* (Philadelphia, 1841), 54.

[37] Ibid., 56.

This was an Assembly not only of pious men, but also consisting of those acquainted with persecution, loss, peril of death. They conclude this appeal by importunately craving,

> your fervent prayers, both public and private, that God would bring salvation to us; that the blessings of truth and peace may rest upon us; that these three nations may be joined as one stick in the hands of the Lord, and that we ourselves, contemptible builders, called to repair the house of God . . . may see the pattern of this house, and commend such a platform of Zerubbabels as may . . . establish uniformity among ourselves; that all mountains may become plains before them and us; that then all who now see the plummet in our hands, may also behold the top-stone set upon the head of the Lord's house among us, and may help us with shouting to cry Grace, grace, to it.[38]

It had also become the practice of the ministers to meet together every Monday to consult together how they might best promote the spread of the gospel. One historian noted that so widespread was the dispersion of piety, that even the military was affected, with the result that, "never was an army in which religious feeling, of one kind or another, so predominated. Frequently their commanding officers preached and prayed in public, and the soldiers were deeply imbued with the same spirit, and spent much of their time, when in quarters, in disputing, or praying."[39] This spirit endowed them with invincible courage and admirable piety.

Preaching and Suffering

Experiential Christianity was a forte of these divines. It almost appears as if, in some way, there was a connection between their suffering and their passionate preaching. For example, one unsympathetic poet wrote describing Assembly member Edmund Calamy's imprisonment for the faith at Newgate as it was exhibited in his preaching style:

> "Dead, and yet preach! these Presbyterian slaves
> Will not give over preaching in their graves. . . .

---

[38] Ibid., 58.

[39] Ibid., 143.

What can't you Nonconformists be content
Sermons to make, except you preach them too?"[40]

According to opponents, it was one thing for the Westminster men to believe, but if believe they must, was it necessary to spread abroad the tidings even in jail?

Samuel Rutherford, a participant of the Assembly, who was also the author of *Lex Rex*, put it well: "The preaching of the word only, if alone without the Spirit, can no more make an hair white or black, or draw us to the Son, or work repentance in sinners, than the sword of the Magistrate can work repentance. What can preaching of man or angel do without God; is it not God and God only who can open the heart?"[41] This same Rutherford, when preaching on Matthew 9:27-31, proclaimed: "As you have need of Christ in your poverty, by faith you accept of him as a Surety to pay your debts when you are broken and cannot pay them yourselves."[42]

Robert Harris was a divine who knew the well-known pulpit axiom: "I preach, as if I ne'er should preach again; And, as a dying man, to dying men." This same Harris, both a Pastor and President of Trinity College, Oxford, was known for excellent order in nurturing his own children in the faith, stating this as his last will: "Also, I bequeath to all my children and their children's children, to each of them a Bible with this inscription, *None but Christ*."[43]

His illnesses were public knowledge, and yet he found sweet delight in the Lord, accounting as his best days, those in which "enjoyed most intercourse with Heaven." After a long testimony

---

[40] Reid, 182-183.

[41] Samuel Rutherford, *A Free Disputation* . . . , 351 as cited in Warfield, *The Westminster Assembly and Its Work* (Edmonton: Still Waters Revival Books, 1992), 221.

[42] Samuel Rutherford, *The Power of Faith and Prayer* (orig. 1713; Isle of Lewis: Reformation Press, 1991), 51.

[43] Reid 2, 21.

to the power of the fellowship of sufferings with Christ, Harris said, "He did not expect much from any man, were his parts ever so great, until he was broken by afflictions and temptations."[44] Harris observed with a keen spiritual eye, "That it was just for God to deny us the comforts of our graces, when we deny him the glory of them," and "That the humblest preachers converted the greatest number of souls, not the most choice scholars while unbroken."[45] Harris had the insight to say, "That a preacher has three books to study: the Bible, himself, and the people . . . that preaching to the people was but one part of the pastor's duty: he was to live and die in them, as well as for them."[46] In sickness he said, "I never in all my life saw the worth of Christ, nor tasted the sweetness of God's love, in so great a measure as I now do."

The lesson has been well-stated: "The heroism of these great men was sublime, their self-abnegation, Christ-like. Not for glory did they brave death, not for honors did they toil, but because they were constrained by the love of Christ and of their fellow-men. I would that you, my spiritual fathers, would read more of these 'living epistles' to your people from your pulpits."[47]

Matthew Newcomen, one of the divines spoke of preaching as "the greater light of heaven," when he charged the Assembly at its outset to have courage:

> Keep no silence, give the Lord no rest until He establish the house . . . except the Lord build the house, reform the Church, it is to no purpose to go about to reform it. . . . I need not tell you how many eyes and expectations there are upon this Assembly . . . what you pray for, contend for...as you pray that God would establish his Church in peace, so labor to work out the Church's peace. And lastly, as you pray that God would make the Church a praise, so endeavor that also; endeavoring . . . that all her ways may be ordered according to the rule of God's Word: that the Gospel may run and be glorified: that those two great illuminating

---

[44] Reid 2, 23.

[45] Reid 2, 23.

[46] Reid 2, 23.

[47] *Anniversary Addresses*, 40.

ordinances of Preaching and Catechizing, which are as the greater and
lesser lights of heaven, may have such liberty, encouragement,
maintenance, that all the earth may be filled with the knowledge of
the Lord.[48]

Many have evaluated that the Puritan preaching of the 1640s
was among the most influential in all of history. During this decade
over 240 sermons (185 of which were on OT texts, and very few
from the Pauline Epistles[49]) were preached to Parliament, and
"Every facet of individual and social life was informed and
understood by a faith that was subject to Scripture."[50] Rather than
modern attempts at humor, levity, drama, and entertainment, these
Puritans knew the power of the pulpit to be the dominant media
apart from such merriment. Robert Norris reminds:

Any philosophy of preaching that forgets the gravity of the task and
neglects the lessons of Westminster will forgo the powerful effects
produced by the preaching of those times. We will not serve the present
generation by neglecting the lessons of the past. And while sacred
eloquence assumes different forms in different generations, and while
no time or church can claim perfection in the manner of presenting
the truth, rarely has any one Christian assembly produced better
counsel backed with the testimony of proven result than the divines
assembled at Westminster.[51]

Another glimpse into the use of the pulpit for spiritual formation
may be seen from a typical (and excellent) ongoing series of
"exhortations." About a decade after the adjournment of the
Assembly, several of the divines joined together to give sermons
at "The Morning Exercises at Cripplegate, St. Giles in the Fields,
and in Southwark." These exhortations, or practical sermons were
given by the Presbyters near London, many of whom had been
supportive of the aims of the Assembly. Even if all of the Morning

---

[48] Cited in *Journal of Presbyterian History,* xxi, nos. 2 and 3, 126-127.

[49] Cf. Robert M. Norris, "The Preaching of the Assembly," in *To Glorify and
Enjoy God: A Commemoration of the Westminster Assembly*, John L. Carson
and David W. Hall, eds. (Edinburgh: Banner of Truth Trust, 1994), 65, 73.

[50] Ibid., 66.

[51] Ibid., 81.

Exercise preachers were not actually involved in the Assembly, there is no evidence that they differed with the ethos of the Assembly. A glance at their topics illumines the practical emphasis on spirituality, as well as the priority of preaching. A sample of the sermons (from Westminster divines) below highlights the spiritual thrust of the preaching: "What Must and Can Persons do Toward Their Own Conversion?" (Ez. 18:32): William Greenhill; "Now is the Time: Or, Instructions for the Present improving the Season of Grace" (2 Cor. 6:1- 2): William Jenkin; "On Sabbath Sanctification" (Is. 63:13-14): Thomas Case; "How Ought We to Bewail the Sins of the Places where we Live?" (2 Pet. 2:7-8): William Jenkin.[52]

Confession of Sins

As noted above, these divines were not afraid to confess their sins. On one occasion, "Palmer rose with the words, 'I desire to begin there,' and opened with the fault of slack attendance, coming late and going early, especially the sparse attendance at committees. It throws a curious light upon their proceedings that he said that during the meetings there was 'reading of news,' 'talking and in confusion; we do not attend at the beginning nor ending for prayer as we ought to do.' His next complaint is also a perennial one: 'On the one hand, some of us are too forward to speak, and some are, I fear too backward.' Finally, he referred to 'unhappy differences and unbeseeming phrases.'"[53]

Charles Herle was not afraid to admit the sins of the Assembly publicly, and organized the offenses of the Assembly, in order to expedite confession as below:

---

[52] Taken from *Puritan Sermons, 1659-1689*, (Wheaton, IL: Richard Owen Roberts, 1981), vols. 1-6. Many other sermons and "cases of conscience" were addressed by the likes of John Owen, Thomas Manton, Robert Trail, Thomas Watson, Richard Baxter, and Stephen Charnock at these preaching sessions.

[53] Carruthers, 76.

I. The sins of the Assembly. 1. Neglect of the service, in slackness in coming and departing at pleasure; 2. By abstaining from prayers; 3. Manifesting a neglect in the time of debate, and neglecting committees; 4. Some speaking too much, and others too little; 5. By irreverent carriage; 6. By haste in debating; 7. Driving on parties; 8. Not serious examination of ministers.

II. Of the armies. 1. Emulation among the officers, causing the loss of many opportunities; 2. Want of ministers; 3. Swearing, drinking, etc., 4. Want of discipline in the army.

III. Of the people. 1. Profaneness, scorn of God's hand upon us; 2. Duties of humiliation 'disfigurated'; 3. Our hearts not humbled upon humiliation; there was 'curling of hair, patching, bare breasts, and painting'; 4. Divisions in opinion and affection among professors; 5. Jealousies, sidings, and tale-bearings; 6. Unthankfulness for God's mercies; 7. Neglect of personal and family reformation; 8. Carnal confidence and general security.

IV. Of Parliament. 1. Not tendering the Covenant to all in their power; 2. Not active in suppressing Anabaptists and Antinomians; 3. Not seeking religion in the first place; 4. Not suppressing state plays, taverns, profaneness, and scoffing of ministers, and even incest itself; 5. Not a free publishing of truths, for fear of losing a party; 6. Oppression by committees, with intolerable fees; 7. Not debts paid; 8. Remissness in punishing delinquents; 9. Private ends aimed at, 'the great incomes of some new invented offices'; 10. Delays in relieving the army; 11. Church lands sold, but not for the maintenance of ministers."[54]

Family Spiritual Formation

Another aspect of spirituality was the undying commitment of these Assemblymen to the spiritual nurture of children, emphasis on family, sabbath, and character-formation. As observed at the 250th anniversary of the Westminster Assembly:

There is a most real and vital connection between belief and conduct, between creed and character. What men believe, that they become. As Bacon says: "Truth and goodness differ but as the seal and the print; for truth prints goodness." The same may be said of error and evil. Evil in conduct and character is ever the imprint of error. Today we are to inquire how the Standards, framed by the Westminster

---

[54] Carruthers, 80.

Assembly, abide this test. How have they stood translation into real life or incarnation in living men and women? Have their practical effects been such as to vindicate their right to survive among the creeds of Christendom? What influence have they exerted upon "the individual, the family, and society," where they have been embraced? . . . The Westminster divines well understood the necessity of training up a child in the way he should go in order to insure against his departing from it in age. They heard and heeded the risen Master's commission to Simon Peter, "Feed my *lambs*." Their very best work, in the judgment of many, is found in the provision which they made for the lambs of the flock. Richard Baxter is quoted as saying: "If the Westminster Assembly had done nothing more than produce the Shorter Catechism they would be entitled to the everlasting gratitude of the Christian church." He further expressed the opinion that, next to the Bible, it was probably the best book in the world. Hence, wherever these doctrines have been received they have brought forth the fruits of righteousness. What Dr. Chalmers said of Scotland is true the world over: "Wherever there has been most Calvinism, men have been most moral."[55]

The beliefs and the practiced spirituality were two sides of the same coin, inseparable for these Westminster forefathers. The "character developed among them was as pure and noble as it was distinct. It is safe to say it has seldom been surpassed in the history of the world. That they had their faults goes without saying. But even their 'failings,' as Burns said of his father's, were such as 'leaned to virtue's side.'"[56]

One of the tell-tale emblems of Westminster spirituality was the honoring and loving of God on a regular, sabbatical basis. Scottish commissioner to the Westminster Assembly, Archibald Johnston, exemplified the spiritual thrust of the Sabbath as he prayed in 1655: "O Lord Jesus, woo Thou their hearts, warme their affections, revive their spirits, gayne their loves; let it be as a resurrection from the dead."[57] On another fast-day,[58] Johnston

---

[55] *Memorial Volume*, 257-258, 260.

[56] *Memorial Volume*, 262.

[57] *The Diary of Sir Archibald Johnston of Wariston* (Edinburgh: Scottish Historical Society, 1940) Third Series, vol. XXXIV, 9.

[58] Johnston frequently refers to fasts (*The Diary of Sir Archibald Johnston of Wariston* (Edinburgh: Scottish Historical society, 1919) Second Series, vol. XVIII, 139, 302, 303) and the Lord's Day (Ibid., 43, 130, 303).

recorded, "I got serveral tymes teares in the church prayers, and between sermons with my wyfe, and then in privat with great freedom."[59] The pitch of spirituality is seen in this prayer and memoir by Lord Wariston: "O Lord, speak graciously to the remnant, and cause our ears to hear Thee. Oh, I feared our abusing the Lord's patience, who has restrayned the rod now from overflowing . . . and has delayed His anger to see if wee would repent and returne."[60] Historian William H. Roberts, commemorating the spiritual disciplines of the divines a hundred years ago made this correlation:

> The family and the Sabbath! The two institutions of Eden which survived the wreck of the fall! They are the two strong supports of all social order, the Jachin and Boaz upon which human society rests. Let them be disintegrated and social chaos inevitably follows. These two institutions our venerable Standards exalt as no others do. For their maintenance the Presbyterian Church has always stood...they have been handed down to us as a precious legacy from God-fearing ancestors . . . a high trust, to be passed on in unimpaired integrity to generations yet to come. . . . These two springs of blessing have been opened for us, at unspeakable cost, by hearts and hands long stilled in death. We have drunk from them and been refreshed. . . . There are no institutions of our holy religion which the great enemy of all good is attacking today with more persistent or subtle malignity and zeal.[61]

We also observe the great thrust toward the family as a primary sphere in which the Westminster faith propagated. One fruit of Westminster is its influence on discipling the family. The role of the family as the chief propagator of the faith can be seen by the extensive use of catechism in instructing the young among Westminster adherents. The Westminster tradition placed a premium on godly parents instructing their covenant children in

---

[59] *The Diary of Sir Archibald Johnston of Wariston* (Edinburgh: Scottish Historical Society, 1919) Second Series, vol. XVII, 16.

[60] *The Diary of Sir Archibald Johnston of Wariston* (Edinburgh: Scottish Historical Society, 1919) Second Series, vol. XVII, 56.

[61] *Memorial Volume,* 268-269.

the principles of the true religion through the catechism. Moreover, family devotionals were a staple for the piety of the Westminster Assembly and great use of family nurture was evident. These made the most of the proverb: "As the twig is bent, the tree is inclined."[62]

On the value of the Catechisms and early memorization, the following was held out one hundred years ago as the potential for the influence of the Catechism on our youth:

> 1. Unless they are learned in childhood and youth, the strong probability is that they will never be learned at all. Not one in five hundred of our people, perhaps, learns them later in life. They must be learned, then, early in life, or never. Are we willing for the latter alternative? Are we willing that our children shall never *accurately* know the great truths of religion? Are we willing that they shall never accurately know what is meant by such doctrines as faith, and repentance, and justification, and sanctification? Would that be wise? Would that be safe?

> 2. We cannot too early impress the great truths of the Catechisms on their minds and hearts . . . in childhood and youth the soul is most susceptible of deep and lasting impressions. In our great museums we sometimes see stone slabs with the marks of raindrops on them that fell before man had any existence, and the impressions of the feet of tiny birds. . . . So, in childhood and youth, the souls of our children are most susceptible of impressions for good or evil; and then, as the years elapse, those souls, with those impressions on them, indurate; and thus those impressions become as lasting, as everlasting, it may be, as the souls themselves. How important it is, then, that these earliest and most enduring impressions should be made in behalf of right and truth and God by the inculcation of the great truths of our Catechisms!

> 3. It is necessary to our success as a denomination that our Catechisms be intelligently and faithfully taught. Our doctrines are constantly and bitterly assailed. In much of the literature of the day, especially in that kind which, unfortunately, our children too much read, they are caricatured as severe, harsh, unreasonable, antiquated; as belonging to a remote and ignorant past; as being entirely out of harmony with the progress that has been made in better views of the benevolence, of the divine nature, of the dignity of man, and of the vastness and freeness of redeeming love.[63]

---

[62] *Anniversary Addresses,* 230.

[63] *Memorial Volume,* 136-137.

A document written contemporaneous with the meeting of the Westminster Confession can also show us most clearly the strong views of the family which were held by the Scottish commissioners. In 1647 the Scottish General Assembly approved a *Directory for Family Worship*. This document reflected the views as well as the sentiments of many of the members of the Westminster Assembly on the importance of family worship. So essential was family worship, not only as a supplement to regular worship on the Lord's Day, that the Scottish Presbyters laid out directions which were to be used to supplement the building up of faith, cherishing piety, the maintaining of unity, and the deterrence of schism among godly families. So important was this family faith that the Scottish General Assembly even called upon Presbyteries to require those within their bounds to carry these things out at the threat of discipline and moreover that every individual family was to practice family worship: "And if any such family be found, the head of the family is to be first admonished privately to amend his fault; and, in case of his continuing therein, he is to be gravely and sadly reproved by the session; after which reproof, if he be found still to neglect Family-worship, let him be, for his obstinacy in such an offence, suspended and debarred from the Lord's supper, as being justly esteemed unworthy to communicate therein, till he amend."

Missionary Zeal

Another mistake of those who are not thoroughly familiar with the Westminster divines is to allege that they had little or no interest in foreign missions. Of course, as early as John Calvin there was interest in evangelizing the Villegagnon Colony (Brazil).[64] As early as 1641, fifteen divines who would become

---

[64] "The Westminster Divines and Foreign Missions," *Journal of the Presbyterian Historical Society*, vol. XXI, June and September, 1943, nos. 2 and 3, 148.

commissioners to the Westminster Assembly joined William Castell in a petition calling for the evangelization of the New World. In addition to these, two of the Scottish divines, Alexander Henderson and Robert Baillie, joined their names to the petition which had seventy signatories. The petition begins with a lament about "the great and general neglect of this kingdome, in not propagating the glorious Gospel in America, a maine part of the world."[65] The petition continues:

> Although some of the reformed religion, English, Scotch, French, and Dutch, have already taken up their habitations in those parts, yet both their going thither (as yet) been to small purpose, for the converting of those nations, either for that they have placed themselves but in the skirts of America, where there are but few natives (as those in New England), or else for want of able and conscionable ministers (as in Virginia) they themselves are become exceeding rude, more likely to turn Heathen, than to turn others to the Christian faith.[66]

The petitioners noted that "there is no great difficulty in the preparation here, or tediousnesse in the passage thither, or hazard when wee come there. . . . It being ordinarily by six weeks sayle, in a sea much more secure for Pirats. . . . And as for our good successe there, wee need not fear it. The natives being now every where more than ever, out of an inveterate hatred to the Spaniard, ready and glad to entertained us."[67]

Signed by Westminster divines R. Brownricke, R. Sanderson, D. Featly, M. Styles, E. Stanton, G. Walker, J. Caryl, E. Calamy, A. Byfield, W. Price, J. White, H. Paynter, S. Marshall, J. Burroughes, and J. Whittaker, this petition to Parliament concluded:

> And which is much more our going with a generall consent in Gods cause, for the promoting of the Gospel, and inlarging of his church, may assure us of a more than ordinary protection and direction. That hitherto, wee have been lesse successfull in our voyage that way, wee may justly impute it to this, that as yet they have not beene

---

[65] Idem.

[66] Ibid., 149.

[67] Ibid., 156.

undertaken with such a generall consent, and with such a full reference to Gods glory as was requisite. And so your Petitioner having delivered his apprehension herein, more briefly, then so weighty a matter might well require, he submits all the premises to your more full deliberation and conclusion, which hee humbly prayeth, may bee with all convenient speed; the onely best way under God to make it the better successfull . . . concerning the propagation of the glorious Gospel of Christ in America.[68]

The Scottish Parliament also received a similar bill, signed by Henderson and Baillie:

The motion made by Master William Castell, Minister of the Gospel, for propagating of the blessed Evangell of Christ our Lord and Savior in American, wee conceive in the generall to bee most pious, Christian and charitable. And therefore worthy to be seriously considered, of all that love the glorious name of Christ, and are zealous of the salvation of soules, which are without Christ, and without God in the world, wishing the opportunity and fit season: the instruments and means. And all things necessary for the prosecution of so pious a worke, to bee considered by the wisedomes of Churches and civil powers, whom God hath called, and enables with Piety, Prudence, and Peace, for matters of publicke concernment, and of so great Importance, And beseeching the Lord to blesse all their consultations and proceedings for the advancing and establishing the Kingdome of Jesus Christ.[69]

Moreover, the work of John Eliot to the American missionaries illustrates that these divines were neither narrow in their concerns nor sterile in their spiritual impulse. About the time of the conclusion of the Assembly, the following pamphlets were published in London: *The Day-Breaking, if not the Sun-rising of the Gospel with the Indians in New-England* (1647); *The Clear Sun-shine of the Gospel, etc.* (1648); *The Glorious Progress of the Gospel, etc.* (1649); *The Light appearing more and more towards the perfect Day, etc.* (1651); *Strength out of Weaknesse* (1652); and *Tears of Repentance* (1653). These demonstrate the pious concern for missions.

---

[68] Ibid., 157.

[69] Ibid., 158-159.

Scripture

No survey of Westminster spirituality would be complete without reference to the admiration of the divines for Scripture, both as the authority for life, and as a devotional staple. The Assembly was so emphatically tied to the Bible that they even proposed a Study Bible. A committee was commissioned to make "The Annotations of the Westminster Assembly." Annotations to the Pentateuch, the OT historical books, Psalms, Proverbs, the major prophets, the Gospels, and Paul's Epistles were compiled. However, these were never published with the sanction of Parliament.

On the views of Assembly members and the Bible, Calamy, one of the most astute professors also commented,

> There are two great Gifts that God hath given to his people. The *Word Christ*, and the *Word of Christ*; Both are unspeakably great; but the first will do us no good without the second. . . . Blessed be God who hath not only given us the book of the Creatures, and the book of Nature to know himself and his will by; but also, and especially the book of Scriptures, whereby we come to know those things of God, and of Christ, which neither the book of Nature nor of the Creatures can reveal unto us. Let us bless God, not only for revealing his Will in his Word, but for revealing it by writing.[70]

One of the participants of the Assembly, Anthony Burgess, wrote in another place on this same topic: "As for that dangerous opinion, that makes God's calling of man to repentance by the Creatures, to be enough and sufficient, we reject, as that which cuts at the very root of free grace: A voice, indeed, we grant they have, but yet they make Paul's trumpet, an uncertain sound; men cannot by them [creational revelation] know the nature of God and his Worship, and wherein our Justification doth consist."[71] John Arrowsmith, another member of the Assembly and one of

---

[70] Edward Calamy, *the Godly Man's Ark*. London, 1672, 55-56, and 90 as cited in Warfield, *The Westminster Assembly and Its Work*, 198.

[71] Anthony Burgess in *Spiritual Refining*, London, 1652, 588 as cited in Warfield *supra*, 197.

the leading theological professors of the time, said similarly: "For to maintain (as some do) that a man may be saved in an ordinary course . . . by any religion whatsoever, provided he live according to the principles of it, is to turn the whole world into an Eden; and to find a Tree of Life in every garden, as well as in the paradise of God."[72]

Even more to the point, Assembly-man, William Bridge stated, "Though Human Reason be a Beam of Divine Wisdom, yet if it be not enlightened with an higher Light of the Gospel, it cannot reach unto the things of God as it should. . . . For though reason be the Gift of God, yet it doth proceed from God as he is God, and General Ruler of the World."[73]

The Scotsman George Gillespie wrote: "The Scripture is known to be indeed the word of God by the beams of divine authority it hath in itself . . . such as the heavenliness of the matter; the majesty of the style; the irresistible power over the conscience; the general scope, to abase man and to exalt God; nothing driven at but God's glory and man's salvation . . . the supernatural mysteries revealed therein, which could never have entered the reason of men; the marvelous consent of all parts and passages (though written by divers and several penmen), even where there is some appearance of difference . . . these, and the like, are characters and marks which evidence the Scriptures to be the word of God."[74]

Calamy attested,

> It is certain that all Scripture is of Divine inspiration, and that the holy men of God spake as they were guided by the Holy Ghost. . . . It transcribes the mind and heart of God. A true Saint loveth the Name, Authority, Power, Wisdom, and Goodness of God in every letter of

---

[72] John Arrowsmith in *A Chain of Principles*, Cambridge, 1659, 128 as cited in Warfield, *supra*, 197-198.

[73] William Bridge, *Scripture-Light, the Most Sure Light*, London, 1956, 32-33, as cited in Warfield, 199.

[74] Cf. Gillespie's *Miscellaneous Questions*, 105-106 (of the Presbyterian's Armory edition, cited by Warfield, 176.

it, and therefore cannot but take pleasure in it. It is an Epistle sent down to him from the God of heaven. . . . The Word of God hath God for its Author, and therefore must needs be full of Infinite Wisdom and Eloquence, even the Wisdom and Eloquence of God. There is not a word in it, but breathes out God, and is breathed out by God. It is...an invariable rule of Faith, an *unerring* (emphasis added) and infallible guide to heaven.[75]

All the Scriptures are *theopneustoi* ["God-breathed" as in 2 Tim. 3:16] by Divine inspiration; and therefore the breathings of God's spirit, are to be expected in this Garden: and those commands of attending to the Scripture only, and to observe what is written, is a plain demonstration that God hath tied us to the Scriptures only: so that as the child in the womb liveth upon nourishment conveyed by the Navel cleaving to it, so doth the Church live only upon Christ by the Navel of the scripture, through which all nourishment is conveyed.[76]

Of the original languages as the authority and without error, Daniel Featley said, "If you will dispute in Divinity, you must be able to produce the Scriptures in the Original Languages. For no Translation is simply Authentical, or the undoubted word of God. In the undoubted word of God there can be no error. But in Translations there may be, and are errors. The Bible translated therefore is not the undoubted Word of God, but so far only as it agreeth with the Original."[77]

Edward Reynolds wrote, "The scriptures . . . are the alone rule of all controversies. . . . So then the only light by which differences are to be decided, is the word, being a full canon of God's revealed will."[78] Samuel Rutherford was of the opinion that, "The Scripture makes it self the judge and determiner of all questions and controversies in religion."[79] Youthful George

---

[75] *The Godly Man's Ark*, 55, 80 as cited in Warfield, 208-209.

[76] Anthony Burgess in *Spiritual Refining*, 152 as cited in Warfield, 208.

[77] Cited by Warfield, 242.

[78] *Works*, v., 152-153, 1826 as cited in Warfield, 256.

[79] *A Free Disputation*, London, 1649, 361 as cited in Warfield, 256.

Gillespie spoke of "the written word of God [as] surer than any voice which can speak in the soul of a man, and an inward testimony may sooner deceive us than the written word can; which being so, we may and ought to try the voice which speaks in the soul by the voice of the Lord which speaks in the Scripture."[80]

The leading scholar at the Assembly of the Bible in its original languages, John Lightfoot, clarified, "How may Christians inquire of God in their doubtings, as Israel did . . . in theirs? I answer briefly, . . . to the written word of God, Search the Scriptures. . . . There is now no other way to inquire of God, but only from his word."[81]

As to the modern question of whether or not the Westminster Confession of Faith advocated the inerrancy of Scripture, the above citations should be sufficient. But if not, a few others could easily be added. Other contemporaries of the Westminster Assembly said the following. Richard Baxter, a leading Puritan of the day, uttered,

> May one be saved who believeth that the Scripture hath any mistake of error, and believeth it not all? . . . He that thinketh that the prophets, sacred historians, evangelists, and apostles, were guided to an infallible delivery and recording of all the great, substantial, necessary points of the gospel, but not to an infallibility in every by-expression, phrase, citation, or circumstance, doth disadvantage his own faith as to all the rest; but yet may be saved, if he believe the substance with a sound and practical belief.[82]

Samuel Rutherford wrote:

> Whereas the means of conveying the things believed may be fallible, as writing, printing, translating, speaking, are all fallible means of

---

[80] *Miscellaneous Questions,* 1649 as cited by Warfield, 256.

[81] *Works of John Lightfoot*, vi, 286 as cited in Warfield, 256.

[82] An excellent summary of these contemporaneous views is set forth in the article, "Inerrancy, Infallibility, and Scripture in the Westminster Confession of Faith" by John Delivuk in the *Westminster Theological Journal*, Fall 1992, vol. 54, no. 2, 349-355.

conveying the truth of old and new Testament to us, and yet the Word of God in that which is delivered to us in infallible, 1. For let the Printer be fallible. 2. The translation fallible. 3. The grammar fallible. 4. The man that readeth the word or publisheth it fallible, yet this hindereth not but the truth itself in the written word of God is infallible.[83]

Edward Reynolds, a member of the Assembly, tied the unfailingness of Scripture to the attributes of God. Wrote Reynolds:

1. That God in his authority is infallible, who neither can be deceived, nor can deceive. 2. That the things, delivered in holy Scriptures are the dictates and truths, which that infallible authority hath delivered unto the church to be believed; and therefore that every supernatural truth, there plainly set down . . . in an unquestionable principle; and everything, but evident consequence and deduction from thence derived, is therefore an undoubted conclusion in theological and divine knowledge.[84]

Furthermore, Reynolds was clear when he said,

First, That God is of infallible authority, and cannot lie nor deceive: which thing is a principle, . . . And, secondly, That this authority, which in faith I thus rely upon, is, indeed and infallibly, God's own authority . . . in regard to our weakness and distrust, we are often subject to stagger, yet, in the thing itself, it dependeth upon the infallibility of God's own Word, who hath said it, and is, by consequence, nearer unto Him who is the fountain of all truth; and therefore must need more share in the properties of truth, which are certainty and evidence. . . . "[85]

John Delivuk concludes,

Edward Reynolds and the other authors of the WCF believed that the Bible was inerrant. This was shown above by the seventeenth-century meaning of the word infallible, the confession writers' use of infallible in contexts where it could be used interchangeably with inerrant, and by their view of Scripture as the product of a perfect God, who had given some his attributes, such as truth and perfection, to his word. The combined evidence of these three points leads one to conclude that the authors of the confession believed strongly in the inerrancy

---

[83] Ibid., 352.

[84] Ibid., 353.

[85] Ibid., 354.

of the Bible. . . . The authors of the confession believed that the Bible is reliable and true in all matters which it addresses, that it is completely free from all errors, falsehoods, or deceits, and that this truthfulness extends to all matters religious and secular.[86]

Final Spirituality

A final attribute of this sophisticated spirituality is bravery: "Courage is another trait which to a marked degree has characterized such as are moulded by this creed. . . .He who believes in an Almighty Father, who has foreordained whatsoever comes to pass, and who through his overruling providence is preserving and governing all his creatures, and all their actions, is made superior to those experiences of life which cause others to quake and fear. Hence, Bancroft says, 'A coward and a Puritan never went together.'"[87]

Such bravery is evident in the death-bed testimonies of some of these divines. On dying in a manner worthy of our Lord, Jeremiah Whittaker put it this way:

'O, my God, break open the prison door, and set my poor captive soul free: but enable me to wait willingly thy time. I desire to be dissolved. Never was any man more desirous of life, than I am of death. When will that time come, when I shall neither sin nor sorrow any more? When shall mortality put on immortality? . . . The soul that would be truly wise, And taste substantial joys, Must rise above this giddy world, And all its trifling toys. Our treasure and hearts with God, We die to all on earth.'[88]

Often the truest measure of Christian vitality is weighed at the conclusion of life. When all is completed, when the quality of fruit is harvested, these divines were some of the most excellent Christians ever, certainly enough to induce us to give a respectful

---

[86] Ibid., 355. Cf. also John Delivuk, "Some Hermeneutical Principles of the Westminster Confession" in *Evangelical Hermeneutics,* Michael Bauman and David W. Hall, eds. (Camp Hill, PA: Christian Publications, 1995).

[87] *Memorial Volume*, 263-264.

[88] Reid, Vol. II, 232-234.

consideration of their words and works. Joseph Caryl was one such member of this Assembly, who though dead still speaketh. About him, as an example of piety, it was eulogized,

> His pious sermons did declare his worth,
> His expositions set his learning forth; . . .
> As in some mirror you might clearly see
> In him, a perfect map of Piety;[89]

Samuel Rutherford was known as an ardent defender of the faith. Flavel commended him for contending against the sectarians of the day, while Robert Baillie boasted of Rutherford as a champion against diverse enemies and specifically against the antinomians. Yet piety was one of his greatest attributes. As he was dying, Rutherford uttered, "I feed upon manna, I have angels' food, my eyes shall see my Redeemer, I know that He shall stand at the latter day on the earth, and I shall be caught up in the clouds to meet Him in the air . . . I sleep in Christ, and when I awake I shall be satisfied with his likeness. O for arms to embrace him."[90] His final words were, "Glory, glory dwells in Emmanuel's land."

In a hymn, Annie Cousins paraphrased the dying words of pious Rutherford, which show the final level of this man's convictions. Perhaps many have sung this without knowing its origin was on the lips of one of the members of the Westminster Assembly.

> Oh! Christ, he is the fountain,
> The deep, sweet well of love;
> The streams on earth I've tasted,
> I'll drink more deep above.
> There to an ocean fullness
> His mercy doth expand,
> And glory, glory dwelleth
> In Immanuel's land.

Many other biographical sketches are available to further these and other lessons in spirituality.

---

[89] Reid, 198-199.

[90] Reid, 2, 357.

Conclusion

These are lives, full of piety, and well worth knowing. They are examples of timeless spirituality, well rounded, balanced, and stable. Most will be spurred on to greater faithfulness in Christian living by a study of such. Reflecting on the value of familiarity with these divines, James Reid noted:

> a brilliant constellation at Westminster . . . [of] sound principles, Christian dispositions, and conversation becoming the gospel of Christ. In these, we may clearly see the power of divine grace shining forth in all its glory in real life, subduing the inbred corruptions of our fallen nature, and animating to every good word and work. In these, we may see pious and learned men eminently zealous in the advancement of true religion, and earnestly contending for the faith which was once delivered unto the saints.[91]

On the benefit of reviving the influence of this spiritual vitality, Robert Coyle urged:

> What we need to multiply conversions, to make our preaching mighty, to kindle our missionary fires, to set every Board free from the incubus of debt, to bring us together, North and South, to unite the entire Presbyterian family, and send us forth upon a new career of conquest and glory, is a revival of loyalty to our King. What is needed is to get away from side issues, away from the catching themes of the hour, away from themes literary, and themes political, and themes social, and themes exploited by the daily press, and lift up the name of our King, and make it pre-eminent above every name. Unless this is done, agnosticism and materialism will win the day. Unless this is done, the pulpit will go into eclipse.[92]

Often overlooked is the fact that these Westminster standards also have influence and potential for unity:

> Some do not like creeds; but our Church has always thought it fair and honorable to state explicitly what it understands the Word of God to teach. Our Creed then is our witness-bearer to the whole world. Indeed, no man can write or preach a sermon without stating in part his creed, and we are bound to contend earnestly for the faith once delivered to the saints. At the same time our Creed is pre-eminently

---

[91] Reid, Vol. 2, 3.

[92] *Anniversary Addresses, 1898*, 145. Note, and it did!!

an irenical document, and we believe the clear, definite statement by the Christian denominations of what they believe, is the very best road to an ultimate agreement of the churches on the fundamental and essential doctrines of our holy religion.[93]

The hope for a unity around biblical summaries in the Confession was expressed:

> Again, with a creed and polity adapted to the conversion of the world to Christ, and to the consolidation of the churches of the world in one grand representative organism, our Church is bent on the gathering of all the friends of Christ into a glorious Solidarity—the Kingdom of God—embracing all the true followers of the King of kings; for it believes that this consummated fact and this unparalleled glory of the Church of Christ are foreordained of God, and that his plan shall not be frustrated by the powers of darkness.[94]

The examples of these divines are of enduring value, and in no way outdated—for they represent God's eternal truths. Moreover, of existing resources among Christians, these practices are still among the best, though most frequently ignored. Rather than continuing such a superficial view, it is helpful for growth in grace to know something of the inner lives of those divines at Westminster. It helps to know what spiritual techniques were used by Christians three and a half centuries ago. Many Christians have already plowed the furrows of spiritual formation. In this discipline, we do not unearth much that is radically new; in the main, we merely dust off a great chapter of history, which is not so different from our own times. Agreeing with Solomon that "There is nothing new under the sun" (Eccl. 1:9), Christians in all ages can instruct those who live later. In turn, much can be learned by standing on the shoulders of those who have gone before. After all, if the "faith was handed down once and for all" (Jude 3), we may expect little change in core biblical truths through the centuries. Since the faith is the same in 1643 or 1993, we find

---

[93] *Anniversary Addresses,* 176.

[94] *Anniversary Addresses,* 188.

some agreement with Chesterton who called the church, a "democracy of the dead," meaning that if we truly understand the unity of the church—both militant and triumphant—we will not want to disenfranchise those in our church, who have gone home to be with the Lord. They, too have much to say in the referenda of today. Though they are dead, they still speak (Heb. 11:4). Perhaps fewer mistakes would be made if we return free expression to those spiritual pioneers who have preceded us.

Measuring the influence of Westminster by its ability to inspire extraordinary spiritual courage and loyalty, one can recall: "Rather than yield their rights of conscience, 2000 English Presbyterian ministers, on St. Bartholomew's Day, 1662, showed the stuff they were made of by leaving their churches, their support, their homes, their weeping flocks, and becoming strangers and wanderers in their native land. It was this doctrine that put into the Presbyterians of Scotland the strength and stability of their own granite hills. . . . Happy will it be for our denomination if this day shall kindle something more of that spirit in us, and send us to our homes and our people to pass it along."[95]

Nor are these merely past sentiments, true only for an earlier age: "These principles are not dead. Principles that involve the glory of the Son of God, the independence of the Church, the infallibility of his Word, the freedom of conscience, the spirituality of worship, can never die. They are the most living issues of this present hour. Today they need ringing out more faithfully than ever."[96]

At a commemoration of the Assembly one century ago, the record was set straight:

> The accusations which their opponents have made against them have, in most instances, been encomiums. They have been criticized for being too strict and uncompromising in their views of life and duty. But all excellence is marked by strictness. Strictness certainly

---

[95] *Anniversary Addresses,* 140-141.

[96] *Anniversary Addresses,* 144.

characterizes everything which truly represents God. The laws of nature are all strict; the laws of hygiene are strict; and the life which would secure their benediction must be a strict life. So with the laws of morals. Like him who ordained them they know "no variableness nor shadow of turning." Any pretended exposition of the moral nature and claims of God which is characterized by looseness, by that very tact brands itself as false. Their narrowness has been unctuously deplored. But after all is it not the narrowness of truth? The Master himself said, "Strait is the gate and narrow is the way which leadeth unto life, and few there be that find it." "Narrowness," it has been said, "is often the badge of usefulness." Great leaders of men have been narrow. Elijah was too narrow to adopt the worship of Baal. Martin Luther was too narrow to include in his creed the errors of the Papacy. Wesley was too narrow to sympathize with the cold ritualism of his age. William Carey was so narrow that he had no sympathy with the anti-mission spirit of his age. Gideon was so narrow that he could not tolerate the idols in his father's house, but rose in his might and tore them down. The narrowness of Calvinists has usually been of the same sort.[97]

---

[97] *Memorial Volume*, 262-263.

The Westminster Shorter and the Heidelberg Catechisms Compared

Joseph H. Hall

Perhaps no introductory remarks could more appropriately frame the comparison of the Westminster Shorter Catechism and the Heidelberg Catechism, than those of Philip Schaff and Benjamin B. Warfield. The former, observing the exact theological precision of the Westminster Shorter Catechism (hereafter WSC), remarked:

> It is full equal to Luther's and to the Heidelberg Catechism, in ability and influence; it far surpasses them in clearness and careful wording, and is better adapted to the Scotch and Anglo-American mind, but lacks their genial warmth, freshness, and childlike simplicity.[1]

Warfield, on the other hand, construed the Heidelberg Catechism (hereafter HC), as not wholly free from a "sort of spiritual utilitarianism, a divine euthumia. . . ." Warfield further declared that the HC,

> Taking its starting point from the longing for comfort, even though it be the highest comfort for life and death, it claims the attention of the pupil from the beginning for its own state. . . . The WC cuts itself free at once from this entanglement with lower things and begins, as it, centers and ends under the illumination of the vision of God in His glory to subserve which it finds to be the proper end of human . . . achievement.[2]

---

[1] Philip Schaff, *Creeds of Christendom* (Grand Rapids: Baker Book House, 1977), 1:787.

[2] Benjamin B. Warfield, *The Westminster Assembly and its Work* (Edmonton: Still Waters, 1991), 379.

Perhaps few would care to argue with Schaff regarding the precise formulation and clarity of the WSC. Some would find arguable the statement that the WSC is "better adapted to the Scottish and Anglo-American mind." Undoubtedly, numbers would take issue with Schaff's statement that the HC surpasses the WSC in "genial warmth freshness, and childlike simplicity."

On the other hand, many would disagree with Warfield that a kind of overly subjective "spiritual utilitarianism" pervades the HC. Moreover, equally as many would find disagreeable Warfield's statement that the WSC "cuts itself free at once from this entanglement with lower things."

Those Important First Questions

There exist no other cathechisms with such splendidly illuminating first questions. Indeed, one may say they summarize the great goals of catechization. But, we ask, are they as polarized as Warfield claims? Is the WSC as absolutely theocentric as Warfield indicates in contradistinction to a supposed anthropocentric theology of the HC?

The WSC, in its first great question, simply asks, "What is the chief end of man?" Answer, "The chief end of man is to glorify God and enjoy Him forever."

The HC poses the equally omnibus question, "What is your only comfort in life and death?" Answer, "That I, with body and soul, both in life and death, am not my own, but belong to my faithful Savior Jesus Christ, Who with His precious blood has fully satisfied for all my sins and delivered me from all the power of the devil. . . . Therefore, by His Holy Spirit, He also assures me of eternal life and makes me wholeheartedly willing and ready henceforth to live for Him."

Warfield, finds immediate foundation for his theocentric approach historically in John Calvin's *Instruction in Faith*. More specifically, Warfield points to Calvin's statement. "It is clear that we all are created in order that we may know the majesty of our Creator, that having known Him, we may esteem Him and honor Him with all fear, love and reverence."[3]

Ultimately, the Princeton professor finds the source of Q/A one of WSC in Augustine's famous statement in his *Confession*: "Thou hast made us for Thyself and our heart is restless till it finds Its rest in Thee."[4]

On the other hand one can find a strong parallel to the HC Q/A one in Calvin's *Institutes*, in the famous section "On the life of the Christian."

> We are not our own: let not our own reason nor our will therefore, sway our plans and deeds. . . . Conversely, we are God's: let us therefore, live for Him and die for Him. We are God's: let His wisdom and will therefore rule all our actions. We are God's: let all parts of our life accordingly strive toward Him as our only lawful goal.[5]

The parallel is unmistakably great! Zacharias Ursinus, chief author of the HC, in his *Commentary on the Heidelberg Catechism*, maintains that the controlling thought of the HC is not comfort as an end in itself but as a means for glorifying God. Comfort, indeed, is necessary to encourage Christians in their walk and, secondly, for worshipping and praising God, "for if we would glorify God in this and a future life, (for which we were created,) we must be delivered from sin and death; and not rush into desperation, but be sustained to the end, with sure consolation."[6]

Is Warfield correct, then, when he charges HC with a sort of "spiritual utilitarianism . . . that claims the attention of the pupil from the beginning for its own state"? While one must honestly

---

[3] John Calvin, *Instruction in Faith* (Philadelphia: Westminster Press, 1949), 17.

[4] Augustine, *Confessions*, 1:1.

[5] John Calvin, *Institutes of the Christian Religion* (Philadelphia: Westminster Press, 1954), 3.7.1

[6] Zacharias Ursinus, *Commentary on the Heidelberg Catechism* (Grand Rapids: Eerdmans, 1954), 20.

beg to be relieved of any possible pejorative intention of the question, nevertheless, one must reply that there exists, indeed, a certain legitimate, objective application of grace that not only comforts but calls forth a subjective response of gratitude. In any event, the term "comfort" was used in a vastly different way by Ursinus than used today: "Comfort is that which results from a certain process of reasoning, in which we oppose something good to something evil, that by a proper consideration of this good, we may mitigate our grief, and patiently endure the evil."[7]

There can be little doubt that the WSC is correct in its theocentric approach that man's chief end is to glorify God. But a balanced interpretation of Q/A one of the WSC must also allow for the enjoyment of God's great salvation as well. Warfield himself allows for the enjoyment of God's gracious salvation in stating, "No man is truly Reformed in his thought . . . unless he conceives of man as destined to be the instrument of divine glory, but also destined to reflect the glory of God in his own consciousness, to exult in God; nay, unless he himself delights in God as the all-glorious One." [8]

We must allow for a divergence of style, rhetoric, and historical nuances in the two catechisms. Certainly it is true that the WSC is clear and crisply exact in its teachings, while infrequently alluding to personal references. The HC, while attempting the same objectivity, employs various motifs which make it a strongly personal catechism. What historical occasions conduced toward these variances, both certainly within the acceptability of the Reformed faith?

Historical Variances Conditioning Each Catechism

Numerous factors converge in the formation of the two catechisms. Chief among these was the fact that the WSC stood

---

[7] Idem, 17-18.

[8] Warfield, 397.

at the very apex of catechetical construction, whereas the HC was written nearer the fountainhead. Scores of Puritan catechisms had been written and published during the fifty years prior to the Westminster Assembly. Moreover, the Westminster Assembly numbered among its constituency at least twelve men who had prepared catechisms or teaching aids prior to 1643. Since these catechists represented at least three pedagogical approaches to catechetical training it is understandable that the Assembly had to settle on a given methodology before writing the catechisms.

Choice might be made from three antecedent Puritan methodologies. One method was called "scriptural catechism," having its answers taken verbatim from Scripture. A second method was that of making paraphrased answers from Scripture. In still a third method, the answer was first given in full as in the second method, but was further divided into subordinate questions which, themselves contained the answer. A simple "yes" or "no" was required for these subordinate questions.[9]

While the Scottish and some English delegates warmly favored the third method, a modification of the third which deleted "yes" and "no" answers prevailed. This chosen method resulted in the most precise catechism ever constructed. Dr. Alexander Mitchell, renown Westminster scholar, remarked concerning the formation of the WSC:

> One can hardly contemplate without a shudder how near we were to missing the most concise, nervous and severely logical catechism in our language had Mr. Palmer and the Scotch Commissioners carried their point and got these subordinate questions and answers inserted in the catechism.[10]

The Westminster Assembly decided in January 1647 to construct two catechisms, a larger and smaller. Ostensibly the

---

[9] Leonard T. Grant, "Puritan Catechising," in *Presbyterian Journal*, XLVI (March 1968): 111.

[10] Alexander F. Mitchell, *The Westminster Assembly, Its History and Standards* (Philadelphia: Presbyterian Board of Publication, 1897), 426.

tension between devising a weighty theological instrument as opposed to the one that would be more teachable to children was the point at issue. The Scot, Samuel Rutherford, very memorably says of the tension, that the committee "found it very difficult to satisfy themselves or the world with one form of catechism; or to dress up milk and meat both in one dish."[11] Both the Larger and Shorter Catechisms were completed in the Spring of 1648.

Certainly the religio/political climate also conduced to the precision of the WSC. The quest for theological homogeneity occasioned by the Solemn League and Covenant for the British Isles, lent itself to the calling by the British Parliament one of the most theologically prestigious largely Puritan convocations ever. What the Assembly sought to do in constructing the Westminster standards, was to present the British Isles with the most biblically sophisticated teaching aids ever devised.

A rich catechetical legacy, a deliberate, painstaking, selection of method, precise collaboration of an average of around sixty scholars for a period of over a year, all conduced to the Westminster catechetical heritage. A highly charged religio/ political situation and a parliamentary mandate fed into its development.

By contrast, within a generation of catechetical development, a solitary Calvinist prince mandated a catechism that was to become the mainstay of the Dutch and German Reformed churches and which today is still beloved for its orthodoxy and warmly personal application.

Prince Frederick III of the Palatinate desired a distinctly Reformed catechetical aid for instruction of his people and thus appointed Zacharias Ursinus and Caspar Olevianus, Heidelberg University professor and court preacher respectively, for the work. They were to receive assistance from the Heidelberg University faculty.

---

[11] Samuel Rutherford, quoted in Mitchell, 429.

The young professor Ursinus became the principal author of the HC. Ursinus had studied with Philip Melanchthon in Wittenberg, Heinrich Bullinger and Peter Martyr in Zurich, and was a friend and acquaintance of Beza and Calvin. It is easy to conclude that his work must have something of an ecumenical flavor, while at the same time, a thoroughly Reformed foundation.

Ursinus had written two catechisms prior to the HC, a *Catechesis Maior* and *Catechesis Minor*, with the latter forming the immediate foundation for the HC. Scholarly consensus today points to a committee of at least seven men, probably most from Heidelberg University, who used the Smaller Catechism of Ursinus as their source for the final draft of the HC.[12]

Without question, the HC is one of the most warmly personal and genial of all catechisms. Comfort in the assurance of salvation and personal application of all loci are the hallmarks of HC. But has it pandered to "spiritual utilitarianism" and thus denigrated the Reformed faith? Not at all. Ursinus, in his *Commentary the Heidelberg Catechism*, maintains the utmost necessity of comfort of faith but ultimately always in the service of God.

Why does the HC differ from Mitchell's "most concise, nervous, and severely logical" WSC? First, the devotional warmth of the HC is shown in its treatment of the Lord's Prayer, in contrast to the straightforward, didactic manner of the WSC. The HC presents each response to the question as an actual prayer to God! Secondly, the personal response is inculcated by creedal questions on the Apostles' Creed (which is relegated to the appendix of the WSC). For example, HC question 26 asks, "what do *you* [italics added] believe when you say, 'I believe in God the Father, Almighty. . . ?' " The answer becomes a very personal response: "The eternal Father . . . is for the sake of Christ His Son *my* God and *my* father in whom *I* so trust. . . ." [emphases added]

---

[12] Bard Thompson, "Historical Background of the Catechism," in *Essays on the Heidelberg Catechism* (Philadelphia: United Church Press,1963), 26.

Finally, the personal warmth of HC is shown by its pastoral nature, especially in preaching. In its use in the Palatine, the HC was divided into nine sections to be read annually to the congregation. Among the Dutch Reformed, the catechism was divided into fifty-two Lord's Days and since the mandate of the Synod of Dordt, many conservative Dutch Reformed churches have faithfully preached the HC once each Sunday as the sermonic foundation. While there exists some record of preaching through the WSC such as Puritan Thomas Watson's *Body of Practical Divinity*, for the most part it has not been the subject of preaching as has the HC.

Structure of Each Catechism

The WSC is structured along the lines of Law, Gospel, Law. From the famous question, "What is sin?" and its definition, "Any want of conformity to, or transgression of the Law of God," WSC carefully shows man's deplorably depraved condition.

However, the WSC presents its exposition proper of the Law only after the soteriological section of the catechism. After presenting the redemptive work of Christ and the benefits for the Christian, WSC proceeds to the Christian's duty, namely, obedience to the Ten Commandments. WSC sets the stage for the covenantal graciousness of law by introducing the position that "because God is the Lord and our God, and Redeemer, therefore, we are bound to keep all his comandments." Thus, after presenting the pedagogical use of the law in leading the person to Christ, the WSC correctly emphasizes obedience as the necessary consequence of redeemed, reconciled sonship. In so doing, the WSC utilizes John Calvin's primary emphasis upon the third use of the Law—as the norm of gratitude for the redeemed.[13]

---

[13] Calvin, *Institutes*, 2.7.12.

Viewing the WSC from its total structure, it is very obviously patterned after the Westminster Confession of Faith, except for the famous introductory question. After the introduction, one encounters the principle of knowledge, Scripture, next theology proper, then anthropology, soteriology, and practical Christian living in obedience to the Law and a life of prayer according to the Lord's Prayer, and a proper use of the sacraments.

The HC is structured, likewise, upon a threefold division Law, Gospel, Law, or as many divide it, Guilt, Grace, and Gratitude. As in the WSC, the Law is the source of my knowledge of sin and misery. Reconciliation comes through the grace of the gospel of Christ and the Holy Spirit's application of redemption. Then, having been redeemed unto good works, I give myself willingly in obedient service. Again, as in WSC, the exposition proper of the Law is found in the soteriological section.

Most interestingly, Ursinus, rather that setting forth a Law, Gospel, Law motif, speaks in his *Commentary* only of a Law and Gospel structure. While certainly willing to allow the Law, Gospel, Law interpretation, Ursinus chooses to include both the pedagogical and normative use of the Law under the one usage.[14]

Viewing the HC from a broader structural perspective, after the famous introductory question, the Law is adduced to show man's misery. In contrast to the loci approach of WSC, the HC omits any comparable treatment of theology proper. Creation, anthropology, and theodicy are treated prior to soteriology proper. The Apostles' Creed is treated in the soteriology section, and is followed by the third section on gratitude which includes the treatment of the Law and the warmly devotional section on the Lord's Prayer.

Theology

Turning from the structure of each catechism, it is appropriate to compare and contrast the theology of each. While both

---

[14] Ursinus, 13.

catechisms are found as bulwarks of Reformed theology, there are theological nuances conditioned in part, by ethnic, chronological, and teleological differences. Four theological loci will be examined: Double Predestination, Covenant, Limited Atonement, and the Lord's Supper.

Double Predestination

Neither the WSC nor HC explicitly teaches double predestination. The WSC Q/A 20 and 21 explicitly teach election unto salvation but fail to teach reprobation. Question/Answer 20 delares that God "elected some to everlasting life," without any reference to the reprobate. In the HC, Q/A 54 teaches election implicitly by declaring that Christ "gathers, defends, and preserves for Himself . . . a Church chosen to everlasting life. . . ."

Moreover, the WSC contains a strongly implicit teaching of reprobation in Q/A 7 on the decrees of God. The decrees of God "are his eternal purpose, according to the counsel of his will, whereby, for his own glory, he has ordained whatever comes to pass." By the strictest logic, we must include reprobation in the absolute "whatever comes to pass."

Likewise in the HC, there exists a strongly implicitly deductive argument from Q/A 26-28 concerning providence. In a famous statement, Christians are exhorted to be "patient in adversity and thankful in prosperity" because God is their faithful Father, from whose love they cannot be separated and, also, because "all creatures are so in His hand that without His will they cannot so much as move." The sovereignty of God here surely includes reprobation.

Why does neither catechism explicitly teach reprobation? Since double predestination is explicitly taught in neither the WSC or Westminster Larger Catechism, but is found in the Westminster Confession, one may legitimately deduce that the doctrine was relegated to a later period of Christian maturity when the child (or adult) could digest strong doctrine. This was indeed the case with Ursinus's HC, for reprobation was taught in his prior Large Catechism from which the HC was partially drawn.[15] It is also possible that Frederick III ruled out the inclusion of reprobation so as not to offend the Lutherans.

Covenant of Grace

The covenant of grace, a hallmark of Reformed theology, is explicitly taught in WSC Q/A 20 and 21 in which election is joined with the covenant of grace. God is shown not only to promise grace through election and covenant, but also shown to act in behalf of His people by the redemptive work of Christ.

But does the HC teach covenant theology? It does, indeed teach election but one looks in vain for such explicit teaching as found in the WSC. Ursinus intended covenant theology to be taught under the rubric of Christ as mediator of the one covenant found in both the Old and New Testaments. In Q/A 15-18, Christ is shown to be the bringer of the new covenant, whereby He "might obtain for us and restore to us righteousness and life."

There exists yet another implicit area of covenant teaching in both catechisms. Both the WSC and HC place the Decalogue in the soteriological section, whereby they intend to teach that the law is covenantal. This is particularly seen in the Prologue to the Law, where God is shown to bring His people from sin's bondage by grace so they might obey the Law from grateful hearts.

Limited Atonement

The WSC is quite explicit on the question, For whom did Christ die? Question 21 asks, "Who is the Redeemer of God's elect?" and answers, "The only Redeemer of God's elect is the

---

[15] Idem, 275.

Lord Jesus Christ. . . ." Question 25 continues, How does Christ execute the office of a priest?" The answer is that Christ did so "in His once offering up of Himself a sacrifice to satisfy divine justice and to reconcile us to God. . . ." In the most unequivocal way, the WSC teaches limited atonement, that is, Christ's death was both purposed by election and effective only for the elect.

The HC, on the other hand, though teaching limited atonement, contains one passage that has been interpreted as teaching universal atonement. Passages very clearly indicating Christ's death on behalf of His people are Q/A 1, 31, 34, 39, 44, 45, 52, 67, 70, 75, and 79.

One passage affording difficulty and possible misinterpretation in the HC is Question 37: "What do you understand by the word suffered?" Answer: That Christ "bore, in body and soul, the wrath of God against the sin of the whole human race, in order that by His passion, as the one atoning sacrifice, He might redeem our body and soul from everlasting damnation, and obtain for us God's grace, righteousness and eternal life."

The phrase in question here is "the sin of the whole human race." Does this denote universal atonement? Several factors indicate a negative to the question. The "whole human race" is limited by the context which specifies the purpose of Christ's atoning work, "that He might redeem our body and soul. . . ." Voetius, opposing a universal interpretation of this passage declares, "the whole human race" must be taken as "people of all sorts, conditions, and nations out of the whole human race."[16] But most important, Ursinus' *Commentary* (although at this point probably written by his successor, David Pareus), makes the distinction between Christ's atonement as sufficient for all men's sin but efficient only for the elect who are in fact redeemed.[17]

---

[16] Voetius, quoted in Roger Nicole, "Year of the *Heidelberg Catechism* (1563-1963)," *Torch and Trumpet* (July-August 1963): 11.

[17] Idem, 12.

The Lord's Supper

One of the real surprises in the WSC is the lack of any mention specifically of the nature of Christ's presence in the Lord's Supper. The surprise is only intensified when one remembers the centrality of the subject in theological debates from Henry VIII forward. The most probable argument is one of silence: that the Puritan framers of Westminster, living three generations later, took the extra-calvinisticum position for granted. Nevertheless, one looks in vain for a statement declaring Christ's presence in heaven and the Spirit's lifting us up to feed upon Him in heaven.

While this is the case, WSC indeed does indicate the nature of the eating; namely, spiritual, and "not after a corporal and carnal manner." (Q/A 96) Moreover, the eating is said to be by faith. (Q/A 97) But the question that so plagued the Continent, and England as well, as to manner of the presence of Christ in the Lord's Supper goes unanswered.

On the other hand, the HC, nearer the fountainhead of Calvinistic development of the Lord's Supper (against the transubstantiation of the Roman Catholics on the one hand and the real presence of the Lutherans on the other), exhibits a solid spiritual presence of the Lord in the elements via the work of the Holy Spirit. Q/A 79 declares that Christians are "really partakers of His true body and blood through the working of the Holy Spirit." Moreover, Q/A 80 underscores Christ's human nature as existing in heaven and the Christian's communing with Him there through the Holy Spirit.

Conclusions

The WSC signals the high-water mark of Reformed catechetical writing, coming after a century of efforts. The Parliamentary mandate, according to the Solemn League and Covenant, was to construct the best Reformed documents possible, with the contribution of the best of the Puritan scholarship, blended with Scotch theological sagacity. The emphasis was upon precision rather than personal devotion or a combination thereof.

The HC, on the other hand, answered the purpose of correcting a formalistic South German church, which though traditionally Lutheran, was in need of embracing the Reformed faith, along with its prince. Thus a prince, rather than a Parliament, desired to bring forth both a Calvinistic creed and true personal piety. Historically, the HC was written in a tumultous period which called for a great amount of personal commitment and assurance.

Whereas, contemporaries of the HC considered it the apex of catechetical writing (Heinrich Bullinger: "I consider it to be the best catechism ever published."[18]), many on this side of Westminster consider the WSC the high-water mark.[19] Both emphases are needed: the precise and genuinely Reformed declarations of WSC and the profoundly Reformed statements of HC integrated with a deeply devotional commitment.

---

[18] Heinrich Bullinger, quoted in Hendrikus Berkhof, "The Catechism in Context," in *Essays on the Heidelberg Catechism*, 14-15.

[19] J. G. Machen, "The Creeds and Doctrinal Advance," in *Scripture and Confession*, ed by John H. Skilton (Philadelphia: Presbyterian and Reformed, 1973), 156.

The Erosion of Calvinist Orthodoxy

I. Hamilton

It was acknowledged by the Puritan framers of the Westminster Confession of Faith that subscription to the Confession could only be, at best, provisional. This is highlighted in rightly memorable words in Chapter 1.10: "The supreme Judge, by which all controversies of religion are to be determined, and all decrees of councils, opinions of ancient writers, doctrines of men, and private spirits, are to be examined, and in whose sentence we are to rest, can be no other but the Holy Spirit speaking in the Scripture." These words underlined the Puritans' conviction that Scripture alone has ultimate and infallible authority for Christians. Whatever else the Confession of Faith was, it was not conceived as an unalterable symbol of Christian truth, a theological "sacred cow." James Bannerman faithfully reflected the thinking and theology of the Confession's framers when he wrote:

> Let any part of them (confessions of faith) be proved from Scripture to be false, and we give it up; for we hold them only because and in so far as they are true. We invite every man to go beyond them if they can. We call upon every student of Gods Word to press forward to fresh discoveries of the truth, and to open up new views of the meaning of Scripture. . . . Those who have studied their Bibles longest and prayerfully are most convinced of that.[1]

---

[1] J. Bannerman, *The Church of Christ* (Edinburgh, 1869), Vol. 1, 320.

The erosion of Westminster Calvinism in those churches which adopted the Westminster Confession as their subordinate standard of faith was a process of some complexity. This complexity is partly seen in the arguments and disputes which preceded every attempt to alter a church's terms of subscription to the Confession. The complexity is more evident, however, in tracing the evolving attachment many ministers and theological teachers exhibited towards their church's subordinate standard of faith. It is a fact, for example, that the men who introduced Higher Criticism into the Scottish Church in the latter half of the nineteenth century all subscribed the Confession of Faith as the confession of their faith simpliciter. We are confronted therefore with a disjunction between what was formally adhered to and what was personally believed. The issue is somewhat further complicated by the view, held most notably by Charles Hodge, that in many of the confessional churches, men were allowed to subscribe the Confession while not subscribing every proposition in it.[2]

Whether Hodge was correct in his understanding of the terms of "The Adopting Act" of 1729 or not, the fact that he believed he was, and no doubt many others concurred in his judgement, means that there probably never was a time when the Confession was subscribed *simpliciter*, without mental, if not verbal or written, reservation at some points by all ministers.

In seeking therefore to chart the erosion of Confessional Calvinism we must acknowledge that we are faced with an inexact science. We can accurately chart when churches publicly and formally altered their subscription to the Confession; but this was always the climax of a period of questioning and disputation.

---

[2] See Charles Hodges article in *The Biblical Repertory and Princeton Review* in 1858 on the "Adoption of the Confession of Faith," and his *The Church and its Polity*, London 1879, 317-335.

The Erosion of Westminster Calvinism within Scottish Presbyterianism[3]

The high point of subscription to the Westminster Confession within Scottish Presbyterianism was Act X of the General Assembly of the Church of Scotland, May 1711.[4] The second question put to ministers at their ordination revealed the extent of the terms of subscription required by the Church to its Subordinate Standard of Faith: "Do you sincerely own and believe the whole doctrine contained in the Confession of Faith . . . to be founded upon the Word of God; and do you acknowledge the same as the confession of your faith. . . . ?"[5]

Although it has been argued that the Church allowed ministers "a certain measure of liberty to depart from the Confessional standard" during the following years,[6] there is no historical evidence to substantiate this claim.[7] The Formula of Subscription imposed on all ministers an unreserved commitment to the "whole doctrine" of the Confession, allowing no written or "mental" qualification.[8] This appears to be markedly different from what prevailed within the American Presbyterian Church from its inception.

Over the next two centuries a number of breaches were made within Scottish Presbyterianism in unqualified subscription to the

---

[3] For a full and thorough discussion see Ian Hamilton, *The Erosion of Calvinist Orthodoxy: Seceders and Subscription in Scottish Presbyterianism* (Edinburgh, 1990).

[4] *Acts of the General Assembly of the Church of Scotland* 1638-1842 (Edinburgh, 1843), 453-456.

[5] Ibid., 455.

[6] See C. G. McCrie, *The Confessions of the Church of Scotland* (Edinburgh, 1907).

[7] See Hamilton, op cit., 4-33.

[8] It is striking that the Formula adopted by the Associate Presbytery in 1737 (the new Presbyterian body formed by the secession of Ebenezer Erskine, William Wilson, Alexander Moncrieff and James Fisher from the National Kirk in 1733), retained the distinctive wording of the 1711 Formula.

Westminster Confession. The first of these breaches came in 1796 when the General Associate Synod effectively qualified its commitment to the Confession by declaring that it only approved of spiritual means for bringing men and women into Christ's Church, notwithstanding the teaching of the Confession regarding the power of the civil magistrate.[9]

The next significant breach occurred in 1847 when the newly formed United Presbyterian Church, a union of the Relief and United Secession Churches, devised a Formula that did not require its ministers to own the Confession of Faith as the confession of their faith. The revised Formula put the following question to ordinands: "Do you acknowledge the Westminster Confession of Faith.. as an exhibition of the sense in which you understand the Holy Scriptures . . . ?"[10]

A. T. Innes believed that by this revised Formula the United Presbyterian Church had "wholly abolished the Formula of Subscription"[11] as a meaningful test of orthodoxy.

The most significant revision of confessional subscription within the Scottish Presbyterian Churches occurred in the United Presbyterian Church's Declaratory Act of 1879. This Act allowed ministers "liberty of opinion . . . on such points in the Standards not entering the substance of the faith."[12] In its new Formula, subscription was to be given to an undefined "substance of the faith." In 1892, the Free Church of Scotland followed suit in redefining its commitment to the Confession in a similar fashion.

Most significantly, in 1905 the Church of Scotland was given power by Parliament to amend its Formula of Subscription to the

---

[9] cf. WCF, Chapter 20.4, and 23.

[10] *Proceedings of the Synod of the United Presbyerian Church 1847-1856* (Edinburgh, 1856), 64

[11] A. T. Innes, *The Law of Creeds in Scotland* (1st ed.; Edinburgh and London, 1867), 438.

[12] *Proceedings,* op cit., 637f.

Westminster Confession. In 1910 a new Formula was adopted: "I hereby subscribe the Confession of Faith, declaring that I accept it as the Confession of this Church, and that I believe the fundamental doctrines of the Christian Faith contained therein."[13] Significantly what was meant by "fundamental doctrines" was never, and until the present day has never been, specified! This "failure" to specify "the substance of the faith" and "the fundamental doctrines" contained in the Confession was a deliberate attempt to hold together, within one church, men of vastly divergent theological views. In essence each man was left to devise his own confession of faith.[14] John Cairns, the chief architect of the United Presbyterian Church Declaratory legislation, recognised the danger inherent in the legislation. He declared: "I humbly trust that, with this qualification allowing liberty, this Church will sacredly and zealously guard this liberty from destroying the very faith it is brought in to strengthen and uphold."[15] At the very moment Cairns was making his plea, the Synod, having condemned the Rev. Fergus Ferguson for heresy, refused to discipline him. Ferguson was an avowed universalist, and had openly challenged the Confession's teaching on a number of doctrines. The refusal of the Synod to discipline him exposed the open-ended nature of the Declaratory legislation. The Synod's refusal to punish Ferguson signalled the final stage in the erosion of Westminster Calvinism within the United Presbyterian Church. Ferguson's biographer, J. D. Leckie, put the matter well: "He (Ferguson) had secured in a measure every one of the ends for which he had fought; increase of liberty, a loosening of ancient

---

[13] Cited in N. M. de S. Cameron, et al, eds., *Dictionary of Scottish History and Theology*, 805-6.

[14] It is interesting that the "liberty of opinion" allowed in the United Presbyterian Declaratory Act was considered to be but a formalising of "the practice hitherto observed in this Church" (*Proceedings*, op cit. 637f).

[15] J. Cairns, *Speech on the Subordinate Standards (With the Report of the Committee and Declaratory Statement)*, (Edinburgh, 1878), 3.

bonds, an opening of the doors of an olden prison-house, a step towards a wider comprehension. . . . In fine, he had achieved the explicit toleration of anti-Calvinistic beliefs within the walls of a Calvinistic Communion."[16] Today there are four Presbyterian bodies in Scotland that subscribe the Confession of Faith without qualification, still requiring ministers to own the Confession as the confession of their faith.[17] In the Church of Scotland, however, the Confession has fallen into desuetude. It remains the Kirk's Subordinate Standard of Faith, but is largely forgotten and rarely studied. Occasionally attempts are made to remove the Confession as the Kirk's Subordinate Standard of Faith, but these have been frustrated by the strange alliance of liberals and conservatives: the one fearful of being asked to subscribe a statement of faith with no "conscience clause"; and the other fearful that a modern statement of faith would have little theological substance, a minimalist reflection of the Kirk's present theological confusion and diversity.

At the present time there is little to suggest that the theology of the Westminster Confession is anything more than an historical relic for the vast majority of Presbyterians in Scotland.

The bare facts of the above, however, do not begin to do justice to the question of the erosion of Westminster Calvinism in the Scottish Church. The passing of Declaratory legislation and qualifying legislation only charts the chronological erosion of Westminster orthodoxy within the Scottish church. More difficult to chart is the erosion of belief that prepared the way for the passing of Declaratory and qualifying legislation.

Within a decade of the Church enacting the 1711 Act, the case of John Simson, Professor of Divinity in the University of Glasgow

---

[16] J. D.Leckie, *Fergus Ferguson, His Theology and Heresy Trial* (Edinburgh, 1923), 262.

[17] i.e.,The Free Church of Scotland, the Free Presbyterian Church of Scotland, and the Associated Presbyerian Churches, and the Free Church of Scotland (Continuing) with a combined membership of around 25,000 (The "Kirk" has a nominal membership of around 750,000).

revealed the presence of "unsound views" within the Kirk. Simson was accused of Socinianism and Arminianism in 1714, and later in 1726 of denying the deity of Christ. It is undeniable that some of Simson's views were wholly contrary to the teaching of the Confession, but although he was eventually suspended from his Chair by the General Assembly, he was never deposed from the ministry. For men like Thomas Boston and Ebenezer Erskine this was a scandal. Earlier, the Assembly of 1717 which found Simson guilty of "some opinions not necessary to be taught in divinity", but which exhonerated him from charges of heresy, condemned the Auchderarder Creed, and in 1720 the *Marrow of Modern Divinity*.

The Age of Moderatism which dominated the Kirk for almost the rest of the century was characterised by formal subscription to the Confession of Faith and a practical (and often public) denial of many of its distinctive Calvinistic doctrines.

The impetus for "confessional revolution"[18] was strengthened during the first half of the nineteenth century by the cases of John McLeod Campbell and John Brown. Campbell was a Church of Scotland minister who was deposed from the ministry in 1831 for teaching, contrary to the Confession, that Christ died for all men, not only the elect, and that assurance belongs to the essence of saving faith (Campbell would later distance himself from a number of orthodox Christian beliefs, including substitutionary, penal atonement and eternal punishment). Although Campbell did not receive much support at the time, his deposition was soon looked upon as something of a sea-change in the Kirk's practical relation to the Confession.[19]

---

[18] See A. C. Cheyne's chapter "The Confessional Revolution" in *The Transforming Of The Kirk* (Edinburgh, 1983). While not a protagonist for Westminster orthodoxy, Cheyne helpfully, if at times sketchily, traces the general course of the confessional revolution within the Kirk.

[19] The refusal of the Assembly to allow Campbell to have his views tried in the light of Scripture (it would only examine them in the light of the Confession) was increasingly seen as an attempt by traditionalists to hide from the new understandings of Scripture coming into the Church.

The universality of God's love which shaped every doctrine for Campbell increasingly became the touchstone to which all confessional statements would be brought.

Brown, a Professor in the United Secession Church, whose exegetical and expository commentaries continue to be in wide circulation, was charged with teaching views of the atonement incompatible with the teaching of the Confession. Between 1841 and 1845, Brown defended his essentially Amyraldian view of the atonement as being consonant with the Confessions teaching on Christ's atonement.[20] Brown was eventually cleared by his Church of teaching views contrary to that of the Confession. Whether an Amyraldian scheme can in any way fit in with the Confession's teaching on the atonement is a moot point (It is interesting, if not significant, that the Amyraldians in the Westminster Assembly felt free to subscribe the Confession's teaching, *simplicter*). What is significant, however, is that the result of this controversy was to make a breach in the Westminster doctrine of limited atonement. "The emphasis placed throughout the Controversy on the love of God to all men acted as something of a harbinger for the revolution in Scottish theology in the 1860's and 1870's, when the love of God to all became the trademark of those dissatisfied with what they considered the narrow exclusivism of the Westminster Standards."[21]

Although we find Robert Candlish as late as 1865 writing about the Westminster Assembly that "its doctrinal decisions, on all the questions fairly before it, will stand the test of time, and ultimately command the assent of universal Christendom,"[22] within twenty years commitment in the Scottish churches to the doctrines of the Confession was altogether more formal than real.

---

[20] See Hamilton. op. cit., 34ff.

[21] Ibid., 74.

[22] R. S. Candish, *The Fatherhood of God* (2nd edn., Edinburgh, 1865), 289.

A further influence for confessional change within the Scottish churches came from an unexpected quarter. The arrival of D. L. Moody, the American evangelist, in 1873 brought to the fore views of doctrine and evangelism which implicitly contradicted the theology of Westminster. One nineteenth century observer believed that Moody's "uncomplicated" gospel "did more to relieve Scotland of the old hyper-Calvinist doctrine of election, and of what the theologians call limited atonement, and to bring home the love of God and the grace of God to all men, than did even the teaching of McLeod Campbell."[23]

By 1910, when the Church of Scotland produced an altered form of subscription which required no more than acceptance of "the fundamental doctrines of the Christian faith contained" within the Confession, "the old exclusiveness (and no doubt the old definiteness and consistency) of Reformed theology was at an end, and the confessional revolution had reached its goal."[24]

The Victorian Age was an age of increasing ferment in the Scottish churches. Rationalism rapidly overtook revelation as the faith of many thinking people. The gathering momentum of criticism directed towards orthodox Christian belief from men and women such as Francis Newman, the novelist George Eliot, and "men of science" like Thomas Huxley, created a new climate of thought with which theology was forced to

---

[23] P. Carnegie Simpson, quoted in Cheyne, op. cit., 83. Even a staunch Westminster man like Revd. Alexander MacRae believed that Moody's preaching was needed in Scotland because "the strictly orthodox character of the preaching of that period . . . failed because it was not evangelistic, not sufficiently personal, pointed, and urgent in seeking to lead souls to Christ." Iain H. Murray, *Revival and Revivalism: The Making and Marring of American Evangelicalism* 1750-1858 (Edinburgh, 1994), 401-402. See also K. R. Ross, "Calvinists in Controversy: John Kennedy, Horatius Bonar and the Moody Mission of 1873-74", *SBET* 9 (1991), 51-63.

[24] Cheyne, op. cit., 85.

grapple. Truth was increasingly seen "no longer as absolute, philosophically static, revealed once for all, but as relative, genetic and evolutionary."[25]

The present situation within the main Scottish Presbyterian churches regarding the Confession is unambiguous. The Free Church, the Free Presbyterian Church, the Associated Presbyterian Churches, and the Free Church of Scotland (Continuing) all subscribe the Confession of Faith simpliciter.[26] The Confession remains the Church of Scotland's Subordinate Standard of Faith *de jure,* but is *de facto* ignored: mentioned in passing at ordinations, but rarely, if ever, examined far less taught.

The legacy inherited from a century and a half of confessional decline is one where theological ambivilence reigns. Most seriously, no longer is the Word of God written viewed as the Christian's final and binding court of appeal and authority. This has been most dramatically seen in the acceptance by the vast majority of evangelical ministers in the Church of Scotland of the General Assembly's declaration regarding the ordination of women. Although most acknowledge that Scripture forbids women to exercise teaching leadership in Christ's Church, it is argued that "other considerations" demand conformity to the Assembly's Act rather than to the plain teaching of Scripture. The core of these "other considerations" seems to be the retention of the pulpit at whatever cost. Barely a generation ago it hardly seemed possible that Reformed evangelicals could adopt such a position. Today, however, the teaching of Scripture is qualified by the pronouncements and enactments of the new infallible

---

[25] N. Annan, "The Strands of Unbelief", in *Ideas and Beliefs of the Victorians* (London, 1949), 151.

[26] In terms of the present-day debate in the Presbyterian Church in America (see Morton H Smith's, *The Case for Full Subscription to the Westminster Standards in the Presbyterian Church in America,* (Greenville, 1992) these churches would be "strict subscriptionists" rather than "system subscriptionists."

authority, the General Assembly.[27] At the present time there are more evangelicals in the Church of Scotland ministry than there has been for over one hundred years. It would be true to say, however, that the evangelicalism in the pulpits, in the main, is no longer distinctively Reformed in its doctrinal convictions. The great Reformation maxim *Sola Scriptura* has been effectively undermined by the willingness, however reluctantly, to put General Assembly enactments above the acknowledged clear teaching of Scripture.[28] It is to be hoped that there may yet be a return to the conviction that Christians are always bound to go where Scripture leads them, whatever the cost. Such a conviction will inevitably prove costly, but it will also secure God's blessing. Then, and not till then, will the doctrines of Westminster occupy a prized place in the Church's life.

---

[27] James Weatherhead, then Principal Clerk to the General Assembly, clarified the law of the Church of Scotland on women's ordination in June 1987: "Any decision by a Kirk Session to the effect that women will not be considered for the eldership is . . . in breach of the law of the Church. . . . While the law stands as it is, there is no provision for conscientious objection to applying it." According to the Church's Procurator, when opposition to women elders is stated as a matter of policy or principle it is *ultra vires*.

[28] See William Philip's article "The Biblical Case for Staying in the Kirk Today," *The Rutherford Journal*, 1.1 (Spring 1994, Edinburgh), 9-12.

Westminster and Establishment: a Scottish Perspective

HUGH M. CARTWRIGHT

This paper considers the teaching of the Westminster Confession on church and state relations in a Christian nation,[1] taking account of Scottish expositions of the subject. The contribution of the Scottish Church and her commissioners at Westminster to its formulation was significant. In Scotland a serious attempt was made to implement the doctrine and secure a spiritually independent Church in friendly connection with a State confessing Reformed Christianity.

The Confession was the fruit of cooperation between church and state. The English Parliament called "an Assembly of learned and godly Divines, and others, to be consulted with by Parliament, for the settling of the government and liturgy of the Church of England, and for vindicating and clearing of the doctrine of the said Church from false aspersions and interpretations."[2] The

---

[1] Strong advocates of church/state separation recognize the concept of a Christian nation as biblical. J. M. Kik, *Church and State: The Story of Two Kingdoms New York*, 1963), 120-130. J. H. Thornwell, *Relation of the State to Christ* in *The Collected Writings of James Henley Thornwell*, Vol. IV (1875; reprint 1974, Banner of Truth Trust), 555: "Our republic will perish like the Pagan republics of Greece and Rome unless we baptize it into the name of Christ."

[2] An Ordinance of the Lords and Commons assembled in Parliament, June

Assembly's aim to "further the union of this Island in one Form of Kirk-government, one Confession of Faith, one Catechism, one Directory for the worship of God"[3] was largely accounted for by the cooperation of Scottish and English civil and religious authorities represented in the 1643 Solemn League and Covenant.[4]

Some editions of the Confession modify statements on church and state without acknowledging deviations from the original. Relevant sections of the text approved by the Assembly[5] follow.

> 20.4. And because the powers which God hath ordained, and the liberty which Christ hath purchased, are not intended by God to destroy, but mutually to uphold and preserve one another; they who, upon pretence of Christian liberty, shall oppose any lawful power, or the lawful exercise of it, whether it be civil or ecclesiastical, resist the ordinance of God. And for their publishing of such opinions, or maintaining of such practices, as are contrary to the light of nature, or to the known principles of Christianity, whether concerning faith, worship, or conversation; or to the power of godliness; or such erroneous opinions or practices, as either in their own nature, or in the manner of publishing or maintaining them, arc destructive to the external peace and order which Christ hath established in the church; they may lawfully be called to account, and proceeded against by the censures of the church, and by the power of the civil magistrate.

> 23.1. God, the supreme Lord and King of all the world, hath ordained civil magistrates to be, under him, over the people, for his own glory, and the public good; and, to this end, hath armed them with the power of the sword, for the defence and encouragement of them that are good, and for the punishment of evildoers.

12th 1643, *The Subordinate Standards and other Authoritative Documents of the Free Church of Scotland* (Edinburgh, 1955), xxiii; *Westminster Confession of Faith* (Free Presbyterian Publications, 1994), 13.

[3] "Commission of the General Assembly to some Ministers and Ruling Elders, for repairing to the Kingdom of England, 19th August 1643," *Subordinate Standards*, 221-226.

[4] "The Solemn League and Covenant" *Subordinate Standards*, 221-226: "The English were for a civil League, we for a religious Covenant"—Baillie to William Spang. 22nd September 1643, *The Letters and Journals of Robert Baille, A. M, Principal of the University of Glasgow,* (Edinburgh 1841), Vol. 2, 90.

[5] The Westminster Confession of Faith, *Subordinate Standards*, I - 48. Cf. S. W. Carruthers, *The Westminster Confession of Faith*, (Manchester, nd).

2. It is lawful for Christians to accept and execute the office of a magistrate, when called thereunto: in the managing whereof, as they ought especially to maintain piety, justice, and peace, according to the wholesome laws of each commonwealth; so, for that end, they may lawfully, now under the New Testament, wage war upon just and necessary occasion.

3. The civil magistrate may not assume to himself the administration of the word and sacraments, or the power of the keys of the kingdom of heaven: yet he hath authority, and it is his duty, to take order, that unity and peace be preserved in the church, that the truth of God be kept pure and entire, that all blasphemies and heresies be suppressed, all corruptions and abuses in worship and discipline prevented or reformed, and all the ordinances of God duly settled, administered, and observed. For the better effecting whereof, he hath power to call synods, to be present at them, and to provide that whatsoever is transacted in them be according to the mind of God.

4. It is the duty of people to pray for magistrates, to honour their persons, to pay them tribute and other dues, to obey their lawful commands, and to be subject to their authority for conscience' sake. Infidelity, or difference in religion, doth not make void the magistrate's just and legal authority, nor free the people from their due obedience to him: from which ecclesiastical persons are not exempted; much less hath the Pope any power of jurisdiction over them in their dominions, or over any of their people; and least of all to deprive them of their dominions or lives, if he shall judge them to be heretics, or upon any other pretence whatsoever.

30.1. The Lord Jesus, as king and head of his church, hath therein appointed a government in the hand of church-officers, distinct from the civil magistrate.

2. To these officers the keys of the kingdom of heaven are committed. . . .

31.1. For the better government, and further edification of the church, there ought to be such assemblies as are commonly called Synods or Councils.

2. As magistrates may lawfully call a synod of ministers, and other fit persons, to consult and advise with about matters of religion; so if magistrates be open enemies to the church, the ministers of Christ, of themselves, by virtue of their office, or they with other fit persons upon delegation from their churches, may meet together in such assemblies.

3. It belongeth to synods and councils ministerially to determine controversies of faith, and cases of conscience; to set down rules and

directions for the better ordering of the public worship of God, and government of his church; to receive complaints in cases of maladministration, and authoritatively to determine the same: which decrees and determinations, if consonant to the word of God, are to be received with reverence and submission, not only for their agreement with the word, but also for the power whereby they are made, as being an ordinance of God, appointed thereunto in his word.

5. Synods and councils are to handle or conclude nothing but that which is ecclesiastical; and are not to intermeddle with civil affairs, which concern the commonwealth, unless by way of humble petition, in cases extraordinary; or by way of advice for satisfaction of conscience, if they be thereunto required by the civil magistrate.

Blessings listed in answer to Question 191 of the Larger Catechism,[6] "What do we pray for in the second petition [of the Lord's Prayer]?, include: "the church furnished with all gospel-officers and ordinances, purged from corruption, countenanced and maintained by the civil magistrate." Principles essential to right interpretation of the Ten Commandments include: "7. That what is forbidden or commanded to ourselves, we are bound, according to our places; to endeavour that it may be avoided or performed by others, according to the duty of their places" (Larger Catechism, 99).

1. The Westminster Doctrine of Church and State.

Unless proved otherwise it may be assumed that the Confession, certainly in the estimation of the distinguished theologians who formulated it, is self-consistent. They were satisfied that no Confessional statement contradicts its claim—fiercely resisted by an Erastian Parliament—that "the Lord Jesus, as king and head of his church, hath therein appointed a government in the hand of church officers, *distinct from the civil magistrate*."[7] Nothing in Chapter 33.3 is inconsistent with its opening statement: "The civil magistrate may not assume to

---

[6] The Larger Catechism, *Subordinate Standards*, 49-112.

[7] Confession, 30.1.

himself the administration of the word and sacraments, or the power of the keys of the kingdom of heaven." Nothing in the Confession is self-evidently inconsistent with Chapter 20.2: "God alone is Lord of the conscience, and hath left it free from the doctrines and commandments of men which are in any thing contrary to his word, or beside it, in matters of faith or worship. So that to believe such doctrines, or to obey such commandments out of conscience, is to betray true liberty of conscience; and the requiring of an implicit faith, and an absolute and blind obedience, is to destroy liberty of conscience, and reason also."[8]

The establishment principle outlined in the Confession can be briefly summarized. Civil government is ordained by God for His glory and the public good. Magistrates should defend and encourage the good and punish evildoers. Christians may be magistrates and Christian magistrates,[9] acting in accordance with the laws of their nation, must aim at maintaining piety, justice and

---

[8] Having "first reclaimed for liberty a large province in which civil and ecclesiastical authorities had previously claimed an absolute and arbitrary sway" they recognised that "there are times when, in the interest of liberty itself, some restraints must be placed on it": *Minutes of the Sessions of the Westminister Divines while engaged in preparing their Directory for Church Government, Confession of Faith and Catechisms (November 1644 to March 1649)*, eds. A. F. Mitchell and J. Struthers (Still Waters Revival Books, 1991 reprint of 1874 edition), lxxii, lxxiii.

[9] R. L. Dabney, *Lectures in Systematic Theology* (1878; Zondervan 1972), 876, caricatures the Principle: "What an absurdity is it for that which is not Christian at all to choose my Christianity for me? Can a Turkish infidel, who has nothing to do with Christianity, confer on one sect a power to persecute another?" Gillespie, *One Hundred and Eleven Propositions (1647; The Works of George Gillespie, One of the Commissioners from Scotland to the Westminster Assembly, with a Memoir of his Life and Writings by W. M. Hetherington*, 1846; Still Waters Revival Books 1991, Vol.1), *Propositions* 68, 69, 95: The Christian magistrate's concern for promoting the Gospel "procedeth not from the nature of his office or function which is common to him with an infidel magistrate, but from the influence of his common Christian calling into his particular vocation, For every member of the church (and so also the faithful and godly magistrate) ought to refer and order his

peace. Nations and rulers are accountable directly to God and not subject in their civil capacity to the church. Ecclesiastical bodies should not meddle with civil affairs.[10] In exceptional circumstances they may petition the authorities or be requested by them to give advice. Church members and officers are subject in civil things to civil authorities. "It is competent to, and incumbent upon, nations, as such, and civil rulers in their official capacity, or in the exercise of their legitimate control over civil matters, to aim at the promotion of the honour of God, the welfare of true religion, and the prosperity of the Church of Christ."[11]

---

particular vocation, faculty, ability, power and honour, to this end, that the kingdom of Christ may be propagated and promoted. . . . Christian magistrates and princes, embracing Christ, and sincerely giving their names to him, do not only serve Christ as men, but also use their office to his glory and the good of the church; they defend, stand for and take care to propagate the true faith and godliness, they afford places of habitation to the church, and furnish necessary helps and supports, turn away injuries done to it, restrain false religion, and cherish, underprop and defend the rights and liberties of the church." T. M'Crie, *Statement of the Difference between the Profession of the Reformed Church of Scotland, as adopted by the Seceders, and the Profession contained in the New Testimony and other Acts, lately adopted by the General Associate Synod* (Edinburgh 1871), 84: "When the body of a nation are agreed in the profession of the true religion and a particular confession of faith, form of worship &c., have been drawn from the Scriptures by those to whom this work immediately belongs, the adding of the civil sanction to them (though this does not give them any spiritual authority, nor make them more binding as ecclesiastical deeds), and their being thus considered as national, may be justified as lawful, expedient and in many cases highly necessary." Christian magistrates, having supernatural revelation, have obligations beyond those which they have simply as magistrates. Cf. Adam Gibb in M'Crie, *Statement*, 106-109.

[10] If "separation of Church and State" . . . "simply means that the Church should not try to supplant the functions of the State" there is no problem, Kik, *Church and State in the New Testament* ("International Library of Philosophy and Theology: Biblical and Theological Studies", Presbyterian and Reformed Publishing Co., 1962), 35. Cf. Ibid., 44: "The Scots Reformers were always careful to point out that the Church must remain in her own ecclesiastical sphere. . . ."

[11] William Cunningham, *Historical Theology* (1862; Banner of Truth 1960), Vol. II, 559, 560. Cf. Vol. I, 391: "an obligation lies upon nations and their

Civil rulers in a Christian state must not exercise authoritative control in the church's spiritual and ecclesiastical affairs, Administration of word, sacraments and discipline is outside their province, as is interference in the free meeting and deliberation of synods.[12] The church, like the family, should be countenanced

---

rulers to have respect in the regulation of their national affairs, and in the application of their national resources, to the authority of God's Word, to the welfare of the Church of Christ, and to the interests of true religion."

[12] Cf. *Act approving the Confession of Faith*, Church of Scotland General Assembly, Edinburgh, 27 August 1647 (*Subordinate Standards*, xxvii, xxviii): "It is further declared, That the General Assembly understandeth some parts of the second article of the thirty-one chapter only of kirks not settled, or constituted in point of government: and that although, in such kirks, a synod of Ministers, and other fit persons, may be called by the Magistrate's authority and nomination, without any other call, to consult and advise with about matters of religion; and although, likewise, the Ministers of Christ, without delegation from their churches, may of themselves, and by virtue of their office, meet together synodically in such kirks not yet constituted, yet neither of these ought to be done in kirks constituted and settled; it being always free to the Magistrate to advise with synods of Ministers and Ruling Elders, meeting upon delegation from their churches, either ordinarily, or, being indicted by his authority, occasionally, and *pro re nata*; it being also free to assemble together synodically, as well *pro re nata* as at the ordinary times, upon delegation from the churches, by the intrinsical power received from Christ, as often as it is necessary for the good of the Church so to assemble, in case the Magistrate, to the detriment of the Church, withhold or deny his consent; the necessity of occasional assemblies being first remonstrate unto him by humble supplication." This Act, advocating friendly association of Church and State, asserting the independence of properly constituted elderships and relieving the Confession of Erastian eisegesis, finds the Confession "to be most agreeable to the word of God, and in nothing contrary to the received doctrine, worship, discipline, and government of this Kirk." In the absence of effective English Church Government Parliament had called the Westminster Assembly. This together with the Erastian history of England constituted a danger to which the Assembly was alert: W. M. Hetherington, *History of the Westminster Assembly of Divines* (Still Waters Revival, 1991), 99, 100. Gillespie, *Propositions* (Works, Vol. 1), Proposition 50f, justifies seeking magistrates' approval for synod meetings as public gatherings within the territory for whose law and order they are responsible and as giving weight to sentences which might otherwise be disregarded by troublers of the Church, though their spiritual authority is not derived from magistrates nor dependent on

and maintained by the magistrate as a positively tolerated part of the civil order of the country.[13] He should aim at preserving unity, peace and truth in the church, suppressing heresies and blasphemies, preventing or reforming abuses in worship and discipline, and securing the settling, administration and observance of all the ordinances of God.[14] He must endeavour to secure these ends in ways competent to him as magistrate— "only in the exercise of his proper jurisdiction in civil things, by exercising his control over person and property, so far as is consistent with the nature of the objects he is to aim at, with the rights of conscience and the liberties of Christ's church"—and

---

them. He expounds the distinct bounds of civil and ecclesiastical authorities when dealing with matters which overlap. "Magistrates shall no less sin in usurping ecclesiastical power, ministering holy things, ordaining ministers, or exercising discipline ecclesiastical, than ministers should sin in rushing into the borders of the magistrate, and in thrusting themselves into his calling" (*Proposition* 79).

[13] James Walker, *The Theology and Theologians of Scotland 1560-1750* (1872; revised edition 1888; Knox Press, Edinburgh, reprint 1982), 149.

[14] Hetherington, op. cit., 330, 331: "The Word of God, in almost innumerable instances, commands the direct encouragement of truth, and also the suppression of certain forms of error,—as of idolatry and blasphemy; but gives no authority to man to judge and punish errors of the mind, so far as these amount not to violations of known and equitable laws, and disturb not the peace of society . . . conscience cannot be compelled. . . . Hence it is evident that it is alike contrary to the Word of God and to the nature of conscience for man to attempt to promote truth by the compulsive suppression of error when that error does not obtrude itself on the public view by open violation of God's commandments and the just laws of the land. But it by no means follows that toleration means, or ought to, mean, equal favour shown to error as to truth. Truth ought to be expressly favoured and encouraged; erring men ought to be treated with all tenderness and compassionate toleration; but error itself ought to be condemned, and all fair means employed for its extirpation. This could never lead to persecution, because it would constantly preserve the distinction between the abstract error and the man whose misfortune it is to be an erring man."

must not usurp spiritual jurisdiction.[15] Synods, to whom ecclesiastical responsibility belongs, should cooperate with his pursuit of these ends.

Against pleas of conscience or Christian liberty in support of resistance to civil or ecclesiastical authorities by citizens or church members the Confession allows persons to be proceeded against by the censures of the church and the power of the magistrate for publishing opinions or maintaining practices contrary to the light of nature, the known principles of Christianity or the power of godliness, or destructive to the external peace and order of the church.[16]

---

[15] William Cunningham, *The Westminster Confession an the Relation between Church and State (Discussions on Church Principles: Popish, Erastian and Presbyterian,* Edinburgh, 1863), 221-227: "But the assertion of the general principle of the right and duty of the civil magistrate to promote these objects, leaves untouched the whole question of the means which he is to employ for effecting these ends; and the Confession, while explicitly asserting the general principle of his right and obligation, does not specify either the nature of the authority he is to exercise, or the character of the means he is to employ, for that purpose. The exercise of any ecclesiastical jurisdiction, the assumption of any right to decide authoritatively ecclesiastical questions . . . would flatly contradict those parts of the Confession which assert Christ's appointment of a distinct government for His church in the hand of ecclesiastical office-bearers, and forbid the assumption by the civil magistrate of the power of the keys," 224, 225; A. Moody Stuart, *Is the 'Establishment of Religion' outside of the Confession?* (Edinburgh 1868; 1900 reprint), 26: "There are seven special duties laid down for him in the Confession regarding religion, and then the particular channel of Church courts is named through which he is to execute these duties;" Gillespie, *Nihil Respondes* (1645; *Works*, 1.13): "There is no banishment in Scotland but by the civil magistrate, who so far aideth and assisteth church discipline, that profane and scandalous persons, when they are found unruly and incorrigible, are punished with banishment or otherwise." Those outwith the church are punishable by the magistrate only for offences against natural law, Gillespie, *Male Audis* (1646; *Works*, 1.7).

[16] Cf.; Gillespie, *Propositions* (*Works*, Vol.1), Proposition 63: "The same sin, therefore, in the same man may be punished one way by the civil, another way by the ecclesiastical power; by the civil power under the formality of a crime, with corporal or pecuniary punishment; by the ecclesiastical power under the notion and nature of scandal, with a spiritual censure." The magistrate punishes idolatry, blasphemy, sacrilege, heresy, profanation of

Reformation creeds and confessions[17] share much of this teaching on church and state, though the care to avoid encroachment on each other's jurisdiction is almost unique.[18] It

---

holy things, and insolent and untamed disturbance of the church as civil crimes. He punishes breaches of "the moral law or Decalogue, as it bindeth all nations (whether Christians or infidels), being the law of the Creator and King of nations," Gillespie, *Aaron's Rod Blossoming*, or, *The Divine Ordinance of Church Government Vindicated* (1646; Sprinkle Publications reprint 1985), 121. Cf. Walker, *op. cit.*, 140: "Non-tolerance of murder and non- tolerance of schism were both purely civil acts, and contemplated directly and primarily civil ends. Everything must somehow become civil before it comes within the magisterial sphere." The Westminster majority dreaded irresponsibility towards God and man, not conscientious difference based on a sense of responsibility to God. Independents enjoyed toleration in Presbyterian Holland and the Scottish Commissioners often supported them at Westminster; the Scottish Church in its ascendancy never persecuted its oppressors; toleration under Cromwell, as advocated by Owen, was by no means universal: cf. Hetherington, *History of the Westminster Assembly of Divines*, 154, 155, 331-336; Alexander F. Mitchell, *The Westminster Assembly. Its History and Standards. Being the Baird Lecture for 1882* (London 1883), 203, 204. George Smeaton, *Preface* to M'Crie's *Statement*, xiii, xiv, criticized the General Associate Synod's position that "the national sanction of one particular profession of Christianity in preference to another, partook of the nature of compulsion, intolerance and persecution. . . . On the contrary, the separating brethren put the question of liberty of conscience on its true ground: that is, they placed it not on the mere metaphysical rights of man, but on the ground that God alone is Lord of the conscience; and that its rights, as derived from Him, can never be alleged as running counter to the authority of God speaking in His word, and commanding nations and rulers to obey Him." Cf. *Minutes*, lxx.

[17] The Westminster Divines were strongly aware of this. Gillespie, *Aaron's Rod Blossoming*, xvi, refers to agreement with *Second Book of Discipline* 1, *Scots Confession* 24, *Helvetic Confession on Magistracy*, *Confession of Bohemia* 16, *French Confession* 39, *Belgic Confession* 36, *Confession of Saxony* 23, *Irish Articles of Religion* 61, 62. These works are also cited in *Jus Divinum Regiminis Ecciesiastici: The Divine Right of Church Government*, by the Ministers of Sion College, London (1646; revised and edited, with an introduction by David W. Hall, Naphtali Press 1995), 79-81.

[18] Ministers interpreting the Word of God and showing the magistrate his duty from it deal not with civil matters but cases of conscience arising from them; magistrates deal not with spiritual matters but with "those external

reflects Calvin's view that the magistrate's concern for "the external regulation of manners" obliges him "to foster and maintain the external worship of God, to defend sound doctrine and the condition of the church, to adapt our conduct to human society, to form our manners to civil justice, to conciliate us to each other, to cherish common peace and tranquillity."[19] He is to ensure "that a public form of religion may exist among Christians and humanity among men."[20] The divines concur in their interpretation of Scripture with Calvin who discusses civil government in his *Institutes of the Christian Religion* "because he is convinced that civil government has a crucial role to perform in advancing the cause of true religion."[21]

While "Church and the State are two distinct societies, independent of each other, each having its own separate functions and objects, and its separate means of executing and accomplishing them, each supreme in its own province, and neither having jurisdiction, or the right of authoritative control, over the other . . . an obligation lies upon the State to aim, in the

---

things which adhere unto and accompany the spiritual things," Gillespie, *Propositions* (1647; Works, Vol. 1), *Propositions* 47, 48. Cf. the arguments for separate functions in *Jus Divinum Regiminis Ecclesiastici*, 82-96. Cf. Kik, *Church and State: The Story of Two Kingdoms*, 3: as a result of the pleas of Gillespie against Erastianism "...we find in *The Westminster Confession of Faith* one of the best delineations of the proper boundaries between, and the separate jurisdictions of Church and State." It requires "a balance between the two, each supreme within its own area of competence", Francis Lyall, *Of Presbyters and Kings. Church and State in the Law of Scotland.* (Aberdeen University Press, 1980), 4. On improvements on previous confessions see *Minutes*, lxix.

[19] *Institutes of the Christian Religion* (Translation by Henry Beveridge, 1962 Printing, London), Book IV, chapter 20, 1, 2.

[20] Ibid., 4.20.3.

[21] Robert Godfrey, *Calvin and Theonomy*, in William Barker and Robert Godfrey, editors, *Theonomy: A Reformed Critique* (Academie Books 1990), 300.

exercise of its proper authority in civil matters, at the welfare of true religion; and . . . there is no consideration which necessarily precludes the Church from entering into friendly union with the State, and of course treating and arranging with it about the terms on which mutual cooperation may take place."[22]

2. Some Historical Considerations.

The Westminster Divines were in constant conflict with the Erastian party in Parliament, largely composed of lawyers who believed "all church government to be a part of the civil and parliamentary power, which nature and scripture has placed in them, and to be derived from them to the ministers only so far as they think expedient."[23] "The Pope and the King were never more earnest for the headship of the Church than the plurality of this Parliament."[24] Parliament's Erastian approach, partly reaction against the former ecclesiastical hierarchy, was illustrated in their insistence on appeal from ecclesiastical to civil courts in disciplinary matters were ecclesiastical courts given any

---

[22] Cunningham, "Royal Supremacy in the Church of England," in *Discussions*, 164, 165. Cf. John Murray, "The Relation of Church and State" in *Collected Writings of John Murray, Vol. One: The Claims of Truth* (Banner of Truth Trust, 1976), 254: "Both church and state are under obligation to recognize this subordination, and the corresponding co-ordination of their respective spheres of operation in the divine institution. Each must maintain and assert its autonomy in reference to the other and preserve its freedom from intrusion on the part of the other. But while this diversity of function and of sphere must be recognized, guarded and maintained, the larger unity within which this diversity exists must not be overlooked. The principle that defines this unity is the sovereignty of God, and the obligation emanating from it is the requirement that both church and state must promote the interests of the kingdom of God."

[23] Baillie to Robert Ramsay, 15th January 1646, *Letters and Journals*, Vol. 2, 336.

[24] Baillie to David Dickson, 17th March 1646, *Letters and Journals*, Vol. 2, 360.

disciplinary function.[25] It attracted Independents concerned for "toleration" and libertines opposed to ecclesiastical discipline[26] and reflected society's developing secularism.[27]

In Scotland, Knox, Melville, Henderson, Rutherford, Gillespie and the church of the first and second Reformations, contended for establishment by the state of a church free to be faithful to the instructions of her Lord in His Word.[28] The Scottish Reformers

---

[25] *Minutes*, 435.

[26] Baillie to Robert Ramsay, 15th January 1646, *Letters and Journals*, Vol. 2. 336.

[27] Robert S. Paul, *The Assembly of the Lord, Politics and Religion in the Westminster Assembly and the 'Grand Debate'* (Edinburgh 1985), 77.

[28] Gillespie, *Propositions* (*Works*, Vol.1): "The Church ought to be governed by no other persons than ministers and stewards preferred and placed by Christ, and after no other manner than according to the laws made by him; and therefore, there is no power on earth which may challenge to itself authority or dominion over the church . . . and it is His will that there be such a government distinct from the civil in all his churches everywhere, as well those which live under Christian, as those under infidel magistrates, even until the end of the end of the world, Heb. xiii. 7, 17; I Tim. v.17, 19; Rom. xii. 28; 1 Thess. v.12; Acts 1.20; Luke xii. 42; 1 Tim. vi. 14; Rev. ii. 25. . . . The orthodox churches believe also, and do willingly acknowledge, that every lawful magistrate, being by God himself constituted the keeper and defender of both tables of the law, may and ought first and chiefly to take care of God's glory, and (according to his place, or in his manner and way) to preserve religion when pure, and to restore it when decayed and corrupted; and also to provide a learned and godly ministry, schools also and synods, as likewise to restrain and punish as well atheists, blasphemers, heretics and schismatics, as the violators of justice and civil peace. . . . Yet the civil power and the ecclesiastical ought not by any means to be confounded or mixed together. Both powers are indeed from God and ordained for his own glory and both to be guided by his word and both are comprehended under the precept, 'Honour thy father and thy mother,' so that men ought to obey both civil magistrates and ecclesiastical governors in the Lord; to both powers their proper dignity and authority is to be maintained and preserved in force; to both also in some way intrusted the keeping of both tables of the law, also both the one and the other doth exercise some jurisdiction, and giveth sentence of judgment in an external court or judicatory; but these and other things of like sort, in which they agree notwithstanding, yet by marvellous vast differences are they distinguished

held that the church owed neither existence, creed nor constitution to the State but legislative recognition and practical support as a body already organized according to God's Word. Moncreiff encapsulates the argument of successive Scottish advocates of establishment that "the special duties of ministers of the Gospel are fixed by Christ, and must be regulated exclusively by the Church Courts interpreting the will of Christ as revealed in His word. When the civil magistrate is satisfied that the Church is acting according to the mind of God, he is justified in countenancing and endowing her; but he is not warranted in fettering her office-bearers in their possession of these endowments by any conditions in relation to their special duties, except that of obedience to their ecclesiastical superiors. If he become dissatisfied with her proceedings the only remedy which he can scripturally apply is a withdrawal of those temporal benefits which he gave."[29]

Powerful anti-Erastian statements, sometimes confirmed by suffering rather than merely theoretical argumentation, came from the strongest advocates of Westminster's Establishment Principle. Scottish Presbyterians suffered fines, imprisonment, banishment and death rather than conform to an Erastianised Church.[30] The

---

the one from the other, and the right of both remain distinct" (*Propositions*, 4, 6, 41, 43). Gillespie's *magnum opus, Aaron's Rod Blossoming*, controverts Erastianism. "Whatever their failings and shortcomings, these men maintained with the cause of ecclesiastical independence that of constitutional liberty and limited monarchy against absolutism and arbitrary power just as truly as the patriots of the Long Parliament and the Westminster Assembly," Mitchell, *The Westminster Assembly*, 282.

[29] Henry W. Moncreiff, *Letter to the Kirk-Session and Congregation of the Established Church, East Kilbride, regarding the late Convocation of Ministers* (Edinburgh, 1843), 5.

[30] "Voluntary Churchmen, out of an Establishment, talk of the independence of the Church—our forefathers, within one, bled and died for it": Charles J. Brown, in *Lectures on Church Establishments* (Glasgow), 15. Cf. G. I. Williamson, *The Westminster Confession of Faith for Study Classes* (Presbyterian and Reformed Publishing Company, 1964), 246.

Scottish Established Church was unwilling to be a state department.[31] Civil and religious freedoms were intimately associated and the dangers to both so real that only a settlement giving civil sanction to God's law and protection to His church could secure both.[32]

Such facts should restrain those who, misunderstanding the divines' position or ignoring their sufferings, attribute Erastianism to them.

3. Destructive Criticism of the Establishment Principle.

Acceptance of the assumption common to Erastians, Voluntaries and Papalists that formal, friendly church/state relations necessitate the subjection of one authority to the other accounts for much criticism.[33]

---

[31] Hetherington, *Memoir of the Rev. George Gillespie (The Works of George Gillespie*, Vol. 1), xi.

[32] Cf. M'Crie, *Statement*, 78. The Scottish experiment challenges the argument that had the Assembly secured the Church government sought "the new establishment could have become one of the most repressive in the history of the reformed churches," Paul, *The Assembly of the Lord*, 539.

[33] Dabney, *Lectures*, deduces from 'Gladstone's theory' of Establishment that "there is no Church. The State is the Church, and ecclesiastical persons and assemblies are but magistrates engaged in one part of their functions," 882. From Chalmers' theory of Establishment he assumes that the State would select preachers, so that the least Evangelical preachers would be appointed, arguing from an abuse against which Chalmers' contended, 884. "This union, on this theory, between Church and State, necessitates the surrender of the Church's spiritual independence. It can no longer preserve its allegiance to Jesus Christ perfect . . . the preachers of this State Church are, in their ministerial functions, State officials, and, of course, should be subordinate, as to these functions, to the State. Responsibility must bind back to the source whence the office comes," 886. Chalmers insisted on the distinction and limitation of the spheres within which Church and State had sovereignty, H. J. Laski, *Studies in the Problem of Sovereignty* (Yale University Press, 1917), Chapter 2: "The Political Theory of the Disruption." Cf. Kik's

Some criticism arises from preoccupation with abuses identified in actual establishments or potential for persecution or infringement of the rights of conscience,[34] though other divinely instituted human relationships affected by sin are not therefore abolished.

Dissatisfaction with Confessional teaching also arises from perceived inability to square it with current concepts of freedom

---

description of Madison leading opposition to the idea that "the establishment of religion as part of the civil administration of the State was necessary to religion itself," *Church and State: The Story of Two Kingdom's*, 115. Kik's misunderstanding of the Westminster relation of Church and State appears in that while opposing it he can write that "they can be mutually helpful; but as to jurisdiction they are independent of each other," Ibid., 140. The Establishment Principle embodies this fact in legislative and institutional structures.

[34] Kik, Ibid., 107, 108: "It was to abolish Erastianism and its incipient dangers that the First Amendment was enacted, binding Congress to 'make no law respecting an establishment of religion, or prohibiting the free exercise thereof.'" Gillespie, *Aaron's Rod Blossoming*, xix: "The best things, whether in church or state, have been actually abused, and may be so again, through the error and corruption of men. The Holy Scripture itself is abused to the greatest mischiefs in the world, though in its own nature it serves for the greatest good in the world. The abuse of a thing which is necessary, and especially of a divine ordinance, whether that abuse be feared or felt, ought not, may not, prejudice the thing itself." M'Crie, *Statement*, 29, 146, 147: "Persons, by fixing their attention unmoveably upon certain evils and abuses which attach to or result from the establishments with which they are acquainted, are in danger of overlooking the more general and extensive good which they are calculated to produce, or may be rendered subservient unto; and instead of seeking the correction of abuses and the redress of grievances they are ready to look forward with big expectations to a total revolution in such matters, without taking into view or being aware of the infinitely greater evils which would arise from the new order of things. . . . It is well known that the power committed by Christ to the office-bearers of his church has been very grossly abused. . . . It is not uncommon with many, from this abuse, to declaim against and decry all church-power." Cf. his discussion of alleged effects of the first establishment of Christianity, 152f. He discusses, pp. 19-30, the practical effects of a "system which would equalise all kinds of religion in the eyes of the law, which proclaims an universal right and liberty in such matters, and deprives religion and its institutions of the countenance and support of human laws."

of religion in multi-racial, multi-faith societies. Barker, controverting theonomic views of church-state relations, undertakes to demonstrate biblical approval for social religious pluralism, "the civil authority recognizing the freedom of religious belief and practice by a variety of groups—including theists, humanists, naturalists, and atheists—with no one such group established or favoured by the state."[35] Error has the same civil rights as truth.[36] Civil authorities should be neutral in the clash between Christianity and secularism.[37]

---

[35] "Theonomy Pluralism and the Bible," in *Theonomy, A Reformed Critique*, 228, 229.

[36] Dabney, *Lectures*, 866, 868: "What then is man's natural liberty? . . . it is freedom to do whatever he has a moral right to do...civil liberty . . . is (under a just government) freedom to do whatever a man has a moral right to do . . . every man is born under obligation to God, to his parents, and to such form of government as may providentially be over his parents." Not every moral evil is properly punishable by society (e.g., prodigality, indolence, gluttony, drunkenness), for it is not the business of society to keep a man from injuring himself but from injuring others, 874, and "no man is to be visited with any civil penalty for his belief as long as he does not directly infringe upon the purpose of the government, which is the protection of the temporal rights of his fellow-citizens," 879.

[37] Cf. Gordon H. Clark, *What do Presbyterians Believe?* (Presbyterian and Reformed, 1965), 213. Cf. Gillespie, *Sermon Preached before the Honourable House of Commons at their late Solemn Fast, Wednesday, March 27, 1644* (Works, Vol.1), 3: "that detestable indifferency or neutrality, abjured in our solemn league." See *A Sermon preached before the Right Honourable the House of Lords, in the Abbey Church at Westminster, August 27, 1645; being the day appointed for Solemn and Public Humiliation* (*Works*, Vol.1), 12: "I beseech you, how can you give liberty of conscience to the heretic and yet refuse liberty of conscience to him that is the conscientious recusant in point of the war? I am sure that there can be no answer given to this argument which will not be resolved into this principle: men's consciences may be compelled for the good of the state, but not for the glory of God; we must not suffer the state to sink, but if religion sink we cannot help it. This is the plain English of it." In *A Treatise of Miscellany Questions* (1649; *Works*, Vol.2), 69, he argues that on the principle that the magistrate ought not to intervene against heretics who do not trouble the state "if the city of London was turning peaceably to Mahometanism or paganism, the

Others oppose the magistrate's support of true religion because (as no Westminster divine questioned) faith is produced only by the blessing of the Holy Spirit on the hearing of the Word.[38]

---

parliament ought not to apply their power to reducing them. . . . But if any magistrates will not have respect to the honour of God and salvation of souls, let them take heed to their own interest. When the church of Christ sinketh in a state, let not that state think to swim. Religion and righteousness must flourish or fade away, stand or fall together. They who are false to God shall not be faithful to men." Conscience relates to more than religion and may be pleaded against laws unrelated to religion. The Divines' awareness of complexity appears from Samuel Rutherford's attitude to Jews or pagans in a Christian community. Neither magistrate nor church can compel them to abandon their religion though they may prevent them from e.g. sacrificing children to their false gods, infecting the church of God or violently impeding pastors from preaching to willing non-Christian hearers, *The Due Right of Presbyteries, or, A Peaceable Plea for the Government of Scotland* (London, 1644), 361-363.

[38] Dabney, *Lectures*, 876; "The Church cannot use persecution to gain her end, which is the belief of religious truth; because penalties have no relevancy whatever to beget belief." Cf. "Civic Ethics" in *Discussions: Philosophical* (1892; Ross House-Sprinkle, 1980), 321. [Equating national recognition of a Church with persecution is gratuitous.] He struggles for consistency: "While the American State is not positively Christian, no state can rightfully be atheistic . . . theism is essential as the basis of civil government. Atheism, if prevalent, would leave civic authority logically baseless . . . no human being has a natural or civic right either to atheism or to live without a Sabbath. These are simply natural iniquities, subversive of social morals as really as incest or murder, though not so greatly. . . . He should no more have the privilege of doing his atheistic work than of attacking the family, which is the secular or earthly foundation of civil society" (*The Sabbath of the State*, in *Discussions: Evangelical and Theological*, Vol.2, 1891; Banner of Truth, 1967), 601-603. Cf. Kik, *Church and State in the New Testament*, 12, 26. The kingdom of Christ is spiritual and promoted by spiritual means (John 18:36). In its visible form it has connections with institutions of human society. The truth of Zechariah 4:6 did not lead Zerubbabel (v 7) to abandon his work or prevent God using the king of Assyria to strengthen their hands (Ezra 6:22, any more than 2 Cor. 10:4 renders external helps, like money (9. 5), inappropriate. Money does not convert souls but can build churches and support ministers! Civil government is another help. M'Crie, *Statement*, 155-158. Rutherford insisted that "fire and sword or war or the coercive power of a magistrate is not God's way of planting the Gospel in a heathen

Abandonment of the Westminster doctrine of church and state, while occasionally seeking scriptural justification, is generally pragmatic.[39] Critics argue circularly from presuppositions originating outside the Bible. Claims that the doctrine was inevitably produced by mediaeval presuppositions and prejudices of men whose idea of the unity of church and state prevented them from separating religion and politics fail to engage with its alleged biblical basis[40] and to sufficiently acknowledge its radically non-mediaeval elements.

James Bannerman[41] considers that were there basis in the Westminster Confession for such concerns this would be "in no small measure fitted to damage the credit due to one of the noblest uninspired expositions of Divine truth anywhere to be found, and to subvert our confidence in it as an accurate and authoritative confession of our faith." Having expounded the lawfulness, duty and necessity of a friendly connection between church and state,[42] he concludes that Erastianism and persecution for conscience' sake can only be read into a Confessional statement "taken out of its connection, and viewed apart without reference to other

---

nation which never heard of the Gospel before;" magistrates cannot force men to believe, though they have powers of compulsion in the area of external conduct and profession in a Christian nation, op. cit., 353-355.

[39] Kik, *Church and State in the New Testament*, 44, 45: noting that "at the beginning of the American revolution nine out of thirteen colonies had an established church which was supported by public funds" because "the early colonists had carried across the ocean inherited views of Church and State alliance," attributes the subsequent separation to "the sturdy individualism engendered by Calvinism," "the multiplicity of denominations" [the view of Jefferson that "several different churches are better than one, as a variety of religious opinions is in the interest of progress and freedom"], and the influence of the Great Awakening which "broke down social rank, created self-respect, and inculcated ideas of self-government within the churches."

[40] Paul, op. cit., 3, 15, 200, 279, 529, 539.

[41] *The Church of Christ*, Vol.1 (Edinburgh 1869), 172.

[42] Ibid., 106-148.

statements in the Confession, and without regard to the use and meaning in their day of the somewhat technical language employed by the authors."[43] Statements should be interpreted in overall context and in the sense common at the time of writing.

4. Sympathetic Elucidation.

Accurate definition is necessary. It is not the case "that in contending for the Establishment principle we are contending for all that Voluntaries are pleased to assert to be included in it."[44]

The Confession affirms Christ's Headship over the church and provision of a structure of church government and discipline. It denies to the civil magistrate any function within that structure. It affirms his responsibility to "exercise his lawful authority in civil things with a view to the promotion of the interests of religion and the welfare of the Church of Christ."[45] The basic principle maintained as scriptural is "that an obligation lies upon nations and their rulers to have respect, in the regulation of their national affairs and in the application of their national resources, to the authority of God's word, to the welfare of the church of Christ, and the interests of true religion."[46] This means "that there is no unwarrantable usurpation on the part of the civil power when it gives the sanction of law, with a view to civil and legal effects, to what may have been agreed on between the parties, respecting the faith, government and worship of the church; and that there is no sacrifice of the church's independence in her pledging herself to adhere to the faith, government and worship which have been agreed upon, and which she believes to be scriptural, so as to be

---

[43] Ibid., 173; cf. 181.

[44] William Balfour, *The Establishment Principle Defended* (Edinburgh, 1873), 6.

[45] Cunningham, *Discussions*, 222.

[46] Cunningham, *Historical Theology*, Vol.1 (Edinburgh, 1862), 391.

tied up from making any change without the consent of the State,—except, of course, in the way of falling back upon her original and essential independence, and renouncing any advantage she may have derived from her State connection. But still the church and the State have their distinct provinces, and each is supreme and independent in its own province."[47] The church is under the magistrate's care, not within the sphere of his jurisdiction.[48]

Denial of any function in administering word, sacrament and discipline coexists with the magistrate's responsibility for the church's well-being in these areas. Dependence upon God for His church's preservation coexists with advocating State support. A later Scottish churchman was in the Westminster tradition when maintaining "that the chief human bulwark of her spiritual independence lay in her own faithfulness and not in the countenance or protection of the civil power. But she has never ceased to assert the duty of the civil power not only to recognise and countenance the church of Christ but to protect her spiritual independence."[49] Following out this principle

---

[47] Cunningham, "Royal Supremacy in the Church of England," in *Discussions*, 179, 180.

[48] Cunningham, "Relation between Church and State," in *Discussions*, 208, 209. A. A. Hodge, *The Confession of Faith* (1869; Banner of Truth 1958), 21: "Although the Westminster Assembly resolutely excluded from their Confession all that they recognised as savouring of Erastian error, yet their opinions as to Church Establishments led to views concerning the powers of civil magistrates, concerning religious things (*circa sacra*), which have always been rejected in America. Hence, in the original 'Adopting Act,' the Synod declared that it did not receive the passages relating to this point in the Confession 'in any such sense as to suppose the civil magistrate hath a controlling power over synods with respect to the exercise of their ministerial authority; or power to persecute any for their religion, or in any sense contrary to the Protestant succession to the throne of Great Britain.'" This argues against Confessional language on the basis of deductions repudiated by its authors and implementers.

[49] Henry Wellwood Moncreiff, *A Vindication of the Free Church Claim of Right* (Edinburgh 1877), 48.

Gillespie [50] asserts that "the power politic or civil is occupied about the outward man and civil and earthly things, about war, peace, conservation of justice, and good order in the commonwealth; also about the outward business or external things of the church, which are indeed necessary to the church, or profitable, as touching the outward man, yet not properly and purely spiritual, for they do not reach unto the souls, but only to the external state and condition of the ministers and members of the church. . . . It is in the power of the magistrate to judge, determine, and give sentence concerning the disposing of their bodies or goods; as also concerning the maintenance of the poor, the sick, the banished, and of others in the church who are afflicted; to regulate (so far as concerneth the civil order) marriage, burials, and other circumstances which are common both to holy and also to honest civil societies; to afford places fit for holy assemblies, and other external helps by which the sacred matters of the Lord may be more safely, commodiously and more easily in the church performed; to remove the external impediments of divine worship

---

[50] *Propositions (Works;* Vol.1), Propositions 45, 46. David C. Lachman, *Preface to Aaron's Rod Blossoming*, ii, iii, summarises Gillespie's position: "As the magistrate rules on God's behalf, he is to enforce the external obedience to the moral law to which all men and nations are obliged by virtue of their relationship to God as their creator. . . . The general principles laid down both by the light of nature and more explicitly in Scripture give guidance. The magistrate is no more free to ignore them in governing the state than we as creatures are free to ignore them in our personal lives. . . . The Christian magistrate ought to be a 'nursing-father' to the church and, under the direction of the ruling officers of the church, should do all in his power 'to advance the kingdom of Christ, and the course of the gospel.' He is at liberty 'to add a civil sanction and strength of a law' to aid 'the exercise of church discipline' if he pleases, though he is not bound to do so. His proper concern, given him by God, is the well-being of the state and its citizens. If he punishes the heretic or adulterer, it is for civil ends and if he sets up and nourishes the true church it is as the church is that which is beneficial to the peace and prosperity of the civil state." Cf. Robert Shaw, *The Reformed Faith. An Exposition of the Westminster Confession of Faith* (1845; 1974 reprint, Inverness), 209, 210.

or of ecclesiastical peace, and to repress those who exalt themselves against the true church and her ministers and do raise up trouble against them." Gillespie saw this as consistent with asserting that Scripture condemns "the spiritualising of the civil power, as well as the secularising of the ecclesiastical power— state papacy as well as a papal state.[51]

Westminster teaches[52] that civil authority "may be lawfully and beneficially employed in the advancement of religion and the kingdom of Christ"—promoting, protecting, propagating— "without encroaching upon the office or business of the church and its officebearers, without compelling their subjects to believe or practise what they do not believe or judge sinful, and without punishing persons who may conscientiously dissent from the authorised and established religion, or depriving them of their natural rights merely on this ground; while at the same time, by using their authority in this way, magistrates do act for the honour of him by whom they rule, for the promotion of religion, the advancement of the kingdom of Christ, and the public good of their subjects." Cunningham's solution to the "acute difficulty"[53] reconciling the first and second parts of the first sentence of Chapter 23.3, is that given the Confession's firm exclusion of the magistrate from ecclesiastical authority the section simply states that the "magistrate is bound to exercise his lawful authority in civil things, with a view to the promotion of the interests of religion and the welfare of the Church of Christ. . . . The civil magistrate is, just like men in general, to use the authority and power competent to him as such—and what that is must be ascertained from other sources—for promoting the interests of religion and

---

[51] *That Excommunication and other Church Censures are appointed by Jesus Christ* (*Works*, Vol II, p.112).

[52] *Statement*, Section VI, 79f. He denies, Section VII, 146f, the deduction of persecution from the principle of national establishment.

[53] Williamson, op. cit., 244.

the purity and prosperity of the church."[54] In promoting the church's welfare in ways competent to him he is excluded from unwarranted interference in her province.

The establishment principle neither promotes persecution nor infringes the rights of conscience. "When a particular profession or confession of faith, form of worship and ecclesiastical government, obtain the formal sanction of civil authority, they are recognized by the legislature as declaratory of that religion which obtains the national countenance and support, and according unto which the legal privileges and emoluments appropriated for this purpose are to be conferred and enjoyed. But this by no means implies that all shall be obliged, under civil pains, to conform unto this establishment or be punished for dissenting from it. There is a wide and essential distinction between the exercise of a compulsive power about religion and compulsion in religion."[55] Why should support of religion or church attract opprobrium when governments legislate and raise taxes for other institutions and activities—arts, sciences, education—without allegations of intolerance or persecution?[56]

The establishment principle is consistent with true liberty of conscience and civil rights. M'Crie[57] shows that absolute uncontrolled liberty is not man's right—every society recognizes in its law enforcement that conscience has no absolute rights. True and extensive freedom is secured when the standard of lawmaking

---

[54] *Discussions*, 222, 225, 226.

[55] *Statement*, 149, 150.

[56] "It is monstrous that the State should be at liberty to spend its money on everything but religion, that is, on everything but the one thing which is most essential to the welfare of its subjects," John Duncan: Kenneth R. Ross, *Church and Creed in Scotland. The Free Church Case 1900-1904 and its Origins* (Rutherford House, Edinburgh, 1988), 64.

[57] *Statement*, Section VIII, 158f. Cf. Bannerman, *The Church of Christ*, 159-171: *Liberty of Conscience: Its extent and limits*.

and conscience is the moral law.[58] An act passed by the Free Church General Assembly of 1846 requiring officebearers to affirm "I do sincerely own and believe the whole doctrine contained in the Confession of Faith, approven by former General Assemblies of this Church to be the truths of God; and I do own the same as the confession of my faith," also declared "that, while the Church firmly maintains the same scriptural principles as to the duties of nations and their rulers in reference to true religion and the Church of Christ, for which she has hitherto contended, she disclaims intolerant or persecuting principles, and does not regard her Confession of Faith, or any portion thereof, when fairly interpreted, as favouring intolerance or persecution, or consider that her office bearers, by subscribing it, profess any principles inconsistent with liberty of conscience and the right of private judgment."[59]

---

[58] J. MacPherson, *The Westminster Confession*. With Introduction and Notes (Edinburgh, 1881), 125: "People were being educated for liberty, but meanwhile they had to be restrained from rushing on to licence."

[59] *The Practice of the Free Church of Scotland in Her Several Courts* (Edinburgh, 1995), 150-154. The position of the Westminster Divines is illustrated by contemporary writings. "We abhor an over rigid urging of uniformity in circumstantial things, and are so far from the cruelty of that giant who laid upon a bed all be took, and those who were too long he cut them even with his bed, and such as were too short he stretched out to the length of it," *Vindication of the Presbyterial Church Government and Ministry*, Provincial Assembly of London, 1649. "But if once the government of Christ were set up among us we know not what would impede it by the sword of God alone, without any secular violence, to banish out of the land those spirits of error, in all meekness, humility, and love, by the force of truth convincing and satisfying the minds of the seduced. Episcopal courts were never fitted for the reclaiming of minds. Their prisons, their fines, their pillories, their nose-slitting, ear-croppings, and cheek-burnings did but hold down the flame to break out in season with the greater rage. But the reformed presbytery doth proceed in a spiritual method eminently fitted for the gaining of hearts; they go on with the offending party with all respect; they deal with him in all gentleness from weeks to months, from months sometimes to years, before they come near any censure," *Dissuasive from the Errors of the Time*, Robert Baillie. Both quoted, Mitchell, *The Westminster Assembly*, 206, 209.

The Confession is not preoccupied with the Church's need but with the responsibility, need and privilege of the State; not primarily with endowment but with recognition. "When we withdraw religion from politics to keep religion pure, what is to keep politics pure, thus separated from religion."[60] Begg found "the American struggle 'peculiarly interesting' as a demonstration that 'the State needs the help of religion much more than religion needs the help of the State.'"[61] As religion lies at the foundation of civil society the expected result of the removal of religious sanctions is that "the swelling torrent of ignorance, irreligion, infidelity, and contempt of divine ordinances, with that profligacy of manners which is their never failing attendant, will overbear all the barriers of civil restraints, fenced with the highest penalties, render their execution fruitless and at last dangerous and impracticable."[62]

Civil government is valid without Christianity, but Christian revelation must be heeded by those possessing it.[63] In a Christian

---

[60] Balfour, *The Establishment Principle Defended*, quoting Professor M'Ilwaine of New York. Cf. Moody Stuart, *Is the 'Establishment of Religion' outside of the Confession?*, 11: "Endowment, however valued, has been secondary, but the establishment of God's truth has ever been held to be a matter of life and death for the nation." Thornwell assumed that the Scottish Church advocated establishment because of endowment, *The General Assembly of 1847* in *Collected Writings*, Vol. IV, 502, 503.

[61] *Preface* by James Begg, in Balfour, op. cit., vii.

[62] M'Crie, *Statement* 116, 117.

[63] Dabney virtually concedes this essential principle of Establishment when he allows the civil legislator with the Bible in his hand to require that in a nation of Christian citizens the first day of the week be recognized as the Sabbath theism provides for human society: "Church and State are independent, but they are not hostile, the state, the organ of earthly righteousness, need not be so jealous of the church, the organ of spiritual salvation, as to refuse to act with her in this one non-essential point, when that God, who is both Creator and Ruler, and also 'the God and Father of our Lord Jesus Christ', honoured his risen Son by transferring the original Sabbath to his resurrection-day . . . the state is bound so to enforce outward rest and quiet, and the cessation of secular labours and public amusements, as to honour God's natural ordinances, and to give the allied institutes, the

State Christian magistrates bring Christian principles to bear on their functions and lend support to the Christian Church.

5. Biblical Basis.

The Westminster Divines proceeded on a principle common to Reformed Confessions, articulated in the *Preface* to the 1560 *Scots Confession*: "protesting that if any man will note in our Confession any chapter or sentence contrary to God's Holy Word, that it would please him of his gentleness and for Christian charity's sake to inform us of it in writing; and we, upon our honour, do promise him that by God's grace we shall give him satisfaction from the mouth of God, that is, from Holy Scripture, or else we shall alter whatever he can prove to be wrong."[64] They sought definitive biblical answers to questions regarding the spheres of church and state in religious matters.[65]

---

family and the church, their proper opportunity for doing their work on the people" (*The Sabbath of the State* in *Discussions: Evangelical and Theological,* Vol.2, 613, 617). Dabney denies any reasonable creature natural right to live without the Sabbath, though granting a natural right to live without the Christian religion. In a predominantly Christian society civil legislators using the Christian Bible are to enforce the Christian Sabbath. To carry this principle as far as the Confession requires he should expect legislation and civil institutions to reflect the Christian revelation when God's blessing on the Gospel so affects society that there is a nominally Christian state with Christian government. Cf. Thornwell, *Relation of the State to Christ* (1861) in *Collected Writings*, Vol. IV, 549-556: "It is not enough for a State which enjoys the light of Divine revelation to acknowledge in general terms the supremacy of God; it must also acknowledge the supremacy of His Son, whom He hath appointed heir of all things, by whom also He made the worlds."

[64] G. D. Henderson and Jams Bulloch, eds., *The Scots Confession 1560* (Edinburgh 1960), 59, 60. Cf. Moody Stuart, *Is the 'Establishment of Religion' outside of the Confession?*, 16: "I set no value whatever on the Confession except in so far as it expresses the truth of the Bible. . . . I defend the Confession . . . on account of the great Biblical truths it contains."

[65] Moncreiff, *A Vindication of the Free Church Claim of Right*, 2, 3.

E. P. Clowney[66] comments: "The old 'proof-text' approach has been much caricatured; its use by men who knew and loved the Scriptures never even approximated the calculated perversion practised by some modern cults. The Westminster divines, for example, were too familiar with their Bibles and with the exegetical labours of John Calvin to ignore the context when they were required to furnish scriptural 'proofs.'"[67] Cunningham held that their views "can be fully established upon scriptural authority, not indeed by express texts which assert them *in termini*, but by fair and legitimate deduction from scriptural statements and principles."[68]

---

[66] *Preaching and Biblical Theology* (First British Edition, London 1962), 17.

[67] Scripture warrant for propositions under consideration was constantly discussed in Committee and Assembly. Proof texts were added to the Confession only at the insistence of Parliament, October 1646. It was suggested officially [Mitchell, *The Westminster Assembly: Its History and Standards*, 368, 369] that proofs were not supplied because a whole volume would be required and Reformed churches generally concurred in the biblical truth of the statements made. Unofficially, there was unwillingness to unnecessarily offend Parliament which would not enact for religious matters on the basis of divine right or Scripture [*The Letters and Journals of Robert Baillie*, Vol.3 (Edinburgh, 1842), p.2]. Baillie suspected that the late demand for proofs was intended to delay completion of the Assembly's business. He conceded that the addition of proofs would strengthen the work. These were carefully debated and reviewed between January and April 1647 [see *Minutes of the Sessions of the Westminster Assembly of Divines*]. Confessional teaching depends on the wide sweep of Scripture and not on isolated texts. Scottish Presbyterian ordinands' unreserved owning and believing "the whole doctrine contained in the Confession of Faith . . . to be the truths of God" [e.g. *Formula, Practice of the Free Church of Scotland*, p.153] has thus traditionally not involved avowed commitment to each use of the proof texts any more than the Assembly intended to commit its members. Study of the proofs on the Divines' principles of interpretation gives insight into the reasoning behind their propositions and their understanding of Scripture and illustrates how firmly based in Scripture scripturally interpreted their teachings are.

[68] *Principles of the Free Church, in Discussions*; 273. Cf. Gillespie, *A Brotherly Examination of some passages of Mr Coleman's late Sermon upon Job XI 20 as it is now printed and published* (1645; *Works*, 6): "Will any divine in

They recognized differences in administration between Old and New Testaments. Their exegesis was based on the essential unity of the Bible. Chapter 19.3, 4, 5 illustrates their sensitivity. While ceremonial laws given to Israel "are now abrogated under the new testament" Christ in the Gospel no way dissolves but much strengthens the obligation of the moral law. "To them, also, as a body politic, he gave sundry judicial laws, which expired together with the state of that people, not obliging any other now, further than the general equity thereof may require." It cannot justly be asserted of the Confession, as has been alleged of theonomy, that it "overemphasises the continuities and neglects many of the discontinuities between the Old Testament and our time." [69] It recognises the distinction between Israel and modern nations in redemptive history. It distinguishes between Jewish polity as a temporary institution and an embodiment of enduring principles.[70] Unlike some modern Calvinists it recognizes the distinction between church and state and church censures and civil punishments in Israel[71] and deduces permanent principles

---

the world deny that it is a divine truth which, by necessary consequence, is drawn from Scripture, as well as that which, in express words and syllables, is written in Scripture?"

[69] *Theonomy: A Reformed Critique*, 11.

[70] Robert C. Craig, *Memorials of the Life and Labours of the Rev. Robert Craig* (Glasgow 1862), 251; cf. Craig, *Theocracy, or, The Principles of the Jewish Religion and Polity adapted to all Nations and Times* (Edinburgh 1848).

[71] *Aaron's Rod Blossoming*, First Book, chapters 2 and 3; cf Tremper Longman III, "God's Law and Mosaic Punishments Today" in *Theonomy. A Reformed Critique*, 46, 48, and Dan G. McCartney, "The New Testament Use of the Pentateuch: Implications for the Theonomic Movement," *ibid.*, 147, 148. The Assembly rejected the view of Selden, Whitelocke, Lightfoot and Coleman that church and state jurisdiction was mixed in Israel and that this is the pattern for NT church-state relations, Hetherington, *History of the Westminster Assembly of Divines*, 288. Neither was it the Assembly's view that church and state are coterminous in NT times: "There may be many subject to the magistrate who are not church members and so not

from the relationship between these distinct though closely allied entities.[72] It does not accept "that 'the Old Testament is not the canon of the Christian Church'" or regard the cooperation of civil and ecclesiastical powers in the theocracy of Israel as a temporary departure from the religious neutrality of the state under the Noahic Covenant.[73] "Take out of these texts all that is typical, ceremonial, Mosaic, local and incidental and there remains this one element in them all: The worship of the true God set up by the whole civil and ecclesiastical power of the nation."[74]

The Confession asserts the biblical truth that church and state have distinct functions and spheres of authority. W. S. Barker[75] explains Matthew 22:15-22 as basic to Romans 13 and 1 Peter 2: "Jesus would not render to Caesar what was God's alone, namely worship and ultimate obedience" and "it was not a compromise of Jesus' commitment to the things of God to pay the tax to Caesar, even with Caesar's blasphemous religion on the coin." It does

---

under the spiritual power," Gillespie, *That Excommunication and other Church Censures are appointed by Jesus Christ*, in *Works*, Vol. 2, 116. "The church may have reason to esteem one as an heathen and a publican that is no church member, whom yet the magistrate in prudence and policy doth permit to live in the commonwealth," Gillespie, *Aaron's Rod Blossoming*, 90. Cf. Paul, *The Assembly of the Lord* 529, 530.

[72] Alexander Moncrieff, *Practical Works,* I, 27, 28, quoted in M'Crie's *Statement*, 95: "Both precepts and examples under the Old Testament are strong and clear to this purpose; and these are not temporary laws but founded upon perpetual and moral grounds, such as the peace of societies, the good of men's souls, the duty of dependent beings to pay homage to their Creator, in the manner Himself has prescribed, and the duty of all magistrates, the ministers and delegates of the great God, to vindicate His honour among men."

[73] John M. Frame (referring to Meredith C. Kline), "The One, the Many and Theonomy" in *Theonomy: A Reformed Critique*, 92-95.

[74] Moody Stuart, *Is the 'Establishment of Religion' outside of the Confession?*, 49.

[75] "Theonomy, Pluralism and the Bible," in *Theonomy. A Reformed Critique*, 235, 236.

not obviously follow that "in the New Testament situation, under a Gentile regime," our Lord "did not expect the civil authority to support the true religion" and that it is not appropriate for it to do so "as it was in the Old Testament theocracy."

The magistrate is to promote the good and terrify the evil (Rom. 13: 3, 4) and to promote external conditions in which "we may lead a quiet and peaceable life in all godliness and honesty" (1 Tim. 2:2).[76]

In *Jus Divinum Regiminis Ecclesiastici* (1646) the magistrate's use of civil power for the "external care of Religion as Nurse-Father (Is. 49:23)" is illustrated by attempts of Hezekiah, Josiah, Asa and Jehoshaphat to "restore the decayed religion, reform the Church corrupted, protect the Church reformed, &c."[77] Biblical warrant is claimed for the idea that as nursing father the magistrate possesses a) "a defensive, protecting, patronising power," b) "a diatectic, ordering, regulating power," c) "a compulsive, coactive, punitive or corrective power" and d) "a cumulative power," all of which is *circa sacra* not *in sacri*— "an objective, external and indirect power about Ecclesiastical

---

[76] "The subordinate end of the civil power is that all public sins committed presumptuously against the moral law may be exemplarily punished, and that peace, justice and good order may be preserved and maintained in the commonwealth, which doth greatly redound to the comfort and good of the church, and to the promoting of the course of the gospel," Gillespie, *Aaron's Rod Blossoming*, 87. Cf. Kik, *Church and State in the New Testament*, 21: "Therefore Christians are to pray for rulers that they may protect religion and provide a peaceful environment for worship and the unhindered propagation of the Gospel. Rulers are appointed by God for the protection of religion as well as the general well-being and peace of society. . . . Of course it is the duty of the Church to make nations aware of this Lordship and urge them and their rulers to 'serve the Lord with fear, and rejoice with trembling, kiss the Son, lest he be angry' (Psalm 2:11,12)."

[77] p. 49. This eminently readable work is described by David W. Hall in his Introduction "as one of the best exegetes of the original intent of the divines at the Assembly on matters of government," xxi.

matters."[78] Isaiah 49:23, Romans 13:3-4, 1 Timothy 2:2, Isaiah 60:10, 16 support the general defensive, protecting and patronising power of the magistrate. His removal of external impediments of true religion is justified by reference to Jehoshaphat, Asa, Hezekiah and Josiah; his encouragement of true religion by these examples (2 Chronicles 15:9-16; 20:7-9; 29-31 and 34, 35) and by the requirement that the king should have a copy of the law by him continually as Protector as well as Practicer thereof (Deuteronomy 17:18-20); his provision of external means and worldly helps (buildings, maintenance, schools) on the basis that they are necessary in New Testament times (1 Timothy 5:17,18; 1 Corinthians 9:6-15; Galatians 6:6) and were provided by Old Testament magistrates (1 Chron. 22; 2 Chron. 29:19; 31:4; 34). The magistrate's regulating power in reforming the Church when corrupt is justified by the example of Moses (Ex. 32), Joshua (Josh. 24), Asa (2 Chron. 15), Jehoshaphat (2 Chron. 17), Hezekiah (2 Kings 18) and Josiah (2 Kings 23; 2 Chron 34); his convening of synods to advise on how the Church is to be reformed by the example of pious magistrates in the Old Testament (1 Chron. 13:1-2; 23:1; 1 Kings 8:1; 2 Chron. 29:4; 2 Kings 23:1-2), the subjection of all to superior powers, who ought to procure the public peace and prosperity of the church (Rom. 13:1-2; 1 Pet. 2:13-17; 1 Tim. 2:2), and the four great Ecumenical Councils called by magistrates; his backing of the laws of God with secular authority by passages such as 2 Chronicles 34:33, Nehemiah 12:12, Daniel 3:28-29 and Daniel 6:26-27; and his care that ecclesiastical matters are duly managed by properly called ecclesiastical persons by 2 Chron. 29:5, 24 and 30:1, 2 Kings 18:6 and Deuteronomy 17:18-20. His power to compel the outward man to external performance of his duties and offices in matters of religion is grounded on Deuteronomy 13 and the relevance of this passage to Gospel times,

---

[78] 72-79.

shown by Calvin and Jeremiah Burroughs.[79] Preaching from Ezekiel 43:11, Gillespie[80] brought Ezekiel 45:8, and 43:7 together with Psalms 52:15, 16, 22, 72:11 and 2:2, and Revelation 17:16, 17 as prophecies concerning the kingdom of Christ[81] and so determinative of practice.

In his classic exposition of the Westminster doctrine of Establishment[82] M'Crie underlines the fact that "the moral law in all its extent is binding upon men, socially as well as individually, and it is the duty of every one according to his place and station to provide that its commandments be regarded."[83] Interpreting

---

[79] Burroughs maintains that as Rom. 13:3-4 and I Pet. 2:13-14 speak generally, we should not distinguish where Scripture does not between evil-doing against the first and second tables of the law, murdering souls by heresy and bodies by the sword, blaspheming God in heaven and kings and rulers on earth.

[80] *Sermon Preached before the Honourable House of Commons at their late Fast, Wednesday, March 27, 1644* (*Works*, Vol. 1), 8.

[81] David Wilson, in his *A Modest Apology for the conduct of Seceders* wonders how the prophecies of Isaiah 60:5, Jeremiah 4:2 and Revelation 11:15 can be accomplished if it is unwarrantable for rulers or representatives of a nation, when they with the concurrence of the greater part of the people embrace the Christian faith, "to authorise the profession of the true religion, and agree to promote the same to the utmost of their power, subordinating all their civil and secular interests to the glory of God" (T. M'Crie, *Statement*, 96). Kik, *Church and State in the New Testament*, 30: the mediatorial kingship of Christ "does not mean, of course, that of kings of the earth and nations cannot serve and worship Christ. . . . Rev. 21:24. . . Rev. 11:15." Thornwell, *Sermon on National Sins* (1860) in *The Collected Writings*, Vol. IV, 516-518: "A commonwealth can no more be organised which shall recognise all religions, than one which shall recognise none. . . . The Christian, the Pagan, the Mohammedan, Jews, Infidels cannot coalesce in one body politic. . . . The service of the Commonwealth becomes an act of piety to God. The State realises its religious character through the religious character of its subjects; and a State is and ought to be Christian, because all its subjects are and ought to be determined by the principles of the Gospel. . . . We are a Christian people and a Christian Commonwealth." How do rulers and nations as such serve Him other than as members of the Church if not in their civic and national character?

[82] *Statement.*

[83] *Statement,* 120.

the Commandments on the principles laid out in the Larger Catechism (99), claiming that "the word of God contains examples to persons in every character and station of life," and illustrating the responsibility of magistrates in connection with the Second, Third and Fourth Commandments, M'Crie argues for the religious responsibilities of magistrates and of nations in their corporate capacity. Shall Christian rulers have less official concern for religion than Persian kings?[84] Israelite magistrates, acting as magistrates as distinct from inspired prophets (as Moses and David), are commended for settling, reforming and encouraging true religion. Though some were divinely inspired and some laws enforced were of national and temporary character the peculiar circumstances of prophets and apostles does not deprive their example of permanent force. "Besides those actions of Old Testament rulers which proceeded upon moral grounds and which had for their object things which are substantially immutable, such as the support of public worship and the prevention of blasphemy, profanation of the name of God, and sabbath-breaking, there is an application of their example in the way of analogy which, while it makes all allowances for the diversity of circumstances and change of dispensation, proceeds upon a general resemblance in certain common principles and ends."[85] The use of "analogy" whereby New Testament practices are argued from Old Testament examples is illustrated from 1 Cor. 9:13, 14, etc. The Jewish Constitution is neither rejected nor adopted wholesale as a model for Christian nations but regarded as an "example of a system of legislation adapted to the state of a

---

[84] *Statement*, 122 : Ezra 6:8-10; Ezra 7:21-23; Is. 60:9-12; Zech. 14:17-19; 2 Sam. 23: 3; Neh. 13: 9-14, 17-18. Cf. Balfour, *The Establishment Principle Defended*, 51, 52: "it was surely no invasion of the divine prerogative for Cyrus to issue a command enforcing the commandment of the God of Israel to build Him a house at Jerusalem" (Ezra 4:3 and 6:14).

[85] *Statement*, 126.

people who were favoured with the true religion" and "a pattern, in those laws which proceed upon moral grounds" whether "immediately connected with religion or with justice and civil order."[86] Non-Jewish magistrates were approved for using their authority for the advancement of the church.[87] "The kingdom of Christ is erected in an external form in the world, and in this respect, as it is subject to injury, restraint and persecution from the men and powers of the earth, so it is capable of receiving and stands in need of protection, encouragement and countenance from them. To these it has a divine claim."[88] From Psalm 2, in conjunction with Psalm 72, illustrative passages elsewhere and prophecies such as Is. 44:23 and 60:10-16, it is noted that promises regarding Gospel times indicate that the Church will enjoy the countenance of civil authorities.[89] Indeed, "the whole tenor of the declarations, promises and predictions of the Old Testament lead to the conclusion that Christianity shall be owned, countenanced and supported in a national way."[90] Those who, in the face of these predictions and the Apostle's assertions (Rom. 13: 3,4), affirm that the magistrate's power is restricted in New Testament times to the Second Table of the law must prove it.[91]

---

[86] *Statement*; 127-129.

[87] *Statement*, 132: Nebuchadnezzar, Darius, Books of Daniel, Ezra, Nehemiah.

[88] *Statement*, 133: Psalm 47:9.

[89] *Statement*, 134f.

[90] *Statement*, 140, 141: Is. 34:1; 41:1, 21-29; 42; Ps. 2:8; 82; Is. 52:15; 49:1; 2:2; Mic. 4:1, 2; Zech. 2:11; 8:20-22; Jer. 4:2; Dan.7:14, 27; Is. 60:6-12; Zech. 14: 20, 21; Ps. 33:12; 145:15; Is. 19:25; Ps. 2: 9, 12; Is. 60:12. N.T. predictions add confirmation: Rev. 11:15; 21:24, 25. Cf. Allan MacKenzie, *What is Wrong with the Confession?* (Religious Tract Society, n.d.), 42: "The doctrine appears in practical application under the Old Dispensation. It is also vividly written in prophetic references to the coming glory of the New Dispensation. It is a doctrine of which any further lengthy elucidation in the New Testament was not required."

[91] *Statement*, 142; cf. Shaw, *The Reformed Faith*, xxi.

Magistrates are bound to promote what Christians are to pray for in 2 Tim. 2:1. The Church's lack of civil countenance during early New Testament centuries no more invalidates the promises and predictions than did the delay in the seed of Abraham inheriting the promised land.[92]

In fulfilling their responsibility civil rulers should follow natural reason and justice and the common law of nations,[93] but Scripture materials bearing on their responsibility "ought to be applied by them as authoritative in regulating their conduct."[94] Natural reason suggests that civil government has responsibility towards God, true religion and the church. Scripture confirms and illustrates this. All social relations are subject to divine law. All ought to employ their talents to promote God's cause in ways appropriate to their position in society. God treats nations as morally responsible. Moral neutrality is impossible. The one divinely ordained state system nurtured the church. Heathen rulers furthered its interests with God's approval. There are areas where church and state, without transgressing bounds of jurisdiction and assuming each other's prerogatives, should be mutually helpful and cooperate in promoting the accomplishment of God's revealed will. What is prophesied and to be prayed for is the duty of rulers to perform. Christ is head over all things in His church's interests. Civil rulers providing for the temporal welfare of citizens cannot ignore religion as the best means to this end.[95] Since church and state are divine institutions, intended in distinctive ways to promote God's glory and the good of society, and their paths properly cross at so many points, the burden of proof lies with those who deny that they should provide mutual assistance.[96]

---

[92] *Statement*, 152, 153.

[93] Calvin, *Institutes*, 4.20.14.

[94] Cunningham, *Relation between Church and State* (*Discussions*, 197).

[95] Cunningham, Ibid., 199. Cf. Smeaton, *Preface*, M'Crie's *Statement*, ix.

[96] Cunningham, *Relation between Church and State* (*Discussions*, 204-206).

6. Practical Experiment.

Has the Westminster doctrine of church and state been translated into practice? Dabney confounds distinct matters: "The separation and independence of Church and State was not only not the doctrine of the Reformation. No Christian nation holds it to this day, except ours."[97] Kik notes that the American Constitutional position "was the achievement of two disparate and almost antagonistic forces that vied for the souls of the new republic" the deeply religious, evangelical and pietistic identified with Edwards, Whitefield and Backus and the sceptical and anti-clerical forces led by Jefferson and Paine.[98] Dabney, *The Sabbath of the State*,[99] reveals the dilemma of a separationist desiring the benefits of the virtual establishment of Christianity if not church (implicated in the Christian principles and practices of the founders of the nation).[100] Attempting to justify church and state separation he opposes unacceptable deductions from separation (taxation of church property; state-controlled secular education;

---

[97] *Lectures*, 880.

[98] "Church and State: The Story of Two Kingdoms," 112, 113. Cf. Mark A. Noll in *Evangelicalism. Comparative Studies of Popular Protestantism in North America, the British Isles and Beyond, 1700-1990*, eds. Mark A. Noll, David W. Bebbington, George A. Rawlyk (Oxford University Press 1994), 117; Philip Schaff, *The Creeds of Christendom*, Vol. 1 (1986 reprint by Baker of 1931 edition by Harper and Row), 800f.

[99] *The Southern Presbyterian Review*, (January 1880); reprinted in *Discussions: Evangelical and Theological*, Vol.2.

[100]Cf. Kik, "The Supreme Court and Prayer in the Public School" (*An International Library of Philosophy and Theology: Biblical and Theological Studies*, Presbyterian and Reformed, 1963), 22, 25, 26: e.g. quote from Justice Joseph Story, *Commentaries on the Constitution of the United States*, 3 Vols., 1833: "An attempt to level all religions, and to make it a matter of state policy to hold all in utter indifference, would have created universal disapprobation, if not universal indignation." In Scotland support for Christianity was equated with support for the one Christian Church. The schismatic notion of denominations was resisted.

abolition of religious oaths; repeal of sabbath laws and laws prohibiting atheistic and blasphemous speech or publication; female franchise).[101]

The principle of "a free church in a free state" which Kik[102] sees safeguarded by the American Constitution rejects attempts to interfere in each others affairs but makes no practical provision for interaction in matters of common interest as appears from his discussions of potential church domination of the state[103] and prayer in public schools.[104] His argument[105] that "the wall of separation is legal . . . not moral or spiritual" and that "there is no reason, under the Constitution of the United States, why the principles of Christianity cannot pervade the laws and institutions of the United States of America," ignores the implications of all religions being equal before the law. Independence in friendly alliance, as distinguished from independence in isolation, was the realistic doctrine of Calvin and Westminster. Cunningham claims that "of all Protestant countries, that in which the scriptural independence of the Church was most strenuously maintained in argument, and most fully realised in practice, was Scotland; and that in which the civil power secured the largest share of unwarranted authority in the regulation of ecclesiastical affairs was England."[106]

---

[101]Thornwell, *Sermon on National Sins* (1860; *Collected Writings*, Vol. IV, 518, 519), seeks separation with benefits of establishment without pluralism.

[102]*Church and State in the New Testament*, 7, 38.

[103]*Ibid.* 10ff. Fear of Church usurping unwarranted power shared by J. H. Thornwell, *Address to all Churches of Christ* (1861; Collected Writings, Vol. IV, 450).

[104]*The Supreme Court and Prayer in the Public School.*

[105]*Church and State: The Story of Two Kingdoms*, 116.

[106]*Royal Supremacy in the Church of England (Discussions*, 167). Hodge, *The Confession of Faith*: the Scottish Church "continued to maintain in a good degree its independence of civil dictation and its integrity as a Presbyterian Church until after King James assumed the throne of England."

In Scotland the Christian faith (expounded in the *Scots Confession*) was established before the church. Attempts were then made to establish a free church in a free state where each party would not be isolated but relate to the other according to mutually acceptable terms. "The attempt to define the limits of authorities basically conceived as distinct is the special contribution of Presbyterianism to the theory of political freedom. . . . It was useless to contend that if state-endowed the Church must be unfree, for it was on the basis of freedom that endowment had been accepted."[107] The distinct but co-ordinate jurisdiction of church and state has been recognized in the constitutions of the Scottish church and nation. The actual implementation of the Constitutional position has frequently been a cause of conflict—e.g., Reformation, Covenants, Disruption—though there have been approaches to the ideal.[108]

7. Modern Application.

The Church of Scotland's *Claim, Declaration and Protest anent the Encroachments of the Court of Session, 1842*,[109] invited office-bearers and members "to unite in supplication to Almighty God, that He would be pleased to turn the hearts of the rulers of this kingdom, to keep unbroken the faith pledged to this Church, in former days, by statutes and solemn treaty, and the obligations, come under to God Himself, to preserve and maintain the government and discipline of this Church in accordance with His Word; or otherwise, that He would give strength to this Church—

---

[107]Laski, *Studies in the Problem of Sovereignty*, 4, 56.

[108]Lyall, *Of Presbyters and Kings*, 71; Ross, *Church and Creed in Scotland*, 104, 105; John R. Young, "Scottish Covenanting Radicalism, the Commission of the Kirk and the Establishment of the Parliamentary Radical regime of 1648-49" (*Records of the Scottish Church History Society*, Vol. XXV, 342-375).

[109]*Subordinate Standards*, 254, 255.

office-bearers and people—to endure resignedly the loss of the temporal benefits of an Establishment, and the personal sufferings and sacrifices to which they may be called, and would also inspire them with zeal and energy to promote the advancement of His Son's kingdom, in whatever condition it may be His will to place them; and that, in His own good time, He would restore to them these benefits, the fruits of the struggles and sufferings of their fathers in times past in the same cause; and, thereafter, give them grace to employ them more effectually than hitherto they have done for the manifestation of His glory."

Secularization, multiplication of professedly Christian denominations, the existence of non-Christian religions—all brought about by sin—affect implementation of biblical principles[110] but do not negate them. God's demands are not modified by human responses.[111] Truth confessed as scriptural may not be abandoned in uncongenial circumstances. Though full implementation is not currently practical, views entertained concerning this principle have real consequences for church and

---

[110]"The Church . . . is no longer coextensive with society; it is no longer a power to be reckoned with. In addition, it is strictly limited to a specific role, and this limitation is an important aspect of the post-Christian era. Spiritual and ethical judgments based on the Christian faith play no role in serious matters. Just as Church has been separated from State, so two spheres are carefully distinguished: on the one side, the social, political, intellectual, scientific and artistic areas in which the Church and Christianity are allowed no voice, since each of these areas follows its own proper laws; and, on the other, the religious, spiritual, and moral areas in which Christianity is allowed a place, even although only as one of many competing ideologies. The Church is carefully limited to these areas. She is not asked to disappear or yield her place, but she is allowed only one seat in the vast ampitheatre of society and she may not budge from it," Jacques Ellul, *The New Demons* (London 1975), 23, quoted in Ross, *Church and Creed in Scotland*, 144.

[111]John Kennedy, *The Disestablishment Movement in the Free Church* (Edinburgh, 1882), 9: "The prospect of success does not determine the question of duty."

state.[112] Christ's comprehensive claims mean that those not for Him are against him. Presuppositions of some kind govern magistrates' attitudes to religious and moral questions encountered in pluralistic, secularised societies. Law's commands are not always in keeping with the moral conviction, or lack of conviction, of citizens.[113] Controversy relates only to the area and method of enforcement, not to the fact. Does Christian revelation provide a greater security than other presuppositions for the freedom of conscientious citizens? "Complete detachment in this area of law itself imports a bias."[114]

This principle should be cherished as a testimony to Christ's supremacy and a rallying point for when the Gospel again leavens society. Sharing benefits with charitable societies helps financially but is not an act of national homage to Christ or truth. Toleration, "an inestimable blessing in its own place," is not national recognition of Christ.[115] Use should be made of facilities available for bringing Scripture truth to bear upon the institutions and life of the nation. Legislative, consultative and material support of the state should be sought for the Christian faith and church. The preaching of the Gospel should envisage not simply personal salvation but the subjection of divinely ordained human institutions to the claims of Christ.

---

[112]Cunningham, *Relation between Church and State (Discussions*, 196); M'Crie, *Statement*; 204: "principles will operate according to their nature and tendency;" Ross, *Church and Creed in Scotland*, 151: "When the April number of the Church of Scotland *Missionary Record* suggested in 1872 that the removal of the privileges of the Established Church might result in, among other things, a secular system of education where the authority of Scripture would not be accepted, profanity being permitted in the press, Bible laws about marriage and divorce being abrogated and in the observance of Sunday being wholly abolished, the Presbyterian for the following month dismissed the suggestion as 'this bosh.'"

[113]Cf. Lyall, *Of Presbyters and Kings,* e.g., 146; MacPherson, *The Westminster Confession of Faith*, 125: "The authority which insists upon the outward observance of the Sabbath, visits the perjurer with punishment, and maintains the sanctity of the marriage bond, deals at once with questions of doctrine and of practice."

[114]Cf. Lyall, op. cit., 147.

[115]Moody Stuart, *Is the Establishment of Religion outside of the Confession*, 10.

Westminster and Worship:
Psalms, Hymns? and Musical Instruments?

NICK NEEDHAM

Any attempt to understand the teaching of the Westminster Confession about worship must begin with what has traditionally been termed the regulative principle. This is the Reformed and Westminsterian equivalent of the grammatico-historical principle in the field of biblical hermeneutics: an overarching meta-concept without which nothing else can be comprehended—the key that unlocks Westminster's liturgical door. It is only in the bright light of the *Confession's* teaching about the regulative principle that we can see our way clearly to grasp its corresponding view of the place of psalms, hymns and musical instruments in Christian worship.

Westminster's formulation of the regulative principle is expressed most succinctly in chapter 21, paragraph 1 of the Confession. This is the chapter headed "Of Religious Worship, and the Sabbath-day." Paragraph 1 states:

> The light of nature sheweth that there is a God, who hath lordship and sovereignty over all; is good, and doeth good unto all; and is therefore to be feared, loved, praised, called upon, trusted in, and served, with all the heart, and with all the soul, and with all the might. But the acceptable way of worshipping the true God is instituted by himself, and so limited by his own revealed will, that he may not be worshipped according to the imaginations and devices of men, or the suggestions of Satan, under any visible representation, or any other way not prescribed in the holy Scripture.

The Confession here distinguishes between those religious truths which can be known (a) from "the light of nature" and (b) from God's "own revealed will"—in other words, general and special revelation. General revelation makes known to us that "there is a God" Who possesses the attributes of lordship, sovereignty and goodness, "and is therefore to be feared, loved, praised, called upon, trusted in, and served" with all our hearts. But general revelation does not make known to us "the acceptable way of worshiping the true God." The Confession is using the word "worship" here in the specific sense of *performing acts whose basic and primary function is to express honour and veneration towards God*. We often hear today that "all life is worship," and this wider definition can be justified from Scripture (e.g., Romans 12:1-2). However, the narrower, more specific sense of the term is equally defensible; we need only recollect that in His discourse on worship in John 4, the Lord Jesus Christ uses the word προσκυνεο, whose original meaning was "to kiss the hand"—a subject kissing the hand of his king in order to express his veneration for the king's regal person. In this narrower sense of the term, not all life is worship. All life is *obedience*; but worship refers to those special acts of obedience directed towards the King of the universe, by which we express the veneration that is appropriate to Him as our God—the spiritual equivalents of kissing His hand. In his *Christian Directory*, Richard Baxter (1615-91) clearly and helpfully makes this distinction between the wider and narrower senses of worship:

> The worshipping of God is the direct acknowledging of his being and perfections to his honour. Indirectly or consequentially he is acknowledged in every obediential act by those that truly obey and serve him; and this is indirectly and participatively to worship him; and therefore all things are holy to the holy, because they are holy in the use of all, and Holiness to the Lord is, as it were, written upon all that they possess or do (as they are holy): but this is not the worship which we are here to speak of; but that which is primarily and directly done to glorify him by the acknowledgment of his excellences.[1]

---

[1] Baxter, *Christian Directory*, 547.

In this more specific sense of the term *worship*, "the acceptable way of worshipping the true God" is not (according to the Confession) made known to us by general but by special revelation, by the Word of God.

One point of interest here is the Confession's statement that the light of nature teaches us that God is to be "called upon." This seems to be a reference to vocal prayer. If so, general revelation does make known at least one component of true worship: special revelation is not necessary to teach people that they ought to offer vocal prayer to their Creator. However, the contradiction is more apparent than real. General revelation may tell people that they *ought* to pray, but it does not tell them *how* to pray. How does God want me to pray? How should I approach and address Him? What should my priorities be? The disciples' question to Christ, "Lord, teach us to pray" (Luke 11:1), is the natural cry of the human heart—the cry prompted by the light of nature. Moreover, by "calling upon" God, the Confession may well (in spite of appearances) be referring to mental rather than vocal prayer—an inward calling on God in feeling, desire and attitude. The reference to "calling upon" God in Confession 21.1 occurs in a list of inward acts of piety, located in the soul's affections, which Westminster says are taught us by the light of nature: God is "to be feared, loved, praised, called upon, trusted in." On this reading, the *Confession* is distinguishing between the inward worship taught by general revelation, and the embodiment of this worship in outward acts which special revelation alone can teach. This is the interpretation pursued by Robert Shaw in his classic commentary on the Confession:

> Religious worship . . . may be viewed as either internal or external; the former consisting in that inward homage which we owe to God, such as loving, believing, fearing, trusting in him, and other elicit acts of the mind; the latter consisting in the outward expression of that homage, by the observance of his instituted ordinances. Concerning the external worship of God, our Confession affirms, *in the first place*, that God can be worshipped acceptably only in the way of his own appointment (etc.).[2]

---

[2] Shaw, *An Exposition of the Confession of Faith*, 200- 201.

Finally on this point, we should reflect that by "the acceptable way of worshipping the true God," the Confession probably has particularly in mind *a system of corporate worship*; and this the light of nature certainly does not reveal. The dean of English Reformed theologians, John Owen (1616-83), followed this line of reasoning in his *A Brief Instruction in the Worship of God*, as well as reinforcing the point made by Shaw about the distinction between inward and outward worship:

These two things all men saw by nature:

First, That God, however they mistook in their apprehensions of him, would be, and was to be, worshipped with some *outward solemn worship*; so that although some are reported to have even cast off all knowledge and sense of a Divine Being, yet never any were heard of that came to an acknowledgment of any God, true or false, but they all consented that he was constantly and solemnly to be worshipped, and that not only by individual persons, but by societies together; that so they might own and honour him whom they took for their God. . . . But beyond this the inbred light of nature could not conduct any of the sons of men; this alone is contained in the first precept [i.e., the first commandment]. That God was to be worshipped they knew, and that he was to be worshipped by ways and means of his own appointment they knew; but what those means were they knew not. These always depended on God's sovereign will and pleasure, and he made them known to whom he pleased, Ps. cxlvii. 19, 20.[3]

The light of nature teaches us that God is to be worshipped, but it does not teach us the form of "outward solemn worship" we should offer, particularly as "societies together." The *how* of worship and the *social dimension* of worship are left undetermined by general revelation. Thus argued Owen, and his argument seems to mirror faithfully the teaching of Westminster Confession 21.1.

We come, then, to the crucial statement of the Confession that

the acceptable way of worshipping the true God is instituted by himself, and so limited by his own revealed will, that he may not be worshipped according to the imaginations and devices of men, or the suggestions of Satan, under any visible representation, or any other way not prescribed in the holy Scripture.

---

[3] Owen, *A Brief Instruction in the Worship of God,* in *Works,* vol. 15, 448-9.

The only acts, forms or rites of worship which God will accept are those "instituted by himself" and "limited by his own revealed will." The "revealed will" of God here refers to special revelation—the Word of God, the Scriptures. This is borne out by the subsequent negative assertion that God must not be worshipped in any way "not prescribed in the holy Scripture." So we could summarize Westminster's teaching on worship in this paragraph thus: *God must be worshiped only in ways He Himself has authorized in Scripture.* If we then ask what acts of worship God has authorized in Scripture for His New Testament Church, the answer of the Confession is found in 21.3-5. Paragraphs 3 and 4 deal with prayer. Paragraph 5 specifies four other acts of corporate worship:

> The reading of the Scriptures with godly fear; the sound preaching, and conscionable hearing of the word, in obedience unto God, with understanding, faith, and reverence; singing of psalms with grace in the heart; as also the due administration and worthy receiving of the sacraments instituted by Christ; are all parts of the ordinary religious worship of God. . . .

The reference to "the sacraments instituted by Christ" means, of course, baptism and the Lord's Supper. However, it can hardly be maintained that baptism is on the same level as the other acts of worship here enumerated by the Confession, for the simple reason that baptism, unlike these other acts of worship, is possible only on special occasions—when there is actually someone to be baptized. For Westminster, then, the basic ingredients of any normal worship service are five:

(a) prayer (1 Timothy 2:1-4, 8);
(b) the public reading of Scripture (Colossians 4:16, 1 Thessalonians 5:27);
(c) preaching (2 Timothy 2:2, 4:2);
(d) the singing of psalms (Ephesians 5:19, Colossians 3:16);
(e) the Lord's Supper (Matthew 26:26ff, Acts 2:42).[4]

---

[4] The Confession does not actually teach that the Lord's supper must be celebrated as a normal part of Sunday worship, i.e., every Sunday. In the *Directory for the Publick Worship of God* we find the following instruction: "The communion, or supper of the Lord, is frequently to be celebrated; but

(We will later investigate what precisely the Confession means by "psalms.") These five things, then, by Westminsterian standards, are the only divinely authorized acts of New Testament worship that flow from the regulative principle. Any church that accepts the meta-concept of the regulative principle, as the Westminster divines understood it, will practise a form of worship habitually marked by these five ingredients, and only these—except on the special occasions that require also the sacrament of baptism.

Almost all important doctrines are forged in the furnace of conflict; and Westminster Confession 21.1 is no exception. The divines of Westminster were, so to speak, fighting on two fronts when they framed this architectonic statement on worship.

(1) On the one hand, they had in view the Roman Catholic Church. Rome claimed God's authorization for all kinds of ceremonies of worship which were admittedly not found in Scripture. Responding to the challenges of the Protestant Reformation, the Council of Trent in the 16th Century had taught that the unwritten traditions of the (Roman) Church were of equal status with Scripture in their divine origin. Roman Catholic apologists could therefore claim that some non-scriptural aspects of Roman worship were nonetheless divinely authorized, because they had been handed down as part of an unwritten apostolic tradition. The *Confession* rejects this understanding of worship by insisting that all the constituent acts of Christian worship must be "prescribed in the holy Scripture." The only apostolic tradition

---

how often, may be considered and determined by the ministers, and other church governors of each congregation on, as they shall find most convenient for the comfort and edification of the people committed to their charge." However, we know that weekly communion was the ideal that Calvin desired (unsuccessfully) to achieve in Geneva (*Institutes* 4.17.43-44), and it was the practice of the early Church in the first few centuries. Acts 20:7 is most naturally interpreted as a reference to weekly communion, and Paul seems simply to assume in 1 Corinthians 11:17ff that when the Corinthian Christians "come together as a church" they will celebrate the Lord's Supper.

the Westminster divines would regard as authoritative was the written tradition of inspired and infallible Scripture.

(2) On the other hand, the Westminster divines also had in view the joint Roman Catholic, Lutheran and Anglican claim that the Church could *itself* institute forms and rites of worship, as long as these forms and rites were not positively forbidden in Scripture. The 39 Articles of the Anglican Church espouse this position in article 20:

> The Church hath power to decree Rites or Ceremonies, and [hath] authority in Controversies of Faith: And yet it is not lawful for the Church to ordain any thing that is contrary to God's Word written. . . .

An example of a religious rite or ceremony decreed by the Anglican Church in the Book of Common Prayer was its instruction to the officiating priest to dip his finger in the baptismal water and trace the sign of the cross on a child's forehead after baptizing him or her. Here is a religious rite nowhere forbidden by Scripture, but nowhere authorized by it either, and it became a focal point for Puritan demands for a more thorough reformation of the Church of England.

This Roman-Lutheran-Anglican view that the Church may institute religious ceremonies as long as they are not prohibited by Scripture was perhaps stated most succinctly by the Roman Catholic Cardinal Nicholas Wiseman (1802-65), in his *Lectures on the Principal Doctrines and Practices of the Catholic Church.* Referring to icons of the "saints" and the practice of praying before them, Wiseman said:

> I may be asked, what warrant there is in Scripture for all this? I might answer, that I seek none; for rather I might ask, what authority there is, to deprive me of such objects: because it is a natural right to use any thing towards promoting the worship of God, which is not in any way forbidden.

> I might as well be asked, what warrant there is in Scripture for the building of churches, for the use of the organ, for the ringing of bells, for music, or for a thousand other things that appertain to the worship of the Church. Do I want a warrant, do I require Scripture, for the use

of the organ? Certainly not: because if the thing be innocent, and serve to raise our hearts towards God we consider that we have a right to use it, and nothing but a positive enactment can deprive us of it.[5]

The Westminster divines, in common with all other Protestants of the Reformed tradition, firmly rejected this Roman-Lutheran-Anglican view. The church possessed no such power of instituting rites and ceremonies of worship. Only God possessed that right. All genuine rites and ceremonies of worship are "instituted by [God] himself" and "prescribed in the holy Scripture."

It would probably be true to say that this second Roman-Lutheran-Anglican view of worship is quite widespread in the evangelical world today, even among congregations within the Reformed tradition. Generally speaking, this does not appear to be because of any self-conscious theological repudiation of the regulative principle. It seems rather to be the product of a broadly prevailing man-centered attitude or mind-set concerning worship. The question which most evangelicals tend to ask of worship-practices is, "Do I find this helpful? Is this meaningful to me? Does this make me feel closer to God?" The question, "Is this how God actually wants to be worshipped?" is rarely raised. In such a hothouse climate of anthropocentricity, the classic Reformed and Westminsterian view of worship has largely vaporized. Certainly the present writer has often encountered an incredulous Wiseman-like rejection of the regulative principle among his fellow evangelicals whenever he has had the temerity to broach the subject. "Where does Scripture say we ought to do

---

[5] Wiseman, *Lectures on the Principal Doctrines and Practices of the Catholic Church*, vol. 2, 128. Wiseman here confuses acts of worship (praying before icons of saints to secure saintly intercession) with circumstances of worship (a church building, the ringing of a bell to summon people to worship). See below for this distinction, and for whether the use of the organ is an act or a circumstance.

this or that in our worship? Why, nowhere! What of it? After all, we do all sorts of things the Bible doesn't tell us to do." It is therefore obvious that Westminster is saying something about worship which many modern evangelicals will find new, challenging and potentially radical in its practical implications.

However, before examining the biblical validity of the regulative principle as the overarching hermeneutic which governs our approach to worship, let us look at what else the Westminster documents have to say about it. To begin with, the Larger and Shorter Catechisms both present this same understanding of worship in their expositions of the Second Commandment. The answer to Question 108 of the Larger Catechism, "What are the duties required in the second commandment?" states:

> The duties required in the second commandment are, the receiving, observing, and keeping pure and entire, all such religious worship and ordinances as God hath instituted in his word. . . .

The religious worship and ordinances to which God has bound us are those "instituted in his word." Negatively, this means we must not add anything to our worship which God has not instituted in His Word. The negative is clearly asserted in the answer to Question 109, "What are the sins forbidden in the second commandment?":

> The sins forbidden in the second commandment are, all devizing, counselling, commanding, using, and any wise approving, any religious worship not instituted by God himself . . . all superstitious devices, corrupting the worship of God, adding to it, or taking from it, whether invented and taken up of ourselves, or received by tradition from others, though under the title of antiquity, custom, devotion, good intent, or any other pretence whatsoever.

A more comprehensive and lucid statement could hardly be imagined. The version of the above contained in the Shorter Catechism, Questions 50 and 51, apart from being briefer, substitutes the word "appointed" for "instituted." Thus, the answer to Question 51, "What is forbidden in the second commandment?" states:

> The second commandment forbiddeth the worshipping of God by images, or any other way not appointed in his word.

This interpretation of the Second Commandment, with its emphatic insistence on God's revealed will as the exclusive source of acceptable worship, lies behind the teaching in Westminster Confession 21.1. (We may perhaps question whether this is really what the Second Commandment means; but few things in church history could be clearer than the fact that this is what the Westminster divines thought it meant.)

There is a further important reference to worship in chapter 1 of the Confession. Paragraph 6 states:

> The whole counsel of God, concerning all things necessary for his own glory, man's salvation, faith, and life, is either expressly set down in Scripture, or by good and necessary consequence may be deduced from Scripture: unto which nothing at any time is to be added, whether by new revelations of the Spirit, or traditions of men. Nevertheless, we acknowledge the inward illumination of the Spirit of God to be necessary for the saving understanding of such things as are revealed in the word; and that there are some circumstances concerning the worship of God, and government of the Church, common to human actions and societies, which are to be ordered by the light of nature and Christian prudence, according to the general rules of the word, which are always to be observed.

As far as worship is concerned, the first part of this paragraph (what we can call 1.6a) is effectively another statement of the regulative principle. It affirms that "all things necessary . . . for man's salvation, faith, and life" are "either expressly set down in Scripture, or by good and necessary consequence may be deduced from Scripture." The "all things" clearly includes worship, unless we wish to adopt the curious position that worship has nothing to do with "man's salvation, faith, and life." Everything necessary for our worship of God, then, is either explicitly or implicitly revealed in Scripture. The paragraph then asserts the negative aspect of this position, that nothing must be added to Scripture's teaching about religious matters "whether by new revelations of the Spirit, or traditions of men." This is the equivalent of the statement in 20.1 that God

> may not be worshipped according to the imaginations and devices of men, or the suggestions of Satan, under any visible representation, or any other way not prescribed in the holy Scripture,

and of the prohibition in Larger Catechism 109 against

> corrupting the worship of God, adding to it, or taking from it, whether invented and taken up of ourselves, or received by tradition from others, though under the title of antiquity, custom, devotion, good intent, or any other pretence whatsoever. . . .

However, in the second part of paragraph 1 of the Confession (what we can call 1.6b), we find the qualifying statement:

> Nevertheless . . . there are some circumstances concerning the worship of God, and government of the Church, common to human actions and societies, which are to be ordered by the light of nature and Christian prudence, according to the general rules of the word, which are always to be observed.

The significant word here is "circumstances." This qualifying statement is not referring to the constituent acts of worship, but to "some circumstances concerning the worship of God." If by "circumstances" of worship the Confession here meant positive, concrete acts of worship, we would be faced with the most explicit and irreconcilable contradiction between Confession 1.6b on the one hand, and on the other, Confession 1.6a and 21.1, Larger Catechism 109, and Shorter Catechism 51. It would be perilous to attribute such wildly nonsensical inconsistency to the Confession, particularly in the space of a single paragraph. The Westminster divines have been accused of many things, but what would amount to a charge of manifest absurdity is stretching the resources of even sanctified credulity a little too far.

Fortunately we do not need to inflict such heartache on ourselves; the appearance of inconsistency, which some have recently professed to find here, exists only in the imaginations of those who profess to find it. A "circumstance" of worship is not a constituent act of worship. This is clear from the descriptive statement that the "circumstances" of worship which the Confession has in mind are "common to human actions and societies." In other words, there are certain things which attach

233

to all kinds of human actions and societies, whether secular or sacred in function, and without which those actions or societies would either not be possible at all, or not be capable of execution in the most effective way. To tease out what the Confession means, let us contemplate circumstances that relate to human societies. If a group of people are going to meet for some purpose, the meeting has to be at a certain time. It does not matter whether the group is gathering to watch a video, discuss politics, eat a meal, or worship Christ: the meeting will have to begin at some particular point in time, on a specified day at a certain hour. This is what the Confession means by a "circumstance." Applying this to worship, the Bible does not tell us at what specific time we ought to meet for worship on the Lord's Day. We ourselves will have to decide on this, guided by "the light of nature and Christian prudence." But the fact that *we* are deciding at what time we will meet for worship does not violate the regulative principle ("all acts of worship must be authorized by Scripture"), because the time of the meeting is not an act of worship but a *circumstance* of worship.

Or again, if a group of people are going to meet for whatever purpose, the meeting has to be in a particular place. The place of meeting is another circumstance "common to human societies." The New Testament does not tell us where to meet for our worship; so again, this is something we will have to decide for ourselves, once more guided by "the light of nature and Christian prudence." But no departure from the regulative principle is involved, because we are not introducing a new act of worship unauthorized by Scripture; we are simply deciding on the circumstance of where we shall meet to carry out the acts of worship which *are* authorized by Scripture.

The same type of reasoning applies to "circumstances common to human actions." For example, if I am going to give a talk on any topic, I may write down the main points and have them in front of me, to refresh my memory and prevent me from wandering and waffling; or I may write out the entire talk; or I may be the kind of speaker who needs no written aids. The

Christian preacher is in no different position. Scripture tells him to preach, but it does not specify that he shall preach with notes, with a fully written-out sermon, or with no written aid at all. The preaching is a divinely commanded act of worship (for the preacher is seeking directly to acknowledge and glorify God by his words, and the congregation is worshiping God by listening to His truth); but whether or not the preacher uses full manuscript or notes is a circumstance of worship, to be regulated by the light of nature and Christian prudence.

The Westminster divines put this theological distinction between acts and circumstances of worship into effect in their *Directory for the Publick Worship of God*, the *Preface* to which states:

> Wherein our care hath been to hold forth such things as are of divine institution in every ordinance; and other things we have endeavoured to set forth according to the rules of Christian prudence, agreeable to the general rules of the word of God. . . .

In dealing with the public reading of Scripture, public prayer, preaching, singing, and admnistering the sacraments, the *Directory* instructs us concerning what belongs to the esse of these worship ordinances—what is "of divine institution" in them. In preaching, for instance, the sermon must be based on the canonical Scriptures. A Protestant clergyman who preached a sermon from *Bel and the Dragon* would be in serious trouble with those to whom he was accountable (one hopes). But given that it is "of divine institution" that Scripture is the minister's sole quarry for sermons, the *Directory* also offers a great deal of heiptirl advice on how to preach a good sermon from Scripture; and this advice, while it is rich in wisdom, is not "of divine institution." It is wise human advice, "set forth according to the rules of Christian prudence, agreeable to the general rules of the word of God."

Here is the same distinction between an act and a circumstance of worship that meets us in Confession 1.6. The *Directory* does not actually use the word "circumstance" to describe the aspects of worship which are not divinely instituted, but it does use the same language that Confession 1.6 employs to say how circumstances of worship must be regulated. Thus, Confession 1:6—circumstances "are to be ordered by the light of nature and *Christian prudence*, according to the general rules of the word"; *Directory*—advice about how best to carry out divinely instituted ordinances of worship is "set forth according to the rules of *Christian prudence*, agreeable to the *general rules of the word* of God." The Directory, then, was manifestly framed in harmony with the theology of worship taught in the Confession; it set out the acts of worship which God has authorized for His New Testament people, explained what constituted the *esse* of these acts, and offered practical advice as to their most effective performance, this advice deriving from "Christian prudence, agreeable to the general rules of the word of God." Divine institution for the acts of worship, wise human advice for their circumstances: here is Confession 1.6 in action. We could express this by the following formula: With reference to the constituent acts of worship, whatever is not authorized is forbidden; but with reference to the circumstances of worship, whatever is not forbidden is lawful (if it is wise and edifying).

This distinction between acts and circumstances of worship was common currency among Reformed divines in the 17th century. John Owen, for example, referred to it at length in his *A Discourse Concerning Liturgies, and their Imposition*. Indeed, the main burden of his argument against an imposed liturgy was that it wrongly changed a circumstance of worship into an act of worship. Owen was a staunch advocate of the regulative principle, as we have seen from his *A Brief Instruction in the Worship of God*, and he would by no means tolerate the centralized imposition of a liturgy by the Anglican establishment, which required pastors to pray in the set liturgical way and no other way. Such an imposition transformed a flexible circumstance of worship (the particular way a pastor prayed) into a necessary act of worship (the pastor was commanded to pray only in one particular way).

Regarding "religious actions in the worship of God," Owen argued:

> Those circumstances . . . which do attend such actions as actions not
> determined by divine institution, may be ordered, disposed of, and
> regulated by the prudence of men. For instance, prayer is a part of
> God's worship. Public prayer is so, as appointed by him. This, as it is
> an action to be performed by man, cannot be done without the
> assignation of time, and place, and sundry other things, if order and
> conveniency be attended to. These are circumstances that attend all
> actions of that nature, to be performed by a community, whether they
> relate to the worship of God or no. These men may, according as
> they see good, regulate and change as there is occasion. . . . There are
> also some things, which some men call circumstances, also, that no
> way belong of themsdves to the actions whereof they are also said to
> be circumstances, nor do attend them, but are imposed on them, or
> annexed unto them, by the arbitrary authority of those who take upon
> them to give order and rule in such cases. . . . The schoolmen tell us
> that that which is made so the condition of an action, that without it
> the action is not to be done, is not a circumstance of it, but such an
> adjunct as is a necessary part.[6]

That is, being interpreted: to impose a set form of prayer on a
minister, forbidding him to pray in any other way, makes the set
form necessary to the very act of public prayer; and this abolishes
a liturgy's circumstantial character, turning it into the *esse* of public
prayer, without which no prayer can be offered. (Owen, in fact, did
not like *any* kind of liturgical prayer; but his basic objection was to
an imposed liturgy which stripped a minister of the freedom to
compose his own prayers.) The relevant point for us is that Owen's
whole discussion of this issue is pivoted around the distinction
between acts of worship, which are necessary and appointed
exclusively by God, and circumstances of worship, which are
inherently flexible and to be regulated by Christian prudence.

Once we grasp this distinction between an act and a
circumstance of worship, we can see how it saves us from tying
ourselves up in knots over whether there is scriptural justification

---

[6] Owen, *A Discourse Concerning Liturgies, and their Imposition*, in *Works*,
vol.15, 35. Owen's appeal to the schoolmen shows that the act-circumstance
distinction was common currency among the theologians of the Middle Ages.

for all kinds of things that accompany our worship, or whether those things should be there if they "aren't in Scripture." In his *Christian Directory*, Richard Baxter usefully listed several examples of circumstances of worship—things neither commanded nor forbidden in Scripture, but necessary to the effective carrying out of the divinely authorized acts of worship, and therefore "to be ordered by the light of nature and Christian prudence, according to the general rules of the word, which are always to be observed." Baxter's list includes the following: The particular text or topic a preacher should choose for any given sermon; the particular method and style of handling that text or topic; the time of the meeting on the Lord's day, and the time of any religious meeting other than on the Lord's day; the place of meeting; the particular sins we should publicly confess, and blessings we should seek or give thanks for; the particular passages of Scripture we should read out; the particular psalms we should sing; the particular translation of Scripture we should use; whether the preacher should use notes; whether the public prayers should be written out; the particular furnishings of a meeting place for worship, *e.g.* pulpits, tables, cushions; gesture and posture in preaching, public reading, and listening; the clothes we wear when we come to worship; and the particular things we use to assist our natural faculties when engaged in the divinely commanded acts of worship, *e.g.* "tunes, musical instruments, spectacles, hourglasses."[7]

It is interesting that Baxter classed musical instruments as a circumstance of worship; we will return to this specific point later on. For our present purposes, we need simply to observe Baxter's classic use of the distinction between an act and a circumstance of worship. His discussion supplies us with a contemporary 17th century English embodiment of what the Westminster divines meant when they made this distinction. Also important is Baxter's insistence that the circumstances of worship are not to be determined by what pleases and excites people, but by the exercise

---

[7] Baxter, *Christian Directory*, 557.

of wisdom—

> by human prudence, not as men please; but as means in order to the
> proper end, according to the general laws of Christ. For Scripture is
> a general law for all such circumstances, but not a particular law.[8]

This could easily be Baxter's gloss on the statement of the
Confession that the circumstances of worship must be in harmony
with "the general rules of the word, which are always to be
observed."

The advance of technology since Baxter's time has added a
number of other circumstances of worship which he did not
specify, *e.g.*, electric lighting, central heating, microphones, and
overhead projectors. The use of these in the place or activity of
worship is not sanctioned by Scripture. But none of these things
is an act of worship. We should use them, not with a view to
"spicing up" our worship or making it more *avant garde*, but
merely to *facilitate* our acts of worship—to remove obstacles
which might hinder the free and ready carrying out of those acts
of worship which are sanctioned by Scripture. Our aim and
intention must always be to regulate the circumstances of our
worship by "the light of nature and Christian prudence, according
to the general rules of the word, which are always to be observed."

The point is also worth making that the distinctions between
acts and circumstances of worship has relevance to an order of
service. Scripture tells us that when we meet together as a church,
God wants our worship to be characterized by prayer, the public
reading of His Word, preaching, psalm-singing and the Lord's
supper. But the precise way we fit together these divinely
authorized acts of worship is not laid down in Scripture. How
many public prayers will there be? How many readings from
Scripture? How many psalms shall we sing? How long will the
sermon be? What order shall we put these things in? The

---

[8] Baxter, Ibid.

construction of an order of service must use only the acts of worship which God has authorized, but the details of construction fall under the category of "circumstance," and are therefore (once again) "to be ordered by the light of nature and Christian prudence, according to the general rules of the word, which are always to be observed." This point is worth emphasizing, because it goes some way towards dispelling the widespread notion that the regulative principle necessarily leads to a rigid, inflexible form of worship with no room for sanctified creativity. The principle *is* rigid and inflexible, and *does* rule out creativity (sanctified or otherwise), as far as the *ingredients* of our worship are concerned; but it equally allows us a measure of Christian liberty in the exact way that we mix or combine those ingredients. Form and freedom are both provided for. No one need fear that adopting the regulative principle will infallibly beget an untouchable, sterile sameness in a church's pattern of worship.

Having established Westminster's clear and consistent espousal of the regulative principle, let us go on to examine its theological rationale. The first point that should be considered is the general one that if we accept the biblical doctrine of a sovereign, transcendent, holy God, the King of kings and Lord of lords, to Whom belongs all authority in heaven and on earth, the regulative principle seems to follow as a matter of course. All we need to do is ask ourselves the question, Are we to worship this God as *we* see fit, regardless of whether we know He approves of our forms of worship? And how can we know He approves, unless He reveals to us in His Word that He does? Scripture makes it clear that the fallen mind of man, left to itself, will devise all kinds of acts and rites of worship which it thinks will please God, but which in fact are unacceptable to Him. We only have to read the apostle Paul's description and excoriation of pagan worship in Romans 1:18-25 to see this. Christ said that some would even think they were offering service or worship λατρεια to God by killing His disciples—further than which, perversity cannot go

(John 16:2). Rather than relying on the independent ideas of our own pious but sinful minds, mere safety counsels that we cleave to God's Word if we would know how to worship Him acceptably.

Furthermore, the Christian's supreme practical motive is his desire to please the Beloved (2 Corinthians 5:9, 2 Timothy 2:4). He will therefore naturally ask, "In what way does it please God that I should worship Him?" Today's hedonistic creed of "Please yourself" cannot apply in Christian worship. True worship is not about what pleases us, but what pleases God. Of course, we will often (but not always) find worship pleasant. But our pleasure, if it is spiritual in nature, will flow from the contemplation of the supreme loveliness of God, which inspires our love for Him, and from the knowledge that we are pleasing the One we love, by worshipping Him as *He* desires to be worshipped. We are therefore again driven back to God's Word to find out what pleases Him in the sphere of our worship.

Finally, if worship is to be an act of faith, it must have God's Word as its basis. All faith is correlative to the Word; it is believing what God says and then acting on it. "For what does the Scripture say? 'Abraham believed God, and it was accounted to him for righteousness'" (Romans 4:3). And "without faith it is impossible to please God" (Hebrews 11:6). If we offer acts of worship to God which are not authorized by His Word, those acts of worship cannot be acts of faith. To deny the regulative principle is, therefore, to create the spectacle of faithless worship, which by definition cannot be pleasing to God.

General religious considerations, then, point us unequivocally to the regulative principle. But what about the explicit teaching of Scripture? Is it one of those things which "by good and necessary consequence may be deduced from Scripture," or is it actually "expressly set down in Scripture"? The answer must surely be the latter: both Old and New Testaments expressly endorse the regulative principle. If we limit ourselves to looking only at the key texts, we may begin in the Old Testament with

Deuteronomy 12:28-32. Here, in the context of giving instructions about worship, God says to Israel:

> Observe and obey all these words which I command you, that it may go well with you and your children after you for ever, when you do what is good and right in the sight of the LORD your God. When the LORD your God cuts off from before you the nations which you go to dispossess, and you displace them and dwell in their land, take heed to yourself that you are not ensnared to follow them, after they are destroyed from before you, and that you do not inquire after their gods, saying, "How did these nations serve their gods? I will do likewise." You shall not worship the LORD your God in that way; for every abomination to the LORD which He hates they have done to their gods; for they burn even their sons and daughters in the fire to their gods. Whatever I command you, be careful to observe it; you shall not add to it nor take away from it.

God instructs the Israelites neither to add to, nor take from, the system of worship which He Himself has given to them (v.32). They will be doing what is good and right in His sight only when they observe and obey all the words which He commands them (v.28). They are not to ask how pagans worship their gods, nor in any way to introduce such forms of worship into their own divine service (v.30). They must keep simply and exclusively to what God has revealed as His way of worship. A more comprehensive statement of the regulative principle could hardly be imagined.

It is important to remember that the entire system of Israelite worship was revealed to God's people under the Old Covenant by God Himself through His Word. At no point did He leave it to His people's reason or imagination to devise the sacrificial system, the Levitical priesthood, the ark, the sabbath, the different festivals, and so on. All these things came via special revelation. The contrast between divine authority and human imagination is vividly expressed in Numbers 15:39-40:

> remember all the commandments of the LORD and do them, that you may not follow the prostitution to which your own heart and your own eyes are inclined, and that you may remember and do all My commandments, and be holy, for I am your God.

In religion, which includes both the object and manner of our worship, if we stray from the path of God's commands to follow after our own hearts and our own eyes, we become guilty of a kind of spiritual prostitution. For if we step outside God's revealed will in our *way* of worship, we are exposing ourselves to the same perils as the idol-maker in distorting the oblect of our worship. By giving free play to our fallen imaginations and inventing our own rites of worship, we will be led, however subtly, into the worship of a god who is less or other than the true God—a reflection of our own minds, which we have substituted for God's mind as our source and standard of worship. And that would be the sin of spiritual harlotry. How do we avoid this fearful danger? Simply by refusing to devise our own acts and forms of worship, and by keeping faithfully and humbly to what God has revealed as His safe, wholesome, acceptable way of worship.

The operation of the regulative principle in Old Testament worship can be seen most strikingly if we consider how God reacted when people offered Him an act of worship which He had not commanded. The classic instance is in Leviticus 10:1-3:

> Then Nadab and Abihu, the sons of Aaron, each took his censer and put fife in it, and offered profane fire before the Lord, which He had not commanded them. So fire went out from the LORD and devoured them, and they died before the LORD. Then Moses said to Aaron. "This is what the LORD spoke, saying: 'By those who come near Me I must be regarded as holy; and before all the people I must be glorified.'" So Aaron held his peace.

The sin of Nadab and Abihu was to offer "profane" or "strange" fire before God "which He had not commanded them." In other words, they offered a worship which God had not told them to offer—unauthorized worship. They had acted according to their own will, not God's will. (The *New International Version* obscures this by translating the phrase "which God had not commanded them" as "contrary to God's command." But the point is not that Nadab and Abihu acted *contrary* to a command from God, but that they acted *without* a command from God. They did not offer a worship explicitly forbidden, but a worship nowhere authorized.)

According to Moses in v. 3, God regarded this as a violation of His holiness. So in order to impress on His people that He would be worshipped according to *His* will, God destroyed Aaron's sons.

Other Old Testament passages could be cited. After the division of the twelve tribes into the dual monarchies, Jeroboam was condemned for instituting his own system of worship in Israel "which he had devised in his own heart" (1 Kings 12:26-33). We find God denouncing the corrupt worship in Judaea in Jeremiah's time in similar terms, a worship "which I did not command or speak, nor did it come into My mind" (Jeremiah 19:5; cf 7:31, 32:35). In both cases Scripture condemns false worship, not so much because it positively contradicted God's revealed will, but because it was of merely human origin.

There can be no doubt, then, about the operation of the regulative principle in Old Testament worship. This brings us to the crucial question: Is the principle carried over into the New Testament? We have every reason to think so. Consider, for example, the Lord Jesus Christ's condemnation of the vain worship of the Pharisees on the grounds of its merely human origin in Mark 7:6-7 (or Matthew 15:1-20):

> "Well did Isaiah prophesy of you hypocrites, as it is written: 'This people honours Me with their lips, but their heart is far from Me. And in vain they worship Me, teaching as doctrines the commandments of men.'"

The reason why this account of Christ's rejection of Pharisaic worship was recorded in the Gospels was (surely) to establish a basic axiom for the worship of His true disciples—unless we wish to put ourselves in the bizarre position of thinking that Christian worship is to be what our Lord condemned in the Pharisees. Authentic worship, Christ teaches, must be of divine, not human origin; God's Word, not (as with the Pharisees) mere human tradition, is the sole ground for all acceptable worship of the living God. The presence of this incident in the Gospels, then, is a clear indication that God intends the regulative principle to operate just as much in New as in Old Testament worship. After all, now that Messiah has come in the flesh and revealed the fulness of saving truth, is God less concerned that we should worship Him according to His will, rather than our own? The notion seems absurd. In the words of John Owen:

> Though these [commands] in the Old Testament had their peculiar respect to the worship that was then instituted, yet they had [respect unto it] not as then instituted, but as the worship which God Himself had appointed. And therefore their general force abides while God requires any worship at the hands of men, unless it may be made to appear that God hath parted with that prerogative of being the appointer of His own worship now under the New Testament, which He so vindicated unto Himself in the Old.[9]

Christians are certainly free from the ceremonial yoke of Mosaic worship (Acts 15:10); but by the same token, we are not free to be a law unto ourselves in the manner of our New Covenant worship. The divine revelation which liberates us from the one, does so by transferring us to the other. The option of man-made worship is never contemplated by either Testament, save as a sin. We have heard Christ condemn it; let us also hear the apostle Paul:

> Therefore if you died with Christ from the basic principles of the world, why, as though living in the world, do you subject yourself to regulations—"Do not touch, do not taste, do not handle," which all concern things which perish with the using—according to the commandments and doctrines of men? These things indeed have an appearance of wisdom in self-imposed religion, false humility, and neglect of the body, but are of no value against the indulgence of the flesh (Colossians 2:20-23).

The phrase translated here by the *New King James Version* as "self-imposed religion" is one Greek word, ἐθελοθπησκιοα, which literally means "will-worship."[10] It means religion, worship or devotion originating in the will of man—"the commandments

---

[9] Owen, *A Discourse Concerning Liturgies*, in *Works*, vol. 15, 38.

[10] The *King James Version* renders it "will worship." *New International Version* renders "self-imposed worship." *New American Standard Bible* renders "self-made religion."

and doctrines of men" (v.22)—worship devised on man's authority rather than God's—volunteered worship, rather than commanded worship. This, Paul says, has "an appearance of wisdom," because of its seeming zeal: imposing acts and forms and exercises of worship on oneself above and beyond what God has required. But such zeal, the apostle advises us, is perverse. It is only an appearance of wisdom, not true wisdom, for it means enthroning mere man-made tradition and authority in God's wisdom, even those "doctrines and commandments of men" which Christ warned against in His criticism of Pharisaic worship.

The great Puritan commentary of Matthew Poole (1624-79) expounds ἐθελοθπησκιοα thus:

> *In will-worship*; In arbitrary superstition, or human invention, or self-willed religion, rather than divine institutions; as all the ancients, and almost all the modems, do interpret that word, it having no good, but an ill character; accounting the compound word here which we render *will-worship*, of no better import, as to the ordainers of worship, than the two simple words of which it is compounded, expressing human arbitrariness and worship. . . . For though a performing those acts of worship willingly, which God Himself hath commanded, be necessary, and commendable in His willing people, Psal. cx.3, and they cannot be acceptable otherwise; yet when the will of man, in contradistinction to the will of God. is considered as constitutive of that worship which is offered to God as of a man's own brain and devizing, without God's warrant, then that will-worship is hateful to God, and the more voluntary the more abominable. It being most just, that not in what way we will and choose, but only in that way which He willeth and chooseth, we should worship Him with acceptance; which should be our greatest care, 2 Cor. v. 9.[11]

The great scriptural truth which lies behind the regulative principle in Christian worship is the Kingship of Christ. The New Testament Church is a theocratic, or (perhaps we should say), a Christocratic community. We are ruled by Christ our King in our doctrine, worship and organization, and have no right to add to, or take from, His royal Word in any of these areas. To quote

---

[11] Poole, *A Commentary on the Holy Bible*, vol. 3, 721.

Richard Baxter again:

> If you think that the Scripture containeth not any law or rule of worship at all, or not so much as indeed it doth, you will deny a principal part of the office of Christ, as the King and Teacher of the church, and will accuse his laws of insufficiency, and be tempted to worship him with a human kind of worship, and to think yourselves at liberty to worship him according to your own imaginations, or change his worship according to the fashion of the age or the country where you are.[12]

The commission Christ gave to the apostles enshrines this truth, that He is His New Covenant people's lawgiver:

> All authority has been given to Me in heaven and on earth. Go therefore and make disciples of all the nations, baptizing them in the name of the Father and of the Son and of the Holy Spirit, teaching them to observe all things that I have commanded you. (Matthew 28:19-20).

All Christ's disciples are under the authority of the One Whose lordship is universal, Who requires us to observe all the commands He entrusted to His apostles. We find here no warrant for the church to think that it is free to invent its own acts or rites by which to worship its King. We are to teach people to observe that Christ has commanded, and not to mingle in those "commandments of men" which our Master said made vain the worship of the Pharisees.

We are now in a position to examine the teaching of the Confession about the place of psalms, hyrnns and musical instruments in New Testament worship. We begin with the following important assumption: in the light of the Confession's full-blooded commitment to the regulative principle, we must take it for granted that *the acts of worship the Confession explicitly authorizes are the only acts for which it finds scriptural justification*. It would be a more than mildly weird state of affairs for a confession of faith to espouse the regulative principle with great force and precision, then to state what its framers believed

---

[12] Baxter, *Christian Directory*, 555.

to be the biblically authorized acts of worship—and yet for there to be other acts of worship, on which the Confession is completely silent, but which its framers believed to be equally divinely authorized. Such a position would be incoherent to the point of unreason. The only logical assumption we can make is that what Westminster actually sets down as the acts of worship authorized by God in Scripture are the *only* acts the Westminster divines believed were thus authorized.

First, then, the Confession clearly teaches that the singing of psalms is a divinely authorized act of New Testament worship. The third ingredient of worship mentioned in Confession 21.5 is "singing of psalms with grace in the heart." *The Directory for the Publick Worship of God* also exhorts us to sing psalms. The section entitled *Of prayer after Sermon* ends with the words, "The prayer ended, let a psalm be sung, if with conveniency it may be done." The last section of the *Directory* is entitled *Of Singing of Psalms*, and says:

> It is the duty of Christians to praise God publicly, by singing of psalms together in the congregation, and also privately in the family. In singing of psalms, the voice is to be tunably and gravely ordered; but the chief care must be to sing with understanding, and with grace in the heart, making melody unto the Lord. That the whole congregation may join herein, every one that can read is to have a psalm book; and all others, not disabled by age or otherwise, are to be exhorted to learn to read. But for the present, where many in the congregation cannot read, it is convenient that the minister or some other fit person appointed by him and the other ruling officers, do read the psalm, line by line, before the singing thereof.

There can be no controversy then, that the Westminster documents regard psalm-singing as a divinely authorized act of Christian worship. And one might have thought that since they mention only psalms, and not hymns, that would settle the question as to whether hymn-singing can be justified by Westminsterian standards. Surely it cannot, in the light of Westminster's lucid espousal of the regulative principle. Only what God has authorized is an acceptable act of worship, and the only thing Westminster says God has authorized is the singing of psalms.

But such a conclusion would, in fact, be premature; for we have yet to ask what the Westminster divines meant by "psalms." There is abundant evidence that in 17th century English, the word "psalm" often meant simply a religious song, with no exclusive reference to the canonical psalms of David being intended. (I will henceforth refer to the 150 psalms of the psalter as "Davidic" to distinguish them from other psalms and songs, even though not all the "Davidic" psalms were actually written by David.) The proof texts in Confession 21.5 for psalm-singing are Colossians 3:16, Ephesians 5:19 and James 5:13; and the first two contain the much-debated Pauline exhortations to sing "psalms, hymns and spiritual songs." Let us see how Matthew Poole's commentary interpreted this exhortation. In this section on Colossians 3:16, the three terms are expounded thus:

> Some would distinguish the three words the apostle here useth from the manner of singing, as well as the matter sung; others, from the Hebrew usage of words expressed by the seventy [*i.e.*, the Septuagint], in the book of Psalms; yet, whoever consults the titles of the Psalms and other places of the Old Testament, they shall find the words used sometimes promiscuously. . . . Hereupon others stand not upon any critical distinction of the three words, yet are inclined to take *psalms* by way of eminency, Luke xxiv. 44; or more generally, as the genus, noting any holy metre, whether composed by the prophets of old, or others since, assisted by the Spirit extraordinarily or ordinarily.[13]

Accepting this latter view that "psalm" means "the genus" of religious song (inspired or not), Poole then goes on to distinguish two kinds of "psalm"—the *hymn*, "whereby we celebrate the excellencies of God and his benefits to man"; and the *ode* or *song*, "of a more ample, artificial, and elaborate composure." Finally, the adjective "spiritual" in "spiritual song" is interpreted to mean "*holy* songs . . . as opposed to carnal, sensual, and worldly ditties."

Poole's commentary, then, clearly takes the third of the three views it sets down, which is why it comes last and is expounded

---

[13] Poole, *A Commentary on the Holy Bible*, vol. 3, 725.

it at such length—namely, that "psalm" meant "any holy metre," whether in the psalter, another part of the Bible, or anywhere else. It then takes "hymn" and "spiritual song" to be two types of psalm, and (crucially) it does not interpret "spiritual" to mean "directly inspired by the Holy Spirit," which would have restricted "spiritual songs" to those found in canonical Scripture. If this is how the most learned and laborious of Puritan commentaries interpreted the word "psalms" in Colossians 3:16, it compels us to think twice before we presume that "psalms" in the Westminster Confession obviously and exclusively mean the psalms of David.

Poole's interpretation of the second of the Confession's proof texts, Ephesians 5:19, is along similar lines:

> *In psalms, and hymns, and spiritual songs*; under these names he comprehends all manner of singing to mutual edification and God's glory. The particular distinction of them is uncertain, but most take psalms to be such as anciently were sung with musical instruments; hymns, such as contained only matter of praise; *spiritual songs*, such as were of various matter doctrinal, prophetical, historical, etc: see on Col. iii. 16.[14]

Psalm is not here defined as any religious song, but one that was "anciently" sung with musical instruments. This is based on the etymology of the Greek verb ψαλλω, which means literally to pluck or twang—hence, a song sung to stringed instrumental accompaniment. There is no reason to think that such songs are limited to the canonical psalter; indeed, there is an excellent example of such a song in Habbakuk chapter 3 (the whole chapter is a religious song and closes in verse 19 with, "To the chief musician. With my stringed instruments"). It is, of course, also significant that once again, as with Colossians 3:16, Poole's commentary does not adopt the exclusive psalmodist interpretation of "psalms, hymns and spiritual songs" as meaning simply the psalter.

The final Confessional proof text, James 5:13 ("Is any merry? Let him sing psalms"), Poole's commentary expounds thus:

---

[14] Ibid., 676.

> express his mirth in a holy manner, by praising God with psalms or
> spiritual songs for mercies received from him. 1 Cor. xiv. 15; Eph. v.
> 19. . .[15]

No definition of a psalm is given here, but his reference to Ephesians 5:19 shows us that once more the psalms of David are not exclusively in mind.

There is one other interesting interpretation of the word "psalm" in Poole's commentary, in the comments on 1 Corinthians 14:26 ("How is it then, brethren? Whenever you come together, each of you has a psalm, has a teaching, has a tongue, has a revelation, has an interpretation. Let all things be done for edification"). The one who "has a psalm" is described as a brother who wants to exercise the gift God has given him "in singing the psalm he has made." So we see again that for Poole the word "psalm" could refer to a newly composed religious song.

Poole's commentary was by no means a lone voice among 17th century Reformed theology in its understanding of what a psalm is. Richard Baxter took the same view. In his *Christian Directory*, Baxter has a section headed *Is it lawful to use David's psalms in our assemblies*? His answer was that it is lawful to take the material of our sung praise from the Davidic psalter; but he nowhere says we must do so. Baxter's argument was not with those who maintained the lawfulness of singing uninspired hymns, but with those who maintained the unlawfulness of singing David's psalms and indeed any other liturgical song in a public assembly.[16] Baxter's response was that it is obligatory to sing praises to God, and the psalms of David are a lawful means to this end. Baxter, like

---

[15] Ibid., 896-7.

[16] Baxter refers to "the sectarian objections against singing David's psalms" (*Christian Directory*, 704). These sectarians were mostly General (i.e., Arminian) Baptists, who rejected all forms of liturgy in all circumstances— "written and set forms of prayer" (ibid.). They feared that an argument in favour of liturgy would stem from admitting that the psalms could be sung in worship; for then a congregation would be using a written and set form of

Poole, clearly uses the word "psalm" to mean any religious song:

> We are commanded in the New Testament to sing psalms; and we are
> not commanded to compose new ones; nor can every one make
> psalms, who is commanded to sing psalms. And if it be lawful to sing
> psalms of our own or our neighbour's making, much more of God's
> making by his Spirit in his prophets.[17]

Baxter here simply assumes that it is "lawful to sing psalms of our own or our neighbour's making." This obviously means that he was using the word "psalm" to mean any religious song. His argument was that the New Testament positively commands us to sing songs to God—here is the thing absolutely required of us as an act of worship. But the New Testament does not positively command us to write our own songs; indeed, not everyone is able to do this—we can all sing, but we are not all song-writers. Therefore it is splendidly reasonable for us to sing the songs that have already been composed by the Holy Spirit, the psalms of David. Such is the logic of Baxter's argument. It is clearly not an argument for exclusive psalmody. Baxter's point was simply that it is "lawful" to sing David's psalms; but then, according to Baxter, it was equally lawful to sing psalms of our own or our neighbour's making."[18] Baxter appears to have taken the attitude that since God commands us to sing, it is lawful for us to save ourselves the trouble of writing our own songs and sing the songs we find in

---

prayer from Scripture, since most of the psalms are prayers. General Baptists held that all set prayers and songs quenched the Spirit, Who worked only through the spontaneous utterances of the individual's own heart. See Davies, *The Worship of the English Puritans*, 77-97, 168-72.

[17] Baxter, Ibid.

[18] Baxter wrote a paraphrase on the Psalms, published posthumously, in the preface to which he explicitly justified the singing of uninspired hymns: "Doubtless Paul meaneth not only David's Psalms, when he bids men sing with grace in their hearts, Psalms, Hymns, and Spiritual songs; yea, it is past doubt, that hymns more suitable to Gospel-times may and ought now to be used." Baxter's own hymns, e.g. "Lord, it belongs not to my care" and "Ye holy angels bright," were his own contribution to these "hymns more suitable to Gospel-times."

the Bible. It is a matter of convenience and expediency. However, Baxter did not by any means deny, but explicitly accepted, the lawfulness of composing "psalms of our own"; and for our purposes, the crucial factor is Baxter's employment of the key term "psalm" in this way to mean any Christian song.

It is clear, then, that Reformed writers in the 17th century were quite capable of using the word "psalm" to denote simply a religious song, whether found in the psalter, another part of the Bible, or composed by uninspired men. This makes us wonder what precisely the Westminster divines meant when they taught in Confession 21.5 that "singing of psalms with grace in the heart" was a divinely sanctioned act of worship. If only they had written "David's psalms," that would be an end of the matter. But they did not write "David's psalms." From a purely linguistic standpoint, it is therefore wholly possible and legitimate to interpret the unqualified word "psalms" in 21.5 either as David's psalms, or as religious songs in general. There is, quite simply, nothing in the Confession 21.5 itself to compel us to understand the "psalms" in the one sense or the other. The proof-texts merely add to the weight of ambiguity, since the "psalms, hymns and spiritual songs" of Colossians 3:16 and Ephesians 5:19 were expounded by an outstanding and representative Puritan commentary like Matthew Poole's to include all types of sung praise, whether inspired or not.

Perhaps further light will be shed on the question if we look at what Churches of the Reformed tradition did actually sing in the 16th and 17th centuries, and what they taught about the materials of sung praise. If history testifies that they sang the psalms of David exclusively, and taught exclusive psalmody as a matter of principle, that would be a strong argument in favour of taking the "psalms" of Confession 21.5 in the narrower Davidic sense. What, then, is the testimony of history?

If we accept Zwingli's Zurich as the birthplace of the Reformed tradition, we find that Zwingli did not incorporate congregational singing into the worship service at all. It is sometimes said that he abolished it, but this is inaccurate; there was no congregational singing for him to abolish in medieval Roman Catholic worship. What Zwingli did was to abolish *choral* singing in *Latin*. He failed to replace it with congregational singing in Swiss German. This failure, however, seems not to have been an absolute rejection by Zwingli of congregational singing as a divinely authorized act of worship; he is on record as having expressed approval in principle of congregational singing. During Zwingli's lifetime, choral singing was replaced by congregational recitation in Swiss German of the psalms of David and the *Gloria in excelsis* (from Luke 2:14). If we assume that Zwingli would have wished people eventually to sing what they were reciting, then the Zurich Reformer's position would seem to have been that

> Scriptural materials of praise, including David's psalms but not excluding other passages, were the appropriate matter for singing.[19]

Zwingli's successor, Bullinger, took the same view; in his *Decades*, the section on singing as an act of worship argues that material from the canonical Scriptures alone (but not the psalter alone) should be sung. Bullinger appealed to the practice of the early Church:

> Ye shall also find this, that by certain decrees of councils it was ordained, that no other thing should be read or sung in holy assemblies but only the canonical Scripture. For even betimes there began neither a mean to be kept in the church, neither the canonical Scripture only to be used, for that certain men intermeddled their own songs.[20]

Bullinger argued that the singing and the reciting of Scripture by the congregation were just two different ways of uttering the Word of God as an act of worship. Every church was at liberty to choose the one way or the other:

> If this uprightness and liberty had remained safe and unaltered; that is to say, if, according to that ancient use of singing, nothing had

---

[19] For a useful summary of Zwingli's views, see R. Christoffel, *Zwingli; or, the Rise of the Reformation in Switzerland*, 150.

[20] Bullinger's *Decades*, vol. 5, 193 (Cambridge, 1852).

been sung but canonical scriptures; if it had been still in the liberty of the churches to sing or not to sing; truly at this day there should be no controversy in the church about singing in the church. For those churches which should use singing after the ancient manner practised in singing, would sing the word of God and the praises of God [*i.e.*, praises inspired by God] only. . . . .[21]

Since Bullinger's *Decades* were widely used in Elizabethan England as the standard textbook of systematic theology, Bullinger's views would probably have had considerable influence on English Protestants in the 16th century.

Calvin's attitude as a Reformer in Strasbourg and Geneva was broadly similar to that of Zwingli and Bullinger, except that the Frenchman was positively committed to congregational singing rather than mere recitation. In 1539, when he was in Strasbourg, he published a song-book which contained metrical versions of seventeen Davidic psalms, the *Nunc dimittis* (Simeon's song Luke 2:29-32), and the Ten Commandments, plus prose chants of Psalm 113 and the Apostles' Creed.[22] The singing of the Ten Commandments was an integral part of the Sunday worship in Calvin's Strasbourg congregation.[23] Calvin's first Genevan liturgy of 1542 contained 39 Davidic psalms, the *Nunc dimittis*, and musical versions of the Ten Commandments, Lord's Prayer and Apostles' Creed. The *Nunc Dimittis* was always sung at the conclusion of the Lord's Supper.[24] However, especially in his second period in Geneva (1541-64), Calvin undoubtedly gave pride of place

---

[21] Ibid., 195.

[22] Julian's *Dictionary of Hymnology*, vol. 2, 932. Calvin may have been influenced by William Farel, his co-Reformer during his first Geneva period. Prior to Calvin's arrival in Geneva, the only singing material Farel had supplied for the newly Protestantized Geneva was the Apostles' Creed and the Ten Commandments set to music. See Baird, *The Presbyterian Liturgies*, 18.

[23] For Calvin in Strasbourg, see Walker, *John Calvin, the Organiser of Reformed Protestantism*, 222-6.

[24] Julian's *Dictionary of Hymnology*, vol. 2, 932-3; Baird, *The Presbyterian Liturgies*, 14-70.

to David's psalms in public worship. His view was expressed succinctly in the preamble to the 1542 Genevan service book:

> Now, what Augustine says is true, namely, that no one can sing anything worthy of God which he has not received from him. Therefore, even after we have carefully searched everywhere, we shall not find better or more appropriate songs to this end than the songs of David, inspired by the Holy Spirit. And for this reason, when we sing them, we are assured that God puts the words in our mouth, as if he himself were singing to us to exalt his glory.[25]

If we look at how Calvin interpreted the scriptural *loci classici* of Colossians 3:16 and Ephesians 5:19, he certainly did not expound them in an exclusive psalmodist manner. He simply distinguished the "psalms, hymns and spiritual songs" into (a) psalms—songs sung to instrumental accompaniment, (b) hymns—any and all songs of praise, and (c) songs or "odes"— songs containing both praise and other matter, e.g. exhortation. He also understood the qualifying term "spiritual" in "spiritual songs" as a reference to the Christian content of the songs, rather than to the Holy Spirit as inspiring author.

> He would have the songs of Christians, however, to be spiritual, not made up of frivolities and worthless trifles.[26]

Calvin's position, then, as demonstrated by his practice, was an acceptance of all suitable Scriptural passages as vehicles of sung praise (including the *Nunc dimittis*, the Ten Commandments and the Lord's Prayer), and even the Apostles' Creed, but within this framework to sanction David's psalms as the jewel in the liturgical crown.

Calvin's encouragement and stamp of approval lay behind the French psalter of 1562, translated by Clement Marot (1497-1544) and Theodore Beza (1519-1605). Marot's first psalter of 1541 contained forty-five metrical Davidic psalms, thirty by Marot

---

[25] Quoted by Ward, *The Psalms in Christian Worship*, 65.

[26] Calvin, *Commentaries on the Epistle of Paul the Apostle to the Philippians, Colossians and Thessalonians*, 217-18

himself. His second psalter of 1542 had only his own thirty psalms; it was condemned by the Sorbonne and prompted Marot's flight to Geneva. His first Genevan psalter of 1543 contained the thirty psalms previously published, nineteen new ones, the *Nunc dimittis*, the *Ave Maria*, musical versions of the Ten Commandments, the Apostles' Creed, and the Lord's Prayer, and two graces to be sung at mealtimes. Marot died the next year, but Beza completed the translation of the psalms into French in 1562. This definitive version contained all one hundred fifty Davidic psalms, the *Nunc dimittis*, and the Ten Commandments set to music.[27]

The French Reformed Church exclusively employed Marot and Beza's psalter after 1562. Certainly uninspired hymns were not used until the early 19th century. However, at the end of the 16th century, French Calvinists did take steps towards singing scriptural songs other than the psalms of David (and, presumably, the *Nunc dimittis*). The national Synod of 1594 agreed to pursue this matter positively, and sent a request to Geneva seeking the assistance of Beza. In 1595 a collection of sixteen songs from Scripture was published. In 1598 the Synod exhorted Church members to familiarize themselves with these songs in family worship, with a view to their use in public worship. The new songs, however, seem not to have caught on, and did not become part of public Huguenot worship. Even so, this interesting historical episode does show that the French Reformed Church was not opposed in principle to the singing of scriptural songs other than those of the psalter, quite apart from the presence of the *Nunc dimittis* and Ten Commandments in the French psalter.[28]

This point is reinforced by the comments of the great French Reformed divine John Daille (1594-1670) in his commentary on Colossians, published in Paris in 1648 (and thus virtually

---

[27] See Julian's *Dictionary of Hymnology*, vol. 2, 932-4.
[28] See H. M. Baird, *Theodore Beza*, 305-6.

contemporary with the Westminster Assembly). On Colossians 3:16, Daille said:

> For the Lord is so good, that He hath provided even for the recreating [recreation] of His children; and knowing, that Song is one of His most natural means, extremely proper both to dilate the contentment of our hearts, and render it full-blown, as also to alleviate, and mitigate their sorrows, He hath not only permitted us, but even commanded us to sing unto Him spiritual songs. And for the forming of us unto so holy, and so profitable an exercise, He hash given us a great number of these Divine Cantides, [such] as the Psalms of *David* and the Hymns of divers other faithful and religious persons, dispersed here and there in the books of the Old and New Testaments.[29]

Daille was inclined to Amyraldianism, but his sentiments on the use of psalms and other scriptural songs in worship were no more than established Huguenot tradition. Thus, then, French Calvinism: essentially psalm-singing in practice, but in principle accepting the lawfulness of singing all the songs of Scripture.

The Reformed Churches of Germany used a translation of the French Reformed psalter, published in 1573. The translator, oddly, was a German Lutheran, Ambrosius Lobwasser (1515-85). Lobwasser included in his German psalter Marot and Beza's metrical versions of the *Nunc dimittis* and the Ten Commandments. His psalter was highly popular with German Calvinists, maintaining its hold on their affections until the 18th century.[30]

The Reformed Church of the Netherlands also used a translation of the French psalter, published in 1566; it contained David's psalms and five other scriptural passages set to music. The Synod of Dort in 1574 (not to be confused with the more famous one forty years later) sanctioned the use of this psalter. In 1612 a plan for liturgical reform was discussed by the Reformed ministers of the province of Utrecht, which if implemented would have revolutionized the worship of the Dutch Reformed Church.

---

[29] Daille, *Sermons of Mr. John Daille*, 95.

[30] Ward, *The Psalms in Christian Worship*, 66-7.

The plan suggested

> That besides the psalms of David and others commonly used already,
> there might be as many other Scriptural hymns relating to our Saviour's
> birth, circumcision, baptism, passion, death, resurrection from the dead,
> ascension into heaven, and the mission of the Holy Ghost, sung in
> churches as, according to the practice of other evangelical reformed
> churches, could be introduced with decency, in order to excite in the
> minds of the people spiritual meditations upon the great benefits
> procured to mankind by Jesus their Saviour, provided such hymns were
> fitly composed, and previously revised by such persons as the States
> should appoint, and not introduced into any church, but by leave of the
> magistrates and consistory of every place.[31]

This plan was never put into effect on a national scale. But it demonstrates that Dutch Reformed divines, like their French brethren, were not opposed in principle to the singing of "other Scriptural hymns" besides the psalms of David. Indeed, the Dutch proposal of 1612 goes beyond its French counterpart of 1594-8 in calling for newly composed songs that enshrine scriptural truths, rather than simply songs already found in Scripture, other than David's psalms. The reference to "the practice of other evangelical reformed churches" is puzzling, unless it is a loose description of other Protestant Churches which would include hymn-singing Lutherans. However, the opening sentence about "the psalms of David and others commonly used already" presents us with another example of the broad definition of the term "psalm."

When the great 1618 Synod of Dort met, it authorized the singing in Dutch Reformed public worship of David's psalms, the Ten Commandments, the Lord's Prayer, the Creed, and the three Gospel "canticles" of the *Nunc dimittis*, the *Magnificat* (Luke 1:46-55), and the *Benedictus* (Luke 1:68-79). Exclusive psalmody was certainly no part of Dutch Calvinism, either in principle or in practice.[32]

The pattern of sung worship in the Continental Reformed

---

[31] Ibid., 67-8.

[32] Ibid., 68.

Churches, then, does not fit into an exclusive psalmodist framework. Nor does it even fit into the broader pattern often described as "inspired materials of praise"—i.e., that only scriptural passages of praise should be sung. Continental Reformed practice went further than this, because the Ten Commandments were sung in worship, and these are not a "praise passage" in Scripture, but simply an important passage of Scripture set to music. The same could be said of the Lord's Prayer, the singing of which was sanctioned by the Dutch Reformed Church; this Scripture passage is petition and intercession, rather than praise. Furthermore, Calvin was not opposed to the chanting of the Creed in public worship, and the Dutch Reformed Church authorized the singing of the Creed, which to all intents and purposes, as sung, is an uninspired hymn.

How then can we categorize the practice of the Reformed Churches in Continental Europe in the 16th and 17th centuries? Probably by describing it as "patristic"—modeled on the liturgical practice of the early Church. This accounts for the specific variety of materials used: David's psalms, other inspired passages of praise, the Ten Commandments, the Lord's Prayer, and the Creed. It is well known that Reformed liturgists in the 16th century consciously went back to the early church fathers for inspiration, and there they would have found the pattern of sung worship sketched above.[33] Certainly the psalms of David occupied the pinnacle of glory in early church worship, but not to the exclusion of other material, especially the New Testament canticles. This "patristic" position seems broadly to have been adopted by the Continental Reformed Churches of the Reformation.

Let us now look briefly at the position in Protestant England and Scotland prior to the Westminster Assembly. The first important English psalter was the 1556 Anglo-Genevan psalter used

---

[33] See Dr. Hughes Oliphant Old, *The Patristic Roots of Reformed Worship*, for a comprehensive and masterly presentation of the evidence.

by the English exiles sheltering in Geneva from the bloody persecution of Queen Mary Tudor (1553-8). This psalter is particularly interesting, in that the English refugees in Geneva were the most radical English Protestant grouping then in existence, proto-Puritans who were more committed to an international vision of Reformed Christianity than the more insular Anglican exiles they had left behind in Frankfort. The two groups parted ways precisely over the question of public worship: the Frankfort party were happy with the Anglican *Book of Common Prayer*, the Geneva party wanted a more full-bloodedly Reformed liturgy. The pastor of the exile church in Geneva was none other than John Knox, soon to be Scotland's revolutionary Calvinist Reformer. The Anglo-Genevan psalter which the Geneva exiles adopted as part of their Reformed liturgy contained fifty-one psalms, forty-four by Sternhold and Hopkins (see below on the Old Version), seven by William Whittingham (1524-79), chief translator of the Geneva Bible. Whittingham also wrote the preface, which stated that

> there are no songs so meet than the Psalms of the Prophet David which the Holy Ghost hath framed to the same use, and commended to the Church, as containing the effect of the where Scripture, that thereby our hearts might be more lively touched.[34]

However, the English Protestants in Geneva do not appear to have been opposed in principle to singing other scriptural passages in worship, for Whittingham appended to the psalter his own metrical version of the Ten Commandments. The 1561 edition also contained Whittingham's renderings of the *Nunc dimittis* and the Lord's Prayer.[35]

---

[34] Quoted by Ward, *The Psalms in Christian Worship*, 71.

[35] Whittingham himself did not practise exclusive psalmody as dean of Durham cathedral from 1563; he was distinguished by his zeal in promoting the choral services to a hitherto unknown level of excellence, using all manner of songs and anthems. Nor had he abandoned his Puritanism; Whittingham offended many by his iconoclasm, and was harried by higher authorities for his nonconforrnity in refusing to wear the cope and surplice. See DNB, vol. 2, 2258-9.

Further editions incorporated musical versions of the Apostles' Creed, "A prayer unto the Holy Ghost to be sung before the Sermon," a post-communion thanksgiving hymn, and several other extra-scriptural compositions.[36] The attitude of the English Genevan exiles can also be gauged from their translation of the Bible, the Geneva Bible (1560), on which Whittingham and Knox both worked, and which became the most popular English translation for the following hundred years. The Geneva Bible's marginal note to Colossians 3:16 did not interpret the "psalms, hymns and spiritual songs" as exclusively the Davidic psalter. It simply said:

> Psalms properly contain complainings to God, narrations, and expostulations; hymns, only thanksgiving; songs contain praises, and thanksgiving, but not so largely and amply as hymns do.[37]

The standard English psalter by Thomas Sternhold (1500-1549) and John Hopkins (d. 1570), edited by the latter, was based on the Anglo-Genevan psalter, and published in 1562 as *The Whole Booke of Psalmes*, later known as "the Old Version." It contained a considerably greater number of non-Davidic songs than the previous version of the Anglo-Genevan psalter had. These included the three Gospel canticles (*Magnificat, Benedictus, Nunc dimittis),* musical versions of the Ten Commandments, the Lord's Prayer, and the Athanasian Creed, and several uninspired hymns, including *The Song of the Three Children* (or *Benedicte Omnia Opera*) from the apocryphal additions to Daniel, the ancient *Veni Creator Spiritus* and *Te Deum*, two "lamentations of a sinner," a Thanksgiving after Holy Communion, the Lutheran hymn "Preserve us, Lord, by Thy dear Word," and three *Glorias*.[38]

---

[36] For the Anglo-Genevan psalter, see Julian's *Dictionary of Hymnology*, 857-8.

[37] Geneva Bible at Colossians 3:16.

[38] Routley, *A Panorama of Christian Hymnody*, 6. The Lutheran hymn "Preserve us Lord" had a rousing first verse, not recommended for our sensitive multi-faith age:

The Sternhold and Hopkins psalter remained definitive in English worship, until the publication in 1696 of the Tate and Brady version ("the New Version"). Tate and Brady's psalter contained the same supplement of non-Davidic songs as Sternhold and Hopkins, except that it dropped the Athanasian Creed and the "Preserve us, Lord," and added a considerable amount of extra material: the Apostles' Creed, a second *Veni Creator*, a second version of the Lord's Prayer, the "Song of the Angels" ("While shepherds watched their flocks by night"), two Easter hymns, two songs from the book of Revelation, and the once well-known "Hymn on the Divine Use of Music."[39] Both of England's standard psalters, then, the Old and New Versions, contained not just the Davidic psalms, but other scriptural material set to music, and uninspired hymns.

Through the efforts of Steinhold and Hopkins, psalm-singing became very popular in Protestant England. However, English Puritans in the pre-Westminster era were not necessarily opposed in principle to the singing of songs other than David's psalms (any more than the proto-Puritan exiles in Geneva had been). Prominent Puritan figures such as Thomas Cartwright (1535-1603) and Paul Bayne (d.1617), in their commentaries on Colossians 3:16 and Ephesians 5:19, accepted the use of non-Davidic songs in public worship. Cartwright, the much-persecuted leader of Elizabethan Puritanism in its Presbyterian form, did not restrict the public singing of Christian songs to the Old Testament psalter. In his comments on Colossians 3:16, he certainly did not interpret "psalms, hymns and spiritual songs" as a reference to the Davidic psalms exclusively. Moreover, he expounded

---

Preserve us, Lord, by Thy dear Word,
From Pope and Turk defend us, Lord;
Both which would thrust out of His throne
Our Lord Christ Jesus, Thy dear Son.

[39] Ibid.

"spiritual songs" to mean, not songs inspired by the Spirit, but songs that excite spiritual as opposed to carnal feelings.

> These must be spiritual songs, viz., holy psalms and songs, not profane and wicked love songs; which condemneth the wicked practice of men and women, that though they have so many excellent psalms, yet sing foolish songs to stir their minds up to wickedness.[40]

In other words, "spiritual" does not refer to the Spirit as author but to the holy sentiments of a song. It is not clear whether such songs in Cartwright's view were only the songs of Scripture or newly written ones. Cartwright also uses the terms "psalms" and "songs" here interchangeably.

Paul Bayne, the successor of the great Puritan divine William Perkins (1558-1602) as lecturer at St Andrews, Cambridge, and the one through whom the heavenly Richard Sibbes (1577-1635) was converted, was as fully committed to Puritanism as Perkins had been; indeed, he suffered for it grievously under the fiercely anti-Puritan Archbishop Bancroft, who sacked him, reducing him to poverty. Payne gave an interpretation similar to Cartwright's of the phrase "spiritual songs19 in Ephesians 5:19:

> It ["spiritual"] is put in by way of distinction, opposite to the sensual songs which profane persons are delighted in. Now there are two kinds, the one extraordinary, such as the Spirit of God did immediately suggest. 2. Ordinary, such as men by benefit of memory could say out of the Scripture, or frame themselves conformable thereto, and both these kinds are here meant.[41]

---

[40] Cartwright, *A Commentary upon the Epistle of St. Paul Written to the Colossians*, 55. In the celebrated controversy between Cartwright and Anglican apologist Richard Hooker (1554-1600), Cartwright apparently did not object to the singing of the Gospel canticles in public worship, but only to their use as daily prayers. See Hooker, *Works,* vol. 2, 554. Hooker referred to the canticles as "psalms of praise and thanksgiving," and throughout this section of his Laws of Ecclesiastical Polity; he uses the terms "psalm," "hymn" and song" with no sharply distinguished meaning.

[41] Bayne, *An Entire Commentary upon the whole Epistle of St. Paul to the Ephesians*, 334.

Bayne, then, explicitly sanctioned newly composed hymns as long as they were based on Scripture. He then attacked Roman Catholic worship because "They have hymns containing matter not grounded in the word."[42] The point, of course, is that Bayne did not condemn Roman Catholic worship for singing hymns rather than Davidic psalms, but for singing hymns that contained doctrinally unsound sentiments.

Other Puritan divines followed in Cartwright and Bayne's footsteps. Nicholas Byfield (1579-1622), the influential Puritan vicar of Stratford-upon-Avon, famous for his ardent Sabbatarianism, expounded the "psalms, hymns and spiritual songs" of Colossians 3:16 thus in his 1615 commentary on that epistle:

> The matter is here three ways to be considered: First, in the ground, foundation, or authority of the Psalms we use, *viz.*, they must be the word of Christ, that is contained in the Scriptures. Secondly in the kinds of *Psalms* there are many sorts of Psalms in Scripture. The Psalms of *Moses, David, Solomon*, and other Prophets: but all are here referred to three heads; they are either *Psalms*, specially so called, or *Hymns*, or *Songs*, great ado there is among Interpreters, to find a difference in these; some would have Psalms to be the songs of men, and Hymns of Angels: some think they differ especially in the manner of music. Some are sung by voice, some played upon instruments; but the plausiblest opinion is not to distinguish them, by the persons that use them, or by the kind of music, but by the matter, and so they says Psalms contain exhortation to manners or holy life. Hymns contain contain praises to God in the commemoration of his benefits. Songs contain doctrine of the chief good, or man's eternal felicity. But I think there needs not any curious distinction: it may suffice us that there is variety of Psalms in Scripture and God allows us the use of every kind. Thirdly, the property of the Psalms, they are *Spiritual* both because they are indited by the Spirit, and because they make us more spiritual in the due use of them.[43]

Byfield clearly interpreted the verse to mean that Christians should sing all the songs of Scripture, not just David's psalms. He says "there are many sorts of Psalms in Scripture," not "many

---

[42] Ibid., 335.

[43] Byfield, *An Exposition upon the Epistle to the Colossians*, 101.

sorts of Psalms in the psalter"; and "God allows us the use of every kind." He even included the "psalms of Solomon." *i.e.*, the Song of Songs (unless he meant psalms 72 and 127). The "psalms of Moses" probably refers to the two songs of Moses in Exodus 15 and Deuteronomy 32 (and perhaps the "prayer of Moses" in Psalm 90). The reference to the "psalms of other Prophets" is obscure; perhaps Byfield meant the psalms of Asaph, Ethan, Heman and the sons of Korah, although these men are not actually called "prophets" in the Old Testament (Asaph is called a "seer" in 2 Chronicles 29:30). On the other hand, if the versifications of George Wither (see below) are anything to go by, Byfield may have had in mind the prophetic songs of Isaiah chapters 5, 12 and 26, Jeremiah's Lamentations, Habakkuk chapter 3, the song of the prophetess Deborah (Judges 5), various prayers of Old Testament prophets, and in the New Testament the songs of Zechariah, Mary and Simeon.[44] At any rate, Byfield obviously did not restrict the psalms, hymns and spiritual songs exclusively to the Davidic psalter: "it may suffice us that there is variety of Psalms in Scripture and God allows us the use of every kind." Byfield, however, did restrict Church singing to the songs of the Bible—a common Reformed position in the 16th and 17th centuries.

Edward Elton, the Puritan incumbent of St Mary Magdelene's, Bermondsey (London), in his highly esteemed commentary on Colossians published in 1620, interpreted the "psalms, hymns and spiritual songs" of Colossians 3:16 thus:

> That by *Psalmes*, we are to understand holy songs in general of what argument soever written, whether precatorie, and containing matter of petition to God for good things, or deprecatorie, containing matter of petition, for turning away of evil things, or consolatorie, containing matter of comfort, or whatsoever, which were wont to be sung to

---

[44] Zechariah, Mary and Simeon are universally understood to have been inspired by the Holy Spirit in uttering their respective Canticles. Zechariah and Simeon are therefore called "prophets" in older writings. The Old Testament passages I have suggested, many of which are actually said to be songs, were all turned into English metrical hymns by Wither.

> God, and sounded out as well with instrument, as with voice. And by *Hymnes* are meant, special songs of praise to God, thanksgiving to God for benefits received. And by *Spiritual songs* are signified, certain special hymnes containing the praises of God for his noble acts, for his great and wonderful workes, which were wont to be sung only with the voice: and such were the songs of *Moses*, Exodus 15; of *Deborah* and *Barak*; Judges 5; and diverse such there be in the book of *Psalmes*, which are therefore called songs, and not Psalmes. The Apostle adds *Spiritual*, thereby understanding such songs as proceed from the Spirit, and are framed by the Spirit, as (namely) such as are either already recorded in the Word, or composed according to the Word, containing spiritual and heavenly matter.[45]

Here we find the use of "psalm" to mean "holy songs in general," and an interpretation of "spiritual songs" which takes in both the non-Davidic songs of Scripture (Exodus 15, Judges 5, etc.), and extra-scriptural hymns "composed according to the Word."

Bayne and Elton might have approved of newly written uninspired worship-songs other than the Davidic psalms, but in fact very few such songs gained popular acceptance English worship between the reign of Queen Elizabeth I and the Commonwealth period. The first complete English collection of newly composed hymns for public worship, poet George Wither's *Hymns and Songs of the Church*, published in 1623, was a commercial flop. Wither (1588-1667) was plunged into protracted controversy with London Stationers' Company over his obtaining of a compulsory order from King James I for the insertion of his hymn collection into all future copies of the Sternhold and Hopkins psalter. The Company regarded this order as an infringement of their privileges, and booksellers refused either to bind up Wither's hymns with the psalter or to sell the hymnbook itself. It was criticized as "popish, superstitious, obscene, and unfit to keep company with David's psalms."[46] Wither and the booksellers did not make peace till 1634. As a result, Wither's

---

[45] Elton, *An Exposition of the Epistle of Saint Paul the Apostle to the Colossians*, 529.

[46] Quoted by Winfred Douglas, *Church Music in History and Practice*, 223.

own translation of the psalms had to be printed in the Netherlands in 1632. However, *Hymnes and Songs of the Church* seems to have enjoyed some popularity with the younger generation, inspired partly perhaps by the specially composed tunes of Orlando Gibbons (1583-1625), one of the finest composers of that period.[47] Wither produced a second book of hymns in 1641, entitled *Hallelujah, or Britain's Second Remembrancer*, described in the title as a collection of *praiseful and penitential hymns, spiritual songs and moral odes*. Critics have appraised this as Wither's finest poetic work far superior to his efforts of 1623. However *Hallelujah* was never actually used in worship as a hymnbook.

It is interesting that Wither, the first would-be English hymnodist, was a committed Sabbatarian, an ardent Parliamentarian in the English Civil War, and when Parliament and army fell out, an equally zealous partisan and publicist of Oliver Cromwell. When the monarchy was restored in 1660, Wither was imprisoned in the Tower of London at his property confiscated. We must therefore not associate uninspired hymn-making in the reign of Charles I and the Commonwealth period with the High Church Royalist "Caroline divines," as is sometimes done.[48]

Thomas Manton (1620-77), one of the most influential Puritans of the mid-17th century, expressed himself very clearly on the subject of sung worship. Before hearing his views, it is well for us to bear in mind that Manton was a leading Presbyterian divine in the city of London at the time of the Westminster Assembly; his reputation was so vast that it was not thought improper for him to write his own introductory "epistle to the reader" as a preface to the printed Confession (even today Manton's epistle is still normally bound with Scottish editions of

---

[47] See Frederick J.Gillman, *The Evolution of the English Hymn*, 146; H. A. L. Jefferson, *Hymns in Christian Worship*, 13; Harry Eskew and Hugh T. McElrath, *Sing with Understanding*, 114.

[48] For Wither, see *DNB*, vol. 2, 2307, and Edward Farr's introduction to the 19th century reprint of the *Hymns and Songs of the Church*.

the Confession). He was also one of the 44 signatories to the Confession's preface "To the Christian reader, especially heads of families." Manton's views on what Christians ought to sing in public worship are to be found in his *A Practical Commentary on the Exposition on the Epistle of James*, published in London in 1653. Addressing the same controversy that we saw Richard Baxter tackling earlier about the propriety of singing David's psalms in Christian worship, Manton said:

> Others question, whether we may sing Scripture-Psalms, the Psalms of *David*; which to me seemeth to look like the cavil of a profane spirit. But to clear this also; I confess we do not forbid other songs; if grave and pious, after good advice they may be received into the Church. *Tertullian* in his Apology sheweth, that in the Primitive times they used this liberty, either to sing Scripture-Psalms, or such as were of private composure.[49]

Manton clearly had no problem in principle with uninspired hymns. He appears to have been speaking for fellow Puritans too—"*we* do not forbid other songs." He also obyiously used the word "psalm" to denote any religious song, which is why he speaks of "Scripture-Psalms" rather than just "Psalms" to refer to the Davidic psalter. We must not misapprehend Manton: he was no strident advocate of uninspired hymns. Indeed, he went on to say that David's psalms were far and away the best songs that Christians could possibly sing in public worship, because they were written by the Holy Spirit:

> Therefore upon the whole matter I should pronounce, That so much as an infallible gift doth excel a common, so much do Scriptural Psalms excel those that are of a private composure.[50]

Nonetheless Manton explicitly endorsed the lawfulness of singing "psalms of private composure" in congregational worship. This outstanding Puritan divine saw no conflict between

---

[49] Manton, *A Practical Commentary or an Exposition on the Epistle of James*, 572.

[50] Ibid., 574.

uninspired hymns and the regulative principle. As if some malign providence were operating to vex exclusive psalmodists among the English-speaking Presbyterian community, the preface to their Confession of Faith was written by a defender of uninspired hymns in public worship.

John Lightfoot (1602-75), a prominent member of the Westminster Assembly, Presbyterian in his views of church office but Erastian in his view of church-state relation, preached in 1660 a sermon on 1 Corinthians 14:26, entitled *Every one hath a psalm.* Lightfoot mentioned the exclusive psalmodist interpretation of Colossians 3:16 and Ephesians 5:19; the words "psalms, hymns and spiritual songs," he said, "are variously, indeed, taken, but very generally for 'the Psalms of David.'" However, he preferred the interpretation

> that by these three are meant the Psalms of David, and other songs in Scripture . . . ["S]piritual songs" were other songs in Scripture besides David's. So you read of "the song of Moses," and "the song of the Lamb," in Rev.15:3.[51]

Thus a leading Westminster divine: all the songs of Scripture may be sung in public worship.

The most thorough treatment of the subject came not from England but from New England, in the treatise of the leading Independent divine John Cotton (1584-1652), *Singing of Psalmes a Gospel Ordinance*, published in London in 1647. Cotton is important because his writings were very influential on English Independents. His position on songs of worship may at first seem confusing. On the one hand, Cotton interpreted the "psalms, hymns and spiritual songs" of Colossians 3:16 as a reference to the Davidic psalter; the three terms were "the very titles of the songs of David, as they are delivered to us by the Holy Ghost himself." So far, Cotton looks like an exclusive psalmodist.

---

[51] Lightfoot, *Works*, vol. 7, 41.

However he then went on to contend that any "spiritual song" found in Scripture could be sung in public worship, and not merely David's psalms:

> [P]re-supposing that God would have the *Psalms of David*, and other Scripture-*Psalms* to be sung of English men . . . then as a necessary means to that end, he would have the Scripture-*Psalms* (which are Poems and Verses) to be translated into English-*Psalms* (which are in like sort Poems and Verses) that English People might be able to sing them.[52]

Here once more we encounter the use of "psalm" to mean a religious song, not just a Davidic one. Cotton further maintained that if a Christian gifted by the Holy Spirit composed a psalm of his own, on some special occasion in the church's public thanksgiving, he could sing it solo to the church (1 Corinthians 14:26). But as far as congregational singing was concerned, Cotton's position was that all the songs of Scripture may be sung, and nothing else.

Other Puritans, however, did adopt the exclusive psalmodist position. For example, George Swinnock (1627-73) took this view. Like Cotton, he interpreted the "psalms, hymns and spiritual songs" of Colossians 3:16 as

> the titles of David's psalms, and the known division of them, expressly answering to the Hebrew words, *Shurim, Telhillim,* and *Miznurim,* by which the psalms are distinguished and entitled, as the learned observe. . . ."[53]

This comment occurred in the context of a discussion of singing as an act of worship. Significantly, Swinnock did not go on, as Cotton did, to say that even though Colossians 3:16 referred specifically to the psalter, other Scriptural songs could also be sung.

Finally, let us consider the evidence of Isaac Watts (1674-1748), the Independent divine often called the father of English

---

[52] Quoted by Davies, *The Worship of the English Puritans,* 167.

[53] Swinnock, *The Christian Man's Calling,* in *Works,* vol. 4, 167.

hymnody. As the 18th century dawned, his *Essay on the Improvement of Psalmody* was a landmark justification of translating David's psalms in a paraphrastic way, replacing typical and ceremonial references by explicit New Testament descriptions of the person and work of Christ. The *Essay* also justified the composing of new uninspired hymns for use in public worship. Watts answered at length all kinds of objections he felt would be made to uninspired hymns by the more liturgically conservative of English Protestants; but what was the position he thought these critics themselves held? It was not exclusive psalmody. Watts made it clear over and again that the position he was combatting was that only the songs of Scripture should be sung in public worship— including David's psalms, but not limited to them. Watts set out

> to prove, that it is proper to use spiritual songs of human composure, as well as the psalms of David, or the words of other songs recorded in Scripture.[54]

Among the "other songs recorded in Scripture," Watts mentioned the Songs of Moses in Exodus 15 and Deuteronomy 32, the Song of Deborah, the Song of Songs, the *Benedictus*, the *Magnificat*, the *Nunc dimittis*, the Song of the Angels, and the songs in the book of Revelation. Apparently his opponents had no problem with these. We may take it that the conservative position Watts was seeking to undermine was nothing other than the early 18th century legacy of Puritan and Nonconformist worship, as it had been conducted since the Restoration of the monarchy and Anglican Church in 1660. It is therefore deeply significant that the conservative Nonconformist view was not exclusive psalmody, but "all the songs of Scripture." Also interesting is Walls' understanding of the word psalm:

> A psalm is a general name for any thing that is sung in divine worship, whatsoever be the particular theme or matter. . . .[55]

---

[54] Watts, *Essay on the Improvement of Psalmody*, in *Works*; vol. 4, 371.

[55] Ibid., 372.

The position in England, then, from the Reformation to the Restoration we can summarize thus. Psalm-singing was the prevailing and popular form of Protestant worship, via the 1562 psalter of Sternhold and Hopkins. But the psalter contained a sizeable supplement with other scriptural material set to music, both poetic and non-poetic passages, and several uninspired hymns. Exclusive psalmody as a liturgical principle was no litmus test of Puritan sympathies; top-rank Puritan spokesmen such as Cartwright, Bayne, Manton, Cotton and Baxter, and others like Byfield, Elton and Lightfoot, justified in principle the singing of songs other than David's psalms, and some of them approved even uninspired hymns. The very word "psalm" was often used to mean any religious song, as is clear from Elton, Manton, Cotton, Baxter, Poole and Watts.

The situation in Scotland was somewhat different. Prior to the first Scottish psalter of 1564, a Protestant collection of songs known as the *Gude and Godlie Ballatis* ("Good and Godly Ballads") had a wide circulation in Scotland. It contained catechetical material in prose (e.g., the Ten Commandments, the Lord's Prayer, the Creed), some of which was also versified, some sixteen songs which are paraphrases of Scripture, some twenty songs which are Christianized versions of popular secular ballads, some twenty Davidic psalms, and some forty anti-papal satirical poems. (The precise number varied from one edition to another.) After the Reformation Parliament of 1560 which made Scotland officially a Calvinist nation, the *Gude and Godlie Ballatis* was reprinted in 1565, 1567, 1578, 1600 and 1621. Some have argued from these many post-1560 reprints that the Reformed Church of Scotland practiced the singing of songs other than the psalms of David in public worship. However there is no evidence that the *Ballatis* were ever used in this way; certainly no General Assembly ever officially sanctioned such a practice. All exclusive psalmodists accept the other songs may be sung in private and family worship, which is almost certainly how the Ballatis were employed.[56]

The Scottish psalter of 1564 became the accepted public praise-book in the Reformed Church of Scotland. Like Sternhold and Hopkins, it was based on the Anglo-Genevan psalter, but it conspicuously omitted all other material save the Davidic psalms in its first edition of 1564. However, some editions printed in and after 1575 did contain other supplementary material, on the pattern of the Anglo-Genevan and Sternhold and Hopkins psalters. The 1575 Scottish psalter had five non-Davidic songs, the 1595 psalter had ten, and the 1634 psalter had fourteen. Nevertheless, competent historical authorities agree that these supplements apparently had no direct authorization from the Church itself through its General Assembly. In actual liturgical practice, the Reformed Church of Scotland was exclusively psalm-singing.[57]

This, of course, does not prove that Scottish Reformed divines were necessarily opposed *in principle* to the singing of other songs in public worship. The conservative Presbyterian divine, Robert Boyd of Trochrigg (1578-1627), who resigned from the principalship of Glasgow University in 1621 owing to his opposition to King James VI's liturgical innovations, defended uninspired hymns in his massive commentary on Ephesians (really a theological compendium, published posthumously in 1652). Taking his cue from the exhortation in Psalm 33:3 to "sing to the Lord a new song," Boyd expostulated with his Church of Scotland colleagues:

> But yet we only sing ancient songs; no new song is heard from our mouth in the Church. Why then do we turn a deaf ear to the admonition of David so often repeated?[58]

---

[56] See Julian's *Dictionary of Hymnology*, 1021-22; *Dictionary of Scottish Church History and Theology,* 379-80.

[57] Julian's *Dictionary of Hymnology,*" 1023.

[58] Quoted by Ward, *The Psalms in Christian in Worship*, 81.

The celebrated Covenanting divine James Ferguson (1621-67) did not go as far as Boyd, but in his commentary on Colossians 3:16 he interpreted "psalms. hymns and spirtual songs" to refer to all the songs of Scripture:

> The psalms of David, and other Scriptural songs in the Old Testament, may, and ought to be sung in this part of gospel-worship. . . .[N]ow all agree that hereby are designed the psalms of David, and other scriptural songs, though there be some difference about the kind of songs which are intended to be expressed by every one of those [terms] in particular.[59]

It is baffling why in the first part of this quotation Ferguson restricts "other Scriptural songs" to those in the Old Testament, a position I have not come across elsewhere. Possibly it was because he considered the *Magnificat, Benedictus* and *Nunc dimittis* as simply poetry rather than true songs; but then, what of the songs in Revelation? Nonetheless, Ferguson's view takes in such Old Testament songs as the two Songs of Moses (Exodus 15:1-18, Deuteronomy 32:1-43), the Song of Deborah (Judges 5:2-31), the Prayer of Habbakuk (Habbakuk chapter 3), the slightly variant form of Psalm 18 found in 2 Samuel 22:2-51, the Davidic song of 1 Chronicles 16:8-36, Isaiah chapter 5:1-7 and chapter 26, possibly the Prayer of Hannah in 1 Samuel 2:1-10 (unless Ferguson regarded this as poetic but not a song), and possibly the Song of Songs interpreted Christologically (George Wither had versified the Song on this basis). Moreover, Ferguson betrayed no sense of violating the Scottish Reformed understanding of the regulative principle, or of setting forth a contentious novelty, in adopting the above view. This seems particularly significant when we reflect that he says these songs not only may but "*ought to be sung in gospel-worship.*"

Some other Scottish divines of this period, by contrast, did interpret the "psalms, hymns and spiritual songs" of Colossians 3:16 and Ephesians 5:19 as referring exclusively to the Davidic

---

[59] Ferguson, *The Epistles of Paul*, 365.

psalter. John Brown of Wamphray (1610-79), for example, espoused this position in 1676 in his *Against the anti-Sabbatarians.*[60] It seems likely that there were differing views within the spectrum of Scottish Reformed orthodoxy, and that no single view was regarded as absolutely binding on Caledonia's Calvinist divines.

We come, then, to the Confession itself, with its authorization of "singing of psalms with grace in the heart" in 21:5. The directly relevant evidence seems to be as follows. First, some of the Westminster divines themselves clearly believed and taught that songs other than those of the Davidic psalter were lawful vehicles of public praise. This was true of those Westminster divines who compiled the vast *Annotations upon all the Books of the Old and New Testament*—usually referred to simply as the "Annotations of the Westminster divines." This was intended to be an authoritative commentary on the whole Bible, clarifying all doubtful points of interpretation. Their exposition of Ephesians 5:19 was:

> [I]t seemeth most probable, that by Psalmes, he meaneth the Psalmes of David set to the harp or psaltery, by Hymnes, certain ditties made upon special occasion; and by spirituall songs, such as were not composed before-hand, and prickt before them with musicall notes, but such as men endited by an extraordinary gift.[61]

This interpretation is immensely interesting. "Psalms" means the Davidic psalms; the authors of the *Annotations* pick up here on the etymology of ψαλλω, to "pluck" or "twang," *i.e.*, on a stringed instrument, a harp or psaltery. Psalms, therefore, are songs set to stringed accompaniment, which the authors identify with "the Psalmes of David." "Hymns" means songs composed on certain special occasions—which the authors appear to distinguish from the psalms of David set to the harp or psaltery, although

---

[60] See Ward, *The Psalms in Christian Worship*, 82.

[61] *Annotations upon all the Books of the Old and New Testament*, at Ephesians 5:19. The comments on Colossians 3:16 and James 5:13 simply refer the reader back to the interpretation of Ephesians 5:19.

there seems no evident reason why a ditty written on a special occasion should not also be set to a stringed instrument. Probably by this description the authors simply meant to separate out these ditties from the Davidic psalms: they were not part of the established regular psalter, but composed at the prompting of some special occasion. This view leaves the identity of the "hymns" indeterminate: were they the other inspired songs of Scripture, outside the psalter, or were they uninspired compositions? Lastly, "Spiritual songs" means songs that were not "composed before-hand" at all, but produced spontaneously, without a pre-set tune, sung by various men who had "an extraordinary gift." Presumably the phrase "by an extraordinary gift" meant "by the special inspiration of the Spirit." This could certainly include some of the other Old Testament songs and the Gospel canticles. At any rate, however we interpret precisely the view here offered by the Westminster divines, it was not exclusive psalmody. At its narrowest, it was the "all the songs of Scripture" position; at its broadest, it took in newly written songs too, as in Manton's view.

We must also consider the actions of the Church of Scotland in authorizing a new psalter at the time of the Westminster Assembly. The English House of Commons, on the Assembly's advice, agreed in 1643 to sanction a new psalter for use throughout the new Reformed English Church. The new version was that of Francis Rous (1579-1659), the zealously Puritan MP for Truro, as revised by himself and the Assembly. It was approved by the Commons in 1646 and printed in April that year. This new "Westminster version" was intended for use in Scotland too, as part of the uniformity of religion designed by the Solemn League and Covenant of 1643, which had bound English Puritans and Scottish Covenanters together in alliance against Charles I. The Scottish divines, however, were not satisfied with the Westminster version, and in 1647 the General Assembly of the Church of Scotland passed an act appointing a committee of revisors to work over Rous's psalter again. Significantly, the same act of Assembly also ordered that

> Mr Zachary Boyd be at the pains to translate the other Scriptural Songs in metre, and to report his travails also to the Commission of the Assembly, that, after their examination thereof, they may send the same to Presbyteries, to be there considered till the next General Assembly.[62]

The next General Assembly of 1648, called upon

> Master John Adamson and Mr Thomas Crawford to revise the labours of Mr Zachary Boyd upon the other Scriptural Songs, and to prepare a report thereof.[63]

The Assembly Commission noted the completion of the task:

> The Commission of Assembly understanding the pains Mr. John Adamson, Mr. Zachary Boyd, and Mr. Robert Lowrie have been at in the translation of the Psalms and other Scriptural songs in metre, and how useful their travails have been in the correcting of the old Paraphrase of the Psalms, and in compiling the new, do therefore return them hearty thanks for these their labours, and that the Moderator show this to Mr. John Adamson, Mr. Robert Lowrie, and write to Mr. Zachary Boyd to this purpose.[64]

What meets us here is the Church of Scotland doing exactly what the French Reformed Church did in 1594: taking steps to authorize a collection of the non-Davidic songs of Scripture. Zachary Boyd (1535-1653), minister of the Barony church in Glasgow, was the cousin of Robert Boyd of Trochrigg, whom we saw earlier defending uninspired hymns. Zachary's own *Psalms of David in Meeter* (1643) contained metrical versions not just of the psalms, but of all scriptural songs of both Testaments. The only plausible interpretation of these events is that the General Assembly intended to have Boyd's translation of the non-Davidic songs of Scripture authorized for use in public worship, just as in 1708 the Assembly authorized its Commission to publish Patrick

---

[62] Julian's *Dictionary of Hymnology*, p.1023

[63] Ibid. Adamson and Crawford were two of the four chief revisors of the Westminster psalter.

[64] Mitchell and Christie, *The Records of the Commissions of the General Assemblies of the Church of Scotland holden in Edinburgh in the years 1648 and 1649*, 339.

Simson's *Spiritual Songs* of 1636 for use in public worship.[65] However, both Boyd's and Simson's efforts drifted through the Assembly's committees into a slow oblivion, perhaps due to public apathy (the common problem encountered by the liturgical innovator), possibly compounded by some opposition from convinced exclusive psalmodists. The point for our present purposes is that the General Assembly's actions in 1647-8 are not easily understood as being consistent with a principled corporate commitment to exclusive psalmody by the Church of Scotland.

Further, it is worth bearing in mind that prior to the Westminster Assembly and the issuing of the *Directory for the Publick Worship of God*, the Reformed Scottish Church had always sung the ancient *Gloria Patri* at the conclusion of each psalm ("Glory be to the Father, and to the Son, and to the Holy Spirit, as it was in the beginning, is now, and ever shall be, world without end, Amen"). The practice was laid aside in deference to English Puritan feeling that a scriptural psalm should not have an uninspired human conclusion tacked on as though it were part of the inspired song. But the *Gloria Patri* was relinquished by Scottish Reformed divines with great reluctance; they had sternly resisted all influence towards its abandonment in the period between the Covenanter takeover of the Scottish Church in 1637 and the Westminster Assembly in 1643 (such influence stemming both from English Puritanism and Irish Presbyterianism). It is impossible to imagine any exclusive psalmodist today accepting the *Gloria Patri* as the conclusion to a publicly sung psalm. Scottish Calvinists in the 16th and early 17th centuries did not share this attitude. Every time they sang a psalm of David in church, they finished the inspired song with an uninspired hymn to the Trinity.[66]

---

[65] Julian's *Dictionary of Hymnology*, 1024.

[66] Warfield, *The Westminster Assembly and its Work*, 47-8.

We must also take into account the actions of the English Presbyterian divines at the Savoy conference in 1661, when they were discussing with the Anglican bishops the form that the Church of England should take under the newly restored monarchy of Charles II. About half of the twelve Presbyterian delegates had also been members of the Westminster Assembly.[67] Much of the discussion at Savoy centred on the place and shape of a liturgy. The Presbyterians were not happy with the Anglican Book of Common Prayer, and their leading spokesman Richard Baxter wrote an alternative which came to be called the "Reformed liturgy." It was accepted by the other Presbyterians and presented to the Anglican bishops for consideration. The Reformed liturgy not only made provision for singing the psalter, but also stipulated that the *Benedictus* and *Magnificat* should be "said or sung" by the congregation, and that the *Te Deum* should be congregationally recited.[68] We therefore see a distinguished number of the Westminster divines sanctioning at Savoy the singing in public worship of Scriptural songs from outside the psalter.

In the light of the above constellation of facts regarding the use of the word "psalm" in 17th century English, the general Reformed interpretation of Ephesians 5:19, Colossians 3:16 and James 5:13, and the liturgical practice of the Reformed Churches on Continental Europe and in Britain, I think the weight of evidence decisively favours interpreting Confession 21.5 as referring to a broader category of song than the Davidic psalter. We could for convenience's sake classify the possible views of what 21.5 means thus:

(a) It is lawful to sing *only and exclusively* the 150 psalms of David in public;

---

[67] See Davies, *The Worship of the English Puritans*, 128.

[68] Reformed Liturgy in Baxter's *Practical Works*, vol.15, 461. For the Savoy conference, see Davies, *The Worship of the English Puritans*, 142-61.

(b) It is lawful to sing *all the songs of Scripture* (whether this includes the Gospel "canticles" of the *Magnificat, Benedictus* and *Nunc dimittis*, which are not act have been sung by Mary, Zechariah and Simeon, would be a moot point);

(c) It is lawful to sing *all the songs and poetic praise passages of Scripture* (this would indisputably include the Gospel canticles and all analogous passages);

(d) It is lawful to sing *any scriptural material* (including e.g., the Ten Commandments and the Lord's Prayer which are not praise passages);

(e) It is lawful to sing *any spiritually edifying material* (including e.g., the Apostle's Creed and extra-scriptural hymns).

I am suggesting that a historical-contextual interpretation of the reference to "singing of psalms" in Confession 21.5 makes (a) the least probable of these five possibilities. As between (b), (c), (d) and (e), the variety and complexity of the evidence make a choice all but impossible. Option (b) is credible in the light of the Church of Scotland's actions in 1647-8 respecting "the other Scriptural songs" to be translated by Zachary Boyd. Options (c) and (d) are credible in the light of the widespread practice of other Reformed Churches. But enough ambiguity exists, I think, to prevent us ruling out (e) as a plausible interpretation: we recollect Calvin's and the Synod of Dort's sanctioning the liturgical use of the Creed.

If we then ask what theological justification can be found for positions (b), (c), (d), and (e), we may argue as follows. The justification for singing all the songs of Scripture is, simply, that these are songs of praise which the Holy Spirit has placed in Scripture. All agree that all the psalms of David are such songs. Yet by what process of reasoning can it be right to sing the psalms of David but wrong to sing the psalm of Habakkuk? Habakkuk chapter 3 begins, "A prayer of Habakkuk the prophet on Shigionoth;" it ends, "To the Chief Musician. With my stringed instruments." Similar wording can be found attached to many of the Davidic psalms. The (probably musical) term "selah," otherwise unique to the psalter, occurs in verses 3, 9 and 13 of

Habakkuk 3.[69] It would require overwhelmingly compelling reasons to persuade us in these circumstances that Habakkuk's psalm was not meant to be sung just as much as David's psalms. Or at least, to phase it differently, it seems a strange and improbable view that the Holy Spirit would inspire such as psalm as Habakkuk 3, and incorporate it in canonical Scripture, and forbid us ever to sing it. The same could be said of the two Songs of Moses (Exodus 15:1-18, Deuteronomy 32:1-43) and the Song of Deborah (Judges 5:2-31). Furthermore, let us consider David's song in 2 Samuel 22:2-51. This is almost but not quite, identical with Psalm 18. But suppose the song had been found only in 2 Samuel. Would we then be forbidden to sing a psalm of David because it was in 2 Samuel rather than in the psalter? And given that the two versions of the psalm are not quite identical, is it sinful to sing the 2 Samuel version, and lawful to sing only the psalter version, merely on the "topographical" grounds that the latter is in the psalter and the former in 2 Samuel? A similar situation obtains with the Davidic song found in 1 Chronicles 16:8-36. It appears to be a compilation from Psalm 105:1-15, 96:1-13, 106:1 and 106:47-8. Are we forbidden to sing this psalm of David merely because it is in I Chronicles rather than in the psalter? Or is it lawful to sing the separate passages of which it is constructed from the psalter, but not to sing the composite construction—because that is in 1 Chronicles?

Hannah's prayer in 1 Samuel 2:1-10, and the three Gospel "canticles" of the *Magnificat* (Luke 1:46-55), the *Benedictus* (Luke 1:68-79) and the *Nunc dimittis* (Luke 2:29-32), have traditionally been understood as songs by all strands of the Christian tradition, including the Puritans (see, for example,

---

[69] The term "shigionoth" at the heading of Habakkuk 3 appears to be the plural of "shiggaion," the title of Psalm 7—"A shiggaion of David," thus rendered in the King James Version and New International Version. The Septuagint translates *shigionoth* as "with a song."

Matthew Poole's exposition). If we accept this tradition, there seems no reason why these should not be sung in our congregational worship. We must once again ask whether we can believe that the Holy Spirit would inspire such beautiful spiritual songs, incorporate them in canonical Scripture, and sternly forbid us ever to sing them in church worship. Also in the New Testament, we have the heavenly songs of Revelation 5:9-10 and 15:3-4. If the citizens of heaven sing these songs, there is no coherent reason why their fellows on earth should not join in. Finally, if we interpret the Song of Songs Christologically, there seems no reason why selected portions could not be versified and sung to Christ, the heavenly Bridegroom, in our public worship (for a 17th century example, see George Wither's ten canticles in his *Hymns and Songs of the Church*).

The broader question of singing other poetic praise passages of Scripture, or any other parts of Scripture, or doctrinally sound hymns that reflect the teaching of Scripture, partly depends on how we understand the "psalms, hymns and spiritual songs" of Colossians 3:16 and Ephesians 5:19. Almost all the Reformed commentators we have looked at failed to interpret these terms as referring to the Davidic psalter alone. Unfortunately they also displayed great variety in trying to differentiate meaningfully between the three words. However, if we adopt the suggestion that the description "spiritual" applies to all three nouns—"psalms, hymns and songs, spiritual" (such is the word order in Greek)—perhaps it becomes unnecessary to discriminate precisely between the three genres of song. We can simply understand Paul to be exhorting us to sing all kinds of songs to God, as long as they are spiritual in content.[70] At a more basic level, if we cannot find an

---

[70] Exclusive psalmodists argue that "spiritual" must mean "produced by the Holy Spirit." But many Reformed expositors of the 16th and 17th centuries did not interpret the word this way. And with good reason, since the apostle Paul uses the same word πνευματικος to refer to "spiritual forces of wickedness" in

exact reference for these three terms, we may fall back on the foundational fact that God has commanded us to praise Him in song. The authorized act of worship is to sing praises to God. What we sing—the genre of song—then comes into the category of circumstance. We could compare it with preaching. God has commanded His ministers to preach; but beyond the fact that the preaching is to be based on Scripture, He has not told them *what* to preach. The specific text and topic and manner of unfolding them are left to the preacher. We are in the realm of circumstance; and in the realm of circumstance, "Whatever is not forbidden is lawful, if it is edifying." So, to apply this to the duty of singing praises to God: God has commanded us to sing, and has nowhere forbidden us to sing the non-Davidic scriptural songs, or Scripture's poetic praise passages set to music, or the Ten Commandments or Lord's Prayer, or even uninspired hymns. Therefore all these are lawful materials of praise, with the important proviso that we choose edfiying Scripture passages and uninspired hymns to sing.[71]

Moreover, all exclusive psalmodists have in fact freely admitted that songs other than the psalms of David, including uninspired hymns, may be sung outside the context of public congregational worship, in "private" worship. But this raises an interesting question: From an exclusive psalmodist viewpoint, what is the scriptural warrant for singing non-Davidic songs in private worship? Presumably the regulative principle does not apply only to public worship; we may not worship God as we

---

Ephesians 6:12. Presumably this does not mean "forces of wickedness produced by the Holy Spirit." Even if we conceded that the term meant "produced by the Spirit," this would not lead to exclusive psalmody, but to the "all the songs of Scripture" position.

[71] Even a passage of Scripture might be unedifying if set to music for worship. E.g., Leviticus 13 or Ezra 2. Conversely, an edifying hymn must be based on Scripture in the same sense that a good sermon is.

please, according to our own ideas, as soon as we leave the public sanctuary. But if the exhortation to sing "psalms, hymns and spiritual songs" is a reference to the psalter alone, where does God authorize us to sing uninspired hymns in worship when we come before Him, not as a church, but as individuals, a family, a group of Christians in a workplace, etc.? I know of a small church that once consisted of one large Christian family and a pastor who lived in the same house. Was this household pleasing God when they sang hymns in family worship, but grievously offending God when the same group of people sang the same hymns in *congregational* worship?

One would also assume that all the well-known pragmatic arguments against uninspired hymn-singing in public worship apply equally to private worship. One could equally condemn private hymn-singing on the grounds that hymns are, after all, merely human compositions, the uninspired words of men liable to error in doctrine and sentiment, etc., and thus liable to pervert the beliefs and spirituality of the singer; how much better, safer, and more reverent to use the words of God in the psalms! Yet exclusive psalmodists have not so argued against hymns in private worship. Perhaps it would be more logical for exclusive psalmody to apply "across the board," to all sung worship, whether public or not. As long as exclusive psalmodists do not thus apply their position, we are faced with what seems the bizarre inconsistency of a group of Christian families being encouraged to sing uninspired hymns in their family worship, but being forbidden to sing those same hymns when they join together to worship as the family of God.

Finally, we should consider that singing to God is simply one mode of addressing God; i.e., it is a mode of prayer. We often make a distinction between "prayer" and "praise," meaning by the latter sung praise. But praise is, of course, a constituent element of prayer. If we contemplate prayer as including praise, thanksgiving, petition, confession and intercession, we may address these to God either in speech or in song. Singing to God is, therefore, one way of praying. Now one assumes that exclusive psalmodists have no objection to a minister composing his own prayer for use in public worship, whether he composes it beforehand or in an extemporary manner. We would not condemn him for using his own words, rather than restricting himself to one of the prayers of the Bible. Nor would we condemn an ordinary member of his congregation for exercising the same liberty in a prayer meeting. The question then arises: Why should we limit this liberty to composing our own prayers in speech, and not extend it to composing our own prayers in song? If it is lawful for us to speak uninspired prayers, is it not lawful for us to sing them too?[72]

It could be objected that this argument justifies only the singing by an individual of his own prayer, while others listen: it does not justify the entire congregation singing together one person's uninspired prayer. However, there can be no problem in principle with a congregation singing together a prayer to God composed by one man, for this is precisely what a congregation does when it sings a psalm by David. And we have already granted the freedom to the individual to compose his own prayer. There seems no cogent reason why a congregation should not join in that prayer vocally, whether the prayer is spoken or sung. Even by simply saying "Amen" to another person's prayer, we have signified our assent to what he has said. Why should we not

---

[72] Some exclusive psalmodists try to turn the force of this argument by insisting on the wide distinction between speech and song, so wide that one cannot legitimately argue from the one to the other. This objection seems difficult to sustain when one reflects that the transition from speech to song is, in fact, not a leap across a chasm, but a graded progression across a spectrum, with chanting occupying the middle ground. If it is lawful to speak uninspired prayers, is it also lawful to chant them? When does speech become chant? And when does chant become song? What about chant-like speech, and song-like chant? Obviously speech and song do differ, just as walking and running differ; but I do not think the distinction is sufficiently absolute in quality to forbid arguing from one to the other, especially when speech, song and chant are all subsets of prayer.

equally signify our assent by praying along with him vocally? Of course, this would require the congregation to know in advance what the person was going to say; his prayer (spoken or sung) would have to be written out and distributed to the other worshippers, or beamed onto a screen by an overhead projector. In other words, it would have to be a "set prayer." If a prejudice is then raised against "set prayer," either spoken or sung, we must merely remind ourselves again that the psalms are set prayers sung to God. The only consistent objection would have to be, not to set prayer in itself but to set prayer that is not inspired. However, I can see no meaningful reason why a set prayer from Scripture should be acceptable when sung to God, but a set prayer not from Scripture (yet enshrining Scriptural truths) should be unacceptable to Him. If the problem is the belief that set prayers somehow "quench the Spirit," that would apply equally to set prayers from Scripture, which is what most of the psalms are, for they are equally "set." And if that is not the problem, what is it?

Finally, we can construct an argument from the purpose or design of singing. Isaac Watts stated this argument classically in his *Essay for the Improvement of Psalmody*:

> [T]he several ends and designs of singing . . . can never be sufficiently attained by confining ourselves to David's Psalms, or the words of any songs in Scripture. The first and chief intent of this part of worship, is to express unto God what sense and apprehensions we have of his essential glories; and what notice we take of his works of wisdom and power, vengeance and mercy; it is to vent the inward devotion of our spirits in words of melody, to speak our own experience of divine things, especially our religious joy; it would be tiresome to recount the endless instances out of the book of Psalms and other divine songs, where this is made the chief business of them. In the texts of the New Testament where singing is required, the same designs are proposed; when the Ephesians are filled with the Spirit, the enlightener and comforter, they are charged to indulge those divine sensations, and let them break out into a spiritual song: *Eph.* 5:19. When any is merry or cheerful, the apostle James bids him express it by singing. Giving thanks unto God, is the command of St. Paul to the saints while he enjoins psalmody on them; and speaking the wonders of his power, justice and grace, is the practice of the church constantly in the visions

of St. John. To teach and admonish one another, is mentioned by St. Paul as another design of singing; the improvement of our meditations, and the kindling divine affections within ourselves, is one of the purposes also of religious melody, if Eph. 5:19 be rightly translated.

Now, how is it possible all these ends should be attained by a Christian, if he confines his meditations, his joys, and his praises, to the Hebrew book of Psalms? Have we nothing more of the nature of God revealed to us than David had? Is not the mystery of the ever-blessed Trinity brought out of darkness into open light? Where can you find a psalm that speaks the miracles of wisdom and power as they are discovered in a crucified Christ? And how do we rob God the Son of the glory of his dying love, if we speak of it only in the gloomy language of "smoke and sacrifices, bullocks and goats, and the fat of lambs"? Is not the ascent of Christ into heaven, and his triumph over principalities and powers of darkness, a nobler entertainment for our tuneful meditations, than the removing of the ark up to the city of David, to the hill of God, which is high as the hill of Bashan. . . . The heaven and the hell that we are acquainted with by the discovery of God our Saviour, give us a more distinct knowledge of the future and eternal state, than all the former revelations of God to men: Life and immortality is brought to light by the gospel; we are taught to look far into the invisible world, and take a prospect of the last awful scene of things: We see the graves opening, and the dead arising at the voice of the archangel, and the sounding of the trump of God: We behold the Judge on his tribunal, and we hear the dreadful and the delightful sentences of decision that shall pass on all the sons and daughters of Adam; we are assured, that the saints shall *"arise to meet the Lord in the air, and so shall we be for ever with the Lord:"* The apostle bids us, *"Exhort or comfort one another with these words*; Thess. iv. 17, 18. Now when the same apostle requires that *"the word of Christ must dwell richly in us in all wisdom, teaching and admonishing one another in psalms and spiritual songs;"* can we think he restrains us only to the Psalms of David, which speak very little of all these glories or terrors, and that in very obscure terms and dark hints of prophecy? Or shall it be supposed, that we must admonish one another of the old Jewish affairs and ceremonies in verse, and make melody with those weak beggarly elements, and the yoke of bondage, and yet never dare to speak of the wonders of new discovery except in the plain and simple language of prose?[73]

---

[73] Watts, *An Essay for the Improvement of Psalmody*, in *Works* vol. 4, 380-1.

It does indeed seem strange that Christians should never be able to sing together in public worship about the doctrine of the Trinity, an explicit presentation of which will not be found in the psalter or even the New Testament songs. Yet the doctrine of the Trinity is the central dogma of the Christian faith. As far as continuing to sing the psalter is concerned, Watts suggested that we should translate it in such a way as to make clear the Christological meaning of its typical references to priesthood, sacrifice, temple, kingship, the Exodus, etc.[74] If we do not do this, the argument becomes so much the stronger that singing the psalter needs to be complemented by singing the songs of the New Jerusalem, lest we find our sung praise locked permanently into the realm of types and shadows.

Theological justification, then, can certainly be offered for the singing of uninspired hymns. Nevertheless, the present writer would be less than candid if he did not place on record at this point his overwhelming conviction that *uninspired hymns should never be allowed to displace from Christian worship the singing of David's psalms and other Scriptural songs*. This is indeed what has largely happened in hymn-singing churches. It is an unnecessary, indefensible, and impoverishing state of affairs. This is especially so at the end of the 20th century, when the charismatic movement has given birth to a prodigious brood of mindless and sentimental ditties which ought frankly to have been aborted in the womb, but which increasingly dominate the singing of so many evangelical congregations. We are becoming progressively cut off from the rich catholic heritage of 2,000 years of Christian worship, as our churches more and more commit themselves to the liturgical lunatic asylum of charismatic choruses (mostly ephemeral and often doctrinally vacuous or erroneous), and ignore to the point of annihilation the majestic sanity, wholesomeness and spiritual beauty of the psalms, the Gospel canticles, the other

---

[74] Ibid., 378-9.

inspired songs of Scripture, and the patristic and Reformation practice of singing the Ten Commandments and the Lord's Prayer.

The interpretation of Westminster Confession 21.5 offered in this chapter should therefore in no way be construed as a passionate plea for more uninspired hymns, nor as an attempt to rationalize and whitewash the man-centred, happy-clappy irreverence of much contemporary evangelical practice. I think uninspired hymns are in principle lawful; I incline to think that the Confession's authorization of "singing of psalms" does not exclude uninspired hymns; but there can be no doubt that the Westminster divines, along with the Reformed tradition in general, saw the singing of scriptural materials of praise, particularly the psalms of David, as occupying pride of place in congregational worship. Neither exclusive psalmody, nor exclusive hymnody, and certainly not exclusive neopentecostal jingles, but an even-handed combination of the best modern translations of the songs of Scripture with the best and soundest extra-scriptural hymns: this is the liturgical wisdom from which I would suggest we need to drink today, if we are not to poison our corporate worship incurably with floods of 20th century charismatic rubbish.[75]

We come now to consider the question of musical instruments in worship. This is a far easier subject to treat than the singing of psalms, given the Westminster Confession's forceful enunciation

---

[75] I am not impressed by the oft-heard counter-argument that many charismatic choruses are simply Scripture set to music. That in itself does not make them edifying. Just because something is Scripture, that does not make it intrinsically good material to be sung in worship; remember Leviticus 13 and Ezra 2. Charismatic Scripture choruses can be highly unedifying for several reasons: (a) they are often so short that they have to be sung three or four or more times, so that their meaningful sense of duration depends on numbing repetition; (b) they frequently lack point and purpose because they are stripped of context and sometimes badly mangled or mutated to fit a tune, rhyme or doctrinal stance; (c) they are often set to sloppy, saccharine music more suited to a nursery rhyme or a popular secular "love" song than to reverent worship of the holy Trinity.

of the regulative principle. As I observed before, we must take it for granted that the acts of worship the Confession explicitly authorizes are the only acts for which it finds and claims scriptural justification. This is axiomatic—indeed, it is the only logical assumption we can make, in the light of Westminster's commitment to the regulative principle as the hermeneutic of acceptable worship. If we grant this, it settles in advance the question of instrumental worship. Thus, what the Westminster divines actually set down in the Confession as the acts of worship authorized by God in Scripture, were the only acts they believed were thus authorized; and they did not set down the playing of musical instruments as an act of worship authorized by God in Scripture for His New Testament Church. The Confession is deafeningly silent on the issue. So are all the other Westminster documents. Clearly the Westminster divines did not believe in the validity of instrumental worship. Indeed, at the same time that the Westminster Assembly was deliberating, the English Puritan-dominated Parliament to which they were accountable decreed on May 9th 1644 that all ecclesiastical organs were to be destroyed:

> Two Ordinances of the Lords and Commons assembled in Parliament for the speedy demolishing of all organs, images and all matter of superstitious monuments in all Cathedrals, and Collegiate or Parish-Churches and Chapels, throughout the Kingdom of England and the Dominion of Wales; the better to accomplish the blessed reformation so happily begun, and to remove all offences and things illegal in the worship of God, do ordain that all organs, and frames or cases wherein they stand, in all churches and chapels, shall be taken away and utterly defaced, and none others hereafter set up in their place.[76]

This should not surprise us. The standard position of the Reformed Churches, from Zwingli and Calvin onwards, had always been that instrumental worship was a feature of Old Covenant worship which had passed away with the coming of Christ and the establishment of the New Covenant. Calvin was outspoken on the matter:

---

[76] K. M. L. Long, *The Music of the English Church*, 206.

> In Popery there was a ridiculous and unsuitable imitation [of the Jews]. While they adorned their temples, and valued themselves as having made the worship of God more splendid and inviting, they employed organs, and many other such ludicrous things, by which the Word and worship of God are exceedingly profaned, the people being much more attached to those rites than to the understanding of the divine Word. We know, however, that where such understanding is not, there can be no edification. . . . What, therefore, was in use under the Law is by no means entitled to our practice under the Gospel; and these things, being not only superfluous but useless, are to be abstained from, because pure and simple modulation is sufficient for the praise of God, if it is sung with the heart and with the mouth. We know that our Lord Jesus Christ has appeared, and by His advent has abolished these legal shadows. Instrumental music [in worship], we therefore maintain, was only tolerated on account of the times and the people, because they were as boys, as the sacred Scripture speaks, whose condition required these puerile rudiments. But in Gospel times we must not have recourse to these, unless we wish to destroy the evangelical perfection, and to obscure the meridian light which we enjoy in Christ our Lord.[77]

The entire Reformed wing of the Reformation, almost without exception, held this view, and accordingly its singing of psalms, hymns and spiritual songs in public worship was not accompanied by musical instrumentation, nor were musical pieces played before, during or after the worship.[78]

Two points should be made about this wholesale rejection of musical instruments in Christian worship by the Reformed Churches. First, it was the very opposite of a strange new position, previously unheard of. On the contrary, Calvinist Reformers were simply returning to the ancient Christian understanding of what was and what was not proper in a service of Christian worship.[79]

---

[77] Calvin, Sermon on 1 Samuel 18:1-9.

[78] Except in the Dutch Reformed Church where, in opposition to the views of most of the ministers, powerful secular interests prevented the total abolition of the organ. Its use, however, was strictly limited to playing pieces before and after the service of worship; in the service itself no instrumental music was played, either by itself or to accompany the singing.

[79] For what follows, see Girardeau, *Musical Instruments in Worship*; Old, *The Patristic Roots of Reformed Worship*; Ward, *The Psalms in Christian Worship*, 58-60; Schaff, *History of the Christian Church*, vol. 4, 439.

Musical instruments were entirely excluded from the worship of the early Church throughout the patristic period. To this day, they are still excluded from the worship of the Orthodox Churches of the East. In the Western Catholic tradition, we first hear of a musical instrument being used in worship in the 8th century, for in the year 757 the Frankish king Pepin presented an organ to the church of St. Corneille in Compiegne. (Some authorities say that the organ was first introduced into church worship slightly earlier by pope Vitalian, whose papacy extended from 657 to 672.) We also, from the 8th century onwards, occasionally find the harp, violin and cithern depicted in some ancient Western musical manuscripts. In the period 900-1100, organs gradually began to become common features of the great Western abbeys and cathedral churches; we know, for instance, that Dunstan, archbishop of Canterbury from 961 to 988, installed an organ in Malmesbury abbey, and several other places in England. This introduction of the organ into Western worship was bound up with contemporary developments in ecclesiastical singing. As the previously established norm of unison plainsong gave way to the more elaborate part-singing, the organ began to be used to accompany and thus sustain the singing in one part (which involved simply playing one line of music), while other instruments were sometimes added (e.g., pipes, comets) to sustain other parts. So we should not think of this initial use of the organ in terms of the playing of complex pieces of music, but as providing, simple accompaniment for the voices of priests, monks and choirs in part-singing.

This "first period" of the organ, 900-1100, did not lead to the widespread use of instruments in ordinary parish churches and thus in normal Western Catholic worship. This is borne out by the fact that mediaeval Western theologians continued to repeat, as a matter of course, the patristic rejection of musical instruments in Christian worship. Thomas Aquinas's statement is well known:

> The Church does not use musical instruments such as the harp or lyre when praising God, lest she should seem to lapse into Judaism. . . . As

> Aristotle says, "Flutes ought not to be introduced into teaching. nor any artificial instrument such as the harp, nor anything of the kind, but only such thing as make men good." For musical instruments usually move the soul more to pleasure than create a good internal disposition. But in the Old Testament, instruments of this kind were used, both because the people were more coarse and carnal, so that they needed to be aroused by such instruments and with temporal promises, and also because these bodily instruments were figurative of something.[80]

Aquinas lived from 1224 until 1274. Clearly in his day, normal public worship was not characterized by instrumental music. In fact, it was not until the 14th and 15th centuries that the playing of musical instruments became a widespread and regular feature of ordinary Western worship, having ceased to perform the merely subservient function of sustaining part-singing. The first great church organist known to history, was Francesco Landino (d. 1390), of the church of St. Lorenzo in Florence. Certainly by the time of the Reformation, the professional playing of complex musical pieces in Western worship had become a scandal to all those who desired a purer, more spiritual Christianity. Erasmus of Rotterdam spoke for many:

> We have brought a cumbersome and theatrical music into our churches, such a confused disorderly chattering of some words, as I think was never heard in any of the Greek or Roman theatres. The church rings with the noise of trumpets, pipes and dulcimers, and human voices strive to bear their part with them. Men run to church as to a theatre, to have their ears tickled. And for this end, organ-makers are hired with great salaries, and a company of boys who waste all their time in learning these whining tones. Pray now compute how many poor people in great extremity might be maintained by the salaries of these singers.[81]

All that the Reformed wing of the Reformation was doing when it repudiated instrumental worship was simply correcting this later Western mediaeval aberration from a previous norm, and returning to the central Christian tradition, both Western

---

[80] Aquinas, *Summa Theologiae*, 2a2ae, 91.

[81] Quoted by Candlish. *The Organ Question*, 118-19.

Catholic and Eastern Orthodox, stretching back to the early Church fathers.

The second point is that our Reformed fathers were not motivated merely by a desire to go back to patristic norms (although this was important to them). As the quotation from Calvin cited above shows, they had theological reasons for rejecting the playing of musical instruments as an act of worship. In brief, they pointed to the difference between the form of worship under the Old and the New Covenants. God had certainly commanded the playing of musical instruments in the worship connected with the ark of the covenant (later the temple). But the Reformed Reformers, following in the theological footsteps of the early Church fathers, saw this instrumental worship as part and parcel of the entire Old Covenant system of worship, which was ceremonial in nature and typical in function. They believed this whole system had passed away with the coming of Christ, the One Whom it had all in various ways foreshadowed. Key texts were John 4:19-26, with its contrast between the old style of worship in Jerusalem" (i.e., the temple) and the new style of worship "in spirit and truth" which Jesus as the Messiah was now introducing; and Hebrews 9:1-10, which describes the outward ceremonial worship of the Old Covenant as "regulations for the body [or 'fleshly ordinances'] imposed until a time of reformation"—the time being the advent of Christ Who is Himself the reformer.

In other words, Calvin and the Westminster divines were insisting that the Church under the New Covenant must derive its pattern of worship from the Scriptures of the New Covenant. There can be no direct appeal to how the Jews worshipped God under the Old Covenant, for we are no longer living under that administration of God's grace. Now that Messiah has come, and the prophecies, types and shadows of Judaism have dissolved into the sunshine of Gospel fulfillment, Messiah's people must consult the New Covenant Scriptures of His apostles for their form of worship and church government.[82] The argument, then, as far as classical Reformed theology was concerned, was simple: Where in the New Covenant Scriptures has God told us to worship Him by playing musical instruments? Nowhere. Therefore we must not offer God a worship He has not told us to offer, lest we incur the condemnation of Nadab and Abihu. What God has told us to do is to *sing* psalms, hymns and spiritual songs. Singing, not playing instruments, is the worship God requires of us. And if anyone today finds this difficult to grasp, having been accustomed to a style of worship steeped in instrumental music, let him simply reflect that the early Church throughout the entire patristic era had no such difficulty, and indeed in its Eastern Orthodox branch has had no difficulty for 2,000 years with the concept of singing but not playing instruments in worship.

Since the New Testament is so obviously lacking in justification for instrumental worship, its advocates have been compelled to appeal to the Old Testament and the worship of the Jerusalem temple to give credibility to their practice. We have seen how this approach breaks itself to pieces on the reefs of the regulative principle: we must worship God only in ways authorized by Himself in the New Testament. However, another interesting point, usually ignored, is that this appeal to the Old Testament actually proves far too much. In Judaic worship, God *commanded* that He be worshiped by the playing of musical instruments, and the instruments were specified. 2 Chronicles 29:25-6 records that king Hezekiah "stationed the Levites in the

---

[82] This accent on the discontinuity between Old and New Covenants does not fragment the unity of God's covenant of grace, which remains the same in all ages of history. The way of salvation is one and indivisible, namely, justification by grace through faith. The internal worship of the heart is also immutable. But the outward forms in which the justified embody their internal worship does change and has changed radically in the transition from Old to New Covenant.

house of the LORD with cymbals, with stringed instruments, and with harps, according to the commandment of David, of Gad the king's seer, and of Nathan the prophet; for thus was the commandment of the LORD by His prophets. The Levites stood with the instruments of David, and the priests with the trumpets." (The trumpets derive from Numbers 10:1-10, where God commands Moses to make two silver trumpets to be blown over animal sacrifices.) The point is that the Jews were not at liberty to worship God by musical instruments apart from His command, nor were they free to choose which musical instruments to use. God explicitly commanded them, through Moses and the prophets, to worship Him on musical instruments, and told them which instruments to use: trumpets, cymbals, harps and certain other stringed instruments. From these strict, specific, divinely imposed Old Covenant stipulations, to argue that we today are free to play any instruments *we* think proper as an act of New Covenant worship, involves a leap of logic so mighty that it sends the mind out of solar orbit. Furthermore, under the Old Covenant, only priests and Levites were authorized to play these instruments. Appealing to the Old Testament would therefore seem to lead us, logically, to instituting a policy of affirmative action to employ only *bona fide* descendants of Levi as instrumentalists in our church bands and orchestras. Yes, I indulge in sanctified sarcasm; but it is richly merited. Trying to base the playing of instruments in Christian worship directly on Old Testament precedent is, as most Christians have seen throughout Church history, a resounding non-sequitur and non-starter.

The playing of musical instruments, then, cannot be a New Testament act of worship, for the simple reason that it lacks New Testament sanction. However, we recollect at this point how Richard Baxter thought that instrumental *accompaniment* of psalm-singing was not an act but a circumstance of worship.[83] Is this valid? Let

---

[83] See Baxter, *Christian Directory*, 557. On 705 he offers several arguments for the lawfulness of instruments in Christian worship. Some are remarkably

us endeavour to appreciate the distinction as it applies to the playing of musical instruments in worship. Under the Old Covenant, when the priests blew the silver trumpets over the sacrifice, that was in itself an act of worship commanded by God. The very noises of the trumpets were what God required. They were not accompaniment. They were themselves the worship. And when Levites clashed their cymbals together and plucked their harps, this too was worship. Hence Psalm 150, "Praise Him with the sound of the trumpet; praise Him with the lute and harp! Praise Him with loud cymbals!" The noise was the worship: an audio-symbolic evocation of the majesty and glory of God. As Aquinas remarked, "these bodily instruments were figurative of something." Such instrumental worship is no longer possible under the New Covenant: it was part of the symbolic, figurative, ceremonial worship of the temple, inextricably intertwined with priesthood and sacrifice, which passed away with the coming of the Lord Jesus Christ, when worship "in Jerusalem" passed over into worship "in spirit and truth." If someone in a church today played a trumpet voluntary as an "act of worship," it might be very competent and beautiful, but it would not be acceptable worship in the eyes of God, and more than any other act which lacked New Testament authorization.

---

weak, e.g., "No Scripture forbiddeth it, therefore it is not unlawful." This is true only if it can be proved that instrumental accompaniment is a circumstance, not an act, of worship, and that its use can helpful and edifying. However, one of Baxter's stronger arguments is that instrumental accompaniment is "a natural help to the mind's alacrity; and it is a duty and not a sin to use the helps of nature and lawful art, though not to institute sacraments, etc., of our own making. As it is lawful to use the comfortable helps of spectacles in reading the Bible, so it is of music to exhilarate the soul towards God." Perhaps "duty" is too strong, unless we take Baxter to mean that in some churches, in certain circumstances, the use of an instrument might be the best way of putting heart and zest into their incompetent and deadly singing, and so would then become a duty for that church at that time.

But what shall we make—not of instrumental *worship*—but of instrumental *accompaniment* under the New Covenant? If the playing of instruments cannot be an act of worship, can it be a *circumstance* of worship, as Baxter suggested? The situation would be thus: the singing alone is the divinely commanded act of worship; the playing of an instrument for the sole purpose of keeping the singing in time and in tune, is a circumstance of worship, "to be ordered by the light of nature and Christian prudence" (Confession 1.6). In other words, this way of using of an instrument is comparable to a minister's using sermon notes: the notes keep his preaching in order, preventing it from wandering; the instrument performs a similar function for the singing. Much ink was spilt in the 19th century over this issue, as Presbyterian advocates of the organ employed the "circumstance" argument to justify its introduction into services of worship, and opponents strove to demonstrate that the playing of an instrument in worship could not be classified as a circumstance.[84] We are here in the realm, not of what the Confession itself actually teaches, but of trying to apply the Confession's teaching. My own thoughts on this contentious issue would be as follows:

(a) It seems to me that if the purpose for which an instrument is used is merely to sustain and regulate the singing—to keep it in time and in tune—then the instrument is performing the same function as (for example) musical notation. If I understand musical notation, and the tune of a psalm is printed in my psalm book, the printed tune helps to keep my singing in good order. The printed tune would be a circumstance of worship. I cannot see why an instrument should not perform the same function, and thus fall into the category of circumstance. Indeed, an instrument so used will be carrying out the same function as a precentor, or a group

---

[84] See for example the arguments of Girardeau in *Musical Instruments in Worship*, and of Begg in *Anarchy in Worship*. Both contend that instrumental accompaniment cannot be considered a circumstance.

of precentors. As long as this is the purpose of the instrument, and it is kept strictly subservient to the singing (which is the *act* of worship), I think that it is possible in certain circumstances to justify the use of a musical instrument, not in order to worship God, but in order to assist the worship of God through song.

(b) This circumstance argument, if valid, can only be employed to justify a *minimal* use of instruments, strictly as accompaniment and nothing more. I cannot see that the argument can legitimately be pressed beyond using a single instrument. It certainly cannot be used to justify bands or orchestras, which by the volume and complexity of sound they generate have clearly passed well beyond the description "accompaniment." As soon as the playing of a musical instrument ceases to be subservient to the singing, it has ceased to be a circumstance and falls under the veto of the regulative principle.

(c) If an instrument is to be justified by the circumstance argument, purely as accompaniment a congregation would need to ask itself: Do we really *need* this instrument to keep our singing in time and in tune? Or is this instrument necessary if we are *most effectively* to sing in time and in tune? My own experience suggests that the larger the congregation, the less it needs any instrumental accompaniment to regulate and sustain its singing. I was for some time a member of a church with some 900 worshippers and an organ. Quite often the minister would instruct us to sing a particular verse of a song unaccompanied; and it was noticeable that when the organ stopped playing, and the congregation's corporate voice was left to its own energies, the quality of the singing improved. We were no longer in competition with the booming instrument. On the other hand, I know of a small church which had no organ and fewer than twenty worshippers, whose inability when singing to keep in time (and possibly in tune) became the despair of the minister. The only practical solution he could come up with was to introduce an electric organ, which, in their case, substantially improved the quality of the singing simply by regulating and sustaining it.

(d) Musical instruments have a way of gradually taking over a service of worship. It may begin innocently enough as pure accompaniment but people may begin to form an emotional and aesthetic bond with the instrument. Tunes are soon being played to which no words are sung, before and after the service, and during the offering or collection. Then one instrument is no longer enough; why not add a few more? Why not have a full-blown band or orchestra? Why not sing songs which have lengthy musical introductions, conclusions and episodes played purely by the instruments? And so the musical instruments take on a life of their own; they are no longer humble bondservants to the singing of God's people, but autonomous generators of elaborate noise. God-centred Christian worship is thus corrupted, by degrees, into aesthetic self-indulgence; "for," as Aquinas said, "musical instruments usually move the soul more to pleasure than create a good internal disposition." This corruption has undoubtedly happened in many evangelical churches, to the extent that the worship of the thrice-holy God is sometimes indistinguishable from a discotheque, where drums and synthesizers beat out sensuous rhythms more likely to stir up erotic than spiritual desire. When one sees or experiences this grossly physical and fundamentally pagan sense-indulgence masquerading as true Christian worship, one feels sympathy for the unexpectedly Puritan sentiments of George Bernard Shaw:

> I am as fond of fine music and handsome building as Milton was, or Cromwell, or Bunyan; but if I found they were becoming the instruments of a systematic idolatry of sensuousness, I would hold it good statesmanship to blow every cathedral in the world to pieces with dynamite, organ and all, without the least heed to the screams of the art critics and cultured voluptuaries.[85]

---

[85] Quoted in Scholes, *The Puritans and Music in England and New England*, 214.

Any congregation that is convinced of the circumstance argument, and thinks it appropriate in its own situation to use an instrument on that basis, must beware of this insidious process by which musical instruments can come to dominate worship. There is no reason why the process should inevitably occur, as long as it is guarded against, any more than the use of a building should inevitably lead to the building becoming an ornate cathedral idol-worshiped by its users. I know churches where a single instrument has long been used, and has been kept strictly in its place as a mere circumstantial aid to the singing. The best way of preserving things in this healthy state is to refuse to allow the instrumentalist to be in charge of what he does or doesn't do: keep him sternly accountable to the minister and elders, and dismiss him if he assumes airs and graces. But if the process of corruption has begun, radical surgery may be necessary to arrest the instrumental gangrene, even to the good, old-fashioned Zwinglian and Calvinist lengths of abolishing the use of the instruments altogether (if not blowing them to pieces with dynamite).

In sum, I think that sometimes the use of a single instrument, purely to keep the singing in time and in tune, can be justified as a circumstance of worship, and thus be consistent with the Confession and its teaching on the regulative principle; but that the ideal to be desired and preferred, if practicable, is the ancient Christian ideal of unaccompanied singing.

Bibliography

Primary source material:

Richard Baxter, *Christian Directory* (Ligonier, PA., 1990) *Practical Works* (23 vols., London, 1830)

Paul Bayne, *An Entire Commentary upon the whole Epistle of St. Paul to the Ephesians* (Edinburgh, 1886)

James Begg, *Anarchy in Worship* (Edinburgh, 1875)

John Brown, *Against the anti-Sabbatarians* (Rotterdam, 1676)

Heinrich Bullinger, *Decades* (5 vols., Cambridge, 1852)

Nicholas Byfield, *An Exposition upon the Epistle to the Colossians* (Cambridge, 1627)

John Calvin, *Commentaries on the Epistles of Paul the Apostle to the Philippians, Colossians and Thessalonians* (Edinburgh, 1851)

R. S. Candlish, *The Organ Question* (Edinburgh, 1856)

Thomas Cartwright, *A Commentary upon the Epistle of St Paul the Apostle to the Colossians* (Edinburgh, 1864)

John Cotton, *Singing of Psalms a Gospel-Ordinance* (London, 1647)

John Daille, *Sermons of Mr. John Daille, on the Epistle of the Apostle St. Paul to the Colossians. The Third Part* (London, 1671)

Edward Elton, *An Exposition of the Epistle of Saint Paul the Apostle to the Colossians* (London, 1620)

James Ferguson, *The Epistles of Paul* (Edinburgh, 1978)

Geneva Bible (Madison, Wisconsin, 1969)

George Gillespie, *Notes of Debates and Proceedings of the Assembly of Divines* (Edinburgh, 1846)

John Girardean, *Musical Instruments in Worship*

Richard Hooker, *Works* (2 vols., Oxford, 1890)

John Lightfoot, *Works* (13 vols., London, 1822)

Thomas Manton, *A Practical Commentary or an Exposition on the Epistle of James* (London, 1653)

John Owen, *Works*, (16 vols., Edinburgh, 1965)

Matthew Poole, *A Commentary on the Holy* Bible (3 vols., London, 1962)

George Swinnock, *Works* (5 vols., Edinburgh, 1868)

Isaac Watts, *Works* (6 vols., London, 1810)

F. E. Wallace and John Giradeau, *The Instrumental Music Question and Instrumental Music in the Public Worship of God* (1980).

Westminster Divines, *Annotations upon all the Books of the Old and New Testaments* (2nd ed., London, 1651)

George Wither, *Hymns and Songs of the Church* (London, 1856)

Secondary reference material:

Charles W. Baird, *The Presbyterian Liturgies: Historical Sketches* (Grand Rapids, Michigan, 1957)

H. M. Baird, *Theodore Beza—The Counsellor of the Franch Reformation 1519-1605* (New York, 1899).

N. M. de S. Cameron (ed.), *Dictionary of Scottish Church History and Theology* (Edinburgh, 1993)

John L. Carson and David W. Hall, *To Glorify and Enjoy God* (Edinburgh, 1994)

R. Christoffel, *Zwingli; or, the Rise of the Reformation in Switzerland* (Edinburgh, 1858)

Horton Davies, *The Worship of the English Puritans* (London, 1948)

Dictionary of National Biography (compact ed. 2 vols., Oxford, 1975)

Winfred Douglas, *Church Music in History and Practice* (London, 1937)

Harry Eskew and Hugh T. McElrath, *Sing with Understanding* (Nashville, Tennessee, 1980)

Frederick J. Gillman, *The Evolution of the English Hymn* (London, 1927)

H .A. L. Jefferson, *Hymns in Christian Worship* (London, 1950)

John Julian, *Dictionary of Hymnology* (2 vols. New York, 1957).

K. R. Long, *The Music of the English Church* (London, 1972)

John McNaugher (ed.), *The Psalms in Worship* (Pittsburgh, PA., 1907)

A. F. Mitchell and J. Christie (eds.), *The Record of the Commissions of the General Assemblies of the Church of Scotland holden in Edinburgh in the years 1646 and 1647* (Edinburgh, 1892)

The Records of the Commissions of the General Assemblies of the Church of Scotland holden in Edinburgh in the years 1648 and 1649 (Edinburgh, 1896)

R. A. Morey, *An Examination of Exclusive Psalmody* (np, nd)

Hughes Oliphant Old, *The Patristic Roots of Reformed Worship* (Zurich, 1975)

James Reid, *Memoirs of the Westminster Divines* (Paisley, 1811)

Erik Routley, *A Panorama of Christian Hymno*dy (Collegeville, Minnesota, 1979)

Philip Schaff, *The History of the Christian Church* (8 vols., Grand Rapids, Michigan, 1994)

Percy Scholes, *The Puritans and Music in England and New England* (New York, 1962)

Robert Shaw, *An Exposition of the Confession of Faith of the Westminster assembly of Divines* (London, nd)

Rowland S. Ward, *The Psalms in Christian Worship* (Melbourne, 1992)

Williston Walker, *John Calvin, the Organiser of Reformed Protestantism* (New York, 1969)

B. B. Warfield, *The Westminster Assembly and its Work* (New York, 1931

W. T. Whitley, *Congregational Hymn-Singing* (London, 1933)

Nicholas Wiseman, *Lectures on the Principal Doctrines and Practices of the Catholic Church* (London, 1847)

W. Young, *The Puritan Principle of Worship, in Servants of the Word* (Puritan Conference papers for 1957)

The Eschatology of the Westminster Confession and Assembly

DEREK THOMAS

The study of eschatology reminds us that the *now* must give way to the *not yet*. History, far from being cyclical in nature, is inexorably moving forward towards its climax—the ultimate and final consummation.

Christ came into the world at Bethlehem to undo the effects of the Fall. When Adam fell, his future fell with him. By eating of the one tree forbidden to him, Adam forfeited the right to eat of the tree of life; his eschatological purpose—that he should "glorify God and enjoy him for ever" (SC 1)—was shattered.[1] Adam did what his progeny have done ever since: he lived for the *now* rather than the *not yet*. This "blindness of mind" (LC 28) is a condition that can only be remedied by, to borrow one of Calvin's word-pictures, the spectacles of God's special revelation. Throughout the course of history, God has been focusing our attention on the way back to Eden.

---

[1] Adam was created with an end in view: to glorify and enjoy God. He was perfect, though in a state of probation "having the law of God written in their power to fulfil it: and yet under a possibility of transgressing, being left to the liberty of their own will, which was subject unto change" (WCF 4:2). His existence was eschatological: though already in paradise and in a condition of sinlessness, his obedience to the 'covenant of works' promised him a confirmation of that existence (WCF 7.3).

The plan of God for the world has had in view the rescuing of his people from this world through faith in his Son. That deliverance continues to this day, and will continue until the return of Christ. Those who argue that there is no evidence of divine intervention in history forget, according to Peter, the story of the Flood (2 Pet. 3:1-7). God erupted into the flow of history then, and will do so again at the *parousia*, the revelation of Jesus Christ in his "royal" visit.

The advent of Christ, which will be personal and physical, visible and triumphant, will end the course of history (c.f. Matt. 24:44; Acts 1:11; Col. 3:4; 2 Tim. 4:8; Heb. 9:28). The last phase of Christ's mediatorial kingdom will witness the raising of the dead, the judgment of the world, the glorification of God's children, and the reconstruction of the universe (c.f. John 5:28-29; Rom. 8:17-21; Col. 3:4; 2 Pet. 3:10- 13). Then the kingdom will be handed over to the Father (1 Cor. 15:24-28). God's signalled triumph over Satan (Gen. 3:15) will then be apparent (Rev. 20:10). The progress of redemption is, in one aspect at least, the triumph of God over Satan. History is witnessing the reversal of the "original corruption" (WCF 6.4). "Redemption from sin," wrote John Murray, "cannot be adequately conceived or formulated except as it comprehends the victory which Christ secured once for all over him who is the god of this world, the prince of the power of the air . . . It is impossible to speak in terms of redemption from the power of sin except as there comes within the range of this redemptive accomplishment the destruction of the power of darkness."[2]

The eschatological features of conquest and renewal—the *triumph* of Christ's rule—is a feature which the Westminster Confession alludes to in its chapter *Of Christ the Mediator*, when it refers to Christ as "the seed of the woman, which should bruise

---

[2] *Redemption—Accomplished and Applied* (London: Banner of Truth, 1961), 50.

the serpent's head" (WCF 8.6).[3] But it is a fatal mistake to think of this eschatological victory as something that is still future, for in a decisive sense, the victory has already been attained! Christ has conquered "him who holds the power of death" (Heb. 2:14). He has been deprived of all authority. He may still attack, of course; but he has no authority to do so. Satan's deception, *in this eschatological age*, is to deceive the children of God into believing

---

[3] A fully adequate doctrine of the atonement recognises that Christ's mediatorial work focuses on God in propitiating His wrath, and on man in obtaining the right to, and means of, bestowing forgiveness, and on Satan in his final overthrow and destruction. The Westminster documents only allude to it in passing and fail to focus on this issue. Anselm of Canterbury's *Cur Deus Homo* had already set the agenda for much of the discussion relating to the work of redemption as far back as 1090, and post-reformation controversy over the atonement raged over different areas. (See Murray, op. cit.). The New Testament gives explicit witness to this theme: "The reason the Son of God appeared was to destroy the works of the devil" (1 John 3:8). "Having disarmed the powers and authorities, [Christ] made a public spectacle of them, triumphing over them in the cross" (Col. 2:15). "Since the children have flesh and blood, [Christ] too shared in their humanity so that by his death he might destroy [or render powerless, disarm] him who holds the power of death—that is, the devil—and free those who all their lives were held in slavery by their fear of death" (Heb. 2:14-15). Reformation and post-reformation analyses of the atonement tended to dismiss debates on Christ's defeat of Satan due, largely, to bizarre notions held and expounded by some of the early Fathers (including Origen and Gregory of Nyssa). Seventeenth century reflections on the work of Christ tended to reflect the Christian's defeat of Satan in his holy war against principalities and powers, rather than Christ's. In the Confession itself, reflecting seventeenth-century pre-occupation with the *ordo salutis*, attention was given to the Christian's triumph over Satan *within,* rather than Christ's triumph over him. However, it has to be conceded that the theological presupposition of the concluding two chapters of the Confession, relating as they do to the certainty of the Christian's glorification and the cosmic judgement of Christ, is that Satan will eventually be, and seen to be, defeated.

This aspect of the atonement needs, however to be stressed. For having "previously compared the cross to a signal trophy or show of triumph, in which Christ led about his enemies," comments Calvin on Colossians 2:14-15, "so he now also compares it to a triumphal car, in which he shewed himself conspicuously to view" (*en grande magnificence*).

that we are still subject to his supremacy. The supreme eschatological moment, is not the second coming, but the cross. It was at Calvary that Christ disarmed "principalities and powers," making a public example of them by triumphing over them in the cross (Col. 2:15).

Inaugurated Eschatology

It is a mistake, however, to think that eschatology concerns itself only with the future. It is part of the wonder of the gospel that something of the age to come has already broken through into this age; that eschatology concerns the present state of the believer and the current phase of the kingdom of God; that believers have already been delivered from this present aeon of evil (Gal.1:4); that we are currently living in the "last days" (Heb. 1:2); that this segment of history is "the end of the ages" (Heb. 9:26); that "the fulfilment of the ages has come" (1 Cor. 10:11). The night is nearly over; the day is almost here (Rom.13:12).

This is a perspective infrequently acknowledged, especially in systematic treatments of the doctrine of eschatology,[4] where attention is drawn merely to the futuristic aspects of death, the intermediate state, the resurrection of the body, and the more general aspects of the millennium, the Second Advent and the Last Judgment. A more balanced perspective is to see the entirety of biblical teaching as having eschatological implications. Thus, Geerhardus Vos, for example, can say with regard to Pauline theology: "to unfold the Apostle's eschatology means to set forth his theology as a whole . . . he views the present soteriological realities of the believer's experience out of a broader

---

[4] E.g., Charles Hodge's treatment of eschatology concerns itself exclusively with 'futuristic' eschatology, *Systematic Theology*, Vol. III (London: James Clarke, 1960), 713-878. The same is true of Louis Berkhof, see *Systematic Theology* (London: Banner of Truth, 1960), 661-751.

eschatological perspective and as themselves the realisation of the *eschaton*."[5] For the Old Testament, the coming "day of the Lord," the distinction between "this age" and "the age to come," was a singular event. But when Messiah arrived, the eschatological process of "the end" is seen to be in two stages: a *first* coming in a "low condition" (SC 27), followed by a *second* coming in glory and power to usher in the final consummation.

The Westminster symbols, do not, of course, allude specifically to a *realized* or *inaugurated*[6] eschatology as such, but unconsciously there are allusions to it in some of its pronouncements. It is the viewpoint of Question 83 of the Larger Catechism, for example: "*What is the answer to communion in glory with Christ which the members of the invisible church enjoy in this life?* The members of the invisible church have communicated to them *in this life the first-fruits of glory with Christ*, as they are members of him their head, and so in him are interested in that glory which he is fully possessed of; and, as an earnest thereof, enjoy the sense of God's love, peace of conscience, joy in the Holy Ghost, and hope of glory; as, on the contrary, sense of God's revenging wrath, horror of conscience, and a fearful expectation of judgment, are to the wicked the beginning of their torments which they shall endure after death (italics added)."

---

[5] *The Pauline Eschatology* (Grand Rapids: Eerdmans, 1972), 11.

[6] The term is used by Anthony A. Hoekema, *The Bible and the Future* (Exeter: Paternoster, 1978), 1. He prefers the term "inaugurated" to "realized," partly because of the latter's association with the unacceptable views of C. H. Dodd, and partly because 'realized' tends to suggest that all eschatological expectations have been fulfilled, something which is patently false. Only a part of the eschatological unfolding of redemptive history has dawned thus far. "Since, however, there remain many eschatological events that have not yet been realised, and since the New Testament clearly speaks of a future as well as a present eschatology, I prefer to speak of 'inaugurated' rather than 'realised' eschatology." Ibid. 17. Jay Adams uses the term "realised millennialism," *The Time is at Hand* (Nutley, NJ: Presbyterian and Reformed, 1970), 9-11, passim.

Clearly, what is in view here is a realization of the fact that something of the future glory (the future *eschaton*) is already present in the consciousness of the believer. As children of God by faith in Christ we live in the light of a vision that has already begun to dawn; even now, in this aeon, we have the "first-fruits of glory with Christ" communicated to us, "and so in him [Christ] are interested in that glory which he is fully possessed of." Our justification has already anticipated the judgment of the Last Day; raised with Christ, as a present spiritual experience, our future bodily resurrection is certain; our salvation, already secured, remains to be completed.[7]

Care must be taken not to limit the scope of eschatology. In one sense, "Christianity is eschatology."[8] From the opening of our Bibles, there is an expectation that, following the fall of

---

[7] In one sense, then, there is an emphasis on eschatology in the New Testament which focuses on what has already happened to us in Christ's coming into the world as our Redeemer; in Christ we are participating in the *eschaton*. One crucial area where the eschatological inauguration manifests itself is in the area of sanctification. In one sense, every Christian is *already* sanctified. Paul tells the Corinthians, "You are sanctified" (1 Cor.1:2). This is relational or positional sanctification. God sanctifies believers once and for ever when he brings them to himself, separating them from the world, delivering them from sin and Satan, and welcoming them into his fellowship (see Heb. 2:11; 10:10,14,29; 13;12). There is an eschatological connection between Christ's resurrection, our union with him and our once-for-all translation into positional (definitive) sanctification (c.f. Rom 6:1-14; Gal.2:20-21; Eph. 2:1-6; Col. 2:6-3:17). It is on the basis of such passages that the Westminster Confession of Faith can say: "They who are effectually called and regenerated, having a new heart and a new spirit created in them, are farther sanctified really and personally, *through virtue of Christ's death and resurrection*, by His Word and Spirit dwelling in them: the dominion of the whole body of sin is destroyed, and the several lusts thereof are more and more weakened and mortified" (WCF 13.1). See "Definitive Sanctification," in *The Collected Writings of John Murray*, Vol. 2, (Edinburgh: Banner of Truth, 1977), 277-284.

[8] Jürgen Moltmann, *Theology of Hope*, Trans. J. W. Leith (New York: Harper and Row, 1967), 16.

mankind, God will come in redemption and power to liberate his people from their bondage to sin, and vindicate himself and his purposes in the covenant of grace. Thus, from this point of view, the centralization of the Westminster Confession on God's eternal decree (WCF 3), which outlines His determination to predestinate some to everlasting life and foreordain others to everlasting death (3.3), foreordaining "all the means thereunto" (3.6),—this is an eschatological statement of immense proportions. Similarly, in the Confession's recognition of God's unified *covenantal* purpose (WCF 7) there are implications for eschatology: throughout history, God has bound himself through the biblical covenants to redeem his people through the death of his Son. The unity of the covenant of grace forces us to read the Bible in such a way that we see the Old Testament as historical witness to an era of preparation in which everything was working towards the coming of the Messiah. It also forces us to read the New Testament as, in part at least, a fulfilment of that covenanted purpose. In one sense at least, the covenantal unity of God's redemptive administration forces us to see the New Testament as God's program of inaugurated eschatology.[9]

Spelling this out, briefly, we are locked into a consideration of the New Testament along the following lines.

From the start, God has been making known what his purpose is about: bringing sinners into a relationship with himself, one defined by the Immanuel formula, "I will be your God, and you will be my people" (e.g., Gen. 17:7; Exod. 6:6,7; 19:4,5; Lev. 11:45; Deut. 4:20; 29:13; Ezek. 34:24; Jer.24:7; 31:33; 32:37f).[10] The New Testament church, by this formula, centering as it does on Christ—

---

[9] This is, of course, in complete contrast to Dispensational eschatology.

[10] For a full treatment of this theme, see O. Palmer Roberston, *The Christ of the Covenants* (Philipsburg, N.J.:Presbyterian and Reformed Publishing Co., 1980), chapter 3.

his coming, dying, rising, ascending to the throne, and pouring out the Spirit—must be seen to have its roots in the Old Testament. The New Testament *ecclesia* is but the Old Testament *qahal* sharpened and fulfilled. Where Israelites took seriously covenantal obedience—relying on God's promises, worshiping, praying, and practicing neighbor-love in accordance with God's law—there, God's Old Testament church was visible. Within this community lay Old Testament expectations of the coming of the kingdom of God (Dan. 7:28-29; Pss. 2; 72), the restoration of Israel (Isa.11:11), and the outpouring of the Holy Spirit (Joel 2:28-29), the day of the Lord (Isa. 2:12,17; 13:9-11; Amos 5:18; Obad. 15-16; Zeph. 1:14-15), the new covenant (Jer. 31:31-32), and the new heavens and the new earth (Isa. 65:17; 66:22).[11]

Just as two mountains blur into a common range of mountains from a distance, even so, from the perspective of the Old Testament, the division of time between the first and second coming of Christ was blurred. "The age to come," wrote Vos, "was perceived to bear in its womb another age to come."[12] From the point of view of the Old Testament, then, the dawning of the New Testament age *is the eschaton*. It is for this reason that New Testament eschatology is divided into two strands: realized (inaugurated) and futuristic.

From one point of view, the eschaton *has* arrived. We are living in the last days (Acts 2:17 [citing Joel 2:28]; 1 Jn. 2:18; Heb.1:2). For this reason alone, it is a mistake to regard "the last days," and eschatology in general, as primarily focused on the period surrounding the second coming of Christ. A recognition of the eschatological nature of the entire interadventual age is crucial for our understanding of both Old and New Testament

---

[11] See, A. A. Hoekema, *The Bible and the Future,* 1-12.

[12] *The Pauline Eschatology,* 36. Vos goes on to speak of the believer now living in "a coexistence of the two worlds," (37).

eschatology. Neither the Confession, nor subsequent Reformed and Puritan analysis has sufficiently recognized this point. The decisive battle against sin and Satan has already been fought by the coming of Christ and his redemptive, mediatorial death on Calvary. To borrow Oscar Cullmann's well-known figure: the coming of Christ, as Old Testament Messiah, was D-day when the forces of Christ landed on the continent of our time. The decisive battle has been won, though ultimate victory (V-day) still awaits us.[13] Several features of this victory are apparent.

1. *The triumph of the rule of God.* Flowing out of the resurrection of Christ are a host of implications for the final victory of God. At the heart of it is the restoration of the cosmos. Among the implications for the final state of the body drawn from the resurrection of Christ, the apostle Paul mentions the following in his prolonged discussion of the theme in 1 Corinthians 15:20-28. In the first place, he mentions the effect Christ's resurrection had on death: "As in Adam all die, so in Christ all will be made alive" (v.22). Secondly, as we have already noted, he mentions the defeat of all his enemies, including "all dominion, authority and power" (v.24). Thirdly, he speaks of Christ handing over the kingdom to the Father (v.24), the Son being "made subject" to the Father (v.28) and finally of God becoming "all in all" (v. 28). Upon the completion of his role as Mediator, Christ brings the recalcitrant cosmos back to the Father.

Clearly, then, an aspect of the resurrection of Christ has implications for God's victory over his enemies. This, at least in part, is underlined in Question 191 of the Larger Catechism: "*What do we pray for in the second petition?* In the second petition,

---

[13] Oscar Cullmann, *Christ and Time*, trans. Floyd V. Filson (Philadelphia: Westminster, 1950), 87.

(which is, *Thy kingdom come*,) . . . we pray, that the kingdom of sin and Satan may be destroyed. . . ." Nor is this to be seen as something which lies wholly in the future. One of the consequences of Christ's resurrection is that the decisive battle against the forces of evil has already been fought, *and won*! The time of prevalent satanic delusion over the Gentiles has passed. Following a sustained campaign by a large band of disciples, Jesus said "I beheld Satan falling from heaven" (Luke 10:18; cf. Matt. 12:29). Satan is bound by a chain (Rev. 20:1). Christ has ransacked his house. As we noted above, there is an aspect of the atonement that is not fully explored in the Westminster Standards: Christ's victory over Satan.

2. *The present reign of Christ*. Christ has, as a consequence of his resurrection, been invested with power (Rom. 1:4). The current reign of Christ is an exercise of his eschatological power, and is something to which the Westminster standards allude, particularly Q. 53 and 54 of the Larger Catechism: "*How was Christ exalted in his ascension?* Christ was exalted in his ascension . . . he, in our nature, and as our head, triumphing over enemies, visibly went up into the highest heavens, there to receive gifts for men, to raise up our affections thither, and to prepare a place for us, where himself is, and shall continue till his second coming at the end of the world." "*How is Christ exalted in his sitting at the right hand of God?* Christ is exalted in his sitting at the right hand of God in that as God-man he is advanced to the highest favour with God the Father, with all fullness of joy, glory, and power over all things in heaven and earth; and doth gather and defend his church, and subdue their enemies; furnisheth his ministers and people with gifts and graces and maketh intercession for them."

3. *The Spirit-anointed community*. A feature of New Testament eschatology is the fact that in the interadventual age in which we live, we have tasted "the powers of the age to come" (Heb. 6:5).

The coming of the Holy Spirit at Pentecost was, according to Peter, the result of Jesus' death and rising again (Acts 2:32-33). By Jesus' death, "he received from the Father the promised Holy Spirit" (c.f. Acts 1:4). Paul says much the same thing when he explains that the essential feature of the Abrahamic covenant was no different from that known to be true of the new covenant era: Holy Spirit baptism. "He redeemed us in order that the blessing given to Abraham might come to the Gentiles through Christ Jesus, so that by faith we might receive the promise of the Spirit" (Gal.3:14). The Holy Spirit's coming on the day of Pentecost is thus seen as "the essence of the entire fulfilment awaited under the old covenant."[14] The presence and ministry of the indwelling Holy Spirit are, then, the first installments of the life of heaven (Rom. 8:23; 2 Cor. 1:22; Eph. 1:13,14; Heb. 6:4,5).

4. *The Church's universal mandate.* As a consequence of Christ's resurrection and in anticipation of his triumphal reign, the church—God's covenanted community—are commissioned to make disciples of "all nations" (Matt. 28:20);[15] they are to go "into all the world," preaching "to the whole creation" (Mark 16:15). There is no limit placed on the extent of the proclamation. This universalism is embryonic in God's covenantal dealing with Abraham. In him all the nations of the earth are to be blessed (Gen. 12:3; 18:18; 22:18). That blessing finds its fulfilment in the coming of Christ. There was no commission, as such, to

---

[14] Richard B. Gaffin, Jr., *Perspectives on Pentecost: New Testament Teaching on the Gifts of the Holy Spirit* (Grand Rapids: Baker, 1979), 17. Vos understood the coming of Spirit as "the element of the eschatological or the celestial sphere, that which characterises the mode of existence and life in the world to come and consequently of that anticipated form in which the world to come is even now realised . . ." *Pauline Eschatology*, 59.

[15] This, in contrast to an earlier commission in which Jesus forbade them enter any Gentile town, but to concentrate instead on the "lost sheep of Israel" (Matt. 10:5-6).

disciple the nations, to win Gentiles for Yahweh, in the Old Testament (though many Gentiles did become believers). Though the hope of one day seeing the nations come to Yahweh was ever present (see Psalms 67, 72 and 100). What happened on the day of Pentecost, when "Parthians, Medes and Elamites, residents of Mesopotamia, Judea and Cappadocia, Pontus and Asia, Phrygia and Pamphylia, Egypt and the parts of Libya near Cyrene; visitors from Rome (both Jews and converts to Judaism); Cretans and Arabs" (Acts 2:9-11) came to faith in Jesus Christ was in essence a fulfilment of the essence of the Abrahamic covenant: *the nations had been blessed.*

5. *Covenantal signs reflecting the dawning of the last days.* There is a redemptive-historical significance to the presence of miracles surrounding the time of Christ's coming, death and resurrection in the world. The expression "the kingdom of heaven has been taken by force" (Matt. 11:12) is meant to signify not only the power with which Jesus preached the gospel; it also alludes to his use of miracles. "Blessed are your eyes, for they see; and your ears, for they hear" (Matt. 13:16; Lk. 10:23). This hearing and seeing refer to both their hearing the gospel and their seeing the miracles which accompanied its initial proclamation. "Jesus miracles reveal the coming of the kingdom of God."[16]

---

[16] H. Ridderbos, *The Coming of the Kingdom* (Philadelphia: The Presbyterian and Reformed Publishing Co., 1975), 65. Jesus' first coming was intimately connected with the casting out of devils, thus once more demonstrating his attack on the kingdom of Satan. It may also be said, with Ridderbos, that disease is considered a "consequence of Satan's rule and that Jesus' struggle against the Evil One is not fought solely in the field of ethics, but in the whole of the physical domain." Ibid, 67. A connection between the church's universal mandate and the covenantal signs reflecting the dawning of the last days can be seen in the phenomenon of "tongues." They were a sign (1 Cor. 14:22) at the inauguration of the new covenant era that God intended to speak to many people ("all nations") as he had promised to do in the Abrahamic covenant. They were a sign of covenantal blessing to the world;

Having traced out the lines of inaugurated eschatology consequent upon Christ's death, resurrection and ascension, we now turn to the main emphasis of Westminster: those aspects of Christ's eschatological victory which are yet to transpire.

Futuristic Eschatology

If the Westminster Standards merely allude to aspects of inaugurated eschatology tangentially, its emphasis upon futuristic eschatology is both clear and precise, though carefully selective. It appears that great attention was given to the parameters of eschatological issues selected for inclusion as well as exclusion.

Two chapters at the close of the Confession deal with futuristic eschatology: one deals with the intermediate state and the future resurrection of the body (Chap. 32 "Of the State of Men after Death, and of the Resurrection of the Dead"), and another deals with the Day of Judgment (Chap. 33 "Of the Last Judgment").[17] One should note that the Second Coming receives only a passing mention in Chapter 33 of the Confession. Linking together the Day of Judgment and the coming of Christ, the Confession warns against "carnal security": "Because they know not at what hour the Lord will come," men ought to be "watchful" and "prepared to say, 'Come Lord Jesus, come quickly. Amen.'"[18]

It would be a mistake to think that this exhausts the eschatological pronouncements of the Westminster Standards. Of enormous significance is Chapter 15.6 of the Confession. In a chapter dealing with the doctrine of the Church, the Confession

---

a sign of covenantal cursing to Israel. God was about to graft in wild stock (Gentiles) to the olive tree, whilst at the same time a sign of breaking off the natural branches (the Jews) of the tree (Rom. 11:11-24).

[17] Parallel sections in the catechisms include Questions 84-90 of the Larger Catechism, and Questions 37 and 38 of the Shorter Catechism.

[18] A reference to Christ's Second Coming also appears in the Larger Catechism in the section on Christ's exaltation (Q. 56).

inserts the well-known formula denying the role of the "Pope of Rome" as head of the Church, claiming instead that he is "that Antichrist, the man of sin, and son of perdition, that exalteth himself, in the Church, against Christ and all that is called God."[19]

Other eschatological issues emerge in the answer given to Question 191 in the Larger Catechism. Dealing with the second petition of the Lord's Prayer ("Thy kingdom come"). In a clear reference to Romans 9-11, the answer includes references to the propagation of the gospel, the calling of the Jews, the gathering of the fullness of the Gentiles and that Christ "would be pleased so to exercise the kingdom of his power in all the world."

A cursory glance at the Standards reveal that the area delineated by futuristic eschatology is personal in nature, dealing as it does with resurrection and judgment, rather than the Second Coming as such. It is, on one level, surprising that the Confession expresses no opinion regarding the Millennium, particularly so since many of its contributors had pronounced views on the matter. George Gillespie, one of the Scottish commissioners to the Assembly, preaching before Parliament on 27 March 1644, chose for his text Ezekiel 43:11, a prophecy concerning the rebuilding of the Temple after the Babylonian exile. Unfolding the text, Gillespie saw a reference to the inauguration of an age of righteousness which would accompany the overthrow of the

---

[19] There appear to be occasions where the Westminster Standards are not wholly consistent with themselves, evidence of the committee structure which lay behind their production. Churches committed to the generic Calvinism of the Confession (e.g. in the USA: the Orthodox Presbyterian, and the Presbyterian Church in America; and in the UK: the Evangelical Presbyterian Church of Ireland), have detected a too-specifically seventeenth century orientation in its identification of the Pope as the antichrist.

It may be asked whether such a specific interpretation of a biblical prophecy is not itself an application of Scripture which goes beyond the doctrinal substance of Scripture and therefore is not only unique in the Confession (the fulfilment of no other NT prophecy receives such specific identification), but also transgresses the Confession's own basic intention.

papacy. With calculations taken directly from the Book of Revelation, Gillespie suggested that 1643 might be the very year in which that new age was to have begun. Although he did not claim to know the exact time of "the rebuilding of this temple," he did claim that "if we reckon from the time that power of the Beast did begin, and withal consider the great revolution and turning of things upside downe in these our dayes, certainly the work is upon the wheele . . . the day of vengeance upon Antichrist, is coming, and is not farre off."[20]

For men like Gillespie, and he was not alone in the belief, the calling of the Westminster Assembly was the first step in the inauguration of the latter day glory. We shall return to this later, but for now it needs to be underlined that, despite such beliefs, great caution was exercised by the Divines in formulating eschatological pronouncements. As R. L. Dabney noted: "Our divines find in the Scriptures the clearest assertions of Christ's second advent, and so they teach it most positively. They find Paul describing with equal clearness one resurrection of the saved and lost just before this glorious second advent and general judgment. So they refuse to sanction a pre-millennial advent. But what is the nature, and what the duration, of that millennial glory predicted in the Apocalypse? Here the Assembly will not dogmatize, because these unfulfilled prophecies are obscure to our feeble minds. It is too modest to dictate a belief amidst so many different opinions."[21]

We now turn our attention to an examination of Chapters 32 and 33 of the Confession together with their parallel statements in the Catechisms.

---

[20] John I. Morgans, "The National & International Aspects of Puritan Eschatology, 1640-1666. A Comparative Study" (Unpublished Ph.D. dissertation, Hartford Seminary Foundation, 1969), 25-26.

[21] *The Westminster Confession and Creeds* (Presbyterian Heritage Publications: Dallas, Texas, 1983), 14.

The Death and Resurrection of the Body

The existence of life after death, whilst fundamental to Scripture and the Westminster Standards, has been of little or no importance to radical theologians of the twentieth century. Schubert Ogden (a process theologian) argues: "What I must refuse to accept, precisely as a Christian theologian, is that belief in our continued existence after death is in some way a necessary article of Christian belief."[22] And Rudolf Bultman could say: "I don't know anything about immortality. The only thing we can know is that our earthly life ends with death. Whether there is another life after this one, we don't know." Paul Tillich argued that there is no immortality in the sense of conscious existence beyond the grave. Only the power of love is immortal and we participate in that love by the return of our self to God.[23] The contrast with the Westminster Standards could hardly be more pronounced.

Several issues are dealt with in this chapter of the Confession, including death, the intermediate state and the resurrection body.

Death

Reflecting the specific language of Hebrews 9:27 and Romans 6:23 and 5:12, death is viewed as a certainty for *all* men; it is sin's *wages*: "Death being threatened as the wages of sin, it is appointed unto all men once to die; for that all have sinned" (LC 84).[24] Death is penal; it is God's judgment upon sin, specifically,

---

[22] Schubert Ogden, *The Reality of God and Other Essays* (New York: Harper & Row, 1966), 229-230, cited by Donald G. Bloesch, *Essentials of Evangelical Theology*, Vol. 2: "Life, Ministry and Hope" (New York:Harper & Row, 1979), 178.

[23] Cited by Bloesch, 204-205.

[24] Whereas it might be thought biblically correct for us say that "all men die apart from those who are alive at the time of Christ's return" (echoing the thought of 1 Thess. 4:16-17), the Catechism makes no mention of Christ's Return at this point.

original sin. Having outlined the misery brought upon all mankind by the fall, including that we are made "liable to all punishments in this world" (LC 27), these punishments include "death itself" (LC 28; SC 19). But it is not only original sin but actual sin that is the cause of death (cf. WCF 6.6: "Every sin, both original and actual, being a transgression of the righteous law of God, and contrary thereunto, doth, in its own nature, bring guilt upon the sinner, whereby he is bound over to the wrath of God , and the curse of the law, and so made subject to death, with all miseries spiritual, temporal, and eternal"). Death (physical as well as spiritual) was God's covenantal curse for Adam's disobedience in the Garden of Eden.[25]

Death is the dissolving of the union between spirit and body: "The bodies of men, after death, return to dust and see corruption: but their souls, which neither die nor sleep, having an immortal subsistence, immediately return to God who gave them . . ." (WCF 32.1; cf. the language of Ecc. 12:7, "the dust returns to the ground it came from, and the spirit returns to God who gave it"). In so doing, God partly un-does what he did at creation when he made man "of the dust of the ground" (LC 17; c.f. Gen. 2:7). Thus death is the severing of two realities which comprise man: body and soul.

Shall all men die? The Larger Catechism answers in the affirmative: "Death being threatened as the wages of sin, it is appointed unto all men once to die; for that all have sinned"[26]

---

[25] The relationship between eschatology and the covenant needs investigating here. Adam was placed under a "covenant of works" (WCF 7.2), or "covenant of life" (SC 12). In his fall, Adam "fell from . . . original righteousness and communion with God, and so became dead in sin, and wholly defiled in all the parts and faculties of soul and body" (WCF 6.2). Had he obeyed the terms of that covenant, it is implied that he would have been confirmed in his original "knowledge, righteousness and holiness" (c.f. SC 10).

[26] The answer is a general one, and does not deny that those who are still alive at the time of Christ's second coming will not die but be immediately translated into Christ's presence (c.f. 1 Thess 4:17; 1 Cor. 15:51-52).

(LC 84). Of interest here is the following question in the Larger Catechism, which asks why it is that Christians are not spared death, seeing that their sins have been atoned for by Christ. The answer given alludes to the fact that death is still advantageous to the believer: "The righteous shall be delivered from death itself at the last day, and even in death are delivered from the sting and curse of it; so that, although they die, yet it is out of God's love, to free them perfectly from sin and misery, and to make them capable of further communion with Christ in glory, which they then enter upon" (LC 85).

Only two are known to have escaped death (Enoch and Elijah); the rest of mankind are not delivered from death apart from those who remain alive at Christ's second coming. What are the advantages? Two are mentioned: i. The sting of death is removed. Death need hold no fear to the justified, for they are assured that death cannot separate them from Christ's love (Rom. 8:38). ii. Their dying is an instance of God's love to them, for through death they are delivered from every last trace of sin and remaining corruption, "the remnants of sin abiding in every part of them" (LC 78). Unless all traces of remaining sin are removed, the believer cannot enjoy the blessedness of the intermediate state. Flesh and blood cannot inherit the kingdom of God (1 Cor. 15:50). The "perishable must clothe itself with the imperishable" (1 Cor. 15:53). This is not to say that the nature of life beyond death will not be physical; rather, it is saying that we cannot in our present body-soul existence inherit the full nature of the blessings of the life to come. Our present bodies need to be changed. In the words of J. A. Schep: "(Man's) human nature must first be changed so that he will be able to live in a world which is completely different from this present world: a new world in which sin, weakness, and death are unknown, where procreation of the human race is no longer needed, where there is no marriage, where the continuation of life depends no longer on eating and drinking and digestion, where heaven and earth are united as never before, and God dwells among and in his people with all the fullness of his Spirit (Isa. 33:24; Matt.22:30; 1 Cor. 15:28; Rev. 7:16; 21:1-4)."[27]

Not only the body, but the soul also needs to be changed so as to be "rendered receptive of the divine glory . . . otherwise it could no more receive the immediate rays of the divine glory, than the weak and distempered eye can look steadily on the sun shining in its meridian brightness."[28]

The Intermediate State

Several objections have been raised against the doctrine of the intermediate state. For some, it is viewed as "individualistic," ignoring the implications of redemption for the cosmos itself. Attributing the *Visio Dei* to the intermediate state makes the broader vision superfluous. But this is misguided. True, more could have been said about the "regeneration of all things." The ultimate reconstruction of the universe, the forming of the "new heavens and the new earth" is something which the Westminster Standards have not chosen to focus upon. The fact, however, that such an emphasis on cosmic renewal *is* biblical does not negate the truth of personal and immediate translation of the believer's soul into the presence of Christ at death.

Of greater import is the anthropological objection which protests against the existence of something incorruptible that survives the death of the body. This, it is argued, is a denial of the psycho-somatic unity of the body. Some have speculated that Paul developed his doctrine of the resurrection, moving away from the possibility of a body-less intermediate state (as envisioned in 1 Corinthians and 1 Thessalonians) to one in which he believed

---

[27] J. A. Schep, *The Nature of the Resurrection Body* (Grand Rapids: Eerdmans, 1964), 204.

[28] Thomas Ridgeley, *Commentary on the Larger Catechism*, Vol. 2 (Edmonton: Still Waters Revival Books, 1993), 230.

that the resurrection body would be given immediately at death. This latter view is thought to be what Paul is arguing in 2 Corinthians 5:1-10.

Both Murray Harris and F. F. Bruce have argued that from the time he wrote 2 Corinthians 5:1-10 Paul believed the resurrection body to be received at death.[29] According to this view, at the Second Coming of Christ, what has been until then a hidden state of embodiment, will be openly revealed. There is still an intermediate state, but an embodied one. This view is incompatible with the Westminster standards which envisions a body-*less* intermediate existence.

Behind this notion lie complex discussions on the nature of time and eternity. In the world to come, it is argued, the sense of time ceases to be, so that an *immediate* consciousness with the last day is created.[30] T.F. Torrance, for example, has argued that the concept of time belongs only to this world, and that at death the person does not belong to our space-time framework any more.

---

[29] As opposed to Paul's view expressed in such passages as 1 Cor. 15:51-58 and 1 Thess. 4:13-18, where he envisages the resurrection body only to be available at the parousia. "2 Corinthians 5:1-10: Watershed in Paul's eschatology?," *Tyndale Bulletin* 22, 1071, 32-57; "Paul on Immortality," *Scottish Journal of Theology* 24, 1971, 457-472. See also Murray Harris', *Raised Immortal: Resurrection and Immortality in the New Testament* (Grand Rapids: Eerdmans, 1985), 165-171 where a long list of scholars taking this position is given, prominent among them is F. F. Bruce. In different forms it is the view taken by Karl Barth, Wolfhart Pannenberg, and Eberhard Jungel. Among Roman Catholics it is held by Hans Kung and A. R. van de Walle, a student of Schillebeeckx; cf. John W. Cooper, *Body, Soul & Life Everlasting: Biblical Anthropology and the Monism-Dualism Debate* (Grand Rapids: Eerdmans, 1989), 117; Ralph P. Martin, *2 Corinthians*, Word Biblical Commentary 40 (Word, 1986), 97-99. But such "development" in Paul's thinking about death and the resurrection body is difficult to sustain when, in a later letter than 2 Corinthians, viz. Philippians, the apostle once more expresses the same view as that of 1 Corinthians and 1 Thessalonians, viz. that only at the coming of Christ will he 'transform our lowly bodies so that they will be like his glorious body' (Phil 3:20, 21).

[30] Cf. the discussion by Berkouwer, *Return of Christ*, 40ff.

Thus when a believer dies he goes to be with Christ and receives his resurrection body. The interval of time between death and resurrection is apparent only from this world's reference point. From the perspective of those who pass on, there is no consciousness of an interval of time.[31]

A brief consideration of 2 Corinthians 5:1-10 will prove helpful here.

2 Corinthians 5:1-10

The section 2 Cor. 4:16-5:10 forms a single unit in which the apostle contemplates that "outwardly" he is "wasting away" (4:16), and that, because of "light and momentary troubles" (4:17). However, in the balance of things, he assures himself that these troubles "are preparing for us an eternal glory that far outweighs them all" (4:17). We need to "fix our eyes on what we cannot see" (4:17). It is then a natural sequence for him to go on to explain to us what he expects to occur when "the earthly tent we live in is destroyed" (5:1).

Referring to the human body as a "earthly tent," Paul asserts that even if it is destroyed we have the assurance of a resurrected body, "an eternal house in heaven, not built by human hands" (5:1). The temporary (the tent) is replaced by the permanent (a house from God). Currently, in this life, "we groan."[32] Present

---

[31] T. F. Torrance, *Space, Time and Resurrection* (Edinburgh: T & T Clark, 1976), 102. Stephen Travis believes that this view involves the "fewest difficulties," *Christian Hope and the Future of Man* (Leicester: IVP, 1980), 112. Others, notably Oscar Cullmann have objected to this concept of eternity, wishing to think of it instead as "endless time." J. A. Schep has also spoken of "a future existence in space and time" as "self-evident." *The Nature of the Resurrection Body* (Grand Rapids: Eerdmans, 1964), 214. See also Paul Helm, *God and Time* (Edinburgh: Paternoster, 2002; *Eternal God: A Study of God Without Time* (Oxford: Claredon Press, 1997).

[32] The same word as in Romans 8:23. Indeed, the whole section of Rom. 8:18-24 is parallel to 2 Cor. 5:1-10.

suffering makes us long for the eschatological completeness of the resurrected body. Paul pictures it as akin to putting on a garment (5:3). The longing is not for the intermediate state of being unclothed, but the final state of resurrected embodiment (5:4).[33] Using two metaphors Paul emphasizes this point: first, he wishes to put on extra clothing to cover the garments already being worn (5:4);[34] and second, he views the "mortal" (i.e., this

---

[33] Paul is establishing a contrast: *first* of being "unclothed," and *then* (at some future point) being "clothed," and *second* of being clothed upon *immediately* (with no experience of being "unclothed"). And the apostle expresses a preference for the latter. As Geerhardus Vos comments: "The preference is a strong one. Under the influence of the uncertainty of its decision Paul groans. Now the question arises: Does this situation fit the case of the bestowal of a new body at the moment of death or the case of the bestowal of it at the parousia? In answer let us make clear to ourselves that the groaning and the strong preference become entirely unintelligible, if we conceive Paul thinking of both members of this alternative as attached to the moment of death. For, how could the resolution of such an alternative *in articulo mortis* become to him a matter of burdensome uncertainty?' By way of an answer, Vos suggests that the real question in Paul's mind is: "would there be or would there not be awaiting him in the near future a *protracted* state of being unclothed, that is 'naked' between his possible death and the arrival of the parousia? The uncertainty, therefore, arising from this can not stand in direct contradiction to the 'we know' in v.1; in other words 'we know' can not, consistently with what follows, carry the meaning: we know that we receive a new body *at the time of death*. Such a conviction would from the outset have rendered all subsequent burdensomeness and groaning out of place." *The Pauline Eschatology*, 190-191.

[34] The NIV simply has "to be clothed with our heavenly dwelling," but this is inadequate. Paul wishes to be "further clothed," "to be clothed *upon*." It is this expression 'further clothed' (*ependusasthai*), "like putting a top-coat over a suit" (P. Hughes, *The True Image*, 396) that begs the question for some: clothed upon *what*? Is Paul anticipating that even at death there is some kind of body, albeit hidden and imperfect, but nevertheless real. Is Paul saying something like, "Even in the event of death and before the general resurrection, we shall not be found absolutely naked?" Confirmation of this is sometimes sought in the fact that Abraham and Lazarus, in Jesus' parable (Luke 16:19-31), exist in bodily form; to white robes given to the martyrs (Rev. 6:11); and the fact that the great multitude in heaven are similarly clothed, having palms in their hands (Rev. 7:9). According to E. A. Litton,

earthly body) as being "swallowed up of life" (i.e., being taken into and transformed by the new order of existence). This is Paul's expectation; it is a confidence based on the certainty of what God has revealed to him (5:6). Even though God may ask him to live in this world a while longer, with all its attendant suffering, Paul is not discouraged, even though he cannot see God in this condition: "as long as we are at home in the body we are away from the Lord. We live by faith, not by sight" (5:6).

Paul's expectation of an immediate transformation following death to a bodily existence, albeit spiritual, can only be fulfilled if he is still alive when Jesus returns. He views that prospect as preferable to that of dying before the parousia. But, Paul is equally sure that it is perfectly possible that he may die before the parousia. Even so, he still expresses the desire to die and pass into the intermediate state: he "would prefer to be away from the body (i.e., death, and in a disembodied state) and at home with the Lord" (5:8).[35] This condition is to be preferred to remaining alive, something which he describes as "being away from the Lord" (5:6). Being "at home with the Lord" (5:8) can hardly refer to the resurrection. As Vos explains: ". . . he would scarcely have expressed himself precisely thus, had he meant that immediately another body would be substituted, for the state in such a body would hardly be describable as the state of one absent from the body."[36]

"to set down all this to poetic imagery is to push the principle of symbolism too far." *Introduction to Dogmatic Theology* (London: T & T Clark, 1960), 564. But as Philip Hughes makes clear in an editorial footnote to the third edition of this work: "to take the visions of the Apocalypse in a literalistic rather than a symbolical sense leads to all kinds of difficulties. Even so, the great multitude of Rev. 7:9 can surely only apply to the multitude of the redeemed *after* they have experienced the resurrection of the body; whereas Rev. 6:9-11 refers specifically to the *souls* of the martyrs." 564 n 2.

[35] Both verbs, "away from" and "present with" are aorist infinitives, signifying once-for-all events.

[36] G. Vos, *The Pauline Eschatology*, 194. Cf. Herman Ridderbos, *Paul: An Outline of His Theology* (Grand Rapids: Eerdmans, 1975), 499-508.

Thus, in 2 Corinthians 5:1-10, Paul envisages the possibility of a body-*less* existence following his death.

It must also be insisted that for Paul it is the resurrection, and not the intermediate state, that forms the ground of the eschatological hope of every Christian. "However much the certainty with which "to be with Christ" is posited as an indication of the bond between Christ and believers that cannot be broken even by death, yet this expectation apparently does not have an "independent existence" for Paul, but is entirely taken up in the hope of the resurrection, and would not exist without it (cf. 1 Cor. 15:18; 1 Thess. 4:13ff.). Some have wanted indeed to conclude from this that Paul knew nothing of a provisional state of blessedness. Otherwise—so it is said—he would surely have comforted the church with it. But this conclusion is not compelling. All that can be inferred from Paul's reasoning is that without the resurrection there is no hope at all for the deceased believers."[37]

What survives death is the soul (or spirit). The Confession speaks of the soul as "having an immortal subsistence" (WCF 32.1). The "immortality of the soul" has occasioned much debate, and is denied in many quarters.[38] The denial of it stems from three points of view:

i. the expression "immortality of the soul" is liable to objection since God alone is immortal in the strict sense of the word (1 Tim. 6:16). The soul has no innate immortality in and of itself. Its immortality is God-given.[39]

ii. The concept of the immortality of the soul is prejudiced by its association with the teachings of the mystery religions of ancient

---

[37] H. Ridderbos, *Paul*, 506.

[38] It is true that of the two Greek words translated 'immortality', *athanasia* and *aphtharsia*, neither is used of the immortality of the *soul*. See, A. A. Hoekema, *The Bible and the Future*, 87-88.

[39] Calvin comment on 1 Timothy 6:16, a passage which suggests that God alone possesses immortality, is: "strictly speaking, immortality does not subsist in the nature of souls, . . . but comes from another source, namely the secret inspiration of God." *Commentary on 1 Timothy,* ad loc.

Greece, and the philosophical expressions of Plato in particular. A view was formulated in which the body was thought to be inferior to the soul—the soul being the rational, and therefore the *real* part of man. The body, according to this view, is the soul's tomb, and death is the soul's release from its incarceration.[40]

iii. The immortality which biblical revelation supports is not that of the soul only, but one which is integrally connected with the body also. Man, as created by God, is essentially a corporeal-spiritual entity. When God warned Adam not to eat of the forbidden tree in Eden, the threat of death applied not merely to his body, thereby suggesting that Adam's soul was untouchable by virtue of some inherent immortality. Some have objected that the intermediate state limits the judgment of God upon sin to the body only. The translation of the soul immediately into God's presence seems to imply that the soul possesses an immunity to the retributive juridical demands of the Fall.[41] "There is no suggestion that a part of him was undying and therefore that his dying would be in part only."[42]

Given this background, it is readily understandable that those wishing to defend biblical truth have sought to distance themselves from the notion of the soul's immortality, particularly since the Bible insists upon the reunion of body and soul in the future resurrection. It is also pointless to deny the influence of Hellenistic philosophy on the Church Fathers. Gregory of Nyssa, for example, argued that since the soul is simple, and not composite, it is incapable of disintegration.

The Westminster divines, though no doubt aware of these philosophical aberrations, nevertheless defended the use of the

---

[40] See *Body Soul & Life Everlasting: Biblical Anthopology and the Monism-Dualism Debate*, by John W. Cooper (Grand Rapids: Eerdmans, 1989), 42-43. Cooper goes to state: "Affirming continuous personal existence does not necessarily commit one to the soul's inherent or essential immortality." 216.

[41] This is the line taken by Helmut Thielicke.

[42] *The True Image: The Origin and Destiny of Man in Christ* (Grand Rapids: Eerdmans, 1989), 400.

term "immortal subsistence" when referring to the soul. The expression is not without its critics. Philip Hughes, for example, thinks the language of the Confession "may be overdogmatic."[43] Some were, no doubt, aware of Calvin's defense of the expression. We may even see traces of philosophical bias in Calvin. He speaks of the soul as man's "nobler part."[44] And sometimes Calvin speaks of the soul, and not the body, as the image of God.[45]

The criticism is, however, without any real foundation. Calvin, who does not appear to be altogether consistent regarding the image of God in man, insists in the *Institutes* that even in man's body "some sparks" of God's image glow.[46] The point being made by the Confession is that *something* survives physical death, and that something is man's soul, the conscious existence of personality in the intermediate state between death and resurrection. The denial of the soul's immortality, then, is indeed, as Calvin suggests at one point, a "brutish error."[47] The soul is not immortal by some inherent indestructibility, or even superiority. This, the Confession denies by

---

[43] Ibid., 394.

[44] *Institutes* 1.15.2.

[45] "Three gradations, indeed, are to be noted in the creation of man; that his dead body was formed out of the dust of the earth; that it was endued with a soul, whence it should receive vital motion; and that on this soul God engraved his own image, to which immortality is annexed." *Commentary on Genesis* 2:7, (Grand Rapids: Baker, 1981) 112. Though it must be noted that earlier, in a comment on Genesis 1:26, Calvin says: "Thus the chief seat of the Divine image was in his mind and heart, where it was eminent: yet was there no part of him in which some scintillations of it did not shine forth." 95.

[46] *Institutes,* 1.15.3.

[47] Ibid., 3.25.6. Calvin did not, however, understand the soul as possessing immortality by some inalienable right, but rather as a gift given by God. "Strictly speaking therefore," Calvin writes, "immortality does not subsist in the nature of souls or angels, but comes from another source, namely, from the secret inspiration of God. . . ." *Commentaries on The Epistles to Timothy, Titus, and Philemon* (Grand Rapids: Baker 1981), Vol. 21, comment on 1 Timothy 6:16.

linking the concept of the soul's survival of physical death with the prospect of future reunion: "their souls, which neither die nor sleep, having an immortal subsistence, immediately return to God who gave them . . . waiting for the full redemption of their bodies."[48]

That this is in keeping with biblical revelation, we need only consider a few passages. In the first instance, there are the words of Jesus to the dying thief: "I tell you the truth, today you will be with me in paradise" (Luke 23:43). Recent suggestions argue that a change in the punctuation alter the meaning of the statement: "Truly, I say to you today, you will be with me in paradise." This removes the assurance of paradise to a future return of Christ rather than an immediate assurance relating to the intermediate state. Its refutation lies along two lines: firstly, the expression, "Truly I say to you" is a characteristic formula used by Jesus in the gospels, a point which makes it unlikely that he would have

---

[48] Hoekema, following Herman Bavinck and G. C. Berkouwer, is reluctant to talk about the immortality of the soul, preferring, instead, to use the expression of man in general: "If we wish to use the word *immortality* with reference to man, let us say that man, rather than his soul, is immortal. But man's body must undergo a transformation by means of resurrection before he can fully enjoy that immortality." Op. cit., 91. But this formula, too, is not without its difficulties for it implies the idea that both body and soul are immortal, even though the body dies to be resurrected again. This, however, contradicts the meaning of the word 'immortal' (meaning 'not mortal'). The body *is* mortal. It dies. What continues to exist after death is the soul, the on-going person. The soul has a God-given quality that the body does not seem to possess, viz. it survives physical death. For this reason, Reformed theologians have expressed agreement with the notion of an "immortal soul." See A. A. Hodge, *Outlines of Theology* (London: Banner of Truth, 1972), 549; William G. T. Shedd, *Dogmatic Theology* (Grand Rapids: Zondervan, nd.), II, 612; Louis Berkhof, *Systematic Theology* (London: Banner of Truth, 1958), 672-8; R. L. Dabney, *Systematic Theology* (Edinburgh: Banner of Truth, 1985), 64-78.

The immortality of the soul did receive special attention in the Scots Confession of 1560 (Art. XVII). The article is not so much concerned with the nature and character of the soul as such, but with 'the nature of continued existence according to Scripture'. G. C. Berkouwer, *Man: The Image of God* (Grand Rapids: Eerdmans, 1962), 271.

added "today" on this occasion; and secondly, the use of the word "today" in an earlier assertion to Peter clearly belongs, not to the introductory formula, but to the assertion itself: "Truly, I say to you, today—yes, tonight—before the rooster crows twice you yourself will disown me three times" (Mark 14:30).[49] The final word from the cross, "Father, into your hands I commit my spirit" (Luke 23:46) would also teach the continuance of the soul after death, though it tells us nothing of the soul's condition after death. John describes the souls of the martyrs crying out for justice, and being told to rest a little longer "until the number of their fellow servants and brothers who were to be killed as they had been was completed" (Rev. 6:9-11). This indicates that the soul is alive and vigilant in the intermediate state. Jesus' exhortation not to fear "those who kill the body but cannot kill the soul," but to fear rather "the One who can destroy both soul and body in hell" (Matt. 10:28), implies that physical death does not imply soul death, though ultimately both body and soul are "destroyed" in hell (that this does not imply annihilation we shall take up below). In addition to 2 Cor. 5:1-10, other passages which confirm this teaching include Paul's desire to "depart and be with Christ" (Phil. 1:24), implying a conscious, even blissful existence, one that is "better" than his present condition.

What happens to the soul after death? The Confession gives a clear answer: "the souls of the righteous, being then made perfect in holiness, are received into the highest heavens, where they behold the face of God, in light and glory, waiting for the full redemption of their bodies. And the souls of the wicked are cast into hell, where they remain in torments and utter darkness, reserved to the judgment of the great day." Several issues are raised by this statement.

---

[49] See, Hughes, Op. cit., 395

Soul-sleep

We have already seen how the Confession insists upon the *conscious* existence of the soul after death. Answer 85 of the Larger Catechism refers to the righteous entering into "communion with Christ in glory" following their death, using the expression "which they then enter upon." The temporal reference, "then," implies an immediacy of consciousness, thus denying any possibility of "soul-sleep."[50]

If the soul of man cannot die; neither can it sleep. The denial of soul-sleep ("their souls, which neither die nor sleep" [WCF 32.1]) needs to be understood in the light of controversies current in the period following the Reformation. The 1553 edition of the Articles of Religion of the Church of England, asserted that those who hold "that the souls of such as depart hence do sleep, being without all sense, feeling, or perceiving until the day of judgment, or affirm that the souls die with the bodies, and at the last day shall be raised up with the same, do utterly dissent from the right belief declared to us in Holy Scripture."

The doctrine was taught by some Anabaptists at the time of the Reformation and strongly refuted by Calvin.[51] It was also

---

[50] The WCF (32.1) and the LC (86) are clearer still, both using the word "immediately" to refer to the conscious existence of the soul with God in fellowship after death.

[51] Soul-sleep had been taught by the Thenopsychites of the third century, and revived by the Anabaptists during the Reformation. Presumably, the Divines were aware of Calvin's attack on soul-sleep in *Psychopannychia*. Written in 1534 in Orléans, and later published in Strasbourg in 1542, the treatise condemned the notion of soul-sleep which had already been condemned by the Fifth Lateran Council in 1513, but continued to have its supporters, particularly amongst the Anabaptists. In *Psychopannychia*, Calvin refers to the heresy of pope John XXII (1316-1334) that the souls of departed saints are not permitted to see the Beatific vision until the resurrection. The issue is briefly alluded to in the *Institutes* (3.25.6). Calvin's point is to suggest that the soul is a "substance," that after death it lives in a state of consciousness (with feeling and rationality). See, W. de Greef, *The Writings of John Calvin: An Introductory Guide*, Trefecca Estate. Lyle D. Bierma (Grand Rapids: Baker, 1989), 165-167.

taught by some Irvingites in the nineteenth century. Support for the doctrine comes from the fact that Scripture does refer to death as "sleep" (Matt. 9:24; 27:52; John 11:11; Acts 7:60; 13:36; 1 Cor. 15:6, 18, 20, 51; 1 Thess. 4:13; 5:10). Then again, certain passages do seem to indicate that the dead are not conscious of their existence (Psa. 6:5; 115:17; Ecc. 9:10; Isa. 38:19).

All these passages are thinking of life from the perspective of this world. It appears to us that the dead, in their graves, do not any longer receive blessings from God, nor give praise to God in return. That this is not the case is manifest in Psalm 115, for after positing this idea: "The dead do not praise the Lord" he goes on in the very next verse to add, "But we will bless the Lord from this time forth and for evermore" (Psa. 115:17-18).

Mention might also be made at this point of the expression "the communion of saints," an expression which followed the doctrine of the church in the Apostles' Creed, and only briefly alluded to in the Westminster documents, not in the Confession's statement on the church (Chap. 25), but in the Larger Catechism's answer to the question, *What are the special privileges of the visible church?* one of which is the enjoyment of the communion of saints (LC 63). This has usually been understood to be a reference affirming the real union of the church "militant here in earth" with the church triumphant, as indicated in Hebrews 12:22-24. In one sense we have a communion with those saints who have died, confirming that whilst we may not be aware of them in any way, our worship here on earth is joined to theirs in heaven. This is evidently not in harmony with a notion of soul-sleep.

Purgatory

The fact that the souls of *all* believers go immediately into God's presence, and that the souls of *all* unbelievers (the "wicked") "are cast into hell, where they remain in torments and utter darkness, reserved to the judgment of the great day" (WCF

32.1), means that there is no such thing as purgatory. The Confession adds a rider: "Besides these two places, for souls separated from their bodies, the Scripture acknowledgeth none." The decisiveness of this pronouncement is all the more noteworthy in view of Augustine's ambivalence over the issue.[52]

At the time of the Assembly, the Church of Rome had accepted the teaching of the Council of Florence (1439), and the Council of Trent (1545-63) endorsing the existence of purgatory.[53] In Roman Catholic theology, purgatory was (and is) a place of *punishment* designed to purify the soul and prepare it for God's final acceptance. According to Romanist dogma, only a few (e.g., the martyrs) are spared purgatory. Whilst those who die in mortal sin, and in a state of impenitence, go to hell, the vast majority, who die in state of grace, must endure the pains of purgatory. Their time in purgatory can be shortened by the works of the living. Prayers[54] and almsgiving can be made for them, and a requiem mass can be offered on their behalf.[55] And the selling of pardoning indulgences on behalf of the dead was a major concern of the Reformation.

---

[52] Augustine thought it not improbable that an intermediate state of purgatorial cleansing may be provided. *Enchiridion*, 109. The view was developed in the Middle Ages by Thomas Aquinas, *Summa Theologica*, Supp.3, q. 69, Art. 2.

[53] The Council of Florence stated that "If any have departed this life in penitence and love of God, before they have made satisfaction for their sins of omission and commission by fruits worthy of repentance their souls are purified after death by purgatorial punishments." The Twenty-fifth Session, on the Decree on Purgatory, of the Council of Trent, whilst admitting certain abuses in the presentation of the dogma, still maintained that "there is a Purgatory and that the souls detained in it are benefited by the prayers of the faithful and especially by the sacrifice of the altar."

[54] Praying for the dead is specifically forbidden in Answer 183 of the Larger Catechism: "For whom are we to pray? *A*. We are to pray for . . . ; but not for dead. . . ."

[55] The "popish sacrifice of the mass" is described in the Confession as "most abominably injurious to Christ's one, only sacrifice, the alone propitiation for all the sins of His elect" (Chap. 29.2).

Appeal was made by Catholic theologians to the apocryphal books, particularly 2 Maccabees, to justify their belief in purgatory. The Confession roundly dismisses their authority: "The books commonly called Apocrypha, not being of divine inspiration, are no part of the canon of the Scripture, and therefore are of no authority in the Church of God, nor to be any otherwise approved, or made use of, than other human writings" (WCF 1.3).[56]

---

[56] The appeal is made to 2 Maccabbes 12:46, a reference to the discovery of some idolatrous symbols of worship under the clothes of some Jewish soldiers who had died in battle. Judas Maccabeus, the leader of the Jewish forces, sent money (2,000 drachmas of silver) to Jerusalem for sacrifice to be offered for the sins of the dead and the comment is added: 'It is therefore a holy and wholesome thought to pray for the dead, that they may loosed from sins.' But this statement proves too much. These men, according to Roman Catholic standards, had died of mortal sin, and as such faced the penalty of hell. Purgatory is only for those who die in penitence and love for God.

The contemporary Catholic theologian, Ludwig Ott, finds support for the doctrine in certain NT passages also. When Paul says, concerning Onesiphorus, "May the Lord grant him to find mercy from the Lord on that Day" (2 Tim. 1:18), it is claimed that Onesiphorus was dead at the time—a claim based on the fact that Paul greets, not Onesiphorus himself, but his 'household' (2 Tim. 1:16). The statement proves nothing except that Paul wished blessing on the entire household of Onesiphorus! Yet another line of reasoning stems from our Lord's words in Matthew 12:32, where Jesus says, "Whoever speaks against the Holy Spirit will not be forgiven, either in this age or in the age to come," leaving open the possibility, according to Ott, that some sins are forgiven in the age to come. This reasoning is false: to say that something will not happen in the age to come does not imply that it might happen in the age to come. Appeal is also made to 1 Corinthians 3:15, where Paul speaks of the judging (testing) of every man's work on the Day of judgement *by fire*. But this takes place at the day of Judgement, as the context makes clear, and can hardly refer to the intermediate time spent in purgatory. Attempts have also been made to understand Peter's preaching "to the spirits in prison" (1 Pet. 3:19) as having some reference to purgatory, but again the context refers to a small group of people the disobedient in the time of Noah. Peter selects this group, no doubt recalling something Jesus himself had said in the Olivet Discourse (Matt. 24:37), to draw a parallel between the day of Noah and the Judgment Day. Just as Christ preached through Noah to a disobedient people who were judged, and are (in Peter's day) dead (i.e., spirits in prison), so all those who reject Christ's on-going preaching through the ages can expect to be judged at the End. It has nothing whatsoever to do with purgatory. See, Ludwig Ott, *Fundamentals of Catholic Dogma*, ed. James Canon Bastible. Trans. Patrick Lynch (St. Louis: Herder, 1955).

Limbus Patrum

There have been those who have held the view that the souls of those who died *before* the resurrection of Christ went to a place of waiting, called the *limbus patrum*.[57] It is held by Roman Catholics that Christ in his soul after death went into the *limbus patrum* in order to announce to the Old Testament saints the salvation which he had procured by his sufferings and to lead them victoriously from the that shadowy abode to the full glory of heaven.[58] The Scriptures, however, teach that the Old Testament saints entered immediately into their glory: e.g., the position of Abraham in the parable of the rich man and Lazarus (Luke 16:22); the reference to the departure of Enoch (Gen. 5:24; cf. Heb. 11:5), and Elijah (2 Kings 2:11—Elijah appears talking with Jesus on the Mount of Transfiguration, Matt. 17:3); and in answer to the scepticism of the Sadducees over the resurrection, Jesus insisted that God had said, "I am the God of Abraham, and the God of Isaac, and the God of Jacob," the present tenses implying "He is not the God of the dead, but of the living" (Matt. 22:32).

---

[57] Catholic dogma has traditionally distinguished between *limbus infantum*, a place where all unbaptized infants go when they die, and *limbus patrum,* were all Old Testament believers went when they died. On the matter of the death of infants generally, the Westminster Confession asserts that "elect infants, dying in infancy, are regenerated, and saved by Christ, through the Spirit, who worketh when, and where, and how he pleaseth" (Chap.10.3).

[58] There are interpretations of Peter's reference to Christ's preaching to the "spirits in prison" (1 Pet. 3:19) that come very close to a *limbus patrum* view.

The souls of believers go immediately into God's presence

Having refuted several matters, we must now turn out attention to what the Westminster symbols *do* say as regards the state of the soul after death. This is described by the Larger Catechism as "communion in glory with Christ (A. 86) which is further expounded in terms of four features:

1. the souls of the righteous are made "perfect in holiness";
2. they are received into the "highest heavens";
3. they experience the beatific vision, beholding "the face of God";
4. it is a state of waiting for the full redemption of their bodies.

1. The souls of the righteous as made "perfect in holiness" after death[59]

It is the testimony of Hebrews 12:23 that believers who have departed this life have been perfected.[60] Roman Catholic interpreters have insisted on the necessity of purgatory for two reasons: to discharge outstanding debts from this life (thus calling into question the sufficiency of the atonement), and to further cleanse the soul from those sinful tendencies with which it leaves this life. Purgatory is not only *forensic*, it is also a means of purification. The fact that the soul is made perfect in holiness is meant to counter this notion. But does this imply that no development of any kind can be attributed to the soul in the intermediate state? The answer is surely negative. Deficiencies can be supplied and weaknesses strengthened without any predication of sin (in the same as Christ is said to have grown in wisdom in his youth, Luke 2:40). Progress and regression are both possible in the intermediate state.

---

[59] (the same expression in all three documents: WCF 32.1; LC 86; SC 37).

[60] τετελειωμένων perfect passive participle of τελειόω (I complete) implying a *lasting* effect.

2. **They are received into the "highest heavens"**

There is a denial here of a view prevalent amongst several of the Church Fathers (including Irenaeus, Tertullian, Epiphanius, Methodius, as well as Jewish writers, e.g., Philo) namely, that the souls of believers at death enter into paradise, but not the "highest heavens." This they do only after the reunion of the glorified body with the soul. The Savior's words to the dying thief: "Today you will be with me in paradise" are understood to imply a difference of meaning between "paradise" and "heaven." Some affirm that the Savior's soul went to paradise after death, but only to heaven following the resurrection.[61]

Amongst the Fathers who adopted this notion was Tertullian, who describes 'paradise' as a place of divine pleasure, encircled by fire designed to keep the wicked out. Others, like Origen, believed "paradise" to be located somewhere on the earth's surface, and the pseudopigraphical writers assumed it to be identical in location to the original garden of Eden.[62] It is thought that this is what Paul refers to when he speaks of being "caught up into paradise" (2 Cor. 12:1); when he speaks, in addition, of having had "visions and revelations" it is supposed that the "vision" is of the glory of heaven and that the "revelation" is of paradise. This seems unwarrantable, for the apostle speaks of being "caught up" into (*as far as*) "the third heaven" (12:2) and in a parallel statement, of being "caught up" into "paradise" (12:4; in both instances the verb is ἁρπάζω "to take by force, carry off"). Thus, it would appear that Paul is describing one experience, not two. As Philip Hughes describes it: "Paradise, then, is not

---

[61] See, Thomas Ridgeley, *Commentary on the Larger Catechism*, Vol. 2 (Still Waters Revival Books, nd), 240.

[62] See references to the *Gospel of Nicodemus, Revelation of Esdras, Revelation of Paul*, and the *Revelation of Moses*, in *Paul's Second Epistle to the Corinthians*, The New International Commentary on the New Testament, by Philip E. Hughes (Eerdmans: Grand Rapids, 1962), ad. loc.

some shadowy waiting-room, but a blissful abode within the very courts of heaven itself. Its glory is that of the ultimate glory, namely, the glory of the presence of the Son of God (cf. Rev. 7:9ff., 22:1ff.). There, in the Paradise of God, the souls of the saints are at home with Christ, the last Adam (1 Cor. 15:45). There they are beyond the reach of sin and suffering, without fear of being driven out, as happened in the first Paradise. There they await the crowning consummation of their redemption, which is the union of soul and resurrection body, when the new heavens and the new earth will be introduced and all God's purposes in creation finally and eternally fulfilled."[63]

3. The *Visio Dei*, or "Beatific Vision"

The souls of the departed are said to "behold the face of God, in light and glory . . ." (WCF 32.1). The language reflects specific New Testament promises to this effect: "Blessed are the pure in heart, for they will see God" (Matt.5:8); "Dear friends, now we are children of God, and what we will be has not yet been made known. But we know that when he appears, we shall be like him, for we shall see him as he is" (1 John 3:2). There is a connection between what we now "see" and what we shall "then" see, as the answer to Question 82 of the Larger Catechism makes clear: "*What is the communion in glory which the members of the invisible church have with Christ?* The communion in glory which the members of the invisible church have with Christ, is in this life, immediately after death, and at last perfected at the resurrection day of judgment." Nevertheless the difference between the two is characterised as the difference between the "imperfect" and "perfection;" between knowing "in part" and knowing "fully;" between seeing one's reflection in a mirror "dimly" and "face to face" (cf. 1 Cor.13:10-12). The beatific vision is an "unveiling," an apocalypse of God.

---

[63] Op. cit., 438.

But is it ever possible to see God? Does not the Confession speak of God as being essentially *invisible*? God is "a most pure spirit, invisible, without body, parts, or passions . . ." (WCF 2.2), reflecting as it does Paul's very word in 1 Timothy 1:17: "Now to the King eternal, immortal, *invisible*, the only God, be honour and glory for ever and ever. Amen." According to the apostle John: "No one has ever seen God" (Jn. 1:18; cf. 1 Jn. 4:12). Paul takes it to the limit when he says of God, "whom no one has seen or can see" (1 Tim. 6:16). In addition there was a certain dread of seeing God: thus Gideon, and Manoah and his wife pointed out the dangers for sinners beholding the face of God (Judges 6:22; 13:22). Yet, Scripture is full of references to folk who *have* seen God, "seen," that is, in some way or another. Thus, God spoke "to Moses face to face, as a man speaks to his friend" (Exod. 33:11). At one point we are told that he saw God's "form" (Numb. 12:8). What was it that Moses saw is made clear, however, in that he was told that he could not see God's "face" but only his "back," as Moses was hidden in the cleft of a rock as the glory of the Lord passed by (Exod. 33:20). Whilst, essentially, God could not be seen, *something* of God was manifested so as to be visible to certain individuals. What is seen in all these cases is left indistinct. Their eyes were open, but God appears under the form of a cloud (cf. Exod. 34:5; 1 Kings 8:11).

Under the Old Covenant, God revealed Himself, little by little, by human analogy and theophany. In Jesus Christ, however, we have One who *exegetes* God to us: No one has ever seen God, but God the One and Only, who is at the Father's side, has made him known (literally, "exegetes" John 1:18). He is "the radiance of God's glory and the exact representation of [God's] being" (Heb. 1:3).

How will we see God in heaven? We shall never be able to "see" or "know" all of God, for God is essentially incomprehensible (Psa. 154:3; cf. John 6:46; 1 Tim. 1:17; 6:16; 1 John 4:12). We shall see the human nature of Jesus (Rev. 1:7). But how will we be able to "see" the divine nature of God the Son, as well as the Father and the Holy Spirit? (cf. Rev. 1:4; 4:2-3,5; 5:6).[64]

4. A state of waiting for the full redemption of the body

Does the Confession not imply that it is the soul that is conscious of *waiting*? Calvin affirms that there is already an "enjoyment of promised glory" yet there is not total fulfilment. For man to be complete, even in a state of glorification, there needs to be a body. Until body and soul are reunited, the condition is one of "waiting" and "wanting." "All things are held in suspense until Christ the Redeemer appear."[65] Calvin admits that "it is difficult to believe that bodies, when consumed with rottenness, will at length be raised up in their season."[66] But, Calvin goes on to add, "Scripture provides two helps by which faith may overcome this great obstacle: one in the parallel of Christ's resurrection; the other in the omnipotence of God."

This leads us, then, to consider the nature of the resurrection body.

The Resurrection Body

When Christ returns the general resurrection will take place; the dead in Christ will be raised and those in Christ who are still alive will be changed, "in a flash" (1 Cor. 15:52). Every believer will be transformed, whether alive or dead. The Confession posits an identity between our bodies, as they are now, and as they will be after the resurrection: "all the dead shall be raised up, with the self-same bodies, and none other (although with different qualities)" (33.2). Behind this statement is the idea that we have

---

[64] cf. the comment of Wayne Grudem: "Perhaps the nature of this 'seeing' will not be known until we reach heaven." *Systematic Theology*, 189.

[65] 3.25.6.

[66] 3.25.3.

already been given an example of the resurrection of the body. Our Lord was the firstfruits of the general harvest of bodies to be raised at the Last Day. Paul speaks of the time when God "will transform our lowly bodies so that they will be like his glorious body" (Phil. 3:21). This connection between our resurrection body and Christ's is crucial, for, as Calvin says: "whenever we consider the resurrection, let Christ's image come before us . . . he is the pledge of our resurrection."[67] Thus, the Larger Catechism speaks: "the self-same bodies of the dead which were laid in the grave, being then again united to their souls for ever, shall be raised up by the power of Christ . . . by virtue of his resurrection as their head, shall be raised in power, spiritual, incorruptible, and made like to his glorious body" (LC 87; cf. WCF 32.3 which speaks of the bodies of the just being "made conformable to [Christ's] own glorious body").

This is in complete harmony with the testimony of Scripture as a consideration of 1 Corinthians 15:12-19 will make clear.

1 Corinthians 15:12-19

The entire argument rests on the connection between Christ's resurrection and that of believers. If Christ has been raised, the general resurrection cannot be denied (v.12) Why not? Because of the organic unity between Christ and his people. Most graphically, in 1 Cor. 15:20, Christ is "firstfruits of those who are asleep" (cf. v. 23). The background lies in Old Testament offerings of grain, wine, cattle etc. (Exod. 23:19; Lev. 23:10; Num. 15:20f.; 18:8, 11f.; Deut. 18:4; 26:2, 10). What is being offered is a token recognition and thanksgiving that the whole has been given by God. It is more, then, than the temporal notion that Christ rose first.

What is in view is an organic relationship between the thing offered and the whole, between Christ's resurrection and that of

---

[67] Ibid.

those for whom he died. "Firstfruits" in relation to Christ's resurrection represents the "beginning of the resurrection of believers."[68] In a context where a *bodily* (somatic) resurrection was being denied by the Corinthians, Paul insists that "the resurrection of Jesus has the bodily resurrection of "those who sleep" as its necessary consequence. His resurrection is not simply a guarantee; it is a pledge in the sense that it is the actual beginning of the general event. In fact, on the basis of this verse, it can be said that Paul views the two resurrections not so much as two events but as two episodes of the same event."[69] "His resurrection and that of his people form an unbreakable unity."[70]

The same point is being made in Col. 1:18ff where Christ is said to be the "firstborn from the dead." On two occasions the word "firstborn" occurs together with "firstfruits" (Neh. 10:36f.; Ezek. 44:30). And it could be thought that Christ's birth (from the dead) is the pledge of many more to come. However, other considerations point to the fact that in Col. 1:15 Christ is said to be the "firstborn of all creation." Here it cannot be thought that Paul is suggesting that Christ is first one born in creation, i.e., the first creature, for he goes on to say the opposite: he is "firstborn" because all things were created by him (v. 16). What is in view is a usage of this term in the Old Testament pointing to uniqueness, status, and dignity "marking anew as the recipient of exceptional favour and blessing."[71] Thus Moses is directed to tell Pharaoh that Israel is his "firstborn" and David is said to be "firstborn, higher than the kings of the earth" (Psa. 88:27). The "firstborn"

---

[68] Richard B. Gaffin, *The Centrality of the Resurrection: A Study in Paul's Soteriology*, 34.

[69] Ibid., 35.

[70] *Paul: An Outline of His Theology*, H. Ridderbos, 538.

[71] Richard B. Gaffin, *The Centrality of the Resurrection: A Study in Paul's Soteriology*, 37.

is to be seen in close connection with "the beginning" which immediately precedes it. Christ is the first, the *First*, not simply in chronological order, but in significance. He is "the Pioneer, the Inaugurator, who opened up the way."[72]

The second point being made here is that of the connection between our future resurrection body and our present body. Paul mentions this resurrection change in 1 Corinthians 15:35ff in answer to a question concerning how the dead are raised and with what kind of body. In answer to the How?, he appeals to a picture from creation itself whereby seeds (which appear to be dead) burst into life and eventually flower (vv. 37). He then elaborates on this metaphor to bring out the point that what emerges in flower is not the same as the seed itself, even though it is derived from that seed (v. 38). So it is in the resurrection. All flesh is of the same classification, but are clearly different species (v. 39). This is true of heavenly bodies also (v. 41). But earthly bodies are different from heavenly bodies (v. 40). The resurrection body belongs to a different order of being than our earthly bodies.

Paul sums it up this way (v. 44): the present body is a natural body (*psuchikon*), which he goes on to explain as perishable, dishonourable and weak; the resurrected body is a spiritual body (*pneumatikon*), which he goes on to describe as imperishable, honourable and powerful. And the prototype here is Christ's resurrection.

Those "different qualities" (WCF 32.2) are, then:

1. The Resurrection body is spiritual (*pneumatikon*).
He does not intend to contrast "flesh" and "spirit" for had he intended to do so he would have chosen the word *sarkikon* and not *psuchikon*.[73] The connection seems to be similar to what is

---

[72] Ridderbos, *Paul*, 56.

[73] See, J. A. Schep, *The Nature of the Resurrection Body: A Study of the Biblical data* (Grand Rapids: Eerdmans, 1964), 200.

said of Christ's resurrection in Romans 1:4. Christ's body was raised by the Spirit *in power* ("it is raised in power" 1 Cor. 15:43). The result of the Spirit's energies in Christ at the resurrection was to translate him from his position of weakness to that of power. Something of that resurrection power (c.f. Phil. 3:10-11) will be the Spirit's endowment in the resurrection body of the believer.

2. The Resurrection body is *glorious*. "It is raised in glory" (1 Cor. 15:43). The Westminster Confession of Faith speaks of the bodies of the just being "made conformable to His (i.e. Christ's) own glorious body" (32.3). It is what Paul alludes to in Romans 8:17, namely that following share in the sufferings of Christ, we may also expect to share in his glory. "Glory," particularly in the Old Testament, carries with it the idea of weight, worth, dignity and splendor. Nowhere is this better seen than in the account of Christ's own glory as it shone on the Mount of Transfiguration. Describing the scene, Peter recalls (many years later) that Christ "received honor and glory from God" (2 Pet. 1:17). And when the apostle John came to recall the scene, he thought of it in terms of the identity of One manifested, the only-begotten of the Father "full of grace and truth'" (John 1:14). Our resurrection bodies will reflect something of that glory.

3. The Resurrection body is the "*self-same*" body (cf. WCF 32.2). It is identifiable, recognisable. The Confession, having noted that the resurrection body possesses different qualities to the natural body, insists that it is the self-same body. (Perhaps it makes this statement in view of Lutheran ideas about the ubiquity of Christ's physical body after the resurrection.) The identity with that of Christ's resurrection is again to be noted (the fact that Mary and the two on the road to Emmaus did not recognise him is due to a sovereign withholding of recognition at the time for particular reasons in each case). There is discontinuity (we are not now of the same classification as what we shall be, as Paul has been

arguing in 1 Cor. 15:40). But there is also continuity: not the continuity of atoms and molecules (that is not true even of our earthly existence), but an identity of being. There is to be recognition in heaven.

The Second Coming and Related Issues

We have had cause to discuss the Confession's understanding of the nature of the resurrection body—it forms an integral part of the soul's anticipation during the period of the intermediate state. The resurrection of the body forms part of the cosmic redemption from sin which culminates in "the regeneration of all things" (Matt. 19:28).

Man and creation are inextricably linked. Made from the dust of the earth, man shares with the animal creation the fact that he is a living soul. Made in the image of God, he transcends creation; but never so as to lose his identity with it. Man was made to display the imprint of God's image in him by ruling and subduing the earth as God's vice-regent (Gen. 1:28).[74] The Fall brought down a curse, not only upon man, but also upon creation. It, too, longs for its liberation from bondage, to be "brought into the glorious freedom of the children of God" (Rom. 8:20-21). Consequently, when the disobedience of Adam is reversed by the obedience of the Last Adam (Rom. 5:12-21) the cosmos will share in it too and bring to fulfilment the great Isaianic vision of the new heavens and the new earth (Isa. 65:17-25). Paul, in describing Christians as a "new creation" (2 Cor. 5:17), suggests that the regeneration at the end-time has already begun. Realised and prospective eschatology are once more inextricably linked. This long-awaited, long-promised event will accompany the return of Christ from heaven (Acts 3:21). Specific mention of the Second Coming of Christ is subsumed in the Confession's teaching

---

[74] WCF 4.2 "dominion over the creatures"; cf. LC 17.

concerning the Day of Judgment. In a warning issued to both believers and unbelievers of the uncertainty as to *when* this judgment will be, the Confession adds that Christians are to "be always watchful, because they know not at what hour the Lord will come." Our duty then is to long for it, saying "Come Lord Jesus, come quickly. Amen" (WCF 33.3).[75]

Every book in the New Testament (apart from Galatians) urges upon us to live in the expectation of Christ's return, his "royal visit," his "appearing" and "coming." The hope relates to a *parousia* that is personal, physical, visible and triumphant (Matt. 24:44; Mark 8:38; Acts 1:11; Col. 3:4; 2 Thess. 1:10; 2 Tim. 4:8; Heb. 9:28; Rev. 1:7). Christ's coming is directed towards the consummation of the purposes of God in redemption through his mediatorial agency: the cosmic redemption of all things accompanied by the raising of the dead, the judgment of the world, the glorification of God's children, the consignment of the ungodly to perdition, a visible victory over the forces of evil, and the reconstruction of the universe. In echoing the closing verses of Revelation: "'Surely I am coming soon.' Amen. Come, Lord Jesus!" (Rev. 22:20), the Confession has captured what is central to New Testament theology.

Samuel Rutherford, writing to Lady Kenmure, in January, 1629 could say: "All is night that is here, in respect of ignorance and daily ensuing troubles, one always making way to another, as the ninth wave of the sea to the tenth; therefore, sigh and long for the dawning of that morning, and the breaking of that day of the coming of the Son of Man, when the shadows shall flee away. Persuade yourself that the King is coming. Read his letter sent before him, (Rev. 3:11) 'Behold, I come quickly.' Wait, with the

---

[75] Cf. LC Q.88: "*What shall immediately follow after the resurrection?* Immediately after the resurrection shall follow the general and final judgement of angels and men; the day and hour whereof no man knoweth, that all may watch and pray, and be ever ready for the coming of the Lord."

wearied night-watch, for the breaking of the eastern sky, and think that ye have not a morrow."[76] The absence of this hope is an indicator that something is wrong in the church.

The caution of the Confession.

Given the precision with which the Divines referred to such issues as the resurrection body and its relation to the resurrection of Christ, it is surprising that no attempt is made to locate the resurrection of Christ within the schema of the end. According to most commentators, this is the great strength of the Confession, taking into consideration the great differences of viewpoint held then, and now, relating to this issue. Robert L. Dabney is typical when he writes: "They were well aware of the movement of the early Millenarians, and of the persistence of their romantic and exciting speculations among several sects. Our divines find in the Scriptures the clearest assertions of Christ's second advent, and so they teach it most positively."[77] But concerning such issues as the millennium the Westminster Standards are praised for their "prudent moderation."[78]

Robert Baillie (1599-1662), professor of divinity at Glasgow, and one of the Scottish representatives in the Westminster Assembly complained that many of the (English) members of the Assembly were millenarians.[79] He later wrote a book exposing "this heresy" by the title: *A Dissuasive from the Errours of the Time: Wherein the Tenets of the principall Sects, especially of the*

---

[76] To Lady Kenmure, Jan. 15, 1629. *Letters of the Rev. Samuel Rutherford*, ed. A. A. Bonar (Edinburgh: Banner of Truth, 1984 [1861]), 42.

[77] R. L. Dabney, *The Westminster Confession and Creeds*, 13.

[78] The 1552 edition of the Thirty-nine Articles contained a stinging rejection of the doctrine of the millennium. C.f. J. A. de Jong, *As the Waters Cover the Sea* (Kampen: J. H. Kok, 1970), 13.

[79] R. Baillie, *Letters and Journals,* ed. D. Laing (Edinburgh: 1841), II, 313.

Independents, are drawn together in one Map, for the most part, in the words of their own Authors, and their maine principles are examined by the Touch-stone of Holy Scriptures (1645). The final chapter of this book is entitled: "The thousand yeares of Christ his visible Raigne upon earth, is against Scripture." In this chapter he castigates the Independents, including Thomas Goodwin[80] and Jeremiah Burroughes[81] for their chiliasm and reckoned it as "all the sparkles of new light wherewith our Brethren doe entertaine their owne and the peoples fancie."[82] Preaching to the House of Commons in March, 1644, Baillie referred to "repairing the breaches and ruines of the Christian Church, and the building up of Zion in her glory, about the time of the destruction of Antichrist,

---

[80] Thomas Goodwin's *A Glimpse of Syons Glory* is singled out for "gross chiliasm." Debate has raged as to whether or not Goodwin is the author of this work. The work itself is a transcription of a sermon preached in Holland at the inauguration of a church in 1641. It is to be found in Nichol's edition of Goodwin's *Works* (1861-66), vol. xii, 62 and 79. That Goodwin is the author of the *Glimpse* has been argued from its similarity with Goodwin's *Exposition of Revelation* (*Works*, III, 198ff, where he openly acknowledges his dependence on Brightman and Mede) in which the millennium, and the events preceding it are given a detailed examination. "Some say [that Antichrist's fall] will be about the year 1650 or 1656" wrote Goodwin, adding that he agreed that these dates were suitable for the conversion of the Jews but preferring 1666 for the fall of Antichrist. Goodwin also defended a physical resurrection of the saints *before* the millennium. *A Sermon of the Fifth Monarchy* (London: 1654), 27-29. See, Bryan W. Ball, *A Great Expectation: Eschatological Thought in English Protestantism to 1660*, Studies in the History of Christian Thought, Vol. XII, ed. Heiko A. Oberman (Leiden: E.J. Brill, 1975), 119-120. For a detailed discussion of the issue of the authorship of *A Glimpse of Syon's Glory*, see *Puritans, The Millennium and the Future of Israel: Puritan Eschatology 1600 to 1660*, ed. Peter Toon, Appendix II, "The Authorship of the 'Glimpse of Syons Glory,'" 131-136. One of the reasons for the ambiguity over the authorship of this document was a written agreement on the part of the Independents and the Presbyterians during the 1630's not to preach about their differences—and certainly not to publish them.

[81] Burroughes' London lectures on Hosea are singled out for criticism.

[82] *Dissuasive*, 241.

and the conversion of the Jewes." Although Baillie does not claim to know the time of the rebuilding of this temple, he does claim that "if we reckon from the time that the power of the Beast did reign and withal consider the great revolution and turning of things upside downe in these dayes, certainly the work is upon the wheele," adding that "the day of vengeance upon Antichrist, is coming, and is not farre off."

Within the ranks of universities and Stuart Puritanism of the seventeenth century there existed a tradition of apocalyptical interpretation of the books of Daniel and Revelation which emphasised an imminent millennium. Chief amongst their number were: Hugh Broughton (d.1612), whose book *A Revelation of the Holy Apocalypse* (1610) became a significant authority, particularly to later dissenters in the Netherlands; Thomas Brightman (d. 1607), whose work *A Revelation of the Apocalypse* (1611) was reprinted during the Assembly's sitting in 1644, together with his *A Most Comfortable Exposition of the Prophecies of Daniel*;[83] and Joseph Mede (sometimes Mead, 1586-1638), Greek lecturer at Cambridge. Two of Mede's works were published posthumously: *The Apostasy of the Latter Times* (1641) and *The Key to Revelation* (1643). Of interest to us here is the fact that William Twisse, the Prolocutor of the Assembly, wrote a preface to Mede's *The Key to Revelation* in which he expressed his cautious, but overall agreement with its publication.[84] Both

---

[83] In these works, Brightman argued that the thousand year reign of Christ began in 1300 and that it would exist in completeness about 1690, when the Dragon (i.e., the Turks) would be destroyed.

[84] Twisse writes: "The book itself gives much light to the understanding of many obscure passages in that sweet and comfortable prophecie, and though Master Mede's opinion concerning the Thousand years of the seventh Trumpet be singular from that which hath been most generally received by Expositors of best esteem, and I conceive he hath no just ground, yet therein delivers his judgement with such modestie and moderation that I think the printing of it will not be perillous. . . ." *The Key of Revelation* (London, 1643),

Brightman and Mede expected a temporal thousand-year reign of Christ. (Brightman believed it had already existed for 300 years).

Other works printed at this time were *A Personal Reign of Christ Upon Earth* (1641, and reprinted in 1642 and 1643), by John Archer, minister of an Independent congregation in Arnheim, Holland. Archer computed that the Jews would be converted in 1650 or 1656, the Pope would be overthrown in 1666 and Christ would come and the thousand year reign begin in 1700. Archer also believed that "Independency is the beginning of Christ's temporal reign on earth," something which the *Glimpse of Syon's Glory* also advocated.

Others could be cited: Henry Wilkinson (1610-1675), canon of Christ Church, Oxford and member of the Assembly, and later Lady Margaret Professor of divinity (1652-1662) preached before the House of Commons in October 1643, in what was to prove to be an astonishingly eschatological sermon. Having reminded the House that their "businesse lies professedly against the Apocalypticall beast, and all his complices" he went to say that "the propheticall calendar in which the time of the ruine of Babylon, and the building of Sion is foretold, seems to intimate that the time is beare approaching both for the one and the other."[85]

Within the ranks of the Assembly was at least one who belonged to the Fifth Monarchy group. Thomas Baylie, rector of Maningford, and described by James Reid as "a zealous covenanter, and an indefatigable preacher" he was ejected in 1662 by the Act of Uniformity, not for his Fifth Monarchy views, but for his non-conformity.[86]

---

page opposite Title Page. Twisse also corresponded with Mede over such matters as the future of Israel (Romans 11), and the colonisation of New England (Twisse had, for a time, entertained the notion that America would be the location of the New Jerusalem). See, J. A. de Jong, *As the Waters Cover the Sea*, 24-25.

[85] His sermon is entitled, "Babylon's Ruine, Jerusalem's Rising."

[86] James Reid, *Memoirs of the Westminster Divines*, 131.

Alexander Henderson, on the other hand, minister at Edinburgh and Commissioner to the Assembly, preached before the House of Lords in May 1645 attacking the millenarian view that the kingdom of God is to come to the earth, saying: "The quality then of the kingdome of Christ, negatively is this, That his kingdome is not of this world: it is not an earthly or worldly kingdome, and therefore by consequence must be a spirituall and heavenly kingdome."[87]

Typical of the overall view of the Westminster Assembly Divines was that of George Gillespie, perhaps the most able delegate amongst them, who, in a sermon preached before Parliament in 1644 from Ezekiel 43:11, suggested that in the prophecy of the rebuilding of the temple he saw an age of righteousness in which the latter day glory would be manifest. It would be symbolised by the overthrow of the Papacy—something which Gillespie suggested from calculations taken from the book of Revelation, could be 1643 itself! "The Westminster Assembly, therefore" comments Samuel Logan, "might be regarded as the first step in the realisation of that latter day glory."[88]

If we are to ask the question as to how the Westminster Divines understood the Coming of Christ's Kingdom, note should be taken of the interpretation of the Second Petition of the Lord's Prayer. "What do we pray for in the second petition?" "In the second petition (which is 'Thy Kingdom come') acknowledging ourselves and all mankind to be by nature under the dominion of sin and Satan, we pray that the kingdom of sin and Satan may be destroyed, the gospel propagated throughout the world, the Jews

---

[87] Sermon before the House of Lord's, 28 May 1645. Henderson, however, did believe in "the greater glory of the kingdome of Christ on earth."

[88] "The Context and Work of the Assembly," by Samuel T. Logan, Jr., in *To Glorify and Enjoy God: A Commemoration of the Westminster Assembly*, edited by John L. Carson and David W. Hall (Edinburgh: Banner of Truth, 1994), 29.

called, the fullness of the Gentiles brought it; the Church furnished with all gospel-officers and ordinances, purged from corruption, countenanced and maintained by the civil magistrate—that Christ would be pleased so to exercise the kingdom of His power in all the world, as may conduce to these ends" (LC 191).

Given this general expectation of the latter day glory, and the prevailing view held by many of the Divines that the Assembly itself was a part of its realisation, it is surprising that the Confession itself contains almost no reference to this dominant eschatology.[89]

By way of contrast, the Savoy Declaration in 1658 was much less modest, embodying their belief in a latter day glory was embodied in their statement concerning the church: "As the Lord in his care and love towards his church hath in his infinite wise providence exercised it with great variety in all ages for the good of them that love him and his own glory; so according to his promise we expect that in the latter days Antichrist being destroyed, the Jews called, and the adversaries of his dear Son broken, the churches of Christ being enlarged and edified through a free and plentiful communication of light and grace, shall enjoy in this world a more quiet, peaceable and glorious condition than they have enjoyed."[90]

---

[89] Robert L. Dabney writes; ". . . we note the caution of the Assembly concerning the millennium. They were well aware of the movement of the early Millenarians, and of the persistence of their romantic and exciting speculations among several sects. Our divines find in the Scriptures the clearest assertions of Christ's second advent, and so they teach it most positively . . . But what is the nature, and what the duration, of that millennial glory predicted in the Apocalypse? Here the assembly will not dogmatise, because these unfulfilled prophecies are obscure to our feeble minds. It is too modest to dictate a belief amidst so many different opinions." *The Westminster Confession and Creeds*, 13-14.

[90] The chief architect of this statement is probably John Owen. In a series of sermons preached before Parliament between 1646 and 1652, Owen was

Given this background of latter-day glory expectations (the 1640s were years of the keenest and most widespread millennial expectancy of any in England and America), it is widely assumed in some circles that the Confession is necessarily postmillennial in its emphasis.[91] One of the difficulties with such pronouncements is an assumed agreement on the relative definitions of the term "postmillennialism." It is fashionable today to distinguish millennial views by using the categories of "optimistic" and "pessimistic," but these are unhelpful and inadequate.[92] Richard

---

careful not to enter into any speculation about the nearness of the latter day glory. Addressing a jubilant House of Commons in October, 1652, at a day of thanksgiving for the victory over the Scots at Worcester, Owen outlined in six points the main characteristics of the forthcoming time of Zion's glory. These included: 1. a time of peace; 2. purity of worship; 3. multitudes of converts; 4. rejection of Arminianism; 5. subjection of the nations to Christ; and 6. and the casting down of all tyrants. See Peter Toon, *Puritans, The Millennium and the Future of Israel*, 39.

[91] Typical of such assertions, on the popular level, is an article called "Confessional Postmillennialism" by Andrew Sandlin (Chalcedon Report, Sept. 1994), 12-13. Sadlin concludes that "the Reformed confessions and Catechisms are not reticent or agnostic about the topic of eschatology and, specifically, the millennium, or the course of God's dealings with the church and the world." On a more sustained level, Kenneth L. Gentry, Jr, asserts: "The Westminster Standards (1640s) set forth a Postmillennial hope."*He Shall Have Dominion: A Postmillennial Eschatology* (Tyler, Texas: Institute for Christian Economics, 1992), 90. Others have concluded a less dogmatic view, e.g., Gordon H. Clark, "The Confession itself asserts neither the postmillennial or premillennial view. Nor does it assert amillennialism," *What Do Presbyterians Believe? The Westminster Confession, Yesterday and Today* (Philadelphia: Presbyterian and Reformed Publishing Company, 1965), 269. J. H. de Jong concludes that the "Westminster's formulation must be seen as a deliberate choice of mild, unsystematized, postmillennial expectations." *As the Waters Cover the Sea*, 38 n 11.

[92] Notable amillennialists, for example, accept the ethnic interpretation of Romans 11 and expect a mass conversion of the Jews. Such a view is hardly pessimistic. In addition, some postmillennialists, especially Reconstructionists, think of the millennium as co-extensive with the entire inter-adventual age. Again "optimism" is hardly the differentiating word

B. Gaffin has helpfully pointed out that in the past, "post"-millennialism distinguished all that was not specifically "pre"-millennial.[93] In *this* sense, it is undoubtedly true to say that the Westminster standards are *post*millennial. But only in this sense. In so far as the Westminster Standards envision the coming of Christ as a single event, dispensational views (which require a two-stage coming of Christ) are not in harmony with it.[94] It is

---

between amilllennial and postmillennial views. John Murray, for example (who is often, wrongly, thought of as embracing a post-millennial view of eschatology due, no doubt, to his interpretation of Romans 11), could hardly have written a more amillennial view in the two representative articles on eschatology he has left us: "The Interadventual Period and the Advent: Matthew 24 & 25," *Collected Writings of John Murray* (Edinburgh: Banner of Truth, 1977), 2:387-400, and "Structural Strands in New Testament Eschatology," *Kerux: A Journal of Biblical-Theological Preaching*, Vol. 6, No. 3 (1991), 19-26. Both of these articles are decidedly amillennial in their point of view. As Richard Gaffin remarks: "With typical incisiveness, Murray shows that the passage covers history down to its consummation and that the decidedly non-"golden" element of tribulation for the church "is represented as characterising the inter-adventual period as a whole," "Theonomy and Eschatology," in *Theonomy: A Reformed Critique*, ed. William S. Baker & W. Robert Godfrey (Grand Rapids: Academie, 1990), 199-200. The judgement of B. B. Warfield with respect to the Westminster Standards, as reported by his friend Samuel G. Craig, was that "he himself [Warfield] freely admitted that a-millenialism, though not known in those days under that name, is the historic Protestant view, as expressed in the creeds of the Reformation period including the Westminster Standards." See, editor's introduction to B. B. Warfield, *Biblical and Theological Studies* (Philadelphia: Presbyterian and Reformed, 1952), xxxix.

[93] *Theonomy*, 200f.

[94] Dispensationalism is not in harmony with the Confession for a much more basic reason than its eschatological views, viz. its refusal to agree with the Confession's covenantal perspective in conveying the unity of the administration of God's plan throughout all ages in terms of the covenant of grace. However, the doctrine of the rapture requires a two-stage "coming" of Christ which finds no support in the Confessional standards. For a critique, see A. A. Hoekema, *The Bible and the Future* (Exeter: The Paternoster Press, 1978), 194-222. It should also be noted that Dispensationalism (especially, L. S. Chafer) advocates two different destinies for God's people: the earthly people of God on earth forever, and the heavenly people of God

also doubtful as to whether premillennial views are in harmony with the Westminster Standards.[95] The return of Christ and the Judgment that follows are represented in the Standards as successive, and there is no hint of any period of time separating the two events (cf. LC 56, 87-90; SC 37-38). Historic premillennialism requires that Christ descend to the earth, after which his millennial kingdom is established where Jesus will visibly rule on the earth for approximately a thousand years.[96] Of particular interest is the idea that the saints, whose souls have been in heaven, should, after the resurrection of the body from the grave, descend to live on earth again, or for that matter, that Christ himself should quit the throne of his glory to live and dwell on earth again is a strain of thought wholly contrary to the general tenor of the Westminster pronouncements. Despite this, some eminent Calvinists, Horatius and Andrew Bonar among them, have espoused premillennial convictions.[97]

Basic to the Westminster perspective is the conviction that Christ is currently manifesting his rule and is not to be thought of in terms of some future reality. The eschatological kingship of

---

(the Church) in heaven forever. The Confession of Faith knows of only one future existence for the righteous: "everlasting life" (WCF 33.2), otherwise called "an everlasting inheritance in the kingdom of heaven" (WCF 8.5). For a critique, see Appendix to *Eschatology: The Doctrine of the Last Things* a position paper adopted by the 118th General Assembly (1978) of the Presbyterian Church in the United States.

[95] R. L. Dabney is quite explicit: 2 ". . . they [the Westminster Divines] refuse to sanction a pre-millennial advent." *The Westminster Confession and Creeds*, 13.

[96] Cf. George Eldon Ladd, *Crucial Questions about the Kingdom of God* (Grand Rapids: Eerdmans, 1956), *The Gospel of the Kingdom* (Eerdmans, 1959), *Commentary on the Revelation of John* (Eerdmans, 1972), *A Theology of the New Testament* (Eerdmans, 1974).

[97] The Bonar brothers were greatly influenced by the teaching of Edward Irving in Edinburgh during the 1820s. See, Iain Murray, *The Puritan Hope* (London: Banner of Truth, 1971), 195.

Christ begins at his coming *the first time*, exercised by the ascended Christ through the ministry of the Holy Spirit. Question 45 of the Larger Catechism, for example, asks, How doth Christ execute the office of a king? The answer? "Christ executeth the office of a king, in calling out of the world a people to himself, and giving them offices, laws and censures, by which he visibly governs them; in bestowing saving grace upon his elect, rewarding their obedience, and correcting them for their sins, preserving and supporting them under all their temptations and sufferings, restraining and overcoming all their enemies, and powerfully ordering all things for his own glory, and their good; and also in taking vengeance on the rest, who know not God, and obey not the gospel." All of these things Christ is doing *now*. One postmillennialist tries to suggest that this answer of the Larger Catechism is a confirmation of a postmillennial interpretation: that the world is becoming increasingly subject to Christ.[98] However, the answer is suggesting something quite different: that ever since Christ's ascension his kingly rule has been visible, not only in the church, but in the Gentle nations also. To cite Gaffin: "for the New Testament the *entire* interadventual period, not just a closing episode, is the 'golden age' of the church; that period and what transpires in it, as a *whole* embodies the church's millennial 'success' and 'victory.'"[99] What gives "optimism" is not an expectation of a future golden age so much as the present realisation of the victory of the exalted Christ which assures God's people of heaven.

Two particular features of Confessional teaching need a comment or two. They are the antichrist (specifically identified in the Confession as "the Pope of Rome" (WCF 25.6) and the Jewish question.

---

[98] Andrew Sadlin, "Confessional Postmillennialism."

[99] "Theonomy and Eschatology," 203.

Unfulfilled Prophecy

Neither Luther nor Calvin expected a future conversion of the Jews. Calvin understood the words of Romans 11:26: "and so all Israel shall be saved" as referring to the salvation of elect Jews and elect Gentiles throughout history.[100] However, Calvin's successor at Geneva, Theodore Beza, taught that Romans 11 leads us to expect a large scale conversion of the Jews at the close of history and *prior* to the return of Christ.[101] In the seventeenth century, belief in the conversion of the Jews was commonplace among the Puritans. George Gillespie[102] and Robert Baillie both preached before Parliament on the theme of unfulfilled prophecy with respect to the Jews. There is evidence in the Larger Catechism of concern for the Jews: the second petition of the Lord's Prayer is said to include the calling of the Jews (LC 191, "the Jews called"). And the *Directory for the Public Worship of God* (section on Public Prayer before the Sermon) insists that prayer be made "for the conversion of the Jews." What is of great significance, however, is that great care was taken in the expressions used at Westminster regarding the future of Israel. The Confessional formula can be subcribed by those who do not hold to a future,

---

[100]See Calvin's comments on Romans 11:26, *Commentary on the Epistle to the Romans*, ad. loc. The problem with Calvin's interpretation lies in the use of the word "Israel" in Romans 11. The term occurs eleven times and in every other instance "Israel" refers to the Jews in distinction from the Gentiles. It is difficult to maintain that in this instance, and this instance only, "Israel" refers to both Jews *and* Gentiles. For Beza's interpretation, see *Annotationes maiores in Novum Dn. Nostri Iesu Christi Testamentum*, n., 1954 (1556), part 2, ad. loc.

[101]The fact that Beza, and those who followed him in the mainstream Puritan period, expected a conversion of the Jews *before* the return of Christ, distinguishes them from the Millenarian movement. Premillennialism is incompatible with this expectation.

[102]"A Sermon preached before The Honourable House of Commons at their late solemn fast," March 27, 1644, *Works of George Gillespie,*(Edmonton: Still Waters Revival, 1991 [1846]), Vol. 1.

large-scale conversion of the Jews. The fact is that those who have a different understanding of Romans 11 and the future of the Jews[103] are also able to speak of "the Jews being called" as well as offer prayer for "the conversion of the Jews." The fact that the majority of the Divines believed in a future, large-scale conversion of the Jews[104] only underlines the care with which these doctrinal statements were written.

What is especially clear in the Westminster Standards relating to the Jewish question, is the expectation that both Jew and Gentile alike are offered the *same salvation*. There is no basis within a subscription to these doctrines for a belief that the Jews are to be saved in any other way but by faith alone in Christ alone and by grace alone. The Reformation slogans: *sola fide*, *sola gratia*, *solo Christo*, are as applicable to the Jew as they are to the Gentile.

Equally clear is the complete lack of any interest in Israel *as a nation*. Israel's future is contemplated only as it occurs within the kingdom of God. Robert Baillie wrote forcefully: "We grant willingly that the nation of the Jews shall be converted to the faith of Christ; and that the fullness of the Gentiles is to come in with them to the Christian Church; also that the quickening of that dead and rotten member, shall be a matter of exceeding joy

---

[103]Two weighty objections have been levelled against the view of a future, large-scale conversion of the Jews. The first objects to the use of the word "all" in the phrase "all Israel shall be saved," limited as it necessarily is by this interpretation to the last generation of Jews living prior to the return of Christ. As a proportion of the total number of Jews (Israel), this would appear to be but a tiny fraction and hardly warrants the use of the word "all." The second objection has to do with the translation of the word *houtós*, sometimes rendered incorrectly, "And *then* all Israel shall be saved." Had Paul wished to convey a temporal idea he would have used a word like *tote* or *epeita*. Thus the understanding of the passage is that "Israel has experienced a hardening in part until the full number of the Gentiles has come in, and *in this way* all Israel will be saved."

[104]See, Iain Murray, *The Puritan Hope* (Edinburgh: Banner of Truth, 1971, 39-51.

to the whole Church. But that the converted Jews shall return to Canaan to build Jerusalem, that Christ shall come from heaven to reign among them for a thousand years, there is no such thing intimated in the Scriptures in hand."[105]

In one area, however, Westminster formulated its belief with precision, and in such a way that seems at odds with the care taken over other eschatological pronouncements. This relates to the identification of the Antichrist as "the Pope of Rome."

The Pope of Rome as the Antichrist

Identification of the papacy with antichrist, having its origins in the medieval era, particularly by certain spiritual Franciscans, Wycliffe, and the Bohemian predecessors of Hus, was almost universally held by the Reformers and Puritans.[106] In the Westminster Confession of Faith, the identification occurs, not in the section on eschatology as we might expect, but in the section dealing with the church and the assumed power of the Roman pontiff. "There is no other head of the Church but the Lord Jesus Christ. Nor can the Pope of Rome, in any sense, be head thereof: but is that Antichrist, that man of sin, and son of perdition, that

---

[105]*A Dissuasive from the Errours of the Time* (1645), chap. 11, "The Thousand Years of Christ his visible reign upon earth is against Scripture." Cited by Iain Murray, op. cit. 50.

[106]No doubt, the Assembly took their cue, in part from Calvin. Referring to both Daniel 9:27 and 2 Thessalonians 2:4, Calvin noted that these passages "foretold that Antichrist would sit in the Temple of God. With us," he concludes, "it is the Roman pontiff we make the leader and standard bearer of that wicked and abominable kingdom." *Inst.* 4.2.12. C.f. 3.20.42; 4.7.4, 25; 4.17.1; Comm. ad. loc. 1 John 2:18. The doctrinal position of the Confession at 25.6 are (1) the Pope is not the head of the Church; (2) he exalts himself as if he were, which (3) proves him to be activated by the anti-Christian spirit which seeks religious veneration (Matt. 23:8-9), persecutes the godly (Rev. 13:6) and illustrates the predicted apostasy in the church (2 Thess. 2:3-4, 8-9). All of which is in complete accord with Scripture. See Rowland S. Ward, *The Westminster Confession of Faith: A Study Guide* (Wantirna: New Melbourne Press, 1996), 165.

exalteth himself, in the Church, against Christ and all that is called God" (WCF 25.6).

Most Presbyterian churches which subscribe the Westminster documents as their confession of faith have either deleted or amended this section; and some have altered their formula of subscription so as to subscribe merely the general doctrine contained in the statement.

It seems evident that the Assembly did not differentiate between "antichrist"—term found only in the epistles of John (1 John 2:18, 22; 4:3; 2 John 7)—and the "man of sin" or, better, "man of lawlessness" (2 Thess. 2:3). We should also note that the appearance of antichrist, in the understanding of the Reformers and Puritans, was not a figure to be looked for at the end of the Christian dispensation but rather a mysterious process of spiritual evil concentrated in the Papacy. The great apostasy, or rebellion which precedes the appearance of antichrist, and out of which antichrist will appear, had already occurred in the centuries of spiritual darkness preceding the Reformation.[107]

Objections to this view have come from two main directions: exegetical and ecumenical. Many interpret this view today in terms of what is thought to be anti-Roman Catholic spirit which pervaded the sixteenth and seventeenth centuries. In a more tolerant and liberal age, such pronouncements against the papacy are seen to be offensive and divisive. Others, whilst maintaining their opposition to Rome as the greatest heresy within Christendom, have been unable, on exegetical grounds, to identify

---

[107]G. C. Berkouwer points out that Luther, in his reading of Psalm 10, "felt that the unrestrained opposition to the believers recorded in it clearly anticipated the situation prevalent in his day . . . Luther believed that the fulfilment of this psalm was taking place in his day . . ." *The Return of Christ* (Grand Rapids: Eerdmans, 1975), 263. Calvin did not identify the antichrist with any individual pope but a system of ecclesiastical opposition which would be maintained throughout the ages. See commentaries at 2 Thess. 2:7; 1 John 2:18; *Inst.* 4.2.12; 4.7.25

as specifically as does the Westminster Confession, the antichrist and the Papacy. A part of that identification involves the identity of the antichrist as a single person, rather than a system. Paul refers to "*the* man of lawlessness . . . the son of perdition" (2 Thess. 2:3). Furthermore, Paul adds that he is *the one who* opposes and exalts himself against every so-called god or object of worship (v.4). *He* takes his seat in the temple of God (v.4), and that something is now restraining *him,* and *he* will be revealed in *his* time (v.6). The Lord Jesus will slay *him* with the breath of his mouth (v.8). And the whole tenor of the passage seems to predict the appearance of the man of lawlessness at a period just prior to the second coming of Christ.[108]

Further difficulties arise from a failure on the part of this pronouncement to see antichrist in anything else save the Papacy, which is contrary to John's explicit warnings that manifestations of it were prevalent in his time (1 John 2:18; 4:3).

When?

Does the fact that certain events must take place before the return of Christ imply that the time of the advent can be ascertained? Despite the fact that a few of the members of the Assembly felt able to speculate when that day was likely to be, and some believed that the end was imminent,[109] it is to their

---

[108]Cf. Hoekema, *The Bible and the Future*, 158-161.

[109]Christopher Hill, for example, asserts that "many in the seventeenth century believed the end of the world was imminent," *Puritanism and Revolution* (1958), 325. However, others have argued that this is a mistaken conclusion, based on a failure to appreciate "the diffusiveness of the seventeenth-century literature which renders it difficult to assess which view-points predominated." Iain Murray, *The Puritan Hope* (Edinburgh: Banner of Truth, 1971), xxiii. Murray goes on to insist that, despite the fact that they believed in, and wrote books on, unfulfilled prophecy, such a belief in the imminence of the end was "not a feature of the mainstream Puritan divines—those whose

immense credit that no such speculations enter the Confessional pronouncements themselves. Indeed, the closing paragraph of the Confession reminds us of the need to be "watchful, because they know not at what hour the Lord will come."[110] Any attempt to predict the Lord's return is futile.[111] As Berkouwer puts it; "The believer is called to an attitude that does not *reckon* but constantly *reckons with* the coming of the Lord."[112] Even if there remain areas of unfulfilled prophecy (e.g., the preaching of the gospel in all the world, the conversion of the Jews as predicted by Romans 11, the personal appearance of Antichrist), it is still impossible to give a prediction of Christ's return even as these prophecies are fulfilled. We have no warrant to believe that the Second Coming is a long way off or very near. All the events yet to be fulfilled could take place in a relatively short space of time.[113]

---

theology is represented by the Westminster Confession (1647) and *The Savoy Declaration* (1658)."

[110]There is nothing in the Confessional statements to warrant the assertion of David Chilton: "This world has tens of thousands, perhaps hundreds of thousands of years of increasing godliness ahead of it, before the Second Coming of Christ." *Paradise Restored* (Tyler, Texas: Reconstruction Press, 1985), 221-222. He may be right, but he has no warrant from Scripture to say so; still less to bind our consciences to believe it.

[111]One of the latest attempts from a Reformed point of view is that Harold J. Camping's *Nineteen Ninety-Four* in which Camping tried to argue that despite the fact that the New Testament tells us that the day and hour of Christ's Second Coming is not given to us, the month and the year may be eschatologically calculable. This betrays a seriously defective hermeneutic.

[112]*The Return of Christ*, 84.

[113]Hoekema comments: "To say therefore that no predicted events need to happen before Christ returns is to say too much. We must be prepared for the possibility that the Parousia may yet be a long way off, and the New Testament data leaves room for that possibility. On the other hand, to affirm with certainty that the Parousia is still a long way off is also to say too much. The exact time of the Parousia is unknown to us. Neither do we know exactly how the signs of the times will intensify. This uncertainty means that we must always be prepared." *The Bible and the Future*, 136. For this reason, Hoekema prefers to speak of the *impending* nature of the

In the death and resurrection of Christ, the stage is set for Christ's return. "History has begun to wind up its lines, but it has not wound them up. The eschatological drama has begun, but it has not yet been consummated. The fact that it has begun plus the fact that it will be consummated charges the present with eschatological imminence. These days are looking for and hastening the advent of the Lord in glory. They fill the present with hope for believers and warning for unbelievers."[114] The warning has in view the Day of Judgment.

The Judgment of God

There is a sense in which the judgment of the eschaton has already erupted into this world. John makes the point that those who believe in Christ are not condemned, whereas those who do not believe in Christ are condemned already (John 3:18). Even now, the believer has escaped the torment of future banishment from God. Everlasting life is promised those who believe on Christ (John 3:16). Not that believers are free from God's judging activity altogether. Paul has to warn Corinthian Christians, who were abusing the Lord's Supper, that some of them had already experienced a judgment in their lives in the form of sickness and even death (1 Cor. 11: 30-31). But the proper focus of God's judgment lies in the parousia of Christ.

Mention needs to be made here of the doom of the wicked. The Confession speaks of their souls being "cast into hell" at death "where they remain in torments and utter darkness, reserved

---

Return rather than its *imminence*. Richard B. Gaffin, on the other hand, prefers to see all the signs of the times as already in the process of fulfilment, asserts that, "A pivotal consideration, it seems, is that according to the New Testament, Christ *could* have returned at virtually any time since the ministry of the apostles." *Theonomy: A Reformed Critique*, 219.

[114] John Murray, "Structural Strands in New Testament Eschatology", *Kerux: A Journal of Biblical-Theological Preaching*, Vol. 6, No. 3 (1991), 21.

to the judgment of the great day," (WCF 32.2), at which time they will be "raised to dishonour" (32.3). There is an increasing uncertainty amongst evangelicals today of the finality of the final condemnation of unbelievers at death. There are two trends that warrant our attention briefly. First, there is a view which posits that after death and before the final Judgment, unbelievers will be given a "second chance." *Post-mortem* evangelism, as it has been called, is something the Confession specifically denies, and this because Scripture and Christian consensus has held to it from the first.[115] The passage in 1 Peter 3:19f cannot be pressed into implying such a thing for the following reason. Whoever, and wherever "the spirits in prison" may be,[116] Peter merely says that

---

[115]Even Herman Bavinck poses the possibility of repentance after death for the many who have been deprived of the gospel. See the discussion in G. C. Berkouwer's *The Church* (Grand Rapids: Eerdmans, 1976), 160.

[116]Wayne Grudem has argued strongly for the view that they represent those who heard Noah preaching before the flood, *1 Peter*, Tyndale New Testament Commentaries (Leicester: Inter Varsity Press, 1988), 203-239. I. Howard Marshall has argued against this view, suggesting that Christ went into Hades proclaiming his victory and God's judgement, *1 Peter*, The IVP New Testament Commentary Series (Leicester: Inter Varsity Press, 1991), 122-129. However, the fact that Christ is said to have preached to spirits who disobeyed in Noah's day makes it difficult to construct a view that he was actually preaching to others.

On 1 Pet. 3:19ff, W. G. T. Shedd comments: "The large amount of matter in Scripture which teaches that the operation of the Spirit in the new birth and its effects belongs only to this life, cannot be invalidated by the lonely text concerning Christ's 'preaching to the spirits in prison': a passage which the majority of exegetes, taking in all ages of the Church, refer to the preaching of Noah and other 'ambassadors of Christ'; but which, even if referred to a personal descent of Christ into an under world, would be inadequate to establish such a revolutionising doctrine as the prolongation of Christ's mediatorial work into the future stage, the preaching of the gospel in sheol, and the outpouring of the Holy Ghost there. For the dogma of a future redemption of all the unevangelised part of mankind is radically revolutionising. It is another gospel, and if adopted would result in another Christendom . . . Heretofore the great Hereafter has been a gulf of darkness for every impenitent man, heathen or nominal Christian, as he peered into

Christ "preached" to "the spirits in prison." This amounts to what is no more than an announcement of his triumph. The verses will not prove universal *post-mortem* evangelism. Here, the Westminster Standards are decisive: "The souls of believers are at their *death* made perfect in holiness, and do immediately pass into glory" (SC 37). "The souls of the wicked are at their *death* cast into hell" (LC 86). Death is a finality.

Then, second, there is a view which goes further than *post-mortem* evangelism to posit an uncertainty about the finality of God's condemnation at the Judgment. The impetus for this uncertainty is the rise of universalism: the doctrine that, in the end, all will be saved. Some Protestants simply pit some universalist-sounding texts of Scripture against others;[117] some

---

it. Now it will be a darkness through which gleams of light and hope are flashing like an aurora. The line between time and eternity, so sharply drawn by the past Christianity and Christendom, must be erased. A different preaching must be adopted. Hope must be held out instead of the old hopelessness. Death must no longer be presented as a finality, but as an entrance for all unevangelised mankind upon another period of regeneration and salvation. Men must be told that the Semiramises and Cleopatras, the Tiberiuses and Neros, may possibly have accepted the gospel in Hades. Children in Sabbath-schools must be taught that the vicious and hardened populations of the ancient world, of Sodom and Gomorrah, of Babylon and Nineveh, of Antioch and Rome, passed into a world of hope and redemption, not of justice and judgement." *Calvinism: Pure and Mixed* (Edinburgh: Banner of Truth, 1893/1986) 120-121.

Shedd also admits the possibility that the unevangelised may be saved, not by a post-mortem work of evangelism and repentance, but by coming to "faith" before they die, even though they have never heard of Christ. "For although the Redeemer has not been presented to him historically and personally as the object of faith, yet the Divine Spirit by the new birth has wrought in him the sincere and longing *disposition* to believe in him." 128-129.

[117]Such passages as John 12:32; Acts 3:21; Rom. 5:18f., 11:32; 1 Cor. 15:22-28; 2 Cor. 5:19; Eph. 1:10; Col. 1:20ff.; Phil. 2:9-11; Heb. 2:9; Tit. 2:11; 1 Tim. 2:4; 1 Jn. 2:2; 2 Pet. 3:9. All these passages posit views which on the surface are capable of universalist interpretations, but only when abandoning Reformed principles of interpretation, viz., that Scripture does not contradict

Roman Catholics, like Karl Rahner, insist that everyone responds in some way to God's grace and are "anonymous Christians."

Then, on the day that God has appointed (Acts 17:31), God will manifest his righteousness[118] in the judgment of the world. This righteousness will be both retributive and remunerative. It will be an apportioning of both curses and blessings, in accordance with covenantal stipulations (Deut. 28), on the whole of mankind, who will "give an account of their thoughts, words, and deeds" (WCF 33.1).

The absolute certainty of final judgment is the sphere in which the New Testament message of redemption is set. In Romans, where the fullest account of the gospel is to be found, Paul sets out the certainty of, and the reasons for, the judgment of God in detail (Rom. 2:5-16).

The judgment will be righteous (2:5). There will be no miscarriages of judgment, no tampering of the evidence, no forced confessions. It will be impartial (2:11-12). God shows no favoritism (2:11), and will take into account the light of revelation each one has received. Those who did not hear the gospel as such had light in their consciences which they either heeded or disregarded (2:12). It will be scrupulously accurate since it is "based on truth" (2:2). It is all-inclusive, detecting "the secrets of men's hearts" (2:16). It is individual, rendering "to every man" (2:6; "every soul," "every man," "to each one" (2:6,9,10), including "apostate angels" (WCF 32.1; see Matt. 8:29; Jude 6), according to his deeds ("what he has done" (2:6); cf. Psa. 62:12;

Scripture. Taken in consideration with other passages which clearly positing the existence of hell, and that hell is not empty, these passages must be taken to mean something else. See, J. I. Packer, "Evangelicals and the Way of Salvation," in *Evangelical Affirmations*, ed. K. A. Kantzer and Carl F. H. Henry (Grand Rapids: Zondervan, 1990), 107-36.

[118]The Confession particularly underlines that the judgement of God will be "in righteousness" WCF 33.1.

Matt.16:27; 2 Cor. 5:10; Rev. 22:12). Each one will give an account of himself to God. It is based on our deeds, "according to what he has done" (2:6). And the standard of judgment will be Christ, into whose hands the Father has committed all judgment (2:16). For the unbeliever, then, the result will be revelation of "the righteous judgment of God" (2:5). There will be "wrath and anger" (2:8). The unregenerate will receive a destiny commensurate with the way of life they have chosen, and its assessment will be based on how much they knew of the will of God, and their consequent response to it. It is in this judgment that God will vindicate himself against the charge that he has ceased to care about what is right (Ps. 50:16-21; Rev. 6:10; 16:5-7; 19:1-5).

Not only unbelievers, but believers also will be brought to judgment on the Last Day ("all persons that have lived upon the earth" WCF 33.1). We must all appear before the judgment seat of Christ (2 Cor. 5:10) where the context is clear that it is to believers that he speaks. The judgment is remunerative as well as retributive. Each one is to be rewarded for whatever he does (Eph. 6:8; cf. Col. 3:24-5). Paul longed for the coming of the this Day, for then he would receive the crown of righteousness which God, as a righteous Judge, would give him (2 Tim. 4:8-10). It is the longing of all who love the appearing of Christ. To return to our previous analysis of 1 Corinthians 15 again, the splendor of one star will differ from that of another star in the world to come (v.41). There is a mistaken egalitarianism within evangelicalism today, and it is based upon an inability, even now, to consider others better than ourselves. When Whitefield was mischievously asked as to whether or not he thought John Wesley would be standing with him in glory, he replied that he thought not. Wesley would be so much nearer the throne than he that he wondered if he would see him at all.

Annhilationism

We must now examine the strong statements made by the Confession on the eternal punishment of the wicked. The relevant statements are these: "The end of God's appointing this day is . . . in the damnation of the reprobate, who are wicked and disobedient . . . the wicked, who know not God and obey not the Gospel of Jesus Christ, shall be cast into eternal torments, and be punished with everlasting destruction from the presence of the Lord, and from the glory of His power." (WCF 33.2). "At the day of judgment, the wicked shall be set on Christ's left hand, and, upon clear evidence, and full conviction of their own consciences, shall have the fearful but just sentence of condemnation pronounced against them; and thereupon shall be cast out from the favorable presence of God, and the glorious fellowship with Christ, his saints, and all his holy angels, into hell, to be punished with unspeakable torments, both of body and soul, with the devil and his angels for ever" (LC 89).

Belief in eternal punishment has been central to the main stream of Christian belief from the start. What needs to be affirmed is the careful and non-speculative tone of the Confession's pronouncements on hell and its nature. There is none of the language of Tertullian, or Aquinas, or for that matter of Jonathan Edwards as we find it in that famous sermon, "Sinners. in the Hands of an Angry God."[119] Nevertheless, the Westminster Standards are unrepentant in their defense of eternal punishment and for their stance, they claim the sanction of Christ himself. As W. G. T. Shedd wrote: "The strongest support of the doctrine of

---

[119]The sermon is found in *The Works of Jonathan Edwards*, ed. E. Hickman (Edinburgh: Banner of Truth, 1974), Vol. 2, 7-12. Edwards' purpose was to awaken sinners to what he saw as the reality of what lay ahead of them. "And now you have an extraordinary opportunity, a day wherein Christ has thrown the door of mercy wide open, and stands in calling, and crying with a loud voice to poor sinners . . . ", 11.

Endless Punishment is the teaching of Christ, the Redeemer of man. Though the doctrine is plainly taught in the Pauline Epistles, and other parts of Scripture, yet without the explicit and reiterated statements of God incarnate, it is doubtful whether so awful a truth would have had such a conspicuous place as it always has had in the creed of Christendom."[120] And Shedd concludes: "Jesus Christ is the Person who is responsible for the doctrine of Eternal Perdition. He is the Being with whom all opponents of this theological tenet are in conflict."[121]

Of interest to us here is the denial of Eternal Punishment by a host of Anglican writers and scholars, particularly some eminent Anglicans of the 20th century: John Wenham, John Stott and Philip Hughes.[122]

---

[120]W. G. T. Shedd, *Dogmatic Theology* (Minneapolis: Klock & Klock, 1979), Vol. 2B, 675. An abridged account of this section has also been published separately under the title, *The Doctrine of Endless Punishment* (Edinburgh: Banner of Truth, 1885/1986). The quotation above can be found on page 12.

[121]*Dogmatic Theology,* 680.

[122]These include: Harold E. Guillebaud who wrote two books for InterVarsity Fellowship, *Moral Difficulties of the Bible*, followed by *The Righteous Judge*; Basil Atkinson in his *Life and Immortality*; John Wenham in his *The Goodness of God*; and John Stott in a relaxed debate with the liberal David L. Edwards in *Essentials: A liberal-evangelical dialogue*, by David L. Edwards and John R. W. Stott (London: Hodder & Stoughton, 1988). Stott finds the idea of everlasting punishment "intolerable," 314. Mention should also be made here of Philip Hughes's comments in *The True Image* (Grand Rapids: Eerdmans, 1989) 398-407. We shall return to Hughes again in this chapter. See also Edward Fudge, *The Fire That Consumes* (1982). Fudge is a member of the Evangelical Theological Society.

It is interesting to note that the thirty nine articles of the Church of England contain no statement whatsoever on the Last Things. Latitude of conscience is therefore compatible with subscription to these articles. Four articles on the Last Things had been prepared by Thomas Cranmer on the eve of the Marian crisis in what was then the Forty-Two Articles, but these were revised by Matthew Parker. The four articles on the last things included one stating that "The Resurrection of the dead is not yet brought to passe . . . but is to be looked for at the laste daie: for then (as Scripture doeth moste manifestlie testifie) to all that bee dead their awne bodies, fleshe, and bone shall be

What are the current arguments in favor of annihilation? The first appears to be a philosophical one.[123] Stott, who believes in the consciousness of the intermediate state and the resurrection of *all* men, continues to argue for the annihilation of unbelievers, insisting that the idea of the soul's immortality is a Greek concept.[124] The question, however, has to be asked: Why does God resurrect the body, only to annihilate it again? The resurrection is a testament to the permanence of the somatic existence of man. Moreover, there is a soteriological objection to annihilation. If annihilation is the ultimate punishment for sin, we have no cause to maintain that Christ has suffered this for us. What Christ endured in our place at Calvary was God-forsakenness, not annihilation. And what Christ has not endured he cannot redeem. If annihilation is true there is nothing in the work of Christ to deliver us from it.

The second argument is an exegetical one. It is argued by annihilationists that certain passages of Scripture have not been exegeted with sufficient care. Thus the word "eternal," so it is argued, really means "belonging to the age to come." Thus when Matthew 25:46 refers to eternal punishment (*aionos*), it does not refer to its duration (eternally enduring punishment), but to its

---

restored, that the whole man maie (according to his workes) haue other rewarde, or punishment, as he hath liued vertuouslie, or wickedlie." (Article XXXIX). Nor did Cranmer evidently believe in conditional immortality (which view denies that the soul survives death), for Article XL went to say: "Thei whiche saie, that the soulles of suche as departe hens doe sleepe, being without al sence, fealing, or perceuiuing, vntil the daie of judgement, or affirme that the soulles die with the bodies, and at the laste daie shalbe raised vp with the same, doe vtterlie dissent from the right beliefe declared to vs in holie Scripture." See, *On the Thirty Nine Articles: A Conversation with Tudor Christianity*, Oliver O'Donovan (Exeter: Paternoster, 1986), 154-155.

[123]I am indebted here to some notes I took from a lecture delivered by Sinclair B. Ferguson in Belfast on the doctrine of Annihilation.

[124]*Essentials*, 316.

quality (the punishment of the age to come, i.e., annihilation). Or when 2 Thessalonians 2:9 uses the same word to refer to the ultimate punishment of the wicked, it does not imply a punishment that goes on and on, but rather to the punishment of the age to come (i.e., annihilation).

Annihilationists have also pointed out that the word "eternal" can mean a result that is enduring in nature. Thus, we find the phrase "eternal salvation" (Heb. 5:9) and "eternal redemption" (Heb. 9:12) where the permanent result of action is view, rather than a continuation of one. Thus, Jesus speaks about the sin against the Holy Spirit as unforgivable; the transgressor is guilty of an "eternal sin" (Mark 3:29). Jesus does not mean that the transgressor goes on and on committing this sin for ever, but that the consequences of his sin last for ever. Annhilationists apply this thought to such passages as Matthew 25:46 which refers to the wicked as going away "to eternal punishment, but the righteous to eternal life." Annihilationists then argue that what is being said here is that the state of affairs brought about at the Judgment is one that is enduring in nature; i.e., unchangeable.

In addition, Philip Hughes suggests that death means "destruction without recall": "everlasting death is destruction without end, that is, destruction without recall, the destruction of obliteration."[125] And this, despite the fact that current scholarship

---

[125] *The True Image*, 405. "Death" in Scripture is the opposite of life-in-communion either with God or man. When John, for example, says that "we know that we have passed from death to life because we love our brothers" (1 John 3:14), he is not suggesting that death is a state of unconscious existence, but rather one of separation from fellowship with God. In Eden, when God pronounced his judicial verdict upon Adam and Eve's rebellion as death, it was not annihilation (or non-being) that they suffered, but a loss of communion with God. We should also note that the use of the word "destruction" does not imply annihilation. Thus, when Jesus speaks of not putting new wine into old wine-skins, or they will be destroyed (Matt. 9:17), he does not imply their complete annihilation but the loss of their original condition. And when in 2 Thess. 1:7-9, mention is made of

insists that *aionos*, as Jesus and the Jews perceived it, meant *unending*.[126] Thus, according to Hughes, we have a view that eternal death means a state of obliteration that is unchangeable in nature. The problem with this is that just because a word *can* mean something, it does not follow that it always has to mean that. The context has to determine the meaning in each case. And the contexts, as well as the imagery, suggest an existence that is both enduring and conscious.[127]

---

being "punished with everlasting destruction and shut out from the presence of the Lord," it can hardly mean annihilation here since the phrase "shut out from the presence of the Lord" would have no meaning. Rather, the construction is a hendiadys: "the 'eternal destruction' consists in exclusion from the presence of him with whom is 'the fountain of life'" F. F. Bruce, *1 & 2 Thessalonians*, Word Biblical Commentary (Waco: Word Books, 1982), 152.

[126]See entry for *aionos* in *A Greek-English Lexicon of the New Testament and Other Christian Literature*, trans. and ed. by W. F. Arndt and F. W. Gingrich (Chicago: The University of Chicago Press, 1957), 27-28. It is true that *aionos* can mean 'pertaining to the age to come' but the age to come was conceived of as being without end and unless given firm grounds to the contrary passages referring to eternal life and eternal death should be thought of in terms of their endless duration.

[127]Thus Jesus speaks of "eternal fire" (Matt. 25:41); "the Gehenna of fire" (Matt.5:22; a particularly striking allusion—Gehenna is the Greek form of an Aramaic expression, meaning "the valley of Hinnom," the valley outside Jerusalem where the smoke of the rubbish on fire rose up day and night, and where once children had been offered in sacrifice to Molech (2 Chron. 28:3; 33:6); "eternal fire" (Matt. 18:9, lit. "the fire that is *aionos*"). He also described hell as "unquenchable," and as a place "where the worm does not die" (Mark 9:43,48; cf. Isa. 66:24). John 3:16 should also be mentioned for its promise to believers that they will "not perish but have everlasting life." The contrast is between "everlasting life" (*zoen aionion*) and "perish(ing)" (*apoletai*). Critics of eternal punishment insist that the Greek word *apollymi* means to annihilate here (Jehovah's Witnesses and Seventh Day Adventists interpret it thus). But the word never means annihilate in any other context: In all three parables in John 15 where something is described as having been "lost" (Son, sheep, coin) it is the word *apollymi* that is used in each case. In the case of Herod's attempt to "kill" the baby Jesus (Matt. 2:13), again it is the word *apollmi* that is used. Herod did not annihilate the babies in Jerusalem. For a fuller treatment of these issues, see A. A. Hoekema, *The Bible and the Future*, 266-273, and John Blanchard, *Whatever Happened to Hell?* (Welwyn: Evangelical Press, 1993), 62-76, 218-249.

Thirdly, there are theological reasons. Hughes' main argument against eternally enduring punishment, the eternal existence of hell, is that it is "incompatible with the purpose and effect of the redemption achieved by Christ's coming."[128] His point is that God's purpose in making us was to perfect us in the image of his Son. God's re-creation of the sin-cursed world involves him in eliminating all traces of sin. Christ has appeared "to put away sin" (Heb. 9:26), and to abolish death (cf. 2 Tim. 1:10; Rev. 21:4). "The conception of the endlessness of the suffering of torment and of the endurance of "living" death in hell stands in contradiction to this teaching."[129] As Packer points out, "this is a kind of universalism in reverse, ensuring not that all who exist will be saved, but that only those who are saved will exist."[130] The logic of this argument is, as Packer insists, that God must save everyone. Only full universalism would meet all the requirements of the problem posed by Hughes. The truth is that within the Biblical portrait of the world to come in the closing chapter of Revelation there is an "outside" (Rev. 22:15). There remains a consciousness in the coming age of a sphere of existence outside the blessedness of fellowship with God.

---

[128]Ibid. 405.

[129]Ibid. 405-406. We should also think of the psychological barrier raised in this connection: How can the righteous be truly happy knowing that others are suffering in hell? And if it is a source of pain and hurt to us, how much more so to God? There is a fundamental misunderstanding of the very nature of God in these sentiments. This is not a paradigm of God (Rev. 19:1ff). Revelation gives us a picture of perfect, sanctified souls praising God for his just judgements. In any case, the hurt envisaged is not altogether removed by knowing that loved ones have been annihilated in this connection. See, Donald MacLeod, *Behold Your God* (Fearn: Christian Focus Publications, 1995), 131-135.

[130]J. I. Packer, *The Problem of Eternal Punishment*, the text of an address delivered for the Evangelical Alliance (Victoria) Australia (Harold Wood Booklets, nd), 14.

Does it matter whether we believe in conditional immortality or not? The answer is surely: yes it does! Conditionalists avoid several essential features: they miss out on the truth that we are made to last for eternity—this is our dignity; they miss out an essential aspect of preaching—telling folk that the future really is bad outside of Christ; and they miss out on an aspect of God's justice, and therefore miss out on the worship and praise that such justice enacted deserves (note the way God's justice is praised in such passages as Rev. 16:5-7 and 19:1-5).

Conclusion

In our survey of Westminster's understanding of eschatology we have had occasion to pin-point certain weaknesses and strengths. By way of weaknesses we may allude to the fact that it concerns itself with the personal, as opposed to the cosmic; and the future as opposed to the inaugurated; and that its avowal of a postmillennial eschatology is to the fore.[131] Yet our Confession of Faith is among the fullest and finest of the Protestant tradition. In the area of its eschatological pronouncements, it is a model of economy and precision. Knowing how divisive the issue of eschatology can be, and that despite an almost unanimous opinion held by the Divines on certain eschatological matters, the Divines chose their words carefully, making no reference whatsoever to issues of major division and misunderstanding (e.g., the millennium), and choosing a formula of expression that comprehensively included several traditions (e.g., the calling of the Jews), as well as denouncing views that were clearly opposed

---

[131]Readers will have noted that there was no distinction made in the seventeenth century between a-millenialism and post-millennialism. A-millennialism, a twentieth century term, was upheld by many in previous centuries, but would have been known as postmillennialism. See, Richard B. Gaffin, "Theonomy and Eschatology: Reflections on Postmillennialism," *Theonomy: A Reformed Critique*, 197ff.

to biblical teaching (e.g., the doctrines of soul-sleep and annihilation). In its criticism of premillennial views, Westminster is a model of gentleness.

The final words of the Confession point us to the Second Coming, urging us to be watchful and expectant and anticipatory. The Confession follows the very Bible itself in its closing pronouncement: "Come, Lord Jesus" (Rev. 22:20). As Matthew Henry (1662-1714) was to write in the conclusion of his Commentary on the Bible: "Thus beats the pulse of the church, thus breathes that gracious Spirit, which actuates and informs the mystical body of Christ; and we should never be satisfied till we find such a spirit breathing in us, and causing us to look for the blessed hope and glorious appearance of the great God and our saviour Jesus Christ. This is the language of the church of the first-born, and we should join with them, often putting ourselves in mind of the promise. What comes from heaven in a promise should be sent back to heaven in a prayer. 'Come, Lord Jesus;' put an end to this state of sin, sorrow and temptation; gather thy people out of this present evil world, and take them up to heaven, that state of perfect purity, peace and joy, and so finish thy great design, and fulfil all that word in which thou hast caused thy people to hope."[132]

---

[132]*An exposition of the Old and New Testaments* (London: Ward, Lock, and Tyler, nd), ad. loc.

The Influence of the Westminster Confession on the Korean Presbyterian Church

CHI MO HONG

Introduction

As the title suggests, this study investigates historically the influence of the Westminster Confession on the Korean Presbyterian church. Foreign missionaries arriving in the late nineteenth century Korea were mainly Americans. As for their denominational background, they were dispatched by the Presbyterian, the Methodist, and the Holiness Churches. The Presbyterians were the most numerous and active among them. Starting with the United States of America, the Presbyterian missionaries also came from Canada and Australia. As soon as they entered Korea, they demonstrated their unity in faith and theology, transcending differences in national and cultural backgrounds. Missionaries manifested not merely an outward coalition and unity as promoted by today's World Council of Churches, but a pure, ecumenical spirit dedicated to founding the true faith and theology, and a single Presbyterian Church. By God's grace, they succeeded in founding one Presbyterian Church and a theological school in Korea.

Once a church is founded, it seeks to consolidate its community of believers and possess a standard, doctrinal confession that expresses the substance of its spirituality.[1] While embodying the public aspect of a community, a confession also possesses significance as an individual believer's response to Christ's calling and as his understanding and acceptance in response to the Word of God.[2] Therefore, according to the former, a confession has the meaning of a community praising the Lord in unison and worshiping Him, while according to the latter, a confession is the criteria for spirituality as possessed by that community. Moreover, because all doctrinal confessions—with the exception of the Apostles' Creed—have been the product of churches that have particularized or externalized spirituality in a given historical setting each confession inevitably embodies a historical dimension.[3] On that ground, a confession has certain temporal limitations. Furthermore, a confession cannot be completely error free like the Scripture. In contrast to the absoluteness of the Scripture, a doctrinal confession is characterized by relativity, because, while the Scripture is God's revelation, a confession is a man's response to the Word of God.[4]

First, this study investigates what doctrinal confession the Korean Presbyterian church has possessed from the time of its founding. Also, the present study seeks to understand the nature of the spirituality and theological background possessed by the missionaries from the U.S. and Australia who played leading roles in founding the Korean Presbyterian church. Secondly, it is mentioned that the articles of faith adopted for the first time by the Korean church were the so-called Twelve Articles. In this context, my study examines the relationship between the Twelve

---

[1] Philip Schaff, *The Creeds of Christendom*, Vol. 1, 6th ed., rev. (Grand Rapids, Michigan: Baker Book House, 1977), 4.

[2] Ibid., 5.

[3] Ibid., 6.

[4] Ibid., 7.

Articles and the Westminster Confession, the characteristics of the newly born General Assembly of Korea Independent Presbytery (*Han'guk tongohoe*) which adopted the Articles instead of the Confession, and the attitude of those missionaries who led and supported the General Assembly.

Lastly, by examining the circumstance in which the mainstream organizations of the Korean Presbyterian church—the Presbyterian Church of Korea (Korean abbreviation: *Tonghap*), the General Assembly of the Presbyterian Church in Korea (*Hapton*) and the General Assembly of the Presbyterian Church of Korea (*Kosin*)—individually adopted the Westminster Confession as their creed after almost a century had passed, the influence of the Westminster Confession on the Korean Presbyterian church is discussed.

I. The Arrival of Foreign Missionaries

The transmission of Protestantism to Korea began fifty years before the signing of the U.S.-Korea Treaty of Amity and Commerce in 1882. The first Protestant missionary to enter Korea was Karl Friderich August Gutzlaff who was renowned for his pioneering missionary activities in China. As a Dutchman of German descent, he belonged to the Netherlands Missionary Society. While working as a hired laborer on an East India Company ship, *Land Amherst*, in 1832, he visited the western Korean coast and distributed Chinese-translation copies of the Bible. Thirty-four years after Gutzlaff's visit, Minister Robert J. Thomas, a British missionary, entered Chinnam-p'o on an American merchant ship, *General Sherman*, journeyed upstream on Taedong River, reached Pyôngyang, and met his martyrdom in 1866. The third attempt at evangelizing Korea was carried out by Alexander Williamson, John Ross, and John Mcintyre, all of whom were from Scotland. Upon meeting the Korean merchants, Sô Sang-ryun and Paek Hong-jun, who were in Manchuria for business, the missionaries had the Koreans translate the Bible into Korean and then distribute copies of the Gospel upon returning to Korea. Since the missionaries themselves could not enter the country; however, their evangelical efforts saw no fruition—only to stop with the contact and translation.

(A) The American Northern Presbyterians

From 1884 after the signing of the US-Korea Treaty, missionary activities of various American denominations began.[5] The American Northern Presbyterian mission in Korea commenced with the arrival of a physician, Horace N. Allen, on September 20, 1884. He laid the foundation for evangelism by earning the trust of the Korean royal family, since he saved the life of Min Yông-ik—an important official and a kinsman of the queen—who suffered a critical injury during the Kapsin Coup in 1884.[6] On Easter morning of April 5 of the following year, an American Northern Presbyterian missionary, Horace G. Underwood, and an American Methodist missionary, Henry G. Appenzeller, arrived in Korea.

Upon John W. Heron's arrival in June 1885, the Northern Presbyterian mission finally came to be organized, and with Seoul as the center, missionary activities through medical care and education got under way. Afterwards, ministers Samuel A. Moffett (1890), William M. Baird (1891), William L. Swallen (1892), and Graham Lee (1892) entered Korea and founded a mission station in Pyôngyang. They were to become the pioneers of evangelism in northwestern Korea. Also, a minister, Frederick S. Miller, established a mission station in Ch'ôngju, while another minister, James K. Adams, did likewise in Taegu. So then, what were the spiritual and theological backgrounds of the Northern Presbyterian

---

[5] Min Kyông-bae, *Han'guk Kidok kychoesa* [History of the Korean Christian church] (Seoul: Taehan Kidokkyo shoe, 1974),105.

[6] L. George Paik, *The History of Protestant Mission in Korea*, 1832-1910 (P'yôngyang: Union Christian College Press, 1929), 95.

ministers who entered Korea by 1920? At the time, A. J. Brown, who was working at the Board of Foreign Missions for the Presbyterian Church in the USA, commented on the Northern Presbyterian missionaries who had come to Korea by 1911 as follows:

> The typical missionary of the first quarter century after the opening of the country was a man of the Puritan type. He kept the Sabbath as our New England forefathers did a century ago. He looked upon dancing and smoking and card-playing as sins in which no true follower of Christ should indulge. In theology and biblical criticism, he was strongly conservative, and he held as a vital truth the premillenarian view of the second coming of Christ. The higher criticism and biblical theology were deemed dangerous heresies. In most of the evangelical churches of America and Great Britain, conservatives and liberals have learned to live and work together in peace: but in Korea the few men who hold "the modern view" have a rough road to travel, particularly in the Presbyterian group of missions.[7]

Harvie M. Conn has said that Brown's commentary, although lacking in sympathy for conservative theology, emphasized frankly the spiritual and theological characteristics of the early missionaries in Korea.[8] Moffett, who empathized much more strongly with his missionary colleagues than did Brown, described the theological trend in 1909 as follows:

> The mission and the Church have been marked preeminently by a fervent evangelistic spirit, a thorough belief in the Scripture as the Word of God, and in the Gospel message of salvation from sin through Jesus Christ.[9]

---

[7] A.J. Brown, *The Mastery of the Far East* (New York: Charles Scribners, 1919), 540, as cited by Harvie M. Conn, "Studies in the Theology of the Korean Presbyterian Church," *Westminster Theological Journal* 29:1 (November 1966): 27.

[8] Conn, 27-28.

[9] As cited by Harriet Pollard, "The History of the Missionary Enterprise of the Presbyterian Church, U.S.A. in Korea with Special Emphasis on the Personnel" (M.A. thesis, Northwestern University, 1927), 26.

A report prepared by the Korean mission office of the American Presbyterian Church in 1922 provides us with a glimpse of the theological background of early missionaries in Korea. At that time, there were seven Americans institutions that had trained the forty Presbyterian missionaries who came to Korea. Of the forty, those from Princeton Theological Seminary were the most numerous, numbering sixteen, and then the next largest group of eleven was from McCormick, with four from San Anselmo and three from New York's Union Theological Seminary. Also, there were about ten Bible schools that had trained the missionaries, among which Moody Bible Institute had produced the most, and the Biblical Seminary of New York had put out the next largest group. Because the majority of missionaries in Korea had been trained by such conservative institutions, they delivered their message from a conservative, Gospel-oriented, Christ-centered attitude when they founded their church in the missionary field of Korea, and their missionary method was the same:[10] To proceed in accordance with the Word of the Scripture was the Truth.

(B) The American Southern Presbyterians

The foreign missionary activities of the American Presbyterian Church were promoted through only one organization until 1861, when the Civil War brought about the division of the Presbyterian Church in the U.S. and the resultant creation of the Southern Presbyterian Church. The Southern Presbyterian Church began its missionary outreach in Korea eight years after the Northern Presbyterians. In October 1891, Underwood returned to the U.S. for his first sabbatical year, and at the annual meeting of the Inter-Seminary Alliance for Foreign Mission in Nashville, he pleaded in behalf of Korean mission. At the time, Yun Ch'i-ho, who was a Korean student studying at Vanderbilt University, was also

---

[10] Conn, 27-28.

attending the meeting and he, too, urged for the mission in Korea.[11]
This led to the appointment of a McCormick student, Lewis B.
Tate, and two students of Union Theological Seminary in
Richmond, William M. Junkin and William D. Reynolds, as
missionaries, and they entered Korea in 1892 As soon as arriving
in Korea, they designated southwestern Korea as the mission zone.
There they set up mission stations in Chônju, Kwangju, Kunsan,
Mokp'o, and Sunch'ôn and began their missionary activities.
Among them, Reynolds was to become a professor of systematic
theology at Pyungyan Seminary where he served for a long time.[12]

(C) The Australian Presbyterians

Australian Presbyterian mission in Korea began with the
arrival of a minister affiliated with the Presbyterian Church of
Victoria named J. Henry Davies and his sister Mary T. Davies in
October 1889. Upon landing in Pusan, they designated the
southeastern region, Kyôngsang-namdo, as their mission zone
and commenced their activities. Davies had originally been a
missionary in India before, but due to bad health, he had to return
home for recovery. Then, with a support from the Presbyterian
Fellowship Union for Bible Study, which was organized in 1888,
he left for Korea as a missionary. From Pusan he went to Seoul
where he engaged in missionary activities for about five months,
and then he left the capital to travel to Kyôngsang-namdo where
he was active as a pioneer missionary. The reason why he left
Seoul was simple: the city already had many active missionaries
there. Tragically, he contracted smallpox during his travel and,

---

[11] Yun was the founder of the Korean Southern Methodist Church and a pioneer
who was active as an ordinary believer. Toward the end of the Japanese
occupation in Korea (1920-1945); however, he succumbed to the pressures
of Japanese authority and compromised his nationalist stance.

[12] Paek Nak-chun, *Han'guk Kaesin 'gyo sa* [History of the Korean Protestant
Church] (Seoul: Yônseidae ch'ulp'anbu, 1973), 198.

adding to his misfortune, also caught pneumonia. He died at James S. Gale's house on April 5, 1890. His death resulted in the dispatch of more missionaries to Korea in the following year. With the establishment of the Australian mission station in Pusan and the official commencement of its missionary activity, stations were also set up in Kôch'ang and other places in the Southeast.

(D) The Canadian Presbyterians

The first Canadian missionary to enter Korea was William J. McKenzie.[13] Having come as an independent missionary in December 1893, McKenzie carried out his mission work for two years until he passed away. With his death, the Canadian Presbyterian Church became more interested in mission work. Before an official dispatch of missionaries to Korea by the Canadian church, another independent missionary took up his post in 1889 with a YMCA sponsorship: he was James S. Gale. That he contributed immensely to the Korean church cannot be overlooked. In 1898, nine years after his arrival, the Canadian Presbyterian Church sent Robert H. Grierson, William R. Foote, and Duncan M. McRae to Korea. Centered in the northeastern regions of Hamgyông-namdo and Hamgyông-pukdo, they commenced their mission activities and established stations in Wônsan, Hamhûng Yongjông, and other places.

II. The Mission Policies of Foreign Missionaries

During the eight years between 1884 and 1892, four missionaries from three countries, the U.S., Canada, and Australia, arrived in Korea, and each set up a mission headquarters. Having four mission headquarters in a small country like Korea necessitated certain fundamental, mutually agreed upon policies

---

[13] Ibid., 196-97.

not only to avoid conflicts, but also, in a more active sense, to make their missionary activities more efficient. The first among such policies was to divide up the country into four mission zones. This proposal was made by an American Southern Presbyterian, William D. Reynolds, and it was adopted.[14]

The next urgent task was to form a collective organization for the mission groups to adjust any differences in their policies and to seek mutual cooperation. As a result, the United Council Of Mission in Korea was formed by Americans and Australians, as soon as the Australian missionary, Davies, arrived in Korea. The Northern Presbyterian missionary, Heron, became the chairman, while Davies became the secretary. This cooperatives body comprised of two groups had lasted four months when Davies died from smallpox, and the United Counsel was dissolved. Upon the establishment of the Southern Presbyterian mission in 1892, the Northern and Southern Presbyterians organized the Council of Missions Holding the Presbyterian Form of Government on January 28, 1893, in order to avoid any unnecessary overlap in their missionary activities.[15] In the same year, the Australian Presbyterians joined this body, and the Canadians followed suit in 1898. The organization of this council by the four missions was for the purpose of founding one theological school and one church in the future. The minutes published by the Northern Presbyterians in 1892 pointed to these goals even before the four missions got together to form the

---

[14] The mission zones were as follows: the American Northern Presbyterians in Seoul, Kyônggi-do, P'yôngan-do, Hwanghae-do, Kyôngsang-pukdo, and Ch'ungch'ông-do, the American Southern Presbyterians in Chôlla-do, the Canadians in Hamgyông-do, and the Australian Presbyterians in Pusan and Kyôngsang-nardo. The eastern central region of Kangwôn-do was not being handled by any group, until it later became the Methodist mission zone.

[15] William M. Baird, "Union of Presbyterian Missions in Korea," in *The Missionary Preview of the World* 6.7 (July 1895); 532.

Council. The minutes stated: "All missionary activities of ours have as their goal to organize one Presbyterian Church in Korea."[16] The Council allowed each member to follow only the instructions from his mission, and it had no standing administrative structure for performing the actual functions of jurisdiction. Paek observed that the body was no more than an unofficial get-together for missionaries to mutually seek and give advice and for fellowship.[17] For the missionaries, this Council acted as the midwife for the future birth of the General Assembly of Korea Independent Presbytery. In light of this fact, what were the important mission policies drafted jointly by the four groups? This writer summarizes them into two: first, the Nevius Mission Plan, and second, theological education through Pyungyang Union Theological Seminary. Through these two vehicles, the missionaries either directly or indirectly imparted in the Korean church both the faith and the theology, both reflected in the Westminster Confession.

(A) The Nevius Mission Plan

The Presbyterian missionaries in Korea sought out various methods for carrying out their mission effectively in Korea. At about that time, the seven young missionaries in Korea decided to invite John I. Nevius, a missionary who was active in China in 1890, to share his experience. Nevius came to Seoul in the spring of 1890 and gave special lectures for two weeks. At the time, he lectured by expanding on the so-called Three Self-Formulas as had been researched and developed collectively by Henry Venn (1796-1873) of Britain and the American mission policy-maker

---

[16] *Minutes of the General Assembly of the Presbyterian Church in the U.S. for 1892*, 532.

[17] Paek, 211; and Charles A. Clark, "Constitutional Law of Korean Presbyterian Church," in *Sinhak chinam* [Korean Theological Quarterly Review] 12.2: 71-72.

[18] R. Pierce Beaver, *The Missionary Between the Times* (Garden City, New York: Doubleday, 1968), 133.

Rufus Anderson (1796-1880).[18] The contents of the lecture were published in *Chinese Recorder* in 1895 and were adopted as the policy for the Korean mission.[19] Sixty-three years later in 1958, the lectures were republished under the title of *The Planting and Development of Missionary Churches* by the Baker Book House in Michigan. The essential concepts of this mission plan were the Self-Support, the Self-Government, and the Self-Propaganda of indigenous churches. Depending on which of the three is emphasized more, there can be some difference in the way the plan as a whole is interpreted. However, Bruce F. Hunt, who wrote the preface for the reprint edition, has related to me that the uniqueness of the Nevius Mission Plan lay in the third element, the Self-Propaganda. Moffett, who may be regarded as the second man of the Korean mission, made the following observation during his commentary at the fiftieth anniversary of Korean mission: "I do not hesitate to state the conviction that the unique and pre-eminent place given to instruction in the Scripture as the very word of God has been the outstanding factor through these fifty years in the evangelization of Korea.[20] The Nevius Plan's strong emphasis on the Bible suggests that the theological background of the Plan itself was conservative. Charles A. Clark, who has researched the Plan's application in Korea, stressed this same point in his book, *The Nevius Plan for Mission Work illustrated in Korea.* Especially in Chapter Six's discussion of the mission methods in Korea from 1893 to 1901, Clark focuses on the Scripture and examines the issue of mission method in the context of Scripture itself:

---

[19] Allen D. Clark, *History of the Korean Church* (Seoul: The Christian Literature Society of Korea, 1961), 115.

[20] *Report of the 50th Anniversary Celebration of the Korean Mission of the U.S.A. Presbyterian Church,* June 30-July 3, 1934, 40, as cited by Conn, 29.

> The Bible itself has been, of course, pre-eminently the greatest factor in the evangelization, as in all other countries, but it has certainly occupied a rather unique position in the work of Korea, and the Korean church . . . has been, as it were, saturated with knowledge of the Bible.[21]

This fact is illustrated by the history of the early Korean church. From 1900 when the missionaries had become fluent in Korean, two-week-long Bible study conferences were held at the presbytery level every summer and winter. There, the missionaries poured all their efforts into teaching the sixty-six books in both the Old and the New Testaments. Such a gathering would be called the "spiritual revival meeting" today in Korea; but up to 1930, it was generally known as the "Bible study conference." Through biblical instructions by the missionaries who had adopted the Nevius Plan, Korean believers came to recognize the unique authority of the Bible, and the Scripture itself was accepted without qualifications as the Word of the living God. Therefore in the early Korean church, the higher criticism was unimaginable. In the end, the Nevius Plan can be said to have contributed tremendously to strengthening of evangelical attitude toward the Scripture.[22] In researching the Nevius Plan, Clark has confirmed the importance of the Bible for the church's growth and education. Linking the Scripture-oriented mission with the early conservative theology is very befitting.[23] To cite another supporting example, the fact that before 1938, Bible instruction occupied more than eighteen hours per week in the curriculum of every grade level at Soong-Eui Girl's High School, a mission school in Pyôngyang, points to the Nevius Plan. On the ground that one sees in the Plan an attitude toward the Scripture identical to that reflected in the

---

[21] *Quarter Centennial Report, Presbyterian North Mission*, Vol 17. as cited by Charles A. Clark, *The Nevius Plan for Mission Work Illustrated in Korea* (Seoul: Christian Literature Society, 1973), 121ff.

[22] Kun Sam Lee, *The Christian Confrontation with Shinto Nationalism* (The Presbyterian and Reformed Publishing Company, 1966), 156ff.

[23] Conn, 30.

title and content of the Westminster Confession's first chapter; that is "Of the Holy Scripture," it cannot be denied that the Nevius Plan was intimately linked to the spirituality of the early Korean Presbyterian church and the formation of its theology.

(B) The Theological Background of Pyungyang Seminary

Theological background of the early Korean Presbyterian church can be discussed in reference to Pyungyang Union Theological Seminary which was officially founded in 1901. In 1900, the Northern Presbyterian mission headquarters gave Moffett permission to found a new theological school and granted the necessary funds. Moffett submitted the proposal to the Council of Missions Holding the Presbyterian Form of Government, and it agreed upon the principle of offering theological education in Korea. In 1901, the Council unanimously approved the establishment of a theological school, and after designating a committee on theological education, P'yôngyang was chosen as the location for the new seminary. From 1906, the four missions in Korea decided to run the school jointly, and they organized a faculty of professors through the dispatch of professors from each mission. Consequently, Pyungyang Union Theological Seminary was opened. In reference to the seminary founded through this process, a missionary, Herbert R. Blair, provided the following description:

> The Bible is the one textbook emphasized and studied. The seminary sets its theological impress upon all pastors alike, has been largely also in the hands of missionary teachers, but is now beginning to be transferred to the control of the General Assembly step by step. Presbyterians, with their historic Calvinistic background, accepting the Westminster standards and Presbyterian form of government have, as of old, unquestionably accepted the Scriptures as the very word of God. On this basis the gospel story centering on the cross of Christ, with its frank Pauline supernaturalistic interpretation has been taught by the missionaries and accepted by the Korean church without reserve.[24]

---

[24] *Report of the 50th Anniversary Celebration lof the Korea Mission of the U.S.A. Presbyterian Church,* 121, as cited by Conn, 35.

The seminary's theology represented America's Old Princeton Theology. The majority of the Presbyterian missionaries in Korea were those who had received training under the influence of Old Princeton Theology. The representative missionaries who influenced the theology at Pyungang Seminary were Moffett, Charles Clark, and Reynolds. Moffett (1864-1939), who entered Korea in 1890, founded Pyungyang Seminary and, as its president from 1901 to 1924, contributed to the development of the school. During his lifetime, he hardly wrote about theology; but his influence in the field was considerable. His theology was conservative and Calvinistic. This writer is certain that what he stated openly during the fiftieth anniversary celebration of Korean mission will be remembered as long as the Korean church exists in this land. He said the following.

> When I first arrived in Korea before starting to spread the Gospel, there was one thing I prayed about and decided. It was that I decided to deliver nothing other than the Way of the Cross, and if I were to deliver anything else, I was to be cursed.

In these words, one can get a glimpse of Moffett's theology.[25]

Clark (1878-1961) was the second person to contribute to the formation of theology in the Korean church. As an American Northern Presbyterian missionary, he was a professor at Pyungyang Seminary from 1908. During his sojourn in Korea, he published more than fifty books in Korean and wrote six works in English. As a practical theologian, his *Sôrgyohak* (homiletics) and *Mokhoehak* (pastoral theology) were used as textbooks until the seminary closed in 1938, and even after it reopened upon the liberation of Korea in 1945, they were once again used as texts. Clark's attitude on theology was fundamentalistic. Active as the editor for *Sinhak chinam* (Korean theological quarterly review)

---

[25] Yang Sun Kim, *History of the Korean Church in the Ten Years Since Liberation (1945-1955)* (Seoul: Religious Education Committee of the Korean Presbyterian Church, 1956), 173.

which first came out in 1918, he was the spokesperson for the theology of Pyungyang Seminary.[26] The third person to contribute to the formation of theology in Korea was Reynolds (1867-1951). He came to Korea as a Southern Presbyterian missionary in 1892 and was active for forty-five years. While he was a traveling missionary and a Bible translator, he was invited in 1924 to become a professor at the Seminary, and there he taught systematic theology until 1937. In an article of his in *Sinhak chinam* 3.1 (1920) entitled "Sinhak pyônjûngnon: sese t'orok sangjon ha'nûn malssûm [Study on theological dogmatism: the word of eternal existence], he strongly emphasized the point that the Scripture had been put together through inspiration. He also made Chia Yu-ming's *Evidence of Christianity* his centerpiece and introduced students to the systematic theology of Charles Hodge and A. A. Hodge, both of whom represented the orthodox American Presbyterian theology of the nineteenth century. The fact that one of the educational missions of Pyungyang Seminary was "to thoroughly infuse the Word of God in order to consolidate theology on the foundation of Truth" indicates what the Pyungyang Seminary's theology was like. Furthermore, the conservative theology introduced in Korea was also evangelical at the same time. Conn points out that the theological background of Pyungyang Seminary before 1938 was based on a precise knowledge of Reformist, Calvinist theology.[27] From the above, it can be guessed that the Korean Presbyterian church inherited the Westminster Confession and the Old Princeton Theology. It is significant also that the curriculum of Pyungyang Seminary included a requirement course entitled "The Creed" which taught the Westminster Confession. Therefore, Clark said at the ceremony celebrating the fiftieth anniversary of the Northern

---

[26] Conn, 37-40.

[27] Ibid., 47.

Presbyterian mission in Korea that such conservative theology was the secret behind God enabling the missionaries to achieve a great success in Korea.[28] This certainly was a most fitting description.

III. The Formation of the Korean Presbyterian Church

As mentioned before, the Northern and Southern Presbyterian missions got together in 1893 to form the Council of Missions Holding the Presbyterian Form of Government. Once the Canadian mission finally joined the Council in 1898, the body became the common discussion forum for all four missions.[29] The Council, however, was merely for the members to promote fellowship and discussion. And because the jurisdiction over the churches established by each mission was still being exercised by the mother church outside Korea,[30] each mission in Korea had to obtain permission from the home church before the Council could assume its own juridical power as the presbytery. As the result of the four missions' requests to their home churches, the Council came to exercise such authority in 1900, and the session during the same year approved the attendance of a Korean delegation starting the following year. From then on, a meeting in Korean language also came to be convened. Nevertheless, converts still had to remain affiliated with the home churches.[31] In 1901, the Council designated the Discussion Committee for Policies on the Establishment of Korean Free Presbytery (*Chosôn chayu changnohoe sôllip pangch'im ûijông ûiwôn*). And in the following year, based on the Committee's report, the organization of the nationwide, united

---

[28] *Report of the 50th Anniversary Celebration of the Korean Mission*, 56.

[29] Charles A. Clark, *Digest of the Presbyterian Church of Korea* (Seoul: The Korea Religious Book and Tract Society, 1918), 607.

[30] Ibid., *Constitutional Law of Korean Presbyterian Church* (1919), 71-72, as cited by *Sinhak chinam* [Korean theological quarterly review] 12.2.

[31] Charles A. Clark, Ibid., 72.

presbytery as the highest-level assembly was approved. The Committee then was asked to prepare the constitution and various regulations for such a presbytery, while each mission in Korea requested permission from its home church for setting up the presbytery in Korea.[32] After receiving answers from their home churches, the four missions got together in 1903 to report on the replies. It turned out that while both the Canadian and the Australian missions had been given the necessary permissions, both the American Northern Presbyterian and the Southern Presbyterian churches had been instructed to defer establishing the national presbytery in Korea for the following reason:

> Setting up the free church in coalition with other churches would be all right in the future, but deferring it is better at the present. The reason for this is as follows. Currently in Korea, local presbyteries are no more than a few throughout the country, and as there still are no Korean ministers, missionaries taking up too much power within a weak, young church may hinder the growth of that weak, young church.[33]

Upon receiving such report, the Council petitioned again and stressed the urgency of establishing the free church in Korea. As of 1901, the Council was seeking to nurture religious workers at Pyungyang Seminary for the future Korean church, and with their imminent graduation, the Council could not stop pushing for the establishment of the Korean church. According to the Presbyterian constitution, a Korean minister had to be ordained as a member of either the home country's presbytery or the new Korean presbytery, and thus both American Presbyterian churches could not avoid approving the establishment of the independent Korean presbytery.[34] After receiving permissions from their home countries, the Council of Missions Holding the Presbyterian Form

---

[32] Charles A. Clark, ed., *Documents of Korean Presbyterian Church History* (Seoul: Korean Christian Book Society, 1918), Korean ed., 21-28.

[33] Paek, 321.

[34] Ibid., 406-7, as cited by Min, 265-65.

of Government met in 1905 and approved the following proposals: the Korean Christian presbytery was to be organized in 1907, Korean pastors were to be appointed as preaching ministers, and a creed was to adopted on behalf of the new Korean church.[35] Finally on September 17, 1907, the first national presbytery of the Korean Presbyterian church was organized at Changdaehyôn Church in Pyôngyang.[36] This makes the year 1907 a turning point in the history of the Korean church, not only because the "Korean" church became officially organized, but also because a spiritual awakening and the Great Revival Movement began at the beginning of that year. Historians usually refer to the Great Revival Movement of 1907 as the "Pentecostal Procession of the Holy Spirit" (*Osunjôl Sôngnyôn kangnim*) in Korea. It was a shocking event during which the Lord Christ—who had been crucified, rose again from the dead in three days, and sits at the right hand of the Father— was met face to face by the faithful through the procession of the Holy Spirit. The Korean Presbyterian church had come to form an organized community and become a part of the Church of the Body of Christ through the great work of the Holy Spirit. Then five years later in 1912, as the church continued to grow and become stronger, seven presbyteries were organized under the General Assembly of Korea Independent Presbytery (*Taehan Yesugyo changnohoe tongnohoe*), and the Independent Presbytery (*Tongnohoe*) dissolved itself, thus giving way to the

---

[35] *Tongnorok, che il-hoe* [The record of the Independent Presbytery, first meeting] (1970), 4. The name *"Tongnohoe"* (Independent Presbytery) is due to the fact that there was only one presbytery in the country. At the meeting Moffett was elected as the president.

[36] Among those at the meeting were 33 foreign missionaries, 36 Korean elders, and seven graduates of Pyungyang Seminary ordained as ministers. Statistics on the Korean Church at the time indicate that Koreans accounted for seven ministers, 53 elders, 859 churches, 19,000 baptized members, and 70,000 other members. Paek, 408.

final, organized body of the General Assembly of the Presbyterian Church in Korea (Taehan Yesugyo changnohoe ch'onghoe).[37]

IV. The Adoption of a Doctrinal Confession by the Korean Presbyterian Church

The collection of documents on the Korean Presbyterian church compiled by Charles A. Clark shows that as of 1901, the Presbyterian Council (*Changnogyo kongûihoe*) was already working on formulating a creed and discussing the constitution.[38] To formulate a creed and a draft for a constitution, the Presbyterian Council chose committee members to translate the Constitution of the World Presbytery. Upon a report by the Discussion Committee for Policies on the Establishment of Korean Free Presbytery, the Council selected members for the constitution preparation committee. The members were to write a constitution which was to be reviewed, adopted, and submitted to the opening national presbytery. Once the Council had received permission from the mother churches to set up the presbytery, it began the process of adopting in advance a church creed for the Korean presbytery in 1905.[39] For three years, the creed preparation committee members had been collecting doctrinal confessions from many countries for study and comparison, and in 1905 they decided that the creed adopted by the Indian church was most suitable. Hoping that the creed would be the doctrinal confession for every Asian Presbyterian church, the Korean Presbyterian church adopted it.[40] This creed is known as the Twelve Articles. In addition, the Independent Presbytery also adopted the

---

[37] Charles A. Clark, *Documents of Korean Presbyterian Church History*, 56-58.

[38] Ibid., 22,24.

[39] Ibid., 41-42.

[40] Paik, 375.

Westminster Shorter Catechism. The reason why the Westminster Confession and the Larger Catechism were not chosen will be discussed later. The Twelve Articles were adopted by the Korean Presbyterian church through the leadership of Presbyterian missionaries in Korea, but the creed had originally been devised by the British Presbyterian missionaries and adopted by the Indian Free Presbyterian Church. Considering the similarities among the mission churches, Presbyterian missionaries in Korea had the Korean Presbyterian church adopt the creed after modifying only the Foreword. For those who may not be familiar with the creed, the Twelve Articles are listed here:

Article I. The Scriptures of the Old and New Testaments are the Word of God, the only infallible rule of faith and duty.

Article II. There is but one God, and He alone is to be worshiped. He is a Spirit, self-existent, omnipresent, yet distinct from all other spirits and from material things; infinite, eternal and unchangeable in His being, wisdom, holiness, justice, goodness, truth and love.

Article III. In the Godhead, there are three Persons, the Father, the Son and the Holy Spirit, and these three are one God, the same in substance, equal in power and glory.

Article IV. All things visible and invisible were created by God by the word of His power; and are preserved and governed by Him so that, while He is in no way the author of sin, He worketh all things according to the counsel of His will, and they serve the fulfillment of His wise and good and holy purpose.

Article V. God created man, male and female, after His own image, in knowledge, righteousness and holiness, with dominion over the creatures. All men have the same origin and are brethren.

Article VI. Our first parents, being free to choose between good and evil, and being tempted, sinned against God; and all mankind, descending by ordinary generation from Adam, the head of the race, sinned in him, and fell with him. To their original guilt and corruption, those capable of so doing have added actual transgressions. All justly deserve His wrath and punishment in this present life and in that which is to come.

Article VII. To save men from the guilt, corruption and penalty of sin, and to give them eternal life, God in His infinite love, sent into the world His eternal and only begotten Son, the Lord Jesus Christ, in whom alone God has become incarnate, and through whom alone men can be saved. The eternal Son became man, and was and continued to be true God and true man, in two distinct natures, and one person forever. He was conceived by the power of the Holy Spirit, and born of the virgin Mary, yet without sin. For sinful men, He perfectly obeyed the law of God, and offered Himself a true and perfect sacrifice to satisfy Divine justice and reconcile men to God. He died on the cross, was buried and rose again from the dead on the third day. He ascended to the right hand of God, where He maketh intercession for His people, and whence He shall come again to raise the dead, and to judge the world.

Article VIII. The Holy Spirit, who proceedeth from the Father and the Son, maketh men partakers of salvation, convincing them of their sin and misery and enlightening their minds in the knowledge of Christ, renewing their wills, persuading and enabling them to embrace Jesus Christ freely offered them in the Gospel, and working in them all the fruits of the righteousness.

Article IX. While God chose the people in Christ before the foundation of the world, that they should be holy and without blemish before Him in love, having foreordained them unto adoption as sons through Jesus Christ, unto Himself, according to the good pleasure of His will, to the praise of the glory of His grace, which He freely bestowed on them in the beloved; He maketh a full and free offer of salvation to all men, and commandeth them to repent of their sins, to believe in the Lord Jesus Christ as their Savior, and to live a humble, and holy life after His example, and in obedience to God's revealed will.

Those who believe in Christ and obey Him are saved, the chief benefits being that they receive justification, adoption into the number of eternal glory. Believers may also in this life enjoy assurance of their salvation. In His gracious work, the Holy Spirit uses the means of grace, especially the Word, the sacraments and prayer.

Article X. The sacraments instituted by Christ are Baptism and the Lord's Supper. Baptism is the washing with water in the name of the Father and of the Son and of the Holy Spirit, and is the sign and seal of our union to Christ, of regeneration, and of the renewing power of the Holy Spirit, and our engagement to be the Lord's. It is administered to those who profess their faith in Christ and to their children.

The Lord's Supper is the partaking of the bread and of the cup as a memorial of Christ's death, and is a sign and seal of the benefits thereof to believers. It is to be observed by His people till He comes in token of their faith in Him and His sacrifice, of their appropriation of its benefits, and of their future engagement to serve Him, of their communion with Him and with one another.

The benefits of the Sacraments are not from any virtue in them or in him who doth administer them, but only from the blessing of Christ and the working of His Spirit in them that by faith receive them.

Article XI. It is the duty of all believers to unite in church fellowship, to observe the sacraments and other ordinance of Christ, to obey His laws, to continue in prayer; to keep holy the Lord's Day, to meet together for His worship, to wait upon the preaching of His word, to give as God may prosper them, to manifest a Christ-like spirit among themselves toward all men, to labor for the extension of Christ's kingdom throughout the world, and to wait for His glorious appearing.

Article XII. At the last day, the dead shall be raised, and all shall appear before the judgment seat of Christ, and shall receive according to the deeds done in the present life, whether good or bad. Those who have believed in Christ and obeyed Him, shall be openly acquitted and received into glory, but the unbelieving and wicked, being condemned, shall suffer the punishment due to their sins.

The contents of the Twelve Articles above may be summarized as follows. The lordship of God, the divinity of Christ, the birth of Christ by a virgin, the atonement for sin, the Holy Spirit, the predestination of the elect, the omnipotent grace of God, the resurrection, and the final judgment are all covered in the confession. It may be said that these Twelve Articles are characterized by a greater degree of universality than the Westminster Confession. So then, why did the four Presbyterian missions in Korea have the Korean church adopt the Twelve Articles of the Indian Free Presbyterian Church rather than the Westminster Confession or the Larger and Shorter Catechisms? There may have been many reasons. Among the most important could have been the belief that, in order for the newly born Presbyterian church of Korea to universally and quickly digest a historical, doctrinal confession of the Christian Church before making the confession its own, the Twelve Articles, characterized by clarity and simplicity, are most suitable for the Korean situation. Moreover, the Twelve Articles may be regarded as an abridged

version of the Westminster Confession. Commenting on the
Twelve Articles, Paek once noted that "the doctrinal confession
itself expresses a strong Calvinistic inclination."[41] Even Song Kil-
sôp, a church historian at the Korean Methodist Theological
School, states that "this doctrinal confession which was prepared
on the basis of moderate Calvinism had received favorable
criticism from the Methodist church at the time and became
accepted without any special sense of objection."[42] Conn notes
that the evangelistic and conservative theology of the early Korean
missionaries is reflected in the Articles adopted by the Korean
Presbyterian church after its establishment in 1907.[43] A historian
asserted that "even if based solely on the fact that there was no
Korean creed" one cannot avoid regarding the confession, which
was adopted upon the mission's decision, as a disgrace to the
founding presbytery.[44] This author, however, believes that it was
too much to require or even to expect the Korean Presbyterian
church with its short history (and just having been established as
an organized church) at the time to put forth an indigenous Korean
confession. Considering that the Westminster Confession was
devised in 1647, which was full 130 years after the Protestant
Reformation in Germany in 1517, a doctrinal confession is not
something that is put together overnight. It has to develop on its
own out of the spiritual experience and maturity of the faithful.
Moreover, a doctrinal confession is made possible even more so,
when all the believers have studied the Scripture in depth and
have made it their own. What cannot be overlooked is the fact

---

[41] Paek, 408.

[42] Song Kiil-sôp, *Han'guk sinhak sasangsa* [History of theological thought in
Korea] (Seoul: Taehan Kidokkyo ch'ulp'ansa, 1987), 164.

[43] Conn, 31.

[44] Min Kyông-bae, "Han'guk kyohoesa wa sinang kobaek" [The spiritual
confession and the history of the Korean Church], in *Kidokkyo sasang* 271
(January 1981): 52.

that the Westminster Shorter Catechism was adopted simultaneously with the Twelve Articles. This catechism was said to be a doctrinal work that must be taught along with the Confession and the Larger Catechism in the Presbyterian church and in its theological seminaries.[45] Even though the Korean Presbyterian church did not officially adopt the Westminster Confession by 1908, this doctrinal confession was being regarded as equivalent to the doctrinal standard of the Korean Presbyterian church. In 1925, Baird translated the revised 1788 edition into Korean and used it as a text for teaching doctrine in the seminary and for the presbytery. As the Korean church formulated and provided spiritual guidelines to the faithful, the average believer gained ownership of an already prepared doctrinal confession without having to wait for an expression of it in his own spiritual experience.[46] Therefore, from the start, the Korean Presbyterian church, through the Bible study conference, read and believed in the Scripture as the Word of God without any qualification. Especially, the Westminster Shorter Catechism was taught and required to be memorized during catechism study sessions. In this fashion, the Korean church was able to grow into a solid church, believing in and living by the Scripture by the fiftieth anniversary of its foundation in 1934.

The year 1934 was another turning point in the history of the Korean church. From that year, there began to emerge within the Korean Presbyterian church those possessing liberal theology and spirituality. The Korean church, however, did not tolerate them. And four years later in 1938, the Korean church was faced with a big crisis, because the Japanese required Christians to perform worshipping ceremonies at Shinto shrines (*sinsa ch'ambae*). The Korean Presbyterian church ended up submitting to the organized,

---

[45] Conn, 31.

[46] Paek, 408.

treacherous policy of the Japanese imperialists. Pyungyang Seminary was closed down by the Japanese authority. By 1941, foreign missionaries were expelled from Korea. Until national liberation in 1945, the Korean church was severely persecuted. Those ministers, presbyters, and preachers who resisted the Shinto worship requirement were imprisoned or even martyred. In contrast, the ministers who collaborated with the Japanese Empire founded a government sponsored seminary in P'yôngyang. In Seoul, too, a similar seminary was established. Professors who began teaching at these two schools were the so-called liberal theologians who had emerged in 1934. From then on, the door was wide open for the liberal theology to enter the Korean church freely.

Upon liberation, the Korean church was drawn into a greater crisis. Firstly, with the North-South division of the country, the church could not avoid organizational division likewise. The church in North Korea lost its religious freedom due to persecution by the Soviet military occupation and by the Communist regime. Fortunately, there was freedom in the South. The situation there, however, was complicated. Above all, there was no repentance and apology at the General Assembly over the issue of Shinto worship which had previously been approved at that level. Secondly, students in Seoul Seminary put forth their dissent in regard to issues of theology and theological education. For this reason, internal fighting ensued every time the General Assembly met. In addition, the ministers who finally were released from prison after refusing to participate in the Shinto worship founded a new theological school in Pusan and declared that it was the successor to the old Pyungyang Seminary. Participating in this movement were the three disciples of Professor Machen and the missionary Hamilton who had previously been a professor at the old Pyungyang Seminary. Ultimately, the Korean Presbyterian Church became divided into four groups: the General Assembly of Presbyterian Church in Korea (Korean abbreviation, *Haptong*), the Presbyterian Church of Korea (*Tonghap*), the General

Assembly of the Presbyterian Church of Korea (*Koryô Theological Seminary*), and the Presbyterian church in the Republic of Korea (*Kijang*). Among the four, the group that continued to espouse, clarify, and teach the doctrines of the Presbyterian church—namely the Westminster Confession and the Catechisms (both the Larger and Shorter)—from 1945 to 1960 was the *Koryô* group. When the American United Presbyterian church devised a new confession in 1967, three organizations of the Korean Presbyterian church, with the exception of the *Kijang* group, sharply criticized the new confession. Before such criticism, the *Haptong* group had decided to adopt the Westminster Confession during its General Assembly meeting in 1963, and the *Tonghap* group had adopted the same confession during its 1968 General Assembly meeting. Finally, the *Koryô* group's approval came during its own General Assembly session in 1972. In this fashion, the Korean Presbyterian church became a Presbyterian church having the Westminster Confession and the Larger and the Shorter Catechisms as its doctrinal confessions.

Conclusion

This author sought to provide a general, historical survey of the formation of the Korean Presbyterian church and the process by which it adopted the Twelve Articles and the Westminster Confession. The Korean Presbyterian church can be said to have grown faster and more soundly than any other mission church in the world. In the background to the quantitative and qualitative growth is the significant fact that the spirituality and theology of early missionaries in Korea were not only evangelistic, but also conservative. What must be assessed very favorably is that the adoption of the Nevius Plan, which emphasized teaching believers to know and love the Scripture, enabled the faithful in the mission church to achieve a speedy, spiritual growth and independence. Finally, the Korean Presbyterian church was able to construct a doctrinal foundation by educating its members in the Westminster Confession and the Larger and the Shorter Catechisms as its standard. When Professor Machen left Princeton Theological Seminary to found Westminster Theological Seminary in 1929, hearts of the Northern and Southern Presbyterian missionaries in Korea were with Machen's theology. Therefore, when the graduates of Pyungyang Union Theological Seminary petitioned to study in the U.S., the missionaries recommended the new Westminster Seminary over Princeton. As a result, both Kim Ch'i-sôn and Pak Yun-sôn became the first Korean students to enter Westminster Theological Seminary.

Oliver Bowles and the Westminster View
of Gospel Ministry

PHILIP GRAHAM RYKEN

The Westminster Divines held the ministry of the gospel in the highest regard. This is not surprising, given that most of them were preachers who considered their calling a sacred trust. Like the apostles, they gave themselves "continually to prayer, and to the ministry of the word" (Acts 6:4; KJV). In their ministry of the word they preached biblical, doctrinal, practical sermons in the plain style. To the clear proclamation of God's word they joined the careful administration of the sacraments. Their diligent attention to these public acts of worship was further complemented by their faithful devotion to private pastoral care.

The immediate origins of this approach to gospel ministry are not hard to find. The Westminster Divines were Puritans, for the most part, and thus shared Puritan sensibilities about ministry in the pulpit and the parish. As far as preaching was concerned, the Puritan view was most fully articulated in *The Art of Prophesying*, a homiletical manual written by William Perkins (1558-1602).[1] When it came to ministry in the parish, the basic handbook was Richard Baxter's (1615-1691) *The Reformed*

---

[1] William Perkins, *The Art of Prophesying* (1606; repr. Edinburgh: Banner of Truth, 1996).

Pastor.[2] For all the theological and ecclesiological differences between Baxter and the men of Westminster, their vision for pastoral ministry was essentially the same.

There is another treatise, however, which sheds even more direct light on the Westminster view of gospel ministry. The book has long been forgotten, due undoubtedly to the fact that it has never been translated from Latin into English.[3] Yet it provides a more comprehensive manual for gospel ministry than either Perkins or Baxter. Unlike *The Art of Prophesying*, it addresses the full range of pastoral duties; unlike *The Reformed Pastor*, it provides detailed instruction in the art of homiletics. The book has the further virtue of having been written by a revered member of the Westminster Assembly, a minister from Bedfordshire named Oliver Bowles. It is called *De Pastore Evangelico Tractatus*, "A Treatise on the Gospel Ministry." A close study of *De Pastore Evangelico Tractatus* broadens our understanding of the Westminster view of gospel ministry. It also reveals a significant truth about the origins of that view. While the Westminster Divines had a thoroughly Reformed understanding of the pastorate, they stood in a much older tradition of pastoral care that stretched back to the early church fathers. The Westminster view of pastoral ministry was not only Puritan, but also catholic, in the best sense of the word.

The Life and Work of Oliver Bowles

Relatively little is known about the life of the venerable Oliver Bowles. He was born around 1577 at Sawtry in Huntingdonshire.

---

[2] Baxter, *The Reformed Pastor* (1656; repr. Edinburgh: Banner of Truth, 1974). Another standard work was *The Faithfull Shepherd* by Richard Bernard (London, 1621).

[3] It is hoped that an English edition may yet be published. I am grateful for the work of Jonathan Rockey in translating the quotations that appear in this essay.

At the age of fifteen or sixteen he matriculated at Queen's College, Cambridge, an institution with strong Puritan loyalties. After receiving his degree, Bowles was named a fellow of the college; he held this position from 1599 to 1606.[4]

As a fellow at Queen's, Bowles' primary responsibility was tutoring undergraduates, and in this he excelled. His most famous pupil—the erudite Puritan theologian John Preston (1587-1628)—considered him "a very holy & learned man, a noted & carefull Tutor."[5] In fact it was Bowles who persuaded Preston to abandon his musical training in order to devote himself to the study of divinity. Eventually Preston succeeded his mentor as a tutor at Queen's and surpassed him as a lecturer in Cambridge University. But by this time Bowles had left the academy for the ministry. Already during his years at Cambridge he had been ordained (Colchester, 1601) and appointed rector in a nearby parish (Abbots Ripton, 1605-1607). In 1607 he was called away from Cambridge to serve the Rectory of Sutton in Bedfordshire, where he remained for the duration of his active ministry.

Oliver Bowles must have enjoyed a favorable reputation beyond Bedfordshire, for he was among the "learned and godly Divines" nominated by the House of Commons to serve in the Westminster Assembly. Since he was approaching seventy when the Assembly convened, Bowles was one of its oldest members. This probably explains why Parliament asked him to preach the sermon which opened the Assembly. The newly-convened Divines, joined by the Houses of Lords and Commons, appointed a fast to dedicate their work to God. The fast-day was honored, in

---

[4] The basic facts pertaining to Bowles' time at Cambridge are outlined in John Venn and J. A. Venn, eds., *Alumni Cantabrigiensis: A Biographical List of all Known Students, Graduates and Holders of Office at the University of Cambridge, from the Earliest Times to 1900, Part 1: From the Earliest Times to 1751*, 4 vols. (Cambridge: Cambridge University Press, 1922), 1:192.

[5] Thomas Ball, *The Life of the Renowned Doctor Preston*, ed. by E. W. Harcourt (1628; repr. Oxford: Parker, 1885), 6.

fine Puritan fashion, with sermons preached at Westminster Abbey. These public sermons were a notable feature of the Long Parliament.[6] Bowles was chosen to preach first, he acknowledged, not because he was the Assembly's most gifted preacher, but out of respect for his age and experience, "that dayes and multitudes of years should speak."[7]

Bowles entitled his sermon—which was subsequently published by order of Parliament—"Zeale for God's House Quickened; or, a Sermon preached before the Assembly of Lords, Commons, and Divines, at their solemn Fast, July 7, 1643, in Abbey Church, Westminster: expressing the Eminency of Zeale required in Church-Reformers." Two features of the sermon are noteworthy. One is its stress on the necessity of an earnest preaching ministry for the spiritual welfare of the church and the nation. "Where Church-reformation is in hand," preached Bowles, "a spirit of zeale should run in the veines of the Reformers."[8] He thus closed by exhorting his colleagues in the gospel ministry to preach "zealously, compassionately, convincingly, feelingly, frequently, and gravely."[9]

Another notable feature of the sermon is the abundance of references Bowles makes to his ecclesiastical predecessors. Some

---

[6] See John F. Wilson, *Pulpit in Parliament: Puritanism during the English Civil Wars, 1640-1648* (Princeton, NJ: Princeton University Press, 1969), and Robert M. Norris, "The Preaching of the Assembly," in *To Glorify and Enjoy God: A Commemoration of the 350th Anniversary of the Westminster Assembly*, ed. by John L. Carson and David W. Hall (Edinburgh: Banner of Truth, 1994), 63-81.

[7] Oliver Bowles, *Zeale for God's House Quickened; or, a Sermon preached before the Assembly of Lords, Commons, and Divines, at their solemn Fast, July 7, 1643, in Abbey Church, Westminster: expressing the Eminency of Zeale required in Church-Reformer* (London, 1643), preface.

[8] Bowles, *Zeale for God's House*, 8.

[9] Bowles, *Zeale for God's House*, 41-47.

of the authors he quotes are Reformers like Martin Luther, Martin Bucer, and John Calvin. This is in keeping with the strong stance he takes against Roman Catholic doctrine and practice. But many more of his references are to patristic and medieval writers such as Eusebius of Caesarea, Basil the Great, Gregory of Nazianzus, Jerome, Chrysostom, Augustine, Gregory the Great, and Bernard of Clairvaux. Bowles was strongly opposed to Popery, but not to catholicity. That is to say, although he squarely rejected the errors of Rome, particularly in the *loci* of soteriology, he firmly believed in the church universal, the worldwide communion of the saints throughout history.

Once the Assembly commenced its regular proceedings, Oliver Bowles was faithful in his daily attendance at Westminster, although he does not appear to have played a major role in the deliberations.[10] Perhaps this was due to his age and infirmity. The date cannot be fixed with certainty, but he seems to have died in 1644, long before the Assembly finished its work.[11]

The only book Oliver Bowles ever wrote was published after his death. Its full title was *De Pastore Evangelico Tractatus: In Quo Universum munus Pastorale, tam quoad Pastoris Vocationem, & Præparationem, quam ipsius muneris Exercitium, accurate proponitur*; that is: "A Treatise on the Evangelical Pastor: in which the whole pastoral office—not only the calling and preparation of the pastor, but also the exercise of the office itself—is carefully set forth." The book was first published in 1649, brought to press by Oliver's son Edward. Bowles had twelve sons

---

[10] James Reid, *Memoirs of the Westminster Divines*, 2 vols. (1811, Paisley; repr. Edinburgh: Banner of Truth, 1982), 1:135.

[11] The *Dictionary of National Biography* maintains that Bowles was succeeded upon his death by Thomas Ford (London: Oxford University Press, 1917ff., 7:425). In his *Lives of the Puritans* (London, 1813, 3:466-68), Benjamin Brook has Bowles dying as late as 1674 (at the age of nearly 100!) and purports to recount the man's dying words. It is unclear where Brook got his information, but it is demonstrably false: the title page for *De Pastore Evangelico Tractatus* proves that the work was published posthumously.

in all, of whom Edward was the most distinguished, having prepared for the gospel ministry at Cambridge under the outstanding Puritan preacher Richard Sibbes (1577-1635). *De Pastore Evangelico Tractatus* went through three editions in England (1649, 1655, 1659) before finding an international readership in the Calvinist communities of Holland (Amsterdam, 1659; Groningen, 1739) and Switzerland (Geneva, 1667).

Given these facts, it cannot be said that Oliver Bowles exercised a demonstrable influence on the writing of the Westminster Standards. His contribution to the deliberations of the Divines was modest, his participation in the Assembly short-lived. Furthermore, his *magnum opus* did not appear in print until after the Assembly's business had been concluded. Nevertheless, *De Pastore Evangelico Tractatus* remains a major source for understanding the Westminster view of gospel ministry. Bowles did not set out to introduce a novel perspective, but to codify the best Puritan convictions about the work of the pastor. *De Pastore Evangelico Tractatus* thus serves as a reliable guide to what the Westminster Divines meant when they spoke of "the ministry of the gospel." Over the course of its four hundred pages, nearly every pastoral duty mentioned in the Westminster *Directory for Public Worship* and *Form of Church-Government* is carefully explained and practically applied.

The Gospel Minister

Oliver Bowles wrote his *De Pastore Evangelico Tractatus* for the benefit of his esteemed fathers and faithful brothers in the gospel ministry. The treatise is divided into three major sections, or books. The first describes the spiritual and intellectual preparation necessary to undertake pastoral work (*De Pastoris praeparatione ad munus Pastorale*); the second analyzes the public and private ministry of God's Word (*De Dispensatione Verbi Pastorali*); and the third discusses the administration of the sacraments and the conduct of pastoral prayer, along with concluding exhortations to faithfulness in pastoral duties (*De Sacramentorum Administratione, Precatione Pastorali & mediis, quibus in munere Pastorali fungendo confirmatur*).

Each section of the treatise offers a host of practical suggestions for ministerial conduct. For example, the manual on preparation for the ministry covers topics as diverse as how to discern a call to pastoral ministry, how to use possessions hospitably and charitably, how most profitably to receive unfavorable criticism, and how to handle one's responsibilities as a husband and father. Chapters later in the treatise address issues such as when it is permissible for a minister to move to a new parish and what it means for an evangelical pastor to minister "under the cross" (*sub cruce*), laboring in a seemingly unproductive parish. From this wealth of practical wisdom emerges the Westminster view of the gospel ministry: a good pastor is a godly, learned, and evangelical shepherd.

The place to begin, of course, is with the minister's personal godliness, which is not so much asserted in the Westminster Standards as it is assumed. The Divines take it for granted that a pastor is a man of superlative spiritual devotion. In his *De Pastore Evangelico Tractatus*, Oliver Bowles paints a portrait of the godly minister after the apostolic sketch in 1 Timothy 3:1-7. By way of warning, Bowles gives particular attention to the sins which most easily destroy a pastoral ministry. The minister must guard against any form of sexual sin, "because most gravely of all does the appearance or even trivial suspicion of this evil wound a man's reputation."[12] In addition to protecting his chastity, the gospel minister must avoid greed, envy, and ambition, which Bowles defines as "an inordinate craving for

---

[12] "Quia omnium gravissime famam ejus vulnerat hujus mali species, vel levior suspicio" (Bowles, *De Pastore Evangelico*, 45).

recognition."[13] The reason these vices are so deadly is that they diminish the minister's appetite for spiritual things: "Any care that comes from an inordinate love of the world oppresses the spirit; as when one is eager for amassing wealth, or ponders his own promotion to a further level of honor, or spends more time on earthly matters than the nature of the business requires; or finally when he is ensnared by whatsoever worldly things the less to raise his soul heavenward."[14]

Although Bowles' treatment of the minister's character is based on a biblical text, it also owes a great deal to descriptions of the moral life in Horace, Seneca, Sophocles, and other classical authors. Besides the vices a minister must avoid, then, there are also the virtues he must embrace. These include godly affections such as zeal, sympathy, humility, reverence, prudence, and holiness. In short, "every Minister of the Word ought to be an *exemplar*, to which when the congregation directs its eyes it may compose its life and character."[15]

One of Bowles' favorite terms for describing the virtuous character of a godly minister is "gravity:" "Let a pastor be revered for his gravity."[16] Bowles had already introduced this term in his fast-day sermon at Westminster Abbey, and it was later to appear in the Westminster Assembly's *Directory for Public Worship*: "The servant of Christ, whatever his method be, is to perform his whole

---

[13] "Ambitio est inordinatus appetitus honoris" (Bowles, *De Pastore Evangelico*, 48).

[14] "Quae a mundi amore inordinato proficiscitur, animum opprimens cura; ut cum quis vel divitiis congerendis studet, vel de se ad ulteriorem honoris gradum promovendo cogitat, vel plus temporis, quam natura negotii exigit, terrenis impendit; vel denique quibuscunque mundanis, quo minus ad caelestia animum attollat, irretitur" (Bowles, *De Pastore Evangelico*, 26).

[15] "[S]ic quilibet Minister Verbi debet esse ut exemplar, ad quod, cum oculos dirigat plebs, vitam moresque componat" (Bowles, *De Pastore Evangelico*, 28).

[16] "Sit Pastor, gravitate reverendus" (Bowles, *De Pastore Evangelico*, 20).

ministry. . . . Gravely, as becometh the word of God; shunning all such gesture, voice, and expressions, as may occasion the corruptions of men to despise him and his ministry."[17] Not that the minister is to be gloomy, of course, but the dignity of his character must convey the sobriety of sacred things. Since the work of the pastor is serious business, writes Bowles, "Let everything that proceeds from him breathe seriousness."[18] He quotes with approval a favorite apothegm of William Perkins, a saying which epitomizes the Westminster view of gospel ministry: "Minister Verbi es, hoc age;"[19] which is as much to say, "You are a minister of the Word . . . get with it!"

In the Puritan tradition, the gospel minister is to be as learned as he is godly. The Westminster *Form of Church Government* thus provides guidelines for the rigorous examination of a candidate for ordination. "He shall be examined," wrote the Divines, "touching his skill in the original tongues, and his trial to be made by reading the Hebrew and Greek Testaments, and rendering some portion of some into Latin; and if he be defective in them, enquiry shall be made more strictly after his other learning, and whether he hath skill in logick and philosophy."[20] In addition, the candidate was to be tested in systematic theology, with particular regard to his ability to defend orthodox doctrine against heresy.

In the section dealing with preparation for the ministry, *De Pastore Evangelico Tractatus* provides detailed recommendations

---

[17] *The Directory for the Publick Worship of God*, in *The Confession of Faith* (Inverness: Publications Committee of the Free Presbyterian Church of Scotland, 1970), 369-94 (p. 381).

[18] "Quaecunque ab eo proficiscuntur, gravitatem spirent" (Bowles, *De Pastore Evangelico*, 23).

[19] William Perkins, quoted in Bowles, *De Pastore Evangelico*, 28.

[20] *The Form of Presbyterial Church-Government and of Ordination of Ministers*, in *The Confession of Faith* (Inverness: Publications Committee of the Free Presbyterian Church of Scotland, 1970), 395-416 (p. 413).

for a candidate's studies in divinity. These studies are to begin and end with holy Scripture, for there is no substitute for a comprehensive knowledge of the Bible in its original languages. Bowles thus quotes Luther with approval: "Although my acquaintance with the Hebrew tongue is scant, still I would not trade it for all the treasures of the whole world."[21] In addition to mastering Hebrew and Greek, the candidate should learn how to use commentaries and other standard tools for biblical interpretation. Bowles also recommends (as one might expect from a former tutor at Cambridge) a broad exposure to the liberal arts, especially rhetoric and history.

As far as systematic theology is concerned, men preparing for the gospel ministry will have to be selective in their reading, and *De Pastore Evangelico Tractatus* helps to set the priorities. The most important theologians to read are the most recent. This is because doctrinal error infected the church almost immediately after the apostolic age. Since pure scriptural doctrine was not fully recovered until the Reformation, "the prize must be granted to the recent authors in matters of Scripture interpretation and in refuting heretics."[22] Nevertheless, the ancients are not to be neglected, and here Bowles practiced what he preached. Since he was a scholar, his treatise was not simply the product of his pastoral experience, but also the fruit of his careful research into the history of pastoral care.

De Pastore Evangelico Tractatus makes frequent reference to the theologians of the Reformation—not only to the magisterial Reformers (Luther and Calvin), but also to other significant Reformers (Philip Melanchthon, Peter Martyr, Heinrich Bullinger)

---

[21] "Quamvis exigua sit mea linguae Hebraicae notitia, cum omnibus tamen totius mundi gazis non commutarem" (Martin Luther, quoted in Bowles, *De Pastore Evangelico*, 77).

[22] "At Neotericis, sive in Scripturis interpretandis, sive in haeresibus refutandis, palma videtur concedenda" (Bowles, *De Pastore Evangelico*, 129).

and to the major theologians of Reformed orthodoxy (Wolfgang Musculus, Jerome Zanchius, Theodore Beza, Zacharias Ursinus, Caspar Olevianus, Thomas Cartwright, Franciscus Junius, William Whitaker, William Perkins, William Ames). Just as extensive as these references to the Reformers, however, are Bowles' citations from the early church fathers: Tertullian, Cyprian, Athanasius, Gregory of Nazianzus, Ambrose, Jerome, Chrysostom, Theodoret, and, of course, Augustine. While acknowledging their limitations, Bowles gives these patristic sources high praise: "It must be admitted that the old fathers did shine in their day as the great lights of the world, as hammers of heretics, fiercest avengers of the sacred truth, and were amply filled with gifts of the Holy Spirit."[23] Bowles also had a healthy appreciation for several later writers, especially Gregory the Great (540-604), who wrote a rule to regulate pastoral care, and Bernard of Clairvaux (1090-1153), the medieval monastic.[24] Bowles even commends the reading of Thomas Aquinas and other scholastic theologians favored by the Roman Catholics, provided one avoids their soteriological heresies.[25]

Bowles' grasp of the history of pastoral care gives the lie to the stubborn stereotype that the Puritans were narrow. On the contrary, the Westminster Divines read widely and had a profound respect for the wisdom of the past. To be sure, they were careful about bringing too much learning into the pulpit. The *Directory for Public Worship* warns against employing "obscure terms of art" and exhorts ministers to preach "plainly, that the meanest

---

[23] "Fatendum illud, antiquos patres ut magna mundi lumina suis temporibus colluxisse, haereticorum malleos, veritatis sacrae acerrimos vindices, Sp. Sancti donis largiter fuisse imbutos" (Bowles, *De Pastore Evangelico*, 129).

[24] On the favorable reception Gregory received among the Reformers, see Hughes Oliphant Old, *The Reading and Preaching of the Scriptures in the Worship of the Christian Church; Vol. 2: The Patristic Age* (Grand Rapids, MI: Eerdmans, 1998), 426-27.

[25] Bowles, *De Pastore Evangelico*, 126-27.

may understand . . . sparingly citing sentences of ecclesiastical or other human writers, ancient or modern, be they never so elegant."[26] Bowles offers similar caveats to the same effect.[27] But the Westminster view of the gospel ministry had an expansive appreciation for the best that Christians anywhere have ever thought or said about the work of the pastor.

The Evangelical Shepherd

The heart of gospel ministry is the gospel itself. Thus nothing mattered more to the Westminster Divines than the faithful exposition of the Bible. According to the *Directory for Public Worship*, "Preaching of the word, being the power of God unto salvation, and one of the greatest and most excellent works belonging to the ministry of the gospel, should be so performed, that the workman need not be ashamed, but may save himself, and those that hear him."[28] The men of Westminster were evangelicals in the sense that they were thoroughly committed to proclaiming the gospel of Jesus Christ.

Not surprisingly, nearly half of *De Pastore Evangelico Tractatus* is devoted to preaching, which Bowles defines as "a divinely instituted means of grace, by which the things of the kingdom of God are publicly explained and applied, unto the salvation and edification of the people."[29] The method he advocates for preaching is identical with the Westminster homiletic and is "circumscribed by these three principles: 1) The interpretation of a given Scripture, 2) The deduction of the doctrine

---

[26] *Directory for Public Worship*, 379, 381.

[27] Bowles, *De Pastore Evangelico*, 160, 197-209.

[28] *Directory for Public Worship*, 379.

[29] "Praedicatio verbi est medium gratiae divinitus institutum, quo res regni Dei publice & explicantur & applicantur, ad populi salutem & aedificationem" (Bowles, *De Pastore Evangelico*, 152).

emerging from it, 3) The application of the doctrine thus deduced."[30] This is the Text-Doctrine-Use structure recommended in the *Directory for Public Worship* and commonly practiced throughout Puritanism. Bowles carefully lays out the considerations in choosing a suitable text, the rules for legitimately deducing and clearly stating a doctrine, and, as we shall see, the factors governing the appropriate application of the doctrine to a particular congregation.

In the Westminster view of gospel ministry, the ultimate goal of preaching is the salvation of souls. "This is what demands our all," writes Bowles: "the salvation of the soul, which is more excellent than this whole universe and which is not acquired without the blood of Christ."[31] The appointed means for saving souls is the preaching of the law and the gospel. Having already defined preaching as the explication and application "of the things pertaining to the kingdom of God," Bowles explains that "the things of the kingdom of God are the Law and the Gospel. The Gospel, as the principal matter, the Law as subservient to it; the Gospel as that by which Christ is displayed unto salvation to anyone so believing that he repents; the Law as that which leads by the hand to Christ, or directs those who are drawn to him."[32]

The way the law leads men to Christ is by showing them that they will surely perish without him. "Make known to the lost sheep the utter misery of their condition outside of Christ. No

---

[30] "Methodus autem concionandi tribus hisce circumscribitur. I. Scripturae datae interpretatione. 2. Doctrinae ex ea emergentis deductione. 3. Doctrinae deductae accommodatione" (Bowles, *De Pastore Evangelico*, 156).

[31] "[N]on quicquid in mundo gloriosum nostram flagitat opellam: Animarum salus, quae toto hoc universo excellentior, & non nisi Christi sanguine acquisita, nos totos vendicat" (Bowles, *De Pastore Evangelico*, 372).

[32] "Res regni sunt Lex & Evangelium. Evangelium, ut quod principale; Lex, ut ei subserviens, Evangelium, ut quo Christus cuivis sic credenti ut resipiscat, in salutem exhibetur: Lex, ut quae vel manuducit ad Christum, vel ad illum adductos dirigit" (Bowles, *De Pastore Evangelico*, 153).

one ever comes to Christ, who stands on his own. The Prodigal does not race back to his father until he has to, lest he perish on his own."[33] While the law shows the sheep that they are lost, only the gospel will bring them home, and thus all preaching is to be evangelistic. The main work of the gospel minister is to preach Christ, who is "the Alpha and the Omega of the ministry."[34] To preach Christ is to take his person, his work, and his benefits and offer them freely to sinners.[35]

It is not surprising that Oliver Bowles should refer to sinners as "lost sheep." While it was not within the purview of the Westminster Assembly to provide a manual for pastoral care, the Westminster Standards make frequent mention of the minister's responsibilities as a shepherd. In the *Directory for Public Worship*, for example, the gospel minister is instructed to walk "before his flock, as an example to them . . . watchfully looking to himself, and the flock whereof the Lord hath made him overseer."[36] Likewise, the *Form of Government* directs him "to pray for and with his flock," "to feed the flock," and to rule "over the flock as a pastor."[37] In the Westminster view of gospel ministry, the minister is truly a "pastor," which is to say, a shepherd.

The role of the pastor as shepherd is introduced on the very first page of *De Pastore Evangelico Tractatus*: "The gospel minister is a man called by Christ through the church to do his

---

[33] "Ovibus perditis sua miseranda extra Christum conditio omnimodo innotescat. Nullus enim ad Christum venit, qui habet de suo in quo subsistat. Prodigus non festinat ad patrem, usque dum aut eundum, aut fame pereundum" (Bowles, *De Pastore Evangelico*, 229).

[34] "Christus sit Alpha & Omega ministerii" (Bowles, *De Pastore Evangelico*, 192).

[35] Bowles, *De Pastore Evangelico*, 236-38, 274-83.

[36] *Directory for Public Worship*, 381.

[37] *Form of Government*, 399-401.

part in feeding the flock by the means necessary for its salvation."[38]
The minister's relationship with his church is thus a *pastoral*
relationship: "It is of the nature of the Church, that every Pastor
have his own portion of the Lord's flock, which he may adorn as
a bridegroom does his bride, for Christ the Chief Shepherd. But
as the flock may be said to be entrusted to a Pastor, so a Pastor is
put over the flock; it is necessary that the pastoral bond exist
between Pastor and people."[39]

Throughout the rest of the treatise, Bowles frequently refers to
God's people as sheep (*ovis*) or as a flock (*grex*). It is the sheep
who need to be preached to, the sheep who need to be prayed for,
the sheep who have spiritual struggles, and so forth. Virtually every
topic Bowles considers is addressed with particular concern for
the needs of God's people, considered as a flock. The reason the
minister must grow in godliness is so he can set a good example;
hence the theme of the fourth chapter: "Let him be an example to
the flock."[40] Hence also the need for a residential ministry. The
Directory for Public Worship assumed that a minister would know
how to apply the Scripture "by his residence and conversing with
his flock."[41] But this was not always the case, since many English
parishes suffered from absentee pastors. This was a major concern
to Oliver Bowles, and he devoted several chapters to defending
the necessity of a residential ministry for the care of God's sheep.[42]

---

[38] "Pastor Evangelicus est persona a Christo per Ecclesiam vocata, ut gregem sibi commissum, mediis ad salutem necessariis, pro parte sua, pascat" (Bowles, *De Pastore Evangelico*, 1).

[39] Denique e re Ecclesiae est, ut quilibet Pastor suam habeat Dominici gregis portionem, quam veluti sponsam, ut pronubus, Christo *arkipoimeni* adornet. Ut vero grex dicatur Pastori commissus, Pastor item gregi praepositus; intercedat oportet, inter Pastorem & populum, vinculum pastorale" (Bowles, *De Pastore Evangelico*, 18).

[40] "Sit Exemplar gregis" (Bowles, *De Pastore Evangelico*, 28).

[41] *Directory for Public Worship*, 380-81.

[42] Bowles, *De Pastore Evangelico*, 92-118.

To take yet another example, consider Bowles' advice to ministers facing persecution. Is it ever permissible for a minister to flee for his life? Yes, provided he is the only person threatened. However, if the entire congregation is endangered, the minister must remain at his post: good shepherds do not abandon their sheep.[43] Or consider finally his discussion of the sacraments. After describing the proper administration of the Lord's Supper, Bowles introduces the need for "inspecting the sheep"—that is, examining them as to their spiritual condition prior to admitting them to the sacrament.[44] In short, every aspect of pastoral ministry requires an affectionate and sympathetic relationship between the pastor and the flock entrusted to his care. A good shepherd knows and loves his sheep.

Nowhere is a minister's knowledge of and affection for his congregation more important than in his ministry of God's Word. Every aspect of this ministry—from the selection of the text to the application of the doctrine—depends on an intimate understanding of the spiritual condition of the flock. The necessity of personal application in preaching is a significant concern of the Westminster *Directory for Public Worship*, which states that the gospel minister is to "divide the word of God aright, to everyone his portion."[45] According to Bowles, this meant that it is the pastor's duty "to allot to each one according to his spiritual condition that which is his."[46] This is simply a matter of good shepherding. Bowles asks, "Would God bear in the shepherd of souls, what no one would permit in a shepherd of sheep? . . . God requires not only that one preach among his people; but it is also necessary that he preach as much as possible concerning his

---

[43] Bowles, *De Pastore Evangelico*, 367.

[44] Bowles, *De Pastore Evangelico*, 345-46.

[45] *Directory for Public Worship*, 378.

[46] "Cuique, pro sua spirituali conditione, tribuere quod suum" (Bowles, *De Pastore Evangelico*, 138).

people's condition. . . . No one is able to address a flock rightly except he who exercises pastoral oversight."[47]

To help pastors analyze the needs of the flock, *De Pastore Evangelico Tractatus* provides several lists describing the various kinds of sheep. "The condition of the sheep of Christ is various," writes Bowles. "Some are healthy, others ill; of these some are strong, some weaker, others lost; some are ignorant, but teachable; some are knowledgeable but not humbled: others are ill: others led astray through errors: others wounded from their falling. Let the pastor make a mental note to which class of these he may assign each one."[48] Or again:

> In dispensing the Word, let him temper his voice according to the varying condition of his hearers. . . . Thus he is to deal one way with those who are nothing but babes in Christ, another way with those who are adults; one way with those who are arrogant, another way with those who are timorous; one way with those who enjoy riches, another way with those who are variously afflicted; one way with those who are spiritual, another way with those who are carnal; one way with those who are carried away with fleshly arrogance, overconfident of salvation, another way with those who are anxious about their spiritual condition; one way with youths, another way with those who are well on in years; one way with city-dwellers, another way with country folk . . . one way with those from the lowest classes, another way with the powerful, who are well off, in a higher position.[49]

---

[47] "Quorsum id ferret Deus in pastore animarum, quod nullus in ovium pastore? . . . . Id exigit Deus, non solum ut apud suos concionetur quis; sed ita concionari oportet, ut maxime e re populi. . . . Nullus potest gregem dextre affari, nisi qui . . . exerceat pastoralem inspectionem" (Bowles, *De Pastore Evangelico*, 107).

[48] "Ovium Christi, varia conditio: aliae sanae, aliae morbidae; quarum hae firmiores, illae infirmiores: aliae perditae; quarum hae ignarae, sed dociles; illae scientes, sed non humiliatae: aliae aegrotae: aliae per errores abactae: aliae e lapsu vulneratae. Animo recognoscat pastor, ad quam harum classem suas revocet" (Bowles, *De Pastore Evangelico*, 139).

[49] "In verbo dispensando, pro varia auditorum conditione sermo temperandus. . . . Aliter itaque agendum cum iis qui non nisi in Christo infantes, aliter cum adultis; aliter cum protervis, aliter cum pusillanimis; aliter cum iis qui rebus prosperis fruuntur, aliter cum iis qui varie affliguntur; aliter cum

One of Bowles' best examples for this type of pastoral classification was Gregory the Great, whose *Liber Regulae Pastoralis* (c. 591) was partly a manual for admonishing various types of parishioners. But these categories are only the beginning. Bowles later conducts a more comprehensive analysis of the spiritual condition of the soul, describing a host of emotional troubles and spiritual anxieties, together with the appropriate pastoral remedy for each one.[50] The point is that, whether he is dispensing the word in public or in private, the minister must adapt his teaching to the capacities and circumstances of his hearers. The term Bowles uses for this is "accommodation": "By the accommodation of the doctrine is meant nothing other than its application, whereby, according to the various conditions of men in spiritual matters, a use is made for the edification of each one."[51] A good pastor not only knows his sheep, but also accommodates his teaching to their spiritual needs.

Accommodation was a characteristic strength of Puritan preaching, which prized the precise application of biblical teaching. This homiletical strategy was something the Puritans inherited rather than invented. As the writings of Oliver Bowles demonstrate, the careful distribution of God's Word to God's sheep was part of the best patristic, medieval, and Reformed tradition of pastoral care. In this respect—as in many others—the Westminster ideal of the pastor as a godly, learned, and evangelical shepherd was not only Puritan, but also catholic.

---

spiritualibus, aliter cum carnalibus; aliter cum iis qui, carnali confidentia abrepti, securi de salute, aliter cum iis qui de spirituali conditione dubitant; aliter cum juvenibus, aliter cum iis qui aetate provectiores; aliter cum urbanis, aliter cum rusticis . . . aliter cum iis qui infimae classis, aliter cum iis qui potentia, opibus valent, loco celsiori sunt" (Bowles, *De Pastore Evangelico*, 215, 217; cf. 154-55, 170, 189).

[50] Bowles, *De Pastore Evangelico*, 258-316.

[51] "Doctrinae deductae Accommodatio nihil aliud quam ejusdem particularis applicatio, qua, pro varia hominum conditione in Spiritualibus, usus ad cujusque aedificationem fit" (Bowles, *De Pastore Evangelico*, 169).

De Pastore Evangelico Tractatus closes with several chapters exhorting pastors to remain faithful to their calling as gospel shepherds. Among the incentives or motivations to diligent pastoral ministry is the following: "That neglectful care of the flock makes us guilty of the most shameful faithlessness towards God."[52] The gospel minister must be a faithful shepherd. Toward that end, Bowles offers this encouragement to every pastor who embraces the Westminster view of the gospel ministry: "Fix your eyes on that eternal and heavenly reward which is reserved for those who feed the flock."[53]

---

[52] "Quod perfidiae in Deum omnium turpissimae nos reos constituit gregis cura negligentior" (Bowles, *De Pastore Evangelico*, 371).

[53] "Praemium illud caeleste & aeternum, quod gregem pascentibus est repositum, in oculis ferendum" (Bowles, *De Pastore Evangelico*, 380).

True Communion with Christ in the Lord's Supper: Calvin, Westminster and the Nature of Christ's Sacramental Presence

LIGON DUNCAN

The point of dispute

The oldest and most fundamental dispute regarding the Lord's Supper in the Protestant churches concerns the nature of the presence of Christ in the Lord's Supper. The Lutherans (and some Anglicans) believe in the real presence. The Reformed, in contrast, believe in the Spiritual[1] presence of Christ. However, since the late nineteenth century there has been a minority report in parts of the Reformed community wanting to claim the language of "real presence" as the Calvinian view and propone it as the central teaching of the Reformed tradition on the presence of Christ in the Lord's Supper.

---

[1] That is, the Reformed believe that the believer enjoys the presence of Christ and communes with him by the power and work of the Holy Spirit. Throughout this essay, when I use "Spiritual" with a capital "S," I am drawing attention to something pertaining to or done by the Third Person of the Trinity, and not identifying something as simply relating to the human spirit, or as "spiritual" as opposed to "physical," or "secular." Hence, when we say that the Reformed believe in the Spiritual presence of Christ, the point is more than a negative denial of the physical presence of Christ, but a positive affirmation of true communion with Christ by the Spirit.

The problem with this is obvious. Real presence is not something that Calvin or any of his Reformed successors taught or believed, and any savvy Lutheran can tell you that.[2] Real presence refers to the actual, local, elemental, corporeal presence of Christ in the Lord's Supper. Calvin, no less clearly or vehemently than Zwingli, rejected this out of hand. Calvin not only objected to the mode of the real presence in Roman Catholicism (transubstantiation) and Lutheranism (consubstantiation), he objected to the idea of the real presence itself. He, rightly, saw that it missed the point of the sacrament.

Nevertheless, because this new Reformed sacramentalism sets itself over against, not simply Zwinglianism so-called, but also over against Cunningham, Hodge, Dabney, Warfield and other faithful expositors of the Westminster tradition, we must now

---

[2]   The *Formula of Concord*, for instance, takes direct aim not only at Zwingli, but especially at Calvin's ("subtle Sacramentarian") view and says: "it is to be noted in the beginning that there are two kinds of Sacramentarians. Some are gross Sacramentarians, who declare in plain German, clear words as they believe in their hearts, that in the Holy Supper nothing but bread and wine is present, and distributed and received with the mouth. Others, however, are subtle Sacramentarians, and the most injurious of all, who partly speak very speciously in our own words, and pretend that they also believe a true presence of the true, essential, living body and blood of Christ in the Holy Supper, however, that this occurs spiritually through faith. Nevertheless they retain under these specious words precisely the former gross opinion, namely, that in the Holy Supper nothing is present and received with the mouth except bread and wine. For with them the word spiritually means nothing else than the Spirit of Christ or the power of the absent body of Christ and His merit, which is present; but the body of Christ is in no mode or way present, except only above in the highest heaven, to which we should elevate ourselves into heaven by the thoughts of our faith, and there, not at all, however, in the bread and wine of the Holy Supper, should seek this body and blood [of Christ] (*Formula of Concord* VII.3-5, translated by F. Bente and W. H. T. Dau in *Triglot Concordia: The Symbolical Books of the Evangelical Lutheran Church* [St. Louis: Concordia, 1921], 503-529; see also *The Book of Concord*, translated and edited by Theodore G. Tappert [Philadelphia: Fortress, 1959]. 482). Note David P. Scaer's apt comments in *Modern Reformation*, Vol. 6 (May/June, 1997).

enumerate at least five views of the presence of Christ in the Lord's Supper identifiable to students of Reformed theology. There is the *Roman Catholic/Greek Orthodox view of the real presence* which asserts that Christ is corporeally, elementally and locally present (via transubstantiation) and corporeally received by all partakers.[3] There is the *Lutheran view of the real presence* which, while denying the sacrificial aspect of the Supper, asserts in a slightly different way that Christ is corporeally, elementally and locally present (via consubstantiation) and corporeally received, even by unbelievers.[4] There is the *memorial view* (often

---

[3] See *The Council of Trent*, especially the seventh and the twenty-second sessions, available in various translations and editions, including *The Council of Trent: The canons and decrees of the sacred and oecumenical Council of Trent*, edited and translated by J. Waterworth (London: Dolman, 1848), the most accessible edition to many Protestant pastors is found in Philip Schaff's *The Creeds of Christendom* (Grand Rapids: Baker, reprint) 1:76-206. See also *Catechism of the Catholic Church* 1333, 1373-1381(San Francisco: Ignatius, 1994), 336, 346-348. The Eastern Orthodox view also strongly affirms real presence and employs the language of transubstantiation (*metousiosis*), but de-emphasizes the mode, stresses that is incomprehensible and a mystery, and highlights both *apotheosis* and *apocatastasis*. Ware says, in *The Orthodox Church* (London: Penguin, 1963), 281 (see also 281-283, and 286-295): "The chief place in Christian worship belongs to the sacraments or . . . *mysteries*." Philaret of Moscow, in *The Doctrine of the Russian Church* says: "the bread truly, really, and substantially becomes the very true Body of the Lord, and the wine the very Blood of the Lord." See also Vladimir Lovsky and Alexander Schmemann for two Orthodox authors that have unhelpful impacts upon underground quadrants in the Reformed and evangelical community. Lovsky says, for instance, "through the sacraments our nature enters into union with the divine nature in the hypostasis of the Son, the Head of His mystical body. Our humanity becomes consubstantial with the deified humanity, united with the person of Christ" in *The Mystical Theology of the Eastern Church* (New York: St. Vladimir's Seminary Press, 1976 reprint), 181. Schmemann provides a good taste current Orthodox thought on the sacraments and Supper in *For the Life of the World* (New York: St. Vladimir's Seminary Press, 1988 reprint), especially 135-151, and 23-46.

[4] See again *The Book of Concord*, translated and edited by Theodore G. Tappert (Philadelphia: Fortress, 1959), 482-486, for instance: VII, 6-7 "1. We believe,

unfairly attributed to Zwingli, who denied it explicitly[5]) which views the Supper as mere remembrance, and treats it as a sign but not a seal, and which typically has a non-theology of the presence of Christ and sacramental efficacy (that is, there has been little theological reflection on those points and hence they are answered only via denials, and any positive affirmations are vague or not forthcoming).[6] There is now what we might call a

teach, and confess that in the Holy Supper the body and blood of Christ are truly and essentially present, and are truly distributed and received with the bread and wine. 2. We believe, teach, and confess that the words of the testament of Christ are not to be understood otherwise than as they read, according to the letter, so that the bread does not signify the absent body and the wine the absent blood of Christ, but that, on account of the sacramental union, they [the bread and wine] are truly the body and blood of Christ." VII, 15-16 "6. We believe, teach, and confess that the body and blood of Christ are received with the bread and wine, not only spiritually by faith, but also orally; yet not in a Capernaitic, but in a supernatural, heavenly mode, because of the sacramental union; as the words of Christ clearly show, when Christ gives direction to take, eat, and drink, as was also done by the apostles; for it is written Mark 14: 23: And they all drank of it. St. Paul likewise says, 1 Cor. 10: 16: The bread which we break, is it not the communion of the body of Christ? that is: He who eats this bread eats the body of Christ, which also the chief ancient teachers of the Church, Chrysostom, Cyprian, Leo I, Gregory, Ambrose, Augustine, unanimously testify. 7. We believe, teach, and confess that not only the true believers [in Christ] and the worthy, but also the unworthy and unbelievers, receive the true body and blood of Christ; however, not for life and consolation, but for judgment and condemnation, if they are not converted and do not repent, 1 Cor. 11:27, 29" (Bente and Dau, trans.).

[5] Zwingli asserted on one occasion "If I have called this a commemoration, I have done so in order to controvert those who would make of it a sacrifice. . . . We believe that Christ is truly present in the Lord's Supper; yea, that there is no communion without such presence. . . . We believe that the true Body of Christ is eaten in Communion, not in a gross and carnal manner, but in a spiritual and sacramental manner, by the religious, believing, and pious heart." See W. P. Stephens extremely helpful survey of Zwingli on the sacraments in *The Theology of Huldrych Zwingli* (Oxford: Clarendon, 1986), 180-193, 218-259.

[6] What is often called Zwinglianism, without respect to the facts of his historic teaching, is simply the generic evangelical tendency, ubiquitously apparent

real presence view within Reformed circles (fostered by the writings of J. W. Nevin, Ronald Wallace, James Jordan, Peter Leithart, Douglas Wilson, and others) that attempts to appeal to Calvin as its theological ancestor, and stresses sacramental efficacy, uses the language of the real presence of Christ in the Supper, and emphasizes the sealing aspect of the sacrament.[7] Finally[8], there is *the true communion with Christ view*, typified in Calvin and the Westminster Confession, which denies any

----

in various ecclesial traditions, and even in some Reformed communions, to downplay the significance and efficacy of the sacraments.

[7] It is now colloquially commonplace in conservative Reformed circles to identify Calvin's view as the "real presence" view, over against, not only Zwinglians, but also Westminster Confession-subscribing Calvinists who do not share all of the particularities of Calvin's position. Even B. A. Gerrish uses the language of "real presence" positively, less careful are the usages and tendencies found in Ronald S. Wallace's *Calvin's Doctrine of Word and Sacrament* (Edinburgh: Oliver and Boyd, 1953), 208; and Douglas Wilson, *Reformed is not Enough* (Moscow: Canon Press, 2002), 113; while Robert Letham more carefully calls Calvin's view the "real spiritual presence" (no doubt, Letham is attempting to avoid the error of ascribing a corporeal presence view to Calvin, but his own titling of Calvin's view still needs some unpacking) in *The Lord's Supper* (Phillipsburg: P&R, 2001), 28. Nevertheless, *realis corporis praesentia* is not language that Calvin endorsed as biblical or employed as the designation of his position. That nagging little fact is run over roughshod by those anxious to make Calvin a proponent of a real presence view, albeit one of a higher order.

[8] Of course, of the enumeration of views there is no end, and one could make a case for different kinds of groupings (for example, the corporeal view [Orthodox, Roman, Lutheran, Anglo-Catholics] or non-corporeal view [Calvin, Zwingli, Bullinger, Westminster, Princeton]). I have enumerated the varying views in the above manner because of two prevalent tendencies: the first—to make a hard distinction between Calvin and Westminster on the sacraments in general and the Lord's Supper in particular, and then propound a contemporary articulation of Calvin's view as the genuine Reformed view over against Westminster; the second—to reinterpret Westminster in light of a contemporary view of Calvin's teaching and then censure those who embrace Westminster (and even Calvin in general) but who do not endorse Calvin in all his particulars which go beyond the affirmations of Westminster.

corporeal (that is, real) presence of Christ in the Supper, and instead asserts a true, Spiritual communion with Christ, by faith, and by virtue of union with Christ, without downplaying the distinction of the sign and the thing signified, the sealing aspect of the ordinance, the indispensable role of faith, the importance of worthy partaking, the dynamic of the Holy Spirit, the correspondence of the grace exhibited in both preaching and the sacraments, and the sanctificational focus of sacramental efficacy. In this view, the presence of Christ in the Supper is understood dynamically, Spiritually and relationally, rather than statically, physically and elementally. This view thus speaks of a Spiritual presence of Christ, the risen and ascended *Logos ensarkos*, to the faith of the believer, by virtue of his union with Christ, in the communion of the Supper.[9]

---

[9] The true communion view (often called other things, such as the "Spiritual presence view") is not monolithic, but represents central Calvinian affirmations, on the one end of this view are those who will occasionally affirm the language of real presence, but (1) with a thorough grasp of the historical problems and nuances of the term, (2) without some of the eccentricities that characterize many of the popular renderings of this position (paedocommunion, baptismal regeneration, etc.), (3) with a high opinion of the Westminster and other Reformed confessional renderings of the doctrine of the sacraments, and (4) without an animus for fellow Reformed men who intelligently and joyfully embrace the affirmations of the Reformed confessions, but not all of Calvin's emphases and speculations, among those characterized by this position are, for instance, R. C. Sproul, Douglas F. Kelly, R. S. Clark, and Michael S. Horton. Still others on this spectrum, we might say in the center, have (1) a tremendous esteem for Calvin, (2) thoroughly understand and generally embrace his view, but are (3) wary of the language of "real presence," and (4) critical of the semi-sacerdotalism pushed under that name and being justified by ahistorical appeals to Calvin, among this group of scholars would be, perhaps, Sinclair B. Ferguson, W. Duncan Rankin, Geoffrey W. Bromiley, and Derek W. H. Thomas. On the other end, would be B. B. Warfield, Donald Macleod, William Cunningham, Robert L. Dabney and others, who would (1) be critical of Calvin at points, though in continuity with him in the main, (2) strongly reject the affirmation of real presence and any hint of sacerdotalism, (3) warmly affirm the emphases of Westminster, but have little time for Nevin, and (4) be less critical of Zwingli, without evacuating the Supper of efficacy or failing to emphasize our Spiritual partaking of Christ.

Our debate pertains to these two latter views. Both views claim to be rooted in Scripture. Both views claim Calvin as antecedent. Both views appeal to the Reformed tradition in general, and yet the real presence view deploys language long avoided in the Reformed tradition, emphasizes certain teachings denied by the Reformed and often comes along with a package of other beliefs (paedo-communion, baptismal regeneration and the like) which find no exposition in the Reformed confessional tradition. In this essay, I will argue for the Spiritual presence view as the legitimate, biblical, confessional and Reformed view.

Some problems with the "Reformed real presence" tendency

Many advocates of the new sacramental realism or what we have called a "Reformed real presence view" of the Lord's Supper appeal to Calvin as the proximate[10] fountainhead of their position and do so, first, by highlighting certain themes in Calvin and the early Reformed tradition that are actually there to be found, but which are generally neglected in contemporary Reformed and evangelical sphragistics.[11] Second, they disproportionately stress these neglected aspects, and furthermore do so without a sufficient appreciation of the contextual debate reflected in the primary

---

[10] I say "proximate" because I do not mean to deny for a moment that the advocates of this view believe their view to be biblical, but one of their central appeals is to the recovery of Calvin's doctrine (as they understand it) for the church today.

[11] Keith Mathison's *Given for You: Reclaiming Calvin's Doctrine of the Lord's Supper* (Phillipsburg: P&R, 2002) is an example of this currently prevalent tendency in Reformed literature on the Supper. However, Mathison's tone and treatment of the subject are significantly different from the works I mention in footnotes below. His work, though I take issue with it at numerous points, is both substantial and pious, and thus deserves sympathetic interaction in a way that much of the material I will cite herein as examples of common current mistakes does not.

sources.[12] Third, they fail adequately to take account of the counterbalancing and qualifying language on the presence of Christ, sacramental efficacy, the sealing aspect of the sacrament, and the distinction between the sign and the thing signified in the earlier Reformed theological and confessional literature which they are imbibing.[13] Fourth, they are often too reliant on modern interpreters of Calvin and the Reformed tradition, and thus unwittingly impose a hermeneutical grid on Calvin that prevents their ascertaining the precise nature of his view.[14] Fifth, they underplay the positive denials of Calvin and the implications of

---

[12] This kind of mistake is evident in Mark Horne's *The Westminster Standards & Sacramental Efficacy* (see http://www.hornes.org/theologia/content/ mark_horne/the_ westminster_standards_and_sacramental_efficacy.htm) and elsewhere in his own historical-theological forays into sphragistics, as well as those of other writers he posts on his website who offer their own views on the historical development of the Reformed doctrine of the sacraments. S. Joel Garver's *Baptismal Regeneration and the Westminster Confession 28.6* is another example of this tendency and problem (see http://www.lasalle.edu/~garver/wcf.htm).

[13] S. Joel Garver's *A Brief Catechesis on Covenant and Baptism* is an example of an attempt to construct a coherent modern, and presumably Reformed, approach to baptism that does not reflect interaction with the historical material (see http://www.lasalle.edu/~garver/cateches.htm and his above-mentioned article).

[14] The influence of, for instance, Ronald Wallace's interpretation of Calvin is evident on many in the contemporary conservative Reformed "real presence school." They would have done well to pay heed to Wallace's own caveats that his book "is not a critical study of Calvin" and that "no attempt has been made to trace in detail the historical development of Calvin's thought in the midst of the various sacramental controversies in which he was involved (*Calvin's Doctrine of Word and Sacrament*, vi and v). It is precisely the failure to consider Calvin in context that has left Wallace vulnerable to projecting his own questions and categories onto Calvin's material, and thus to reshaping Calvin's thought, even whilst using his own words. Furthermore, when one sees how Wallace depicts Calvin's doctrine of revelation and God's word written, one ought to be on guard from what he does with the sacraments. The Barthian influence and grid is apparent to any careful reader.

those denials on the makeup of his overall position.[15] Sixth, they blur the important distinction of outward sign and inward reality, in an effort to highlight the actuality of the sacrament.[16] Seventh, they understress Calvin's emphatic teaching on the sacramental analogy, and thus vest too much in the sacrament rather than focusing on what it points to.[17] Eighth, they underemphasize faith, especially by failing to accent that faith is the way we get Christ in the sacrament and that the sacrament is nothing and of no benefit whatsoever without it.[18] Ninth, conscious as they are of the

---

[15] As Gerrish has pointed out, many interpreters of Calvin on the Supper have claimed to know "what Calvin really believed in his heart." The Lutheran scholastics thought that Calvin was, deep-down, just a disingenuous Zwinglian. But they were wrong, precisely because they ignored what he said and chose to read him according to their grid. The modern Scoto-Barthians and their heirs, think that even though Calvin explicitly denied real presence, he really believed it. But they are wrong too. All we have to go on is what Calvin said. That testimony is perplexing enough without projecting on top of it speculations as to what he really thought though it is contrary to his written expressions of his view and his summary statements of it.

[16] This is evident in what is being called the "Auburn Avenue Theology" which fails to make an adequate distinction between water baptism and the reality to which it points in saying "By baptism one is joined to Christ's body, united to Him covenantally, and given all the blessings and benefits of His work" in *Summary Statement of AAPC's Position on the Covenant, Baptism, and Salvation*, 7. This is a position statement issued by a Presbyterian Church in American Session, but is contrary to the *Westminster Standards* teaching.

[17] While Calvin calls sacraments "appendages" of the Gospel, more and more modern would be Calvinian sacramentarians speak of "giving the sacraments a central place in worship." If that means moving the regular focus of our worship to the ordinary means of grace (public reading of Scripture, preaching of Scripture, administration of the sacraments and prayer) and away from the manmade clutter that fills many modern evangelical and even Reformed worship services, then it is perfectly Calvinian. If it means creating a symmetry between word and sacrament in the worship of the church, or worse, exalting the sacraments as the apex of our worship experience, then it is thoroughly unCalvinian. The sacraments confirm the center, which is the word, not vice versa.

[18] Because the question "what does the Lord's Supper do/accomplish/effect/ convey?" drives the agenda of so many neo-Reformed sacramentarians (in

constant evangelical stress on the inefficacy of the sacraments (that is, explanatory rubrics that say only what the sacraments don't mean and accomplish), they propone a view of sacramental efficacy which is discontinuous with Calvin, and based upon a scriptural exegesis precariously like unto a non-Protestant sacramental realism.[19] Tenth, in their frustration with non-answers even in the Reformed community as to the nature of the sealing aspect of the sacraments, they foster a novel view of sacramental sealing and fail to note the simple and repeated emphasis and explanation of Calvin on the nature of the sealing function of the sacraments.[20]

---

their desire to recover what they call "the objectivity of the covenant") and because the answer they long to give is that it "does something objectively," they are reticent to admit and generally downplay what Calvin emphasized: (1) that we feed on Christ *only* by faith and (2) that what the Lord's Supper does is precisely to nourish the faith of worthy recipients. In other words, the kind of "objectivity" that they ascribe to the Supper is a different kind of objectivity than Calvin asserted.

[19] See again Garver, *A Brief Catechesis on Covenant and Baptism*; Peter Leithart, *Sacramental Efficacy* (http://www.hornes.org/theologia/content/peter_leithart/sacramental_efficacy.htm); Rich Lusk, *Baptismal Efficacy and the Reformed Tradition: Past, Present, and Future* (http://www.hornes.org/theologia/content/rich_lusk/baptismal_efficacy_the_reformed_tradition_past_present_future.htm); Mark Horne, *John Calvin and Paedocommunion* (http://www.hornes.org/theologia/content/mark_horne/john_calvin_paedocommunion.htm).

One of the ways one can easily detect the serious discontinuity with Calvin among so many who appeal to his doctrine of the Lord's Supper as the foundation of their own is to note what they say about Calvin when it comes to paedocommunion and the issue of worthy partaking. Calvin explicitly and deliberately rejects paedocommunion and upholds the idea that communion is for worthy participants (which means more than simply believing on Christ— *contra* the Lutheran view in the *Formula of Concord*). Both of these views cut at the new sacramental objectivism of being proponed by Garver, Wilson, Lusk, Horne, Leithart and others, and reveal that their view of the nature of the sacraments is fundamentally hyper-Calvinistic and not genuinely Calvinian.

[20] One notes, with not a little amusement, how every reference to the "sealing" aspect of the sacraments found in Calvin or some other magisterial Reformer, is taken by our covenantal objectivist friends to be yet another proof that

Calvin himself warns against just these kinds of mistakes in his *Harmony of the Gospels* where he says:

"But there are three mistakes against which it is here necessary to be on our guard; first, not to confound the spiritual blessing with the sign; secondly, not to seek Christ on earth, or under earthly elements; thirdly, not to imagine any other kind of eating than that which draws into us the life of Christ by the secret power of the Spirit, and which we obtain by faith alone. First, as I have said, let us always keep in view the distinction between the sign and the thing signified, if we do not wish to overturn every thing; for otherwise we shall derive no advantage from the sacrament, if it do not, according to the measure of our small capacity, lead us from the contemplation of the earthly element to the heavenly mystery. And therefore, whoever will not distinguish the body of Christ from the bread, and the blood from the wine, will never understand what is meant by the Lord's Supper, or for what purpose believers use these symbols."[21]

---

the Reformers held to the views they are now purveying in their names. "Seal" is taken to mean that the recipient is endowed with all the benefits exhibited in the sacrament (based, in part, upon the neo-Reformed sacramentarian reading of passages like Hebrews 6:1-6, which supposedly teaches, according to them, that in water baptism and at the Lord's Supper all recipients are enlightened, taste of the heavenly gift, are made partakers of the Holy Spirit, taste of the good word of God and the powers of the age to come). This is not what the Reformers or the confessions teach however. Calvin makes it amply clear in what sense the Lord's Supper is a seal. The sacraments are seals, Calvin says, in that they confirm God's promises and thus nourish faith. The sacraments are "not so much needed to confirm God's truth as to establish it in us" (*Institutes* (1536), [IV.A.1], 87; *Calvini Opera*, hereafter, *CO* XXIX, 102 [that is, *Iohannis Calvini opera quae supersunt omnia*, edited by Wilhelm Baum, Eduard Cunitz and Eduard Reuss, 59 vols. {*Corpus Reformatorum*, vols. 29-87} (Brunswick: C. A. Schwetschke and Son, 1863-1900), 29:102]. In other words, as signs, the sacraments represent and exhibit to us the Lord's gracious promises because of the weakness of our faith, as seals, the sacraments actually nourish our trust in God's promise as we receive them in faith, and thus objectively ground us in assurance and confident hope. Sacraments are seals, for Calvin, in that they objectively contribute to the assurance of those who receive them by faith.

[21] See John Calvin, *A Harmony of the Gospels*, A. W. Morrison, trans. David W. Torrance and Thomas F. Torrance, eds. (Grand Rapids: Eerdmans, 1972), 3:136; *CO* LXXIII, 708. The translation quoted above is the old Calvin Translation Society version found in *Harmony of the Evangelists* (Grand Rapids: Baker), 3:209.

Hence, we will summarize the Reformed teaching on this area, offer an outline of historical issues related to this discussion and then proceed to make a scriptural and historical argument for the Spiritual presence view.

A Summary of the Central Reformed Teaching on the Sacraments and Christ's Presence in the Supper

Since there are new claims being made as to what constitutes the central Reformed teaching on the nature of the sacraments and the presence of Christ in the Supper, perhaps we should summarize the Reformed consensus here. Reformed confessional teaching on the nature of the sacraments may be epitomized as follows: God's sacraments or covenant signs/seals are "visible words" (Augustine). In them we see with our eyes the promise of God. Indeed, in the sacraments we see, smell, touch and taste the word. In the public reading and preaching of Scripture, God addresses our mind and conscience through the hearing. In the sacraments, he uniquely addresses our mind and conscience through the other senses. In, through and to the senses, God's promise is made tangible. A sacrament is a covenant sign and seal, which means it reminds us and assures us of a promise. That is, it points to and confirms a gracious promise of God to his people. Another way of saying it is that a sacrament is an action designed by God to sign (symbolize) and seal (ratify) a covenantal reality, accomplished by the power and grace of God, the significance of which has been communicated by the word of God, and the reality of which is received or entered into only by faith. Hence, the weakness, the frailty of human faith welcomes this gracious act of reassurance. The sacraments are by nature supplemental to and confirmatory of the promises held out in the word, and the grace conveyed by them is the same grace held out via the means of preaching. The sacraments are efficacious for the elect and the elect only, since their benefits are sanctificational and received by faith, and for them provide effectual and objective nourishment of faith.

The consensus of Reformed teaching on the way in which Christ is present in the Lord's Supper may be summarized as follows: there is absolutely no corporeal presence of Christ whatsoever in the Lord's Supper. The believer does not corporeally partake of Christ in the Supper. Christ is not elementally, spatially or locally present in the Supper in any way. There is no change or conversion of the elements in the Supper. The believer does indeed receive Christ in the Supper, but not by the mouth, rather by faith. Nor does Christ's humanity come down to the believer, but by the Spirit the believer is raised in heart to receive Christ in his ascended glory. To put it in the language of the Westminster Confession, the Spiritual presence of Christ in the Lord's Supper may be summarized as follows: (1) the outward elements of the Lord's Supper (bread and wine) sustain such an analogy to Christ crucified that they may truly, but only sacramentally, be called by the name of the things they represent, that is, the body and blood of Christ; nevertheless in their substance and nature they are truly and only bread and wine (see Westminster Confession 29.5). (2) Worthy recipients who outwardly partake of the visible elements of Lord's Supper also inwardly by faith, really and truly, though not carnally and corporeally but rather spiritually, receive and feed upon Christ crucified and all benefits of his death. (3) The body and blood of Christ are not in any way corporeally or carnally in, with, or under the bread and wine; nevertheless Christ crucified is really, but spiritually, present to the faith of believers, in the Supper, just as the elements themselves are to their outward senses (see Westminster Confession 29.7). (4) The grace which is exhibited in or by the sacrament rightly used, is not conferred by any power in the elements or ritual. (5) The efficacy of the sacrament is utterly dependent upon the work of the Spirit, in accordance with the word of covenant promise (and hence the necessity of the words of institution, which contain both the dominical precept authorizing the Supper and a covenant promise of benefit to worthy receivers) (see Westminster Confession 27.3).

Meanwhile, Calvin's own positive view of the presence of Christ in the Supper (difficult as its precise apprehension has proven to be, even by those friendly to Calvin), entails the following emphases:

(1) the sign of the Lord's Supper and the thing signified must be distinguished (*Institutes*[22] 4.17.1; 2:1359-1361; *CO* XXX, 1002-1003);

(2) we feed on Christ in the Lord's Supper [though not corporeally], there is a true and Spiritual communion with Christ beyond our full comprehension (4.17.1; 2:1359-1361; *CO* XXX, 1002-1003);

(3) the believer's partaking of the Lord's Supper is a means of grace and especially a means of assurance and Christian growth (4.17.2; 2:1361-1362; *CO* XXX, 1003);

(4) the sacramental analogy leads us to ponder the Spiritual reality to which it points (4.17.3; 2:1362-1363; *CO* XXX, 1003-1004);

(5) the chief purpose of the sacrament of the Lord's Supper is to confirm/seal to us the promise established by the cross of Christ (4.17.4; 2:1363-1364; *CO* XXX, 1004-1005);

(6) the grace conferred in the Lord's Supper is received by faith alone, and without faith not received at all (4.17.5; 2:1364-1365; *CO* XXX, 1005-1006);

---

[22] The references here are to the Ford Lewis Battles translation of John Calvin's *Institutes of the Christian Religion* (Philadelphia: Westminster, 1960). The first set of numbers refers to the book, chapter and section of the Institutes, the second set refers to the volume and page number for the Battles edition. I have also cited the *Calvini Opera Omnia*, abbreviated here and elsewhere as *CO*. It should be here noted that a helpful exercise is learning the heart of Calvin's view of the sacraments is to begin by reading the 1536 edition (available in English in a Ford Lewis Battles translation, of the *Institutes of the Christian Religion* [London: Collins, 1975], 87-123; *CO* XXIX, 102-140), and then through each successive edition up to the 1559 edition. It allows the student to detect the repeated and unaltered core of Calvin's view, without the accouterments that accompany the final rendition, and perhaps confuse the unwary reader.

(7) in a mysterious, inexplicable and non-corporeal way we partake of the humanity of Christ, and not just of the Spirit, in the Lord's Supper (4.17.7; 2:1366-1368; *CO* XXX, 1007);

(8) the Supper uniquely witnesses to the incarnation and enfleshment of the Second Person of the Trinity, and thus highlights the role of his humanity in our redemption (4.17.8; 2:1368-1369; *CO* XXX, 1007-1008);

(9) Christ's humanity is a life-giving force to his people (4.17.9; 2:1369-1370; *CO* XXX, 1008-1009);

(10) Christ's humanity, then, is made present to us in the Supper, by the Spirit, and received only by faith and by faith alone (4.17.10; 2:1370-1371; *CO* XXX, 1009-1010);

(11) we must retain the distinction between the sign and the thing signified in the Lord's Supper, without denigrating the sacramental efficacy (4.17.11; 2:1371- 1372; *CO* XXX, 1010);

(12) the idea of a "real," spatial, local, elemental, corporeal presence of Christ in the Supper is a preposterous and blasphemous medieval Roman Catholic heresy (4.17.12; 2:1372-1373; *CO* XXX, 1010-1011);

(13) though the Roman medieval scholastic theologians try to state their teaching on the real presence carefully, they fail, because the fundamental concept is flawed (4.17.13; 2:1373-1374; *CO* XXX, 1011-1012);

(14) the idea of the conversion of the elements produced the fiction of transubstantiation (4.17.14; 2:1374-1376; *CO* XXX, 1012-1013);

(15) the error of transubstantiation is founded on the errors of the corporeal presence of Christ and our corporeal feeding on Christ (4.17.15; 2:1376-1378; *CO* XXX, 1013-1015);

(16) the Lutheran view of consubstantiation is wrong too, based on the erroneous doctrine of the ubiquity of Christ's humanity (4.17.16; 2:1379; *CO* XXX, 1015);

(17) the doctrine of ubiquity is Marcionite in tendency because it makes Christ's earthly humanity a temporary apparition (4.17.17; 2:1379-1380; *CO* XXX, 1015- 1016); and

(18) rather than being brought down from heaven to us in the sacrament, by the Spirit, our hearts are lifted up to heaven to feed on Christ by faith in the Lord's Supper (4.17.18; 2:1380-1381; *CO* XXX, 1016-1017).

It is vital to understand then, that Calvin's view of the Lord's Supper is not about real presence but about true communion. The central distinctive affirmations of Calvin's view of the Supper are: (1) in the Lord's Supper there is a true, Spiritual communion of the soul with the risen and ascended Christ; (2) because the risen and ascended Christ is *Logos ensarkos*, we may and indeed must speak of the believer's partaking of the humanity of Christ in the Supper, for that is the only way that one can commune with Christ who is everlastingly a theanthropic person;[23] (3) nevertheless, the "real presence" of Christ in the Supper is not only an error but a blasphemy; (4) true communion in the Lord's Supper is both objective and subjective: objectively accomplished by the Spirit, subjectively received by faith; (5) in the Supper we feed by faith, but faith is not the same thing as feeding (communing);[24] (6) the Supper is both sign and seal, and hence objectively both (a) points to the meaning of the death of Christ and the divine reality of communion with Christ, and (b) assures and nourishes us in the reality to which it points; (7) the Supper is an instrument[25] whereby we experience on earth a foretaste of the glorious communion of the heavenly consummation; (8) the

---

[23] See the interesting and suggestive discussion in Sinclair B. Ferguson's *The Holy Spirit* (Downer's Grove: IVP, 1996), 200-205.

[24] In his commentary on John 6:35 for instance, Calvin says: "Those who infer from this passage that to eat Christ is faith, and nothing else, reason inconclusively. I readily acknowledge that there is no other way in which we eat Christ than by believing; but the eating is the effect and fruit of faith rather than faith itself. For faith does not look at Christ only as at a distance, but embraces him, that he may become ours and may dwell in us. It causes us to be incorporated with him, to have life in common with him, and, in short, to become one with him (John 17:21). It is therefore true that by faith alone we eat Christ, provided we also understand in what manner faith unites us to him." See *The Gospel According to John*, translated by T. H. L. Parker (Grand Rapids: Eerdmans, 1961), 1:159; *CO* LXXV, 145. The above translation is the old Calvin Translation Society version.

[25] I am well aware of the debate on Calvin's view of the Supper as *instrumentum*. See Gerrish, *Grace and Gratitude*, e.g., 11-12.

difference between Calvin and Zwingli on the Supper, based upon the primary data, seems to be one of emphasis, expression, detail and sophistication rather than fundamental divergence; (9) Calvin's view is more specific, speculative, and semantically complex than Westminster's but may in fact be wholly consonant with it; (10) Calvin explicitly denied that the Supper is the only place we experience the Spiritual presence of or communion with Christ. As B. A. Gerrish has rightly noted ". . . Calvin certainly believed that a man would be equally deceived if he supposed that any thing less is offered in a sermon than is conferred through a sacrament."[26]

In light of this, a more suitable name for Calvin's view than "real presence" would be the "true, Spiritual and mysterious presence" view, or better yet the "true, Spiritual, and mysterious communion" view. This denomination picks up on four vital positive Calvinian emphases: (1) we truly commune with Christ through the Supper; (2) we only commune with Christ by the Spirit; (3) this communion is incomprehensible in many of its details; and (4) the language of communion better captures Calvin's stress on the experience of the believer in the Supper than does presence, which can be misleading and send one off on rabbit trails.[27]

---

[26] B. A. Gerrish, *Tradition and the Modern World: Reformed Theology in the Nineteenth Century* (Chicago: University of Chicago Press, 1978), 63.

[27] For Calvin, *praesentia* always serves the end of *communio* (see, e.g., *Institutes* 4.17.12; 2:1373). This is a key aspect of Calvin's "virtualism" (see Gerrish, *Grace and Gratitude*, 177-78, Ferguson, *Holy Spirit*, 201-203, and *Institutes* 4.17.18; 2:1381; *CO* XXX, 1016-1017). Yes, Calvin's language of presence is sometimes so strong that it provokes his friends to accuse him of double-talk, incomprehensibility, confusion and even crypto-Romanism (as Cunningham and Bullinger did, for instance!), nevertheless, close attention to the way Calvin speaks of Christ's *praesentia in virtute et efficacia*, will divulge Calvin's attempt to do a brilliant end run around the "real presence" debate by an appeal to Patristic and especially post-Nicene Greek participationist language.

A Summary of Important Historical Issues
in this Debate

There is a current and popular mythology in some quarters regarding the history of the Reformed view of the presence of Christ in the Lord's Supper, and so it will be helpful to consider some of the more salient aspects of it at the outset of this exchange.[28]

1. "Real Presence" is language that Calvin never uses to describe his own view of the presence of Christ in the Lord's Supper, but rather to describe the Roman Catholic view (and by implication the Lutheran view) he is criticizing. Hence, "real presence" rather than being an apt descriptor of the Reformed understanding of the Supper in general and the presence of Christ in the Supper in particular, is instead Calvin's term for a medieval, Roman, blasphemous error. It is imprudent in the extreme, then, to apply it as a title for his own teaching.

2. The trend towards using the language of "real presence" as a description of Calvin's view originated with Nevin (and his infamous *The Mystical Presence: A Vindication of the Reformed or Calvinistic Doctrine of the Holy Eucharist*) and Mercersburg in America and with Scoto-Catholic presbyterians in Britain. This language entered into the backwaters of conservative Reformed thought in the third quarter of the twentieth century primarily through Ronald Wallace's book *Calvin's Doctrine of the Word and Sacrament*, a tome that reflects the then current Scoto-Barthian thinking on this *locus*, arguing for a view based in part upon a mistranslation of Calvin's Latin which turns him into a real presence Lutheran—a misstep devastatingly exposed by David Willis-Watkins of Princeton in his excellent work *Calvin's Catholic Christology*.[29]

---

[28] Geoffey W. Bromiley's *Sacramental Teaching and Practice in the Reformed Churches* (Grand Rapids: Eerdmans, 1957; and recently reprinted by Wipf and Stock) is not a bad brief introduction to this terrain.

[29] The full title is *Calvin's Catholic Christology: The Function of the So-Called Extra Calvinisticum in Calvin's Theology* (Leiden: E. J. Brill, 1966).

3. The best current book available on Calvin's doctrine of the sacraments is B. A. Gerrish's *Grace and Gratitude* (Philadelphia: Fortress Press, 1993). It originated as the Cunningham Lectures at the University of Edinburgh, New College in 1990 and is the most important monograph on the subject in English in 25 years. Gerrish is far from antagonistic to Nevin and Wallace. Nevertheless, he distills nuances in Calvin's view to which both of them were oblivious and offers a far more balanced picture of Calvin's overall thought.

4. In the second half of the nineteenth century there was a significant debate between Charles Hodge of Princeton and J. W. Nevin of Mercersberg on the Calvinian doctrine of the Lord's Supper. Many contemporaries judged Hodge right and Nevin wrong, but Hodge in some measure conceded Calvin to Nevin (arguing that Calvin's views were not essential to his system or followed by his successors). In the late twentieth century, under the influence of the Barthian school of Calvin interpretation, general judgment was reversed and many argued that Nevin was right and Hodge wrong, and that Nevin's view was the genuine Calvinian approach to the Supper. In fact, however, Hodge and Nevin, both, were partly right and partly wrong. Each misunderstood aspects of Calvin's teaching on the nature of the presence of Christ in the Supper and sacramental efficacy.

5. Hence, the view that is often attributed to Calvin today is in fact Nevin's view (or Wallace's view) of Calvin, that is, a part for the whole view of Calvin in which aspects of Calvin's view are extracted and emphasized outside the contour of his total presentation in its rhetorical and historical-theological context. The best mainstream Calvin scholars of our time (exemplified in B. A. Gerrish) would find these approaches to Calvin in need of considerable refinement.

6. Though I take fiendish delight in Dabney's quip that Calvin's view is "not only incomprehensible, but impossible," and believe that he and the Southern Presbyterian theologians in

general (especially Thornwell) understood Calvin's view better than did Hodge, I must in the end disagree with Dabney's assessment of Calvin, too. Calvin does have a discernable view, but it is extremely subtle. Friends and foes alike have stumbled over it for four centuries, and only those with a full knowledge of post-Chalcedonian patristic Christology ever get close to it. Nevertheless, it would be nigh unto impossible to prove that the Mercersburg theology had a better grasp of or better represents Calvin's view in the main than the Westminster Assembly.

7. The previous point notwithstanding, it should be remembered that the great nineteenth-century Reformed critics of the Calvinian view, on both sides of the Atlantic, Charles Hodge, Robert Lewis Dabney and William Cunningham among them, all had views of the Lord's Supper that were perfectly consonant with the Westminster Confession (and thus ought to be esteemed as part of the Reformed consensus on the Supper) and their counterparts (like Nevin) held views that went beyond the Confession. When Hodge, Dabney or Cunningham criticized Calvin, they did so precisely in areas in which the doctrine of the Supper was unspecified in the Confession.

8. For ascertaining the central Reformed view on the Supper, ecclesial confessions are far more important than the formulations of individual theologians (however prominent), since they reflect a churchly consensus. All of us, of course, ought ultimately to appeal to Scripture and justify our positions from thence, but then there needs to be respect shown especially to the didactic authority of our confessions. "Such and such a theologian said this about the presence of Christ in the Lord's Supper" does not carry as much weight, even if that theologian is Calvin, as does "churches in England, Scotland, Wales, Ireland, the Americas, Korea, Africa and beyond have embraced this position on the presence of Christ in the Supper as the biblical view and have described it in their corporate confession of their collective faith." Both the *Consensus Tigurinus* and the Westminster Confession, then, have a right to

be taken seriously as reflective of the sixteenth and seventeenth century Reformed consensus, influential to this day, and the latter especially since it serves as the public theology of most presbyterians in our own time.

9. The Westminster Confession gives no comfort to any approach to the Supper that wants to call itself the "real presence" view. The Confession does not state its position using the word "real" for a reason. The English "real" is based upon the Latin *res*—that is, "the thing." So "real presence" means "the thing is present" and "the thing" being referred to is the physical body of Christ. Hence, the Confession only uses the word adverbially, and always with the qualification "yet spiritually" in order to distance itself from what every good Reformed Scholastic theologian worth his salt knew was a medieval Roman Catholic heresy, rather than a shorthand description of the Calvinian view! As we have asserted above, Calvin knew this too and so it is important to note his language (and very often it is what he does not say that you have to watch). Despite Calvin's verbal pyrotechnics to exalt the Spiritual presence of Christ in the Supper, the Lutherans are correct—he did not teach a real presence of Christ. Real presence always has and always will mean corporeal presence, and neither Calvin's view nor Westminster's can rise to that level, even under the most strained of exegesis. In the Westminster Confession, then, "really" means "truly" (not bodily or physically). Hence, all confessional Calvinists, simply on that point, are barred from communion in all conservative confessional Lutheran churches, precisely because the Lutherans correctly understand that we do not believe in the "real presence." It is most amusing that, in spite of this, contemporary Reformed folk are anxious to claim that label.

10. When people who have grown up under the influence of generic evangelicalism and its non-doctrine of the sacraments discover Bucer, Calvin, Vermigli, Bruce and the Reformed Confessions, they are immediately struck by assertions about the reality of the believer's reception of Christ, the affirmation of

sacramental efficacy, the strongly actualist language, and the emphasis on the sealing function of the signs. That is to say, they are gripped by those things which are absent in their own traditions (and even within the Reformed community today). If they resonate with these emphases, they also tend to extract them from their context, emphasize them disproportionately and fail to appreciate tacit messages and qualifying language in the material. In light of this, Richard Muller's warning regarding current interpretation of Calvin is apropos here, that the Reformers' teaching is so often lodged in a sixteenth-century polemical and exegetical contexts that "modern synthesizing or dogmatic" approaches tend to "distort or lose much of its meaning and implication."[30]

The Teaching of Scripture

Of course, the major question here is "what does the Bible teach?" We can engage in an interesting historical debate and it may prove enlightening and clarifying in many ways, but Scripture is our final authority, and so it is to Scripture that we must turn to settle the question of the nature of Christ's presence in the Supper.

Several general points should be made. First, exegetically speaking, the fundamental meaning and significance of the Supper is found in the dominical institutional words recorded in the Synoptics and 1 Corinthians; nevertheless, the doctrine of the presence of Christ in the Supper must be sought elsewhere than the references to the body of Christ in the Supper narratives. We will demonstrate this point momentarily. Second, the doctrine of the presence of Christ in the Supper must also be sought elsewhere than the biblical doctrine of covenant signs and seals. One will be hard-pressed to name any covenant sign/seal of the old or new covenants (apart from the disputed Supper) *in which* we may speak

---

[30] Richard A. Muller, *The Unaccommodated Calvin* (New York: Oxford University Press, 2000), 7.

of God being specially present. Third, we cannot get a doctrine of the presence of Christ in the Supper directly from John 6. There are indirect lessons for us that may be gleaned from John 6 but a direct application will be necessarily problematic and is more typical of sacerdotal approaches to the Supper. Fourth, positively, the biblical view of the presence of Christ in the Supper is grounded in the larger biblical doctrine of the covenantal presence of God, the dominical ecclesial presence promises (for instance in Matthew 18 and 28), the doctrine of union with Christ and the communion of the saints, and in the distinct reality signified, experienced in and confirmed but not created by the Supper as a covenant sign.

That being said, any proper understanding of the nature of the presence of Christ in the Lord's Supper must begin with an understanding of the biblical doctrine of the sacraments in general. Since biblical sacraments are, precisely, covenant signs and seals, we must refer to their function in the covenant relationships of Scripture if we are to do them justice. As can be seen from Genesis 17 and Romans 4, sacraments are actions designed by God to sign and seal (that is represent and ratify) a covenantal reality which has already been communicated and conveyed by the word of God. Hence, they are essentially acts of divine reassurance to us.

This is easily seen, for instance, in the context of the institution of the sign of circumcision. God has already entered into a covenant relationship with Abraham entailing blessings and obligations (Genesis 12), he has ratified that covenant relationship ritually (Genesis 15), Abraham after long waiting for the as-yet-unfulfilled promise has attempted to bring about realization of God's promises through sinful human designs (Genesis 16). In this context, God in his mercy grants Abraham a sacrament. In Genesis 17, God institutes an abiding mark, circumcision, to remind Abraham of his covenantal promises.

After reviewing his promises to Abraham (Genesis 17:2-8), God gives Abraham a sign designed to remind, teach, mark, seal and assure him of the certainty of the fulfillment of those promises. "God said further to Abraham, 'Now as for you, you shall keep *My covenant*, you and your descendants after you throughout their generations. *This is My covenant*, which you shall keep, between Me and you and your descendants after you: *every male among you shall be circumcised*. And you shall be circumcised in the flesh of your foreskin, and it shall be *the sign of the covenant* between Me and you'" (Genesis 17:9-11, emphases mine).

Notice that whereas God's covenant promises began with the words "As for me," now Abraham's obligations are stressed with the words "As for you." In this structure and phraseology we see, in the context of a gracious covenant, a stress on the mutuality of the covenant relationship.[31] The prime thing God asks of Abraham is faith, which evidences itself in commitment. Kidner observes: "The striking feature of the stipulations is their lack of detail. To be *committed* was all. Circumcision was God's brand; the moral implications could be left unwritten (until Sinai), for one was pledged to a Master, only secondarily to a way of life."[32]

In this context, the closest possible association is made between the sign and the covenant itself. They are so related that the sign is said to be the covenant and the covenant is the sign: "This is My covenant . . . every male among you shall be circumcised" (10); "it shall be the sign of the covenant between Me and you" (11); "thus shall My covenant be in your flesh for

---

[31] "The promise to Abraham and his descendants came in the form of a covenant which also placed definite responsibilities upon them. In verse 4 we read, 'As for me, this is my covenant with you.' Now we have the other side of the covenant announced in, 'As for you, you must keep my covenant.' This reveals the very nature of the covenant. Although it was one-sided in the sense that God set up all the terms, there were two parties in this covenant, as there are in every covenant." G. C. Aalders, *Genesis* (Grand Rapids: Zondervan, 1981), 1:308.

[32] Derek Kidner, *Genesis: An Introduction and Commentary* (Downers Grove: IVP, 1967), 129.

an everlasting covenant" (13). Nevertheless, this language makes it clear that the covenant and the sign of the covenant are two different things. They are identified, but without being confused or losing their distinguishability. This vital, exegetically derived distinction between the sign and the thing signified becomes a controlling hermeneutical principle for a proper understanding of the language of passages like Galatians 3:27, Romans 6:1-4, 1 Peter 3:21, and Colossians 2:11-12.

What does the sign itself do? By itself, nothing. Ishmael alone is ample proof of that. But in conjunction with the Word (which it confirms) and our faith (which it assures) it does much: 1. It provides an outward sign of entrance into the external covenant community. 2. It signifies the need for cleansing from sin and the availability of that cleansing. 3. It also has the significance of marking the member as the possession of God and of guaranteeing the promises for those who do not reject the covenant (or to put it positively, to those who keep the covenant). Thus the sign seals the elect for the possession of eternal life. The elect are sealed into the certainty of ultimate possession of the promises. 4. Because it signifies and seals inclusion in the external community of the covenant of Grace, circumcision does not lead to presumption but to personal responsibility. 5. The covenant sign/seal itself does not bring about covenantal blessing. It evidences (signs) and completes (seals) the fact of a covenantal relationship, which always entails responsibility to the one with whom one has covenanted. That covenantal relationship may thus be fulfilled in either blessing or curse. If the person who has received the sign of the covenant, rejects the covenant (by refusing to have faith and repent), he is sealed to double curse. 6. The covenant sign/seal does not inaugurate, effect or create the covenant relationship, but ritually acknowledges and confirms it (which is inherent in the language of sign and seal).

It is a failure to understand these rudimentary truths regarding biblical covenant signs that leads to unhelpful sacramental realism, cultivates an unhealthy view of sacramental efficacy and produces an ungrounded doctrine of the real presence of Christ in the sacraments. Nevertheless, sacraments, which are outward signs of inward Spiritual realities, are truly means of grace and far more than empty tokens. Calvin explains their function and efficacy this way:

> While we believe the word of God, we ought not to despise the aids which he has been pleased to add for the purpose of strengthening our faith. For instance, the Lord offers to us in the gospel everything necessary for salvation; for when he brings us into a state of fellowship with Christ, the sum of all blessings is truly contained in him. What then is the use of Baptism and the Lord's Supper? Must they be regarded as superfluous? Not at all; for any one who shall actually, and without flattery, acknowledge his weakness, of which all from the least to the greatest are conscious, will gladly avail himself of those aids for his support. We ought indeed to grieve and lament, that the sacred truth of God needs assistance on account of the defect of our flesh; but since we cannot all at once remove this defect, any one who, according to his capacity shall believe the word, will immediately render full obedience to God. Let us therefore learn to embrace the signs along with the word, since it is not in the power of man to separate them.[33]

So, Calvin says, covenant signs are given to us by God to bolster our flagging faith. And when God says you need something, you need it! Nevertheless, proponents of sacramental realism will be at loss to derive any doctrine of the presence of Christ from the biblical teaching on the sacraments in general.

There are at least five passages that any doctrine of the presence of Christ, must come to grips with (Matthew 26:26-27; Mark 14:22-24; Luke 22:19-20; 1 Corinthians 11:23-29; and John 6:41-58), and there are explicit exegetical reasons for four of them to be read in light of Old Testament covenant thought and implicit reasons for the fifth of them to be understood

---

[33] Calvin, *Commentary on Isaiah*, translated by William Pringle (Grand Rapids: Baker, 1981 reprint), 1:240-241; *CO* LXIV, 152, but see the larger, helpful discussion from 1:239-242; *CO* LXIV, 151-153.

covenantally.[34] As we approach the three Supper accounts found in the Synoptics, as well as Paul's record of the words of institution and John's discourse on faith in Christ, it will be our purpose to discern the theological significance of these texts for the doctrine of the presence of Christ in the Supper.[35]

In general, we should note the following about these passages as they come to bear on our understanding of the Supper. First, the synoptic accounts all emphasize the Supper as pre-explanatory of the meaning of the death of Christ and hence indicative of the significance of the believer's participation in the covenantal benefits which accrue from Christ's saving work. In light of this, Jesus' language about his body and blood, rather than drawing attention to his physical body, is designed to move the disciples to contemplation of his death as a sacrifice for a broken covenant by speaking of the two component parts of old covenant atoning sacrifices: body and blood. Second, Paul's account in 1 Corinthians, while picking up this same theme, is placed squarely in the context of a larger discussion of what it means to

---

[34] R. V. Moss calls the Supper accounts "the *locus classicus* of covenant thought in the tradition of the sayings of Jesus," "The Covenant Conception in Early Christian Thought" (PhD Diss., University of Chicago, 1964), 93; and H. A. A. Kennedy observes that the usage of the covenant concept in the eucharistic narratives "is in many respects the most remarkable and the most difficult instance of the Covenant-idea in the New Testament" in "The Significance and Range of the Covenant Conception in the New Testament," *Expositor*, 8th ser. 10 (1915):395. John W. Pryor has argued compellingly for the importance of the covenant idea in the Gospel of John, see *John: Evangelist of the Covenant People* (Downers Grove: IVP, 1992), esp. 157-180.

[35] I will not, here, engage in the historical debate concerning the origins of the accounts and the precise chain of events at the Last Supper, for an introduction to which see I. H. Marshall, *Last Supper and Lord's Supper* (Exeter: Paternoster, 1980), esp. 13-75,107-146; J. Jeremias, *The Eucharistic Words of Jesus*, 3rd ed., trans. N. Perrin (London: SCM, 1966); A. J. B. Higgins, *The Lord's Supper in the New Testament* (London: SCM, 1952); and N. Clark, *An Approach to the Theology of the Sacraments* (London: SCM, 1956), 36-59.

be part of Christ's church, and thus points to the communion that flows from union with Christ and hence the communion of the saints that ought to characterize believers' communion with Christ in the Supper. That is the significance of his call for us to discern the body. Which means, not discerning a mystical and special presence of Christ's humanity in the Supper, but rather the discernment of the church as the body of Christ, and hence a discernment that our union with Christ establishes a communion with his people, his ecclesial body, that must be practically manifested in community, mutual love and concern, and accountability. Finally, John's account of Jesus' bold discourse in John 6 is manifestly anchored in a larger discussion of faith in Christ. Hence Jesus' graphic language about our eating and drinking his body and blood must be taken as descriptive of the act of faith, rather than explanatory of some kind of fleshly presence of Christ in the Lord's Supper (a topic that never even remotely appears in the context of John 6 or in the rest of the Gospel). Now, to the specific passages.

The Matthean form of the eucharistic words is usually taken to be a slight revision of Mark's account.[36] Matthew's bread-word (in 26:26) is "While they were eating, Jesus took *some* bread, and after a blessing, He broke *it* and gave *it* to the disciples, and said, 'Take, eat; this is My body.'" The breaking and giving are significant and relate to the fulfillment of Isaiah 53 (as we shall see in more detail in out treatment of Luke). The assertion "this

---

[36] See D. P. Senior, *The Passion Narrative According to Matthew: A Redactional Study* (Leuven: Leuven University Press, 1975), 76-88; Jeremias, *Eucharistic Words*, 184; and Marshall, *Last Supper*, 33, 99-101. The priority of Mark has been recently questioned by a number of scholars (W. R. Farmer, B. Orchard, and H. H. Stoldt), see the *International Standard Bible Encyclopedia (ISBE)* 3:281, but we are simply following the canonical order in our discussion here. Matthew's Gospel has been dated between 70 and 115 (most commonly in the 80s) and was far more frequently cited by the fathers than Mark and Luke, see the *Interpreter's Dictionary of the Bible (IDB)* 3:312-313.

is my body" clearly points to the death of Christ in the flesh (over against all patripassian and Gnostic interpretations), and the directives "take, eat" indicate the vital role of the disciples' believing on Christ's person and trusting in his work on the cross.

In Matthew's narrative the cup-word reads as follows: "Drink from it, all of you; for this is My blood of the covenant (τὸ αἷμά μου τῆς διαθήκης), which is poured out for many for forgiveness of sins" [Matt. 26:27b, 28]. There are at least three observations worth mentioning concerning the covenantal background to this passage.

First, the phrase "this is my blood of the covenant" recalls the words of the sacrificial inauguration of the Sinaitic covenant recorded in Exodus 24:8 "Behold, the blood of the covenant (τὸ αἷμά τῆς διαθήκης[LXX]), which the Lord has made with you."[37] Here, Moses sacrificed young bulls and, after the reading of the book of the covenant in the presence of the people, sprinkled the blood of the slaughtered beasts on the people, declaring it to be the blood of the covenant. Thus the covenant was ratified. In the Matthean eucharistic narrative then, the significance of the cup (or its contents) is explicitly related to the blood sprinkled in ratification of the Mosaic covenant. Second, and following on this point, we may note that Matthew's text differs from the LXX in the addition of μου, to the phrase "the blood of the covenant," so that the cup is said to represent not simply *the* blood of the covenant, but *Christ's* ("My") blood of the covenant. This explicit connection between Jesus' blood and the blood sprinkling at Sinai points to an understanding of Jesus' death as one of covenantal sacrifice.[38] Third,

---

[37] Some have argued for Zech. 9:11 as the source of the cup-word, see for instance B. Lindars, *New Testament Apologetic: The Doctrinal Significance of the Old Testament Quotations* (London: SCM, 1961), 132-133; but see also D. J. Moo's effective response in *The Old Testament in the Gospel Passion Narratives* (Sheffield: Almond, 1983), 301-311.

[38] For more detailed corroboration of this view see Marshall, *Last Supper*, esp. 91-93; Moo observes that "the covenant sacrifice (Ex. 24:8) is a unique and foundational event, implying perhaps the taking away of sins as a

the Matthean cup-word alone includes the phrase "for forgiveness of sins (εἰς ἄφεσιν ἁμαρτιων)," which serves to indicate the purpose of the shedding of the blood of the covenant and may be suggestive of Isaiah 53:12 or Jeremiah 31:34.[39] Here we have a direct connection between the covenant idea and forgiveness of sins.[40]

Mark's bread-word (found in 14:22) runs "While they were eating, He took *some* bread, and after a blessing He broke *it*, and gave *it* to them, and said, 'Take *it*; this is My body.'" We find here the eucharistic component in the presence of the "blessing" (though this is clearer in Luke), the ritual breaking of bread which harkens back to Isaiah 53 and the assertion we have already met in Matthew that "this is my body"—in other words, read in light of the Isaianic allusion, Christ is saying in effect: "this bread represents the colossally important reality of my human death, which I will render tomorrow, on your behalf, because of the Father's and my love for you, as a covenantal sacrifice, on account of your sin."

The Marcan form of the cup-word is as follows: "This is My blood of the covenant (τὸ αἷμά μου τῆς διαθήκης), which is poured out for many." As we have previously mentioned, it seems

---

necessary prelude to a relationship between man and God, but emphasizing more strongly the establishment of fellowship. It has been pointed out that the narrative of Exodus 24 is the only sacrificial ritual recorded in the OT in which the blood was sprinkled on the *people*, signifying '*eine direkte und reale Gemeinschafte mit dem bundesstiftenden Altargeschehen.*' Furthermore, Jewish tradition ascribed atoning sacrifice to this blood. It is not, therefore, with an ordinary sacrifice that Jesus connects his death, but with a unique atoning sacrifice that emphasizes the ultimate involvement of those who participate." *Passion Narratives*, 311.

[39] Moo, *Passion Narratives*, 306; and Marshall, *Last Supper*, 92-93,100.

[40] Marshall says: "This is a fresh theological concept. Since there is already a reference to the covenant in the cup-saying, which alludes to the new covenant in Jeremiah 31:31-34, it is likely that the reference to forgiveness of sins takes up the last promise in that passage, 'for I will forgive their iniquity, and I will remember their sin no more.'" *Last Supper*, 100.

to be the precursor of the Matthean cup-word and shows signs of Hebrew or Aramaic origins.[41] We may again note the presence of the allusion to Exodus 24:8 and the addition of μου,, "which is essential to the allusion."[42] The phrase, "which is poured out for many (ἐκχυννόμενον ὑπὲρ πολλῶν)," though it too is found in Matthew's account. It has been suggested that this is a word of explanation, reminiscent of Isaiah 53:12 (MT rather than LXX),[43] pointing to the imminent,[44] vicarious (ὑπὲρ) death of Jesus that would establish the covenant.

When we turn to the Lucan account, we encounter a textual problem that warrants brief consideration. In a small number of texts Luke 22:19b-20 is omitted, and despite strong MSS support for the longer reading, many scholars prefer the shorter reading.[45] The shorter reading is probably the harder of the two readings

---

[41] Jeremias, *Eucharistic Words*, 187; and Marshall, *Last Supper*, 33. It is common to date Mark's gospel in the 60's (see the discussions of C. E .B. Cranfield in *IDB* 3:268 and R.P. Martin in *ISBE* 3:253-254).

[42] Moo, *Passion Narratives*, 304.

[43] Moo, *Passion Narratives*, 130-132; Jeremias, *Eucharistic Words*, 178; and Marshall, *Last Supper*, 43.

[44] Jeremias notes: "The striking present tense is explained by the fact that, contrary to Greek, Hebrew and Aramaic possess no participial forms which distinguish time. The participle is atemporal. Its time sphere is determined by the context. In Aramaic the participle is often used for an event expected in the near future. . . . Our passage will therefore have to be translated: '(my blood) that (soon) *will* be shed'. Failure to notice this fact has led to serious misunderstandings, especially to the view that Jesus speaks of a pouring out of his blood at the Supper–not on the Cross!" in *Eucharistic Words*, 178-179.

[45] Moo explains: "Verses 19b-20 in this passage were omitted by Westcott and Hort as a "Western non-interpolation," this cumbersome term coined by them to describe the rare occasions when (according to them) the Western text preserved a shorter, and presumably earlier, reading than the other MSS traditions (and especially and B). Although considerable doubt now exists as to the validity of this judgment regarding "non-Western interpolations," a great number of scholars continue to regard vv. 19b-20 as secondary." *Passion Narratives*, 127-128.

and so reasonably favored according to the canons of textual criticism ("a shorter reading is preferred, and a more difficult reading is given priority").[46] However, on behalf of the longer reading, we may point out the weakness of the MSS evidence for the shorter reading[47] and the strength of MSS support for the longer version.[48] Additionally, it can be argued that the presence of two cups in the longer form of the Lucan eucharistic narrative constitutes as difficult a reading as the reversal of the bread-cup order in the shorter form and may indeed account for the existence of the shorter reading.[49] Hence, it is not unreasonable to support the longer reading as the original form. Our consideration, then, of the Lucan institutional words will proceed on the presupposition of the authenticity of Luke 22:19b-20.

Luke's record of our Lord's institutional words over the bread are chock full of meaning. While the disciples still had the taste of the passover lamb in their mouths, Christ takes bread and breaks

---

[46] See Jeremias, *Eucharistic Words*, 152-159; Moo, *Passion Narratives*, 128; and Marshall, *Last Supper*, 37.

[47] Marshall says: "A point of particular importance is that manuscript evidence for the short text is poor. It consists of only one Greek MS (D) and some Latin versions, together with some Syriac and Coptic evidence for rearranging the verses, and a variant reading with only one Greek MS (a decidedly erratic one!) in its favour is decidedly weak." *Last Supper*, 37. See also Jeremias, *Eucharistic Words*, 142-152.

[48] "The Long Form is attested: (1) by all the Greek MSS. (the earliest being at present P[75], AD 175/225) except D, (2) by all the versions with the exception of the Old Syriac (syr^cur sin, see below, pp. 143f.) and a part of the Itala, and (3) by all early Christian writers, beginning with Marcion, Justin and Tatian." Jeremias, *Eucharistic Words*, 139. He goes on to say that "the decisive argument in favour of the Long Text is its overwhelming attestation." *Eucharistic Words*, 159. A. R. Eagar refers to the MSS testimony as "overwhelming external evidence." "St. Luke's Account of the Last Supper: A Critical Note on the Second Sacrament," *Expositor* 7th ser. 5 (1908):343.

[49] Moo concludes: "The traditional explanation remains the most satisfactory: the longer text has been shortened by a scribe who found the mention of two cups difficult; in the process, v. 19b has been omitted as well." *Passion Narratives*, 129-130.

it, and says: "This is My body which is given for you; do this in remembrance of Me." It is obvious that "this is my body" is to be read symbolically or figuratively here, as Calvin himself does,[50] for at least three reasons. One, Jesus is in their immediate presence physically as he distributes the bread, it would have occurred to none of them that he was, or was going to eventually be, somehow physically present in the bread—an idea utterly alien to the whole covenantal sacramental tradition of the Old Testament. Two, the whole thrust of the passage is prophetic and pre-explanatory of his death on the morrow. He is providing them a covenantal theology of the atonement, not a sacramental theology of elemental-corporeal presence. Three, Jesus figurative references to himself regarding salvific roles had become commonplace to his disciples by this time. They were used to him saying things like "I am the door" (John 10:7, 9). The concussive impact of his bold metaphor itself would have clued the disciples into the symbolic nature of his words and actions.

Hence, the significance of Luke's bread-word is not transubstantiation, consubstantiation or real presence, but rather (1) Christ's pre-explanation of the meaning of his death—"my body given for you"—points to substitutionary atonement. (2) Christ's anchoring of that pre-explanation in the fulfillment of Scripture. He explicitly connects his death to the bruised servant of Isaiah 53 as part of the pre-explanation of his death (that is, he indicated that the broken and given bread related forward to his immolated body and back to the crushed servant). So, "my body for you," signified his fulfillment and realization of covenantal righteousness for all his people through his singular redemptive

---

[50] Calvin says "the bread is called body because it is the symbol of the body" and "No one with a moderate acquaintance of Scripture will deny that sacramental expression must be taken as metonymy," in *A Harmony of the Gospels*, (Torrance/Eerdmans edition), 3:134. See his larger discussion in *A Harmony of the Gospels*, 3:132-139; *CO* LXXIII, 704-708.

suffering. (3) Christ's call for the covenantal memorialization of his death. He tells his disciples to memorialize the reality pointed to by the sign. Indeed, Christ's call to remembrance—"Do this in remembrance"—will be echoed and exegeted in 1 Corinthians by Paul's assertion that when we remember we "proclaim the Lord's death until he comes" (11:26b).

In fact, Luke's bread-word establishes a connection between the covenant idea and Passover as related to the Lord's Supper. In Luke, as in the other Synoptic eucharistic narratives, Jesus' words "My body" and "My blood" appear. Jeremias has argued that these words designate the component parts of a slaughtered sacrificial animal (cf. Lev. 17:11,14; Deut. 12:23; Ezek. 39:17-19; Heb. 13:11,12).[51] So when Jesus applies these words to Himself, He is speaking of Himself as a sacrifice.[52] Furthermore, it is likely, given the context of a Passover meal,[53] that Jesus is referring to Himself as a paschal lamb.[54] If this is the case, then it is possible to argue that the Synoptists' understand Jesus' death

---

[51] Jeremias, *Eucharistic Words*, 221-222; and Moo, *Passion Narratives*, 306-308.

[52] "He is applying to himself *terms from the language of sacrifice*, as is also the case with the participle ἐκχυννόμενον ('poured out', Mark 14:24). Each of the two nouns presupposes a slaying that has separated flesh and blood. In other words: *Jesus speaks of himself as a sacrifice.*" Jeremias, *Eucharistic Words*, 222.

[53] Of course, it has been much disputed whether or not the Last Supper was a Passover meal. For detailed discussions of this important matter see Marshall, *Last Supper*, 57-75; and Jeremias, *Eucharistic Words*, 15-84. In our subsequent discussion we shall assume that Marshall and Jeremias are correct in their arguments that the Supper was indeed a Passover meal.

[54] "With the words *den bisri*, 'this is my (sacrificial) flesh', and *den idmi*, 'this is my (sacrificial) blood', Jesus is therefore most probably speaking of himself as the paschal lamb. He is *the eschatological paschal lamb*, representing the fulfillment of all that of which the Egyptian paschal lamb and all the subsequent sacrificial paschal lambs were the prototype." Jeremias, *Eucharistic Words*, 223. Additionally, Moo observes: "It would not be surprising if Jesus and the evangelists appealed to the Passover traditions in their explication of Jesus' passion, inasmuch as this tradition was supremely influential in Jewish theology and often regarded as a prefigurement of the eschaton." *Passion Narratives*, 311.

as a paschal sacrifice that establishes the new covenant.[55] As Jeremias says so well:

> Jesus describes his death as this eschatological passover sacrifice: *his vicarious* (ὑπέρ) *death brings into operation the final deliverance,* the new covenant of God. Διαθήκη ('covenant') is a correlate of βασιλεία τῶν οὐρανῶν ('kingdom of heaven'). The content of this gracious institution which is [mediated] by Jesus' death is perfect communion with God (Jer. 31.33-34a) in his reign, based upon the remission of sins (31.34b).[56]

The Lucan cup-saying reads as follows: "This cup which is poured out for you is the new covenant in My blood (ἡ καινὴ διαθήκη ἐν τῷ αἵματί μου)" [Luke 22:20]. We may make two observations relating to the presence of Christ and the covenantal background to Luke's cup-word. First, the Lucan account includes the emphasis on the vicarious nature of Jesus'

---

[55] "By comparing himself with the eschatological paschal lamb Jesus describes his death as a *saving death*. . . . The blood of the lambs slaughtered at the exodus from Egypt had *redemptive power* and made *God's covenant* with Abraham operative." Jeremias, *Eucharistic Words*, 225. It is worth noting that Jewish interpretation understood the blood of the Passover lamb to be "covenant-blood" which brought about the deliverance from Egypt. For instance, Dalman has pointed out that the Targum on Zech. 9:11 ("because of the blood of My covenant with you, I have set your prisoners free from the waterless pit") connects this passage with the Exodus: "'Also ye, for whom an "agreement" over blood was appointed, I have redeemed from slavery of Egypt'. At the same time, the direct reference is to the blood of the Passover lambs, which brings into fruition God's 'covenant' at the redemption from Egypt. . . . All the occurrences at the Exodus meant an 'agreement' with the God of Israel, and it was not a far-fetched thought to consider the Paschal blood as the blood of this 'agreement'." G. Dalman, *Jesus-Jeshua: Studies in the Gospels*, trans. P. R. Levertoft (London: SPCK, 1929), 166-167.

[56] Jeremias, *Eucharistic Words*, 226; the brackets are mine where the quotation reads "mediated," because the book reads "meditated" which is, presumably, a typographical error.

action ("for you"), as do Matthew and Mark ("for many").[57] This idea, as we have previously seen, relates to Jesus as covenantal sacrifice.

Second, and in distinction from the Matthean and Marcan forms, Luke identifies the cup with the *new* covenant, apparently looking back to Jeremiah 31:31-34.[58] The significance of this is that Christ's death is seen as fulfillment and realization of Jeremiah's new covenant prophecy and promise. At first glance, this allusion to Jeremiah 31 in the cup-word may seem to set the Mark/Matthew tradition (which is, arguably, drawing on Exodus 24:8) over against that of Paul/Luke. Jeremias, however, sees Luke's wording "the new covenant in My blood" as explanatory of "My blood of the covenant" rather than contradictory of it.[59] And Moo observes that "while the covenant in Matthew/Mark is not specifically identified as 'new,' it is idle to deny that the

---

[57] For discussion of the origin and significance of ὑπὲρ in the Supper narratives, see Jeremias, *Eucharistic Words*, esp. 195-196,178-182.

[58] Some have attempted to deny this connection [e.g., Grässer, *Der Alte Bund im Neuen: Exegetische Studien zur Israelfrage im Neuen Testament* (Tübingen: J. C. B. Mohr, 1985), 115-126], however the scholarly consensus remains firmly behind the relation between the Pauline/Lucan cup-word and Jeremiah's new covenant prophecy. See Y. K. Yu, "The New Covenant: The Promise and its Fulfillment" (Ph.D.Diss., Durham University, 1989), 183-184.

[59] See Jeremias, *Eucharistic Words*, "Likewise explanatory is the further definition of the 'covenant' by 'new' (Paul/Luke), a reference to Jer. 31:31-34. The addition is certainly pre-Pauline, as the agreement of Paul with Luke shows, but presumably first arose on hellenistic soil, since the position of the adjective 'new' before 'covenant' is unsemitic" [171-172]. "In the process of transformation, whose result is the Pauline formulation, there are different, partly overlapping, motives at work, which may be briefly summarized: . . . A tendency towards clarification may be recognized: the semitisms εὐλογήσας (p. 175) and πολλῶν (pp. 179ff.) could be misunderstood by non-Jews and were replaced. The second 'this' was clarified by 'cup', 'covenant' by 'new'" [187]. ". . . the thought of the new covenant was not far from [Jesus'] thoughts, even when it is not otherwise attested in the tradition of his words" [195].

concept is implicitly present in Jesus' claim that a covenant in *His* blood is about to be ratified."[60] It seems likely then that Jeremiah 31:31-34 is in the background of the Mark/Matthew cup-sayings, as well as Luke's.[61] Furthermore, we may note that the Lucan allusion to Jeremiah's new covenant prophecy in the cup-word neither excludes the possibility of reference to Exodus 24:8[62] nor prevents him from elsewhere explaining Christ's death in relation to the Mosaic economy. For instance, in the Lucan transfiguration narrative Jesus appears in glory, talking with Moses and Elijah. Here, Luke seems to be looking to the Exodus event when he says that they "were speaking of His exodus (τὴν ἔξοδον αὐτοῦ) which He was about to accomplish in Jerusalem" [Luke 9:31].[63]

John 6 has long been a playground for sacerdotalism and real presence advocates. The key section is 48-58, where Jesus says:

> "I am the bread of life. Your fathers ate the manna in the wilderness, and they died. This is the bread which comes down out of heaven, so

---

[60] Moo, *Passion Narratives*, 305.

[61] Y. K. Yu has noted: "With regard to the close connection between the new covenant of Jer 31:31ff and that in the NT, it is important to note that the OT allusions in the cup-word indicate that the writers of the Synoptic Gospels and Paul understand the new covenant established by the blood of Jesus by relating the event not to Jer 31:31ff alone but to Jer 31:31ff in combination with other OT texts. In other words, the fulfillment of the promise of the new covenant of Jer 31:31ff in the NT does not seem to have been conceived of as a one (Jer. 31:31ff) to one (the new covenant established at the Last Supper) correspondence. Rather, this fulfillment can be understood by relating the significance of the death of Jesus to Jer 31:31ff through the process of interpretation in the light of other OT texts." "New Covenant," 292.

[62] See Moo, *Passion Narratives*, 305.

[63] The context argues that more is meant by ἔξοδον than "departure" as it is usually translated, see Moss, *Covenant Conception in Early Christian Thought*, 86 and Moo, *Passion Narratives*, 324; for further discussion of the evangelists' appeal to the Exodus event in interpreting Jesus' life and ministry, cf. J. Marsh, *The Fulness of Time* (London: Nisbet, 1952), 84-90; see also J. Daniélou, *From Shadows to Reality* (London: Burns and Oates, 1960), 153-166; and Moss, *Covenant Conception*, 82-83.

that one may eat of it and not die. I am the living bread that came down out of heaven; if anyone eats of this bread, he will live forever; and the bread also which I will give for the life of the world is My flesh."

Then the Jews *began* to argue with one another, saying, "How can this man give us *His* flesh to eat?"

So Jesus said to them, "Truly, truly, I say to you, unless you eat the flesh of the Son of Man and drink His blood, you have no life in yourselves. He who eats My flesh and drinks My blood has eternal life, and I will raise him up on the last day. For My flesh is true food, and My blood is true drink. He who eats My flesh and drinks My blood abides in Me, and I in him. As the living Father sent Me, and I live because of the Father, so he who eats Me, he also will live because of Me. This is the bread which came down out of heaven; not as the fathers ate and died; he who eats this bread will live forever."

Roman Catholic interpreters cite this passage as grounds for the doctrine of the corporeal eucharistic presence of Christ and for the idea of transubstantiation. Obviously, all Protestant interpreters reject the latter, but Lutherans affirm the former. Calvin rejects a "real presence" interpretation of this passage and, though he sees indirect significance of this passage for our understanding of the Lord's Supper, he stands squarely in the Reformed tradition of interpretation when he declares: "This sermon does not refer to the Lord's Supper, but to the continual communication which we have apart from the reception of the Lord's Supper."[64] Indeed, whatever Christ is speaking of here is of the essence of salvation. Any interpretation of this passage that makes Christ's words primarily referent to or explanatory of the Supper must view the Supper as necessary for salvation.

The passage's meaning is clear enough, however pregnant and suggestive the language may be.[65] Christ's references here to

---

[64] *Commentary on John*, Parker trans. (Eerdmans), 1:169; *CO* LXXV, 154. It is interesting to note that the Westminster Assembly, consonant with this observation of Calvin's, does not cite John 6 in the Scripture references illustrative of its teaching on the Supper.

[65] See F. F. Bruce's helpful overview in *The Hard Sayings of Jesus* (Downers Grove: IVP, 1983), 21-25.

the necessity of eating and drinking his body and blood, point to two grand realities: (1) the absolute necessity of his person and work for communion with God ("unless you eat the flesh of the Son of Man and drink His blood, you have no life in yourselves"), and (2) the absolute necessity of faith (which is graphically portrayed here as eating and drinking).[66] Hence, Augustine said: *Crede et manducasti*.[67] The whole context of this passage in the flow of John's Gospel confirms these interpretive points. J. I. Packer concurs in this assessment and says:

> Jesus' sermon (John 6:35-58) about himself as the Bread of Life, and the need to feed on him by eating his flesh and drinking his blood, was preached before the Supper existed and is better understood as being about what the Supper signifies (i.e., communion with Christ by faith) than about the Supper itself.[68]

Turning now to 1 Corinthians,[69] we will briefly attend Paul's account of the Lord's Supper. He gave us the term (see 11:20). Paul's record of the dominical bread-word in 1 Corinthians 11:24 tells us that when Jesus had given thanks, he broke it and said, "This is My body, which is for you; do this in remembrance of Me." Once again we have three distinct components to the explanatory rubric: (1) the language of atoning sacrifice "this is my body," (2) the assertion of vicarious or substitutionary sacrifice "which is for you," and (3) a call to covenantal memorialization "do this in remembrance of me."

---

[66] See A. A. Hoekema, *Saved By Grace* (Grand Rapids: Eerdmans, 1989), 136-138, esp. 137.

[67] *Homilies on John*, 26.1. See *Nicene and Post-Nicene Fathers*, edited by Philip Schaff (Grand Rapids: Eerdmans, 1983 reprint), 7.168.

[68] *Concise Theology* (Wheaton: Tyndale, 1993), 218.

[69] The Corinthian letters are commonly dated in the mid-50s (55, argues S. Gilmour, *IDB* 1:692 & 698), see L. Morris for discussion *ISBE* 1:777 & 780; First Corinthians is the first NT book to be cited along with the name of its author (1 Clement), and Ignatius and Polycarp quote from it as well; Second Corinthians was first quoted by Polycarp.

The Pauline cup-word in 1 Corinthians 11:25 reads: "This cup is the new covenant in my blood (ἡ καινὴ διαθήκη ἐστιν ἐν τῷ ἐμῷ αἵματι); do this, as often as you drink it, in remembrance of Me." The first clause is close to the reading in Luke 22:20.[70] The second is a distinctive part of Paul's cup-word. Here, as in the Lucan word of explanation, the cup is said to represent the inauguration of the new covenant by the blood (death) of Christ.[71] Hence, Paul's account also manifests the allusion to the covenant inauguration by sacrifice in Exodus 24:8[72] and to the fulfillment of Jeremiah's new covenant.[73] Paul's cup-word, however, does not include a phrase parallel to Luke's "poured out for you" (which indicated explicitly the vicarious nature of Jesus' death). Nevertheless, the concept of Jesus' vicarious death is clearly implied, both by comparison with Paul's bread-word [11:24, "for you"] and in Paul's understanding of Jesus as the eschatological Paschal lamb, which is made evident in 1 Corinthians 5:7 ("For Christ our Passover also has been sacrificed").[74]

---

[70] Paul's cup-word includes ἐστιν in contrast to Luke, and there is a textual variant behind the phrase "in my blood." The preferred reading in Nestle-Aland, ἐμῷ αἵματι, is supported by ℵ B D F 𝐆 Ψ and many of the small manuscripts. The reading which is in harmony with the Lucan wording, αἵματ μου, is supported by P[46] A C and p [33],p[365],p[1175],p [1241s].

[71] "In this context the *new covenant* is understood to have been ratified *by* the blood of Christ, which means by his death." W. F. Orr and J. A. Walther, *1 Corinthians (Anchor Bible)* (Garden City: Doubleday, 1976), 267.

[72] See C. K. Barrett, *First Corinthians* (London: Black, 1968), 268-269; P. S. Liao observes of the Pauline eucharistic account: "It seems plain . . . that the event of the Last Supper is a clear recollection of the covenant-event at Sinai. . . . Not only is there a resemblance in words used in the two events, there is also a correspondence in situation." "The Place of the Covenant in the Theology of the Apostle Paul" (Ph.D. Thesis, Hartford Seminary, 1973), 52-52.

[73] See Yu, "New Covenant," esp. 183-186.

[74] Jeremias says of 1 Cor. 5:7b: "the lamb is interpreted as the symbol of the Messiah who was sacrificed as the unblemished lamb." *Eucharistic Words*, 60.

As we previously mentioned, "do this in remembrance of Me" is unique among the cup-sayings, though found in both Paul's and Luke's bread-words. A. R. Millard sees in this memorial emphasis a recollection of the ancient covenant formula.[75] Whatever the case may be, it serves to remind that the Supper is about the significance of the Lord's death, which is reiterated by Paul in the phrase "as often as you eat this bread and drink this cup, you proclaim the Lord's death until He comes" [11:26].

A Summary of the Biblical Testimony

The emphases of the key scriptural passages on the sacraments in general and Lord's Supper in particular are clear. (1) Sacraments, or covenant signs/seals, do not inaugurate or effect a covenant relationship, rather they represent and confirm a previously existing, grace-established, Father-initiated, Spirit-bestowed, Christ-grounded, faith-received, covenant relationship.

---

[75] Millard, looking for evidence of the covenant scheme (the basic elements of which are "preamble, historical prologue, stipulations, blessings and curses") [Millard is following K. Baltzer's study, *The Covenant Formulary*, trans. D. E. Green (Oxford: Blackwell, 1971)] in 1 Corinthians, finds a number of traces, especially in the eucharistic narrative. On the subject of the Supper as a remembrance (in dissent from Jeremias' view), he says: "Each time the Corinthian Christians shared the Lord's Supper they purported to show their allegiance to the covenant it symbolized, and therefore could not but expect its provisions to be active upon them for good or for ill. This follows the ancient pattern in which the regular reiteration of the covenant terms by vassals was a condition. . . . Two purposes were accomplished by this prompting of memory: thanksgiving which involved renewal of loyalty to the gracious Suzerain, and recollection of the commitments undertaken in response (well illustrated in Jos. 24:16-18). . . . Remembrance of the establishment of the covenant was, therefore, an integral feature of this pattern. . . . This similarity with the ancient covenant form is important for the interpretation of 11:24-25. . . . Paul's words mean that the Supper of the Lord was initiated to remind the disciples of the Lord of the work he had done." "Covenant and Communion in First Corinthians," in *Apostolic History and the Gospel*, ed. W. Gasque and R. P. Martin (Exeter: Paternoster, 1970), 241-248.

(2) Sacraments are part of the divine program of assurance. They are given to buttress and grow faith in the covenantal promises of God. It is this area that relates to the idea of sacraments as seals. (3) God is not present "in" any sacrament, but the sacramental analogy in every sacrament points to the glorious, gracious, covenantal, communional, promise of the presence of God, and by the Spirit we know something of this presence. That is, through the sacrament, and especially through the ongoing and repeated Lord's Supper, we are pointed to and experience a foretaste of the glorious communion of the ultimate covenant promise "I will be your God and you will be my people," and the ultimate covenant hope "God with us," and the ultimate covenant fellowship "to recline at his table." (4) There is an objective and subjective aspect to the sacraments, as well as an inward and outward. Any refusal to come to grips with the distinction between the sign (outward) and the thing signified (inward), utterly overthrows the sacrament, as Calvin noted. Furthermore, the objective is for the subjective in the sacrament. So to talk about sacramental efficacy in the absence of the key subjective instrument (faith) and effects (strengthened faith, growth in grace, assurance) is to miss the whole point of Spirit's use of and goal for the sacrament. (5) Following on this, sacramental sign's do not bestow the sacramental reality. The sacraments are efficacious in the sense that the accomplish God's purpose, but they not invariably efficacious. There are always Ishmael's and Simon's. Those who want an invariable objective efficacy will have to go to Rome or Constantinople, and without the slightest support from biblical covenant thought. (6) Not one of the Lord's Supper narratives focuses our attention on the bodily presence of Christ in the Supper. The language of body and blood clearly points us to contemplation of the covenantal sacrifice of Christ.[76] (7) Positively,

---

[76] Donald Macleod puts it forcefully "The question of the Lord's presence in the Sacrament is not raised by the New Testament material itself." *Priorities for the Church* (Fearn, Ross-shire: Christian Focus, 2003), 122.

the Supper narratives press us (a) to give thanks to God for the salvation we have by Christ; (b) to commemorate Christ's death, as the new covenant exodus, in a covenant meal; (c) to proclaim or set forth the incalculable significance and glorious meaning of his saving death; and (d) to commune with him and with his people, which is his body.

Pastoral Theological Observations

In light of this summary of the scriptural teaching, a few pastoral theological comments relating to our approach to Christ's presence in the Supper are in order. (1) Any view of the sacraments as instruments of grace which obscures the truth that we come to God through Christ alone is deficient. (2) The sacraments are appendices to the gospel. When people speak of the sacraments as "central" to our worship, they are failing to grasp this Calvinian principle. (3) One can only understand the nature, force, office and fruit of the sacraments by starting with Christ. (4) Spiritual communion in the sacrament is enjoyed only by those who are united to Christ. (5) Spiritual communion with Christ makes every believer a partaker of all the blessings which reside in him. Both preaching and the sacraments testify to this. (6) The sacraments are (a) marks and badges of Christian profession and our community or brotherhood, and (b) means of grace to incite us to thanksgiving and exercises of faith and godly living and to be contracts binding us to this. But especially, through them, God represents, seals, confirms and ratifies his grace to us. (7) God grants within us by his Spirit that which the sacraments figure to our eyes and other senses. (8) The distinction between the signs and the things signified must be maintained, though not disjoined. (9) The essence of the sacrament is not the bare signs but rather reality exhibited in and the promise attached to them. (10) The wonder of the sacraments is that of the reality to which they point, not the signs themselves. The sacraments, separated from Christ, are nothing. Their message is: "hold fast to none other than Christ alone and to seek the grace of salvation nowhere else." (11) There is no inherent virtue in the sacraments. God uses them as helps and instruments of ministry, but their efficacy is not intrinsic and derives only from the Holy Spirit. (12) The sacraments are efficacious, but efficacious in such a way that their whole efficacy is attributed to God alone rather than seen as inherent, and that their efficacy is understood to be Spiritually administered, faith received, sanctificationally focused. (13) The grace of the sacrament resides in the thing signified rather than the sign, and only by Christ and his Spirit can the realities signed in the sacrament be effected. Christ alone fulfils what the sacraments figure, and he employs the sacraments in such a way that the whole effect of them rests upon the work of his Spirit. (14) The sacraments are seals in the sense that they nourish, confirm and promote faith. Yet they are seals proximately, while the Spirit is the seal ultimately. (15) Only the elect, by the secret virtue of his Spirit, receive what the sacraments offer. (16) Nothing is received in the sacraments except by faith, and thus not all who receive the sign receive the thing itself. (17) This does not undermine the proper objectivity of the sacrament in the least. It accomplishes what the Lord please and we each receive according to the measure of faith. (18) Communion with Christ is not confined to the sacraments. (19) Thus the benefit which we receive from the sacraments is not to be restricted to the time at which they are administered to us. (20) Every variation of the idea of a local presence of Christ in the Supper should be emphatically rejected. (21) "This is my body" and "this is my blood" are to be taken figuratively, so that the bread and wine are said to be that which they signify. The this the natural, biblical meaning of these phrases. (22) The way in which we commune with Christ in the Supper is by drawing life from his body and blood once offered as a sacrifice of atonement, by virtue of the Spirit, through faith. (23) Transubstantiation rather than being a pious mystery, is absurd. (24) Because our Lord Christ is *Logos ensarkos*, and thus his human body is physically and spatially at the right hand, he is bodily and corporeally separated from us as the third heaven is from earth. (25) To "adore" the elements of the Supper under any pretense is to confuse the sign and the thing signified, to miss the point of the sacramental analogy and in fact to commit idolatry.[77]

Conclusion

It should be patently obvious by now that the central Reformed consensus on the presence of Christ in the Supper is not the "real presence" view, that Calvin did not hold to a real presence view (whatever our final assessment of him may be[78]), and, more importantly, that Scripture does not support a real presence view.

---

[77] Observant readers will have already noted that this advice is, in the main, simply a paraphrastic rendering of the *Consensus Tigurinus*.

[78] Keith Matthison and Sinclair Ferguson have recently rendered positive verdicts on Calvin's teaching, Donald Macleod (Cunningham *redivivus!*) gives a negative judgment: "Calvin never really shook off the legacy of the mediaeval doctrine." *Priorities for the Church*, 122. Indeed, any assessment of Calvin's view has to ask the question: Do the Supper narratives of the New Testament warrant Calvin's focus on our partaking of Christ's humanity? Is that really the point, or even part of the point of those narratives? Exegesis can't yield the question of Christ's presence once you have said, as Calvin did, that "the *is* of 'this is my body . . . my blood' means 'represents,' not 'constitutes'" (see Packer, *Concise Theology*, 218-219). So, the question has to be raised from elsewhere, from some broader biblical theological reality. We have already suggested where one might go for this, but one must still ask: was Calvin unduly influenced by the larger traditional medieval theological categories of discussion on this issue, or influenced by the hope of unity with the Lutherans?

Accordingly, appeals to the church to go "back to Calvin" on the real presence,[79] fail on every count. If we go back to Calvin, that's not what he taught. It is certainly not the teaching of the great Reformed confessions. And the New Testament Supper narratives don't get us anywhere near it.

It is better to stick with the confessional expressions of the meaning and significance of this great covenant meal. Surely, the modern Reformed church has far enough to go to understand and truly embrace and teach them. It would be a shame to further divide the Reformed community over Calvin's precise view of the presence of Christ in the Supper or some neo-real presence view read back onto him.

No, what the Reformed community has always agreed upon, whatever differences we may have harbored on the exact nature of Christ's presence in the Supper, is that the worthy recipient truly communes with Christ, by faith, by the Spirit. The Westminister Assembly summarized it as carefully, clearly and biblically as has ever been done:

> The outward elements in this sacrament, duly set apart to the uses ordained by Christ, have such relation to him crucified, as that, truly, yet sacramentally only, they are sometimes called by the name of the things they represent, to wit, the body and blood of Christ; albeit, in substance and nature, they still remain truly and only bread and wine, as they were before.

> That doctrine which maintains a change of the substance of bread and wine, into the substance of Christ's body and blood (commonly called transubstantiation) by consecration of a priest, or by any other way, is repugnant, not to Scripture alone, but even to common sense, and reason; overthroweth the nature of the sacrament, and hath been, and is, the cause of manifold superstitions; yea, of gross idolatries.

---

[79] We hear this often, for instance, David E. Holwerda of Calvin Seminary characterizes Keith Matthison's *Given for You* as a cogent argument for "returning to Calvin's richly nuanced view of the real presence of Christ in the sacrament."

Worthy receivers, outwardly partaking of the visible elements, in this sacrament, do then also, inwardly by faith, really and indeed, yet not carnally and corporally but spiritually, receive, and feed upon, Christ crucified, and all benefits of his death: the body and blood of Christ being then, not corporally or carnally, in, with, or under the bread and wine; yet, as really, but spiritually, present to the faith of believers in that ordinance, as the elements themselves are to their outward senses.[80]

---

[80] *Westminster Confession of Faith* 29.5-7. I would argue that Calvin's view is not contrary to this view, but rather consonant with it. It is certainly more detailed (as you would expect). If Calvin differs from Westminster it is in the fact that his view is more speculative, more specific and more sibylline. I grant that many of Calvin's characteristic emphases are muted or ignored in the *Consensus Tigurinus* but I would also argue that: (1) the *Consensus Tigurinus* is more reflective of late sixteenth century Reformed consensus than the highly nuanced view of Calvin; (2) the *Consensus Tigurinus* is perfectly consonant with the Westminster Confession; (3) the fact that Calvin was willing to co-draft and sign the *Consensus Tigurinus* is an example of his spiritual maturity, his heart for the unity of the church and his polemical magnanimity—three qualities often utterly lacking in some who have taken up his name in support of their own neologies.

The Westminster Confession and Lapsarianism:Calvin and the Divines

J. V. Fesko

Introduction

From the earliest days of the Reformation with Desiderius Erasmus' (c. 1469-1536) criticism of Martin Luther's (1483-1546) doctrine of election in his *Bondage of the Will* to the Arminian Remonstrance at the Synod of Dort (1618-19), the Reformed doctrine of predestination has never been short of critics.[1] The same holds true today of the Reformed tradition as it comes through the Westminster Confession (1647) and its contemporary critics. There have been a handful of critics who assert that after John Calvin (1509-64), Reformed theologians of both Early (1565-1630/40) and High Orthodoxy (1630/40-1700) distorted his doctrine of predestination.[2] The divines moved predestination

---

[1] This is revised and updated material that appears in J. V. Fesko, *Diversity within the Reformed Tradition: Supra- and Infralapsarianism in Calvin, Dort, and Westminster* (Greenville: Reformed Academic Press, 2003), 257-96. Archaic spelling in quotations has been updated throughout.

[2] The four major theological periods in the sixteenth, seventeenth, and eighteenth centuries are as follows: the Reformation, 1517-64; Early Orthodoxy, 1565-1630/40; High Orthodoxy, 1630/40-1700; and Late Orthodoxy, 1700-1790 (Richard A. Muller, *Post-Reformation Reformed*

away from soteriology, where Calvin had placed it, and moved it into the doctrine of God, which produced supralapsarianism. Among the modern critics Brian Armstrong and Basil Hall contend that supralapsarianism led to the doctrines of a limited atonement and the immediate imputation of original sin, teachings that were foreign to Calvin.[3] J. B. Torrance makes similar critical comments more specifically about the Westminster Confession and Theodore Beza (1519-1605), Calvin's successor at Geneva:

> Thus the doctrine of the decrees of God in the tradition of Theodore Beza and William Perkins becomes the major premise of the whole scheme of creation and redemption . . . When the doctrine of the decrees becomes the major premise, what happens?...[it] gives rise to the feeling of 'Legalism' in the documents . . . It leads logically to the Bezan and Post-Reformation doctrine of a 'limited atonement' and a particular redemption.[4]

Hence Armstrong, Hall, and Torrance argue that supralapsarianism, particularly that of Theodore Beza, created negative side effects: definite atonement, imputed guilt, and legalism. This means, therefore, we should ask, Did supralapsarianism bring these negative side effects as these critics claim? These general and specific charges can be tested against

---

Dogmatics, vol. 1, *Prolegomena to Theology* [Grand Rapids: Baker, 1987], 40-52). Muller relies upon the brief but well-balanced survey of Reformed Orthodoxy by Otto Weber, *Foundations of Dogmatics*, vol. 1, trans. Darrell L. Guder (Grand Rapids: Eerdmans, 1981), 112-27.

[3] Brian G. Armstrong, *Calvinism and the Amyraut Heresy: Protestant Scholasticism and Humanism in Seventeenth Century France* (Madison: University of Wisconsin Press, 1969), 41-42; Basil Hall, "Calvin Against the Calvinists," in *John Calvin*, Courtenay Studies in Reformation Theology, vol. 1, ed. G. E. Duffield (Appleford: Sutton Courtenay Press, 1966), 27.

[4] J. B. Torrance, "Strengths and Weaknesses of the Westminster Theology," in *The Westminster Confession in the Church Today*, ed. Alasdair I. C. Heron (Edinburgh: Saint Andrew Press, 1982), 46-47; cf. idem, "The Concept of Federal Theology – Was Calvin a Federal Theologian?" in *Calvinus Sacrae Scripturae Professor: Calvin as Confessor of Holy Scripture*, ed. Wilhelm H. Neuser (Grand Rapids: Eerdmans, 1994), 18-20.

the Westminster Confession through the investigation of lapsarianism in the Confession and then seeing whether it is guilty of propounding the so-called negative supralapsarian side effects as the critics claim. Let us first define the various lapsarian terms with which we will interact.

Definitions of Terms

There are several lapsarian variants that we will encounter in the course of our investigation: supralapsarianism, infralapsarianism, and Amyraldianism. One must first realize that all of the following definitions are logical prioritizations of the decrees *sub specie aeternitatis*, not a chronological order of events. This is an essential factor to note because all of the lapsarian variants temporally, or *sub specie temporis*, unfold in the same order. There are two main characteristics that the investigator must look for to classify properly the lapsarian nature of a doctrine of predestination: (1) theologians often give an explicit *ordo decretorum*, which is the formal cause of a lapsarian view; and (2) a theologian will identify the object of predestination as either *homo creabilis et labilis*, man as creatable and liable to fall, or *homo creatus et lapsus*, man as created and fallen, which is the material cause of a lapsarian view. The main difference between the views is not just about the order of the decrees but rather whether a theologian will take into consideration the fall and original sin in his doctrine of predestination. In other words, is man "elected or rejected *homo creabilis et labilis*, or is he *homo creatus et lapsus*?"[5]

---

[5] Karl Barth, *Church Dogmatics*, vol. 2, *The Doctrine of God*, pt. 2, ed. G. W. Bromiley and T. F. Torrance, trans. G. W. Bromiley, et al. (Edinburgh: T & T Clark, 1957), 127.

Supralapsarianism

Supralapsarianism, from *supra lapsum*, literally, "above the fall," argues that *electio* and *reprobatio* are "positive, coordinate decrees of God by which God chooses those who will be saved and those who will be damned, in other words, a fully double predestination, or *praedestinatio gemina*."[6] The supralapsarian *ordo decretorum*, therefore, is as follows:

1. The decree to save some and condemn others.
2. The decree to create both the elect and reprobate.
3. The decree to permit the fall of both classes.
4. The decree to provide salvation only for the elect.[7]

While the *ordo decretorum* is the formal cause of supralapsarianism, the material cause is *homo creabilis et labilis* as the object of the decree of predestination. In other words, one should not simply look for an *ordo decretorum*; rather, one must pay particular attention to the idea that supralapsarians typically speak of predestined man as one who has not fallen nor has been created. This means that the supralapsarian will discuss election and reprobation apart from any consideration of the fall or original sin. Supralapsarianism is also typically associated with *praedestinatio gemina* because in this formulation predestination contains two separate decrees: election and reprobation.

Infralapsarianism

Infralapsarianism, on the other hand, from *infra lapsum*, literally, "below" or "subsequent to the fall," argues that predestination is the "positive decree of God by which he chose in Christ those who will be his eternally, but they view *reprobatio*

---

[6] Richard A. Muller, *Dictionary of Latin and Greek Theological Terms: Drawn Principally from Protestant Scholastic Theology* (Grand Rapids: Baker, 1985), 235.

[7] Millard Erickson, *Christian Theology* (Grand Rapids: Baker, 1985), 917.

as a negative act or passing over of the rest of mankind, leaving them in their sins to their ultimate *damnatio*."[8] The infralapsarian *ordo decretorum* is as follows:

1. The decree to create human beings.
2. The decree to permit the fall.
3. The decree to save some and condemn others.
4. The decree to provide salvation only for the elect.[9]

The material cause of infralapsarianism is *homo creatus et lapsus* as the object of predestination. In other words, infralapsarians typically speak of predestined man as already created and fallen. This means that the infralapsarian typically speaks of mankind as sinful and for this reason is in need of salvation. Infralapsarianism is often called *praedestinatio ad vitam*, or single-predestination, because there is only one decree of predestination: the decree of election. Those who are non-elect are simply passed by in the decree of election, or are not elect by default, and are left in their sin unto their ultimate damnation. There are, however, two points that one must note regarding single-predestination.

First, the term *single* refers to the number of decrees. Stated simply, double-predestination has two decrees of predestination: election and reprobation. Single-predestination has only one decree of predestination: election. The non-elect are not the subject of God's specific predestinating will but instead the subject of God's general will, or providence. It must be noted that single-predestination is not a denial of the concept of reprobation.[10] One

---

[8] Muller, *Dictionary*, 234-35.

[9] Erickson, *Christian Theology*, 918.

[10] This point must be made in light of attempts by Neo-Orthodox theologians to refute the idea of double-predestination. For example, Brunner writes that the "Bible teaches that all salvation is based on eternal Election of God in Jesus Christ, and that this eternal Election springs wholly and entirely from God's sovereign freedom. But whenever this happens, there is no mention of a decree of rejection" (Emil Brunner, *The Christian Doctrine of God*, Dogmatics, vol. 1, trans. Olive Wyon [Philadelphia: The Westminster

can illustrate this point by imagining a group of people who want to choose teammates for a game. Team captains are assigned and the captains begin the selection process. Single-predestinarians would say, "I pick you, I pick you, and I pick you." Some people are chosen and others are simply passed by. Double-predestinarians, on the other hand, would say, "I pick you, I reject you, I pick you, and I reject you." Both groups of people are directly selected and rejected. First, one must realize that the end result is the same with single- or double-predestination; namely, both affirm eternal election and rejection. Nonetheless, this is a distinction that theologians employ when discussing predestination. Second, there are theologians who are infralapsarians but will speak of *praedestinatio gemina*; some theologians will speak of an infralapsarian *ordo decretorum* but specify that there are two decrees of predestination: election and reprobation. Hence, while supralapsarian formulations will always be *praedestinatio gemina*, infralapsarianism comes in two variants: double- and single-predestination. One must be aware of these nuances to be able to distinguish accurately between the various positions and not mistake infra- for supralapsarianism.

Amyraldianism

Lastly, it is necessary to define Amyraldianism because the investigation will come across proponents of this position. Amyraldianism, or Hypothetical Universalism, was most notably put forth by Moïse Amyraut (1620-64) as an alternative view to supra- and infralapsarianism. He specifically wanted to

---

Press, 1949], 326). Infra- and supralapsarianism both have two aspects, election and rejection, regardless of the number of decrees. See R. C. Sproul, "Double Predestination," in *Soli Deo Gloria: Essays in Reformed Theology: Festschrift for John H. Gerstner*, ed. R. C. Sproul (Philadelphia: Presbyterian & Reformed, 1976), 63-72.

accommodate a universal atonement.[11] The Amyraldian *ordo decretorum* is, therefore, as follows:

1. The decree to create human beings.
2. The decree to permit the fall.
3. The decree to provide salvation sufficient for all.
4. The decree to choose some to receive salvation.[12]

The idea behind this conception of the decrees is that God first, *sub specie aeternitatis*, saw that man would fall and hence sent His Son to atone for the sins of all mankind through His work as the Messiah. God, however, also knew that man would reject this offer of forgiveness and therefore was required to appoint some to receive salvation. So, Amyraldianism has a universal atonement but is still monergistic in its formulation of predestination.

Caveat Regarding Equal Ultimacy

Regarding all of these variants of predestination, one major caveat must be noted. All of them generally argue that the fall of man is a permissive decree. This means that none of the aforementioned lapsarian positions are expressions of what is called hyper-Calvinism, hyper- supralapsarianism, or the doctrine of equal ultimacy. Equal ultimacy is the idea that God positively works evil in the hearts of the non-elect in the same way He positively works righteousness in the elect (i.e., God is the author of sin).[13] None of the aforementioned positions teach equal ultimacy. Stated positively,

---

[11] See Armstrong, *Calvinism and the Amyraut Heresy, passim.*

[12] Erickson, *Christian Theology*, 918. It is important to note that some contemporary works such as that of Erickson call Amyraldianism, *sublapsarianism*. This term, however, is not desirable for two reasons: (1) *sub-* and *infra-* are synonymous prefixes, literally "subsequent" or "below"; and (2) in older theological works prior to the twentieth century *infralapsarianism* and *sublapsarianism* are used interchangeably. Hence, to avoid confusion the term *Amyraldianism* will be used in lieu of *sublapsarianism.*

[13] Sproul, "Double Predestination," 72.

all of the proponents of the above mentioned positions deny that God is the author of sin. We may now proceed to our investigation of the lapsarian debates at Westminster.

The Lapsarian Debates

As with any topic, especially the doctrine of predestination, theologians are bound to disagree on how it should be stated. The Westminster divines were certainly no exception to this rule. Robert Baillie (1602-1662), one of the Scottish advisors, noted in a letter: "We had long and tough debates about the decrees of election."[14] We can get some idea of the nature of the debates on the decrees of election from the minutes of the assembly.[15] In tracking the debates over the various issues, however, one must recognize that the assembly used James Ussher's (1580-1655) *Irish Articles* (1615) as a starting point for the composition of the Confession. This provides the investigator with a frame of reference to know the approximate starting point for the debates over predestination.

From a survey of the minutes it appears that the topic of predestination occupied the assembly for close to one month.[16] The committee assigned to the composition of the third chapter of the Confession presented their work before the assembly in

---

[14] Robert Baillie, *The Letters and Journals of Robert Baillie: Principal of the University of Glasgow 1637-1652*, 3 vols., ed. David Laing (Edinburgh: Robert Ogle, 1841), vol. 2, 325. Lifespans for the Westminster divines are taken from William S. Barker, *Puritan Profiles: 54 Influential Puritans at the time when the Westminster Confession of Faith was written* (Fearn: Christian Focus Publications, 1996).

[15] Alexander F. Mitchell and John Struthers, eds., *Minutes of the Sessions of the Westminster Assembly of Divines* (Edinburgh: William Blackwood and Sons, 1874).

[16] B. B. Warfield, "The Making of the Westminster Confession, and Especially of its Chapter on the Decree of God," *Presbyterian and Reformed Review* 6 (1901), 260-61; Sinclair B. Ferguson, "The Teaching of the Confession," in *The Westminster Confession in the Church Today*, ed., Alasdair I. C. Heron (Edinburgh: Saint Andrew Press, 1982), 31.

session 494 on August 29, 1645. The divines quickly began dissecting this article; there was a debate over the title of the article. Ussher's title for the chapter on predestination is called "Of God's Eternal Decree and Predestination." We do not know whether this was the title that the drafting committee presented to the assembly. However, given that the final version of the title is "Of God's Eternal Decree," there were obviously some delegates who did not want the term *predestination* included the chapter title.[17] In session 520 on October 20, 1645, there were debates concerning the decree and its relation to the fall of Adam. On this day it appears that there was disagreement between the infra- and supralapsarians over the number and nature of the decrees. For example, Lazarus Seaman (c. 1607-1675) asserted: "If those words 'in the same decree' be left out, will involve us in a great debate." To this assertion Samuel Rutherford (1600-1661), a Scottish advisor and supralapsarian, responded: "All agree in this, that God decrees the end and means, but whether in one or more decrees is not . . . Say God also hath decreed. . . . It is very probable but one decree, but whether fit to express in a Confession of Faith. . . ."[18] After several others spoke, Edward Reynolds (1599-1670) added his opinion concerning the decrees: "Let not us put in disputes and scholastical things into a Confession of Faith." One of the last recorded comments during this debate was a question regarding the *obiectum praedestinationis*; Edmund Calamy (1600-1666) inquired: "I question that 'to bring this to pass'; we assert

---

[17] Mitchell, *Minutes*, 126. For the *Irish Articles* and the Westminster Confession, see Philip Schaff, *The History of the Creeds of Christendom*, 3 vols., (London: Hodder & Stoughton, 1877), vol. 3, 528, 608. Westminster Confession of Faith hereafter abbreviated as WCF.

[18] Mitchell, *Minutes*, 150; on Rutherford's supralapsarianism see John MacLeod, *Scottish Theology: In Relation to Church History Since the Reformation*, Lectures Delivered in Westminster Theological Seminary (Edinburgh: Publications Committee of the Free Church of Scotland, 1943), 70.

massa pura in this . . . I desire that nothing may be put in one way or other; it makes the fall of man to be *medium executionis decreti*."[19] This was an objection to supralapsarianism; Calamy believed it made the fall of man merely a means unto an end. We see, then, that the debates in this session were over the number of decrees, the object of predestination, and whether such subjects were even suitable to be mentioned in the Confession at all.

Debates over predestination continued in session 521 on October 21, 1645 regarding the fall of man and the decree. It was decided that "those words 'to bring this to pass' shall not stand."[20] There was, however, further debate in this session over this same issue because Reynolds offered the following suggestion for the paragraph on predestination: "As God hath appointed the elect unto glory, so hath He by the same eternal and most free purpose of His will foreordained all the means thereunto, which He in His counsel is pleased to appoint for the executing of that decree; wherefore they who are endowed with so excellent a benefit, *being fallen in Adam*, are called in according to God's purpose."[21] As one can see, there was reluctance to place the fall of Adam in a direct relationship to the divine decree. Hence Reynolds suggested that assembly specify that man was "fallen in Adam." Along similar lines, in session 522 on October 22, 1645, Calamy asserted that *homo creatus et lapsus* was the object of predestination: "I am for special election; and for reprobation, I am for *massa corrupta*."[22] The discussions on the decrees continued for several more days; there was a debate between the Amyraldians and other members of the assembly on how the decrees related to the extent of the atonement. Additionally, there was also some debate over

---

[19] Mitchell, *Minutes*, 151.

[20] Mitchell, *Minutes*, 151.

[21] Mitchell, *Minutes*, 151-52; emphasis.

[22] Mitchell, *Minutes*, 153.

the desire of one of the divines to see the reference to reprobation deleted.[23] Beyond these sketchy details of the debates we do not have any more information that sheds light on the specifics of the disagreements regarding infra- and supralapsarianism. Nevertheless, we can compare specific points of the Confession with the *Irish Articles* and see in what way the divines resolved these issues.

The Lapsarian Outcome

The Confession begins with a chapter on the Holy Scriptures and then proceeds to a second chapter on God and the Holy Trinity. It is in the third chapter that the Confession treats the subject of "God's Eternal Decree." Much like the *Irish Articles*, the Confession asserts: "God from all eternity did, by the most wise and holy counsel of his own will, freely and unchangeably ordain whatsoever comes to pass; yet so as thereby neither is God the author of sin, nor is violence offered to the will of the creatures, nor is the liberty or contingency of second causes taken away, but rather established" (3.1).[24] This paragraph is almost identical to its corresponding paragraph in the *Irish Articles*. There was, however, one modification to Ussher's original statement; the Westminster divines add the phrase "neither is God the author of sin." They were aware that with the affirmation of the sovereignty of God critics would bring the accusation that they made God the author of sin. The divines, therefore, denied this charge from the very outset of their exposition of the decree. The divines also

---

[23] Mitchell, *Minutes*, 152-61; Warfield, "Westminster Confession," 267.

[24] Eph. 1.1; Rom. 11.33; Heb. 6.17; Rom. 9.15, 18; James 1.13, 17; 1 John 1.5; Acts 2.23; Matt. 17.12; Acts 4.27-28; John 19.11; Prov. 16.33. Cf. Larger Catechism, Q. 12, and the Shorter Catechism, Q. 7 (The Larger and Shorter Catechism, in *The Confession of Faith, Together with The Larger and Shorter Catechism with Scripture Proofs* [Atlanta: The Committee for Christian Education & Publications, 1990]); hereafter abbreviated as LC and SC.

wanted to avoid the charges of fatalism; they retained Ussher's use of the scholastic distinction of primary and secondary causality. Moreover, throughout various chapters of the Confession, the divines emphasized and affirmed the free will of man. For example, they write: "God hath endued the will of man with that natural liberty, that is neither forced nor by any absolute necessity of nature determined to good or evil" (9.1).[25] The divines consistently affirmed the sovereignty of God and human responsibility; they held these two doctrines in tension.[26]

Paragraph 3.2 states: "Although God knows whatsoever may or can come to pass upon all supposed conditions, yet hath he not decreed any thing because he foresaw it as future, or as that which would come to pass upon such conditions" (3.2).[27] To this second paragraph there is no corresponding passage in the *Irish Articles*.[28] This, however, is not a point of contention. On the contrary, one must keep in mind that there were greater doctrinal and polemical demands upon the Westminster divines; they added this paragraph

---

[25] Matt. 17.12; James 1.14; Deut. 30.19. Cf. LC, Q. 21; SC, Q. 13.

[26] Paul Helm, "Of God's Eternal Decree," paper presented at the 1997 Edinburgh Dogmatics Conference, 17. One study examines how this tension was manifested in the sermons of the divines before Parliament. The author argues that the divines were not just concerned with reaching the next world but they also had a concern for this world (James C. Spalding, "Sermons Before Parliament (1640-1649) as a Public Puritan Diary," *Church History* 36 [1967], 24-35). Another example of how the divines maintain this tension is demonstrated in their treatment of the fall: "This their sin, God was pleased, according to His wise and holy counsel, *to permit*, having purposed to order it to His own glory" (WCF 6.1; emphasis). They similarly write in the LC that our "first parents being left to the freedom of their own will through the temptation of Satan, transgressed the commandment of God" (LC, Q. 21; cf. SC, Q. 13). The chapters in the Confession on providence, for example, also maintain this careful tension (see WCF 5.1-7; LC, QQ. 18-20; SC, QQ. 11-12).

[27] They cite the following: Acts 15.18; 1 Sam. 23.11-12; Matt. 11.21, 23; Rom. 9.11, 13, 14, 18.

[28] Warfield, "Westminster Assembly," 265.

as a specific refutation of Arminianism and Molinism. The Synod of Dort refuted Arminianism in 1619, yet it was still alive and spreading in the 1640s. The divines denied one of the main Arminian tenets of its soteriology with the assertion that God has "not decreed any thing because he foresaw it as future."[29] The second half of this passage refutes the views of Luis de Molina (1535-1600).[30] Certain Continental theologians, such as the Jesuits, asserted that God based His eternal decrees upon *scientia media*, or middle knowledge. *Scientia media* refers to God's knowledge of how individuals will react to every imaginable situation. With this reactionary catalog of information, God then arranges history in such a way that each person freely responds to the situations brought before Him. Hence God can arrange a person's salvation, not based upon an absolute decree or based upon foreknowledge of future events, but instead upon this catalog of free responses. Nevertheless, the divines also rejected this theory with the phrase "Yet hath he not decreed any thing because . . . [it] would come to pass upon such conditions."[31]

---

[29] See James Arminius, *The Works of James Arminius*, vol. 3, trans. William Nichols (1875; Grand Rapids: Baker, 1996).

[30] Luis de Molina, *On Divine Foreknowledge*, Part IV of the *Concordia*, trans. Alfred J. Freddoso (Ithaca: Cornell University Press, 1988).

[31] Helm, "Of God's Eternal Decree," 13; Mitchell, *Minutes*, lii-liiii. Reformed theologians rejected middle knowledge and its use because "in general, Reformed writers held that God, in his ordination of all things, had ordained some things to occur necessarily and others contingently. Since the existence of contingents thus depended directly on the divine will, the divine foreknowledge of future contingents could be explained as belonging to the *scientia libera seu visionis*, without recourse to any concept of a *scientia media*" (Richard A. Muller, *God, Creation, and Providence in the Thought of Jacob Arminius: Sources and Directions of Scholastic Protestantism in the Era of Early Orthodoxy* [Grand Rapids: Baker, 1991], 154-55). A common response to the idea of middle knowledge is that of Gisbert Voetius (1589-1676) who writes: "(1) – This view posits the absurdity of absurdities, that in created things there is given a fixed futurition prior to every divine decree and that it suffices to produce futurition that a decree be

Paragraph 3.3 deals with one of the main issues for the decree: predestination. The *Irish Articles* and the Confession state:

Irish Articles §11	Westminster 3.3
By the same eternal counsel God hath predestinated some unto life, and reprobated some unto death: of both which there is a certain number, known only to God, which can neither be increased nor diminished.	By the decree of God, for the manifestation of his glory, some men and angels are predestinated unto everlasting life, and others are foreordained to everlasting death.

Although both passages appear very similar, there are several important differences between the two. First, recalling the debates over the decrees, one can see that the assembly decided that the phrase "By the same eternal counsel," found in the *Irish Articles*, should not remain in the Confession; they simply maintained that election and rejection were by the "decree of God." However, one should not too quickly assume that the divines decided that there was only one decree given their affirmation of the "decree of God." In the Larger Catechism, for example, the answer to question thirteen states: "God, by an eternal and immutable *decree* ... hath elected some angels to glory," while the very next question says, "How doth God execute his *decrees*? A. God executeth his *decrees*. . . ." Hence this oscillation between *decree* and *decrees*

---

posited on the condition laid down or a decree accompanying the object of this knowledge, not actual but possible *ad modum.* – (2) In a like class it lays down something else not less seriously absurd, that there still remains after the divine determination some futurition of what is in every way a non-futurition of things. – (3) From this knowledge we on our part will be able to assign the reason and cause of divine predestination. – (4) Thus, predestination as regards this knowledge will have to be called postdestination rather than predestination, as regards the temporary object" (Voetius, *Selectarum Disputationum theologicarum*, I, 320, as cited in Heinrich Heppe, *Reformed Dogmatics: Set Out and Illustrated from the Sources*, ed. Ernst Bizer, trans. G. T. Thomson [London: George Allen & Unwin Ltd., 1950], 80). Cf. Francis Turretin, *Institutes of Elenctic Theology*, 3 vols., trans. George Musgrave Giger, ed. James T. Dennison (Phillipsburg: Presbyterian & Reformed, 1992-97), 3.13.1-23, vol. 1, 212-20.

illustrates the assembly's desire not to render a decision upon this point.[32] The second point of difference lies in the language used for predestination.

The *Irish Articles* maintain that "God hath *predestinated* some unto life, and *reprobated* some unto death." The assembly, on the other hand, did not state predestination in such terms; the Confession states that God "*predestinated* unto everlasting life, and others *foreordained* to everlasting death." This difference represents a significant modification of Ussher's original statement. How? Had the divines been satisfied with Ussher's language they would have simply repeated his use of *predestination* and *reprobation*. However, the terms *predestination* and *reprobation* as they are found in the *Irish Articles* reflect *praedestinatio gemina*.[33] On the other hand, the use of the term *foreordain* in lieu of *reprobate* by the Westminster divines demonstrates a movement from *gemina* to single-predestination. Some may disagree and argue that *foreordain* is a synonym for *predestine*. Nevertheless, when one examines how the divines employ the term *foreordain* in a subsequent paragraph, it does not justify this claim. In paragraph 3.6, for example, the divines assert that the elect are appointed unto glory and that God has "*foreordained* all the means thereunto" (emphasis). If *foreordain* is synonymous with *predestine*, then this means that paragraph 3.6 could be read as "[predestined] all the means thereunto." This is not in harmony with the way in which the divines use the term *predestine*; this term is used in their soteriology, not in their explanations of the doctrine of providence. This is further demonstrated in the Larger and Shorter Catechisms.

---

[32] LC, QQ. 13 & 14; emphasis. See also David A. S. Fergusson, "Predestination: A Scottish Perspective," *Scottish Journal of Theology* 46 (1993), 465.

[33] B. B. Warfield, "Predestination in the Reformed Confessions," in *Studies in Theology*, ed. Ethelbert Warfield, et al. (New York: Oxford University Press, 1932), 143.

The Larger Catechism, question twelve, asserts: "What are the decrees of God?" The catechism replies: "God's decrees are the wise, free, and holy acts of the counsel of his will whereby, from all eternity, he hath, for his own glory, unchangeably *foreordained whatsoever comes to pass in time*, especially concerning angels and men" (emphasis).[34] This question mirrors the eighteenth question of the catechism, which states: "What are God's works of providence?" The catechism replies: "God's works of providence are his most holy, wise, and powerful preserving and governing all his creatures; ordering them, and all their actions, to his own glory."[35] These parallels confirm that *foreordain* is not a synonym for *predestine* but that it is instead a term for God's *providence*.[36] This nomenclature reflects the idea that predestination is a subset of the overarching category of providence. Hence the *Irish Articles* speaks of *praedestinatio gemina*, or election and reprobation, whereas the Confession only speaks of predestination and foreordination. The non-elect are not the specific subject of a decree of reprobation; they are instead the subject of God's providence. In fact, the Confession does not use the term *reprobation* in any of its articles.[37] This structure mirrors the formulations of other

---

[34] Eph. 1.1; Rom. 9.14-15, 18; 11.33; Eph. 1.4, 11; Rom. 9.22-23; Ps. 33.11.

[35] Ps. 145.17; 104.24; Heb. 1.3; Ps. 103.19; Matt. 10.29-31.

[36] Sinclair Ferguson, "Introductory Essay," in Robert Shaw, *An Exposition of the Westminster Confession of Faith* (1845; Fearn: Christian Focus, 1998), 18-19; J. G. Vos, *The Westminster Larger Catechism: A Commentary*, ed. G. I. Williamson (Phillipsburg: Presbyterian & Reformed, 2002), 30-31,

[37] Robert Shaw, *An Exposition of the Confession of Faith of the Westminster Assembly of Divines* (1845; Lochcarron: Christian Focus, 1980), 57; Mitchell, *Westminster Assembly*, 376.

single- predestinarians such as Augustine (354-430), Thomas Aquinas (1224/5-74), or Heinrich Bullinger (1504-75).[38]

Paragraph 3.4 states: "These angels and men, thus predestinated and foreordained, are particularly and unchangeably designed; and their number is so certain and definite that it can not be either increased or diminished."[39] This section merely repeats the same sentiments found in the latter half of the eleventh paragraph in the *Irish Articles*. Continuing on, both confessions mirror each other on the explanation of the destiny of the elect. They both affirm that the elect are the recipients of the grace of God and their destiny is to be made into vessels of God's mercy.[40] There is, however, another difference that arises between paragraph 3.6 and Ussher's work:

Irish Articles §15	Westminster 3.6
Such as are predestinated unto life, be called according unto God's purpose (his Spirit working in due season), and through the grace they obey the calling, they be justified freely, they be made sons of God by adoption, they be made like the image of his only begotten Son Jesus Christ, they walk religiously in good works, and at length, by God's mercy, they attain to everlasting felicity.	As God hath appointed the elect unto glory, so hath he, by the eternal and most free purpose of his will, foreordained all the means thereunto. Wherefore *they who are elected being fallen in Adam*, are redeemed in Christ by his Spirit working in due season; are justified, adopted, sanctified, and kept by his power through faith unto salvation. Neither are any other redeemed by Christ, effectually called, justified, adopted, sanctified, and saved, but the elect only.

---

[38] Augustine, *Enchiridion*, in *Nicene and Post-Nicene Fathers*, vol. 3, ed. Philip Schaff, trans. J. F. Shaw (Grand Rapids: Eerdmans, 1956), chp. XCVIII, 268; cf. Charles *Systematic Theology*, 3 vols. (1880; Grand Rapids: Eerdmans, 1993), vol. 2, 316; Thomas Aquinas, *Summa Theologiae*, vol. 5 (Ia. 19-26), God's Will and Providence, trans. Thomas Gilby, Blackfriars edition (London: Eyre & Spottiswoode, 1963), Ia. 23, 3, 117; cf. Jacques Maritain, "St. Augustine and St. Thomas Aquinas," in *Saint Augustine*, trans. Fr. Leonard (Cleveland: World Publishing, 1957), 215; Heinrich Bullinger, et al., "Second Helvetic Confession" in *Reformed Confessions Harmonized*, eds. Joel R. Beeke & Sinclair B. Ferguson (Grand Rapids: Baker, 1999), § 10.1-2; cf. Cornelius Venema, *Heinrich Bullinger and the Doctrine of Predestination* (Grand Rapids: Baker, 2002), 53, 68-69, 98.

[39] 2 Tim. 2.19; John 13.18.

[40] See *Irish Articles*, §§13, 14, and WCF 3.5. Eph. 1:4, 9, 11; Rom. 8:30; 2 Tim. 1:9; 1 Thess. 5:9; Rom. 9:11, 13, 16; Eph. 1:6, 12.

The two statements are virtually synonymous, though there are slight variations in nomenclature, in their outline of the effects of election. There is, however, one important point to note: the Westminster divines specify the object of predestination as *homo creatus et lapsus* with the phrase "wherefore they who are elected being fallen in Adam." Like Ussher before them, they specified that fallen man is the object of predestination.[41] Calamy, therefore, had his request met and approved by the rest of the assembly that predestination refer to a *massa corrupta*.[42] It should be noted, though, that nowhere in the third chapter of the Confession is a specific *ordo decretorum* mentioned, neither supra- nor infralapsarianism is referenced. Nevertheless, the identification *sub specie aeternitatis* of the object of predestination in this passage as *homo creatus et lapsus* demonstrates the Confession favors the infralapsarian position. G. D. Henderson notes that supralapsarianism "did not carry at Westminster anymore than the same views when advanced by

---

[41] *Irish Articles*, § 13: "Predestination to life is the everlasting purpose of God whereby before the foundations of the world were laid, he hath constantly decreed in his sacred counsel to deliver from curse and damnation those who he hath chosen in Christ out of mankind." To see the lapsarian development in both the *Irish Articles* and the Confession, we must also take note of the *Lambeth Articles* (1595). Ussher appropriated the Lambeth Articles into his article on predestination (R. Buick Knox, *James Ussher Archbishop of Armagh* [Cardiff: University of Wales Press, 1967], 18). The Lambeth Articles state: "God from eternity hath predestinated certain men unto life; certain men he hath reprobated." In the second article Lambeth states: "The moving or efficient cause of predestination unto life is not the foresight of faith, or of perseverance, or of good works, or of any thing that is in the person predestinated, but only the good will and pleasure of God" (Schaff, *Creeds*, vol. 3, 523-24). We can see that Lambeth makes no mention whatsoever of the object of predestination or the fallen condition of man. There is genuine ambiguity on this matter and it has no bias towards either supra- or infralapsarianism.

[42] Mitchell, *Minutes*, 153.

Gomarus at Dort."[43] This is also the conclusion of A. A. Hodge (1823-86), Robert Shaw (c. 1845), Charles Hodge (1797-1878), and W. G. T. Shedd (1820-94).[44] Shedd, in fact, notes: "The Westminster Assembly, in common with the Calvinistic creeds previously made, adopted the infralapsarian order."[45] This, however, is not the last distinction between the two documents.

The *Irish Articles* do not elaborate upon the subject of reprobation. It merely says that "God hath predestinated some unto life, and reprobated some unto death."[46] The Westminster

---

[43] G. D. Henderson, *Religious Life in Seventeenth-Century Scotland* (Cambridge: Cambridge University Press, 1937), 95.

[44] Warfield is correct when he writes that in the Canons of Dort the "definition of election emphasizes its eternity, immutability, and absolute freedom. *Its object is said to be fallen men*, and its end redemption" ("Predestination in the Reformed Confessions," 145; emphasis). He goes on to specify that it is infralapsarian because it is among the confessions that "explicitly declare that the discrimination which God made among men was made *in massa corrupta*" (229). He also correctly argues that in *Lambeth* and the *Scotch Confession* of 1560 "the lines are so drawn that it is impossible to discover that there is an advantage given to either party to the debate over [infra- and supralapsarianism]" (229-30). He mistakenly writes, however, that the *Irish Articles* and Westminster share this same peculiarity with Lambeth and the Scots Confession; he argues they give no advantage to either party (230). The difference between the Lambeth Articles and the Westminster Confession is plainly evident; the Westminster divines identify the object of predestination as *homo creatus et lapsus* whereas Lambeth has definite lapsarian ambiguity (see Schaff, *Creeds*, 523-35; also above, n. 43). For example, Shaw writes that the "Father chose a definite number of mankind *sinners* to eternal life" (Confession, 56; emphasis). Likewise, another prominent Reformed theologian comments: "The decree of God determines that *out of the mass of fallen humanity* certain individuals shall attain to eternal salvation, and that the rest shall be left to be dealt with justly for their sins" (A. A. Hodge, *The Confession of Faith: A Handbook of Christian Doctrine Expounding The Westminster Confession* [London: Banner of Truth, 1958], 70; emphasis). Charles Hodge also argues that the confession is infralapsarian (Hodge, *Systematic Theology*, vol. 2, 317).

[45] W. G. T. Shedd, "The Meaning and Value of the Doctrine of Decrees," *The Presbyterian and Reformed Review* 1 (1890), 4.

[46] *Irish Articles*, §12.

divines, however, apparently wanted to elaborate and define the nature of non-election. They write in paragraph 3.7: "The rest of mankind, God was pleased, according to the unsearchable counsel of his own will, whereby he extendeth or withholdeth mercy as he pleaseth, for the glory of his sovereign power over his creatures, to pass by, and to ordain them to dishonour and wrath for their sin, to the praise of his glorious justice" (emphasis).[47] While this definition and elaboration might be viewed as a desire to emphasize non-election, it should not be taken as such; rather, it is a further clarification of how the non-elect are rejected. The Westminster divines stipulate that non-election is not the exact logical coordinate of predestination. God predestines certain people to salvation; on the other hand, they assert, in terms of Augustinian preterition that God passes by those whom He does not choose. In fact, the Latin translation of the Confession asserts that "Reliquos humani generis Deo . . . praeterire . . ." (3.7).[48] A second point to note is that while election to salvation is absolute and is not based upon any action of man, the non-elect are ordained "to dishonour and wrath for their sin" (3.7). In other words, non-election is not absolute; it is based upon the wickedness of man's sin. On this point, A. A. Hodge elaborates the twofold nature of non-election; Hodge writes that non-election is:

> (1.) Negative, inasmuch as it involves a determination to pass over these, and to refuse to elect them to life. (2.) Positive, inasmuch as it involves a determination to treat them on the principles of strict justice, precisely as they deserve. In its negative aspect, *reprobation is simply not election*, and is absolutely sovereign, resting upon his good pleasure alone, since those passed over are no worse than those elected. In respect to its positive element, *reprobation is not in the least sovereign, but purely judicial*, because God has determined to treat the reprobate precisely according to their deserts in view of absolute justice.[49]

---

[47] Matt. 11:25-26; Rom. 17-18, 21-22; 2 Tim. 2:19-20; Jude 4; 1 Pet. 2:8.

[48] Schaff, *Creeds*, vol. 3, 610.

[49] Hodge, *Confession*, 75; emphasis.

In other words, the Confession is very careful to protect the righteousness of God. The judicial nature of non-election is even more manifest when one reads the answer to the nineteenth question in the Shorter Catechism: "All mankind by their fall lost communion with God, are under his wrath and curse, and so made liable to all miseries in this life, to death itself and to the pains of hell for ever."[50] Hence, according to the divines, God observes, *sub specie aeternitatis*, the fallen human race and predestines certain people out of the corrupt mass; others are passed by and ordained to wrath for their sin.[51]

Summary

While the Westminster divines largely follow Ussher's *Irish Articles*, they made several key modifications that not only rejected Arminianism and Molinism but also codify infralapsarianism. However, they deleted references to reprobation and replaced them with the term *foreordain*. This outcome, however, raises the question, Why did infralapsarianism prevail at Westminster?

Why Did Infralapsarianism Prevail?

After the analysis of the Confession, some might wonder why the divines specified the object of predestination. Does the identification of the object of predestination represent a rejection of supralapsarianism? First, the majority of the divines were infralapsarians.[52] Second, the supralapsarians in the assembly were willing to concede some of these points; they were not dogmatic and uncompromising. For example, Rutherford said in the debates

---

[50] SC, Q. 19; Hodge, *Systematic Theology*, vol. 2, 317.

[51] See LC, Q. 30.

[52] Mitchell, *Westminster Assembly*, 338; idem, *Minutes*, 150-51; Warfield, "Westminster Assembly," 374; Hodge, *Systematic Theology*, vol. 2, 317.

that including the number of decrees was not suitable for a confession of faith.[53] Rutherford's Scottish colleague Robert Baillie also made similar observations when he wrote: "It will be my endeavor that our assembly meddle not with such subtle questions, but leave them to the schools."[54] Hence infra- and supralapsarians alike were not adamant about inserting an *ordo decretorum* in the Confession. However, for those like Rutherford, would not the affirmation of the infralapsarian object of predestination be a negation of his own supralapsarianism?

While this might be a possibility, it is ruled out when one examines the statements of two of the assembly's supralapsarians on issues related to this question. First, Rutherford did not always state his doctrine of predestination in the most uncompromising supralapsarian terms. Rutherford writes in his catechism *The Sum of Christian Religion*:

> Q. What decrees has God concerning mankind?
> A. Two, the decrees of election and reprobation.
>
> Q. What is God's decree of election?
> A. It is the Lord's free appointment setting some men apart for glory and making them his sons in Christ, for the praise of his glory.
>
> Q. What is the decree of reprobation?
> A. It is God's free appointment whereby he decreeth to pass by some and to leave them to the hardness of their own heart.
>
> Q. What moveth God to make this difference?
> A. Neither good nor evil in man, but only the good pleasure of his will.[55]

---

[53] Mitchell, *Minutes*, 150.

[54] Baillie, *Letters and Journals*, vol. 3, 6.

[55] Samuel Rutherford, *The Sum of Christian Religion*, chp. 4, in Alexander F. Mitchell, *Catechisms of the Second Reformation* (London: James Nisbet & Co., 1886), 163. He cites the following: Eph. 1.5-6; John 17.6; 2 Thess 2.13; Jude 4; 1 Pet. 2.8; 1 Thess. 5.8; Rom. 9.22; 2 Pet 2.12; Rom. 9.11. It is equally difficult to notice Rutherford's supralapsarianism in other works. For example, see Samuel Rutherford, *The Covenant of Life Opened: or A Treatise of the Covenant of Grace* (Edinburgh: Andro Anderson, 1655), 13.

While Rutherford's treatment resonates with supralapsarianism, it is not stated in the strictest terms, nor is an *ordo decretorum* stated. Moreover, one should note that Rutherford defines reprobation in terms of preterition, which is typical nomenclature for infra- rather than supralapsarians. So, in this catechism Rutherford did not reveal all of the tenets of his supralapsarianism. This characteristic is further illustrated by William Twisse (1578-1646), a supralapsarian and moderator of the assembly, when he writes about the differences between infra- and supralapsarianism:

> Now the authors of these several opinions have no reason to go together by the ears about these three opinions, but with brotherly love to entertain one another: First, because the difference herein is not so much in divinity, as in Logic and philosophy; difference in opinion about the order in intentions, being merely logical, and to be composed according to the right stating of the end intended, and of the means conducing to the end; it being generally confessed that the intention of the end is before the intention of means conducing thereunto. And that look what is first in intention, the same must be last in execution. Secondly, the authors of these several opinions about the object of predestination, do agree in two principal points. 1. That all men, before God's eternal predestination and reprobation are considered as equal in themselves, whether as uncreated, or as created, but not corrupted, or lastly, whether created or corrupted. 2. That God's grace only makes the difference, choosing some to work them to faith, and repentance, and perseverance therein; while he rejecteth others, leaving them as he find them, and permitting them to finish their days in sin, whereby is upheld and maintained.[56]

In other words, Twisse believed the major disagreement between the two camps was not theological but rather over logic and philosophy. Second, while the infra- and supralapsarians did not agree on the object of predestination, Twisse believed that they both agreed on two important points regarding predestination: (1) all men are equal in the eyes of God whether they were *creabilis et*

---

[56] William Twisse, *The Riches of God's Love unto the Vessells of Mercy Consistent with His Absolute Hatred or Reprobation of the Vessells of Wrath or An Answer unto a book entitled God's Love unto Mankind, manifested by Disproving His Absolute Decree for their Damnation* (Oxford: 1653), bk. 2, 10.

labilis or *creatus et lapsus*; and (2) that God's gracious election is the difference in who receives salvation and who is rejected.

This is important evidence regarding how a supralapsarian viewed logic and philosophy. Twisse, contra charges of rationalism leveled against supralapsarians, did not view logic and philosophy as a foundation to theology; he was no rationalist. He saw the two disciplines as instruments for theology whose role was strictly ancillary, and he was willing to set these disciplines aside for the sake of theological unity with his infralapsarian brethren. In other words, Twisse considered logic and philosophy subservient to theology. Hence, when one considers that supralapsarians did not always express themselves in the strictest of terms, such as Rutherford, and they were willing to set aside issues concerning logic, like Twisse, it is easy to understand how they allowed the object of predestination to be *homo creatus et lapsus*. This compromise was additionally possible because the Confession did not sanction a specific *ordo decretorum* nor did it specifically mention infra- or supralapsarianism by name, nor were there any negative statements against supralapsarianism as there were against Molinism and Arminianism.[57] Charles Hodge on this point notes: "The symbols of that Assembly, while they clearly imply the infralapsarian view, were yet so framed as to avoid offence to those who adopted the supralapsarian theory."[58] One should also

---

[57] Fergusson, "Predestination," 464-65; Mitchell, *Minutes*, lv; Warfield, "Westminster Assembly," 374-75.

[58] Hodge, *Systematic Theology*, vol. 2, 317. The same cannot be said, however, about the *Consensus Formula Helvetica* written by Francis Turretin during the period of High Orthodoxy. In the *Forumla* there is a specific endorsement of the infralapsarian *ordo decretorum*. Turretin writes: "So indeed, God, determining to illustrate His glory, decreed to create man perfect, in the first place, then, permit him to fall, and finally pity some of the fallen, and therefore elect those, but leave the rest in the corrupt mass, and finally give them over to eternal destruction" (*Formula Consensus*, § 4, in Martin I. Klauber, "The Helvetic Consensus (1675): An Introduction and Translation," *Trinity Journal* 11 [1990], 116). Concerning this endorsement

keep in mind the political situation that weighed upon the divines. The English wanted unity for the sake of a military alliance and the Scots wanted unity for the sake of a theological alliance.[59] While political elements were not the major factor in the outcome, they nevertheless should not be ignored; this situation undoubtedly fostered a spirit of compromise among the divines. These conclusions, therefore, lead to the next question, How does the Confession compare with John Calvin? Do the charges of the modern critics withstand the test of close scrutiny?

Calvin and Westminster on Predestination

Lapsarian Views Compared

There is ample evidence to demonstrate Calvin's supralapsarianism; it is also evident that the Confession asserts an infralapsarian doctrine of predestination.[60] These differences can

---

of infralapsarianism Hodge comments: "In the 'Formula Consensus Helvetica,' drawn up . . . in 1675 . . . there is a formal repudiation of the supralapsarian view" (Hodge, *Systematic Theology*, vol. 2, 317). This difference demonstrates that the Westminster divines did not want to condemn supralapsarianism.

[59] B. B. Warfield, "The Westminster Assembly and its Work," *Princeton Theological Review* 6/2 (1908), 193-95.

[60] See John Calvin, *The Epistle of Paul the Apostle to the Romans and Thessalonians*, Calvin's New Testament Commentaries, ed. David W. Torrance and T. F. Torrance, trans. Ross Mackenzie (Grand Rapids: Eerdmans, 1995), Rom. 9.11, 11.7-8, 200-01, 244; idem, *Concerning the Eternal Predestination of God*, trans. J. K. S. Reid (Cambridge: James Clark, 1961), § 8.5, 121; idem, "Articuli de Praedestinatione," in *Opera Calvini*, vol. 9, 713 and, in Schaff, *Creeds*, vol. 3, 524; Barth, *Dogmatics*, vol. 2.2, 127-28; Edward Dowey A., *The Knowledge of God in Calvin's Theology* (Grand Rapids: Eerdmans, 1994), 186-87; Fesko, *Supra- and Infralapsarianism*, 57-150, esp. 88-95, 142-47; J. K. S. Reid, Introduction," in *Concerning the Eternal Predestination of God*, 12-13; G. C. Berkouwer, *Divine Election*, trans. Hugo Bekker (Grand Rapids: Eerdemans, 1985), 89; cf. Henri Blocher, "Calvin infralapsaire," *La Revue Réformée* 31 (1980), 273; Turretin, *Institutes*, vol. 1, 4.9.30, 349-50. When we compare Calvin's definition of predestination with the notoriously

be illustrated when the two respective expressions are compared:

Calvin	Westminster
We call predestination God's eternal decree, by which he determined with himself what he willed to become of each man. For all are not created in equal condition; rather, eternal life is foreordained for some, eternal damnation for others. Therefore, as any man has been created to one or the other of these ends, we speak of him as predestined to life or to death.[61]	By the decree of God, for the manifestation of his glory, some men and angels are predestinated unto everlasting life, and others to everlasting death. . . Wherefore they who are elected, being fallen in Adam, are redeemed by Christ . . . the rest of mankind God was pleased, according to the unsearchable counsel of his own will . . . to pass by, and ordain them to dishonour and wrath for their sin (3.3-7).

At first glance the two definitions appear to have more in common than first realized due to the use of *foreordain* in both statements. Nevertheless, Calvin uses *foreordain* synonymously with *predestine*, whereas Westminster differentiates between the two. This coincidence aside, Calvin speaks of individuals who are created towards the specific end of election or reprobation: *praedestinatio gemina*. Westminster, on the other hand, speaks only of single-predestination and specifies the object of predestination as *homo creatus et lapsus*. This is not to argue that Westminster denies reprobation. Both Calvin and Westminster's views on predestination have two aspects: election and rejection. Calvin states rejection in terms of a decree of "predestination to death," whereas Westminster speaks of rejection in terms of preterition. Shedd notes on this point that in

---

supralapsarian Theodore Beza, there is virtually no difference between the two definitions (cf. John Calvin, *Institutes of the Christian Religion*, Library of Christian Classics, vols. 20-21, ed., John T. McNeill, trans., Ford Lewis Battles [Philadelphia: The Westminster Press, 1960], 3.21.5, 926; and Theodore Beza, *A Brief Declaration of the Chiefe Poyntes of Christian Religion set Forth in a Table* [London: n. d.]).

[61]B. B. Warfield, "The Westminster Assembly and its Work," *Princeton Theological Review* 6/2 (1908), 193-95.

preterition, God repeats, in respect to an individual, the act which He performed in respect to the race. He permitted the whole human species to fall in Adam in such a manner that they were responsible and guilty for the fall, and He permits an individual of the species to remain a sinner and to be lost by sin, in such a manner that the sinner is responsible and guilty for this.[62]

Hence Calvin uses reprobation as a specific decree that is hedged by primary and secondary causality in order to deny that God is the author of sin; he denied the use of the permissive will of God.[63] The divines, however, used the idea of the permissive will of God with the idea of preterition. Shedd notes that preterition "is a branch of the permissive decree, and stands or falls with it."[64] This moderation by the Westminster divines is further illustrated when one compares what they write about non-election to Calvin's expressions.

Calvin did not shy away from stating both decrees of predestination: election and reprobation. This is certainly evident in his definition of predestination, but it is especially evident in Calvin's exegesis of Romans 9. Calvin, for example, writes on Romans 9.11:

In order, however, to prevent any doubt from remaining, as though Esau's condition had been worse because of some vice or fault, it was expedient for Paul to exclude sins no less than virtues. It is true that the immediate cause of reprobation is the curse which we all inherit from Adam. *Nevertheless, Paul withdraws us from this view, so that we may learn to rest in the bare and simple good pleasure of God*, until he has established the doctrine that God has sufficiently just cause for election and reprobation in His own will.[65]

Elsewhere Calvin makes similar comments regarding Romans 11.7-8:

Indeed, the cause of eternal reprobation is so hidden from us, that we can do nothing else but wonder at the incomprehensible counsel of

---

[62] Shedd, "The Doctrine of Decrees," 5.

[63] Calvin, *Institutes*, 1.18.1, 230; 1.17.5, 217.

[64] Shedd, "The Doctrine of Decrees," 5.

[65] Calvin, *Comm.*, Rom. 9.11, 200; emphasis.

> God, as we shall see at length from Paul's conclusion. It is foolishness to try to conceal beneath the garb of immediate causes, as soon as we hear them mentioned, this first cause which is hidden from our notice, as though God had not freely determined before the fall of Adam to do what He thought best with the whole human race.[66]

In other words, Calvin unabashedly proclaims that not only is election absolute, but reprobation is also absolute; original sin is not a determining factor in his doctrine of reprobation. The Confession, on the other hand, does not use the term *reprobation* in the document. Second, they do not state non-election in terms of an absolute decree as Calvin does. The Confession states that the non-elect are passed by and ordained to dishonor and wrath "for their sin" (3.7). Hence Torrance's claim that the Puritan federal scheme is established upon a double-decree like that of Beza and William Perkins (1558-1602), in other words, supralapsarianism, is not tenable in light of the comparison of the two explanations of predestination. Simply stated, Torrance erroneously argues that the Confession teaches the supralapsarianism of Beza. On the contrary, the predestination of the Confession is a moderated view in comparison with that of Calvin and Beza and instead reflects the views of infralapsarians such as Augustine, Aquinas, and Bullinger.[67] In fact, regarding this point Charles Hodge calls the Westminster divines Augustinians, not Calvinists: "Such has been the doctrine of the great body of Augustinians from the time of Augustine to the present day."[68] The modern critics make much of the placement of the doctrine of predestination. What about the placement of predestination in Calvin and Westminster?

---

[66] Calvin, *Comm.*, Rom. 11.7-8, 244.

[67] John Leith, *Assembly at Westminster: Reformed Theology in the Making* (Richmond: John Knox Press, 1973), 68-69; A. T. B. McGowan, "Was Westminster Calvinist?" paper presented at the 1997 Edinburgh Dogmatics Conference, 8.

[68] Hodge, *Systematic Theology*, vol. 2, 317.

Placement of Predestination

The modern critics base a large part of their argument of distortion upon the placement of the doctrine of predestination. They argue that when the divines treat predestination in the doctrine of God, it becomes the determinative principle for the rest of the Confession.[69] For example, Armstrong writes: "While a simple relocation of the doctrine of predestination may not at first sight seem momentous, it in fact is. It makes the most profound difference whether one approaches theology via predestination or simply discusses the doctrine as an implicate of grace."[70] Is this true? Does the decree function as the *central dogma* of the Confession? First, as previously noted, the Confession was based upon the *Irish Articles*. Ussher treated predestination after the headings of Scripture and the Trinity. Ussher's placement was not new; it was the traditional doctrinal structure that had its roots in Peter Lombard (c. 1095-1169) and Aquinas. Moreover, Lombard's order, and the Confession for that matter, is not synthetic, rather it is chronological. Lombard, for example, used the chronological order of the history of salvation: God, Creation, Redemption, Sacraments, and Eschatology.[71] The reason predestination is covered after the doctrine of God and before creation is because the decrees chronologically precede creation. Additionally, neither Aquinas, who is infralapsarian just as the Confession, nor Lombard have been accused of making predestination a determinative principle for their theology as the Confession has for following this order of presentation.

Second, if we take Torrance and Armstrong's claim about the

---

[69] Torrance, "Strengths and Weaknesses," 45. See similar assertions in Armstrong, *Calvinism and the Amyraut Heresy*, 127-39.

[70] Armstrong, *Calvinism and the Amyraut Heresy*, 40.

[71] Karl Rahner, ed., "Scholasticism," in *Sacramentum Mundi: An Encyclopedia of Theology*, 6 vols. (London: Burns & Oates, 1970), vol. 6, 26.

placement of predestination in the Confession to its logical conclusion, then predestination is not the determinative principle for the document. Rather, the doctrine of Scripture is the *central dogma* of the Confession given the fact that it is placed prior to all other doctrines. In fact, Mitchell notes this very point regarding the placement of the article on the Holy Scriptures: "The Westminster divines, like the Irish, place this Article at the head of their Confession. This, and not the doctrine of the Decree, is the point from which their whole system is sought to be evolved, although that doctrine is placed by them, as it had been by the Irish divines, in its logical rather than in its natural order."[72]

Third, Torrance and Armstrong do not take consideration of genre when they compare Calvin's *Institutes* with the Confession. Calvin's *Institutes* is not a systematic theology; it is an instruction manual for students that covers basic doctrinal *loci*. Therefore, comparing a catechetical doctrinal work with a confession that is modeled on a medieval doctrinal structure, namely Ussher's appropriation of Lombard's order of doctrines, and concluding distortion based upon order alone is questionable.[73] To illustrate further this point using Torrance's method of comparison based strictly on form, one might easily conclude that the Confession is far superior to Calvin's *Institutes* because the divines treat the doctrine of Scripture, whereas Calvin has no formal *locus* for this doctrine.[74] This conclusion, however, should be rejected because no one seriously argues that Calvin considered the doctrine of Scripture unimportant just because he did not devote a specific *locus* for it in his work. Rather, one simply searches the *Institutes* to see what Calvin has to say on the topic. Therefore, given the

---

[72] Mitchell, *Minutes*, xlix. Cf. Leith, *Assembly at Westminster*, 71, 89.

[73] Richard A. Muller, *The Unaccommodated Calvin: Studies in the Foundation of a Theological Tradition* (New York: Oxford University Press, 2000), 118-39.

[74] Ferguson, "The Teaching of the Confession," 35.

different architectonic aims of the two works, it seems more appropriate to compare the two in their content rather than form.

One must, therefore, reject the notion that order alone determines the significance of a doctrine. Moreover, the concept of a *central dogma* is theologically anachronistic for the seventeenth century. This theory rests upon eighteenth-century Wolffian rationalism that "points away from the *locus* method of the sixteenth- and seventeenth century orthodox theologians. Indeed, the theory presents a late eighteenth and nineteenth century view of the organization of theological systems, what Bauke called a 'systematic monism,' that is ultimately quite incompatible with sixteenth and seventeenth century dogmatics."[75] However, there are some who might argue that the formal starting point for the Confession is Scripture, but the material starting point is predestination. If this were true, one would then expect to find that the divines would speak of predestination throughout all of their works. Yet, Karl Barth (1886-1968) argues that this is not the case:

> And even in the *Westminster Confession* and the theologians mentioned, it was not a matter of deducing all dogmatics from the doctrine of predestination. They did bring the doctrine into direct relationship with the doctrine of God. They placed it at the head of all other doctrines. And this meant, of course, but meant only, that in it they found the first and decisive word which we have to receive and proclaim in respect of the will of God in relation to creation; the word of which we have always to take account in everything that follows. *If we read their expositions connectedly we are more likely to get the impression that from the standpoint of its systematic range and importance they gave to the doctrine too little consideration rather than too much.*[76]

Hence Torrance and Armstrong's second point of criticism, distortion by placement, lacks cogency on several levels in light

---

[75] Richard A. Muller, *After Calvin: Studies in the Development of a Theological Tradition* (New York: Oxford, 2003), 94.

[76] Barth, *Dogmatics*, vol. 2.2, 77; emphasis; Helm, "On God's Eternal Decree," 1.

of a close consideration of the evidence. The Confession, therefore, is not a distortion of Calvin's doctrine of predestination. On the contrary, the Confession is infralapsarian and Calvin is supralapsarian. Westminster represents a step down from Calvin's position. This portion of the investigation has cleared the Confession, then, of the charge that it distorted Calvin's doctrine of predestination. There are, however, still the supposed effects of supralapsarianism that must be dealt with, namely definite atonement, legalism, and imputed guilt. We need to investigate these issues to determine whether the Confession infected Reformed theology with these "negative supralapsarian by-products."

Supralapsarian Side Effects?

Definite Atonement

As previously noted, Armstrong and Hall claim that the doctrine of a definite atonement was foreign to Calvin's thought, and was a post-Reformation innovation as a result of Theodore Beza's supralapsarianism. There are others, such as R. T. Kendall, who make similar claims: "Fundamental to the doctrine of faith in John Calvin (1509-64) is his belief that Christ died indiscriminately for all men." Kendall then marches out various passages from Calvin's works to substantiate his claim; M. Charles Bell argues along the same lines as Kendall in his *Calvin and Scottish Theology*.[77] Specifically with the Confession, Torrance argues that since the Confession subordinated grace to election, it "leads logically to the Bezan and post-Reformation doctrine of a 'limited atonement' and particular redemption."[78] First, while the Confession teaches a doctrine of a

---

[77] Kendall, *Calvin and English Calvinism*, 13; see 13-18. Similar claims are made by M. Charles Bell, *Calvin and Scottish Theology: The Doctrine of Assurance* (Edinburgh: The Handsel Press, 1985), 13-18.

[78] Torrance, "Strengths and Weaknesses," 47. Also see T. F. Torrance, *Scottish Theology: John Knox to John McLeod Campbell* (Edinburgh: T & T Clark, 1996), 146.

definite atonement, it does not do so in the most uncompromising terms. The Confession states: "Wherefore they who are elected being fallen in Adam, are redeemed by Christ; are effectually called unto faith in Christ by his spirit working in due season; are justified, adopted, sanctified, and kept by his power through faith unto salvation. Neither are any others redeemed by Christ, effectually called, justified, adopted, sanctified, and saved, but the elect only" (3.6). This is the passage that theologians argue contains a doctrine of a definite atonement. Hodge comments that the word *redeem* in this passage of the Confession is synonymous for *atone* in seventeenth century English. Hodge notes: "In the time that this Confession was written, the phrase 'to redeem' was used in the same sense in which we now use the phrase 'to make atonement for.'" He goes on to argue "first, positively, that Christ was eternally appointed to make atonement as a means of executing the purpose to save the elect; and second, negatively, that he has made atonement for none others."[79] There are several other phrases in the Confession that validate this claim; for example, in chapter 29.2 it states: "The popish sacrifice of the mass (as they call it) is most abominably injurious to Christ's one, only sacrifice, *the only propitiation for all the sins of His elect*" (emphasis). Nevertheless, the Confession demands a very careful reading in order to see where the divines define the extent of the atonement. The moderation of the divines is especially evident when one compares Westminster with a confession that specifically refutes Amyraldianism, namely the *Helvetic Formula Consensus* (1675), written by Francis Turretin (1623-87).

---

[79] Hodge, *Confession*, 73. Shaw makes similar comments: "Our Confession first asserts, positively, that *the elect are redeemed by Christ*; and then, negatively, that *none other are redeemed by Christ but the elect only*. If this does not affirm the doctrine of particular redemption, or of a limited atonement, we know not what language could express that doctrine more explicitly" (Shaw, *Confession*, 55). Cf. Mitchell, *Minutes*, xx; T. F. Torrance, *Scottish Theology*, 146.

On the atonement, the Consensus argues that in light of the work of Christ they

> can hardly approve the opposite doctrine of those who affirm that of his own intention and counsel and that of the Father who sent him, Christ died for each and every one upon the condition, that they believe. We also cannot affirm the teaching that he obtained for all a salvation, which, nevertheless, is not applied to all, and by his death merited a salvation and faith for no one individually, but only removed the obstacle of divine justice, and acquired for the Father the liberty of entering into a new covenant of grace with all men.[80]

One can immediately see from this statement that Turretin denies the legitimacy of a universal atonement. This same clarity and explicit disapprobation of Amyraldianism is not present in the Confession. Moreover, one must recall that the Amyraldians participated in the writing of the Confession. For example, Edmund Calamy argued during the debates that

> Christ did pay a price for all,—absolute intention for the elect, conditional intention for the reprobate in case they do believe,—that all men should be *salvabiles, non obstante lapsu Adami* . . . that Jesus Christ did not only die sufficiently for all, but God did intend, in giving of Christ, and Christ in giving Himself, did intend to put all men in a state of salvation in case they do believe.[81]

Given this statement, Calamy would be excluded from the strict statement of the Consensus, yet he was welcome at the Westminster assembly, though he was an Amyraldian. This means, therefore, *if* Calvin held to a universal atonement, as Armstrong, Kendall, Bell, and Torrance maintain, it becomes quite impossible to argue that Westminster distorted his doctrine of the atonement given the Amyraldian presence at the assembly. Could not Calvin also affirm the Confession with the like-minded Amyraldians?[82]

---

[80] Formula Consensus, § 16, in Klauber, "The Helvetic Formula," 119.

[81] Mitchell, *Minutes*, 152.

[82] This is not to say that the Confession embodies Amyraldianism but that those who held to the position were welcome at the assembly (see A. Craig Troxel, "Amyraut 'At' The Assembly: The *Westminster Confession of Faith* and the Extent of the Atonement," *Presbyterion* 22/1 [1996],pp. 43-56). The supposed chasm between Calvin and Westminster is therefore negated.

This, however, assumes that the critics' claim is true. Did Calvin hold to a universal atonement?

The Confession does not state the doctrine of a definite atonement in the strictest terms and is therefore at harmony with the pronouncements of the Synod of Dort on the same subject. Dort does not teach a strict definite atonement; it simply uses the medieval distinction between sufficiency and efficiency: "The death of the Son of God is the only and most perfect sacrifice and satisfaction for sin; is of infinite worth and value, abundantly *sufficient* to expiate the sins of the whole world . . . the quickening and saving *efficacy* of the most precious death of his Son should extend to all the elect."[83] Westminster can accommodate this medieval distinction.[84] What does Calvin have to say about this distinction? Commenting on 1 John 2:2, Calvin writes:

> But here the question may be asked as to how the sins of the whole world have been expiated. I pass over the dreams of the fanatics, who make this a reason to extend salvation to all the reprobate and even to Satan himself. Such a monstrous idea is not worth refuting. *Those who want to avoid this absurdity have said that Christ suffered sufficiently for the whole world but effectively only for the elect. This solution has commonly prevailed in the schools. Although I allow the truth of this*, I deny that it fits this passage. For John's purpose was only to make this blessing common to the whole Church. Therefore, under the word 'all' he does not include the reprobate, but refers to all who would believe and those who were scattered through various regions of the earth.[85]

---

[83] Canons of Dort, 2.3, 8, in Schaff, *Creeds*, vol. 3, 586-87; emphasis. Cf. Peter Lombard, *Liber Quatuor Sententiarum*, in *Patrologia Latina*, vol. 192, ed., J. P. Migne (Paris: 1852), lib. 3, dist. 20.3; col. 799.

[84] Fergusson, "Predestination," 463.

[85] John Calvin, *The Gospel of St. John 11-21 and The First Epistle of John*, trans. T. H. L. Parker, eds., David W. Torrance and T. F. Torrance (Edinburgh: Oliver and Boyd, 1961), 1 Jn. 2:2, 244; emphasis added. T. F. Torrance misreads Calvin on this specific point. Torrance bases his argument upon the following passage in Calvin: "Georgius thinks he argues very acutely when he says: Christ is the propitiation for the sins of the whole world; and hence to those who wish to exclude the reprobate from participation in Christ

Hence Calvin believed the medieval distinction does not apply to 1 John 2:2, but he does affirm the validity of the distinction when he says, "I allow the truth of this." This, by resistless logic, means that Calvin would not only affirm the Canons of Dort on their explanation of the atonement, but he would also be comfortable with the pronouncements of Westminster.[86] Hence, due to the Amyraldian presence at the assembly and Calvin's own approbation of the medieval distinction of sufficiency/efficiency, it appears that

---

must place them outside the world. *For this the common solution does not avail, that Christ suffered sufficiently for all, but efficaciously only for the elect.* By this great absurdity, this monk has sought applause in his own fraternity, but it has no weight with me" (Calvin, *Eternal Predestination*, 9.5, 148; emphasis). From this quote Torrance concludes: "That 'common solution', as it was called, had already been rejected by Calvin" (*Scottish Theology*, 64). Yet, what Calvin simply argues that the "common solution" does not apply to 1 John 2.2; he *does not*, however, reject the validity of the distinction. Calvin argues that "the great absurdity" is Georgius' argument, *not* the medieval sufficient/efficient distinction. This is especially evident in light of his assertions in his comments on 1 John 2:2 quoted above. There are those, however, who in light of this passage still argue that Calvin held to a universal atonement (see Kendall, *Calvin and English Calvinism*, 13- 20, esp. 16, n. 2; and Bell, *Calvin and Scottish Theology*, 13-19, esp. 14-15). There are passages in Calvin that might lead one to agree that Calvin is contradictory on this point. Muller, however, based upon Calvin's use of vocabulary, argues: "Calvin's usage of an unlimited *expiatio* or *satisfactio* and a limited *reconciliatio, redemptio,* or as we shall see *intercessio,* follows closely the old distinction between sufficiency and efficiency and well fits what is loosely called 'limited atonement' not only in Calvin's thought but also in later Reformed theology" (Richard A. Muller, *Christ and the Decree: Predestination and Christology From Calvin to Perkins* [Grand Rapids: Baker Book House, 1986], 34). In the light of the evidence, Muller's explanation appears superior to those of Kendall and Bell.

[86] Although Barth does not hold to a doctrine of a definite atonement, regarding Calvin and the atonement, he notes: "The grim doctrine (which does logically follow from Calvin's conception of predestination) that Christ did not die for all men but only for the elect" (Karl Barth, *Church Dogmatics*, vol. 4, *The Doctrine of Reconciliation*, pt. 1, trans., G. W. Bromiley, eds., G. W. Bromiley and T. F. Torrance [Edinburgh: T & T Clark, 1956], 57). Also see Paul Helm, *Calvin and the Calvinists* (1982; Edinburgh: The Banner of Truth Trust, 1998), 13-23, 32-50.

Calvin and the Confession are at consonance at this point.

Where the modern critics go astray is they assume that a definite atonement is a by-product of supralapsarianism. Yet, supralapsarians were not the first advocates of a definite atonement. Rather, among the earliest advocates of a definite atonement were Gottschalk of Orbais (c. 803-69) and his colleagues, moderate infralapsarians, in the ninth century.[87] One must recall that this was long before the ascendancy of Aristotle, scholasticism, supralapsarianism, or any discussions of an *ordo decretorum*. Stated simply, a definite atonement is not strictly related to supralapsarianism, nor was it introduced to Reformed theology by Theodore Beza. A definite atonement was intertwined with predestination for over seven hundred years prior to Westminster or the existence of Beza. To argue that Beza's supralapsarianism introduced the "post-Reformation doctrine of a limited atonement" ignores the historical facts to the contrary. What about the second supposed negative side effect of supralapsarianism: legalism?

Legalism: Covenant or Contract?

Torrance argues that a covenant is a "promise binding two people or two parties to love one another *unconditionally*." He defines a contract as a "*legal* relationship in which two people or two parties bind themselves together on mutual *conditions* to effect some future result. It betokens a mutual bargain, a compact, a business deal . . . It takes the form, 'If . . . if . . . then . . . ,' as in the business world."[88] He goes on to argue that first- generation Reformers such as Calvin and John Knox (1514-72) understood salvation in terms

---

[87] See, e.g., Remigius, *Liber de Tribus Epistolis*, in *Patrologia Latina*, vol. 121, ed. J. P. Migne (Paris: 1852), chp. 16, col. 1015.

[88] J. B. Torrance, "Covenant or Contract?: A Study of the Theological Background of Worship in Seventeenth-Century Scotland," *Scottish Journal of Theology* 23 (1970), 54.

of a covenant of grace, not a contract. He writes about this covenant: "It is not conditioned by anything in man, but is founded solely on the love of God." He believes that if any conditions are introduced into the covenant of grace, it violates the unconditional nature of the promise.[89] As previously noted, Torrance argues that this was a result of supralapsarianism, which he argues subsumed grace to law. Torrance believes this supralapsarian reversal was accomplished by post-Reformation theologians through the introduction of the covenant of works. He writes:

> This distinction between a Covenant of Works and a Covenant of Grace was unknown to Calvin and the Reformers—nor indeed would Calvin ever have taught it. The very distinction implies the confusion between a *covenant* and a *contract*—the one Latin word *foedus* meaning both and hence obscuring the distinction . . . For Calvin, all God's dealings with men are those of grace, both in Creation and in Redemption.[90]

Does Calvin ever speak of conditions to the covenant of grace?

When Calvin set forth the covenant of grace, it is undisputed that he explained it in the most unconditional and gracious terms as Torrance asserts. All one has to do is read Calvin's statements on predestination and it is not long before one is struck by his robust monergism. Yet, did this strong monergism preclude Calvin from speaking of conditions to the covenant? In the *Institutes* Calvin writes that

> in all covenants of his mercy *the Lord requires of his servants in return uprightness and sanctity of life*, lest his goodness be mocked or someone, puffed up with empty exultation on that account, bless his own soul, walking meanwhile in the wickedness of his own heart. Consequently, in this way he wills to keep *in their duty* those admitted

---

[89] Torrance, "Covenant or Contract?," 55-56.

[90] Torrance, "Covenant or Contract?" 62. See similar comments in Fergusson, "Predestination," 466; T. F. Torrance, *Scottish Theology*, 62; Holmes Rolston III, *Calvin Versus the Westminster Confession* (Richmond: John Knox Press, 1972), 16.

> to the fellowship of the covenant; nonetheless the covenant is at the outset drawn up as a free agreement, and perpetually remains as such.[91]

In this passage Calvin sets forth the gracious nature of the covenant with his use of terms such as "mercy" and "free agreement." Nevertheless, Calvin also describes the same gracious covenant with terms such as "duty" and "requires;" he speaks of conditions of the covenant. Why does Calvin do this? Does this not compromise the gracious nature of the covenant as Torrance asserts? Plainly and simply, as Calvin notes in this passage, conditions to the covenant ward off antinomianism. In fact, this is not the only place where Calvin speaks of conditions to the covenant. If we read Calvin's sermons on Deuteronomy, we find the same emphasis upon conditionality. For example, Calvin states:

> And let us note, that seeing we made God to speak so, that is to say, to grant us liberty to come unto him, and to require him to accomplish his promises; *we must at least while mutually bound unto him, and he take promise of us, that we will be his people*, that is to say, that because he hath redeemed us by the blood of his only son, we will hue no longer after our own lusts and fleshly desires, but be ruled by him.[92]

Elsewhere he writes: "For God adopteth us with this condition; that his glory should shine forth in us."[93] Calvin, however, explains in his somewhat typical brusque manner that "as soon as the ignorant sort do hear of the word condition, they bear themselves in hand that God maketh some payment, and that when he showeth us any favor, he doth it in recompense of our deserts."[94] Calvin goes on to argue that the conditions of God's covenant merely spur believers

---

[91] Torrance, "Covenant or Contract?" 55-56.

[92] John Calvin, *Sermons on Deuteronomy*, trans., Arthur Golding (London, Henry Middleton, 1583; Reprint; Edinburgh: The Banner of Truth Trust, n. d.), Serm. 148, Deut. 26.16-19; 913b; emphasis.

[93] Calvin, Serm. 183, Deut. 32.20-22, 1134a.

[94] Calvin, Serm. 54, Deut. 7.11-15, 322a.

to show forth the Spirit of God through their good works: "Seeing that God hath adopted us, we must live as his children, so as we may show that he hath not called and invited us to that heavenly life in vain."[95] In other words, Calvin did not minimize the gracious nature of the covenant nor its conditions.[96] Far from unique, Calvin, like any other theologian who treated this subject, placed emphasis upon both the mono- and dipleuric aspects of the covenant.[97] The mono- and dipleuric aspects of the covenant(s) is a feature that is found in both Reformation and post-Reformation infra- and supralapsarian theologians such as William Tyndale (1494-1536), Heinrich Bullinger, Wolfgang Musculus (1497-1563), William Perkins (1558-1602), and Robert Rollock (1555-99).[98]

---

[95] Calvin, Serm. 54, Deut. 7:11-15, 323b.

[96] Calvin's sermons on Deuteronomy are replete with references to the conditions of the covenant; for example: "But rather they must understand that all the promises which God hath given in his law, import a condition..." (Serm. 45, Deut. 5.1-4; 268a); "But yet for all that, look that you walk warily, for the covenant is made with condition, that you must be found and have a right meaning heart" (Serm. 53, Deut. 7.7-10, 317a); also 267b, 300a, 321a, 454b, 480a, 563b, 913b, 915b, 922b, 923b-24a, 955a, 1075b. See also Anthony A. Hoekema, "The Covenant of Grace in Calvin's Teaching," *Calvin Theological Journal* 2 (1967), 133-61.

[97] Peter A. Lillback, "The Continuing Conundrum: Calvin and the Conditionality of the Covenant," *Calvin Theological Journal* 29 (1994), 42-74.

[98] William Tyndale, *Doctrinal Treatises and Introductions to Different Portions of the Holy Scriptures*, Parker Society, ed. Henry Walter (Cambridge: Cambridge University Press, 1848), 470; Heinrich Bullinger, *A Brief Exposition of the One and Eternal Testament or Covenant of God (1534)*, ed. and trans. Charles McCoy and J. Wayne Baker, in *Fountainhead of Federalism: Heinrich Bullinger and the Covenantal Tradition* (Louisville: Westminster / John Knox Press, 1991), 111; Wolfgang Musculus, *Common Places of Christian Religion*, trans. John Man (London: Henry Bynneman, 1578), 287b-88b; William Perkins, *A Golden Chain*, in *Workes*, vol. 1 (London: 1612), 31b-32a, 70a-b; Robert Rollock, *A Treatise of God's Effectual Calling*, in *The Select Works of Robert Rollock*, ed. William M. Gunn, 2 vols. (Edinburgh: Woodrow Society, 1849), vol. 1, 39-41.

Consequently, Calvin and Westminster are not at odds when it comes to the proper comprehension of the term *covenant*. In fact, even with the covenant of works, the divines emphasize its benevolent nature: "The distance between God and the creature is so great that although reasonable creatures do owe obedience unto him as their Creator, yet they could never have any fruition of him as their blessedness and reward but *by some voluntary condescension on God's part*, which he hath been pleased to express by way of covenant" (7.1; emphasis).[99] Moreover, the catechisms do not always use the term *covenant of works*; they describe the first covenant as a "covenant of life."[100] Hodge elaborates upon these facts when he writes: "This covenant was also in its essence a covenant of grace, in that it graciously promised life in the society of God as the freely granted reward of an obedience already unconditionally due."[101] Granted, the covenant of works carried more emphasis upon dipleuricism than the covenant of grace. Nevertheless, one should not diminish its monopleuric aspects. This means that Torrance's claims that Westminster theology places emphasis on law over grace does not stand because the divines assert that the covenant of works is an act of divine condescension. The Westminster Confession, therefore, still maintains the priority of grace in God's redemption of fallen man in consonance with Calvin.

---

[99] See Hodge, *Confession*, 121-22; 128; Muller, *After Calvin*, 175- 90; David B. McWilliams, "The Covenant Theology of the *Westminster Confession of Faith* and Recent Criticism," *Westminster Theological Journal* 53 (1991), 112-14.

[100]LC, Q. 20; SC, Q. 12.

[101]Hodge, *Confession*, 122. This is unrelated to the question of merit in the covenant of works. On this matter cf. Lee Irons, "An Examination of Medieval Presuppositions in Covenant Theology," in *Creator, Redeemer, Consummator: A Festschrift for Meredith G. Kline*, eds. Howard Griffith and John R. Muether (Greenville: Reformed Academic Press, 2000), 253-70; John Murray, *Collected Writings*, vol. 2, *Systematic Theology* (1977; Edinburgh: Banner of Truth, 1996), 47-59.

What is interesting to note about Torrance's claims that Bezan supralapsarianism produced legalism, is that J. Wayne Baker makes the exact opposite claim. Baker argues that the double-predestinarian scheme, or supralapsarianism, yielded antinomianism, not legalism.[102] The examination of both Calvin and the Confession demonstrates that they were not guilty of either antinomianism, as evidenced by their focus on the dipleuric aspects of the covenant(s), or legalism, as evidenced by the monopleuric aspects of the covenant(s). Both the supralapsarian Calvin and the infralapsarian Westminster were able to avoid the Scylla and Charybdis of these two extremes. Granted, after Westminster there were undoubtedly individuals who distorted this careful balance, but this cannot be said of Calvin or Westminster.[103] Hence, contra Torrance, there is no connection between supralapsarianism and legalism. What, however, of the last of the supposed supralapsarian side effects: imputed guilt?

Imputed Guilt: the Covenant of Works

It is claimed by Hall, for example, that as a result of Beza's supralapsarianism, he "taught the imputation of Adam's sin to all mankind with precision, whereas Calvin, not finding this to be clear in Scripture, had avoided the point."[104] The primary means by which Westminster deals with the fall and its effects is under the covenant of works. For example, the Confession states that the "first

---

[102] J. Wayne Baker, *Heinrich Bullinger and the Covenant: The Other Reformed Tradition* (Athens: Ohio University Press, 1980), 214.

[103] After Westminster, there were disruptions of the careful doctrinal balances contained in the confession (Richard A. Muller, "Covenant and Conscience In English Reformed Theology: Three Variations on a 17th Century Theme," *Westminster Theological Journal* 42 [1979-80], 334). For another example, see coverage on the "Marrow Controversy" in Scotland; see MacLeod, *Scottish Theology*, 139-66; T. F. Torrance, *Scottish Theology*, 204-20; and A. T. B. McGowan, *The Federal Theology of Thomas Boston* (Carlisle: The Paternoster Press, 1997).

[104] Hall, "Calvin Against the Calvinists," 27.

covenant made with man was a covenant of works, wherein life was promised to Adam, and in him to his posterity, upon condition of perfect and personal obedience" (7.2). Torrance contends that this concept is not contained in Calvin's writings. On the same note Holmes Rolston also writes: "Indeed, it has seldom been realised by those reared in the Reformed tradition that the two-covenant concept which dominates the organisational sub-structure of all later Reformed dogmatics is totally absent from Calvin." He goes on to argue that the "double covenant fabric not only modifies; it reverses much of Calvin's thought about man's primal relation to his God."[105] Hence one may determine whether Westminster suffers from the supposed supralapsarian side effect of imputed guilt by an examination of the Confession and Calvin on the concept of the covenant of works.

It is undisputed: Calvin does not speak of a covenant of works. This term marks a definite distinction between Calvin and the Confession. One must ask, however, does this difference mark a departure from Calvin's thought as Rolston and Torrance claim? The easiest way to verify their claim is to determine if there are contradictory concepts between the Confession and the reformer. Therefore, if we place the term *covenant of works* aside and examine its predicate, "life was promised to Adam, and in him to his posterity, upon the condition of perfect and personal obedience," we can then see if these concepts are found in Calvin. Within this phrase there are two concepts: (1) life is promised to Adam in the garden upon the condition of obedience; and (2) he is the federal head of humanity. Can we find these concepts in Calvin?

First, did Calvin affirm that life was promised to Adam upon the condition of obedience? Calvin writes in the *Institutes* about the fall of man:

---

[105] Holmes Rolston III, "Responsible Man in Reformed Theology: Calvin versus the *Westminster Confession*," *Scottish Journal of Theology* 23 (1970), 129, 142-43.

> Adam was denied the tree of the knowledge of good and evil to test his obedience and prove that he was willingly under God's command. The very name of the tree shows the sole purpose of the precept was to keep him content with his lot and to prevent him from becoming puffed up with wicked lust. But the promise by which he was bidden to hope for eternal life so long as he ate from the tree of life, and conversely, the terrible threat of death once he tasted of the tree of the knowledge of good and evil, served to prove and exercise his faith.[106]

In this passage on Adam's state in the garden, Calvin states the same concepts that one finds in the Confession. Here Calvin asserts that the tree of life contains "the promise by which he was bidden to hope for eternal life." Adam was required to pass the test of obedience and "prove that he was willingly under God's command." Along similar lines, Calvin comments on Genesis 2:16:

> To the end that Adam might the more willingly comply, God commends his own liberality. 'Behold,' he says, 'I deliver into thy hand whatever fruits the earth may produce, whatever fruits every kind of tree may yield: from this immense profusion and variety I except only one tree,' Then by denouncing punishment, he strikes terror, *for the purpose of confirming the authority of the law*.[107]

In other words, Calvin did not simply argue that God's pronouncement was strictly a command; on the contrary, the command of God was law. This means that Adam and Eve were under a state of law in the garden according to Calvin. Therefore, Calvin and Westminster agree on these points. Did Calvin consider Adam the federal head of mankind? Did he impute Adam's guilt upon mankind?

Calvin argues in the *Institutes* that Adam's fall did not only affect his own state, but it also affects the circumstance of all his offspring. Calvin writes:

---

[106]Calvin, *Institutes*, 2.1.4, 245.

[107]John Calvin, *Commentary on Genesis*, vol. 1, trans. John King, Calvin's Commentaries (Grand Rapids: Baker Book House, 1993), Gen. 2:16, 126-27; emphasis.

> Adam was not only the progenitor but, as it were, the root of human nature; and that therefore in his corruption mankind deserved to be vitiated. . . . Adam so corrupted himself that infection spread from him to all his descendants. . . . Hence, rotten branches from a rotten root, which transmitted their rottenness to the other twigs sprouting from them. For thus were the children corrupted in the parent, so that they brought disease upon their children's children. That is, the beginning of corruption in Adam was such that it was conveyed in a perpetual stream from the ancestors into their descendants.[108]

In this passage Calvin argues that Adam was the root of all mankind; if the root is corrupt, then so is the rest of the tree. Westminster echoes this same point: "They being the *root* of all mankind, the guilt of this sin was imputed, and the same death in sin and corrupted nature conveyed to all their posterity descending from them by ordinary generation" (6.3; emphasis).[109] Hence corruption passed to subsequent generations through the natural propagation of the race. Some might argue, however, that while the Confession speaks of Adam and Eve as the *root* of mankind, Calvin does not *impute* Adam and Eve's guilt to their offspring. Does Calvin speak of imputed guilt? Calvin does indeed speak of the guilt of Adam's fall in terms of imputation. Calvin writes: "For the contagion does not take its origin from the substance of the flesh or soul, but *because it had been so ordained by God* that the first man should at one and the same time have and lose, both for himself and for his descendants, the gifts that God had bestowed upon him."[110] Consequently, Calvin affirmed that Adam's guilt passed onto his offspring primarily by divine ordination. This is consonant with the Westminster affirmations of imputed guilt.

Therefore, first, the Confession and Calvin both affirm that Adam, had he obeyed God, would have been able to attain eternal

---

[108]Calvin, *Institutes*, 2.1.6-7, 248-50.

[109]Cf. LC, QQ. 26-27; SC, Q. 16.

[110]Calvin, *Institutes*, 2.1.7, 250; see similar comments in idem, *Comm.*, Rom. 5:12, 111-12. See also Paul Helm, "Calvin and the Covenant: Unity and Continuity," *The Evangelical Quarterly* 55 (1983), 72.

life. Moreover, Adam's condition in the garden was governed by law. Second, both Calvin and Westminster affirm that Adam and Eve were not only the physical progenitors of sin, but the guilt of their sin was ordained by God, in the case of Calvin, and imputed, in the case of Westminster, to the rest of mankind. Though Calvin and the Confession contain these parallels, this is not to argue that the two are exactly synonymous. The Confession does represent further development, a greater degree of precision, and tighter organization of similar concepts found in Calvin. The Westminster divines, however, do not assert anything antithetical to the theology of Calvin on these specific doctrines. Therefore, it is legitimate to assert that the Confession and Calvin are consonant on the doctrine of the covenant of works and more specifically imputed guilt.[111] This then means that imputed guilt was not a supralapsarian innovation as the modern critics claim. Both Westminster, which is infralapsarian, and Calvin, who is supralapsarian, taught that Adam's sin was passed onto his offspring through natural generation and divine ordination and imputation. Hence the last of the supposed supralapsarian distortions has been dismissed. We may now draw some conclusions about Calvin's influence upon the lapsarian development in High Orthodoxy and the claims of the modern critics.

Conclusion

The reconnaissance of the *Irish Articles* and the Westminster Confession demonstrates that the Westminster divines offered an explicitly infralapsarian explanation of predestination. They reflected the common Reformed confessional position,

---

[111] Everett H. Emerson, "Calvin and Covenant Theology," *Church History* 25 (1956), 142; Jens Møller, "The Beginnings of Puritan Covenant Theology," *Journal of Ecclesiastical History* 14 (1963), 61; Peter A. Lillback, "Ursinus' Development of the Covenant of Creation: A Debt to Melanchthon or Calvin?" *Westminster Theological Journal* 43/2 (1981), 288.

infralapsarianism, by replacing the word *reprobation* with *foreordain* and *to pass by*, and they identified the object of predestination as *homo creatus et lapsus*. This yields some important conclusions when we consider the claims of the modern critics.

First, the modern critics have the unchecked presupposition that Calvin is the regulative theologian for the Reformed tradition. This presupposition is why the critics argue that Early and High Orthodox Reformed theologians distorted Calvin's doctrine of predestination. Yet, we must realize that Calvin did not wield as great an influence upon post-Reformation theology as some might think. At the time of the creation of the Confession there appears to have been a great number of other Reformed theologians wielding influence upon English, Scottish, and Irish theologians. For example, Peter Martyr Vermigli (1499-1562) taught at Oxford, Martin Bucer (1491-1551) taught at Cambridge, Heinrich Bullinger's works were translated and diffused through these nations, and, even in the debates at the assembly, names as diverse as Dort and Amyraut were mentioned.[112] In fact, even those divines such as William Twisse, whose doctrine of predestination was very similar to Calvin and Beza, did not see roots of his own supralapsarianism in these two Genevans. For example, Twisse writes:

> Now judge I pray with how little judgment, or modesty this author intimates Beza to be the author of the doctrine of absolute reprobation. Perhaps he will say his meaning is, that he was the author of the upper-way, as touching the making of the object of Predestination mankind not yet created. But to this I answer, that Beza does so indeed, but he was never called to a conference hereabouts, and consequently he never declined it. And that which was declined, he makes to be declined by the abettors, as well as the authors; which cannot be understood of this nice and logical point, as touching the object of reprobation. The main question is, whether there be any cause of reprobation, as touching the act of God reprobating: the negative whereof, was maintained very generally among the school-divines before Beza was born.[113]

---

[112]Mitchell, *Westminster Assembly*, 336-37; idem, *Minutes*, 152-53.

[113]Twisse, *Riches of God's Love*, bk. 1, 61.

In other words, Twisse argues that the doctrine of absolute reprobation did not find its origin in Beza; rather, it had roots in medieval theology. On a similar note, in defense of his doctrine of predestination, Twisse argues that his explanation of "this doctrine is not only approved by Dr. Whitaker Doctor of the Chair in the University of Cambridge . . . but [it is] justified and confirmed by a variety of testimonies both of schoolmen, as Lombard, Aquinas, Bannes, Peter of Alliaco, Gregory of Rimini . . . Bucer at Cambridge, by Peter Martyr at Oxford."[114] Whether or not Twisse's claim is correct is beside the point; what is of interest is the host of names he quotes, especially that of Gregory of Rimini (c. 1330-58), a fourteenth century supralapsarian. It should also be noted that Twisse edited *De Causa Dei*, the work by another fourteenth-century supralapsarian, Thomas Bradwardine (1290-1349).[115] It should also be noted whose name Twisse does not cite; he does not mention Calvin. One must also recall that the structure of the *Irish Articles* reflects medieval models found in the works of Peter Lombard and Thomas Aquinas. All of this evidence shows that there

---

[114]Twisse, *Riches of God's Love*, bk. 2, 10-11.

[115]Leith, *Assembly at Westminster*, 39. Another unchecked assumption that the modern critics assert is the idea that Beza is the source of supralapsarianism. There is ample evidence, however, that proves that supralapsarianism originated in the middle ages in the theology of Bradwardine and Rimini. See Thomas Bradwardine, "The Cause of God Against the Pelagians," in *Forerunners of the Reformation: The Shape of Late Medieval Thought*, ed. Heiko Augustinus Oberman, trans Paul L. Nyhus (London: Lutterworth Press, 1967), 78; cf. Heiko A. Oberman, *Archbishop Thomas Bradwardine A Fourteenth Century Augustinian: A Study of His Theology in Its Historical Context* (Utrecht: Drukkerijen en UitgeversMaatschappij v/h Kemink & Zoon N.V., 1957), 220; Gregory of Rimini, *Super Primum et Secundum Sententiae*, Franciscan Publications Text Series no. 7, ed. Elgius M. Buytaert (1522; St. Bonaventure: Franciscan Institute, 1955), I. D. 40 & 41, q. 1, a. 1, 158 B-C; Frank A. James III, "A Late Medieval Parallel in Reformation Thought: Gemina Praedestinatio in Gregory of Rimini and Peter Martyr Vermigli," in *Via Augustiniana: Augustine in the Later Middle Ages, Renaissance and Reformation*, eds. Heiko A. Oberman and Frank A. James (Leiden: E. J. Brill, 1991), 31.

were numerous influences contributing to the lapsarian development during High Orthodoxy in England, Ireland, and Scotland.

This is a factor that the modern critics appear to miss. They assume that the Reformed tradition is totally synonymous with Calvin's theology. Yet, Calvin's own theology was not entirely his own; it bore the marks of medieval and contemporary influence.[116] Hence, why would Westminster theologians be any different than Calvin? Again, one must remember that Reformed theologians did not see their roots strictly in Calvin. Rather, they saw their roots in the catholic church. This meant that they read other theologians beyond Calvin and often incorporated their insights.[117] When one reads Calvin's *Institutes*, for example, one finds a host of patristic and medieval names in the index. This is why, then, that Calvin is only one name out of a throng of medieval, Reformation, and post-Reformation authors who influenced the development of lapsarianism during High Orthodoxy.

The Westminster Confession did not distort Calvin's supralapsarianism. Rather, they put forth a moderate expression in comparison to Calvin. Even in the supposed supralapsarian side effects such as definite atonement, legalism, and imputed guilt, Calvin and Westminster were found in essential harmony. Despite the attempts of modern scholars to drive a wedge between Calvin and Westminster, we have seen that though there are some discontinuities, the overwhelming continuities between the Genevan and the Divines are evident. Far from the claims of the critics, Calvin and Westminster stand together with the great body of Reformed luminaries and herald the sovereign grace of God.

---

[116]See A. N. S. Lane, *John Calvin: Student of the Church Fathers* (Grand Rapids: Baker, 1999).

[117]See Willem J. van Asselt, "The Fundamental Meaning of Theology: Archetypal and Ectypal Theology in Seventeenth-Century Reformed Thought," *Westminster Theological Journal* 64/2 (2002), 319-36.

Index

A

Aalders, G. C., 452n.31
Abbot, George, 8, 14
Abihu, 80, 243, 296
Abraham, 216, 241, 317, 339, 451-52
Adam, 307, 323, 331, 342, 349, 519-22
Adams, James K., 384
affections, 225, 288, 316, 416
Ahlstrom, Sidney, 120
Alexander, Archibald, 33-35
Alexander, J. W., 37
almsgiving, 337
Amyraldians, 176, 258, 482-83, 486, 509-12
Amyraut, Moïse, 482-83
Anabaptists, 335
Anderson, Rufus, 390
angels, 63, 97, 104, 113, 122, 272, 370, 372, 490-93, 502
Anglicans, 229, 373, 429
annihilationism, 372-78
Anselm of Canterbury, 309n.3
antinomianism, 515
Apostles' Creed, 81, 96, 161, 255-57, 263, 281, 336
Appenzeller, Henry G., 384
Aquinas, Thomas, 293-94, 298, 301, 419, 492, 504-5, 524
Archer, John, 354

Arminians, 7-9, 57, 489, 497, 500
Armstrong, Brian, 478, 505-8
Arrowsmith, John, 113, 123, 130, 144-45
atheism, 198n.38
"Auburn Affirmation", 60-61
Augustine, 114-15, 157, 337, 467, 492, 504

B

Baillie, Robert, 142, 150, 205n.59, 208n.67, 351, 361-63, 484, 498
Baird, William M., 384
Baker, J. Wayne, 518
Bannerman, James, 169, 199
baptism, 88-91, 227
Barker, W. S., 210
Barth, Karl, 507, 512n.86
Baxter, Richard, 147, 224, 238-39, 247, 251-53, 269, 280, 297, 409
Baylie, Thomas, 354
Bayne, Paul, 263-67
beatific vision, 342-44
Bell, M. Charles, 508
Bellarmine, Cardinal, 65
Benedictus, 259, 262, 272, 275, 280, 282
Berkouwer, G. C., 364n.107, 366
Beza, Theodore, 1, 93, 256-57, 361, 478, 504, 508, 513, 523-24

About the Editors and Contributors

Ligon Duncan, PhD, is the Senior Minister of the historic First Presbyterian Church (1837), Jackson, Mississippi, and Adjunct Professor of Theology at the Reformed Theological Seminary (RTS). He was formerly the John R. Richardson Professor of Systematic Theology at RTS. He is a Council Member of the Alliance of Confessing Evangelicals.

W. Duncan Rankin, PhD, is Professor of Systematic Theology at Reformed Theological Seminary in Jackson, Mississippi, and Minister of the Lebanon Presbyterian Church in Learned, Mississippi.

Derek W. H. Thomas, PhD, is the John E. Richards Professor of Pastoral and Systematic Theology at Reformed Theological Seminary. He is also Minister of Teaching at the First Presbyterian Church in Jackson, Mississippi.

Robert C. Cannada, Jr., DMin, is the President of Reformed Theological Seminary which has US campuses in Jackson, Mississippi; Orlando, Florida; Charlotte, North Carolina; Washington, DC; and Atlanta, Georgia.

Stephen R. Berry, PhD (cand.), is the former Archivist of the Reformed Theological Seminary Library, winner of the G. Aiken Taylor Award for American Presbyterian Church History and doctoral candidate at Duke.

Stephen E. Tindall, BA, Biblical and Theological Studies, Gordon College, is a student at Reformed Theological Seminary in Jackson, MS, and currently serves as intern for the Senior Minister at First Presbyterian Church. He is happily married to Sara.

Joel Beeke, PhD, is President and Professor of Systematic Theology and Homiletics at Puritan Reformed Theological Seminary, pastor of the Heritage Netherlands Reformed Congregation in Grand Rapids, Michigan, editor of *Banner of Sovereign Grace Truth*, editorial director of Reformation Heritage Books, president of Inheritance Publications, and vice-president of the Dutch Reformed Translation Society.

Hugh M. Cartwright, MA, was formerly Minister and Professor of Church History and Church Principles in the Free Church of Scotland; now Minister and Tutor in New Testament, Catechetics and Church Practice, Free Presbyterian Church of Scotland, Edinburgh.

David B. Calhoun, DPhil, is Associate Professor of Church History at Covenant Theological Seminary in St. Louis, Missouri. He is also a minister of the Presbyterian Church of America. He has taught at Covenant College, Columbia Bible College (now Columbia International University), and Jamaica Bible College (where he was also principal).

R. Scott Clark, DPhil, is Professor of Historical and Systematic Theology at Westminster Theological Seminary in California. He has also taught at Reformed Theological Seminary, Wheaton College, and Concordia University (Irvine). He also serves as associate pastor of the Oceanside United Reformed Church in Oceanside, California.

J. V. Fesko, PhD, is the pastor of Geneva Orthodox Presbyterian Church in Marietta, Georgia. He is a visiting lecturer in Systematic Theology at Reformed Theological Seminary in Atlanta.

Douglas F. Kelly, PhD, is the J. Richard Jordan Professor of Systematic Theology at Reformed Theological Seminary in Charlotte, North Carolina. He is serving with David Wright of the University of Edinburgh as a general editor for a revision of *Calvin's Old Testament Commentaries*. In addition, he is co-editor for a twenty-volume dogmatics series, for which he is writing a volume on the Trinity.

David W. Hall, PhD, is the Senior Minister of the Midway Presbyterian Church in Powder Springs, Georgia. He was formerly Senior Fellow of the Center for the Advancement of Paleo-Orthodoxy (CAPO), and Minister of the Covenant Presbyterian Church in Oak Ridge, Tennessee.

Joseph H. Hall, ThD, is currently in retirement writing a history of the Reformation while continuing to develop a third-world theological library. He has taught at Mid-America Reformed Seminary, Knox Theological Seminary, Covenant Theological Seminary and Sangre de Christo Seminary.

Ian Hamilton is minister of Cambridge Presbyterian Church. He was the minister of Loudoun Church of Scotland, Newmilns, Ayrshire, serving there for almost twenty years. He also serves as a Trustee of the Banner of Truth.

Paul Helm, PhD, is the J.I.Packer Chair in Philosophical Theology at Regent College, Vancouver. Previously, he held the Chair in the History and Philosophy of Religion at King's College, London, and prior to that position was Reader in Philosophy at the University of Liverpool.

Chi Mo Hong, DLitt, is currently Professor Emeritus at Chongshin University, where he has served as both professor (since 1977) and vice president (from 1991 until 1994). He has also served as the president of the Korean Church History Society.

Nick Needham, PhD, is Lecturer in Church History and joint coordinator of postgraduate research at The Highland Theological College. He also was Assistant Pastor of Central Baptist Church, Walthamstow, London and Lecturer in Church History at Samuel Bill Theological College Nigeria as well as a part-time lecturer in Systematic Theology at Scottish Baptist College, Glasgow.

Philip G. Ryken, DPhil, is Senior Minister of Tenth Presbyterian Church in Philadelphia, Pennsylvania. He is a Council Member of the Alliance of Confessing Evangelicals and Bible Teacher for *Every Last Word*.

Other books of interest
from
Christian Focus

The Westminster Confession into the 21ˢᵗ Century

Volume One

Edited By Ligon Duncan

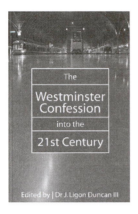

Contributors include:
Michael Horton, Mark Dever,
Timothy George, Richard Gaffin,
David F. Wright

Ligon Duncan has assembled an impressive array of contributors from a variety of ecclesiastical backgrounds. The aim is simple - to enable the 21st Century to understand the confession more fully, and so bring about the same kind of rugged, vigorous, intelligent and self-sacrificing Christianity that was the result of its initial publication over 350 years ago.

In the first of four volumes, the topics covered include:-

Baptists and the Westminster Confession
Finney's attack on the Westminster Confession
The Holy Spirit and the Westminster Confession

'...a most worthy undertaking and, to my mind, one that is quite timely not only because of the anniversary of the Assembly but also because of the clear need in Presbyterian and Reformed circles for scholarly work on the Reformed tradition and its confessions.'

Richard A. Muller, PhD
P.J. Zondervan Professor of Historical Theology
Calvin Theological Seminary, Grand Rapids, Michigan

ISBN 1-85792-862-8

The Practical Calvinist

An introduction to the
Presbyterian and Reformed Heritage
In Honor of D. Clair Davis' Thirty Years at
Westminster Theological Seminary

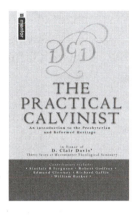

Contributors include:
Sinclair B. Ferguson, Robert Godfrey,
Edmund Clowney,
Richard Gaffin, William Barker

For Thirty Years D. Clair Davis taught Church History at Westminster Theological Seminary in Philadelphia. His influence will not be fully known until the next life, but as a measure of the esteem that he is held in this remarkable volume has been prepared.

'A marvellous collection of superb essays by some of the leading scholars of the Reformed tradition. Here is scholarship and pastoral theology at its best — both done in the service of the church.'

Timothy George,
Beeson Divinity School, Birmingham , Alabama

'Anyone concerned to understand and to maintain the heritage of conservative Reformed Christianity will find many engaging essays that fit their interests.'

George M. Marsden
University of Notre Dame, Indiana

'...a feast, both appetizing & satisfying, of contemporary reflection on the Presbyterian & Reformed heritage. Articles from a galaxy of scholars lead us into matters historical, theological, homiletical & pastoral.'

Edward Donnelly
Reformed Theological College, Belfast

ISBN 1- 85792-814-8

A Faith To Live By

Understanding Christian Teaching

Donald Macleod

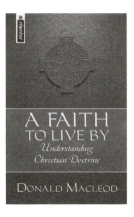

'...a master of making difficult things seem simple, without compromising their profundity...Macleod is simultaneously an able apologist and a world class exegete (one does not hesitate to mention his name alongside Warfield and Murray in exegetical competence). Read the book. Learn from Macleod. Argue with Macleod. And then bow the knee to your Saviour, the Lord Jesus Christ, and worship!'

**J. Ligon Duncan III,
First Presbyterian Church, Jackson, Mississippi**

'...one of the finest theologians Scotland has produced in a long time. Professor Macleod displays an originality of thought and sharp clarity of expression which will enable a new generation of readers to enter sympathetically into an understanding of the Reformed Faith.'

A.T.B. McGowan, Highland Theological College

'I have always valued Donald Macleod's writings, his great learning, his respect for those with whom he disagrees, the absence of foolish dogmatism and the presence of a pastoral heart. Here we have first rate Christian theology, exceedingly encouraging...'

Dick Lucas, The Proclamation Trust

Donald Macleod is Principal of the Free Church College, Edinburgh. Recognised as a leading systematic theologian, he has developed this reputation by being able to explain complex thoughts with simplicity and clarity.

ISBN 1-85792-428-2

Samuel Rutherford
A New Biography of the Man and his ministry
Kingsley G. Rendell

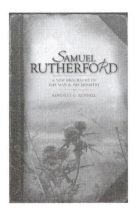

Rutherford played a major role as a reformer at the Westminster Assembly and was also a crucial figure in the establishment of Presbyterianism for Scotland in 1689. Rutherford's 'Lex Rex' heavily influenced John Locke and in turn, the framers of the US Constitution and Declaration of Independence.

Several biographies have been written to eulogise Samuel Rutherford but little has been done to consider the man and his work critically. Kingsley Rendell uses Rutherford's writings and contemporary material to present a comprehensive picture of him from his student days to his death in 1661.

'Readers who know little of the life of Samuel Rutherford in its tangled and political context will find a reliable guide in Kingsley Rendell. This is no uncritical hagiography... Those who have never encountered this relentless controversialist and master-wordsmith should start here.'
David Wright, University of Edinburgh

'Kingsley Rendell's study provides the welcome service of putting this important and interesting figure in the context of his times and of the church controversies in which he was involved.'
William Barker, Westminster Theological Seminary, Philadelphia

Kingsley Rendell was a distinguished teacher of theology and an able historian. This volume is a tribute to his abilities as both. Sadly Dr. Rendell died after completing this book but before its publication.

ISBN 1-85792-262-X

Treatises on the Sacraments

Calvin's Tracts translated by Henry Beveridge

John Calvin

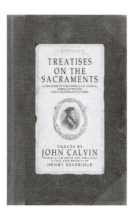

A key figure in the Protestant Reformation, Calvin's legacy remains immensely strong, with hundreds of thousands gaining insights from his works on major doctrines such as the interaction between the Sovereignty of God and Man's Free Will. Countless analyses and critiques of Calvin's work have been released over the centuries, and a huge number of Churches and denominations hold to Calvin's teaching to varying degrees. Calvin's name is thrown about in theological discussions covering a broad spectrum, we may know the Calvinist's view, but what does Calvin himself say?

One of the key issues that led to the reformation and the birth of Protestantism was Rome's treatment of the Lord's Supper. This is the main subject of this collection of Calvin's tracts. Calvin and the Reformers believed the Catholic Mass was founded on a grave error that needed to be corrected. According to Rome's doctrine of transubstantiation the bread and wine supernaturally became Christ's body and blood. Calvin on the other hand held that they were symbolic and to say otherwise bordered on idolatry and diminished Christ's once for all sacrifice on the cross. This key point of difference remains to this day and Calvin's writings have become a starting point from which Reformed Theologians have gone on to defend and develop the Protestant stance.

This unedited collection of sermons allows you to read John Calvin's own ideas on issues relating to the sacraments, catechisms, forms of prayer and confessions of faith.

ISBN 1-85792-725-7

Matthew Henry's Unpublished Sermons on The Covenant of Grace

Matthew Henry

Edited by Allan Harman

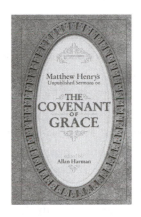

Matthew Henry's commentary on the Bible is legendary. Used by literally millions it has stood the test of time, and remains a testament to his desire to make the whole Bible and its teaching reach the ordinary man.

Fifty years ago Allan Harman was given a small, well-worn book of handwritten sermon notes. It was clear that what he had was Matthew Henry's own handwritten notes, from a series of sermons he preached to his Chester congregation during 1691 and 1692. Harman knew these sermons needed to reach a wider audience and started turned these long forgotten sermons into what you hold in your hand today – a revealing, and deeply spiritual work that allows us to read Matthew Henry on that most fundamental of doctrines – God's promise of unmerited favour to mankind. Harman filled in the shorthand gaps, added footnotes to help with passages obscure to our contemporary ears and translated the Greek, Hebrew and Latin quotes. He also provides a biographical introduction to help us picture Henry and see the context in which these sermons were preached.

'He studied the Scriptures intently (All but four of the Biblical Books are referred to) and organised his material methodically. Constantly he illustrates, not be lengthy stories but by phrases and references which crystallize his points... I can testify to the blessing they have been to me.'

Allan Harman

Allan is a Research Professor at the Presbyterian Theological College, Melbourne.

ISBN 1-85792-796-6

Standing Forth
Collected Writings of Roger Nicole
Roger Nicole

Long regarded as one of the pre-eminent theologians in America, Roger Nicole has devoted a lifetime to defending the orthodox belief on wide range of issues under attack including the inspiration of scripture, the nature of the atonement, the existence of hell, and more recently the openness of God issue.

'a masterful systematic theologian, poised for logical-exegetical pincers movements against muddles and mistakes.'
J. I. Packer, Regent College, Vancouver

'Nicole is one of God's great gifts to the church. His careful study and thoughtful analysis serve as models of evangelical scholarship.'
**R. Albert Mohler Jr., President,
Southern Baptist Theological Seminary, Louisville**

'This is a marvelous book, a treasure trove of godly wisdom from one of the master theologians of our times.'
**Timothy George, Executive Editor, Christianity Today
Dean of Beeson Divinity School, Birmingham, Alabama**

'...one of the premier Reformed theologians of our time. Dr. Roger Nicole, whose encyclopedic knowledge of the entire theological discipline most of us can only dream of acquiring, has for many years been a winsome apologist for biblical inerrancy and the Reformed faith. This volume contains the 'cream of the crop' of his literary output...the reader has several rich hours of reading in store for him.'
**Robert L. Reymond,
Knox Theological Seminary, Fort Lauderdale, Florida**

ISBN 1-85792-646-3

The Saints' Everlasting Rest

Richard Baxter

Throughout his life, Richard Baxter suffered from ill-health and it was during one of the more serious periods of illness that he began writing *The Saints' Everlasting Rest*. His intention was to provide suitable meditations on the theme of heaven. The book was published in 1650 and it became one of the most best-known of his writings and has continued to be so to the present day.

Richard Baxter (1615-1691) was a leader in the Puritan movement in Britain. His successful ministry in the town of Kidderminster, England, was outstanding even in that period of eminent pastors and preachers, and his book *The Reformed Pastor* explains many of the principles he practised there.

Richard Baxter was a prolific author, writing over sixty books. When he was dying, a friend comforted him with the reminder of the benefit many had received from his writings. He replied, 'I was but a pen in God's hand, and what praise is due to a pen?'

ISBN 1-85792-389-8

The Bond Of Love
God's Covenantal Relationship with His Church
David McKay

'*Covenant Theology is a way of understanding the entire biblical message from Genesis to Revelation as essentially one theme. It covers everything, and anyone who writes on it must not only be familiar with biblical themes, but must also be able to integrate historical, systematic and practical theology in such a way that what results is comprehensive and comprehensible. McKay manages to all of this with breathtaking ease. I have been waiting for over twenty years for such a book. This is it.*'

Derek W. H. Thomas, Reformed Theological Seminary, Jackson, Mississippi

'*Particularly useful is McKay's treatment of contemporary issues from a covenant perspective: e.g., neo-orthodoxy, the New Age Movement, feminism, evolutionism, the "open view of God," etc. He interacts with an amazing range of Reformed authors, from Calvin to the Puritans to Murray, Van Til, and Reymond. I enthusiastically commend this work, and will use it in my Seminary courses.*'

**Wayne R. Spear,
Reformed Presbyterian Theological Seminary,
Pittsburgh, Pennsylvania**

David McKay is Professor of Systematic Theology, Ethics and Apologetics at the Reformed Theological College, Belfast.

ISBN 1-85792-641-2

Covenant Theology
The Key of Theology in Reformed Thought and Tradition
Peter Golding

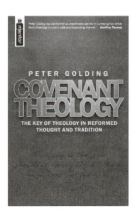

'*Peter Golding has performed an inestimable service in surveying this whole field of theology in such a safe and fascinating manner. One feels one's own ministry has been superficial compared to this gripping and profound introduction to Covenant Theology.*'

**Geoffrey Thomas,
Aberystwyth, Wales**

Is there an accessible and consistent interpretative framework we can use to understand the Bible? - or is it essentially a disconnected set of concepts?

The lack of a consistent approach to the study of the Bible has reduced the level of understanding of God's revelation as a whole. The 'lazyology' that has resulted is a key ingredient in the lack of clarity that has made the church 'off-message' to our society.

Help is at hand. Peter Golding gently takes us on a trip through time and unfolds the Big Picture that is Covenantal Theology. The Big Picture that gives you a vision of a Bigger God.

This unique study surveys, analyses, and evaluates the main streams of Reformed thinking in this field, and offers a gentle critique from an orthodox stance. It gives the reader a well-documented synthesis of historical, biblical and systematic theologies on the Covenant, and demonstrates its contemporary relevance and the abiding hope it provides for the future.

Peter Golding pastored Hayes Town Congregational Chapel for over 30 years and has served on the Board of Governors at the London Theological Seminary since 1984.

ISBN 1-85792-923-3

Puritan Profiles

*54 Members and Contemporaries
of the Westminster Assembly*

William Barker

"Will Barker's love of biography, historian's eye for detail, his personal devotion to Christ and Scripture make these pages an expertly guided tour of the varied characters and remarkable personalities drawn together by the Westminster Assembly'.

**Sinclair B. Ferguson,
Westminster Theological Seminary,
Dallas Campus, Texas**

...insightful, wise and encouraging! Read them, and come away a stronger person.'

**The Late James Boice,
Tenth Presbyterian Church, Philadelphia**

'For those who admire the confessional statements [of the Westminster Assembly] but know little of their origins, this is a wonderful introductory volume. The diversity of the assembly participants with their immense commonalities is amazing. Also of interest are the enormous energy of involved in the debates, the participants' struggles to understand the Bible and freedom to vent disagreement at high decibels while maintaining a spirit of unity.'

John D. Hannah, Bibliotheca Sacra

William Barker is vice-president for academic affairs and Professor of Church History at Westminster Theological Seminary, Philadelphia. He is an ordained minister in the Presbyterian Church in America. His keen interest in contemporary culture and politics ensures that this book is relevant today.

ISBN 1-85792-191-7

An Exposition of the Westminster Confession of Faith

Robert Shaw

Foreword by Sinclair B. Ferguson

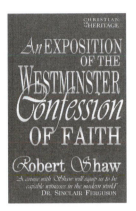

'The fullest and most carefully constructed exposition of the Christian Faith ever written'
**Sinclair B. Ferguson,
Westminster Theological Seminary,
Dallas Campus, Texas**

'...one of the best written and helpful expositions ever to appear. ...each category of doctrine is opened up with clarity and applied with warmth and spirituality. It is a handsome volume and is recommended highly.'
Evangelical Times

The Westminster Confession of Faith is the standard of Church beliefs for the Reformed churches worldwide. It is also the most comprehensive statement of biblically based Christian belief available. Hence you have an excellent manual for Christian Doctrine, expertly unpacked by Robert Shaw.

This book is a practical aid to help us understand and apply material in the Confession to our lives - making us live out our confession as individual Christians and as members of a world-wide church.

This book is the recognised companion volume to the Westminster Confession of Faith.

ISBN 0-90673-104-6

Christian Focus Publications

publishes books for all ages

Our mission statement –

STAYING FAITHFUL

In dependence upon God we seek to help make His infallible word, the Bible, relevant. Our aim is to ensure that the Lord Jesus Christ is presented as the only hope to obtain forgiveness of sin, live a useful life and look forward to heaven with Him.

REACHING OUT

Christ's last command requires us to reach out to our world with His gospel. We seek to help fulfill that by publishing books that point people towards Jesus and help them to develop a Christ-like maturity. We aim to equip all levels of readers for life, work, ministry and mission.

Books in our adult range are published in three imprints.

Christian Focus contains popular works including biographies, commentaries, basic doctrine, and Christian living. Our children's books are also published in this imprint.

Mentor focuses on books written at a level suitable for Bible College and seminary students, pastors, and other serious readers. The imprint includes commentaries, doctrinal studies, examination of current issues, and church history.

Christian Heritage contains classic writings from the past.

For a free catalogue of all our titles, please write to
Christian Focus Publications, Ltd
Geanies House, Fearn,
Ross-shire, IV20 1TW, Scotland, United Kingdom
info@christianfocus.com

For details of our titles visit us on our website
www.christianfocus.com